The Oxford Handbook of Leader–Member Exchange

OXFORD LIBRARY OF PSYCHOLOGY

Editor in Chief PETER E. NATHAN

The Oxford Handbook of Leader–Member Exchange

Edited by

Talya N. Bauer

Berrin Erdogan

OXFORD
UNIVERSITY PRESS

OXFORD
UNIVERSITY PRESS

Oxford University Press is a department of the University of
Oxford. It furthers the University's objective of excellence in research,
scholarship, and education by publishing worldwide.

Oxford   New York
Auckland   Cape Town   Dar es Salaam   Hong Kong   Karachi
Kuala Lumpur   Madrid   Melbourne   Mexico City   Nairobi
New Delhi   Shanghai   Taipei   Toronto

With offices in
Argentina   Austria   Brazil   Chile   Czech Republic   France   Greece
Guatemala   Hungary   Italy   Japan   Poland   Portugal   Singapore
South Korea   Switzerland   Thailand   Turkey   Ukraine   Vietnam

Oxford is a registered trademark of Oxford University Press
in the UK and certain other countries.

Published in the United States of America by
Oxford University Press
198 Madison Avenue, New York, NY 10016

Library of Congress Cataloging-in-Publication Data
The Oxford handbook of leader-member exchange / edited by Talya N. Bauer, Berrin Erdogan.
    pages cm.—(Oxford library of psychology)
Includes bibliographical references and index.
ISBN 978–0–19–932617–4 (hardback)
1. Leadership.   2. Industrial relations.   3. Organizational behavior.   4. Psychology, Industrial.   I. Bauer, Talya N., editor.
II. Erdogan, Berrin, editor.
HM1261.O945 2015
303.3′4—dc23
2015024089

9 8 7 6 5 4 3 2 1
Printed in the United States of America
on acid-free paper

SHORT CONTENTS

Oxford Library of Psychology   vii

About the Editors   ix

Acknowledgments   xi

Contributors   xiii

Contents   xvii

Chapters   1–422

Index   423

The *Oxford Library of Psychology,* a landmark series of handbooks, is published by Oxford University Press, one of the world's oldest and most highly respected publishers, with a tradition of publishing significant books in psychology. The ambitious goal of the *Oxford Library of Psychology* is nothing less than to span a vibrant, wide-ranging field and, in so doing, to fill a clear market need.

Encompassing a comprehensive set of handbooks, organized hierarchically, the *Library* incorporates volumes at different levels, each designed to meet a distinct need. At one level is a set of handbooks designed broadly to survey the major subfields of psychology; at another level are numerous handbooks that cover important current focal research and scholarly areas of psychology in depth and detail. Planned as a reflection of the dynamism of psychology, the *Library* will grow and expand as psychology itself develops, thereby highlighting significant new research that will have an impact on the field. Adding to its accessibility and ease of use, the *Library* will be published in print and, later, will be published electronically.

The *Library* surveys the principal subfields of psychology with a set of handbooks that captures the current status and future prospects of those major subdisciplines. This initial set includes handbooks of social and personality psychology, clinical psychology, counseling psychology, school psychology, educational psychology, industrial and organizational psychology, cognitive psychology, cognitive neuroscience, methods and measurements, history, neuropsychology, personality assessment, developmental psychology, and more. Each handbook undertakes to review one of psychology's major subdisciplines with breadth, comprehensiveness, and exemplary scholarship. In addition to these broadly conceived volumes, the *Library* also includes a large number of handbooks designed to explore in depth more specialized areas of scholarship and research, such as stress, health and coping, anxiety and related disorders, cognitive development, or child and adolescent assessment. In contrast to the broad coverage of the subfield handbooks, each of these latter volumes focuses on an especially productive, more highly focused line of scholarship and research. Whether at the broadest or most specific level, however, all of the *Library* handbooks offer synthetic coverage that reviews and evaluates the relevant past and present research and anticipates research in the future. Each handbook in the *Library* includes introductory and concluding chapters written by its editor to provide a roadmap to the handbook's table of contents and to offer informed anticipations of significant future developments in that field.

An undertaking of this scope calls for handbook editors and chapter authors who are established scholars in the areas about which they write. Many of the nation's and world's most productive and best-respected psychologists have agreed to edit *Library* handbooks or write authoritative chapters in their areas of expertise.

For whom has the *Oxford Library of Psychology* been written? Because of its breadth, depth, and accessibility, the *Library* serves a diverse audience, including graduate students in psychology and their faculty mentors, scholars, researchers, and practitioners in psychology and related fields. Each will find in the *Library* the information he or she seeks on the subfield or focal area of psychology in which he or she works or is interested.

Befitting its commitment to accessibility, each handbook includes a comprehensive index, as well as extensive references to help guide research. And because the *Library* was designed from its inception as an online as well as a print resource, its structure and contents will be readily and rationally searchable online. Furthermore, once the *Library* is released online, the handbooks will be regularly and thoroughly updated.

In summary, the *Oxford Library of Psychology* will grow organically to provide a thoroughly informed perspective on the field of psychology, one that reflects both psychology's dynamism and its increasing interdisciplinarity. Once published electronically, the *Library* is also destined to become a uniquely valuable interactive tool, with extended search and browsing capabilities. As you begin to consult this handbook, we sincerely hope you will share our enthusiasm for the more than 500-year tradition of Oxford University Press for excellence, innovation, and quality, as exemplified by the *Oxford Library of Psychology*.

Peter E. Nathan
Editor-in-Chief
Oxford Library of Psychology

ABOUT THE EDITORS

Talya N. Bauer and Berrin Erdogan

Talya N. Bauer (Ph.D., Purdue University) and Berrin Erdogan (Ph.D., University of Illinois, Chicago) are Fellows of SIOP. Both are well-known scholars in the area of leader–member exchange (LMX). Since 1996 they have been engaged in understanding how LMX relationships form, develop, and evolve. In addition, they have examined important boundary conditions related to understanding LMX. Talya serves as an Associate Editor for the *Journal of Applied Psychology* and Berrin serves as an Associate Editor for *Personnel Psychology*.

ACKNOWLEDGMENTS

This book has truly been a team effort. First, a big thank you goes to all the authors who committed their time to writing chapters for this handbook. They shared their unique and diverse perspectives as well as ideas for future research. Every chapter was a pleasure to read, and, as a collection, it is a powerful body of work. We appreciate authors' enthusiasm in saying "yes" when we approached them to contribute a chapter as well as their timely delivery of high-quality manuscripts.

Our advisors Steve Green and Bob Liden were our first introduction to Leader Membership Exchange (LMX) theory, and we value the high-quality LMX relationship we developed with them over the years. We also thank our colleagues at Portland State University (PSU) for their continued collegial support. The School of Business at PSU has continued to provide an empowering and enriching research environment.

Many hands helped to copyedit this book at Oxford Press and PSU, including our graduate assistants Jay Cornelius and Didem Karpuzcu. In addition, Jay also created the graphics included in Chapter 1. We are grateful for their support. The editorial guidance of Anne Dellinger and Abby Gross over the course of this project was wonderful. This book would not have been possible without their vision and support.

Finally, we thank our families for fully supporting both the joys and demands of our profession every step of the way, from helping to lighten burdens when they can as well as celebrating successes along the way!

CONTRIBUTORS

Smriti Anand
Stuart School of Business
Illinois Institute of Technology
Chicago, IL

Neal M. Ashkanasy
UQ Business School
University of Queensland
Brisbane, Australia

Stacy L. Astrove
Henry B. Tippie College of Business
University of Iowa
Iowa City, IA

Talya N. Bauer
School of Business Administration
Portland State University
Portland, OR

Gabriela Burlacu
HCM Practices Manager
SuccessFactors/SAP

Aarn Xiaoyun Cao
Department of Managerial Studies
University of Illinois at Chicago
Chicago, IL

David V. Day
Department of Leadership and
Management
University of Western Australia
Business School
Crawley, Australia

Cécile Emery
Department of Management
London School of Economics
London, UK

Olga Epitropaki
ALBA Graduate Business School at the
American College of Greece, and
Aston University
Birmingham, UK

Berrin Erdogan
School of Business Administration
Portland State University
Portland, OR

Caren Goldberg
Department of Psychology
George Mason University
Washington, D.C.

Vicente González-Romá
Idocal Research Institute
University of Valencia
Valencia, Spain

Maria L. Kraimer
Henry B. Tippie College of Business
University of Iowa
Iowa City, IA

Jared C. Law-Penrose
Department of Management
Purdue University
West Lafayette, IN

Marcia L. Lensges
Carl H. Lindner College of Business
University of Cincinnati
Cincinnati, OH

Robert C. Liden
Department of Managerial Studies
University of Illinois at Chicago
Chicago, IL

Drew B. Mallory
Department of Psychological
Sciences
Purdue University
West Lafayette, IN

Robin Martin
Manchester Business School
University of Manchester
Manchester, UK

Suzanne S. Masterson
Carl H. Lindner College of Business
University of Cincinnati
Cincinnati, OH

Fadel K. Matta
Eli Broad Graduate School of
Management
Michigan State University
East Lansing, MI

Patrick F. McKay
School of Management and Labor
Relations
Rutgers, the State University of
New Jersey
Piscataway, NJ

Darja Miscenko
School of Business and Economics,
Organisation and Strategy
Maastricht University
Maastricht, the Netherlands

Jennifer D. Nahrgang
W.P. Carey School of Business
Arizona State University
Tempe, AZ

Hae Sang Park
Department of Managerial Studies
University of Illinois at Chicago
Chicago, IL

Ekin K. Pellegrini
College of Business Administration
University of Missouri-St. Louis
St. Louis, MO

Alexander Pundt
Department of Work and Organizational
Psychology
University of Mannheim
Mannheim, Germany

Deborah E. Rupp
Department of Psychological Sciences
Department of Management
Purdue University
West Lafayette, IN

Birgit Schyns
Durham University Business School
Durham University
Durham, UK

Scott E. Seibert
Henry B. Tippie College of Business
University of Iowa
Iowa City, IA

Jungmin Jamie Seo
W.P. Carey School of Business
Arizona State University
Tempe, AZ

Sabine Sonnentag
Department of Work and Organizational
Psychology
University of Mannheim
Mannheim, Germany

Raymond T. Sparrowe
Olin Business School
Washington University in St. Louis
St. Louis, MO

David L. Taylor
Department of Psychology
Wake Forest University
Winston-Salem, NC

Pamela Tierney
School of Business Administration
Portland State University
Portland, OR

Ashlea C. Troth
Griffith Business School
Griffith University
Brisbane, Australia

Donald M. Truxillo
Department of Psychology
Portland State University
Portland, OR

Herman H. M. Tse
Griffith Business School
Griffith University
Brisbane, Australia

Linn Van Dyne
Eli Broad Graduate School of
Management
Michigan State University
East Lansing, MI

Prajya R. Vidyarthi
Department of Management
University of Texas at El Paso
El Paso, TX

Mo Wang
Department of Management
University of Florida
Gainesville, FL

Sandy J. Wayne
Department of Managerial Studies
University of Illinois at Chicago
Chicago, IL

Kelly Schwind Wilson
Department of Management
Purdue University
West Lafayette, IN

Junfeng Wu
Department of Managerial Studies
University of Illinois at Chicago
Chicago, IL

Le Zhou
Department of Management
University of Minnesota
Gainesville, FL

CONTENTS

Part One • Foundations of Leader–Member Exchange (LMX)

1. Leader–Member Exchange (LMX) Theory: An Introduction and Overview   3
   Talya N. Bauer and *Berrin Erdogan*
2. Leader–Member Exchange (LMX): Construct Evolution, Contributions, and Future Prospects for Advancing Leadership Theory   9
   David V. Day and *Darja Miscenko*
3. Leader–Member Exchange Measurement   29
   Robert C. Liden, Junfeng Wu, Aarn Xiaoyun Cao, and *Sandy J. Wayne*
4. Leader–Member Exchange (LMX) from the Resource Exchange Perspective: Beyond Resource Predictors and Outcomes of LMX   55
   Jared C. Law-Penrose, Kelly Schwind Wilson, and *David L. Taylor*
5. Leader–Member Exchange and Justice   67
   Suzanne S. Masterson and *Marcia L. Lensges*

Part Two • Antecedents of LMX

6. How and Why High Leader–Member Exchange (LMX) Relationships Develop: Examining the Antecedents of LMX   87
   Jennifer D. Nahrgang and *Jungmin Jamie Seo*
7. Leader and Follower Personality and LMX   119
   Birgit Schyns

Part Three • Consequences of LMX

8. LMX and Work Attitudes: Is There Anything Left Unsaid or Unexamined?   139
   Olga Epitropaki and *Robin Martin*
9. Leader–Member Exchange and Performance: Where We Are and Where We Go from Here   157
   Fadel K. Matta and *Linn Van Dyne*
10. LMX and Creativity   175
    Pamela Tierney
11. Leader–Member Exchange from a Job-Stress Perspective   189
    Sabine Sonnentag and *Alexander Pundt*
12. Leader–Member Exchange and Emotion in Organizations   209
    Herman H. M. Tse, Ashlea C. Troth, and *Neal M. Ashkanasy*
13. Leader–Member Exchange and Newcomer Adjustment   227
    Le Zhou and *Mo Wang*

14. Consequences of High LMX: Career Mobility and Success 241
    Maria L. Kraimer, Scott E. Seibert, and *Stacy L. Astrove*

Part Four • LMX Beyond the Dyad

15. LMX Differentiation: Understanding Relational Leadership
    at Individual and Group Levels 263
    Smriti Anand, Prajya R. Vidyarthi, and *Hae Sang Park*
16. Tracing Structure, Tie Strength, and Cognitive Networks in
    LMX Theory and Research 293
    Raymond T. Sparrowe and *Cécile Emery*
17. Leader–Member Exchange and Organizational Culture and Climate 311
    Vicente González-Romá

Part Five • Issues in LMX

18. "Good" Leadership: Using Corporate Social Responsibility to Enhance
    Leader–Member Exchange 335
    Drew B. Mallory and *Deborah E. Rupp*
19. Relational Leadership through the Lens of International
    LMX Research 351
    Ekin K. Pellegrini
20. Diversity and LMX Development 381
    Caren Goldberg and *Patrick F. McKay*
21. Does Age Matter to LMX and Its Outcomes? A Review and
    Future Research Directions 397
    Donald M. Truxillo and *Gabriela Burlacu*
22. Leader–Member Exchange Theory: A Glimpse into the Future 413
    Berrin Erdogan and *Talya N. Bauer*

PART 1

Foundations of Leader–Member Exchange (LMX)

Leader–Member Exchange (LMX) Theory: An Introduction and Overview

Talya N. Bauer *and* Berrin Erdogan

Abstract

Leader–member exchange (LMX) is the foremost dyadic, relational approach to leadership. Findings in LMX show that leaders are more inclusive and communicative with some members compared to others. Thus, leaders form high-quality, trust, affect, and respect-based relationships with a subset of their team, whereas they tend to have a lower-quality social exchange that is limited to the employee and the leader's job description with other members. This handbook consists of 22 chapters representing a comprehensive review of the LMX literature written by leading LMX scholars on five key aspects of LMX. Throughout the handbook, authors offer summations of the theoretical underpinnings of LMX, discuss the measurement of LMX quality, review in detail the antecedents and consequences of LMX, and explore more recent developments aimed at examining group level implications of LMX. Future research directions and recommendations for best practices for research methods and dyadic relationship nomenclature are also addressed.

Key Words: leader–member exchange, LMX, relational leadership, dyadic leadership, social exchange

Leader–member exchange (LMX) theory is the foremost dyadic theory in the leadership literature (Erdogan & Liden, 2002; Liden, Sparrowe, & Wayne, 1997). Whereas contemporary leadership theories, such as transformational, servant, or authentic leadership theories, are focused on the effects of leader behaviors on employee attitudes, motivation, and team outcomes, LMX theory views the dyadic relationship quality between leaders and members as the key to understanding leader effects on members, teams, and organizations. According to the LMX approach, leaders are closer, friendlier, more inclusive, and more communicative with some members who report to them. In other words, leaders form high-quality, trust, affect, and respect-based relationships with a subset of their team, whereas they tend to have a lower-quality exchange that is limited to the employee and the leader's job description with other members. Since its early beginnings as Vertical Dyad Linkage (VDL) theory

(Dansereau, Graen, & Haga, 1975), LMX theory has been the subject of hundreds of studies (Dulebohn, Bommer, Liden, Brouer, & Ferris, 2012; Gerstner & Day, 1997).

When we were asked by David Day to contribute a chapter on LMX to his *Oxford Handbook of Leadership and Organizations* (Erdogan & Bauer, 2014), we were excited for the opportunity to review the literature and take stock of where we have been and where we are going. As we examined the literature in depth, we were both struck by two specific things. The first was the realization that LMX has become a mature research area. It did not feel like so long ago that LMX as a research area was "wide open." However, over the years, researchers have made much progress in establishing LMX as a key construct in the leadership realm. Our second, and perhaps related, observation was the explosive growth in research attention and publications that LMX has experienced. It has been simply stunning to see the increase in activity.

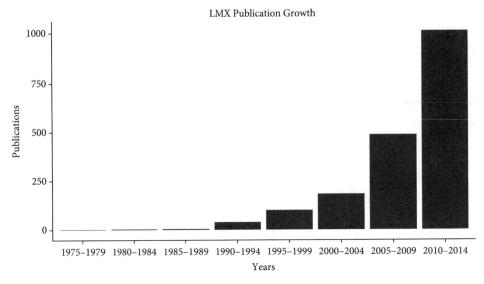

Fig. 1.1 Frequency count of articles containing LMX in the title, key words, and/or abstract in 5-year increments from 1975 to 2014 from the Web of Science database.

For example, as can be seen in Figure 1.1, as of December 31, 2014 the Web of Science database, a major online collection of abstracts and citations in the behavioral sciences, contained 1,824 articles with leader-member exchange (LMX) as a key word in the title, abstracts, and/or key words. In addition, the research pace in this area is currently accelerating, as we found that 1,010 articles (or 55% of the total number of articles identified) were published between 2010 and 2014. Similarly, the growth in citations of LMX articles has also been growing exponentially as indicated in Figure 1.2. Given the overwhelming amount of interest in this theory in the past four decades, we believe that taking stock of the literature to examine its roots, what is currently known, what research gaps may exist, and what areas are in need of the most urgent research attention is needed in order to further stimulate future studies and open up new research streams. In established fields such as LMX, the large number of studies in the literature may make it difficult to see what remains to be done or to identify areas in which little progress has been made. Moreover, the rapid growth of the literature makes it difficult for new scholars to appreciate the main contributions in the field. In this handbook, it is our intention to summarize the major developments in LMX literature so that scholars interested in this field will find it easier to get up to speed quickly and efficiently.

We organized this handbook into five sections. We start with a summary of the foundations of LMX, including its history, measurement, and key theoretical underpinnings. We next present a set of chapters that provides an overview of the literature examining antecedents. This is followed by chapters reviewing the consequences of LMX quality. Next, we summarize the recent efforts to examine the effects of LMX beyond the dyad, at the team level. The final section of the handbook includes a set of chapters that encompasses key issues of our time related to LMX.

Oxford Handbook for LMX by the Numbers

Figure 1.3 contains a summary of this handbook "by the numbers." As shown in this infographic, this handbook includes 22 chapters, contains over 180,000 words, and is written by 44 authors from 7 countries and 26 universities.

Oxford Handbook of LMX Chapter Overviews

More specifically, this handbook begins with a discussion of some of the foundations of LMX. Figure 1.4 depicts a visual summary of the 22 chapters included in this handbook. Day and Miscenko (2015) discuss the evolution of the construct of LMX, the overall contributions that have been made to date, and future prospects for the field. David Day is in a unique position to assess the place of LMX within the constellation of leadership theories, as he recently completed his role as Editor of the *Oxford Handbook of Leadership and Organizations* (Day, 2014). He also co-authored the first meta-analysis of LMX back in 1997. Those looking for an excellent overview of many

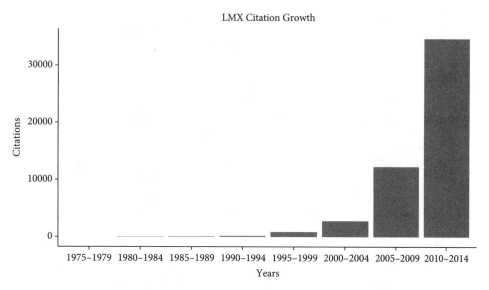

LMX Citation Growth

Fig. 1.2 Frequency count of citations to LMX articles in 5-year increments from 1975 to 2014 from the Web of Science database.

of the issues (both new and old) are encouraged to read this chapter to quickly get up to speed, and even those experienced with LMX research will likely find some new information, as this chapter takes a wide perspective. Day and Miscenko's chapter also includes a table that lists the top 30 most highly cited publications on LMX to date. It was exciting for us to see how many of the authors of those papers were also authors of chapters included in this handbook. Another foundational article in this handbook is Liden, Wu, Cao, and Wayne (2015). Their article traces the history of LMX since 1972. Reading the insider's perspective from Bob Liden, who was involved with LMX as a research topic from its beginning, feels like going back

Fig. 1.3 Handbook infographic.

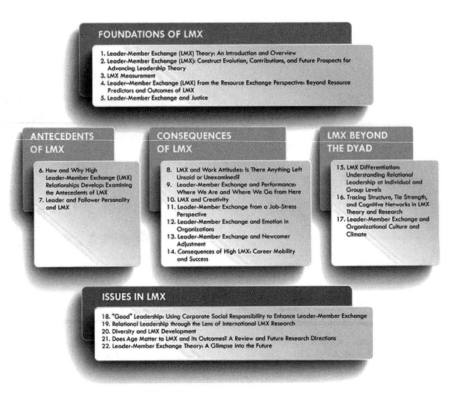

Fig. 1.4 Visual summary of *Oxford Handbook of LMX* chapters.

in time to watch the theory and research evolve. We anticipate that this article will be highly useful to present and future scholars in the area of LMX for many reasons, but one major reason is that the authors have compiled an appendix of *every* measure of LMX identified in the published literature. This treasure trove of LMX measures is now our "go to" article for any measurement questions, as we have found that having all of this information in one place is invaluable. In their chapter on the resource exchange perspective, Law-Penrose, Wilson, and Taylor (2015) delineate the specific resources that are exchanged between leaders and their subordinates. Drawing upon work by Foa and Foa (1980), and inspired by Wilson, Sin, and Conlon (2010), the authors review the literature on both antecedents and consequences that could be characterized as resources. This chapter is an important complement to the later sections of the handbook, which cover antecedents and consequences with a broader approach. Finally, Masterson and Lensges (2015) complete the handbook's foundational chapters of the LMX section with a discussion of LMX and justice. After almost 20 years, researchers are still not certain *exactly* how LMX and justice are related, but there is no doubt that there is a strong connection between the two constructs. Interested readers will benefit from this thorough review of the

many potential paths through which LMX and justice may influence one another.

Understanding the antecedents to LMX is a critical part of understanding LMX theory as a whole and helping dyads to form positive and strong relationships. However, as you will see in the review of the key antecedents by Nahrgang and Seo (2015), more work remains to be done in this area. For those looking for a fruitful area of research, we recommend focusing on key antecedents of LMX and starting by reviewing this chapter to quickly gain an understanding of the past research and conceptualization of LMX development and formation. For a more in-depth look at LMX antecedents, Schyns (2015) delves specifically into the relationship of leader and follower personality and LMX. Her focus on both negative as well as positive aspects of personality should inspire a great deal of research on this topic, a prospect that we welcome.

As LMX theory has evolved, its focus has clearly been tipped in favor of the consequences of LMX. The section of this handbook that focuses on consequences begins with a chapter by Epitropaki and Martin (2015), who delve into the black box of LMX and work attitudes relationships. We found this chapter provocative and suspect others will as well. Matta and Van Dyne (2015) review the work to date on LMX and performance, including both in-role and extra-role behaviors. Readers will find that the authors have keenly and thoroughly identified the key topics in this area, making it a "must read" for scholars interested in how LMX affects what is often considered the "bottom line" for organizations. Tierney (2015) reviews the literature on LMX and creativity and then expertly extends this discussion further by exploring how key potential mediators such as self-efficacy, identity, motivation, sensemaking, and justice may affect creative behaviors, making this a "one stop shop" for those interested on focusing on creativity and LMX. Stress is another research area that has seen explosive growth. In their chapter, Sonnentag and Pundt (2015) explain how LMX is related to stress and well–being at work as well as in a broader work–family context. Readers will find that the chapter is a good way to survey the research to date and think about research in the future. Similarly, Tse, Troth, and Ashkanasy (2015) wrote a chapter that provides an important step toward understanding how LMX and emotions interface. Although emotions have not been a major research direction to date, we see this chapter as inspiring future researchers to consider the potential this research stream has to offer the field. In their chapter on LMX and adjustment, Zhou and Wang (2015) consider the research on new employee socialization and LMX in multiple contexts, including expatriates. This is a topic that has many potential avenues for future research. Finally, Kraimer, Seibert, and Astrove (2015) review the literature on LMX and career mobility and success which continues to be an important, yet understudied aspect of psychology and management research.

The next section of the handbook includes LMX chapters that address research beyond the dyadic level. It begins with a great chapter by Anand, Vidyarthi, and Park (2015) who review the burgeoning literature on LMX differentiation. Sparrowe and Emery (2015) examine the interconnections between LMX theory and social network analysis. The figures and conceptualizations presented in this chapter should help readers unfamiliar with social network analysis to connect it with LMX. Gonzàlez-Romà (2015) examines LMX and organizational culture as well as climate. We believe that these three chapters are especially important for researchers considering where to take their next steps in the field of LMX.

Finally, we wanted this handbook to address a number of key emerging issues in the context of their implications for LMX. Mallory and Rupp (2015) set the stage by offering, "one may wonder who invited social responsibility (CSR) to the [LMX] party?" That would be us! Given the importance of corporate social responsibility (CSR) and the ways in which leaders affect CSR behaviors, we thought this was a vitally important topic to cover, and this chapter does an excellent job of laying out key issues and related literatures. In her chapter on international LMX research, Pellegrini (2015) provides a detailed account of the key issues and findings from an international perspective. Her summary table of antecedents and consequences in non-U.S. contexts is an efficient way to see what has (and has not) been examined to date. Similarly, diversity in organizations has never been more salient than it is today, and we believed it was an important issue to be specifically covered in this handbook. Goldberg and McKay (2015) do a masterful job of introducing the key issues and implications surrounding diversity and LMX. Finally, Truxillo and Burlacu (2015) bring their expertise on age and the aging worker to their chapter on LMX and its relationship to issues surrounding age and aging workers. This is truly a chapter on the cutting edge of both theory and practical issues. They conclude their chapter with a set of research questions that should serve to spark related research for years to come. Additional avenues for future research appear in the last chapter of the book (Erdogan & Bauer, 2015).

Conclusion

We set out to provide a handbook that would serve as a comprehensive primer for those new to the LMX literature, as well as a detailed summary and ideas for future research for LMX research veterans. As we noted earlier, the growth in the LMX literature has been explosive as researchers and business leaders alike begin to realize the impact LMX can have on important job outcomes such as job satisfaction, turnover, and performance. Further understanding LMX's antecedents is the key to unlocking the full potential of LMX at the dyadic, group, and organizational levels. Given its prevalent place in the context of organizational life, we also view understanding the key societal issues and implications for LMX as an important topic for inclusion and exploration. We hope that the readers of this edited volume will find the content useful, stimulating, and comprehensive. We are looking forward to witnessing and participating in the next decades of research on LMX theory.

Author Note

Material in this chapter is partially adapted, with permission from Oxford Press, from Erdogan, B., & Bauer, T. N. (2014). Leader–member exchange (LMX) theory: The relational approach to leadership. In D. Day (Ed.), *Oxford Handbook of Leadership and Organizations*. Oxford, England: Oxford University Press.

References

Anand, S., Vidyarthi, P. R., & Park, H. S. (2015). LMX differentiation: Understanding relational leadership at individual and group levels. In T. N. Bauer & B. Erdogan (Eds.), *The Oxford handbook of leader–member exchange*. Oxford, England: Oxford University Press.

Dansereau, F., Graen, G., & Haga, W. J. (1975). A vertical dyad linkage approach to leadership within formal organizations: A longitudinal investigation of the role making process. *Organizational Behavior and Human Performance*, 13, 46–78.

Day, D. (Ed.). (2014). *Oxford handbook of leadership and Organizations*. Oxford, England: Oxford University Press.

Day, D. V., & Miscenko, D. (2015). Leader–member exchange (LMX): Construct evolution, contributions, and future prospects for advancing leadership theory. In T. N. Bauer & B. Erdogan (Eds.), *The Oxford handbook of leader–member exchange*. Oxford, England: Oxford University Press.

Dulebohn, J. H., Bommer, W. H., Liden, R. C., Brouer, R. L., & Ferris, G. R. (2012). A meta-analysis of antecedents and consequences of leader–member exchange integrating the past with an eye toward the future. *Journal of Management*, 38, 1715–1759.

Epitropaki, O., & Martin, R. (2015). LMX and work attitudes: Is there anything left unsaid or unexamined? In T. N. Bauer & B. Erdogan (Eds.), *The Oxford handbook of leader–member exchange*. Oxford, England: Oxford University Press.

Erdogan, B., & Bauer, T. N. (2014). Leader–member exchange (LMX) theory: The relational approach to leadership. In D. Day (Ed.), *Oxford handbook of leadership and organizations*. (pp. 407–433). Oxford, England: Oxford University Press.

Erdogan, B., & Bauer, T. N. (2015). Leader–member exchange theory: A glimpse into the future. In T. N. Bauer & B. Erdogan (Eds.), *The Oxford handbook of leader–member exchange*. Oxford, England: Oxford University Press.

Erdogan, B., & Liden, R. C. (2002). Social exchanges in the workplace: A review of recent developments and future research directions in leader–member exchange theory. In L. L. Neider & C. A. Schriesheim (Eds.), *Leadership* (pp. 65–114). Greenwich, CT: Information Age Press.

Foa, E. B., & Foa, E. G. (1980). Resource theory. In K. J. Gergen, M. S. Greenberg, & R. H. Willis (Eds.), *Social exchange* (pp. 77–94). New York, NY: Springer.

Gerstner, C. R., & Day, D. V. (1997). Meta-analytic review of leader–member exchange theory: Correlates and construct issues. *Journal of Applied Psychology*, 82, 827–844.

Goldberg, C., & McKay, P. F. (2015). Diversity and LMX development. In T. N. Bauer & B. Erdogan (Eds.), *The Oxford handbook of leader–member exchange*. Oxford, England: Oxford University Press.

Gonzàlez-Romà, V. (2015). Leader–member exchange and organizational culture and climate. In T. N. Bauer & B. Erdogan (Eds.), *The Oxford handbook of leader–member exchange*. Oxford, England: Oxford University Press.

Kraimer, M. L., Seibert, S. E., & Astrove, S. L. (2015). Consequences of high LMX: Career mobility and success. In T. N. Bauer & B. Erdogan (Eds.), *The Oxford handbook of leader–member exchange*. Oxford, England: Oxford University Press.

Law-Penrose, J. C., Wilson, K. S., & Taylor, D. (2015). Leader–member exchange (LMX) from the resource exchange perspective: Beyond resource predictors and outcomes of LMX. In T. N. Bauer & B. Erdogan (Eds.), *The Oxford handbook of leader–member exchange*. Oxford, England: Oxford University Press.

Liden, R. C., Sparrowe, R. T., & Wayne, S. J. (1997). Leader–member exchange theory: The past and potential for the future. *Research in Personnel and Human Resources Management*, 15, 47–119.

Liden, R., Wu, J., Cao, A. X., & Wayne, S. J. (2015). LMX measurement. In T. N. Bauer & B. Erdogan (Eds.), *The Oxford handbook of leader–member exchange*. Oxford, England: Oxford University Press.

Mallory, D. B., & Rupp, D. E. (2015). "Good" leadership: Using corporate social responsibility to enhance leader–member exchange. In T. N. Bauer & B. Erdogan (Eds.), *The Oxford handbook of leader–member exchange*. Oxford, England: Oxford University Press.

Masterson, S., & Lensges, M. (2015). Leader-member exchange and justice. In T. N. Bauer & B. Erdogan (Eds.), *The Oxford handbook of leader–member exchange*. Oxford, England: Oxford University Press.

Matta, F. K., & Van Dyne, L. (2015). Leader–member exchange and performance: Where we are and where we go from here. In T. N. Bauer & B. Erdogan (Eds.), *The Oxford handbook of leader–member exchange*. Oxford, England: Oxford University Press.

Nahrgang, J. D., & Seo, J. J. (2015). How and why high leader–member exchange (LMX) relationships develop: Examining the antecedents of LMX. In T. N. Bauer & B. Erdogan (Eds.), *The Oxford handbook of leader–member exchange*. Oxford, England: Oxford University Press.

Pellegrini, E. K. (2015). Relational leadership through the lens of international LMX research. In T. N. Bauer & B. Erdogan (Eds.), *The Oxford handbook of leader–member exchange*. Oxford, England: Oxford University Press.

Schyns, B. (2015). Leader and follower personality and LMX. In T. N. Bauer & B. Erdogan (Eds.), *The Oxford handbook of leader–member exchange*. Oxford, England: Oxford University Press.

Sonnentag, S., & Pundt, A. (2015). Leader–member exchange from a job-stress perspective. In T. N. Bauer & B. Erdogan (Eds.), *The Oxford handbook of leader–member exchange*. Oxford, England: Oxford University Press.

Sparrowe, R. T., & Emery, C. (2015). Tracing structure, tie strength, and cognitive networks in LMX theory and research. In T. N. Bauer & B. Erdogan (Eds.), *The Oxford handbook of leader–member exchange*. Oxford, England: Oxford University Press.

Tierney, P. (2015). LMX and creativity. In T. N. Bauer & B. Erdogan (Eds.), *The Oxford handbook of leader–member exchange*. Oxford, England: Oxford University Press.

Truxillo, D. M., & Burlacu, G. (2015). Does age matter to LMX and its outcomes? A review and future research directions. In T. N. Bauer & B. Erdogan (Eds.), *The Oxford handbook of leader–member exchange*. Oxford, England: Oxford University Press.

Tse, H. H. M., Troth, A. C., & Ashkanasy, N. M. (2015). Leader-member exchange and emotion in organizations. In T. N. Bauer & B. Erdogan (Eds.), *The Oxford handbook of leader–member exchange*. Oxford, England: Oxford University Press.

Wilson, K. S., Sin, H. P., & Conlon, D. E. (2010). What about the leader in leader–member exchange? The impact of resource exchanges and substitutability on the leader. *Academy of Management Review*, 35, 358–372.

Zhou, L., & Wang, M. (2015). Leader–member exchange and newcomer adjustment. In T. N. Bauer & B. Erdogan (Eds.), *The Oxford handbook of leader–member exchange*. Oxford, England: Oxford University Press.

Leader–Member Exchange (LMX): Construct Evolution, Contributions, and Future Prospects for Advancing Leadership Theory

David V. Day *and* Darja Miscenko

Abstract

Leader–member exchange (LMX) is a highly influential leadership theory that has continued to evolve over the past four decades. Compared with other scholarly approaches in the study of leadership, LMX stands out with its focus on the (potentially) unique relationship between a leader and a follower. The purpose of this essay is to give an overview of important developments within LMX research as indicated by highly cited publications and to understand how LMX theory relates to other active approaches to leadership (specifically, personality-based, contextual, information processing, and new leadership schools). Finally, the essay provides future directions for the LMX theory-building and research by suggesting that the latest methodological tools, as well as the theoretical roots of LMX, can inform and stimulate deeper understanding and study of the relational leadership.

Key Words: Leader–member exchange, relational leadership, vertical dyad linkage, leadership theories, research methods, multilevel models

Across a time span of more than four decades, leader–member exchange (LMX) theory has made many valuable contributions to advancing the scholarly leadership literature. Research and theory development related to LMX represent a highly active area of study that continues to evolve well into the 21st century. LMX has outlived approaches such as contingency theories and behavioral theories of leadership, which are presently inactive in terms of ongoing research (Day & Antonakis, 2012). Research based on LMX theory has also spawned thus far four meta-analyses examining antecedents, consequences, and correlates of LMX (Dulebohn, Bommer, Liden, Brouer, & Ferris, 2012; Gerstner & Day, 1997; Ilies, Nahrgang, & Morgeson, 2007; Rockstuhl, Dulebohn, Ang, & Shore, 2012). What is remarkable about LMX as a subfield of leadership research is that it has gone

through several evolutions that have taken it from its origins as a vertical dyad linkage approach to what is presently conceptualized as relational leadership theory (see Erdogan & Bauer, 2014).

LMX theory stands out among the many scholarly leadership approaches with its unique focus on the leader–follower (or supervisor–subordinate) dyad. As noted by others, LMX theory is "the foremost dyadic theory in the leadership literature" (Erdogan & Bauer, 2014, p. 407). Other leadership theories tend to emphasize the individual leader (i.e., leader–centric in focus) and study the effects of a leader on employee attitudes, motivation, and performance. More recently, interest is emerging in shared leadership (Pearce & Conger, 2003) and broader conceptualizations of a shared leadership capacity (Day, Gronn, & Salas, 2004) that can develop in teams and organizations and transcends the effects associated with any individual leader. By focusing on the dyad, LMX occupies a unique space between the many individual-level leadership theories (e.g., leader traits and behavior, transformational leadership, servant leadership) and the more nascent forms of shared and collective leadership. This is also important because LMX is the only leadership theory that focuses tightly on the relationship between a leader and his or her followers. As suggested by Gerstner and Day (1997) the relationship with one's boss is a lens through which the entire work experience is viewed. Although this may come across as hyperbole, there is ample evidence to suggest that it has evidence-based support.

Another unique feature of LMX theory as compared to other leadership theories is its foundation in differentiated relationships with followers. A key premise that spawned the development of LMX theory was that leaders tend to have high-quality relationships with only some of their employees (Erdogan & Bauer, 2014). As research evolves to include a focus on LMX differentiation (i.e., within group variation of exchange quality) and its effects on individual- and workgroup-level outcomes, there is a new trend toward situating exchange relationships within the broader group context. In this way LMX is broadening its horizons beyond a focus on dyadic exchange to more relational approaches that consider dyads relationally within a group context. This is a relatively new development in LMX theory that will be revisited later in this essay.

In providing an overview of theoretical developments and the positioning of LMX among the broader constellations of leadership theory, the purpose of this essay is to highlight the contributions of LMX theory to the leadership field, understand its position relationally with other active approaches to leadership, highlight important developments within the field of LMX research, and to look to the future as to what are likely additional developments and needs with regard to theory-building and research.

The first section of this essay will summarize in a decade-by-decade fashion the major contributions made to LMX theory and research as indicated by citation counts in the literature. The most active schools of leadership research are those that publish the most and attract the most citations. LMX is considered to be one of those highly active schools of research over the previous 40+ years (Day & Antonakis, 2012). In referencing citation counts there is always some degree of potential historical bias to consider in that everything equal older

articles are cited more than recent ones (Antonakis, Bastardoz, Liu, & Schriesheim, 2014). Nonetheless, it may be of interest to see which of the many LMX articles have had relatively more impact on the field by virtue of the number of citations received. The narrative focus will be on those articles receiving 100 or more citations as noted by Thomson Reuters Web of Science™ statistics with the acknowledgment that this provides an advantage to those articles published earlier in the lifespan of the theory. In recent research on highly cited articles published in *The Leadership Quarterly* (Antonakis et al., 2014) it was noted that only approximately 6% of the articles published in that journal had 100 or more citations. Thus, we will review articles that have achieved what could be considered the elite levels of the publication distribution in the leadership field.

The second section of this essay will adopt a relational perspective in examining LMX in the context of other active leadership approaches. In particular, the review will focus on LMX in relation to trait or personality-based approaches to leadership; contextual approaches that include aspects of culture, diversity, and levels of analyses; the so-called new leadership approaches that include neocharismatic/transformational/visionary leadership; and information processing approaches that include topics such as implicit leadership theories, leadership prototypes, and categorization and social theories. These approaches were chosen as referents because they remain very active—along with LMX—in terms of ongoing research and theory building. Behavioral, contingency, and skeptics of leadership approaches will not be considered because they are generally inactive in terms of 21st century research (Day & Antonakis, 2012).

The third and final section of this essay will look at recent developments in LMX theory and research, and will provide a glimpse into the future by suggesting where researchers need to focus to make further contributions to the leadership field in general, and LMX theory, in particular. This will help provide a foundation on which other essays in this handbook can build in terms of understanding the myriad facets of LMX theory and its place within the broader constellation of leadership theories.

The Evolution of LMX

Erdogan and Bauer (2014) noted in their review of LMX theory that there are more than 700 references to articles with *leader–member exchange* in the title or as a key word in the abstract. What is remarkable is that nearly 50% of the articles in the PsycInfo database were published in the years 2006–2010. It appears from these data that interest in LMX is not only sustained over the previous four decades but is getting stronger.

The present approach to tracking the evolution of LMX theory and research over time is different from what was conducted by Erdogan and Bauer (2014). Specifically, this essay will provide an overview of scholarly impact of the LMX literature as measured by citation counts to individual articles as indexed in the Web of Science. Figure 2.1 plots the citations by year of those published articles demonstrating the largest impact in terms of citations (as of February 2014). From 1975 until 2000, only those articles with at least 100 citations are plotted. From 2000 to 2012, most of the articles included in the review had 100 or more citations, but this time period also includes a few articles with 50 or more citations. Those in the latter category were considered to offer novel insights such as applying LMX in a new domain or offering new theoretical extensions to the theory. The cutoffs with regard to minimum citation numbers are admittedly somewhat arbitrary, but doing so provides an overview snapshot of those articles that seem to have made significant impact (approximately the 95th percentile in terms of citation counts) on the direction of the LMX field.

As presented in Figure 2.1, there are four publications that have received 500 or more citations,

respectively. Collectively these might be considered the "Big 4" of LMX scholarship, having shown the most impact in shaping the field. Leading the way with 965 citations is a narrative review of LMX theory (Graen & Uhl-Bien, 1995), which also happens to be the most cited article across the 25 years that *The Leadership Quarterly* has been in publication (Antonakis et al., 2014). The next most cited piece with 683 citations is an empirical article examining the relationships between perceived organizational support and LMX (Wayne, Shore, & Liden, 1997). Third on the list of the Big 4 with 680 citations is the foundational article establishing the vertical dyad linkage (VDL) approach to leadership within formal organizations (Dansereau, Graen, & Haga, 1975). As elaborated in a subsequent section of this essay, one of the major evolutions in the history of LMX theory is the transition from VDL approaches to what became LMX beginning in the early 1980s. Rounding out the Big 4 list with 597 citations is the first published meta-analytical review of LMX theory constructs and correlates (Gerstner & Day, 1997).

Other notable contributions to the LMX literature according to citation counts include an early narrative review and critique of the theory (403 citations; Dienesch & Liden, 1986), a longitudinal study of the early development of LMXs (308 citations; Liden, Wayne, & Stilwell, 1993), another article examining social exchanges in organizations

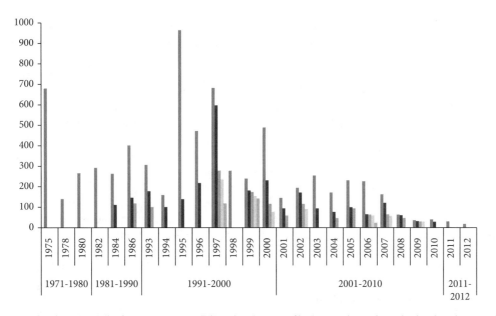

Fig. 2.1 Most cited articles (Web of Science citations) dedicated to the topic of leader–member exchange by decade and year. Each bar represents an article published in the respective year (i.e., in 1997 there were five highly cited articles published). The *y*-axis represents the number of times each article has been cited.

linking perceived organizational support (POS) with LMX (472 citations; Settoon, Bennett, & Liden, 1996), and an article examining the role of procedural and interactional justice on social exchange relationships as measured by LMX (490 citations; Masterson, Lewis, Goldman, & Taylor, 2000). Table 2.1 presents a list of the top 30 most highly cited LMX publications and a brief summary of the respective contribution for each article.

A critical question is whether these citation counts are indicative of major impact on the field, in general, as compared with other leadership theories. That might be worth considering in a broader treatment of leadership literature, but the point is not whether LMX has had a major impact relative to other theories but rather what are some of the most important concerns that have helped to sustain interest in the topic for nearly a half century. Not surprisingly, reviews (quantitative and narrative) are highly represented on this list of most cited LMX articles. Perhaps more surprising is the influence that articles integrating LMX with constructs such as POS and justice have had in terms of impact. Although an early longitudinal study is represented in the second half of this most-cited list, it is also the case that longitudinal approaches to studying LMX are still desperately underrepresented in the leadership literature (Day, 2014).

It is also the case that citation counts alone do not tell the entire story with regard to quality or impact of a particular article; however, citation counts do provide a ready proxy for estimating some degree of impact, indicating a particular level of interest and influence in shaping the field. Although it may be possible for a paper to be cited for all the wrong reasons such as making claims that are not subsequently supported (but none such articles come readily to mind) for the most part high levels of citations indicates a disproportionate level of impact on the development of a discipline relative to low or moderately cited pieces. Nonetheless, it should also be noted that there are plenty of other papers that have shaped the LMX field—or will shape the field in the future—that may not have been cited as much as some other pieces.

In order to provide a more complete overview or overall picture of the LMX field since inception, Figure 2.2 charts the number of highly cited (100 or more) LMX publications from 1975 through 2012 along with the number of citations during that same time span. What is interesting to note is the general climb in both the number of highly cited publications and the number of citations spiking in 1997.

There was a drop in highly cited LMX publications in 1998 but a return to a strong level of publication output from 1999 through 2002 and then spiking again in 2006. Despite this publication output of influential works the number of citations has not returned to 1997 levels. It is difficult to understand the reasons for this drop in citations relative to publication other than it being attributable to an historical artifact (i.e., bias for older articles to draw more citations as compared with more recent articles). It is also the case that two of the so-called Big 4 articles were published in 1997 (Gerstner & Day, 1997; Wayne et al., 1997). The overview of the evolution of LMX theory in this essay will next focus on what are some of the more influential or pivotal pieces of LMX scholarship by decade from the 1970s to the present. This is presented as a way of potentially providing deeper insights into the evolution of LMX theory.

The 1970s

The origins of LMX theory can be traced to the introduction of VDL theory in the mid-1970s (Dansereau et al., 1975). Most of the early work is focused on developing the theoretical foundation for VDL and establishing its construct validity (Graen & Schiemann, 1978; Liden & Graen, 1980). A novel insight offered by Dansereau et al. (1975) was that traditional leadership theory rested on two assumptions, neither of which seemed legitimate. The first assumption was that members of a group or organizational unit reporting to the same supervisor (i.e., leader) are relatively homogenous in terms of their perceptions, interpretations, and reactions such that they could be considered as a single entity or work group (this was well before what we know today about aggregation statistics). A second assumption is that a supervisor behaves in the same prescribed manner toward each of his or her subordinates (i.e., they develop undifferentiated exchanges with their direct reports). This is the so-called *average leadership style* assumption that is characteristic of most leadership approaches and epitomized in the behavioral descriptions from the Ohio State leadership studies (Stogdill & Coons, 1957). Indeed, Dansereau et al. (1975) claimed that after decades of active research organizational leadership models "have failed to develop beyond rather primitive levels" (p. 47). Thus, an appropriate focus theoretically and analytically is on each of the dyadic relationships within a workgroup. This recommendation was made before greater insights were developed regarding potential biases and other

Table 2.1. Review and Summary of Top 30 Highly Cited LMX Publications.

Rank	Citations	Reference	Summary
1	965	Graen and Uhl-Bien (1995)	Narrative review of LMX theory tracing the development of LMX and proposing a new taxonomy of approaches to leadership in which LMX is positioned as a relationship-based approach.
2	683	Wayne et al. (1997)	Proposed a model of the relationship between LMX and perceived organizational support (POS) based on social exchange theory. Findings suggested that LMX and POS have unique antecedents and differentially relate to the outcome variables.
3	680	Dansereau et al. (1975)	Foundational article that established the vertical dyad linkage (VDL) approach to leadership. Based on the results of longitudinal investigation, authors proposed that superiors develop different exchange relationships with their members.
4	597	Gerstner and Day (1997)	First published meta-analytical review of LMX theory constructs and correlates, including job performance, satisfaction, and turnover intentions. In addition, authors examined issues related to LMX measurement and leader–member agreement.
5	490	Masterson et al. (2000)	Empirical study showing interactional justice affecting supervisor-related outcomes via LMX mediation, whereas procedural justice affects organization-related outcomes via POS.
6	472	Settoon et al. (1996)	Based on social exchange theory and the norm of reciprocity, study demonstrates that LMX is associated with citizenship and in-role behavior, whereas POS is associated with organizational commitment.
7	403	Dienesch and Liden (1986)	An early review of LMX literature highlighting a number of methodological and theoretical issues; multidimensional conceptualization of LMX proposed along with associated developmental process.
8	308	Liden et al. (1993)	Longitudinal study on the early development of LMX showing that affective variables such as expectations and perceived similarity predict LMX better than subordinate performance ratings.
9	294	Graen et al. (1982)	Field experiment showing that LMX condition results in significant gains in satisfaction and productivity, whereas job design condition had no effect.
10	281	Liden and Maslyn (1998)	Developed and validated a multidimensional measure of LMX with four dimensions: affect, loyalty, contribution, and professional respect.
11	280	Liden et al. (1997)	Narrative review and categorization of LMX antecedents and consequences. Authors also discussed a number of suggestions to improve LMX theory and empirical research.
12	267	Liden and Graen (1980)	Empirical study establishing the validity and generalizability of VDL approach to leadership showing that the quality of relationship with one's supervisor is positively related to subordinate performance.
13	264	Scandura and Graen (1984)	Field experiment testing how initial LMX quality moderates the effects of a leadership intervention on productivity, satisfaction, and supervisor support; the initially low-LMX group showed significantly higher gains across outcomes compared to initially high-LMX group.
14	256	Hofmann et al. (2003)	Building on role theory, social exchange, and organizational citizenship in the context of safety climate, results suggested the relationship between LMX and subordinate citizenship role definitions was moderated by climate.

(continued)

Table 2.1. Continued

Rank	Citations	Reference	Summary
15	241	Tierney et al. (1999)	Development and test of a multidomain, interactive creativity model, suggesting that LMX and the interaction between LMX and employee cognitive style positively relate to employee creative performance.
16	236	Sparrowe and Liden (1997)	Using insights from social network analysis, a conceptual LMX process and structure model is proposed that more fully encompasses reciprocity and differentiation beyond the formal leader–subordinate relationship.
17	233	Liden et al. (2000)	LMX and team–member exchange (TMX) directly relate to organizational commitment; contrary to expectations, this relationship was not mediated by empowerment.
18	231	Wang et al. (2005)	In a sample of Chinese employees, LMX fully mediates the relationship between transformational leadership and task performance, as well as organizational citizenship behaviors (OCB).
19	227	Piccolo and Colquitt (2006)	Structural model proposed and tested in which the relationships between transformational leadership and task performance, as well as OCB, were significantly stronger for followers with high perceived LMX.
20	218	Bauer and Green (1996)	Longitudinal study examining the development of LMX with a sample of new subordinates; results suggest that LMX quality is related to positive affectivity similarity, performance, and delegation, but not gender similarity.
21	194	Cropanzano et al. (2002)	Support found for the proposition that procedural justice associated with reactions to organization, whereas interactional justice associated with reactions toward one's supervisor, with LMX mediating the latter relationship.
22	182	Hofmann and Morgeson (1999)	Extending the application of LMX into safety domain showing that LMX quality is positively and significantly related to safety communication, safety commitment, and accidents.
23	179	Judge and Ferris (1993)	Model of the performance-rating process proposed and tested including several social and situational variables, with results suggesting that LMX is related to supervisor's rating of subordinate's performance via mediation of supervisor's affect toward subordinate.
24	175	Schriesheim et al. (1999)	Narrative review of theoretical, measurement, and analytical adequacy of LMX studies; conclusion that disparity of definitions and measurements of LMX may have undermined research findings.
25	173	Janssen and Van Yperen (2004)	In a sample of Dutch employees, LMX quality mediates the relationship between a mastery orientation and in-role job performance, as well as job satisfaction.
26	173	Wayne et al. (2002)	Antecedents and consequences of LMX and POS examined with results suggesting that contingent reward was related to LMX, whereas LMX predicted performance ratings.
27	164	Ilies et al. (2007)	Meta-analytical review reporting a strong, positive relationship between LMX and OCB; LMX was a stronger predictor of individual-targeted than organizational targeted behaviors.
28	159	Scandura and Schriesheim (1994)	Empirical study suggesting that LMX and mentoring are distinct constructs from supervisor's perspective, but not subordinate's; LMX and mentoring each found to account for incremental variance in performance and promotion rate.

(*continued*)

Table 2.1. Continued

Rank	Citations	Reference	Summary
29	154	Howell and Hall-Merenda (1999)	Based on a longitudinal study, LMX positively relates to transformational leadership, and that the effects of LMX on follower performance are positive irrespective of physical distance.
30	148	Duchon et al. (1986)	Data from a longitudinal field study suggesting sociometric assessment of LMX converges with conventional measures; demographic variables predict LMX quality but unrelated to job enrichment and satisfaction.

Note. Citation counts from Thomson Reuters Web of Science™ as of March 17, 2014.

problems with data nonindependence where multiple followers report to the same leader (Bliese & Hanges, 2004). An emerging theme in this narrative review is that advances in theory and research related to levels-of-analyses issues have been particularly helpful in advancing LMX theory.

Another unique feature of VDL theory was its focus on the role making process. Specifically, the degree of latitude that a supervisor provides a subordinate in negotiating a work role was found to be related over time to subsequent behavior on the part of both the supervisor and the subordinate. This notion of *negotiating latitude* was defined as the extent to which a supervisor was willing to consider requests from a subordinate on matters concerning role development. Those subordinates who had latitude to negotiate their roles were thought

to hold an important resource in the form of negotiating latitude strength. What has not been examined is whether having greater negotiating latitude strength by virtue of being in a leader's in-group also enhances something like role breadth self-efficacy or the perceived capability of carrying out a broader set of work tasks (Parker, 1998).

The 1980s

During the 1980s the theoretical focus shifted from VDL to LMX, bringing with it the first empirical tests of the latter construct (Graen, Novak, & Sommerkamp, 1982). What differentiates these two leadership constructs is subtle with VDL emphasizing the notion of differentiated exchanges and LMX focusing primarily on relational domains of jobs in addition to task domains. In other words, someone's

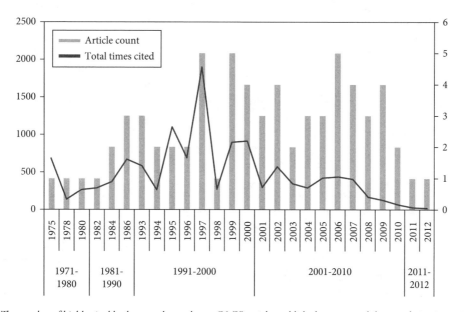

Fig. 2.2 The number of highly cited leader–member exchange (LMX) articles published per year and the cumulative times cited (Web of Science citations). Each bar shows the number of articles per given year (on a secondary *y*-axis). The primary *y*-axis and the line represent the total times cited for the articles published in the given year. For example, in 2000 there were a total of four highly cited LMX articles published and cumulatively those were cited 916 times.

response to a job is a function of relational variables (especially the relationship with a leader or supervisor), job variables, and their interactions. In this manner early manifestations and tests of LMX were considered to be extensions of job design frameworks, especially the job characteristics model (Hackman & Oldham, 1976).

This decade was a transitional one in terms of theoretical focus, with nearly an equal number of articles focusing on VDL (Duchon, Green, & Taber, 1986; Liden & Graen, 1980; Vecchio & Gobdel, 1984) as on LMX (Graen et al., 1982; Scandura & Graen, 1984; Scandura, Graen, & Novak, 1986). Notable among these publications is the finding that 90% of the time leaders develop differentiated exchanges with their followers (Liden & Graen, 1980). Also notable in this decade was the publication of the first highly cited review and critique of LMX theory (Dienesch & Liden, 1986).

The 1990s

The LMX literature started coming into its own during this decade and by the mid-1990s there was an accumulated body of scholarship that could be quantitatively reviewed using meta-analytic techniques (Gerstner & Day, 1997), which among other things allows researchers to estimate effects across studies and to correct for sampling error. In the beginning of the decade, the construct of organizational citizenship behavior (OCB) was integrated into LMX literature (Deluga, 1994; Wayne & Green, 1993), followed by perceived organizational support (POS) in later years (Hofmann & Morgeson, 1999; Hui, Law, & Chen, 1999; Settoon et al., 1996; Wayne et al., 1997).

During this decade there were a couple of articles examining the development of LMX over time (Liden et al., 1993; Bauer & Green, 1996); however, this research preceded advances in the areas of growth modeling (Singer & Willett, 2003) that offer more accurate and robust approaches to modeling change over time. In terms of cross-sectional research, LMX was examined as a predictor of employee work outcomes such as organizational commitment, turnover intention, and job satisfaction (Major, Kozlowski, Chao, & Gardner, 1995); performance ratings (Howell & Hall-Merenda, 1999; Judge & Ferris, 1993); and employee creativity (Tierney, Farmer, & Graen, 1999).

Several review papers were published in the second half of the decade, starting with the highly cited qualitative narrative review of the relation-based approach to leadership (Graen & Uhl-Bien, 1995). This was followed by a quantitative review in the form of a meta-analysis (Gerstner & Day, 1997), and three additional narrative reviews (Liden, Sparrowe, & Wayne, 1997; Schriesheim, Castro, & Cogliser, 1999; Sparrowe & Liden, 1997). In terms of the relationship between LMX and job attitudes, Gerstner and Day (1997) reported an average corrected correlation of .46 between LMX and job satisfaction and .35 for organizational commitment. These findings suggest some very robust relationships between LMX and job attitudes; however, because both LMX and the attitudinal variables tended to be measured from the perspective of the follower, these estimated effects are likely upwardly biased to some extent due to common source issues. Another interesting finding to emerge from this meta-analysis was that the average correlation between the leader's and the member's rating of the same exchange quality was only around .30. This is a provocative finding in that it suggests only around 10% of the variance in exchange quality can be explained by the shared leader–member perceptions, which remains as an issue to be fully understood more than two decades later (Sin, Nahrgang, & Morgeson, 2009).

2000–Present

The new millennium has seen even greater research interest in LMX. Rather than losing its appeal, researchers are discovering new and interesting ways of integrating LMX with different constructs, theories, and processes. For example, researchers have integrated LMX with areas such as trust building (Brower, Schoorman, & Tan, 2000), attribution theory (Dasborough & Ashkanasy, 2002; Davis & Gardner, 2004), social network perspectives (Sparrowe & Liden, 2005), nonlinear effects (Harris & Kacmar, 2006), and employee voice (Burris, Detert, & Chiaburu, 2008). In addition, several articles investigated LMX in conjunction with organizational justice (Masterson et al., 2000; Cropanzano, Prehar, & Chen, 2002; Erdogan, Liden, & Kraimer, 2006; Walumbwa, Cropanzano, & Hartnell, 2009) and empowerment (G. Chen, Kirkman, Kanfer, Allen, & Rosen, 2007; Z. Chen, Lam, & Zhong, 2007; Gómez & Rosen, 2001).

LMX researchers also continued to propose and examine models that combined LMX and its well-known correlates. OCB and POS remained as popular constructs to study in conjunction with LMX across a variety of contexts (Dulac,

Coyle-Shapiro, Henderson, & Wayne, 2008; Erdogan & Enders, 2007; Erdogan, Kraimer, & Liden, 2004; Hofmann, Morgeson, & Gerras, 2003; Kraimer, Wayne, & Jaworski, 2001; Piccolo & Colquitt, 2006; Wang, Law, Hackett, Wang, & Chen, 2005; Wayne, Shore, Bommer, & Tetrick, 2002). At the same time, some articles proposed novel antecedents of LMX, such as effort (Maslyn & Uhl-Bien, 2001), implicit leadership theories (Epitropaki & Martin, 2005), as well as how personality and performance shape the development of LMX relationships over time (Nahrgang, Morgeson, & Ilies, 2009).

A promising development in the second half of the decade involved the construct of LMX differentiation (i.e., variability in LMX quality among members of a workgroup). This harkens back to the foundations of VDL/LMX theory in terms of leaders differentiating relationships with followers (Henderson, Wayne, Shore, Bommer, & Tetrick, 2008; Liao, Liu, & Loi, 2010; Liden, Erdogan, Wayne, & Sparrowe, 2006). This is an especially important development in the LMX literature because it widens the lens to consider multilevel and group effects asociated with LMX. This not only advances LMX theory but also provides opportunities for researchers to use state-of-the-art procedures in modeling LMX effects across levels. Although results to date suggest that LMX differentiation does not appear to have a universally positive or negative effect on group or team outcomes, this is a topic that will certainly be the focus of research attention in the coming years. Of particular interest is the link between LMX differentiation and fairness perceptions among members of a workgroup (Erdogan & Bauer, 2014).

Given the rapidly developing literature on LMX it is not surprising that two additional meta-analyses were published during this time. The first provided a meta-analytic review of the relationship between LMX and citizenship behaviors enacted by employees (Ilies et al., 2007). Results suggested a strong, positive relationship between LMX and OCB that was significantly stronger when the target of the citizenship behavior was at the individual as compared with the organizational level. More recently, an update and extension of the Gerstner and Day (1997) LMX meta-analysis concluded that "results demonstrated that LMX frequently plays a mediating role in the relationships where mediation could be tested" (Dulebohn et al., 2012, p. 1716). In addition to demonstrating significant mediating effects there is a need to more fully develop process

models of leadership that examine not just LMX as a measure but identify and test the underlying role-making processes that mediate between antecedents and outcomes (Day & Antonakis, 2013).

The previous section reviewed the evolution of LMX theory and research focusing on the most highly cited works in a decade-by-decade manner. What has always been central to the unique focus of LMX is the notion of differentiated relationships with followers. After more than 40 years this issue is starting to gain research traction through interest in LMX differentiation in groups using multilevel modeling procedures. In this way LMX is evolving from mainly an individual and dyadic focus to one that crosses dyad-group levels. Advances in multilevel modeling techniques have helped researchers in taking their ideas to the next level (pun intended) in extending the LMX literature.

The next section takes a relational perspective with regard to LMX. That is, the focus is on examining how LMX theory and research has been informed by other prominent (and currently active) leadership approaches including trait theories, contextual approaches, and "New Leadership" theories. A purpose in doing this is to potentially foster more integrative leadership approaches and more integrative ways of researching leadership. To further widen the lens in terms of literature that is reviewed, the following section does not consider only highly cited articles but includes relevant research regardless of impact.

LMX in Relation to Other Leadership Theories

Trait Theories of Leadership

The so-called "great man" [sic] or trait-based perspective is the oldest approach to studying leadership. The approach is characterized by its attempt to identify the core traits of effective leaders. The trait approach to leadership has waxed and waned (and waxed again) as an active field of research (Day & Antonakis, 2012). Of interest in this essay section is reviewing the research that has attempted to link leader/follower personality with LMX.

One development that has reinvigorated trait-based approaches to leadership is the introduction and adoption of the Big Five factors of personality (*viz.* conscientiousness, agreeableness, neuroticism, openness to experience, and extraversion). This personality framework has given researchers a common language and measurement approach to the study of human personality. Although the personality traits of leaders are at the core of the trait-based approach, more studies have investigated follower rather than leader traits as antecedents of LMX quality. The most recent meta-analysis of LMX noted 11 studies examining follower extraversion as a predictor of LMX, but only four studies have looked at leader extraversion (Dulebohn et al., 2012). Nevertheless, this same meta-analysis showed that leader extraversion and agreeableness have significant positive relationships with LMX quality. For example, a longitudinal study that examined the development of LMX quality over time found that leader agreeableness was positively associated with LMX at the time of initial interaction (Nahrgang et al., 2009). Similarly, leader agreeableness was found to predict subordinates' perception of LMX quality and this relationship was mediated by liking of the leader (Sears & Hackett, 2011). Overall, this is somewhat consistent with meta-analytic findings that extraversion is the most consistent correlate of leadership (Judge, Bono, Ilies, & Gerhardt, 2002) and that it has some effect in shaping the quality of exchange that develops between a leader and a follower.

Apart from Big Five personality traits, a leader's locus of control has been found to be positively related to LMX quality (Barbuto, Weltmer, & Pennisi, 2010) with other leader traits predicting subordinates' LMX ratings only in certain contexts. For example, leader self-efficacy and optimism predicted subordinates' ratings of LMX quality only for female supervisors (Murphy & Ensher, 1999). As noted, there are fewer studies in the literature that have examined leader (compared with follower) traits in relation to LMX, which is somewhat surprising given that trait and relational theories are among the most influential and longstanding of those in the scholarly leadership literature. One area for future research consideration might be investigating whether LMX potentially mediates the relationship between leader traits and employee outcomes or leadership effectiveness.

Another area that has been examined concerns the notion of leader–follower personality similarity and its effect on LMX quality. Leader–follower differences in emotional stability, intellectual openness, agreeableness, and conscientiousness were found to be negatively related to employees' perceived LMX quality (Bernerth, Armenakis, Feild, Giles, & Walker, 2008). In addition, similarity in leader–follower emotional intelligence was associated with higher employee reports of exchange quality (Sears & Holmvall, 2010), whereas leader–follower congruence in proactive personality was

related to higher-quality LMX, which was associated in turn with higher levels of job satisfaction, affective commitment, and performance (Zhang, Wang, & Shi, 2012). Nonetheless, it should be noted that some studies have found a negative relationship between personality similarity and LMX (e.g., Oren, Tziner, Sharoni, Amor, & Alon, 2012). These findings suggest a potential need for more nuanced research in distinguishing what personal aspects are most important in terms of their similarity when it comes to enhancing overall exchange quality. Another potential application of trait theory with LMX would involve examining how leader traits moderate the relationship between certain contextual variables and LMX. For example, physical distance and interaction frequency were found to have a negative effect on LMX, but this relationship was buffered by a leader's psychological capital (Story, Youssef, Luthans, Barbuto, & Bovaird, 2013).

Contextual Schools of Leadership

Emerging as a leadership approach extending, and to some extent replacing, contingency theories of leadership, the contextual schools conceptualize various factors that are thought to enhance or inhibit particular leadership behaviors or their dispositional antecedents (Liden & Antonakis, 2009). Of particular interest to LMX researchers have been the contextual factors of national culture, levels of analyses (workgroup and organization), and LMX as a contextual variable itself.

National culture. Research suggests that national culture moderates relationships between LMX quality and some of its correlates. In other words, LMX may operate somewhat differently depending on the culture in which it is studied. Differences were shown to exist between individualistic and collectivistic cultures in terms of relationships between LMX and OCB, justice perceptions, job satisfaction, and turnover intentions (Rockstuhl et al., 2012). But this meta-analysis found that national culture does not alter the relationships between LMX and task performance, organizational commitment, or transformational leadership. Although it is not always easy to draw meaningful inferences from null findings, taken together these results suggest that there may be some cultural universals as well as culturally contingent effects with regard to LMX similar to what was demonstrated in the Project GLOBE research (House, Hanges, Javidan, Dorfman, & Gupta, 2004).

Even across what might be considered relatively similar cultures there is evidence of differences in the effects of LMX. For example, a comparison of research in United States and Germany revealed that antecedents are related to LMX to a lower degree in Germany and consequences to a higher degree (Schyns, Paul, Mohr, & Blank, 2005). The research evidence suggests that that some differences might also exist across Eastern cultures. For example, a recent study showed that LMX quality had a significant negative relationship with work turnover intentions in China but not in Korea (Kim, Lee, & Lee, 2013). An interesting avenue of research in relation to national culture is to consider LMX in the context of non-Western leadership styles, such as paternalistic leadership. Initial evidence suggests that paternalism mediates the relationship between LMX and employee outcomes in Turkish culture (Pellegrini & Scandura, 2006).

Workgroup level. An interesting development regarding LMX research is the perspective that LMX cannot be considered independent of other relationships that occur within the workgroup. This perspective has motivated a stream of research looking into the effects of various contextual variables on LMX quality at the workgroup level. In terms of coworker exchange (CWX)—or the exchange quality between coworkers reporting to the same supervisor—it was found that employees with similar levels of LMX quality relationship (high or low) experienced a higher quality CWX than those with dissimilar LMX relations (Sherony & Green, 2002). But if a follower with high-quality LMX perceived a co-worker to have an unfairly low-quality LMX with their supervisor, the CWX was higher in comparison to instances when the co-worker's low LMX was perceived to be just (Omilion-Hodges & Baker, 2013). Thus, distributive justice appears to moderate the relationships between LMX and CWX.

Workgroup size and cohesiveness are significantly related to LMX at the group level, although there is within-group variation (Cogliser & Schriesheim, 2000). In addition, workgroup climate was shown to moderate the relationship between LMX and safety citizenship role definitions (Hofmann et al., 2003), but a team's empowerment climate negatively moderated the effects of LMX on negative feedback-seeking behavior (Z. Chen et al., 2007). Procedural and distributive justice climate moderated the relationship between LMX differentiation and employee work attitudes and withdrawal behavior (Erdogan & Bauer, 2010) and between outcome favorability and OCB (Sun, Chow, Chiu, & Pan, 2013). Taken together, these insights from the research integrating across workgroup variables and

CWX suggest that the development and effects of LMX might not solely depend on the characteristics of a focal leader and follower, but rather are influenced (strengthened and neutralized) by the quality of relationships with others as well as by the overall workgroup climate.

Organizational level. Organizational climate and culture appear to influence relationships between LMX quality and employee outcomes. For example, a learning organizational culture positively moderates the relationships between LMX quality and in-role job performance (Joo & Ready, 2012). Perceived organizational support (POS), a construct that has often been studied in relation to LMX, was shown to moderate the relationships between LMX, job satisfaction, and job performance. Consistent with expectations, POS strengthened the positive relationship between LMX and job satisfaction. Interestingly, LMX was related to performance only when manager's POS was high (Erdogan & Enders, 2007). Organizational culture also diminishes the importance of LMX on work-related outcomes, as the quality of LMX relationships was found to be relatively less important for individuals employed in organizations with "respect for people" cultures as opposed to cultures characterized as "aggressive" (Erdogan et al., 2006).

Several studies proposed that a leader's position and status in the organization will have an effect on LMX quality. For example, the positive LMX relationship between a leader and the leader's boss has a moderating effect on the relationship between LMX quality and the employees' attitudes toward the organization and its customers (Tangirala, Green, & Ramanujam, 2007). Similarly, having a leader who is highly influential in the organization's network (as measured by network centrality) is beneficial, as a leader's centrality positively moderates the relationship between LMX and member's influence in the network (Sparrowe & Liden, 2005). Overall, it seems that similar to variables at the workgroup level, organizational variables moderate relationships between LMX and employee outcomes. Although a number of studies have investigated the joint effects of LMX and POS, the nature of the relationship between these variables at different levels is not entirely clear. This suggests a need for more research that adopts available multilevel methodologies to simultaneously consider dyad, workgroup, and organizational levels in the development and effects of LMX.

LMX as contextual variable. LMX quality itself has been proposed as a contextual variable that helps to explain the effects of employee antecedents on outcomes such as performance. As example, LMX was found to positively moderate the relationship between performance goal orientation and career satisfaction (Joo & Ready, 2012) and to compensate for low levels of employee conscientiousness in predicting contextual performance (Jawahar & Carr, 2007). Similarly, a high-quality relationship with one's leader can reduce the effect of employee perceptions of negative work conditions on performance. Under low LMX conditions it was found that perceptions of distributive injustice had a negative effect on employee performance (Rosen, Harris, & Kacmar, 2011). Overall, LMX has been shown to strengthen the positive relationships between employee characteristics and work outcomes and to mitigate some of the negative relationships.

A relevant critique of the LMX literature is that evaluating exchange quality ratings by their absolute value is flawed in that it is more likely that followers evaluate their LMX quality with reference to their perception of others' LMX relationships (Avolio, Walumbwa, & Weber, 2009). It is also the case that differentiated leader–follower relationships require some sort of social context (e.g., workgroup) to understand fully. Someone's absolute level of exchange quality might be average (for example) but if the rest of the workgroup has poor exchanges with the same leader, in a relative sense an average LMX rating is good. For these reasons, absolute ratings of LMX have been proposed to moderate relationships between group-level variables including relative LMX. In this spirit, one study showed that while controlling for individual level perceptions of LMX quality, relative LMX positively predicted psychological contract fulfillment (Henderson et al., 2008). These results help demonstrate how a social context created by LMX differentiation processes are related to employee outcomes.

Another extension of LMX theory was proposed in studies examining group-level (i.e., aggregated) LMX and within-group variance in LMX ratings. In one study the positive relationship between diversity and group turnover was weaker when the group mean on LMX was high or when group differentiation on LMX was low (Nishii & Mayer, 2009). Another study demonstrated that LMX differentiation was positively related to team commitment and performance only in teams with a low-quality LMX median (Le Blanc & González-Romá, 2012). Difference in LMX ratings can also arise at the dyadic level (i.e., leader–member disagreement in

LMX quality), with leader ratings of LMX moderating the relationship between follower's LMX ratings and job performance, job satisfaction, and organizational commitment. These results suggest that a higher LMX rating provided by either a leader or follower is associated with better follower work outcomes, with the best performance achieved when both the leader and a given follower rate their relationship as high (Cogliser, Schriesheim, Scandura, & Gardner, 2009). Overall, these findings indicate that LMX can and probably should be considered as a contextual variable (i.e., boundary condition) at higher analysis levels, as well as a predictor of various work outcomes. In addition, whereas LMX differentiation has been studied mainly as a direct predictor of various work outcomes and moderated by individual perceptions of LMX quality with one's supervisor, initial results suggest that it can be an important contextual variable at the workgroup level. For example, LMX differentiation was found to attenuate the direct effects of LMX quality on self-efficacy and the indirect effect on creativity (Liao et al., 2010).

New Leadership (Neocharismatic/Transformational/Visionary) School

The so-called New Leadership school extends the foundational work on leader behavior (e.g., Ohio State studies on consideration and initiating structure) promoting transformational, charismatic, and visionary leadership, which have also been considered under the heading of Neocharismatic approaches (Day & Antonakis, 2012). Collectively, these approaches represent the most dominant focus in leadership research over the past decade or so. Of particular interest for the present review is how LMX has been studied in combination with the various approaches that make up the New Leadership school.

Recent meta-analyses have shown that across studies there is a robust, positive association between transformational leadership and LMX quality (Dulebohn, et al., 2012). However, since transformational leadership is a complex construct consisting of several dimensions (i.e., individual consideration, intellectual stimulation, inspirational motivation, idealized influence; Bass & Riggio, 2006), it is possible that certain dimensions of transformational leadership are more strongly related to LMX; that is, it might be that relations-oriented aspects of transformational leadership have more influence on LMX than the change-oriented aspects (Yukl, O'Donnell, & Taber, 2009). This suggests that a more nuanced approach to examining the relationship between LMX and the components of transformational leadership might be needed.

In a related stream of research, LMX quality has been proposed as a mediator of the relationships between transformational leadership and employee outcomes; however, in general such studies report mixed results. In one study LMX was found to fully mediate the relationship between transformational leadership and task performance as well as organizational citizenship behaviors (Wang et al., 2005). But a different study suggested that whereas transformational leadership and LMX quality were strongly related, LMX did not mediate the relationship between transformational leadership and turnover intentions but the relationship was mediated by organization-based social exchange (i.e., affective commitment; Tse, Huang, & Lam, 2013). This suggests that a transformational leader may influence followers by building high-quality personalized exchange relationships and also by inspiring them to work for collective interests. Thus, organizational context should be considered as a potential moderator between transformational leadership, LMX quality, and employee outcomes. Other contextual factors might also play into this relationship. For example, one study showed that although LMX is positively related to transformational leadership, those leadership constructs are differentially related to follower performance under geographically close and distant conditions. Specifically, LMX predicted performance regardless of distance, whereas transformational leadership was found to be effective only under low distance conditions (Howell & Hall-Merenda, 1999).

LMX quality was also proposed to moderate the relationships between transformational leadership and employee behaviors and perceptions. For example, relative LMX (defined as the level of divergence between an individual's exchange quality and the average of others' exchange qualities in the workgroup; Hu & Liden, 2013) moderated the relationship between transformational leadership and employee influence tactics. Specifically, employees reporting to a transformational leader with high relative LMX were more likely to use soft influence tactics rather than hard (i.e., rational) influence tactics (Epitropaki & Martin, 2013). In addition, the relationship between transformational leadership and task performance/core characteristics perceptions was more positive for employees with higher LMX quality (Piccolo & Colquitt, 2006). Thus, LMX quality appears to strengthen the positive

effect of transformational leadership on followers. Finally, it is possible to consider the moderating role of LMX quality on the relationship between transformational leadership and its outcomes in more specific contexts. For instance, in the context of a crisis situation, LMX quality was shown to strengthen the positive relationship between transformational leadership and value congruence (Zhang, Jia, & Gu, 2012). Overall, it seems that LMX and transformational leadership are closely related constructs, although some of the relationships seem to hold only in specific contexts. Given the conceptual similarity between transformational and charismatic leadership, it was surprising to find no publications that combined charismatic leadership and LMX.

Information Processing School

The final active school to be considered is the Information Processing school, which arose from the initial work of Lord and colleagues on leadership categorization theory (Lord, Foti, & De Vader, 1984). The focus of this research has been on understanding how and why a leader is accorded influence through categorization and prototype matching processes of followers, as well as understanding how cognition and emotion are related to the enactment and interpretation of leadership.

One of the first studies that looked into cognitive factors associated with LMX quality found that perceived attitudinal similarity and liking predict both supervisor and subordinate LMX ratings (Engle & Lord, 1997). However, the same study showed that the effect of implicit leadership theory congruence on LMX ratings was much stronger for supervisors than subordinates. In contrast, a later study showed that followers' perceived prototype difference (in terms of implicit theory versus actual leader's traits) had a significant negative impact on LMX quality and seemed to matter independent of contextual influence (Epitropaki & Martin, 2005). There are several initial suggestions to explain this apparent controversy. First, initial evidence suggests that leaders and members tend to form different relational schemas of their partners: Leaders focus on work-related issues whereas members focused on interpersonal concerns (Huang, Wright, Chiu, & Wang, 2008). Second, though unrelated to LMX, one study showed that followers use mental representations and expectations of previous leaders to evaluate new leaders (Ritter & Lord, 2007). This suggests that the information processing involved in evaluating LMX quality will differ between leaders and followers and requires further theoretical consideration and empirical testing.

Another rich area of leadership research has examined LMX within the domains of social identity and identification. At the individual level, leader and follower identities have been shown to predict LMX quality (Jackson & Johnson, 2012). This study also demonstrated that the fit between leader and follower identities and the interactions among fit at different self-identity levels also predict LMX quality. This echoes the arguments about the importance of leader and follower similarity in establishing high-quality LMX. In addition, leader relational identity was found to moderate relationships of LMX with subordinate performance and OCB. Specifically, leader relational identity mitigated the effect of low-quality LMX on performance (Chang & Johnson, 2010). In addition, identification with organization and the group were found to mediate relationships between LMX and job satisfaction (Loi, Chan, & Lam, 2014), and job performance (Tse, Ashkanasy, & Dasborough, 2012). Overall, there is some evidence that leader and follower identities play important roles in the development and maintenance of LMX and also link LMX with important work outcomes.

Emotions also have been found to be related to LMX quality. Emotional regulation is important in the workplace and especially so in managing hierarchical relationships. But when emotional regulation takes the form of emotional masking by subordinates, it has been shown to be detrimental with regard to LMX quality (Xu, Liu, & Guo, 2014). Similar findings suggest that suppressing and faking emotions correlates negatively with the relationship between LMX and job satisfaction, and positively with health complaints among leaders and followers. Surprisingly, the same study reports higher level of emotion regulation among supervisors (Glasø & Einarsen, 2008). Another study showed that members in high-quality LMX relationships were negatively affected by leader's surface acting (expressing faked emotion), when predicting members' prosocial behavior (Fisk & Friesen, 2012). This suggests that emotional regulation not only predicts LMX quality, but also potentially moderates the effects of LMX on employee behavior. Interestingly, followers' perception of LMX quality also relates to the emotions followers experience about their co-workers. In this vein, one study demonstrated that a group member is more likely to experience contempt for a co-worker when perceiving to have a higher or lower LMX as compared with the co-worker, than when the perceived level of LMX is similar between the two (Tse, Lam, Lawrence, & Huang, 2013).

Summary

Across four domains of leadership research considered to be very active over the previous two decades or more (i.e., trait, contextual, new leadership, information processing), there have been varied and various findings suggesting that LMX informs leadership from different theoretical approaches as well as the reverse. These findings argue for a more integrative approach to leadership research. The field of leadership studies may have reached a saturation point in terms of what any singular approach to leadership—including LMX—might be able to illuminate. Rather than arguing for some sort of grand unified theory of leadership, future research might be well-served by examining leadership processes across various levels of analyses (e.g., individual, dyad, group/team, organization) and across time. These and other themes are discussed in the final section proposing future directions for LMX research.

Future Research Directions

Just as the history of LMX theory and research is relatively long the future is very bright. As a theory, LMX is positioned uniquely as a dyadic and relational approach to leadership. It has not always been studied as such (Schriesheim et al., 1999) perhaps because of historical limitations in terms of data analysis and modeling approaches that no longer pose these problems. Although it is easy to claim that a theory is dyadic, analyzing data in a truly dyadic manner requires techniques that are not the norm in leadership research. But times have changed and there are accepted techniques for conducting multilevel modeling, longitudinal analyses, as well as testing moderated mediation and mediated moderation models. LMX research will continue to benefit from all of these methodological and analytic advances.

In terms of future research directions and needs, low hanging fruit has been harvested for the most part. Meaningful contributions in the future will come from taking longer perspectives, adopting true process modeling approaches, and becoming less measurement-bounded in research. These and other related issues are discussed in this final section.

Longitudinal Perspectives on LMX

The role of time in the development of LMX remains an underresearched area (Day, 2014). The

Japanese career progress studies of Graen and colleagues provide one example of a research program where more long-term perspectives were taken with regard to the career implications of LMX (Graen, Dharwadkar, Grewal, & Wakabayashi, 2006; Wakabayashi & Graen, 1984; Wakabayashi, Graen, Graen, & Graen, 1988). This program of longitudinal research—some of which considered the career implications of LMX over more than 20 years (Graen et al., 2006)—demonstrated that the ability to develop high-quality relationships with a supervisor (leader) predicts subsequent exchange quality relationships with different supervisors. Furthermore, those employees (followers) who are effective in developing positive relationships progress faster throughout their careers relative to those who have difficulty negotiating positive leadership exchanges. This research is an interesting juxtaposition to research that has examined LMX in academic classroom settings under much shorter time periods (Nahrgang et al., 2009).

Over the course of a professional career it is likely that someone will work with many different bosses (leaders). Thus, from a career perspective the relative impact of a single exchange quality relationship may be less important than the ability to consistently forge high-quality exchanges with different superiors. Although previous research has demonstrated a positive relationship across serial leader–member exchanges, identifying and testing potential dispositional antecedents to developing consistently positive relationships with leaders offers one avenue for potentially interesting research. But from the perspective of a single LMX, considering the most appropriate time scale (Zaheer, Albert, & Zaheer, 1999) in which to study development and change, research may need to take a more intensive approach than has been previously adopted (i.e., involving many more waves of data) in order to understand and predict the underlying dynamics of any relationship, including that between a leader and follower(s). This highlights a potential need to think more carefully about the likely time scales involved and to design longitudinal LMX research accordingly, depending on whether something like a career or a relationship with a single leader is the intended focus of study.

Process Models

What tends to get overlooked not just in LMX research but leadership research in general is that leadership is a process and not a person or a position—or even a particular relationship. As

such, we should be proposing and testing the most appropriate models that capture relevant underlying processes. With regard to LMX, given its foundation in role-making processes (Graen & Cashman, 1975) it makes particular sense to design research that rigorously examines underlying causes that drive important variables and relationships in better understanding such processes from both the leader and member perspectives. This includes adopting more sophisticated research designs that take temporal issues into account more fully.

Another advantage of incorporating a process perspective in the study of LMX is that doing so allows researchers to identify and test the deep determinants that are thought to cause observable behaviors, which shape the development of leader–member relationships. This can serve as an effective check for the problems associated with introducing endogeneity (i.e., where a predictor correlates with the model's error term), which undermines any possible causal inferences that might be drawn (Antonakis, Bendahan, Jacquart, & Lalive, 2014). Such models can also incorporate mediation and moderation where appropriate and in doing so helping to incorporate relevant contextual variables. Proposing and testing these kinds of process models is an important future direction in LMX research because they allow researchers to identify causal effects associated with role-making processes in the development of leader–member exchanges.

Measurement

In many leadership domains including LMX there is an unsettling trend toward becoming measurement bound. By that it is meant that LMX becomes whatever a purported LMX scale is supposed to measure rather than focusing on the actual processes that compose the construct. Others have noted that the many different definitions of LMX and various scales used to measure it have clouded an overall picture as to the meaning of its underlying construct (Schriesheim et al., 1999). It is also the case that much is still unknown about the evolution of LMX and how the role-making process actually occurs. Researchers should keep in mind that a map (i.e., measure) is not the territory (i.e., leadership). Labeling any survey questionnaire a "leadership measure" does not mean it actually measures leadership (Day, 2012).

Something that has plagued the leadership field—and the LMX area is no exception—is that when a relatively brief, easy-to-administer questionnaire is designed and published researchers will surely use it. But it is important to remember that such "quick and dirty" approaches to measuring leadership are likely to be both deficient and contaminated. The field needs to do better and by that become less reliant on survey questionnaire methods and focus more on the underlying processes that unfold over time often in a dynamic manner.

In conclusion, LMX continues to be the focus of research interest for more than 40 years after its introduction into the leadership literature. There are several reasons for this long-lived interest, including: (a) the dynamic and developmental nature of LMX; (b) the unique focus on the relationship between a leader and a follower, which has spawned interest in broader theories of relational leadership (Uhl-Bien, 2006); (c) the inherent multilevel nature of LMX incorporating individuals, dyads, and more recently, workgroups and organizations; and (d) the importance of followers' relationships with their respective leaders that provides "a lens through which the entire work experience is viewed" (Gerstner & Day, 1997, p. 840).

The field of LMX research has produced many highly cited articles that have been instrumental in the development of broader leadership research. Four decades later, the nomological net of the LMX construct includes many studied antecedents, outcomes, contextual and process variables. Furthermore, LMX has been integrated with other influential leadership schools that highlighted potential overlaps for fostering deeper insights into leadership phenomena. Nevertheless, the present review suggests the need for more research, especially studies focused on using modern methodological approaches and incorporating process models in examining LMX at its roots as a role-making process.

References

Antonakis, J., Bastardoz, N., Liu, Y., & Schriesheim, C. A. (2014). What makes articles highly cited? *The Leadership Quarterly*, *25*(1), 152–179.

Antonakis, J., Bendahan, S., Jacquart, P., & Lalive, R. (2014). Causality and endogeneity: Problems and solutions. In D. V. Day (Ed.), *The Oxford handbook of leadership and organizations* (pp. 93–117). New York: Oxford University Press.

Avolio, B. J., Walumbwa, F. O., & Weber, T. J. (2009). Leadership: Current theories, research, and future directions. *Annual Review of Psychology*, *60*, 421–449.

Barbuto, J. E., Jr., Weltmer, D. F., & Pennisi, L. A. (2010). Locus of control, sources of motivation, and mental boundaries as antecedents of leader-member exchange quality. *Psychological Reports*, *106*(1), 175–188.

Bass, B. M., & Riggio, R. E. (2006). *Transformational leadership* (2nd ed.). Mahwah, NJ: Erlbaum.

Bauer, T. N., & Green, S. G. (1996). Development of leader-member exchange: A longitudinal test. *Academy of Management Journal*, *39*(6), 1538–1567.

Bernerth, J. B., Armenakis, A. A., Feild, H. S., Giles, W. F., & Walker, H. J. (2008). The influence of personality differences between subordinates and supervisors on perceptions of LMX: An empirical investigation. *Group & Organization Management*, *33*(2), 216–240.

Bliese, P. D., & Hanges, P. J. (2004). Being too liberal and too conservative: The perils of treating grouped data as though they were independent. *Organizational Research Methods*, *7*(4), 400–417.

Brower, H. H., Schoorman, F. D., & Tan, H. H. (2000). A model of relational leadership: The integration of trust and leader–member exchange. *The Leadership Quarterly*, *11*(2), 227–250.

Burris, E. R., Detert, J. R., & Chiaburu, D. S. (2008). Quitting before leaving: the mediating effects of psychological attachment and detachment on voice. *Journal of Applied Psychology*, *93*(4), 912–922.

Chang, C.-H. D., & Johnson, R. E. (2010). Not all leader–member exchanges are created equal: Importance of leader relational identity. *The Leadership Quarterly*, *21*(5), 796–808.

Chen, G., Kirkman, B. L., Kanfer, R., Allen, D., & Rosen, B. (2007). A multilevel study of leadership, empowerment, and performance in teams. *Journal of Applied Psychology*, *92*(2), 331–346.

Chen, Z., Lam, W., & Zhong, J. A. (2007). Leader-member exchange and member performance: a new look at individual-level negative feedback-seeking behavior and team-level empowerment climate. *Journal of Applied Psychology*, *92*(1), 202–212.

Cogliser, C. C., & Schriesheim, C. A. (2000). Exploring work unit context and leader–member exchange: a multi-level perspective. *Journal of Organizational Behavior*, *21*(5), 487–511.

Cogliser, C. C., Schriesheim, C. A., Scandura, T. A., & Gardner, W. L. (2009). Balance in leader and follower perceptions of leader–member exchange: Relationships with performance and work attitudes. *The Leadership Quarterly*, *20*(3), 452–465.

Cropanzano, R., Prehar, C. A., & Chen, P. Y. (2002). Using social exchange theory to distinguish procedural from interactional justice. *Group & Organization Management*, *27*(3), 324–351.

Dansereau, F., Jr., Graen, G., & Haga, W. J. (1975). A vertical dyad linkage approach to leadership within formal organizations: A longitudinal investigation of the role making process. *Organizational Behavior and Human Performance*, *13*(1), 46–78.

Dasborough, M. T., & Ashkanasy, N. M. (2002). Emotion and attribution of intentionality in leader–member relationships. *The Leadership Quarterly*, *13*(5), 615–634.

Davis, W. D., & Gardner, W. L. (2004). Perceptions of politics and organizational cynicism: An attributional and leader–member exchange perspective. *The Leadership Quarterly*, *15*(4), 439–465.

Day, D. V. (2012). Leadership. In S. W. J. Kozlowski (Ed.), *The Oxford handbook of organizational psychology* (Vol. 1, pp. 696–729). New York: Oxford University.

Day, D. V. (2014). Time and leadership. In A. J. Shipp & Y. Fried (Eds.), *Time and work* (Vol. 2, pp. 30–52). New York: Psychology Press.

Day, D. V., & Antonakis, J. (2012). Leadership: Past, present, and future. In D. V. Day & J. Antonakis (Eds.), *The nature of leadership* (2nd ed., pp. 3–25). Los Angeles, CA: Sage.

Day, D. V., & Antonakis, J. (2013). The future of leadership. In H. S. Leonard, R. Lewis, A. M. Freedman & J. Passmore (Eds.), *The Wiley-Blackwell handbook of the psychology of leadership, change, and organizational development* (pp. 221–235). London: Wiley-Blackwell.

Day, D. V., Gronn, P., & Salas, E. (2004). Leadership capacity in teams. *The Leadership Quarterly, 15*, 857–880.

Deluga, R. J. (1994). Supervisor trust building, leader-member exchange and organizational citizenship behaviour. *Journal of Occupational and Organizational Psychology, 67*(4), 315–326.

Dienesch, R. M., & Liden, R. C. (1986). Leader-member exchange model of leadership: A critique and further development. *Academy of Management Review, 11*(3), 618–634.

Duchon, D., Green, S. G., & Taber, T. D. (1986). Vertical dyad linkage: A longitudinal assessment of antecedents, measures, and consequences. *Journal of Applied Psychology, 71*(1), 56.

Dulac, T., Coyle-Shapiro, J. A., Henderson, D. J., & Wayne, S. J. (2008). Not all responses to breach are the same: The interconnection of social exchange and psychological contract processes in organizations. *Academy of Management Journal, 51*(6), 1079–1098.

Dulebohn, J. H., Bommer, W. H., Liden, R. C., Brouer, R. L., & Ferris, G. R. (2012). A Meta-analysis of antecedents and consequences of leader-member exchange: Integrating the past with an eye toward the future. *Journal of Management, 38*(6), 1715–1759.

Engle, E. M., & Lord, R. G. (1997). Implicit theories, self-schemas, and leader-member exchange. *Academy of Management Journal, 40*(4), 988–1010.

Epitropaki, O., & Martin, R. (2005). From ideal to real: a longitudinal study of the role of implicit leadership theories on leader-member exchanges and employee outcomes. *Journal of Applied Psychology, 90*(4), 659–676.

Epitropaki, O., & Martin, R. (2013). Transformational–transactional leadership and upward influence: The role of relative leader–member exchanges (RLMX) and perceived organizational support (POS). *The Leadership Quarterly, 24*(2), 299–315.

Erdogan, B., & Bauer, T. N. (2010). Differentiated leader–member exchanges: The buffering role of justice climate. *Journal of Applied Psychology, 95*(6), 1104–1120.

Erdogan, B., & Bauer, T. N. (2014). Leader-member exchange (LMX) theory: The relational approach to leadership. In D. V. Day (Ed.), *The Oxford handbook of leadership and organizations* (pp. 407–433). New York: Oxford University Press.

Erdogan, B., & Enders, J. (2007). Support from the top: Supervisors' perceived organizational support as a moderator of leader-member exchange to satisfaction and performance relationships. *Journal of Applied Psychology, 92*(2), 321–330.

Erdogan, B., Kraimer, M. L., & Liden, R. C. (2004). Work value congruence and intrinsic career success: The compensatory roles of leader-member exchange and perceived organizational support. *Personnel Psychology, 57*(2), 305–332.

Erdogan, B., Liden, R. C., & Kraimer, M. L. (2006). Justice and leader-member exchange: The moderating role of organizational culture. *Academy of Management Journal, 49*(2), 395–406.

Fisk, G. M., & Friesen, J. P. (2012). Perceptions of leader emotion regulation and LMX as predictors of followers' job satisfaction and organizational citizenship behaviors. *The Leadership Quarterly, 23*(1), 1–12.

Gerstner, C. R., & Day, D. V. (1997). Meta-analytic review of leader–member exchange theory: Correlates and construct issues. *Journal of Applied Psychology, 82*(6), 827.

Glasø, L., & Einarsen, S. (2008). Emotion regulation in leader–follower relationships. *European Journal of Work and Organizational Psychology, 17*(4), 482–500.

Gómez, C., & Rosen, B. (2001). The leader-member exchange as a link between managerial trust and employee empowerment. *Group & Organization Management, 26*(1), 53–69.

Graen, G. B., & Cashman, J. F. (1975). A role making model of leadership in formal organizations. In J. G. Hunt & L. L. Larson (Eds.), *Leadership frontiers* (pp. 143–165). Kent, OH: Kent State University.

Graen, G., Dharwadkar, R., Grewal, R., & Wakabayashi, M. (2006). Japanese career progress: an empirical examination. *Journal of International Business Studies, 37*, 148–161.

Graen, G. B., Novak, M., & Sommerkamp, P. (1982). The effects of leader-member exchange and job design on productivity and satisfaction: Testing a dual attachment model. *Organizational Behavior and Human Performance, 30*, 109–131.

Graen, G., & Schiemann, W. (1978). Leader–member agreement: A vertical dyad linkage approach. *Journal of Applied Psychology, 63*(2), 206–212.

Graen, G. B., & Uhl-Bien, M. (1995). Relationship-based approach to leadership: Development of leader-member exchange (LMX) theory of leadership over 25 years: Applying a multi-level multi-domain perspective. *The Leadership Quarterly, 6*, 219–247.

Hackman, J. R., & Oldham, G. R. (1976). Motivation through the design of work: Test of a theory. *Organizational Behavior and Human Performance, 16*, 250–279.

Harris, K. J., & Kacmar, K. M. (2006). Too much of a good thing: the curvilinear effect of leader-member exchange on stress. *The Journal of Social Psychology, 146*(1), 65–84.

Henderson, D. J., Wayne, S. J., Shore, L. M., Bommer, W. H., & Tetrick, L. E. (2008). Leader-member exchange, differentiation, and psychological contract fulfillment: A multilevel examination. *Journal of Applied Psychology, 93*(6), 1208–1219.

Hofmann, D. A., & Morgeson, F. P. (1999). Safety-related behavior as a social exchange: The role of perceived organizational support and leader–member exchange. *Journal of Applied Psychology, 84*(2), 286–296.

Hofmann, D. A., Morgeson, F. P., & Gerras, S. J. (2003). Climate as a moderator of the relationship between leader-member exchange and content specific citizenship: Safety climate as an exemplar. *Journal of Applied Psychology, 88*(1), 170–178.

House, R. J., Hanges, P. J., Javidan, M., Dorfman, P. W., & Gupta, V. (Eds.). (2004). *Culture, leadership, and organizations: The GLOBE study of 62 societies*. Thousand Oaks, CA: Sage.

Howell, J. M., & Hall-Merenda, K. E. (1999). The ties that bind: The impact of leader–member exchange, transformational and transactional leadership, and distance on predicting follower performance. *Journal of Applied Psychology, 84*(5), 680–694.

Hu, J., & Liden, R. C. (2013). Relative leader-member exchange within team contexts: How and when social comparison impacts individual effectiveness. *Personnel Psychology, 66*(1), 127–172.

Huang, X., Wright, R. P., Chiu, W. C., & Wang, C. (2008). Relational schemas as sources of evaluation and misevaluation of leader–member exchanges: Some initial evidence. *The Leadership Quarterly*, *19*(3), 266–282.

Hui, C., Law, K. S., & Chen, Z. X. (1999). A structural equation model of the effects of negative affectivity, leader-member exchange, and perceived job mobility on in-role and extra-role performance: A Chinese case. *Organizational Behavior and Human Decision Processes*, *77*(1), 3–21.

Ilies, R., Nahrgang, J. D., & Morgeson, F. P. (2007). Leader-member exchange and citizenship behaviors: a meta-analysis. *Journal of Applied Psychology*, *92*(1), 269.

Jackson, E. M., & Johnson, R. E. (2012). When opposites do (and do not) attract: Interplay of leader and follower self-identities and its consequences for leader–member exchange. *The Leadership Quarterly*, *23*(3), 488–501.

Janssen, O., & Van Yperen, N. W. (2004). Employees' goal orientations, the quality of leader-member exchange, and the outcomes of job performance and job satisfaction. *Academy of Management Journal*, *47*(3), 368–384.

Jawahar, I., & Carr, D. (2007). Conscientiousness and contextual performance: The compensatory effects of perceived organizational support and leader-member exchange. *Journal of Managerial Psychology*, *22*(4), 330–349.

Joo, B.-K. B., & Ready, K. J. (2012). Career satisfaction: the influences of proactive personality, performance goal orientation, organizational learning culture, and leader-member exchange quality. *Career Development International*, *17*(3), 276–295.

Judge, T. A., Bono, J. E., Ilies, R., & Gerhardt, M. W. (2002). Personality and leadership: a qualitative and quantitative review. *Journal of Applied Psychology*, *87*(4), 765–780.

Judge, T. A., & Ferris, G. R. (1993). Social context of performance evaluation decisions. *Academy of Management Journal*, *36*(1), 80–105.

Kim, T. G., Lee, J. K., & Lee, J. H. (2013). Do interpersonal relationships still matter for turnover intention? A comparison of South Korea and China. *The International Journal of Human Resource Management*, *24*(5), 966–984.

Kraimer, M. L., Wayne, S. J., & Jaworski, R. A. A. (2001). Sources of support and expatriate performance: The mediating role of expatriate adjustment. *Personnel Psychology*, *54*(1), 71–99.

Le Blanc, P. M., & González-Romá, V. (2012). A team level investigation of the relationship between Leader–Member Exchange (LMX) differentiation, and commitment and performance. *The Leadership Quarterly*, *23*(3), 534–544.

Liao, H., Liu, D., & Loi, R. (2010). Looking at both sides of the social exchange coin: A social cognitive perspective on the joint effects of relationship quality and differentiation on creativity. *Academy of Management Journal*, *53*(5), 1090–1109.

Liden, R. C., & Antonakis, J. (2009). Considering context in psychological leadership research. *Human Relations*, *62*(11), 1587–1605.

Liden, R. C., Erdogan, B., Wayne, S. J., & Sparrowe, R. T. (2006). Leader-member exchange, differentiation, and task interdependence: Implications for individual and group performance. *Journal of Organizational Behavior*, *27*(6), 723–746.

Liden, R. C., & Graen, G. (1980). Generalizability of the vertical dyad linkage model of leadership. *Academy of Management Journal*, *23*(3), 451–465.

Liden, R. C., & Maslyn, J. M. (1998). Multidimensionality of leader-member exchange: An empirical assessment through scale development. *Journal of Management*, *24*(1), 43–72.

Liden, R. C., Sparrowe, R. T., & Wayne, S. J. (1997). Leader-member exchange theory: The past and potential for the future. In G. R. Ferris (Ed.), *Research in personnel and human resources management* (Vol. 15, pp. 47–119). Greenwich, CT: JAI Press.

Liden, R. C., Wayne, S. J., & Sparrowe, R. T. (2000). An examination of the mediating role of psychological empowerment on the relations between the job, interpersonal relationships, and work outcomes. *Journal of Applied Psychology*, *85*(3), 407–416.

Liden, R. C., Wayne, S. J., & Stilwell, D. (1993). A longitudinal study on the early development of leader-member exchanges. *Journal of Applied Psychology*, *78*(4), 662–674.

Loi, R., Chan, K. W., & Lam, L. W. (2014). Leader–member exchange, organizational identification, and job satisfaction: A social identity perspective. *Journal of Occupational and Organizational Psychology*, *87*(1), 42–61.

Lord, R. G., Foti, R. J., & De Vader, C. L. (1984). A test of leadership categorization theory: Internal structure, information processing, and leadership perceptions. *Organizational Behavior and Human Performance*, *34*, 343–378.

Major, D. A., Kozlowski, S. W., Chao, G. T., & Gardner, P. D. (1995). A longitudinal investigation of newcomer expectations, early socialization outcomes, and the moderating effects of role development factors. *Journal of Applied Psychology*, *80*(3), 418–431.

Maslyn, J. M., & Uhl-Bien, M. (2001). Leader–member exchange and its dimensions: Effects of self-effort and other's effort on relationship quality. *Journal of Applied Psychology*, *86*(4), 697–708.

Masterson, S. S., Lewis, K., Goldman, B. M., & Taylor, M. S. (2000). Integrating justice and social exchange: The differing effects of fair procedures and treatment on work relationships. *Academy of Management Journal*, *43*(4), 738–748.

Murphy, S. E., & Ensher, E. A. (1999). The effects of leader and subordinate characteristics in the development of leader–member exchange quality. *Journal of Applied Social Psychology*, *29*(7), 1371–1394.

Nahrgang, J. D., Morgeson, F. P., & Ilies, R. (2009). The development of leader-member exchanges: Exploring how personality and performance influence leader and member relationships over time. *Organizational Behavior and Human Decision Processes*, *108*(2), 256–266.

Nishii, L. H., & Mayer, D. M. (2009). Do inclusive leaders help to reduce turnover in diverse groups? The moderating role of leader–member exchange in the diversity to turnover relationship. *Journal of Applied Psychology*, *94*(6), 1412–1426.

Omilion-Hodges, L. M., & Baker, C. R. (2013). Contextualizing LMX within the workgroup: The effects of LMX and justice on relationship quality and resource sharing among peers. *The Leadership Quarterly*, *24*(6), 935–951.

Oren, L., Tziner, A., Sharoni, G., Amor, I., & Alon, P. (2012). Relations between leader-subordinate personality similarity and job attitudes. *Journal of Managerial Psychology*, *27*(5), 479–496.

Parker, S. K. (1998). Enhancing role breadth self-efficacy: The roles of job enrichment and other organizational interventions. *Journal of Applied Psychology*, *83*(6), 835–852.

Pearce, C. L., & Conger, J. A. (Eds.). (2003). *Shared leadership: Reframing the hows and whys of leadership*. Thousand Oaks, CA: SAGE.

Pellegrini, E. K., & Scandura, T. A. (2006). Leader–member exchange (LMX), paternalism, and delegation in the Turkish business culture: An empirical investigation. *Journal of International Business Studies*, 37(2), 264–279.

Piccolo, R. F., & Colquitt, J. A. (2006). Transformational leadership and job behaviors: The mediating role of core job characteristics. *Academy of Management Journal*, 49(2), 327–340.

Ritter, B. A., & Lord, R. G. (2007). The impact of previous leaders on the evaluation of new leaders: an alternative to prototype matching. *Journal of Applied Psychology*, 92(6), 1683–1695.

Rockstuhl, T., Dulebohn, J. H., Ang, S., & Shore, L. M. (2012). Leader–member exchange (LMX) and culture: A meta-analysis of correlates of LMX across 23 countries. *Journal of Applied Psychology*, 97(6), 1097–1130.

Rosen, C. C., Harris, K. J., & Kacmar, K. M. (2011). LMX, context perceptions, and performance: An uncertainty management perspective. *Journal of Management*, 37(3), 819–838.

Scandura, T. A., & Graen, G. B. (1984). Moderating effects of initial leader–member exchange status on the effects of a leadership intervention. *Journal of Applied Psychology*, 69(3), 428.

Scandura, T. A., Graen, G. B., & Novak, M. A. (1986). When managers decide not to decide autocratically: An investigation of leader–member exchange and decision influence. *Journal of Applied Psychology*, 71(4), 579.

Scandura, T. A., & Schriesheim, C. A. (1994). Leader–member exchange and supervisor career mentoring as complementary constructs in leadership research. *Academy of Management Journal*, 37(6), 1588–1602.

Schriesheim, C. A., Castro, S. L., & Cogliser, C. C. (1999). Leader–member exchange (LMX) research: A comprehensive review of theory, measurement, and data-analytic practices. *The Leadership Quarterly*, 10(1), 63–113.

Schyns, B., Paul, T., Mohr, G., & Blank, H. (2005). Comparing antecedents and consequences of leader–member exchange in a German working context to findings in the US. *European Journal of Work and Organizational Psychology*, 14(1), 1–22.

Sears, G. J., & Hackett, R. D. (2011). The influence of role definition and affect in LMX: A process perspective on the personality–LMX relationship. *Journal of Occupational and Organizational Psychology*, 84(3), 544–564.

Sears, G. J., & Holmvall, C. M. (2010). The joint influence of supervisor and subordinate emotional intelligence on leader–member exchange. *Journal of Business and Psychology*, 25(4), 593–605.

Settoon, R. P., Bennett, N., & Liden, R. C. (1996). Social exchange in organizations: Perceived organizational support, leader–member exchange, and employee reciprocity. *Journal of Applied Psychology*, 81(3), 219–227.

Sherony, K. M., & Green, S. G. (2002). Coworker exchange: Relationships between coworkers, leader-member exchange, and work attitudes. *Journal of Applied Psychology*, 87(3), 542–548.

Sin, H.-P., Nahrgang, J. D., & Morgeson, F. P. (2009). Understanding why they don't see eye-to-eye: An examination of leader-member exchange (LMX) agreement. *Journal of Applied Psychology*, 94(4), 1048–1057.

Singer, J. D., & Willett, J. B. (2003). *Applied longitudinal data analysis: Modeling change and event occurrence*. Oxford, UK: Oxford University Press.

Sparrowe, R. T., & Liden, R. C. (1997). Process and structure in leader-member exchange. *Academy of Management Review*, 22(2), 522–552.

Sparrowe, R. T., & Liden, R. C. (2005). Two routes to influence: Integrating leader-member exchange and social network perspectives. *Administrative Science Quarterly*, 50(4), 505–535.

Stogdill, R. M., & Coons, A. E. (Eds.). (1957). *Leader behavior: Its description and measurement*. Columbus, OH: Ohio State University, Bureau of Business Research.

Story, J. S., Youssef, C. M., Luthans, F., Barbuto, J. E., & Bovaird, J. (2013). Contagion effect of global leaders' positive psychological capital on followers: Does distance and quality of relationship matter? *The International Journal of Human Resource Management*, 24(13), 2534–2553.

Sun, L.-Y., Chow, I. H. S., Chiu, R. K., & Pan, W. (2013). Outcome favorability in the link between leader–member exchange and organizational citizenship behavior: Procedural fairness climate matters. *The Leadership Quarterly*, 24(1), 215–226.

Tangirala, S., Green, S. G., & Ramanujam, R. (2007). In the shadow of the boss's boss: Effects of supervisors' upward exchange relationships on employees. *Journal of Applied Psychology*, 92(2), 309–320.

Tierney, P., Farmer, S. M., & Graen, G. B. (1999). An examination of leadership and employee creativity: The relevance of traits and relationships. *Personnel Psychology*, 52(3), 591–620.

Tse, H. H., Ashkanasy, N. M., & Dasborough, M. T. (2012). Relative leader–member exchange, negative affectivity and social identification: A moderated-mediation examination. *The Leadership Quarterly*, 23(3), 354–366.

Tse, H. H., Huang, X., & Lam, W. (2013). Why does transformational leadership matter for employee turnover? A multi-foci social exchange perspective. *The Leadership Quarterly*, 24(5), 763–776.

Tse, H. H., Lam, C. K., Lawrence, S. A., & Huang, X. (2013). When my supervisor dislikes you more than me: The effect of dissimilarity in leader–member exchange on coworkers' interpersonal emotion and perceived help. *Journal of Applied Psychology*, 98(6), 974–988.

Uhl-Bien, M. (2006). Relational leadership theory: Exploring the social processes of leadership and organizing. *The Leadership Quarterly*, 17, 654–676.

Vecchio, R. P., & Gobdel, B. C. (1984). The vertical dyad linkage model of leadership: Problems and prospects. *Organizational Behavior and Human Performance*, 34(1), 5–20.

Wakabayashi, M., & Graen, G. B. (1984). The Japanese career progress study: A 7-year follow-up. *Journal of Applied Psychology*, 69(4), 603–614.

Wakabayashi, M., Graen, G. B., Graen, M. R., & Graen, M. G. (1988). Japanese management progress: Mobility into middle management. *Journal of Applied Psychology*, 73(2), 217–227.

Walumbwa, F. O., Cropanzano, R., & Hartnell, C. A. (2009). Organizational justice, voluntary learning behavior, and job performance: A test of the mediating effects of identification and leader-member exchange. *Journal of Organizational Behavior*, 30(8), 1103–1126.

Wang, H., Law, K. S., Hackett, R. D., Wang, D., & Chen, Z. X. (2005). Leader-member exchange as a mediator of the relationship between transformational leadership and followers' performance and organizational citizenship behavior. *Academy of Management Journal*, *48*(3), 420–432.

Wayne, S. J., & Green, S. A. (1993). The effects of leader-member exchange on employee citizenship and impression management behavior. *Human Relations*, *46*(12), 1431–1440.

Wayne, S. J., Shore, L. M., Bommer, W. H., & Tetrick, L. E. (2002). The role of fair treatment and rewards in perceptions of organizational support and leader-member exchange. *Journal of Applied Psychology*, *87*(3), 590–598.

Wayne, S. J., Shore, L. M., & Liden, R. C. (1997). Perceived organizational support and leader-member exchange: A social exchange perspective. *Academy of Management Journal*, *40*(1), 82–111.

Xu, J., Liu, Y., & Guo, Y. (2014). The role of subordinate emotional masking in leader–member exchange and outcomes: A two-sample investigation. *Journal of Business Research*, *67*(2), 100–107.

Yukl, G., O'Donnell, M., & Taber, T. (2009). Influence of leader behaviors on the leader-member exchange relationship. *Journal of Managerial Psychology*, *24*(4), 289–299.

Zaheer, S., Albert, S., & Zaheer, A. (1999). Time scales and organizational theory. *Academy of Management Review*, *24*(4), 735–741.

Zhang, Z., Jia, M., & Gu, L. (2012). Transformational leadership in crisis situations: Evidence from the People's Republic of China. *The International Journal of Human Resource Management*, *23*(19), 4085–4109.

Zhang, Z., Wang, M., & Shi, J. (2012). Leader-follower congruence in proactive personality and work outcomes: The mediating role of leader-member exchange. *Academy of Management Journal*, *55*(1), 111–130.

Leader–Member Exchange Measurement

Robert C. Liden, Junfeng Wu, Aarn Xiaoyun Cao, *and* Sandy J. Wayne

Abstract

Over the history of leader–member exchange (LMX) research, dating from 1972, many measures have been used to assess the construct, ranging from the initial two-item negotiating latitude scale to the LMX-7 and the multidimensional (LMX-MDM) scales, which are those most frequently used today. In more recent years, additional measures have been introduced as replacements or supplements to the two prominent LMX measures. The purpose of our essay is to present an overview of LMX measures as well as scales that are relevant to LMX research. As a service to researchers, the complete text of all items from past versions of LMX and related scales are presented in Appendix 1, and items for the current standard measures (LMX-MDM and LMX-7) are provided in Appendix 2.

Key Words: Leader–member exchange (LMX), vertical dyad linkage (VDL), measurement, scale development, social exchange, relative LMX (RLMX), social comparison, leader–member exchange social comparison (LMXSC)

Introduction

Given that leader–member exchange (LMX) is thoroughly defined in other essays of this volume, we begin our discussion of LMX measurement with the assumption that readers are familiar with the framework of LMX theory. Even those familiar with the construct, however, may not be acquainted with the history of LMX measurement, which extends back to 1972, when the idea of differentiated leader–follower relationships was discovered by Graen, Dansereau, and Minami in a study of leader behaviors assessed with the Leader Behavior Description Questionnaire (LBDQ). It was noticed that there was substantial variance across followers of the same leaders on responses to LBDQ items (Dansereau, Graen, & Cashman, 1973; Graen et al., 1972). Previously, such variability across followers was treated as error variance. Dansereau, Graen, and their colleagues reasoned that rather than reflecting error in measurement, this variance may be reflective of actual differences in follower perceptions of the leader. That is, the variance is valid and thus should not be treated as error. Indeed, further exploration demonstrated that

analyzing the data at the dyad level rather than averaging across followers (often referred to as the "average leadership style approach") to arrive at an overall measure of leader behavior/style, explained additional variability in outcomes. They chose the name "vertical dyad linkage" (VDL) to capture the focus on dyads composed of a supervisor and subordinate. "Vertical" captures the fact that leaders occupy a higher position in the structure of the organization. At this point in the evolution of the theory, relationship quality was simplified as either in-group or out-group.

The term leader–member exchange (LMX) was introduced in a book chapter (Graen & Cashman, 1975) that referred to both VDL and LMX. By 1982, the change from VDL to LMX was established. The change in terms was intended to put more emphasis on the interplay between leader and follower, including the exchange of resources and support between the two parties of the exchange. But in addition to the change in names, VDL is distinctly a dyadic construct, whereas LMX has evolved to become a multilevel approach. Also, as observed by Dansereau, Seitz, Chiu, Shaughnessy, and Yammarino (2013,

p. 809), whereas VDL continues to focus "primarily on negotiating latitude and delegation, . . . LMX has developed conceptually . . . as . . . relationship quality," including such factors "as competence, interpersonal skill, trust (Graen, 1976), attention, sensitivity (Cashman, Dansereau, Graen, & Haga, 1976), support, reward, and satisfaction with the leader (Graen & Ginsburgh, 1977)."

Past VDL and LMX Measures
Negotiating Latitude (Measuring VDL)

Given the success of the first two studies that were based on the LBDQ (Dansereau et al., 1973; Graen et al., 1972), Dansereau and his colleagues (Dansereau, 1972; Dansereau, Graen, & Haga 1975) wrote two items that reflected what they thought represented the essence of differentiated leader–follower relationships (see Appendix 1 to view a summary of all scale items). These items were based on their definition of negotiating latitude as, "the extent to which a superior is willing to consider requests from a member concerning role development" (p. 51). As presented by Dienesch and Liden (1986), this two-item scale introduced by Dansereau et al. (1975) was subsequently used in several of the initial studies (Cashman et al., 1976; Graen & Ginsburgh, 1977). In the studies using the two-item VDL measure, which used 4-point response scales, scores from the two items were summed to form a composite with possible scores ranging from 2 to 8. A median split was used to identify the out-group and the in-group. In the Dansereau et al. (1975) data, the out-group consisted of subordinates with scores from 2 to 7, and the in-group was made up of those with a score of 8. These results clearly indicated that to better capture the variability in leader–member relationships the scale needed to contain more than two items.

VDL/LMX

The two-item negotiating latitude/VDL scale was augmented to four items by Graen and Schiemann (1978) and by Liden and Graen (1980) to better capture the domain of the construct and to capture additional variance in relationships between leaders and followers. Added to the original two items was a third item to capture loyalty, "To what extent can you count on your supervisor to "bail you out," at his expense, when you really need him?" The new fourth item, "How often do you take your suggestions regarding your work to your supervisor?" was intended to capture subordinates' contributions to the relationship. In Liden and Graen's (1980) study,

although artificial subgrouping was still used, a middle-group was added to the original out-group and in-group based on dividing the sample roughly into thirds based on their VDL scores.

LMX

Following Graen and Cashman (1975), who introduced the term "leader–member exchange," Graen and Schiemann (1978) were the first to label the measurement scale leader–member exchange. Interestingly, despite the name change, the four items used to measure LMX were essentially the same items used to capture VDL (e.g., Liden & Graen, 1980). Subsequently, Graen, Liden, and Hoel (1982) added a fifth item designed to provide an overall assessment of relationship quality. The method for utilizing LMX in the analyses was novel, however. Rather than using the traditional approach of averaging all of the LMX items, Graen, Liden, and Hoel (1982) operationalized LMX as the difference between a focal individual's LMX score and the average LMX score across his or her workgroup. They referred to this operationalization as "deviation LMX." The goal was to more clearly illustrate the difference between examining leadership at the dyadic level as opposed to the more traditional "average leadership style" approach (captured in the average LMX score across group members). To our knowledge, aside from Ferris's (1985) replication of Graen, Liden, and Hoel (1982), despite the appeal of this operationalization, the approach lay dormant until Henderson, Wayne, Shore, Bommer, and Tetrick (2008) brought it back to life and referred to it as "relative LMX," or RLMX. Following Henderson et al.'s (2008) revival of this operationalization, a number of studies have appeared on RLMX (Epitropaki & Martin, 2013; Hu & Liden, 2013; Tse, Ashkanasy, & Dasborough, 2012; Vidyarthi, Liden, Anand, Erdogan, & Ghosh, 2010).

A 12-item LMX Scale was used in a 13-year longitudinal study that was reported in Wakabayashi and Graen (1984) and in Wakabayashi, Graen, Graen, and Graen (1988). However, none of the items were provided in either of these articles and, to our knowledge, the scale was not used in subsequent studies. In addition, a 13-item LMX scale was used in Settoon, Bennett, and Liden (1996) and Liden, Erdogan, Wayne, and Sparrowe (2006). This was a preliminary version of the LMX-Multidimensional Measure (LMX-MDM) that was supplanted by the 12-item LMX-MDM scale presented in Liden and Maslyn (1998).

Current LMX Measures

Although some researchers still use earlier versions of the scale, the LMX-7 version presented by Graen and Uhl-Bien (1995) and the LMX-MDM (Liden & Maslyn, 1998) are the two measures most frequently used in LMX research (Dulebohn, Bommer, Liden, Brouer, & Ferris, 2012). The 1995 version of the LMX-7 scale contains slight changes to the items and response scales that were presented by Scandura and Graen in 1984 (although Graen, Novak, and Sommercamp (1982) reported using a seven-item measure of the leader–member relationship, they did not report the items). Many researchers, though, have found the varied response anchors for the LMX-7 (Graen & Uhl-Bien, 1995; Scandura & Graen, 1984) to be cumbersome, and have instead chosen to use adapted versions of the scale that can accommodate a strongly disagree to strongly agree response scale (Bauer & Green, 1996; Liden, Wayne, & Stilwell, 1993).

Gerstner and Day (1997), in their meta-analysis of LMX and its outcomes recommended that researchers use the LMX-7 scale. However, shortly after their article was published, Liden and Maslyn's (1998) LMX-MDM scale was introduced. In subsequent years, the LMX-MDM has been used in many studies. It has been noted that the LMX-MDM was created through an extremely rigorous scale development process (Joseph, Newman, & Sin, 2011), whereas the LMX-7 evolved through a piecemeal process over a number of years. Keller and Dansereau (2001) empirically demonstrated that *ad hoc* additions and deletions of items from scales can alter psychometric properties. The LMX-MDM does not suffer from this problem as it was developed through an integrated scale development process. An additional advantage of the LMX-MDM is that through the integration of theory (Dienesch & Liden, 1986) with critical incident interviews and content validation involving expert judges, the LMX-MDM does a better job of capturing the domain of the LMX construct, as reflected in four dimensions—affect, loyalty, contribution, and professional respect—that emerged through the scale development process. Support for a higher-order confirmatory factor analysis (CFA) demonstrated that each of the four dimensions factor as theorized and all fall under the global LMX construct. This evidence provides support for use of the LMX-MDM to assess the separate dimensions of LMX, or as a global LMX assessment by combining all 12 items (Liden & Maslyn, 1998). Despite these theoretical and empirical advantages, the empirical evidence shows that when assessing global LMX, the LMX-7 and LMX-MDM measures are highly correlated (Joseph et al., 2011) and related in similar ways to both antecedents and outcomes (Dulebohn et al., 2012). Nevertheless, it is no longer meaningful to justify use of the LMX-7 scale based on the recommendation of Gerstner and Day (1997) that predates the introduction of LMX-MDM.

Supervisor Versions of LMX

As a dyadic approach to leadership, LMX concerns both subordinates' and leaders' perceptions of the relationship (Dansereau et al., 1975; Graen & Cashman, 1975; Graen et al., 1982; Graen & Uhl-Bien, 1995). As such, it has been suggested that LMX research should include data collected from both parties of the dyad rather than only from the subordinate's perspective (Scandura & Schriesheim, 1994; Schriesheim, Neider, & Scandura, 1998). In reviewing the extant supervisor versions of LMX measures, we observe that researchers usually transform subordinate versions of LMX measures to make the corresponding supervisor versions of LMX scales.

To modify subordinate reported LMX items to assess LMX from a supervisor's perspective, researchers have generally used two approaches—the mirroring approach and the parallel approach. For the mirroring approach, supervisor version LMX items are "mirrors" of the items measured from a subordinate's perspective (e.g., Graen & Uhl-Bien, 1995; Liden et al., 1993). For example, an item from the subordinate reported LMX measure is "I can count on my supervisor to 'bail me out,' even at his or her own expense, when I really need it" (Liden et al., 1993, p. 666). A corresponding supervisor reported LMX item mirroring this subordinate LMX item is "I would be willing to 'bail out' my subordinate, even at my own expense, if he or she really needed it" (Liden et al., 1993, p. 666). In fact, the LMX item from the subordinate's perspective and the LMX item from the supervisor's perspective are capturing the same information. That is, the extent to which the supervisor would be willing to "bail out" a subordinate. Most of the extant supervisor versions of LMX measures used the mirroring approach to reflect how the supervisor treats the subordinate. Greguras and Ford (2006) suggested a parallel approach to capture the exchanges in the dyadic relationship between leader and follower. Specifically, they suggested that measuring the supervisor's view of LMX should focus on how subordinates treat the supervisor. Maslyn and Uhl-Bien (2001, p. 701) used such an approach with parallel supervisor items, such as "Regardless of the amount of formal authority your employee has, what are the chances that he/she would 'bail you out' at his/

her expense?" In the following section, we review the extant supervisor versions of LMX measures.

Supervisor Versions of LMX-7

Graen and Uhl-Bien (1995) provided a mirrored supervisor version of the LMX-7 measure (SLMX-7) by changing the wording of the subordinate reported LMX-7. An example LMX-7 item is, "How well does your leader understand your job problems and needs?" and the corresponding supervisor-reported (SLMX-7) item is, "How well do you understand your follower's job problems and needs?" (Graen & Uhl-Bien, 1995, p. 237). Graen and Uhl-Bien (1995) did not provide psychometric properties for this SLMX-7 scale. Later studies using this scale found acceptable reliabilities (e.g., .78 in Huang, Wright, Chiu, & Wang, 2008; .83 in Schriesheim, Castro, & Yammarino, 2000).

Maslyn and Uhl-Bien (2001) offered a different version of SLMX-7 based on Graen and Uhl-Bien's (1995) LMX-7. In particular, they worded the items to capture "what the manager receives from the subordinate in the relationship" (p. 701). The way in which they adapted the LMX-7 items was consistent with the parallel approach (Greguras & Ford, 2006). In other words, the items were created to assess, from the supervisor's perspective, how subordinates interact with him or her. In their study, the Cronbach α for the SLMX-7 was .92 and it had a correlation of .46 with subordinate reported LMX.

Liden and colleagues (1993) also provided an alternative version of the seven-item supervisor LMX scale. Using a mirroring approach, their SLMX-7 items mirrored their seven-item member LMX scale. This SLMX-7 had satisfactory internal consistency with Cronbach's αs ranging from .79 to .81 for the total sample measured at three time points. Moreover, factor analysis indicated that SLMX-7 was distinct from leader reported liking of the member and expectations of the member.

Supervisor Versions of Multidimensional LMX

Building on Liden and Maslyn's (1998) multidimensional subordinate LMX measure, Greguras and Ford (2006) developed the multidimensional supervisor LMX scale. To capture the mutual exchange nature of the LMX relationship, Greguras and Ford converted Liden and Maslyn's (1998) LMX-MDM items into SLMX-MDM items in a parallel fashion. In so doing, the SLMX-MDM items assess supervisor's liking, contribution, and respect toward the subordinate and subordinate's loyalty toward the supervisor. Similarly, they also created a parallel version of the SLMX-7 based on Scandura and Graen's (1984) LMX-7 scale, with items such as, "How well do you feel that this subordinate understands your problems and needs?" Consistent with Liden and Maslyn's (1998) LMX-MDM, Greguras and Ford's SLMX-MDM consists of four dimensions, including affect, loyalty, contribution, and professional respect, and this four-dimension structure was supported by CFAs. Correlation analyses showed that the correlation between SLMX-MDM and SLMX-7 was .76, supporting the convergent validity of SLMX-MDM. Regression results showed that the dimensions of SLMX-MDM related differently with the criterion variables and after controlling for LMX-MDM and SLMX-7, respectively; SLMX-MDM explained incremental variance for important outcomes, such as in-role performance and organizational citizenship behaviors. The SLMX-MDM measure demonstrated reliabilities of .90 (Greguras & Ford, 2006) and .86 (Olsson, Hemlin, & Pousette, 2012) for its global construct and reliabilities ranging from .75 to .91 for its four sub-dimensions (Greguras & Ford, 2006; Olsson et al., 2012).

Another four-dimension supervisor LMX-MDM scale was created by Liden, Sparrowe, Erdogan, Gavino, and Maslyn (2006) and used in Sparrowe, Soetjipto, and Kraimer (2006). This scale was based on Liden and Maslyn's (1998) multidimensional subordinate LMX measure as well. The items for affect, loyalty, and professional respect are similar to the items in Greguras and Ford's (2006) measure, but the items for contribution are different. Specifically, the contribution dimension items in Greguras and Ford's measure capture the supervisor's contribution to the subordinate from the supervisor's perspective. In contrast, Liden et al.'s (2006) contribution dimension items reflect the subordinate's contribution to the supervisor.

Leader–Member Agreement

Depicting an exchange relationship between leader and subordinate, LMX delineates leader and subordinate's mutual trust, liking, respect, and obligation (Dienesch & Liden, 1986; Graen & Scandura, 1987; Graen & Uhl-Bien, 1995). As a result, the quality of the relationship is mutually perceived and employees' reported LMX and supervisors' reported LMX should converge. In a meta-analysis with 64 independent studies, Sin, Nahrgang, and Morgeson (2009) found that after correcting for measurement errors, the population estimate correlation between LMX and SLMX was .37, which shows a moderate level of agreement. Notably, Sin et al. (2009) compared the studies using mirroring versions of SLMX (i.e., supervisors report what they provide to a certain subordinate) and the studies using parallel versions of SLMX (i.e., supervisors report what they receive from a certain subordinate) and did not find differences for the true score correlations between studies using different types of SLMX. Using multitrait-multimethod (MTMM) analyses, Joseph and colleagues (2011) showed that leader LMX and member LMX, including leader reports vs. member reports of leader provisions and leader reports of leader provisions vs. member reports of member provisions, appear to be independent constructs.

Exploratory Measures

LMX-24. Current LMX measures are not balanced with respect to the number of items capturing what the leader and member bring to the exchange. For example, all but one item of the LMX-7 deal with what the leader provides to the follower. Only one item, "I have enough confidence in my immediate supervisor that I would defend and justify his or her decisions if he or she were not present to do so," captures what the follower brings to the relationship. Three of the four LMX-MDM dimensions refer to what the leader provides to the follower, whereas the three items contained in the contribution dimension all depict follower behaviors provided for the leader. Chaudhry, Vidyarthi, Glibkowski, Liden, and Wayne (2012) attempted to rectify this imbalance by developing scales based on the LMX-MDM that contain an equal number of items with each referent for assessing both LMX and SLMX. There are 12 LMX items, all of which ask followers to report what the leader provides to them. Similarly, the 12 items used to measure SLMX all capture what the follower provides to the leader.

Leader–member *guanxi* (LMG). Recent years have witnessed the growing acceptance and popularity of the indigenous concept of *guanxi* in the English academic literatures of sociology, social psychology, and business and management (e.g., Bian, 1997; Tsui & Farh, 1997). *Guanxi*, as a cultural phenomenon in China, refers to informal, personal and particularistic relationships at the dyadic level (see Chen & Chen, 2004, for review). In particular, leader–member *guanxi* (LMG, or supervisor–subordinate *guanxi*) has been defined as "a dyadic, particular and sentimental tie that has potential of facilitating favor exchanges between the parties connected by the tie" (Bian, 2006, p. 312). Scholars (Hui & Graen, 1997; Law, Wong, Wang, & Wang, 2000; Lin, 2002) have suggested that *guanxi* and social exchanges are theoretically related but nonequivalent. Although substantial findings regarding LMX theory have been replicated

in Chinese contexts, the construct of LMG emphasizes a unique set of Confucian ideology and social identification processes that may influence personal relationships between a leader and his or her subordinate in Chinese contexts (Farh, Tsui, Xin, & Cheng, 1998). Empirical research has also provided evidence that LMG can explain additional variance when controlling for LMX, and that LMG demonstrates unique association patterns concerning important individual and organizational outcomes (Chen, Friedman, Yu, Fang, & Lu, 2009; Law et al., 2000). Below, we briefly discuss two measures of LMG in light of existing research.

Farh and colleagues (1998) examined LMG based on a categorical approach that views *guanxi* as given, based on particularistic ties. They measured eight specific ties: former classmate, relative, same last name, same natal origin, former colleague, former teacher/student, former boss/subordinate, and former neighbor. They asked subordinates to indicate whether each of these eight ties is present between them and their immediate supervisors. Supervisors were also asked to indicate whether those ties were present between them and their subordinates. Both subordinates and supervisors were given a checklist with a yes/no response format. The presence of *guanxi* in a dyad was recorded only when both parties independently recognized the tie. A dichotomous score was obtained on the *guanxi* variable, with 0 indicating the absence of and 1 indicating the presence of *guanxi*. This measure has two major limitations. First, it is impossible to identify all categories of ties due to the particularistic nature of *guanxi*, as well as to avoid potential overlap among categories. Second, even though the eight categories could be fundamental in relationship building and development in Chinese contexts, this measure cannot provide a direct assessment of the *guanxi* quality between supervisor and subordinate (Chen et al., 2009).

Building on a dynamic process model of *guanxi* development, Chen and coauthors (2009) conceptualized LMG as a multidimensional construct, and conducted three studies using multiple diverse Chinese samples to validate a three-dimensional supervisor-subordinate *guanxi* measure. The three dimensions, including affective attachment, personal-life inclusion, and deference to supervisor, capture the changes that occur when a work relationship between leader and subordinate becomes family-like. Each of the three dimensions has four items. All 12 items were based on 6-point Likert scales, with response options from 1 ("strongly disagree") to 6 ("strongly agree"). In their factor analyses

(Chen et al., 2009), the three-factor model demonstrated good fit, compared with both one- and two-factor models. The reliabilities of the three *guanxi* dimensions ranged from .79 to .89. In addition, the three dimensions strongly correlated with each other, ranging from .61 to .80. Although the correlations between the three *guanxi* dimensions with LMX are high (i.e., .87, .81, and .57, for affective attachment, deference to supervisor, and personal-life inclusion, respectively), Chen and colleagues found support for the discriminant validity of this scale with respect to LMX (LMX-MDM, Liden & Maslyn, 1998) in their studies 2 and 3. By presenting formal psychometric support for the measure, Chen and her colleagues addressed one of the major criticisms of *guanxi* research, though further confirmation of the scale's validities and reliabilities in a wider range of samples is needed. It should be noted that Chen and colleagues' theoretical model focused primarily on the infusion of family-like relations into work relations and paralleled the quality of *guanxi* to the notion of "tie strength" (2004). This dimensional conceptualization of *guanxi* is different from the categorical view, which posits that different *guanxi* bases define different types of relationships and trigger different principles of interaction. Given that there is not a clear conceptual understanding of this Chinese social and cultural phenomenon, we echo other scholars' view (e.g., Yang, 2001) that construct building represents a serious limitation in Chinese *guanxi* theory and research, as well as in these pioneer studies on LMG.

Related Measures

Because relationships between individuals are complex, there are many ways to examine them both conceptually and empirically (Ferris et al., 2009). We present in this section measures selected for their relevance to LMX and the measurement of leader–follower relationships.

Relative LMX. Relative LMX (RLMX) refers to one's own LMX quality as compared with the average LMX quality within a workgroup (Henderson et al., 2008). RLMX concerns the individual-within-group analysis of LMX theory, which helps answer how one's LMX relative to others' LMXs in the workgroup affects the focal employee's attitudes and behaviors (Henderson et al., 2008; Schriesheim, Castro, Zhou, & Yammarino, 2001). Extant studies show that RLMX predicts employee turnover (Graen et al., 1982), in-role performance, organizational citizenship behaviors, job satisfaction, psychological contract fulfillment, and self-efficacy after controlling for LMX (Henderson et al., 2008; Hu &

Liden, 2013; Tse et al., 2012; Vidyarthi et al., 2010). Two approaches have been used to operationalize RLMX. The first approach obtains RLMX scores by subtracting the mean individual-level LMX score in a workgroup from the focal employee's LMX score (Epitropaki & Martin, 2013; Graen et al., 1982; Henderson et al., 2008; Tse et al., 2012). The second approach applies the polynomial regression technique (Edwards, 1993, 1994; Edwards & Parry, 1993) and uses the divergence between individual-level LMX and group mean LMX to operationalize RLMX (Hu & Liden, 2013; Vidyarthi et al., 2010). The second approach is advantageous in considering the interdependence and interactions between individual-level LMX and group mean LMX (Edwards, 1993, 1994; Hu & Liden, 2013).

LMX Social Comparison. LMX social comparison (LMXSC) captures the perceptions of one's own LMX relative to the LMXs of coworkers (Erdogan, 2002; Vidyarthi et al., 2010). Erdogan (2002) developed the six-item LMXSC measure that reflects whether one has a better and more effective relationship with the supervisor, compared with coworkers' LMXs. She further validated the scale and showed that LMXSC was distinct from LMX and controlling for LMX, LMXSC was able to explain interactional justice. Vidyarthi et al. (2010) further showed that after controlling for LMX and RLMX, LMXSC positively related to employee in-role and extra-role performance. LMXSC, as perceived by employees, mediated the effects of RLMX, as operationalized by the incongruence between one's own LMX and group mean LMX, on employee job performance and citizenship behaviors. Across the studies in Erdogan (2002) and Vidyarthi et al. (2010), the LMXSC measure demonstrated high reliabilities, ranging from .84 to .86.

Perceived LMX Variability. Hooper and Martin (2008) developed a single-item measure of LMX distribution to assess subordinates' relationship quality with the leader. This item correlated as high as .75 with the LMX-7 scale. Using this single-item measure, employees were asked to rate their relationship quality and every other team member's relationship quality with the leader. Using these scores reported by the focal employee, a perceived LMX variability score for the focal employee was obtained by calculating the coefficient of variation (i.e., dividing the standard deviation of LMX relationships within the team by the team mean as reported by the focal employee). By so doing, employees each have their own perceived LMX variability scores. Results show that perceived LMX variability negatively associates with employee job satisfaction and well-being and one's perceived relational team conflict mediates the effect of perceived LMX variability on employee job satisfaction and well-being. In a recent study, for example, the LMX distribution scale was used to capture and operationalize perceived LMX differentiation (Zhao, Kessel, & Kratzer, 2013).

Social and Economic Exchange. In order to gauge the general forms of employee exchange relationships with the organization from employees' perspectives, Shore, Tetrick, Lynch, and Barksdale (2006) introduced the social and economic exchange measures. The social exchange measure focuses on the social-emotional side of the exchange relationship between employee and employer while the economic exchange measure reflects the financial and material exchange relationship. The final social exchange scale and economic exchange scale each include eight items, and show acceptable internal consistency (α = .87 for social exchange; α = .78 for economic exchange). A series of CFAs demonstrated that social exchange and economic exchange were two distinct constructs and they were distinct from other exchange related constructs, e.g., perceived organizational support, affective commitment, and continuance commitment. Since it was published, the social and economic exchange measures have been used, in their original forms or with modifications, together or individually, in a number of studies in the arena of social exchange theory and beyond (e.g., Hom, Tsui, Wu, Lee, Zhang, Fu, & Li, 2009; Rousseau, Hornung, & Kim, 2009; Shore, Bommer, Rao, & Seo, 2009; Song, Tsui, & Law, 2009).

Social LMX and Economic LMX. Instead of treating the exchange relationship between leader and subordinates as a continuum ranging from low to high quality, Kuvaas, Buch, Dysvik, and Haerem (2012) developed items adapted from Shore and colleagues' (2006) social/economic exchange scale to measure two aspects of the exchange relationship between leader and subordinate—social LMX (SLMX) and economic LMX (ELMX). SLMX, similar to the traditional conceptualization of LMX, refers to an exchange relationship that is characterized by mutual trust, diffuse obligation, long-term orientation, and social-emotional exchanges (Kuvaas et al., 2012). ELMX, on the other hand, refers to an exchange relationship that is transactional, short-term, and economic- and contract-based (Kuvaas et al., 2012). According to the definitions, SLMX and ELMX are two theoretically distinct constructs that assess two sides of the leader–subordinate exchange relationship. After deleting cross-loaded items from the original 16 items adapted from Shore

and colleagues (2006), Kuvaas et al. (2012) retained four items measuring SLMX (α = .78) and four items assessing ELMX (α = .74). CFAs showed that the two-factor model fit the data well, supporting the distinctiveness of SLMX and ELMX. They also found that SLMX related positively with, whereas ELMX associated negatively with, work performance and organizational citizenship behavior.

Leader–Member Social Exchange. To implicitly measure the exchange nature in LMX, Bernerth, Armenakis, Field, Giles, and Walker (2007) created the leader–member social exchange (LMSX) scale. They coined the term LMSX as "the perception held by subordinates as to whether or not voluntary actions on their part will be returned by the supervisor in some way" (Bernerth et al., 2007, p. 985). Consistent with Liden, Sparrowe, and Wayne (1997), Bernerth and colleagues (2007) noted that previous LMX scales did not fully reflect the exchange notion that underlines LMX theories. To address this issue, following Blau's (1964) social exchange theory, they generated and validated eight items that directly delineated the global exchanges between leader and subordinate. These eight items loaded on a single factor and showed high internal consistency (α = .92). Correlational analyses indicated that LMSX was highly correlated with LMX-7 (r = 0.86, p < .01) and LMX-MDM (r = 0.79, p < .01). Confirmatory factor analyses, however, demonstrated that LMSX was distinct from LMX and LMX-MDM, respectively. In terms of predictive power, controlling for LMX-7, LMSX explained additional variance for quit intentions, organizational commitment, and contextual performance, but not task performance. Controlling for LMX-MDM, LMSX explained additional variance for organizational commitment, contextual performance, task performance, but not quit intentions. It is noted that controlling for LMSX, LMX-MDM was able to explain unique variance for quit intentions and organizational commitment. Overall, the results provided evidence to support the criterion validity of LMSX. The LMSX scale was adopted in a recent study by Gooty and Yammarino (in press) to assess LMX from leader and follower perspectives and the reliabilities were .92 for both sources.

Reciprocity. While LMX is based on the notion of reciprocity, most measures of LMX do not directly assess this aspect of exchange (Liden et al., 1997). That is, reciprocity is a critical component of high-quality exchange relationships; however, the majority of LMX measures attempt to measure the quality of the relationship rather than the degree of reciprocity. Addressing this gap in the literature, Uhl-Bien and Maslyn (2003) developed a measure of subordinate perceptions of reciprocity in their relationship with their manager. Relying on the work of Gouldner (1960), reciprocity is defined as "the pattern of exchange through which the mutual dependence of people, brought about by the division of labor, is realized" (pp. 169–170). This pattern of exchange is impacted by what Gouldner describes as a generalized norm of reciprocity. The norm of reciprocity is manifested when an individual develops obligations or indebtedness towards another based on past behaviors, which drives the individual to repay the other party. Liden and colleagues (1997) and Sparrowe and Liden (1997) integrated the work of Gouldner (1960) and Sahlins (1972) on forms of reciprocity with LMX, which, in turn, formed the basis for the Uhl-Bien and Maslyn (2003, p. 519) measure: (a) equivalence (the extent to which what is given is equivalent to what was received); (b) immediacy (the amount of time between the receipt of an exchange and reciprocation); and (c) interest (whether the dyadic partner's motive for the exchange is based on self-interest, mutual-interest, and other-interest). While Uhl-Bien and Maslyn (2003) link each dimension of reciprocity to member and leader perceptions of relationship quality, their study also employs a configurational approach by examining the dimensions concurrently through cluster analysis. Subordinate reports of immediacy, equivalence, and self-interest were negatively associated with relationship quality whereas mutual-interest was positively associated. Support was also found for hypotheses based on the reciprocal configurations, such as high-quality exchanges (characterized by low equivalence, low immediacy, and mutual- and other-interest) being related to desirable work outcomes. The Uhl-Bien and Maslyn measure is best suited when attempting to assess differences in manager-employee relationships based on reciprocation processes.

Test of Negative Social Exchange. Ruehlman and Karoly (1991) contend that social relationships are comprised of both positive and negative elements. However, they state that measures based on social exchange tend to emphasize positive aspects of the relationship and do not capture negative elements. Addressing this need, they developed an instrument to capture dimensions of negative social interaction, which they labeled the Test of Negative Social Exchange (TENSE). Items were developed to capture a broad range of negative social interactions. The resulting measure consisted of four dimensions: hostility/impatience, insensitivity, interference, and ridicule. While the majority of leader–member relationship measures focus on social exchange, they tend to capture the positive end of the continuum but not the negative end, representing negative exchange. TENSE fills this gap by capturing negative interactions within the relationship. Another approach to capturing negative exchanges in leader-follower relationships is provided by Zahn and Wolf (1981; also see Liden et al., 1997).

Perceived Supervisor Support. With social exchange theoretical underpinnings for predicting employee attitudes and behaviors, organizational support theory (Eisenberger, Huntington, Hutchison, & Sowa, 1986) supposes that employees develop global impressions of the degree to which the organization appreciates their contributions and cares about their well-being (perceived organization support [POS]). Research indicates that employees differentiate between support received from the organization versus that received from their supervisors (Kottke & Sharafinski, 1988). Perceived supervisor support (or PSS; Kottke & Sharafinski, 1988) refers to employees' general perceptions concerning whether their supervisor values their contributions and cares about their well-being. Perceived supervisor support may impact relationship formation and development and serve as an important assessment of the relationship quality from employees' perspectives, given that the quality of exchange relationships is influenced by each party's perceived contributions to the exchange (Dienesch & Liden, 1986). Consistent with Kottke and Sharafinski (1988), Rhoades/Shanock and her colleagues (Rhoades, Eisenberger, & Armeli, 2001; Shanock & Eisenberger, 2006) created the PSS scale by selecting four POS items with high factor loadings and "conveyance, in their adapted form, of general indications concerning a supervisor's positive valuation of the employees' contributions and care about the employees' well-being." (p. 828). Then they modified these four POS items by replacing the word "organization" with "supervisor." Their work demonstrated that psychometric characteristics of PSS mirrored POS. A critical element missing from the development of this scale, however, was an assessment of convergent validity, such as testing the association with LMX and evaluating whether PSS explains incremental variance in outcomes beyond that explained by LMX.

Trust. Trust plays a significant role in high quality relationships (Mayer, Davis, & Schoorman, 1995). Blau (1964) argued that mutually beneficial social exchange relationships require trust. The expectation that one's contribution will be reciprocated sometime in the future is essential to the exchange relationship. The significance of trust in leadership has also been emphasized repeatedly in past decades (see Dirks & Ferrin, 2002, for a review). With respect to LMX, Dienesch and Liden (1986) acknowledged the possibility of other dimensions being involved in developing and maintaining leader–member relationships, besides contribution, loyalty, and affect. Trust was identified as a dimension of LMX in the critical incident interviews conducted by Liden and Maslyn (1998), an initial phase of their development of the LMX-MDM. However, during the content validation phase, content experts were unable to differentiate items intended to capture the loyalty dimension versus items designed to assess trust. Liden and Maslyn resolved the problem by retaining only the loyalty dimension.

LMX has been shown to be positively associated with trust in the supervisor (Gómez & Rosen, 2001). However, contrary to LMX and social exchange theories, trust is not necessarily reciprocal or mutual (Schoorman, Mayer, & Davis, 2007). As suggested by Schoorman and colleagues (2007), this inconsistency may "present a fruitful area for future research" (p. 347). The concept of trust is enormously rich and complex. Scholars in this area have defined trust differently, and the measurement of trust varies accordingly.

McAllister (1995) developed a two-dimensional measure of trust (see Appendix 1). This measure consists of 11 items. Six cognition-based trust items were designed to capture the sense of reliability and dependability and the expectations of competence and responsibility. Five affect-based trust items were designed to capture the emotional bonds between individuals (i.e., emotional investments, genuine concern for the other, and belief in the intrinsic virtue of the relationship). In this scale development study, the respondents used a 7-point Likert scale, ranging from 1 ("strongly disagree") to 7 ("strongly agree"). Factor analyses supported the two-dimensional conceptualization of trust. The Cronbach's αs for the cognition- and affect-based trust measures were .91 and .89, respectively. Recent studies distinguishing between the cognition- and affect-based trust often adapted McAllister's (1995) measure, and have demonstrated promising evidence for the scale's psychometric properties. For instance, Colquitt and colleagues (Colquitt, LePine, Piccolo, Zapata, & Rich, 2012) adapted this scale to measure employees' cognition- and affect-based trust in supervisor, and found coefficient αs of .88 and .93 for cognition-based and affect-based trust, respectively. Their CFA also supported the 2-dimensional model of trust. However, other researchers (Yang

& Mossholder, 2010) cautioned that McAllister's (1995) measure was developed for trust between peer managers, and "more work needed to be done regarding a measure of trust using a bases-and-foci framework" (p. 54). Therefore, Yang and Mossholder (2010) developed a new 20-item instrument (see Appendix 1) assessing the two principal foundations of trust (cognition and affect) and two foci (management and immediate supervisor). A 5-point response format was used for the instrument in this study, ranging from 1 ("strongly disagree") to 5 ("strongly agree"). Their results demonstrated acceptable reliability for all five-item measures (cognitive trust in management α = .95, affective trust in management α = .94, cognitive trust in supervisor α = .94, and affective trust in supervisor α = .95). Exploratory factor analyses and CFAs both suggested good fit of the four-factor trust model.

In contrast with the two-dimensional conceptualization, other scholars following the definition given by Mayer and colleagues (1995), defined "trust" as the willingness to be vulnerable to another party. Schoorman and colleagues (2007) provided a brief review of measures of trust, including four-item (Schoorman, Mayer, & Davis, 1996), five-item (Mayer & Gavin, 2005), seven-item (Schoorman & Ballinger, 2006), and 10-item (Gillespie, 2003) measures. As they pointed out, empirical studies revealed low internal consistency reliability of the original four-item measure (Schoorman et al., 1996), which is understandable and acceptable for such a "complex construct that has maximum validity" (Kline, 1986). Among the more recent scale development efforts, Schoorman and Ballinger's (2006) seven-item scale was considered the most promising measure to date. Using a 5-point Likert response scale and a sample of veterinary hospital employees, Schoorman and Ballinger (2006) produced an α level of .84. This seven-item scale, capturing the willingness to be vulnerable to one's supervisor, is included in Appendix 1.

Interpersonal Reactivity Index. Drawing from various theoretical perspectives, Colbert, Bono, and Purvanova (2008) identified mutual caring and concern as one of the central characteristics of high-quality supervisory relationships. The role of empathic concern and perspective taking has been highlighted in transformational leadership (Kuhnert & Lewis, 1987). Goleman (1995) stated that empathy is an important leadership skill, because it can inspire and motivate others. Although few LMX studies directly examined shared concerns or goals, the LMX literature assumes the concept of mutuality (Baumeister & Leary, 1995) in high-quality

LMXs. Empathy skills allow leaders to better understand subordinates' perspectives and opinions, making the mutuality and communal norms possible. Regardless of theoretical background, most theorists posit that perspective-taking and empathic concerns are essential components of successful social interactions (Parker & Axtell, 2001).

Davis (1980) developed the Interpersonal Reactivity Index (IRI, see Appendix 1), which has become a frequently used measure for empathy. Davis considered empathy as a set of distinct constructs related in that they all concern the reactions of one individual to the observed experiences of another. The 28-item IRI is self-reported and consists of four seven-item subscales: perspective-taking, empathic concern, personal distress, and fantasy. In the interests of this essay, we focus only on the first two dimensions. The perspective-taking scale assesses the tendency to view the world through others' eyes. The empathic concern scale measures sympathy feelings and concern for others. Davis (1980, 1983) found support for the internal consistency for the subscales. Although the two subscales, perspective-taking and empathic concern, are well suited to capture the general groundings of perspective-taking behaviors, we need to point out that Davis' (1980) scale is a more dispositional assessment of empathy. It is more appropriate for measuring an individual's stable tendency and capacity to take others' perspectives and show concern for others. Moreover, studies using IRI need to be aware of problems with single time point self-report data.

Perspective Taking. Parker and Axtell (2001) made an attempt to simplify the measurement of perspective taking with two indicators: *feelings of empathy* and *making positive attributions* about behaviors and outcomes. Their measure consists of three items for each of the indicators. A 5-point Likert response scale, ranging from 1 ("strongly disagree") to 5 ("strongly agree"), was used. Their results suggested acceptable reliabilities (.78 for empathy, and .71 for positive attributions), and supported their proposed factor structure. This measure is distinct from the IRI, because Parker and Axtell (2001) theorize perspective taking as a cognitive-affective experience that is target specific.

We note that both the IRI and Parker and Axtell's measures were designed for horizontal (i.e., same-level employee) interactions. In order to adapt these measures to supervisor-subordinate relationships, researchers need to take into account the hierarchical and dyadic nature of supervisory relationships.

Social Network Analysis and Measures. Sparrowe and Liden (1997) view social network analysis and LMX theory as complementary. The first aspect of social network elements that closely relates to LMX is the strength of network ties. Social network literature defines tie strength as the linear combination of amount of time, emotional intensity, intimacy, and reciprocity (Granovetter, 1973). Krackhardt (1992) further propounded the idea of tie strength as the quality of relationship that involves interaction, affection, and time. In addition to tapping into dyadic relationship quality, social network analysis provides the means to reflect the structure of exchange relationships. In pioneering studies that integrate leadership theory and network analysis, two network measures have been used: centrality and density. Sparrowe and colleagues (Sparrowe, Liden, Wayne, & Kraimer, 2001) have provided detailed description of these two network measures. Other examples include Burt (2001), Ibarra (1993), as well as Sparrowe and Liden (2005).

Centrality refers to "the extent to which a given individual is connected to others in a network" (Sparrowe et al., 2001, p. 316). It is a structural property associated with instrumental outcomes such as power (Brass, 1984). Centrality is important when social interaction is not solely determined by formal structures. Thus, it complements LMX, which focuses on leader–member dyads. Centrality is often assessed as the number of network ties per focal network member relative to the number of ties of others in the network (Sparrowe et al., 2001). High variance in centrality suggests that some individuals have proportionately more ties than others, and therefore interactions are more concentrated in these individuals.

Density is defined as "the ratio of the number of relationships that exist to the total number of possible ties in the network, if each member were tied to each other" (Wasserman & Galaskiewicz, 1994, p. 101). Greater network density indicates a higher overall level of interaction among network members (Sparrowe et al., 2001). Density, a group-level variable, has been associated with social support (Ibarra, 1995) as well as identification and feelings of belonging (Podolny & Baron, 1997). While LMX measures focus on the quality of dyadic relationships between leaders and subordinates, social networks address the nested and interacting exchange relationships within organizations.

Suggestions for Future Research and Development

Since 2000 LMX research has seen the introduction of an array of new measurement approaches (Bernerth et al., 2007; Henderson et al., 2008;

Hooper & Martin, 2008; Hu & Liden, 2013; Kuvaas et al., 2012; Shore et al., 2006; Uhl-Bien & Maslyn, 2003; Vidyarthi et al., 2010). Perhaps the most promising of these is the LMXSC (Vidyarthi et al., 2010), which is based on the predominant force within most individuals to assess their status and position based on their perceived ranking relative to peers. Perceived relative standing appears to be more important to most individuals than absolute possession of desired tangible or intangible resources. Thus, relationship quality as assessed with the LMX-MDM and LMX-7, may take a back seat to focal individuals' perceptions of how their relationships with the leader compare with the relationships that coworkers have with the leader. Although the currently available LMXSC measure has shown acceptable internal consistency reliability, convergent, and criterion-related validity, the scale was not developed following the full set of recommended scale development procedures, such as used in the development of the LMX-MDM (qualitative methods and assessment of theory in order to define the domain of the construct, content validation, assessment of susceptibility to social desirability response sets, etc.). Therefore, future research may endeavor to create a more psychometrically sound measure of LMX social comparison.

Perhaps due to consistent evidence of positive associations between LMX quality and personal outcomes (Dulebohn et al., 2012; Gerstner & Day, 1997; Ilies, Nahrgang, & Morgeson, 2007), it is typically assumed that all individuals desire a high LMX relationship. This assumption neglects the acknowledgement by LMX theorists (Dienesch & Liden, 1986; Graen, 1976; Graen & Scandura, 1987) that some followers may reject leaders' "offers" of high-quality LMX relationships. This suggests that implicit theories concerning the "desire for high quality LMX relationships" should be taken into consideration. One possibility is to develop a measure that captures followers' implicit theories regarding LMX. Specifically, it may be useful to assess the degree to which individuals, in general, wish to have high-quality LMX relationships. For example, as Dienesch and Liden (1986) commented, if followers feel that they are "being used" by a leader, they may be reluctant to enter a special (high LMX) relationship with that leader. Such a measure of desire for a high LMX relationship may serve an important role as a moderator of relationships between LMX and outcomes.

Summary and Conclusions

After a development period of about 25 years, LMX research has come to consistently rely on either the LMX-7 or LMX-MDM measures. Although the LMX-7 was developed in piecemeal fashion compared with the rigorous scale development procedures used in the development of LMX-MDM, the two measures correlate highly and show a consistent pattern of relationships with both antecedents and outcomes (Dulebohn et al., 2012). Updating the advice of Gerstner and Day (1997), we recommend that LMX research employ the LMX-MDM, due to empirical evidence of its psychometric properties and its capability for addressing research questions dealing both with LMX dimension as well as global LMX. Perhaps the most promising of the new measures of LMX is the LMXSC, which has been shown to explain variance in outcomes beyond LMX per se (Vidyarthi et al., 2010). Indeed, although "raw" LMX quality is salient, followers appear to be influenced more by the way their relationship quality with the immediate leader compares to the perceived relationship quality that peers have with the leader. This social comparison approach to assessing LMX may play an increasingly important role in future LMX research.

References

Bauer, T. N., & Green, S. G. (1996). The development of leader-member exchange: A longitudinal test. *Academy of Management Journal, 39,* 1538–1567.

Baumeister, R. F., & Leary, M. R. (1995). The need to belong: Desire for interpersonal attachments as a fundamental human motivation. *Psychological Bulletin, 117,* 497–529.

Bernerth, J. B., Armenakis, A. A., Feild, H. S., Giles, W. F., & Walker, H. J. (2007). Leader–member social exchange (LMSX): Development and validation of a scale. *Journal of Organizational Behavior, 28,* 979–1003.

Bian, Y. (1997). Bringing strong ties back in: Indirect ties, network bridges, and job searches in China. *American Sociological Review, 62,* 366–385.

Bian, Y. J. (2006). Guanxi. In J. Beckert & M. Zafirovski (Eds.), *International encyclopedia of economic sociology* (pp. 312–314). New York: Routledge.

Blau, P. M. (1964). *Exchange and power in social life.* New York: Wiley.

Brass, D. J. (1984). Being in the right place: A structural analysis of individual influence in an organization. *Administrative Science Quarterly, 29,* 518–539.

Burt, R. S. (2001). Structural holes versus network closure as social capital. In Lin, N., Cook, K. S., & Burt, R. S. (Eds.), *Social capital: Theory and research* (pp. 31–56). New Brunswick, NJ: Transaction Publishers.

Cashman, J., Dansereau, F., Graen, G., & Haga, W. J. (1976). Organizational understructure and leadership: A longitudinal investigation of the managerial role-making process. *Organizational Behavior and Human Performance, 15,* 278–296.

Chaudhry, A., Vidyarthi, P., Glibkowski, B., Liden, R. C., & Wayne, S. J. (August, 2012). *It Takes Two to Tango: Examining the Effects of Convergence in Leader and Member Perceptions of LMX.* Paper presented at annual meeting of the Academy of Management, Boston, MA.

Chen, X. P., & Chen, C. C. (2004). On the intricacies of the Chinese *guanxi*: A process model of *guanxi* development. *Asia Pacific Journal of Management, 21*, 305–324.

Chen, Y., Friedman, R., Yu, E., Fang, W., & Lu, X. (2009). Developing a three-dimensional model and scale for supervisor-subordinate Guanxi. *Management and Organization Review, 5*, 375–399.

Colbert, A. E., Bono, J. E., & Purvanova, R. K. (2008). Generative leadership in business organizations: Enhancing employee cooperation and well-being through high-quality relationships. In B. A. Sullivan, M. Snyder, & J. L. Sullivan (Eds.), *Cooperation: The political psychology of effective human interaction* (pp. 199–217). Oxford: Blackwell Publishing.

Colquitt, J. A., LePine, J. A., Piccolo, R. F., Zapata, C. P., & Rich, B. L. (2012). Explaining the justice–performance relationship: Trust as exchange deepener or trust as uncertainty reducer? *Journal of Applied Psychology, 97*, 1–15.

Dansereau, F. (1972). *The invisible organization*. Doctoral dissertation, University of Illinois at Champaign-Urbana.

Dansereau, F., Graen, G., & Cashman, J. (1973). Instrumentality and equity theory as complementary approaches in predicting the relationship of leadership and turnover among managers. *Organizational Behavior and Human Performance, 10*, 184–200.

Dansereau, F., Jr., Graen, G., & Haga, W. J. (1975). A vertical dyad linkage approach to leadership within formal organizations: A longitudinal investigation of the role-making process. *Organizational Behavior and Human Performance, 13*, 46–78.

Dansereau, F., Seitz, S. R., Chiu, C. Y., Shaughnessy, B., & Yammarino, F. J. (2013). What makes leadership, leadership? Using self-expansion theory to integrate traditional and contemporary approaches. *The Leadership Quarterly, 24*, 798–821.

Davis, M. (1980). A multidimensional approach to individual differences in empathy. *JSAS Catalog of Selected Documents in Psychology, 10*, 85.

Davis, M. H. (1983). The effects of dispositional empathy on emotional reactions and helping: A multidimensional approach. *Journal of Personality, 51*, 167–184.

Dienesch, R. M., & Liden, R. C. (1986). Leader–member exchange model of leadership: A critique and further development. *Academy of Management Review, 11*, 618–634.

Dirks, K. T., & Ferrin, D. L. (2002). Trust in leadership: Meta-analytic findings and implications for research and practice. *Journal of Applied Psychology, 87*, 611–628.

Dulebohn, J. H., Bommer, W. H., Liden, R. C., Brouer, R., & Ferris, G. R. (2012). A meta-analysis of the antecedents and consequences of leader-member exchange: Integrating the past with an eye toward the future. *Journal of Management, 38*, 1715–1759.

Edwards J. R. (1993). Problems with the use of profile similarity indices in the study of congruence in organizational research. *Personnel Psychology, 46*, 641–665.

Edwards, J. R. (1994). The study of congruence in organizational behavior research: Critique and a proposed alternative. *Organizational Behavior and Human Decision Processes, 58*, 51–100.

Edwards, J. R., & Parry, M. E. (1993). On the use of polynomial regression equations as an alternative to difference scores in organizational research. *Academy of Management Journal, 36*, 1577–1613.

Eisenberger, R., Huntington, R., Hutchison, S., & Sowa, D. (1986). Perceived organizational support. *Journal of Applied Psychology, 71*, 500–507.

Epitropaki, O., & Martin, R. (2013). Transformational–transactional leadership and upward influence: The role of Relative Leader–Member Exchanges (RLMX) and Perceived Organizational Support (POS). *The Leadership Quarterly, 24*, 299–315.

Erdogan, B. (2002). *Leader–member exchange differentiation fairness: Evidence for a new construct*. Retrieved from Dissertation Abstracts International. (UMI No. AAT 3058101).

Farh, J., Tsui, A. S., Xin, K., & Cheng, B. (1998). The influence of relational demography and *guanxi*: The Chinese case. *Organization Science, 9*, 471–488.

Ferris, G. R. (1985). Role of leadership in the employee withdrawal process: A constructive replication. *Journal of Applied Psychology, 70*, 777–781.

Ferris, G. R., Liden, R. C., Munyon, T. P., Summers, J. K., Basik, K. J., & Buckley, M. R. (2009). Relationships at work: Toward a multidimensional conceptualization of dyadic work relationships. *Journal of Management, 35*, 1379–1403.

Gerstner, C. R., & Day, D. V. (1997). Meta-analytic review of leader–member exchange theory: Correlates and construct issues. *Journal of Applied Psychology, 82*, 827–844.

Gillespie, N. (2003). *Measuring trust in work relationships: The Behavioral Trust Inventory*. Paper presented at the annual meeting of the Academy of Management, Seattle.

Goleman, D. (1995). *Emotional intelligence: Why it can matter more than IQ?* New York: Bantam Books.

Gómez, C., & Rosen, B. (2001). The leader-member exchange as a link between managerial trust and employee empowerment. *Group & Organization Management, 26*, 53–69.

Gooty, J., & Yammarino, F. J. (in press). The leader-member exchange relationship: A multisource, cross-level investigation. *Journal of Management*.

Gouldner, A. W. (1960). The norm of reciprocity: A preliminary statement. *American Sociological Review, 25*, 161–177.

Graen, G. (1976). Role-making processes within complex organizations. In M. D. Dunnette (Ed.), *Handbook of industrial and organizational psychology* (pp.1201–1245). Chicago: Rand McNally.

Graen, G., & Cashman, J. F. (1975). A role-making model of leadership in formal organizations: A developmental approach. In: J. G. Hunt & L. L. Larson (Eds), *Leadership frontiers* (pp. 143–165). Kent, OH: Kent State University Press.

Graen, G., Dansereau, F., & Minami, T. (1972). Dysfunctional leadership styles. *Organizational Behavior and Human Performance, 7*, 216–236.

Graen, G., & Ginsburgh, S. (1977). Job resignation as a function of role orientation and leader acceptance: A longitudinal investigation of organizational assimilation. *Organizational Behavior and Human Performance, 19*, 1–17.

Graen, G., Liden, R. C., & Hoel, W. (1982). The role of leadership in the employee withdrawal process. *Journal of Applied Psychology, 67*, 868–872.

Graen, G. B., Novak, M. A., & Sommerkamp, P. (1982). The effects of leader-member exchange and job design on productivity and satisfaction: Testing a dual attachment model. *Organizational Behavior and Human Performance, 30*, 109–131.

Graen, G. B., & Scandura, T. A. (1987). Toward a psychology of dyadic organizing. *Research in Organizational Behavior, 9*, 175–208.

Graen, G., & Schiemann, W. (1978). Leader-member agreement: A vertical dyad linkage approach. *Journal of Applied Psychology, 63*, 206–212.

Graen, G. B., & Uhl-Bien, M. (1995). Relationship-based approach to leadership: Development of leader–member exchange (LMX) theory of leadership over 25 years: Applying a multi-level multi-domain perspective. *The Leadership Quarterly, 6,* 219–247.

Granovetter, M. S. (1973). The strength of weak ties. *American Journal of Sociology, 78,* 1360–1380.

Greguras, G. J., & Ford, J. M. (2006). An examination of the multidimensionality of supervisor and subordinate perceptions of leader-member exchange. *Journal of Occupational and Organizational Psychology, 79,* 433–465.

Henderson, D., Wayne, S. J., Shore, L. M., Bommer, W. H., & Tetrick, L. E. (2008). Leader-member exchange within the work group and psychological contract fulfillment: A multi-level approach. *Journal of Applied Psychology, 93,* 1208–1219.

Hom, P. W., Tsui, A. S., Wu, J. B., Lee, T. W., Zhang, A. Y., Fu, P. P., & Li, L. (2009). Explaining employment relationships with social exchange and job embeddedness. *Journal of Applied Psychology, 94,* 277–297.

Hooper, D. T., & Martin, R. (2008). Beyond personal leader–member exchange (LMX) quality: The effects of perceived LMX variability on employee reactions. *The Leadership Quarterly, 19,* 20–30.

Hu, J., & Liden, R. C. (2013). Relative leader–member exchange within team contexts: How and when social comparison impacts individual effectiveness. *Personnel Psychology, 66,* 127–172.

Huang, X., Wright, R. P., Chiu, W. C., & Wang, C. (2008). Relational schemas as sources of evaluation and misevaluation of leader–member exchanges: Some initial evidence. *The Leadership Quarterly, 19,* 266–282.

Hui, C., & Graen, G. (1997). Guanxi and professional leadership in contemporary Sino-American joint ventures in mainland China. *The Leadership Quarterly, 8,* 451–465.

Ibarra, H. (1993). Personal networks of women and minorities in management: A conceptual framework. *Academy of Management Review, 18,* 56–87.

Ibarra, H. (1995). Race, opportunity, and diversity of social circles in managerial networks. *Academy of Management Journal, 38,* 673–703.

Ilies, R., Nahrgang, J. D., & Morgeson, F. P. (2007). Leader-member exchange and citizenship behaviors: A meta-analysis. *Journal of Applied Psychology, 92,* 269–277.

Joseph, D. A., Newman, D. A., & Sin, H. (2011). Leader–Member Exchange (LMX) measurement: Evidence for consensus, construct breadth, and discriminant validity. In D. Ketchen & D. Bergh (Eds.), *Research Methodology in Strategy and Management* (vol. 6, pp. 89–135). Bingley, UK: Emerald Group Publishing Limited.

Keller, R., & Dansereau, F. (2001). The effect of adding items to scales: An illustrative case of LMX. *Organizational Research Methods, 4,* 131–143.

Kline, P. (1986). *A handbook of test construction: Introduction to psychometric design.* London: Methuen.

Kottke, J. L., & Sharafinski, C. E. (1988). Measuring perceived supervisory and organizational support. *Educational and Psychological Measurement, 48,* 1075–1079.

Krackhardt, D. 1992. The strength of strong ties: The importance of philos in organizations. In N. Nohria & R. G. Eccles (Eds.), *Networks and organizations: Structure, form and action* (pp. 216–239). Cambridge, MA: Harvard Business School Press.

Kuhnert, K. W., & Lewis, P. (1987). Transactional and transformational leadership: A constructive/developmental analysis. *Academy of Management Review, 12,* 648–657.

Kuvaas, B., Buch, R., Dysvik, A., & Haerem, T. (2012). Economic and social leader–member exchange relationships

and follower performance. *The Leadership Quarterly, 23,* 756–765.

Law, K. S., Wong, C. S., Wang, D. X., & Wang, L. H. (2000). Effect of supervisor–subordinate guanxi on supervisory decisions in China: An empirical investigation. *International Journal of Human Resource Management, 11,* 715–730.

Liden, R. C., Erdogan, B., Wayne, S. J., & Sparrowe, R. T. (2006). Leader-member exchange, differentiation, and task interdependence: Implications for individual and group performance. *Journal of Organizational Behavior, 27,* 723–746.

Liden, R. C., & Graen, G. (1980). Generalizability of the vertical dyad linkage model of leadership. *Academy of Management Journal, 23,* 451–465.

Liden, R. C., & Maslyn, J. M. (1998). Multidimensionality of leader-member exchange: An empirical assessment through scale development. *Journal of Management, 24,* 43–72.

Liden, R. C., Sparrowe, R. T., Erdogan, B., Gavino, M., & Maslyn, J. M. (2006, August). *The role of proactive personality and behaviors on social exchange relationships in the workplace.* Paper presented at the national meetings of the Academy of Management, Atlanta, GA.

Liden, R. C., Sparrowe, R. T., & Wayne, S. J. (1997). Leader-member exchange theory: The past and potential for the future. In G. R. Ferris, & K. M. Rowland (Eds.), *Research in personnel and human resources management* (Vol. 15, pp. 47–199). Greenwich, CT: JAI Press.

Liden, R. C., Wayne, S. J., & Stilwell, D. (1993). A longitudinal study on the early development of leader-member exchanges. *Journal of Applied Psychology, 78,* 662–674.

Lin, Y. M. (2002). Beyond dyadic social exchange: Guanxi and third-party effects. In G. Thomas, D. Guthrie, & D. Wank (Eds.), *Social connections in China: Institutions, culture, and the changing nature of guanxi* (No. 21, pp. 57–76). Cambridge University Press.

Maslyn, J. M., & Uhl-Bien, M. (2001). Leader-member exchange and its dimensions: Effects of self-effort and other's effort ton relationship quality. *Journal of Applied Psychology, 86,* 697–708.

Mayer, R. C., Davis, J. H., & Schoorman, F. D. (1995). An integrative model of organizational trust. *Academy of Management Review, 20,* 709–734.

Mayer, R. C., & Gavin, M. B. (2005). Trust in management and performance: Who minds the shop while the employees watch the boss? *Academy of Management Journal, 48,* 874–888.

McAllister, D. J. (1995). Affect- and cognition-based trust as foundations for interpersonal cooperation in organizations. *Academy of Management Journal, 38,* 24–59.

Olsson, L., Hemlin, S., & Pousette, A. (2012). A multi-level analysis of leader–member exchange and creative performance in research groups. *The Leadership Quarterly, 23,* 604–619.

Parker, S. K., & Axtell, C. M. (2001). Seeing another viewpoint: Antecedents and outcomes of employee perspective taking. *Academy of Management Journal, 44,* 1085–1100.

Podolny, J. M., & Baron, J. N. (1997). Resources and relationships: Social networks and mobility in the workplace. *American Sociological Review, 62,* 673–693.

Rhoades, L., Eisenberger, R., & Armeli, S. (2001). Affective commitment to the organization: The contribution of perceived organizational support. *Journal of Applied Psychology, 86,* 825–836.

Rousseau, D. M., Hornung, S., & Kim, T. G. (2009). Idiosyncratic deals: Testing propositions on timing, content, and the employment relationship. *Journal of Vocational Behavior, 74*, 338–348.

Ruehlman, L. S., & Karoly, P. (1991). With a little flak from my friends: Development and preliminary validation of the test of negative social exchange (TENSE). *Psychological Assessment: A Journal of Consulting and Clinical Psychology, 3*, 97–104.

Sahlins, M. (1972). Stone age economics. New York: Aldine De Gruyter.

Scandura, T. A., & Graen, G. B. (1984). Moderating effects of initial leader-member exchange status on the effects of a leadership intervention. *Journal of Applied Psychology, 69*, 428–436.

Scandura, T. A., & Schriesheim, C. A. (1994). Leader-member exchange and supervisor career mentoring as complementary constructs in leadership research. *Academy of Management Journal, 37*, 1588–1602.

Schoorman, F. D., & Ballinger, G. A. (2006). *Leadership, trust and client service in veterinary hospitals*. Working paper, Purdue University, West Lafayette, IN.

Schoorman, F. D., Mayer, R. C., & Davis, J. H. (1996). *Empowerment in veterinary clinics: The role of trust in delegation*. Presented in a symposium on trust at the 11th Annual Conference, Society for Industrial and Organizational Psychology (SIOP), San Diego, CA.

Schoorman, F. D., Mayer, R. C., & Davis, J. H. (2007). An integrative model of organizational trust: Past, present, and future. *Academy of Management Review, 32*, 344–354.

Schriesheim, C. A., Castro, S. L., & Yammarino, F. J. (2000). Investigating contingencies: An examination of the impact of span of supervision and upward controllingness on leader–member exchange using traditional and multivariate within-and between-entities analysis. *Journal of Applied Psychology, 85*, 659–677.

Schriesheim, C. A., Castro, S. L., Zhou, X., & Yammarino, F. J. (2001). The folly of theorizing "A" but testing "B": A selective level of analysis review of the field and a detailed leader–member exchange (LMX) illustration. *The Leadership Quarterly, 12*, 515–551.

Schriesheim, C. A., Neider, L. L., & Scandura, T. A. (1998). Delegation and leader-member exchange: Main effects, moderators, and measurement issues. *Academy of Management Journal, 41*, 298–318.

Settoon, R. P., Bennett, N., & Liden, R. C. (1996). Social exchange in organizations: Perceived organizational support, leader-member exchange, and employee reciprocity. *Journal of Applied Psychology, 81*, 219–227.

Shanock, L. R., & Eisenberger, R. (2006). When supervisors feel supported: Relationships with subordinates' perceived supervisor support, perceived organizational support, and performance. *Journal of Applied Psychology, 91*, 689–695.

Shore, L. M., Bommer, W. H., Rao, A. N., & Seo, J. (2009). Social and economic exchange in the employee-organization relationship: The moderating role of reciprocation wariness. *Journal of Managerial Psychology, 24*, 701–721.

Shore, L. M., Tetrick, L. E., Lynch, P., & Barksdale, K. (2006). Social and economic exchange: Construct development and validation. *Journal of Applied Social Psychology, 36*, 837–867.

Sin, H. P., Nahrgang, J. D., & Morgeson, F. P. (2009). Understanding why they don't see eye to eye: An examination of leader-member exchange (LMX) Agreement. *Journal of Applied Psychology, 94*, 1048–1057.

Song, L. J., Tsui, A. S., & Law, K. S. (2009). Unpacking employee responses to organizational exchange mechanisms: The role of social and economic exchange perceptions. *Journal of Management, 35*, 56–93.

Sparrowe, R. T., & Liden, R. C. (1997). Process and structure in leader-member exchange. *Academy of Management Review, 22*, 522–552.

Sparrowe, R. T., & Liden, R. C. (2005). Two routes to influence: Integrating leader-member exchange and social network perspectives. *Administrative Science Quarterly, 50*, 505–535.

Sparrowe, R. T., Liden, R. C., Wayne, S. J., & Kraimer, M. L. (2001). Social networks and the performance of individuals and groups. *Academy of Management Journal, 44*, 316–325.

Sparrowe, R. T., Soetjipto, B. W., & Kraimer, M. L. (2006). Do leaders' influence tactics relate to members' helping behavior? It depends on the quality of the relationship. *Academy of Management Journal, 49*, 1194–1208.

Tse, H. H. M., Ashkanasy, N., & Dasborough, M. T. (2012). Relative leader–member exchange, negative affectivity and social identification: A moderated-mediation examination. *The Leadership Quarterly, 23*, 354–366.

Tsui, A. S., & Farh, J. L. (1997). Where Guanxi matters: Relational demography and guanxi in the Chinese context. *Work and Occupations, 24*, 56–79.

Uhl-Bien, M. & Maslyn, J. M. (2003). Reciprocity in manager-subordinate relationships: Components, configurations, and outcomes. *Journal of Management, 29*, 511–532.

Vidyarthi, P., Liden, R. C., Anand, S., Erdogan, B., & Ghosh, S. (2010) Where do I stand? Examining the effects of leader-member exchange social comparison on employee work behaviors. *Journal of Applied Psychology, 95*, 849–861.

Wakabayashi, M., & Graen, G. (1984). The Japanese career progress study: A seven year follow-up. *Journal of Applied Psychology, 69*, 603–614.

Wakabayashi, M., Graen, G., Graen, M., & Graen, M. (1988). Japanese management progress: Mobility into middle management. *Journal of Applied Psychology, 73*, 217–227.

Wasserman, S., & Galaskiewicz, J. (1994). *Advances in social network analysis: Research in the social and behavioral sciences*. Thousand Oaks, CA: Sage.

Yang, C. F. (2001). A critical review of the conceptualization of *guanxi* and *renqing*. In C. F. Yang (Ed.), *The interpersonal relationship, affection, and trust of the Chinese: From an interactional perspective* (pp. 3–26). Taipei: Yuan Liou Publishing. (In Chinese).

Yang, J., & Mossholder, K. W. (2010). Examining the effects of trust in leaders: A bases-and-foci approach. *The Leadership Quarterly, 21*, 50–63.

Zahn, G. L., & Wolf, G. (1981). Leadership and the art of cycle maintenance: A simulation model of superior-subordinate interaction. *Organizational Behavior and Human Performance, 28*, 26–49.

Zhao, H., Kessel, M., & Kratzer, J. (2013). Supervisor-subordinate relationship, differentiation, and employee creativity: A self-categorization perspective. *Journal of Creative Behavior, 48*, 165–184.

Appendix 1: Past Versions of VDL and LMX Scales and Related Measures

Negotiating Latitude (two-items)

Reprinted from *Organizational Behavior and Human Performance, Vol. 13,* Dansereau, F., Jr., Graen, G., &

1. How flexible do you believe your supervisor is about evolving changes in your job activity structure? (he sees no need for change = 1; he sees little need for change = 2; he is lukewarm about change = 3; he is enthused about change = 4)

2. Regardless of how much formal authority your supervisor has built into his position, what are the chances that he would be personally inclined to use his power to help you solve problems in your work? (no chance = 1; he might or might not = 2; he probably would = 3; he certainly would = 4)

Note. No reliability information for this measure was provided.

Negotiating Latitude (four-items)

1. How flexible do you believe your supervisor is about evolving changes in your job? (supervisor sees no need to change = 1; he sees little need to change = 2; he is lukewarm about change = 3; he is enthused about change = 4)

2. Regardless of how much formal authority your supervisor has built into his position, what are the chances that he would be personally inclined to use his power to help you solve problems in your work? (not at all = 1; he might or might not = 2; he probably would = 3; he certainly would = 4)

3. To what extent can you count on your supervisor to "bail you out", at his expense, when you really need him? (not at all = 1; he might or might not = 2; he probably would = 3; he certainly would = 4)

4. How often do you take your suggestions regarding your work to your supervisor? (never = 1; seldom = 2; usually = 3; almost always = 4)

Note. Items were summed to form a composite and then divided into lower (out-group) third, middle third (middle-group), and higher third (in-group). Reliability was estimated based on a test-retest correlation (3-month separation) of .75.

Vertical Exchange (four-items)
Graen, G. (1980).Generalizability of the vertical dyad linkage model of leadership. *Academy of Management Journal, 23,* 451–465.

1. How flexible do you believe your supervisor is about evolving change in your job duties and responsibilities?

2. Regardless of how much formal organizational authority your supervisor has built into his position, what are the chances that he would be personally inclined to use his power to help you solve a problem in your work?

3. How often do you take your suggestions regarding your work to your supervisor?

4. To what extent can you count on your supervisor to "bail you out" at his expense when you really need him?

Note. The first scale referred to as measuring LMX (Graen & Schiemann, 1978) contained 4 items that closely resemble the VDL four-item measure (Liden & Graen, 1980). Reliability from test-retest correlations between time periods were provided for "pattern agreement" across all scales included in the study of agreement between leader and follower, but reliability information specific to LMX was not provided.

Leader-Member Exchange (five-items)

1. How flexible do you believe your supervisor is about evolving change in *your* job? (4 = Supervisor is enthused about change; 3 = Supervisor is lukewarm to change; 2 = Supervisor sees little need to change; 1 = Supervisor sees no need for change)

2. Regardless of how much formal organizational authority your supervisor has built into his/her position, what are the chances that he/she would be personally inclined to use his/her power to help *you* solve problems in your work? (4 = He certainly would; 3 = Probably would; 2 = Might or might not; 1 = No)

3. To what extent can *you* count on *your* supervisor to "bail you out", at his/her expense, when *you* really need him/her? (4 = Certainly would; 3 = Probably; 2 = Might or might not; 1 = No)

4. How often do *you* take suggestions regarding *your* work to *your* supervisor? (4 = Almost always; 3 = Usually; 2 = Seldom; 1 = Never)

5. How would *you* characterize *your* working relationship with *your* supervisor? (4 = Extremely effective; 3 = Better than average; 2 = About average; 1 = Less than average)

Note. A fifth item was added to provide an overall assessment of relationship quality (Graen et al., 1982). Cronbach's coefficient α was .80.

LMX-7

1. Do you usually feel that you know where you stand; do you usually know how satisfied your immediate supervisor is with what you do? (4 = Always know where I stand; 3 = Usually know where I stand; 2 = Seldom know where I stand; 1 = Never know where I stand)

2. How well do you feel that your immediate supervisor understands your problems and needs? (4 = Completely; 3 = Well enough; 2 = Some but not enough; 1 = Not at all)

3. How well do you feel that your immediate supervisor recognizes your potential? (4 = Fully; 3 = As much as the next person; 2 = Some but not enough; 1 = Not at all)

4. Regardless of how much formal authority your immediate supervisor has built into his or her position, what are the chances that he or she would be personally inclined to use power to help you solve problems in your work? (4 = Certainly would; 3 = Probably would; 2 = Might or might not; 1 = No chance)

5. Again, regardless of the amount of formal authority your immediate supervisor has, to what extent can you count on him or her to "bail you out" at his or her expense when you really need it? (4 = Certainly would; 3 = Probably would; 2 = Might or might not; 1 = No chance)

6. I have enough confidence in my immediate supervisor that I would defend and justify his or her decisions if he or she were not present to do so. (4 = Certainly would; 3 = Probably would; 2 = Maybe; 1 = Probably not)

7. How would you characterize your working relationship with your immediate supervisor? (4 = Extremely effective; 3 = Better than average; 2 = About average; 1 = Less than average)

Note. Cronbach's coefficient α was .86 at Time 1 and .84 at Time 2.

LMX-7 and SLMX-7

1. Do you know where you stand with your leader ... do you usually know how satisfied your leader is with what you do? (Does your member usually know)
Rarely; Occasionally; Sometimes; Fairly Often; Very Often

2. How well does your leader understand your job problems and needs? (How well do you understand)
Not a Bit; A Little; A Fair Amount; Quite a Bit; A Great Deal

3. How well does your leader recognize your potential? (How well do you recognize)
Not at All; A Little; Moderately; Mostly; Fully

4. Regardless of how much formal authority he/ she has built into his/ her position, what are the chances that your leader would use his/ her power to help you solve problems in your work? (What are the changes [*sic*] that you would)

None; Small; Moderate; High; Very High

5. Again, regardless of the amount of formal authority your leader has, what are the chances that he/she would "bail you out," at his/ her expense? (What are the chances that you would)
None; Small; Moderate; High; Very High

6. I have enough confidence in my leader that I would defend and justify his/ her decision if he/she were not present to do so? (Your member would)
Strongly Disagree; Disagree; Neutral; Agree; Strongly Agree

7. How would you characterize your working relationship with your leader? (Your member)
Note. Item responses were Extremely Ineffective; Worse Then[*sic*] Average; Average; Better Than Average; Extremely Effective

Continuous scale of sum of 5-point items (1 left to 5 right). Leader's form consists of same seven items asked about member of (leader in parentheses). Expected agreement between leader and member reports is positive and strong and used as index of quality of data.

Reliability information was not provided in the paper.

LMX-7

1. Regardless of how much power he/she has built into his/her position, my supervisor would be personally inclined to use his/her power to help me solve problems in my work.

2. I can count on my supervisor to "bail me out" even at his or her own expense, when I really need it.

3. My supervisor understands my problems and needs.

4. My supervisor recognizes my potential.

5. My supervisor has enough confidence in me that he/she would defend and justify my decisions if I were not present to do so.

6. I usually know where I stand with my supervisor.

7. My working relationship with my supervisor is effective.

Note. Item responses ranged from 1 ("strongly disagree") to 7 ("strongly agree").

Coefficient α reliabilities ranged from .80 to .90 across two samples and three time periods.

LMX-8

This scale is the same as Liden et al. (1993) above, except that instead of dropping the second half of item #1 in Scandura and Graen (1984) as did Liden et al (1993), they divided it into two items: "I usually know where I stand with my manager," and "I usually know how satisfied my manager is with me." These authors also changed the wording of the last item: "I would characterize the working relationship I have with my supervisor as extremely effective." Coefficient α reliability for this scale was .94.

LMX-MDM

1. I respect my manager's knowledge of and competence on the job.

2. My manager would defend me to others in the organization if I made an honest mistake.

3. My manager is the kind of person one would like to have as a friend.

4. I do not mind working my hardest for my manager.

5. My manager would come to my defense if I were "attacked" by others.

6. I like my manager very much as a person.

7. I do work for my manager that goes beyond what is expected of me in my job.

8. I admire my manager's professional skills.

9. My manager defends (would defend) my work actions to a superior, even without complete knowledge of the issue in question.

10. My manager is a lot of fun to work with.

11. I am willing to apply extra efforts, beyond those normally required, to meet my manager's work goals.

12. I am impressed with my manager's knowledge of his/her job.

Note. Item responses ranged from 1 = strongly disagree to 7 = strongly agree. The items presented above are the same as the original, except that item #7 has been revised given that many of today's workers either do not have a formal job description or are not familiar with it. The scale assesses 4 dimensions: Professional Respect (1, 8, 12), Loyalty (2, 5, 9), Affect (3, 6, 10), and Contribution (4, 7, 11). The same response scale is used for all 12 items. Coefficient α reliabilities from the organizational samples (including extra analyses from the addendum of the article) were .90 for affect, .78 for loyalty, .77 for contribution, and .92 for professional respect.

SLMX-7 (Liden et al., 1993)

1. Regardless of how much power I have built into my position, I would be personally inclined

to use my power to help my subordinate solve problems in his or her work.

2. I would be willing to "bail out" my subordinate, even at my own expense, if he or she really needed it.

3. I think that I understand my subordinate's problems and needs.

4. I think that I recognize my subordinate's potential.

5. I have enough confidence in my subordinate that I would defend and justify his or her decisions if he or she were not present to do so.

6. I usually let my subordinate know where he or she stands with me.

7. My working relationship with my subordinate is effective.

Note. Item responses ranged from 1 = strongly disagree to 7 = strongly agree.

Coefficient α reliabilities ranged from .75 to .84 across two samples and 3 time periods.

SLMX-7

1. Do you know where you stand with this subordinate ... do you usually know how satisfied this subordinate is with what you do? (1 = Rarely; 2 = Occasionally; 3 = Sometimes; 4 = Fairly Often; 5 = Very Often)

2. How well does this subordinate understand your job problems and needs? (1 = Not a Bit; 2 = A Little; 3 = A Fair Amount; 4 = Quite a Bit; 5 = A Great Deal)

3. How well does this subordinate recognize your potential? (1 = Not at All; 2 = A Little; 3 = Moderately; 4 = Mostly; 5 = Fully)

4. Regardless of how much formal authority he/she has built into his/her position, what are the chances this subordinate would use his/her power to help you solve problems in your work? (1 = None; 2 = Small; 3 = Moderate; 4 = High; 5 = Very High)

5. Again, regardless of the amount of formal authority this subordinate has, what are the chances that he/she would "bail you out" at his/her expense? (1 = None; 2 = Small; 3 = Moderate; 4 = High; 5 = Very High)

6. I have enough confidence in this subordinate that I would defend and justify his/her decision if he/she were not present to do so? (1 = Strongly Disagree; 2 = Disagree; 3 = Neutral; 4 = Agree; 5 = Strongly Agree)

7. How would you characterize your working relationship with this subordinate? (1 = Extremely Ineffective; 2 = Worse than average; 3 = Average; 4 = Better than average; 5 = Extremely Effective)

Note. Coefficient α reliability was .92. Schriesheim, Wu, and Cooper (2011) provided a similar version of SLMX-7.

SLMX-MDM

Affect dimension:

1. I like my subordinate very much as a person.

2. My subordinate is the kind of person one would like to have as a friend.

3. My subordinate is a lot of fun to work with.

Loyalty dimension:

1. My subordinate defends my decisions, even without complete knowledge of the issue in question.

2. My subordinate would come to my defense if I were "attacked" by others.

3. My subordinate would defend me to others in the organization if I made an honest mistake.

Contribution dimension:

1. I provide support and resources for my subordinate that goes beyond what is specified in my job description.

2. I am willing to apply extra efforts, beyond those normally required, to help my subordinate meet his or her work goals.

3. I do not mind working my hardest for my subordinate.

Professional respect:

1. I am impressed with my subordinate's knowledge of his/her job.

2. I respect my subordinate's knowledge of and competence on the job.

3. I admire my subordinate's professional skills.

Note: Item responses ranged from 1 = strongly disagree to 5 = strongly agree.

Coefficient α reliabilities were .85 for affect, .85 for loyalty, .75 for contribution, and .91 for professional respect.

SLMX-MDM

From Liden, R. C., Sparrowe, R. T., Erdogan, B., Gavino, M., & Maslyn, J. M. (2006, August). The role of proactive personality and behaviors on social exchange relationships in the workplace. Paper presented at the national meetings of the Academy of Management, Atlanta, Georgia. Reprinted by permission of the authors of original article.

1. I like this employee very much as a person.

2. This employee does work for me that goes beyond what is specified in his/her job description.

3. I am impressed with this employee's knowledge of his/her job.

4. This employee is the kind of person one would like to have as a friend.

5. This employee would defend my work actions to others in the organization, even without complete knowledge of the issue in question.

6. This employee is a lot of fun to work with.

7. I seek out this employee's opinion on important job-related matters.

8. This employee would come to my defense if I were criticized by others.

9. This employee does not mind working his/her hardest for me.

10. This employee would defend me to others in the organization if I made an honest mistake.

11. I admire this employee's work-related skills.

12. This employee is willing to apply extra efforts, beyond those normally required, to meet my work goals.

Note: Item responses ranged from 1 = strongly disagree to 7 = strongly agree.

The scale assesses 4 dimensions: Professional Respect (3, 7, 11), Loyalty (5, 8, 10), Affect (1, 4, 6), and Contribution (2, 9, 12). The same response scale is used for all 12 items.

LMX-24

From Chaudhry, A., Vidyarthi, P., Glibkowski, B., Liden, R. C., & Wayne, S. J. (August, 2012). It Takes Two to Tango: Examining the Effects of Convergence in Leader and Member Perceptions of LMX. Paper presented at annual meeting of the Academy of Management, Boston, Massachusetts. Reprinted by permission of the authors of original article.

Employee Survey Items:

Affect:

1. I am the kind of person my manager would like to have as a friend.

2. My manager likes me very much as a person.

3. My manager believes I'm a lot of fun to work with.

Contribution:

4. My manager does not mind working his/her hardest to support me.

5. My manager is willing to apply extra efforts, beyond those normally required, to meet my work goals.

6. My manager does work for me that goes beyond what is normally required.

Loyalty:

7. My manager would come to my defense if I were "attacked" by others.

8. My manager defends (would defend) my work actions to a superior, even without complete knowledge of the issue in question.

9. My manager would defend me to others in the organization if I made an honest mistake.

Professional Respect:

10. My manager respects my knowledge of and competence on the job.

11. My manager admires my professional skills.

12. My manager is impressed with my knowledge of my job.

Manager Survey Items:

Affect:

1. I am the kind of person this employee would like to have as a friend.

2. This employee likes me very much as a person.

3. This employee believes I'm a lot of fun to work with.

Contribution:

4. This employee does not mind working his/her hardest for me.

5. This employee is willing to apply extra efforts, beyond those normally required, to meet my work goals.

6. This employee does work for me that goes beyond what is specified in his/her job description.

Loyalty:

7. This employee would come to my defense if I were "attacked" by others.

8. This employee defends (would defend) my work actions to others, even without complete knowledge of the issue in question.

9. This employee would defend me to others in the organization if I made an honest mistake.

Professional Respect:

10. This employee respects my knowledge of and competence on the job.

11. This employee admires my professional skills.

12. This employee is impressed with my knowledge of my job.

Note: Item responses ranged from 1 = strongly disagree to 7 = strongly agree.

Supervisor–Subordinate Guanxi

Copyright © 2009 by John Wiley and Sons. From Chen, Y., Friedman, R., Yu, E., Fang, W., & Lu, X. (2009). Developing a three-Dimensional model and scale for supervisor-subordinate Guanxi. *Management and Organization Review, 5*(3), 375–399. Reprinted by Permission of John Wiley and Sons.

Affective Attachment:

1. My supervisor and I always share thoughts, opinions, and feelings toward work and life.

2. I feel easy and comfortable when I communicate with my supervisor.

3. I would feel sorry and upset if my supervisor decided to work for another company.

4. If my supervisor has problems with his/her personal life, I will do my best to help him/her out.

Deference to Supervisor:

5. I am willing to obey my supervisor unconditionally.

6. While I disagree with my supervisor, I would still support his/her decisions.

7. I am willing to give up my goals in order to fulfill my supervisor's goals.

8. I am willing to sacrifice my interests in order to fulfill my supervisor's interests.

Personal-life Inclusion:

9. My supervisor would ask me to help him/her deal with some family errands.

10. During holidays, my supervisor and I would call each other or visit each other.

11. After office hours, I have social activities together with my supervisor, such as having dinner together or having entertainment together, which go beyond work duties.

12. I am familiar with the family members of my supervisor and have personal contact with these members.

Note: Item responses ranged from 1 = strongly disagree to 6 = strongly agree.

Coefficient α reliabilities for affective attachment ranged from .85 to .89 across three studies; coefficient α reliabilities for personal-life inclusion ranged from .79 to .87 across three studies; coefficient α reliabilities for deference to supervisor ranged from .84 to .87 across three studies.

LMXSC

Copyright © 2010 by the American Psychological Association. Reproduced with permission from Vidyarthi, P. R., Liden, R. C., Anand, S., Erdogan, B., & Ghosh, S. (2010). Where do I stand? Examining the effects of leader–member exchange social comparison on employee work behaviors. *Journal of Applied Psychology, 95*(5), 849–861. doi:10.1037/a0020033. No further reproduction or distribution is permitted without written permission from the American Psychological Association.

1. I have a better relationship with my manager than most others in my work group.

2. When my manager cannot make it to an important meeting, it is likely that s/he will ask me to fill in.

3. Relative to the others in my work group, I receive more support from my manager.

4. The working relationship I have with my manager is more effective than the relationships most members of my group have with my manager.

5. My manager is more loyal to me compared to my coworkers.

6. My manager enjoys my company more than he/she enjoys the company of other group members.

Note: Item responses ranged from 1 = strongly disagree to 5 = strongly agree.

Coefficient α reliability ranged from .84 to .86 across three studies.

Perceived LMX Variability

Reprinted from The Leadership Quarterly, Vol. 19, Hooper, D. T., & Martin, R., Beyond personal leader–member exchange (LMX) quality: The effects of perceived LMX variability on employee reactions, pp. 23–24, Copyright (2008), with permission from Elsevier.

Social/Economic Exchange

Copyright © 2006 by John Wiley and Sons. From Shore, L. M., Tetrick, L. E., Lynch, P., & Barksdale, K. (2006). Social and economic exchange: Construct development and validation. *Journal of Applied Social Psychology, 36,* 837–867. Reprinted by Permission of John Wiley and Sons

Economic Exchange:

1. My relationship with [my organization] is strictly an economic one—I work and they pay me.

LMX distribution measure (Hooper & Martin, 2008)

Instructions

The boxes below represent different quality relationships that may exist between members of your work team and your immediate supervisor. Please indicate in each box the number of members in your work team whose working relationship with the supervisor falls within each category (please include yourself in this count). The boxes should add together to equal the number of people in your work team. If unsure, please make a reasonable estimate.

Very poor	Poor	Satisfactory	Good	Very good

The quality of the working relationship between myself and my supervisor is… (please circle the appropriate response)

Very poor	Poor	Satisfactory	Good	Very good

Example response:

Very poor	Poor	Satisfactory	Good	Very good
0	1	3	0	0

Very poor	Poor	Satisfactory	(Good)	Very good

This response shows that within a work team of 4 people, 1 person has a poor relationship with the supervisor, and 3 people have a good relationship with the supervisor. The respondent is one of the 3 team members with a good quality relationship with the leader.

---

2. I do not care what [my organization] does for me in the long run, only what it does right now.

3. I only want to do more for [my organization] when I see that they will do more for me.

4. I watch very carefully what I get from [my organization], relative to what I contribute.

5. All I really expect from [my organization] is that I be paid for my work effort.

6. The most accurate way to describe my work situation is to say that I give a fair day's work for a fair day's pay.

7. My relationship with [my organization] is impersonal—I have little emotional involvement at work.

8. I do what [my organization] requires, simply because they pay me.

Social Exchange:

1. [My organization] has made a significant investment in me.

2. The things I do on the job today will benefit my standing in [this organization] in the long run.

3. There is a lot of give and take in my relationship with [my organization].

4. I worry that all my efforts on behalf of [my organization] will never be rewarded. [R]

5. I don't mind working hard today—I know I will eventually be rewarded by [my organization].

6. My relationship with [my organization] is based on mutual trust.

7. I try to look out for the best interest of [the organization] because I can rely on my organization to take care of me.

8. Even though I may not always receive the recognition from [my organization] I deserve, I know my efforts will be rewarded in the future.

Note: Item responses ranged from 1 = strongly disagree to 5 = strongly agree. [R] indicates item is reverse-scored.

Coefficient α reliability was .87 for social exchange scale and .78 for economic exchange scale.

Social/Economic LMX

Reprinted from The Leadership Quarterly, Vol. 23, Kuvaas, B., Buch, R., Dysvik, A., & Haerem, T., Economic and social leader–member exchange relationships and follower performance, p. 763, Copyright (2012), with permission from Elsevier.

Economic LMX:

1. The most accurate way to describe my relationship with my store manager is that I do what I am told to do.

2. I do what my store manager demands from me, mainly because he or she is my formal boss.

3. My relationship with my store manager is mainly based on authority, he or she has the right to make decisions on my behalf and I do what I am told to do.

4. All I really expect from my store manager is that he or she fulfils his or hers formal role as supervisor or boss.

Social LMX:

1. My relationship with my store manager is based on mutual trust.

2. My store manager has made a significant investment in me.

3. I try to look out for the best interest of my store manager because I can rely on my store manager to take care of me.

4. The things I do on the job today will benefit my standing with my store manager in the long run.

Note: Item responses ranged from 1 = strongly disagree to 5 = strongly agree.

Coefficient α reliability was .74 for ELMX and .78 for SLMX.

Leader–Member Social Exchange

Copyright © 2007 by John Wiley and Sons. Bernerth, J. B., Armenakis, A. A., Feild, H. S., Giles, W. F., & Walker, H. J. (2007). Leader–member social exchange (LMSX): Development and validation of a scale. *Journal of Organizational Behavior, 28,* 979–1003. Reprinted by Permission of John Wiley and Sons.

1. My manager and I have a two-way exchange relationship.

2. I do not have t o specify the exact conditions to know my manager will return a favor.

3. If I do something for my manager, he or she will eventually repay me.

4. I have a balance of inputs and outputs with my manager.

5. My efforts are reciprocated by my manager.

6. My relationship with my manager is composed of comparable exchanges of giving and taking.

7. When I give effort at work, my manager will return it.

8. Voluntary actions on my part will be returned in some way by my manager.

Note: Item responses ranged from 1 = strongly disagree to 7 = strongly agree.

Coefficient α reliability was .92.

Reciprocity

Copyright © 2003 by SAGE Publications. From Uhl-Bien, M. & Maslyn, J. M. (2003). Reciprocity in manager-subordinate relationships: Components, configurations, and outcomes. *Journal of Management, 29,* 511–532. Reprinted by Permission of SAGE Publications.

Immediacy:

1. If my manager and I do favors for one another we want to return them as soon as possible so we do not feel indebted to one another.

2. If my manager and I do a favor for one another, we expect the other to return it right away.

3. When I do something extra for my manager I watch for him/her to pay me back.

Equivalence:

4. When exchanging favors my manager and I pay attention to what we get relative to what was given.

5. We expect each other to give back exactly what was given.

Self-interest:

6. I have learned to look out for myself in this relationship.

7. My manager looks out for him/herself first.

Other-interest:

8. I am more concerned that my manager gets what he/she needs than I am about satisfying my own interests.

9. If necessary, I would place my manager's needs above my own.

10. If necessary, my manager would place my needs above his/her own.

Mutual-interest:

11. My manager and I try to do what's best for each other.

12. If one of us saw that the other needed something we would do it for the other without being asked.

13. My manager and I look out for one another.

14. My manager and I would do just about anything for the other.

Note. Response scale ranged from 1 = strongly disagree to 5 = strongly agree. Reliabilities were .75 for immediacy, .71 for equivalence, .79 for self-interest, .79 for other-interest, and .84 for mutual-interest.

Test of Negative Social Exchange (TENSE)

Copyright © 1991 by the American Psychological Association. Adapted with permission from Ruehlman, L. S., & Karoly, P. (1991). With a little flak from my friends: Development and preliminary validation of the Test of Negative Social Exchange (TENSE). *Psychological Assessment: A Journal of Consulting and Clinical Psychology, 3*(1), 97–104. doi:10.1037/1040-3590.3.1.97. No further reproduction or distribution is permitted without written permission from the American Psychological Association.

Hostility/Impatience:

1. Lost his or her temper with me
2. Yelled at me
3. Was angry with me
4. Was impatient with me
5. Nagged me
6. Disagreed with me

Insensitivity:

7. Took me for granted
8. Took advantage of me
9. Was inconsiderate
10. Ignored my wishes or needs
11. Took my feelings lightly

Interference:

12. Distracted me when I was doing something important
13. Was too demanding of my attention
14. Invaded my privacy
15. Prevented me from working on my goals

Ridicule:

16. Made fun of me
17. Laughed at me
18. Gossiped about me

Note. Respondents indicated how often the people in their lives engaged in each of the behaviors listed below over the previous month. A 5-point response scale ranging from 0 (not at all) to 4 (about every day) was used. Reliabilities were .83 for Hostility/Impatience; .82 for Insensitivity; .75 for Interference; .70 for Ridicule.

Perceived Supervisor Support

1. My supervisor cares about my opinions.
2. My work supervisor really cares about my well-being.
3. My supervisor strongly considers my goals and values.
4. My supervisor shows very little concern for me. (R)

Note: Item responses ranged from 1 = strongly disagree to 7 = strongly agree. (R) indicates the item is reverse scored. Coefficient α reliability was .90.

Trust

Affect-based trust:

1. We have a sharing relationship. We can both freely share our ideas, feelings, and hopes.
2. I can talk freely to this individual about difficulties I am having at work and know that (s)he will want to listen.
3. We would both feel a sense of loss if one of us was transferred and we could no longer work together.
4. If I shared my problems with this person, I know (s)he would respond constructively and caringly.
5. I would have to say that we have both made considerable emotional investments in our working relationship.

Cognition-based trust:

1. This person approaches his/her job with professionalism and dedication.
2. Given this person's track record, I see no reason to doubt his/her competence and preparation for the job.
3. I can rely on this person not to make my job more difficult by careless work.
4. Most people, even those who aren't close friends of this individual, trust and respect him/her as a coworker.
5. Other work associates of mine who must interact with this individual consider him/her to be trustworthy.
6. If people knew more about this individual and his/her background, they would be more concerned and monitor his/her performance more closely. (R)

Note: Item responses ranged from 1 = strongly disagree to 7 = strongly agree. (R) indicates the item is reverse scored.

Coefficient α reliabilities were .89 for affect-based trust and .91 for cognition-based trust.

Trust

Cognitive trust in supervisor:

1. I can depend on my supervisor to meet his/her responsibilities.

2. I can rely on my supervisor to do what is best at work.

3. My supervisor follows through with commitments s(he) makes.

4. Given my supervisor's track record, I see no reason to doubt his/her competence.

5. I'm confident in my supervisor because (s)he approaches work with professionalism.

Affective trust in supervisor:

1. I'm confident that my supervisor will always care about my personal needs at work.

2. If I shared my problems with my supervisor, I know (s)he would respond with care.

3. I'm confident that I could share my work difficulties with my supervisor.

4. I'm sure I could openly communicate my feelings to my supervisor.

5. I feel secure with my supervisor because of his/her sincerity.

Note: Item responses ranged from 1 = strongly disagree to 5 = strongly agree.

Coefficient α reliabilities were .94 for cognitive trust in supervisor and .95 for affective trust in supervisor.

Trust

1. My supervisor keeps my interests in mind when making decisions.

2. I would be willing to let my supervisor have complete control over my future in this company.

3. If my supervisor asked why a problem occurred, I would speak freely even if I were partly to blame.

4. I feel comfortable being creative because my supervisor understands that sometimes creative solutions do not work.

5. It is important for me to have a good way to keep an eye on my supervisor.

6. Increasing my vulnerability to criticism by my supervisor would be a mistake.

7. If I had my way, I wouldn't let my supervisor have any influence over decisions that are important to me.

Note: Item responses ranged from 1 = strongly disagree to 5 = strongly agree.

Interpersonal Reactivity Index (IRI)

Empathic Concern Scale:

1. When I see someone being taken advantage of, I feel kind of protective toward them.

2. When I see someone being treated unfairly, I sometimes don't feel very much pity for them. (-)

3. I often have tender, concerned feelings for people less fortunate than me.

4. I would describe myself as a pretty soft-hearted person.

5. Sometimes I don't feel sorry for other people when they are having problems. (-)

6. Other people's misfortunes do not usually disturb me a great deal. (-)

7. I am often quite touched by things that I see happen.

Perspective-taking Scale:

1. Before criticizing somebody, I try to imagine how I would feel if I were in their place.

2. If I'm sure I'm right about something, I don't waste much time listening to other people's arguments. (-)

3. I sometimes try to understand my friends better by imagining how things look from their perspective.

4. I believe that there are two sides to every question and try to look at them both.

5. I sometimes find it difficult to see things from the "other guy's" point of view. (-)

6. I try to look at everybody's side of a disagreement before I make a decision.

7. When I'm upset at someone, I usually try to "put myself in his shoes" for a while.

Note: Item responses ranged from 0 = does not describe me well to 4 = describes me very well. (-) indicates the item is reverse scored. Standardized α coefficients for Empathic Concern Scale were .68 for males and .73 for females; Standardized α coefficients for Perspective-taking Scale were .71 for males and .75 for females.

Perspective Taking

Copyright © 2001 by the Academy of Management. Reproduced with permission from Parker, S. K., & Axtell, C. M. (2001). Seeing another viewpoint: Antecedents and outcomes of employee perspective taking. *Academy of Management Journal, 44,* 1085–1100.

Empathy:

1. I feel concerned for my suppliers if they are under pressure.

2. It pleases me to see my suppliers doing well.

3. I understand the problems my suppliers experience.

Positive Attributions:

1. They are doing the best they can, given the circumstance.

2. If they make mistakes, it's usually not their fault.

3. They work just as hard as we do.

Note: The reliability for empathy was .78; the reliability for positive attributions was .71. Item responses ranged from 1 = strongly disagree to 5 = strongly agree.

Appendix 2 : Recommended (Standard and Most Frequently Used) LMX Measures

LMX-MDM

Copyright © 1998 by SAGE Publications. From Liden, R. C., & Maslyn, J. M. (1998). Multidimensionality of leader-member exchange: An empirical assessment through scale development. *Journal of Management, 24,* 43–72. Reprinted by Permission of SAGE Publications.

1. I respect my manager's knowledge of and competence on the job.

2. My manager would defend me to others in the organization if I made an honest mistake.

3. My manager is the kind of person one would like to have as a friend.

4. I do not mind working my hardest for my manager.

5. My manager would come to my defense if I were "attacked" by others.

6. I like my manager very much as a person.

7. I do work for my manager that goes beyond what is expected of me in my job.

8. I admire my manager's professional skills.

9. My manager defends (would defend) my work actions to a superior, even without complete knowledge of the issue in question.

10. My manager is a lot of fun to work with.

11. I am willing to apply extra efforts, beyond those normally required, to meet my manager's work goals.

12. I am impressed with my manager's knowledge of his/her job.

Note. Item responses ranged from 1 = strongly disagree to 7 = strongly agree. The items presented below are the same as the original, except that item #7 has been revised given that many of today's workers either do not have a formal job description or are not familiar with it. Also, in item #9, "(would defend)" was added for clarification. The scale assesses 4 dimensions: Professional Respect (1, 8, 12), Loyalty (2, 5, 9), Affect (3, 6, 10), and Contribution (4, 7, 11). The same response scale is used for all 12 items. Coefficient α reliabilities from the organizational samples (including extra analyses from the addendum of the article) were .90 for affect, .78 for loyalty, .77 for contribution, and .92 for professional respect.

LMX-7*

Copyright © 1984 by the American Psychological Association. Reproduced with permission from Scandura, T. A., & Graen, G. B. (1984). Moderating effects of initial leader–member exchange status on the effects of a leadership intervention. *Journal of Applied Psychology, 69*(3), 428–436. doi:10.1037/0021-9010.69.3.428. No further reproduction or distribution is permitted without written permission from the American Psychological Association.

1. Do you know where you stand with your leader . . . do you usually know how satisfied your leader is with what you do?

Rarely; Occasionally; Sometimes; Fairly Often; Very Often

2. How well does your leader understand your job problems and needs?

Not a Bit; A Little; A Fair Amount; Quite a Bit; A Great Deal

3. How well does your leader recognize your potential?

Not at All; A Little; Moderately; Mostly; Fully

4. Regardless of how much formal authority he/she has built into his/ her position, what are the chances that your leader would use his/ her power to help you solve problems in your work?

None; Small; Moderate; High; Very High

5. Again, regardless of the amount of formal authority your leader has, what are the chances that he/she would "bail you out," at his/ her expense?

None; Small; Moderate; High; Very High

6. I have enough confidence in my leader that I would defend and justify his/ her decision if he/ she were not present to do so?

Strongly Disagree; Disagree; Neutral; Agree; Strongly Agree

7. How would you characterize your working relationship with your leader?

Extremely Ineffective; Worse Than Average; Average; Better Than Average; Extremely Effective

Note. Continuous scale of sum of 5-point items (1 left to 5 right).

Reliability information was not provided in the paper. Typo in item 7 was corrected.

*Many researchers use these items modified to accommodate a strongly disagree to strongly agree response scale for all items, such as used by Bauer and Green (1996) and Liden et al. (1993) and these modified items appear in Appendix 1.

Leader–Member Exchange (LMX) from the Resource Exchange Perspective: Beyond Resource Predictors and Outcomes of LMX

Jared C. Law-Penrose, Kelly Schwind Wilson, *and* David L. Taylor

Abstract

This chapter investigates the quality of leader–member exchange (LMX) in relation to specific resources that are exchanged between leaders and their subordinates. Drawing on the findings from a number of empirical studies that focus on LMX, we consider how various resources affect and result from LMX relationships within organizations. We also examine the view that LMX itself is a resource for some leader and member dyads, along with the implications of this approach for individual employees including both leaders and members. The chapter outlines six types of resources (money, goods, services, status, information and affiliation) and assigns the studies under review to each of the six categories. Finally, we discuss avenues for future research, with an emphasis on more complete or two-way exchange relationships (that is, resources are provided by, or exchanged between, the leader and the member).

Key Words: leader–member exchange, resources, leaders, members, money, goods, services, status, information, affiliation

From early on, leader–member exchange (LMX) research has discussed the resources that leaders and employees exchange within their working relationship (Graen & Cashman, 1975; Graen & Scandura, 1987; Liden & Maslyn, 1998). As the LMX literature grew, social exchange theory began to provide the theoretical foundation for the investigation of the exchange process shared between individuals, in this case a leader and his or her subordinates or members (Blau, 1964; Liden & Maslyn, 1998). While recent research has incorporated other resource-related theories into the LMX literature including the job demands-resource model (JD-R) and conservation of resources theory or COR (Harris, Wheeler, & Kacmar, 2011; Loi, Ngo, Zhang, & Lau, 2011), these studies examine resources more broadly. The JD-R suggests that burnout occurs if high job demands lead to overtaxing or a lack of resources hinders meeting job demands (Demerouti, Bakker, Nachreiner, &

Schaufeli, 2001). Loi and colleagues (2011) state that employees "can obtain abundant resources and support from their supervisors"(p. 671), however, the type of resources obtained are not specified. Harris and colleagues (2011) examine the relationships between LMX, job embeddedness and work attitude outcomes. Although this work describes embeddedness as involving resources (e.g., links, fit, and sacrifice), the focus is on the general relationship between LMX and embeddedness, with the latter representing a broad group of valuable resources that, according to COR, employees strive to accumulate within their job or organization (Harris et al., 2011). On the other hand, the purpose of the present chapter is to examine what we know about the relationships between LMX quality and specific resources that are exchanged between a leader and member. Therefore, the present chapter will focus on what can be learned from the LMX literature with regard to how various resources impact and result from LMX relationships within organizations, as well as how LMX itself may be viewed as a resource for some leader-member dyads and the implications of this approach for individual employees including both leaders and their followers.

Before reviewing the findings in the literature, we will provide a review of some of the key theoretical pieces that are relevant for research regarding LMX and resources. Graen and Scandura (1987) outlined a number of positional and personal resources that leaders exchange with members including information, influence, tasks, latitude, support and attention. Using information as an example, according to Graen and Scandura (1987) information includes planning for the future in terms of identifying problems and opportunities as well as visibility into the workings of top management teams or the organization's leadership. Some research assumes that "because managerial positions are designed to have higher status and greater authority than do the positions of members, managerial positions are given greater organizational resources than are those of members" (Graen & Scandura, 1987, p. 182). Such research then tends to focus on the resources supervisors or leaders share, and not what resources members can provide to leaders. Going back to the information example, some might then believe that "though the member 'grapevine' is an alternative medium, it is generally a poor second to the superior's information sources" (Graen & Scandura, 1987, p. 183). Unfortunately, deemphasizing resources that members can provide to leaders ignores the fundamental notion of social *exchange* involved in the LMX relationship.

Social exchange is defined by Blau (1964) as the voluntary actions individuals provide another individual or group based on the returns they would expect to receive. In other words, social exchange entails a give and take among all individuals involved. A recent advancement in LMX has recognized the importance of taking a "bidirectional perspective" when examining resources (Wilson, Sin, & Conlon, 2010, p. 359) and examining the resources both leaders and members provide and receive. The most popular and potentially comprehensive classification of resources utilized in the social exchange and LMX literatures follows Foa and Foa's resource theory (1974, 1980; Cropanzano & Mitchell, 2005; Wilson et al., 2010). Cropanzano and Mitchell (2005) note that within the organizational literature, Foa and Foa's resource categories are usually collapsed into two dimensions, economic and socioemotional resources, and as a result

most of the resources "have not been fully appreciated by organizational scientists" (p. 881). New research in LMX has begun to address this need for research (e.g., Wilson et al., 2010), but first we will summarize Foa and Foa's ideas.

Foa and Foa (1974, 1980) define a *resource* as anything that can be transacted or exchanged between individuals and proposed six basic categories or types of resources. These types include money, goods, services, status, information and affiliation (originally labeled as love). Affiliation refers to expressions of affection, regard, support or comfort; information involves advice, opinions, instruction or enlightenment; status is a judgment that conveys high or low esteem or prestige; services involve labor activities or the labor one performs for another; goods are tangible objects, products or materials; and money consists of any coin or currency that has some standard value (Donnenworth & Foa, 1974; Foa & Foa, 1974). Foa and Foa also argue that these resource categories can be organized along two dimensions—whether the resource is concrete or abstract and whether it is particular or universal. Concrete resources involve a tangible product or activity such as goods and services, whereas abstract resources are more symbolic and may be conveyed by verbal or other communication-related behaviors. More abstract resources include status and information. Particularistic resources depend on the identity of the source or the importance of who provides the resource, whereas universal resources are those in which the source or exchange member's identity is irrelevant. Thus, affiliation resources are highly particularistic and status and services also rank high on particularism, whereas, money is universal along with information and goods (Foa & Foa, 1974).

Wilson and colleagues' (2010) theoretical work applies Foa and Foa's (1974) resource theory and taxonomy to LMX and focuses primarily on the resource outcomes leaders receive from their resource exchanges with members. Following Foa and Foa's (1974) tenet that individuals typically exchange the same resource type (e.g., leaders receive status in exchange for status, affiliation in exchanged for affiliation), Wilson et al. (2010) also recognize that constraints impact members' access to certain types of resources and that members may be unable to frequently or directly exchange goods and money types of resources with leaders. In addition, this research examines resource substitutes that members are likely to provide leaders when they cannot exchange the same type of resource as well as how the quality of the LMX relationship impacts the value leaders place on the various resources received from members. For example, Wilson et al. (2010) propose that leaders place more value on receiving affiliation and status types of resources from high-quality LMX members compared to low-quality LMX members.

Finally, scholars have addressed the multidimensionality and measurement of LMX (including the multidimensional measure of LMX or the MDM; Liden & Maslyn, 1998). Support for the multidimensionality of LMX includes findings from social exchange theorists who have "identified numerous material and non-material goods that may be exchanged" between leaders and members, which suggests that "exchange relationships between individuals appear to be multidimensional" (Liden & Maslyn, 1998, p. 44). In other words, taking a specific resource exchange perspective allows researchers to examine multiple dimensions of LMX. Liden and Maslyn (1998) conclude that there are four key dimensions of LMX: affect, loyalty, contribution, and professional respect. As we will describe subsequently, these LMX dimensions overlap with Foa and Foa's (1974) resource categories reviewed above. Therefore, research that takes a multidimensional approach to investigating LMX (i.e., uses the MDM measure) allows one to view LMX itself as a resource. In the following sections, the findings we will review from the LMX literature regarding resources will be organized or categorized by the six types of resources (money, goods, services, status, information and affiliation) outlined in Foa and Foa (1974). Additionally, Table 4.1 summarizes which studies fall under each of the six categories. The table was compiled by comparing the independent and dependent variables in each published study with Foa and Foa's definitions of the six resource categories (provided previously). First, we will discuss research that examines specific resources as predictors of LMX. Second, we will summarize research that examines specific resources as outcomes of LMX. Finally, we will examine research that measures LMX using the MDM and what implications the dimensions or overarching resources involved in LMX hold for leaders, members and potentially organizations as a whole.

Resources as Antecedents of LMX

In a classic article, Gouldner (1960) offered a conceptual framework of reciprocity. He argued specifically that there are two underlying assumptions of reciprocity: "(1) people should help those who have helped them, and (2) people should not injure those who have helped them" (p. 171). In an organizational context, "help" could be thought of as anything outside of the scope of the normal job expectations. To more directly apply the concept of reciprocity to LMX we could rewrite the first assumption as: people should give resources to those who have given them resources. These assumptions are critical for understanding resources as antecedents of LMX. As resources are exchanged between a leader and member that are outside of the normal work role, the recipient of the resource feels indebted to the other party (Blau, 1964). The receiving party is then obligated to reciprocate by providing a resource in kind. Gouldner's "norm of reciprocity" provides a theoretical foundation for predicting LMX relationships as a result of resources exchanged. In this section we explore and

Table 4.1. LMX Research Organized by Resource Categories.

Status Resources	Affiliation Resources	Service Resources
Bauer & Green (1996)	Masterson, Lewis, Goldman & Taylor (2000)	Liden, Wayne & Stilwell (1993)
Venkataramani, Green & Schleicher (2010)	Bauer & Green (1996)	Bauer & Green (1996)
	Wayne, Shore & Linden (1997)	Settoon, Bennett & Liden (1996)
	Dockery & Steiner (1990)	Graen, Novak & Sommerkamp (1982)
	Wayne & Ferris (1990)	Hofmann, Morgeson & Gerras (2003)
	Van Vianen, Shen & Chuang (2011)	Wayne, Shore & Liden (1997)
		Wayne & Ferris (1990)
		Liden, Wayne & Sparrowe (2000)
		Wang. Law. Hackett & Chen (2005)
		Sparrowe, Soetjipto & Kraimer (2006)

Information Resources	Money Resources	Goods Resources
Vidyarthi, Erdogan, Anand, Liden & Chaudhry (2014)	Wayne, Shore & Liden (1997)	Note: Many companies have fromal gift policies that prevent goods related exchanges, which may explain why little research exists regarding goods (Donnelly, 2010)

summarize the extant LMX literature that uses specific resources as predictors of LMX. We follow the framework from Foa and Foa (1974) and review the literature here along the same resource dimensions (status, affiliation, services, information, money, and goods; the first three are the most particularistic resources and the latter three are the most universal resources based on Foa and Foa's dimensions). Because it is often difficult for a follower to repay a leader with the same type of resource (Wilson et al., 2010), the existing research has evaluated predictors of LMX that are more easily reciprocated.

In a study testing the distinctiveness of perceived organizational support (POS) and LMX, Wayne, Shore, and Liden (1997) build on Gouldner's work and argue in favor of three distinct antecedents of LMX; leader ratings of liking, salary expectations, and dyad tenure. Each of these predictors was significant in explaining LMX. LMX then significantly predicted employee performance, organizational citizenship behaviors (OCBs), and favor doing. Liking was measured using items that highly relate to Foa and Foa's (1974) definition of affiliation (e.g., "I think this employee would make a good friend" and "I like this employee very much"). Salary expectation was operationalized by asking supervisors the pay grade they expected their employee to reach at the end of five years. Modeling Foa and Foa (1974) and Gouldner (1960), Wayne et al. (1997) demonstrates that when affiliation (liking) and money (salary expectation) are given to an employee, LMX increases and the employee responds by providing services to the leader through favors and OCBs.

Foa and Foa's concept of affiliation is one of the most common resource antecedents of LMX. Affiliation has been typically operationalized using the construct of "liking." Dockery & Steiner (1990) found that liking between employee and leader was a significant predictor of LMX. Their study operationalized liking through a four-item measure that evaluated the affiliation of employees with their leaders. Wayne and Ferris (1990) used both a lab and field study to test the impact of liking on exchange quality and also concluded that liking significantly predicts LMX.

In a study integrating justice and social exchange, Masterson, Lewis, Goldman, and Taylor (2000) measure affiliation using interactional justice and show that interactional justice predicts LMX. In a similar study, Aryee, Budhwar, and Chen (2002) validated a mediation model where affiliation (measured as interactional justice) increased trust in the supervisor (a proxy for LMX) and resulted in increased OCBs. Bies and Moag (1986) suggest that an individual's judgment of fairness is highly related to interpersonal interactions during the justice process (calling it interactional justice). Because interactional justice is measured using items that evaluate interpersonal interactions it is consistent with Foa and Foa's conceptualization of affiliation—increased ratings of interpersonal interactions should be related to increased regard or support. Both Masterson and colleagues (2000) and Aryee and colleagues (2002) hypothesized that interactional justice (i.e., affiliation) is an antecedent of LMX. By distinguishing between procedural and interactional justice Masterson et al. (2000) and Aryee et al. (2002) demonstrate that LMX is a result of affiliation (among other resources) as opposed to perceived fairness of procedures. Regardless of operationalization, affiliation is a clear predictor of LMX.

In a different approach to studying LMX, Liden, Wayne, and Stilwell (1993) use a longitudinal approach to look at the development of LMX over time. In their study they looked at performance as a predictor of LMX (among other things). They argue that when leader-member dyads operate reciprocally, mutual trust and LMX develop. Specifically, employees perform certain aspects of their jobs with the belief that their leaders will reciprocate. When both parties perform their expected roles, LMX will follow. In this sense, employee performance is a service that employees provide to their leaders. Consistent with Foa and Foa, employee performance is a service-related resource. As performance or service between leader and member is reciprocated, LMX is strengthened as a result of the exchange (of service resources). Liden et al. (1993) corroborate previous work by Wayne and Ferris (1990) and demonstrate that service (i.e., employee performance) positively predicts LMX.

Responding to a call to test the way in which LMX develops over time, Bauer and Green (1996) conducted a longitudinal study that looked at the salience of different factors on LMX over time. Based on earlier work (Dienesch & Liden, 1986), they hypothesized, first, that early in the LMX tenure demographic factors (affiliation) were more salient resources and second, as tenure of the dyad increases the combination of employee performance (service) and supervisor delegation (status) becomes a more dominant predictor of LMX. They used supervisor reports to measure employee performance. Delegation was measured using the items from the Management Practices Survey (Yukl,

1990). Demographic factors in this study were used as a proxy for affiliation. When similarity of demographic factors is high there is typically increased affiliation. Measuring delegation to employees coincides with Foa and Foa's explanation of status as providing an individual with esteem. As more tasks are delegated to a subordinate the leader is making a judgment of the capability of the member and therefore providing or denying status. Bauer and Green (1996) found general support for their hypotheses that the relative importance of specific resources on LMX changes as the tenure of the dyad increases.

Venkataramani and colleagues (2010) examined whether leaders' social networks within their organizations impact the quality of their LMX relationships and in turn, the influence of LMX on subsequent member outcomes including attitudes. This study specifically investigated the relationship between members' perceptions of leaders' status and LMX quality. The findings suggest that leaders' status is positively related to LMX. Additionally, this relationship between leaders' status and LMX was moderated by member centrality such that the relationship was stronger for employees who were less central in their own peer networks. Overall, this study suggests that leaders' status-related resources may be an important antecedent of LMX, especially for members with low network centrality.

Throughout this section we have tried to identify key studies relating to specific resources as defined by Foa and Foa (1974) that positively predict LMX. A clearer understanding of the antecedents of LMX allows more effective placement of leaders in the appropriate level or team within an organization. The most common resource addressed in the studies we review here is affiliation. Affiliation is commonly measured as the degree to which a leader or member like the other person. This type of resource is likely the most commonly studied because, in addition to being relatively easy to measure, it is also easily given (i.e., affiliation is not a limited resource like money). Whereas if an individual exchanges a more universal resource such as money or goods (Foa & Foa, 1974) there is greater risk that those resources will not be reciprocated (given they are limited and that leaders and members may lack access to such resources; see Wilson et al., 2010).

In the studies summarized above, information and goods were not studied as specific antecedents of LMX. It is likely that information and goods are still antecedents of LMX but are more difficult to operationalize and/or observe. Wilson et al.

(2010) noted that certain resources are more easily exchanged between leaders and members because it is often difficult for a member to reciprocate the same resource. Future research should address this gap in the literature and evaluate the salience of information and goods (if applicable, which we will discuss in more detail later) as predictors of LMX.

Resources as Outcomes of LMX

An alternative way to apply resource theory to LMX is to address resources as outcomes of LMX. In this section we summarize key pieces from the existing literature that look at resources as outcomes of LMX. The majority of LMX outcomes in the articles reviewed in this section in some way operationalize Foa and Foa's definition of services and/or affiliation. First, in a randomized sample of 254 nonsupervisory hospital workers nested in 28 work groups, Settoon, Bennett, and Liden (1996) clarified the role of LMX in promoting both job performance and citizenship behaviors. They found that LMX significantly predicts job performance (operationalized as in-role behavior) and citizenship behaviors. The particularistic nature of each of these variables corresponds with services as defined by Foa and Foa. Settoon and colleagues' (1996) study contributes to our understanding of the role of exchange relationships between leaders and members and the resources (i.e., services) that members produce for the organization as a result of LMX.

In a study cited earlier, Wayne, Shore, and Liden (1997) tested specific resources as both antecedents and outcomes of LMX. They hypothesized that affiliation and money (liking and salary expectations respectively) would result in LMX and that LMX would result in increased job performance, OCBs, and favor doing. Each of the outcomes they evaluated relate to Foa and Foa's (1974) resource category of services. Moreover, these outcomes in Wayne and colleagues' (1997) model are highly particularistic—they are specific and concrete as described by Foa and Foa (1974). This study is unique in that Wayne et al. (1997) demonstrate a complete resource exchange relationship through LMX. Wayne and colleagues (1997) show that LMX is a mediator of resource reciprocity between leader and follower.

In another study that tests antecedents and outcomes of LMX, Aryee and colleagues (2002) demonstrated another type of resource exchange from beginning to end. They tested a mediation model where affiliation from the supervisor (measured as interactional justice) increases trust in the leader (a proxy for LMX) resulting in increased services (measured as OCBs) from the member. Such studies are important given that they demonstrate both antecedents and outcomes of LMX in the same model. Masterson et al. (2000) and Aryee et al. (2002) demonstrate Gouldner's principle of reciprocity (1960) in that when employees are given resources, LMX between the leader and member increases and employees seek to return resources. These two studies also demonstrate how the reciprocated resources may be of a different type—potentially as a result of constraints on the employee (Wilson et al., 2010).

In a field experiment, Graen, Novak, and Sommerkamp (1982) explored the value of LMX in garnering improved employee performance. In their experimental condition, they conducted training with the participants aimed at improving LMX. The training they facilitated resulted in increased LMX across the participating leader and member dyads. Graen et al. (1982) used an objective measure of productivity (i.e., number of cases completed per hour) in assessing employee performance. Their study found that as LMX increased employee productivity also increased. Productivity increased 16.3 percent without a loss in quality for the experimental group that received LMX training. Because employees in their study had control over their rate of production, we can extrapolate that the employee was providing a particularistic in-role behavior—consistent with Foa and Foa's definition of services. The participants in this study responded to an increase in LMX by offering service as a resource. As one of the first studies specifically looking at outcomes of LMX, it provides a framework for understanding the value of LMX in harvesting resources from employees.

Taking a slightly different approach, Hofmann, Morgeson, and Gerras (2003) examined specific safety citizenship behaviors as outcomes of LMX. They hypothesized that increased LMX would positively predict safety-related behaviors. Safety citizenship behaviors were measured using supervisor ratings of specific extra-role behaviors of employees. Because this measure is a highly particularistic evaluation of specific behaviors, it is consistent with Foa and Foa's concept of service resources. Hofmann et al. (2003) found support for their hypothesis and concluded that LMX resulted in increased service resources in the form of safety citizenship behaviors.

Wang, Law, Hackett, Wang, and Chen (2005) tested task performance and citizenship behaviors as outcomes of LMX. Like many of the other studies summarized here, Wang et al. (2005) hypothesized that LMX would result in increased task performance and citizenship behaviors. They measured task performance using a scale from Tsui, Pearce, Porter, and Tripoli (1997) and citizenship behavior with a translated version of a scale validated by Podsakoff and colleagues (1990). Their results indicated that LMX positively predicts citizenship behaviors and task performance. Both of these outcome measures are consistent with service resources as conceptualized by Foa and Foa (1974).

Liden, Wayne, and Sparrowe (2000) tested the relationship between LMX, job performance, and organizational commitment. They hypothesized that psychological empowerment mediates the relationship between LMX and employee job performance. To test their theory they sampled 337 employees and their immediate supervisors. Contrary to their hypothesis, the relationship between LMX and employee job performance was not mediated by psychological empowerment. Unlike earlier experiments (Graen et al., 1982), this study operationalized job performance by supervisor ratings of specific job characteristics defined by the human resource department. Although relying on organization-specific ratings alone may not be the best measure of job performance, it is consistent with the category of services as a resource. In addition to this finding, Liden et al. (2000) found that employee organizational commitment, measured using the Meyer and Allen (1984) scale, increased as a result of LMX. Referring back to Foa and Foa's six resource types, organizational commitment is consistent with affiliation. When LMX increased the employees in this study had greater support and affect for their organization. Overall, this study is important in that it demonstrates that LMX directly results in the exchange of services as well as affiliation toward the organization as a whole.

More recently, Van Vianen, Shen, and Chuang (2011) examined employee commitment as an outcome of LMX in a Chinese context. They hypothesized that the relationship between supervisor and employee perceptions of person-supervisor fit and commitment are mediated by LMX. In their model, supervisory commitment and organizational commitment are hypothesized as outcomes of LMX. This study operationalized commitment using the scale from Cheng et al. (2003) which uses items that are theoretically similar to Foa & Foa's concept of affiliation. Using a Taiwanese sample from a variety of industries, Van Vianen et al. (2011) found support for commitment as an outcome of LMX. The relationship between LMX and commitment is constant across cultures. Rockstuhl, Dulebohn, Ang, and Shore (2012) meta-analyzed the results of 282 LMX studies and concluded that the relationship between LMX and commitment does not vary as a function of culture. This suggests that a resource view of LMX can be effectively applied cross-culturally.

Each of the studies summarized in this section evaluate service or affiliation resources as outcomes of LMX. Although each of the studies may operationalize these resources in a slightly different way (i.e., task performance, safety behaviors, citizenship behaviors), each outcome is consistent with Foa and Foa's categories of service and affiliation resources. As noted by Wilson and colleagues (2010), certain constraints may limit the resources that subordinates can exchange with their leader. This requires us to think about Gouldner's norm of reciprocity differently. The studies reviewed in this section suggest that it may not be possible for employees to exchange the same type of resource with their leader resulting in the employee reciprocating with one or more of their available resources—services or affiliation. It is clear that services are commonly exchanged as an outcome of LMX, however, less is known about other types of resources members exchange with leaders. More research should be done to determine the implications of LMX on other types of resource exchanges.

LMX as a Resource Itself

Much early research on LMX was dedicated to understanding the role-making process that forms the leader-follower (also described as member) relationship (e.g. Dansereau, Graen, & Haga, 1975; Graen & Cashman, 1975). The underlying assumption is that both leaders and members enter into relationships with one another for the purposes of exchanging valuable resources that each hold (Graen & Cashman, 1975) and each value. More recent research does not focus on the development process involving leader-member dyads, but such a focus would be a fruitful avenue for research striving to uncover the resources that exist in early leader-member dyads. For example, "leaders hold a variety of positional resources, such as the assignment of interesting tasks, the distribution of valuable information, and opportunities to speak favorably about subordinates to others in the organization" (Wilson et al., 2010). Subordinates also hold resources in the form of their work effort, commitment, initiative and

proactive behaviors (Liden, Sparrowe, & Wayne, 1997) that their leaders value. Research also suggests that the quality of those relationships differ between leaders and subordinates, and that leaders often develop different "styles" (Liden & Masyln, 1998) based on the relationship or exchange between individual subordinates (Dansereau, Graen, & Haga, 1975; Graen & Cashman, 1975; Graen & Scandura, 1987; Liden & Graen, 1980). Differing levels of relational quality influence what types and levels of resources are contributed to the relationship and as such, influence the creation of certain outcomes.

Theory and research now assumes that the LMX process is a multi-dimensional construct that considers several components of the complex relational exchange process (Dienesch & Liden, 1986). Outcomes such as turnover (Graen, Liden, & Hoel, 1982), organizational commitment (Duchon, Green, & Taber, 1986), job satisfaction and satisfaction with supervision (Schriesheim & Gardiner, 1992), satisfaction with work (Vecchio & Gobdel, 1984), and advancement (Wakabayashi, Graen, Graen, & Graen, 1988) are linked to the LMX relationship that develops between leaders and members. The expression of these different dimensions serves as antecedents to particular outcomes. The theoretical foundations supporting the multi-dimensionality of LMX are based in role theory and social exchange theory (Graen, 1976). Role theory provides that the relational role forming process between leaders and members develops over time through a series of interactions and tests. Further, role theory asserts that roles are multi-dimensional (Katz & Kahn, 1978) and may fulfill a range of relational needs faced by both parties in the relationship. For example, some roles are based exclusively on tasks and work-related duties, whereas other roles may form based on social interaction alone (Liden & Maslyn, 1998). Thus, certain dimensions of the relationship may emerge as significant factors influencing the transaction of resources, benefits or outcomes given the intended or expected quality of the exchange. Leaders' and members' roles may also be negotiated based on the resources exchanged in the role making process. Moreover, those individual roles that develop may go beyond work- or task-related behaviors to encompass a broader social interactivity (Diensch & Liden, 1986).

Specifically, LMX relationships may be based on three domains of exchange, or as Dienesch and Liden

Table 4.2. LMX Dimensions and Resource Category Overlaps.

Liden and Maslyn's (1998) LMX Dimensions	Foa and Foa's (1974) Resource Categories
Affect: mutual affection within the dyad based on interpersonal attraction (e.g., friendship)	*Affiliation*: expressions of affection/liking, warmth or comfort
Loyalty: expression of public support for the goals and character of the other dyad member	*Affiliation*: see above
Contribution: work-oriented activity each member of dyad puts forth toward mutual goals	*Services*: activities that constitute labor for another
Professional Respect: perceptions of each dyad member's reputation for excelling at his/her work	*Status*: expressions of evaluation or judgments that include high/low prestige or esteem

(1986) suggest, as "three currencies of exchange" described as task-related behaviors (e.g., contribution), loyalty and liking (e.g., affect). Dienesch and Liden assert that an exchange relationship may be based on one, two or all three domains. A richer understanding of the LMX construct therefore, helps us to understand not only how relationships develop and are maintained, but also the scope of how those resources affect both leader and member outcomes.

Liden and Maslyn (1998) extended these assumptions to empirically support the multi-dimensionality of the LMX construct. Their research proposes that the LMX construct encompasses four dimensions. First, affect is defined as the mutual affection members share in the dyad (e.g., friendship). Second, loyalty is defined as the "expression of public support for the goals and personal character of the other member in the dyad" (Liden & Maslyn, 1998, p. 50). Third, contribution is defined as the level of work-related or task-related activity each member exerts towards the mutual goals of the relationship. And fourth, professional respect refers to the perceived reputation that one builds inside or outside the organization related to one's line of work (Liden & Maslyn, 1998).

As previously mentioned, by integrating Foa and Foa's (1974) resource theory, Wilson and colleagues (2010) suggest that leaders and members have access to six categories of resources that they can contribute to the exchange relationship with their member or leader respectively. Mapping the "currencies of exchange" as proposed by Dienesch and Liden (1986), we assert that task-related behaviors (contribution) may be considered "service," and liking (affect) and loyalty may be considered "affiliation." Further, the MDM dimensions of affect (i.e., affiliation), loyalty (i.e., affiliation), contribution

(i.e., service) and professional respect (i.e., status) map onto the more particular domains as described by Foa and Foa (1974; Table 4.2 provides a summary of these ideas). The more "universal" forms of resources, such as goods, money and information, represent possible extensions of additional bases of exchange that support the creation of distinct outcomes.

As described, most research describes the role making and exchange process of LMX based on what Foa and Foa (1974; 1980) would describe as more "particular" forms of resources (e.g. status, affiliation and service). Thus, in many ways, the MDM measure captures the essence of the relational or particular forms of resources shared within the dyad, yet fails to consider the broader scope of the tools or access to resources that a manager has at his or her disposal. Future research may seek to better understand how these types of resources affect not only the role-making process but also serve as resources involved in specific leader and member outcomes.

Selected Empirical Research Using the MDM-LMX

The work by Wang, Law, Hackett, Wang, and Chen (2005) integrates both the one-on-one relational and interpersonal aspects of LMX with the behavioral approach of transformational leadership theories with the outcomes of member's task performance and OCBs. According to theory, the "heightened outcomes associated with transformational leadership" (Wang et al., 2005, p. 422) are the consequence of the resource exchange or the role making process of LMX (Deluga, 1992). Transformational leaders create an environment that enriches the LMX process and thus supports important outcomes such as task performance and improved

OCBs. In this way, transformational leadership is an antecedent to the creation of an enduring, strong LMX relationship. In their research, Wang et al. (2005) found this to be true by empirically demonstrating that the MDM measure of LMX fully mediates the relationship between transformational leadership and task performance and organizational citizenship behaviors.

Similarly, Sparrowe, Soetjipto, and Kraimer (2006) found that when the member perceives LMX as low, leaders' use of inspirational appeal/exchange is negatively related to members' helping behaviors. When members perceived their LMX as high, leader's exchange tactics were positively related to member's behaviors. We can draw the conclusion from this evidence that the MDM measure of LMX serves as an anchor from which to interpret member behavior.

Other work using the MDM measure of LMX also indicates the role of the exchange process and the resources themselves in creating beneficial member-related outcomes. In particular, Atwater and Carmeli (2009) showed that high quality relationships, as measured by the LMX-MDM, resulted in increased creative work involvement. Laschinger, Finegan, and Wilk (2009) found that the MDM measure of LMX positively influenced psychological empowerment and organizational commitment at the individual level. Overall, the research reviewed suggests that leader-member dyads with high affect, loyalty, contribution and professional respect, or in other words, dyads that share the resources of affiliation, status and service, appear to report increased performance, OCBs, and commitment among other outcomes. Most of the outcomes examined within these studies, therefore, focus on service-related resources (performance and OCBs).

A recent study in 2014 examined employees who work with two leaders and therefore have two LMX relationships. Specifically, the employees are consultants and have an agency leader from their own company who is responsible for project assignments and performance management and a client leader who is responsible for various aspects of the project, schedules and duties (Vidyarthi, Erdogan, Anand, Liden, & Chaudhry, 2014). Communication frequency was examined, which is related to information resources, and the research found that "employees with low-quality LMX-client had more positive outcomes when their LMX-agency was high and there was a high degree of communication with the agency leader, indicating that high levels of communication with the leader who plays a long-term role over the career of the individuals can compensate for a low-quality exchange with the leader who shapes the daily tasks of the individual" (Vidyarthi et al., 2014, p. 12). Based on these findings, information may be a valuable resource in some leader-member dyads and future research should examine not only information frequency but also information content or quality and how such communication influences LMX development and quality.

Future Research

The research reviewed suggests a number of avenues for future research, some of which have already been mentioned previously. Furthermore, future research should explore more complete or two-way exchange relationships (i.e., exchanges in which both the leader and the member provide or exchange resources). Only two of the studies reviewed above demonstrate a full structural equation model that demonstrates the flow of resources from leader leading to increased LMX, which in turn results in the return of resources from the member (Aryee et al. 2002; Wayne et al. 1997). In addition, future research should specifically look at non-service types of resources. In testing a full exchange model (a resource predicting LMX which then predicts a resource), scholars should explore the magnitudes of the effects of different types of leader given resources in increasing specific member behaviors. Not to mention, LMX may not always be the intervening mechanism for increasing member behaviors. In addition to LMX, measures of felt obligation should be included. It is possible that the recipient (typically the member) of the initial resource feels indebted to the giver (typically the leader). While certain resources may be antecedents and/or outcomes of LMX, more work needs to be done to incorporate the work of Gouldner (1960). It is possible that resources (i.e., services) are outcomes of the exchange process because the recipient of the resource feels obligated to perform for the other party.

Another specific area that future research should explore is the differences in leader-member behavior when the flow of resources begins with the subordinate. The studies reviewed in this chapter that evaluate the antecedents of LMX all seem to make an assumption that the resources first flow from a leader to a member. For example, a leader may initially provide their members with affiliation which results in LMX. The member then reciprocates by providing services (e.g., increased task performance,

OCBs, etc.) to the leader or organization. There is an implicit assumption that resources exchanges must begin with the leader, as they are the more "powerful" partners in the relationship. The leader may have a wider selection of resource types that they can provide to their members (e.g., money, services, affiliation, information, status, etc.), whereas, the member is typically limited in the types of resources they can provide their leader (Wilson et al., 2010). It appears that in most situations, a member is only able to provide their leader with service resources (e.g., task performance, OCBs, etc.). Even though a member is more constrained in the types of resources they can provide they may still initiate the exchange process. In essence, current research has largely ignored member initiated exchanges with leaders. Future research could explore the nature of LMX relationships that are initiated by the member. If the member initiates a resource exchange, does it impact the quality of LMX? As noted above, members are usually constrained to offering service resources. Given this, the leader may view the resource provided as an in-role behavior and may view the service as reciprocity for pay. If a leader does not view the service as an actual resource, we would not expect the quality of LMX to increase. Answering such questions in future research could elucidate a critical aspect of LMX research and demonstrate that LMX relationships are fundamentally initiated by the leader.

An additional question that should be explored in future research relates to the differentiation of resources from the organization and the leader. The research reviewed in this chapter explores LMX from a resource perspective and the extant research has evaluated resources from the leader. The organization is an alternative source of resources. Some resources may frequently come from an organization, while others may more frequently be provided by the leader. For example, an organization is typically the source of monetary resources (i.e., salary, bonuses, etc.) whereas the leader is more typically the source of affiliation resources. Similarly, the leader and the organization may both offer the same resources such as status. Some existing research has looked at perceived organizational support as an outcome of specific leader given resources. Extant research, however, has not explored the impact of different resource suppliers on LMX relationships and member behaviors. One question that remains includes whether the source of the resource matters for LMX, leader, and member outcomes. Specifically,

future research should determine if a resource provided by the organization increases LMX between the member and the leader. It is possible that the member does not differentiate between the leader and the organization as resource exchange partners. As a result, the LMX relationship may improve regardless of the resource exchange partner. This research could be incredibly valuable for organizations in that it would provide a framework for understanding which types of resources should come from a leader and which types of resources should come from the organization.

Our review of existing LMX research highlights that leader-member dyads experiencing high levels of affect, loyalty, contribution, and professional respect have relationships based on the exchange of resources that are more relational or particular in nature: affiliation, status and service. Outcomes from these exchanges appear to report increased performance, OCBs, and commitment as the primary product of high-performing LMX relationships. While it is accepted that LMX is a relational model of leadership, managers do have access to more universal forms of resources that may be utilized when developing member and organization-level types of outcomes (e.g., work unit performance, innovation, return-on-assets, etc.). Moreover, it is likely that managers have discretionary power over member access and allocation to those more universal and organization-level resources. Future research should examine the processes through which the multiple dimensions of LMX impact universal types of resource outcomes.

We also propose that research should consider how members' view the discretionary role managers have in determining how resources are allocated to members in their work group or team. It is likely that the perceived discretionary role leaders have can influence outcomes beyond those already empirically determined (e.g., OCBs, performance, commitment, etc.). This link between leaders total resource exchanges with all employees may describe more macro-level outcomes such as team performance, for example. In addition, we may also consider how leaders with perceived power, or access to more universal resources, are responsible for determining the quality of the LMX relationship. Would we see that leaders who are perceived to have greater organizational authority and discretionary power over a broader network of resources are viewed as more powerful and thus "beyond" the ability to form close dyadic relations with members (where LMX is not relevant)?

Finally, as noted in Table 1, goods have not been the focus of empirical research regarding LMX as far as we are aware. This may be due to the fact that many organizations have gift policies that prohibit employees from accepting certain gifts or goods from others (Donnelly, 2010). Studies could take a qualitative approach to examining whether goods exchanges still take place between leaders and members without the organization's awareness and what implications such exchanges hold for LMX quality. As discussed throughout this review, Table 1 also highlights the need for much more research on a number of the resource categories (e.g., status and information) outlined by Foa and Foa (1974) and the leader-member exchange relationship.

Conclusion

Herein, we reviewed a number of key empirical studies that have investigated various antecedents and outcomes of LMX, with a focus on antecedents and outcomes that could be classified as resources. Overall, we concluded that a great deal of research has studied affiliation-related resources as the main antecedents of LMX, whereas service-related resources appear to be the main outcome of LMX. We also reviewed research that investigated LMX using the MDM and framed this multidimensional approach to LMX as viewing LMX itself as a resource. Again, service-related resources appeared to be a key outcome of LMX. Future research will hopefully continue to examine resources and LMX, especially different types of resources (e.g., status and information) and how they affect the LMX relationship, as well as begin to address the question of whether high-quality LMX relationships throughout an organization can be utilized as a beneficial resource for organizations in terms of firm performance, innovation, or other organization-level outcomes.

References

Aryee, S., Budhwar, P. S., & Chen, Z. X. (2002). Trust as a mediator of the relationship between organizational justice and work outcomes: test of a social exchange model. *Journal of Organizational Behavior, 23,* 267–285. doi: 10.1002/job.138

Atwater, L., & Carmeli, A. (2009). Leader-member exchange, feelings of energy, and involvement in creative work. *The Leadership Quarterly, 20,* 264–275.

Bauer, T. N., & Green, S. G. (1996). Development of leader-member exchange: A longitudinal test. *Academy of Management Journal, 39,* 1538–1567.

Bies, R. J., & Moag, J. S. (1986). Interactional justice: Communication criteria of fairness. In R. J. Lewicki, B. H. Sheppard, & M. H. Bazerman (Eds.), *Research on negotiation in organizations*: Vol. 1, 43–55. Greenwich, CT: JAI Press.

Blau, P. M. (1964). *Exchange and power in social life.* New York: John Wiley.

Cropanzano, R., & Mitchell, M. S. (2005). Social exchange theory: An interdisciplinary review. *Journal of Management, 31,* 874–900.

Dansereau, F., Graen, G., & Haga, W. (1975). A vertical dyad approach to leadership within formal organizations. *Organizational Behavior and Human Performance, 13,* 349–354.

Deluga, R. J. (1992). The relationship of leader-member exchanges with laissez-faire, transactional, and transformational leadership. In K. E. Clark, M. B. Clark, & D. R. Campbell (Eds.), *Impact of leadership*: 237–247. Greensboro, NC: Center for Creative Leadership.

Demerouti, E., Bakker, A. B., Nachreiner, F., & Schaufeli, W. B. (2001). The job demands: resources model of burnout. *Journal of Applied Psychology, 86,* 499–512.

Dienesch, R. M., & Liden, R. C. (1986). Leader-member exchange model of leadership: A critique and further development. *Academy of Management Review, 11,* 618–634.

Dockery, T. M., & Steiner, D. D. (1990). The role of the initial interaction in leader-member exchange. *Group and Organizational Studies, 15,* 395–413.

Donnelly, T. (2010). How to set an employee gift policy. Retrieved from http://www.inc.com/guides/2010/12/how-to-set-an-employee-gift-policy.html

Donnenworth, G. V., & Foa, U. G. (1974). Effects of resource class on retaliation to injustice in interpersonal exchange. *Journal of Personality and Social Psychology, 29,* 785–793.

Duchon, D., Green, S. G., & Taber, T. D. (1986). Vertical dyad linkage: A longitudinal assessment of antecedents, measures, and consequences. *Journal of Applied Psychology. 71,* 56–60.

Foa, U. G., & Foa, E. B. (1974). *Societal structures of the mind.* Springfield, IL: Charles C. Thomas.

Foa, E. B., & Foa, U. G. (1980). Resource theory: Interpersonal behavior as exchange. In K. J. Gergen, M. S. Greenberg, & R. H. Willis (Eds.), *Social exchange* (pp. 77–94). New York: Plenum Press.

Gouldner, A. W. (1960). The norm of reciprocity: A preliminary statement. *American Sociological Review, 25,* 161–178.

Graen, G. (1976). Role-making processes within complex organizations. *Handbook of industrial and organizational psychology. Chicago: Rand McNally.*

Graen, G. B., & Cashman, J. F. (1975). A role-making model of leadership in formal organizations: A developmental approach. In J. G. Hunt & L. L. Larson (Eds.), *Leadership frontiers* (pp. 143–166). Kent, OH: Kent State University.

Graen, G., Liden, R. C., & Hoel, W. (1982). Role of leadership in the employee withdrawal process. *Journal of Applied Psychology, 67,* 868–872.

Graen, G., Novak, M. A., & Sommerkamp, P. (1982). The effects of leader-member exchange and job design on productivity and satisfaction: Testing a dual attachment model. *Organizational Behavior and Human Decision Processes, 30,* 109–131.

Graen, G. B., & Scandura, T. A. (1987). Toward a psychology of dyadic organizing. *Research in Organizational Behavior, 9,* 175–208.

Harris, K. J., Wheeler, A. R., & Kacmar, K. M. (2011). The mediating role of organizational role embeddedness in the LMX-outcomes relationship. *The Leadership Quarterly, 22,* 271–281.

Hofmann, D. A., Morgeson, F. P., & Gerras, S. J. (2003). Climate as a moderator of the relationship between leader-member exchange and content specific citizenship: Safety climate as an exemplar. *Journal of Applied Psychology, 88*, 170–178. doi: 10.1037/0021-9010.88.1.170

Laschinger, H. K. S., Wilk, P., Cho, J., & Greco, P. (2009). Empowerment, engagement and perceived effectiveness in nursing work environments: Does experience matter? *Journal of Nursing Management, 17*, 636–646.

Liden, R. C., & Graen, G. (1980). Generalizability of the vertical dyad linkage model of leadership. *Academy of Management Journal, 23*, 451–465.

Liden, R. C., & Maslyn, J. M. (1998). Multidimensionality of leader-member exchange: An empirical assessment through scale development. *Journal of Management, 24*, 43–72.

Liden, R. C., Wayne, S. J., & Sparrowe, R. T. (2000). An examination of the mediating role of psychological empowerment on the relations between the job, interpersonal relationships, and work outcomes. *Journal of Applied Psychology, 85*, 407–416. doi: 10.1037//0021-9010.85.3.407

Liden, R. C., Wayne, S. J., & Stilwell, D. (1993). A longitudinal study on the early development of leader-member exchanges. *Journal of Applied Psychology, 78*, 662–674.

Liden, R. C., Sparrowe, R. T., & Wayne, S. J. (1997). Leader-member exchange theory: The past and potential for the future. *Research in Personnel and Human Resources Management, 15*, 47–119.

Loi, R., Ngo, H. Y., Zhang, L., & Lau, V. P. (2011). The interaction between leader member exchange and perceived job security in predicting employee altruism and work performance. *Journal of Occupational and Organizational Psychology, 84*, 669–685.

Katz, D., & Kahn, R. L. (1978). *The social psychology of organizations,* (2nd Ed.). New York: Wiley.

Masterson, S. S., Lewis, K., Goldman, B. M., & Taylor, M. S. (2000). Integrating justice and social exchange: The differing effects of fair procedures and treatment on work relationships. *Academy of Management Journal, 43*, 738–748.

Meyer, J. P., & Allen, N. J. (1984). Testing the "side-bet theory" of organizational commitment: Some methodological considerations. *Journal of Applied Psychology, 69*, 372–378.

Podsakoff, P. M., MacKenzie, S. B., Moorman, R. H., & Fetter, R. (1990). Transformational leader behaviors and their effects on followers' trust in leader, satisfaction, and organizational citizenship behaviors. *Leadership Quarterly, 1*, 107–142.

Rockstuhl, T., Dulebohn, J. H., Ang, S., & Shore, L. M. (2012). Leader–member exchange (LMX) and culture: A meta-analysis of correlates of LMX across 23 countries. *Journal of Applied Psychology, 97*, 1097–1130. doi: 10.1037/a0029978

Schriesheim, C. A., & Gardiner, C. C. (1992). An exploration of the discriminant validity of the leader-member exchange scale (LMX 7) commonly used in organizational research. In *Proceedings of the southern management association* (pp. 91-93).

Settoon, R. P., Bennett, N., & Liden, R. C. (1996). Social exchange in organizations: Perceived organizational support, Leader-Member Exchange, and employee reciprocity. *Journal of Applied Psychology, 81*, 219–227.

Sparrowe, R. T., Soetjipto, B. W., & Kramer, M. L. (2006). Do leaders' influence tactics relate to members' helping behavior? It depends on the quality of the relationships. *Academy of Management Journal, 49*, 1194–1208.

Tsui, A. S., Pearce, J. L., Porter, L. W., & Tripoli, A. (1997). Alternative approaches to the employee-organization relationship: Does investment in employees pay off? *Academy of Management Journal, 40*, 1089–1121.

Van Vianen, A. E. M., Shen, C., & Chuang, A. (2011). Person-organization and person-supervisor fits: Employee commitments in a Chinese context. *Journal of Organizational Behavior 32*, 906–926.

Vecchio, R. P., & Gobdel, B. C. (1984). The vertical dyad linkage model of leadership: Problems and prospects. *Organizational Behavior and Human Performance. 34*, 5–20.

Venkataramani, V., Green, S. G., & Schleicher, D. J. (2010). Well-connected leaders: The impact of leaders' social network ties on LMX and members' work attitudes. *Journal of Applied Psychology, 95*, 1071–1084.

Vidyarthi, P. R., Erdogan, B., Anand, S., Liden, R. C., & Chaudhry, A. (2014). One member, two leaders: Extending leader–member exchange theory to a dual leadership context. *Journal of Applied Psychology.* Advance online publication. doi: 10.1037/a0035466

Wakabayashi, M., Graen, G., Graen, M., & Graen, M. (1988). Japanese management progress: Mobility into middle management. *Journal of Applied Psychology, 73*, 217–227.

Wang, H., Law, K. S., Hackett, R. D., Wang, D., & Chen, Z. X. (2005). Leader-member exchange as a mediator of the relationship between transformational leadership and followers' performance and organizational citizenship behavior. *Academy of Management Journal, 48*, 420–432.

Wayne, S. J., & Ferris, G. R. (1990). Influence tactics, affect, and exchange quality in supervisor-subordinate interactions: A laboratory experiment and field study. *Journal of Applied Psychology, 75*, 487–499.

Wayne, S. J., Shore, L. M., & Liden, R. C. (1997). Perceived organizational support and leader-member exchange: A social exchange perspective. *Academy of Management Journal, 40*, 82–111.

Wilson, K. S., Sin, H. P., & Conlon, D. E. (2010). What about the leader in leader-member exchange? The impact of resource exchanges and substitutability on the leader. *Academy of Management Review, 35*, 358–372.

Yukl, G. P. (1990). *Managerial Practices Survey.* Manus Associates.

Leader–Member Exchange and Justice

Suzanne S. Masterson *and* Marcia L. Lensges

Abstract

Researchers have been investigating leader–member exchange (LMX) and justice variables jointly for almost two decades, although there is still no definitive agreement on the nature or form of their relationship. This chapter reviews the LMX–justice literature, categorizing the research into several main approaches: LMX as antecedent to justice, LMX differentiation as antecedent to justice, justice as moderating the relationship between LMX and outcomes, justice as antecedent to LMX, and LMX as moderating the relationship between justice and outcomes. A model is proposed that reconciles some of these multiple perspectives by incorporating event-based, entity-based, and anticipatory justice perceptions with both LMX and supervisor LMX. The chapter ends with a discussion of future directions for LMX–justice research.

Key Words: leader–member exchange (LMX), organizational justice, distributive justice, procedural justice, fairness

Introduction

Researchers have been investigating leader–member exchange (LMX) and justice variables jointly for almost two decades, although there is still no definitive agreement on the nature or form of their relationship. Given that LMX represents the quality of the social exchange relationship between a supervisor and an employee (e.g., Scandura, 1999) and given that social exchange theory has been used as a theoretical lens for explaining the impact of justice perceptions on ensuing attitudes and behaviors (e.g., Moorman, 1991; Shore & Shore, 1995), this attention to the relationship between the two is not surprising. Research has examined LMX as an antecedent of justice perceptions (e.g., Dulebohn, Bommer, Liden, Brouer, & Ferris, 2012; Pillai, Scandura, & Williams, 1999); justice perceptions as antecedent to LMX (e.g., Cropanzano, Prehar, & Chen, 2002; Masterson, Lewis, Goldman, & Taylor, 2000); and LMX (or justice) as moderating between justice (or LMX) and other variables (e.g., Piccolo, Bardes, Mayer, & Judge, 2008; Rosen, Harris, &

Kacmar, 2011), among other conceptualizations. Moreover, fairness issues come into play when LMX differentiation is studied (e.g., Erdogan & Bauer, 2010; Ma & Qu, 2010). Across this research, it is clear that there exists a robust correlation between LMX and justice variables, although the nature of the relationship is still in dispute.

In this chapter, we review the many ways in which LMX and justice have been studied in relation to one another and propose a process model incorporating LMX and multiple forms of justice (event-based, entity-based, and anticipatory) as a means of reconciling these multiple perspectives. Our model also incorporates both subordinate LMX perceptions and SLMX (supervisor LMX) perceptions of the same relationship to more fully represent the dyadic nature and the way that actions by each party to the relationship impact perceptions and reactions of the other. Our chapter ends with a discussion of future research needs in the LMX–justice literature. To begin, however, we provide a very brief overview of LMX and justice, before conducting a detailed review of the multiple ways that LMX and justice have been studied jointly.

Leader–Member Exchange

LMX can be defined as "the unique relationship-based social exchange between leaders and members" (Scandura, 1999, pp. 25–26). As Dulebohn et al. (2012) noted, although originally based in role theory, over time LMX research has more heavily relied on social exchange theory (e.g., Erdogan & Liden, 2002). High LMX relationships are characterized by feelings of mutual trust and reciprocity and broader social exchanges of support, loyalty, and commitment, while low LMX relationships are more limited to economic exchange focusing on the formal elements of employment contracts (e.g., Anand, Hu, Liden, & Vidyarthi, 2011; Cropanzano & Mitchell, 2005; Dulebohn et al., 2012).

Much research over the past several decades has focused on identifying antecedents and consequences associated with LMX, as well as contextual factors that may change the nature of LMX's relationship with other variables. In a recent meta-analysis of the LMX literature, Dulebohn et al. (2012) found evidence across studies for LMX antecedents including follower characteristics (such as competence and positive affectivity), follower personality characteristics (including agreeableness and conscientiousness), leadership behaviors (including contingent reward and transformational leadership), leader personality characteristics (including agreeableness and extraversion), and interpersonal relationship variables (such as perceived similarity, liking, and trust). Similarly, Dulebohn et al. (2012) found support for consequences ranging from performance and organizational citizenship behavior to attitudes such as organizational commitment and job satisfaction. Justice perceptions have been modeled as both an antecedent (e.g., Colquitt, Scott, Rodell, Long, Zapata, Conlon, & Wesson, 2013) and consequence (e.g., Dulebohn et al., 2012) of LMX.

Recent LMX research has focused on LMX differentiation, or the extent to which leaders form relationships of varying quality (high to low) with different members within a work group or unit (e.g., Erdogan & Bauer, 2010; Henderson, Wayne, Bommer, Shore, & Tetrick, 2008). This perspective is different from earlier work which focused on the dyadic relationship between a leader and member in isolation in that it takes into account the members' awareness that different quality relationships exist. These divergent LMX relationships provide

clear opportunities for justice perceptions to play a role when LMX differentiation is considered (e.g., Erdogan & Bauer, 2010).

Justice Perceptions

Studies of organizational justice focus on employees' perceptions of fairness within organizations (e.g., Colquitt, Conlon, Wesson, Porter, & Ng, 2001). Early justice research focused on the fairness associated with outcomes received in organizations, beginning with Adams' (1965) equity theory, and is labeled as distributive justice. Distributive justice perceptions may be formed using one of several different fairness rules, including equity, equality, and need. When individuals apply an equity-based justice rule, they compare their own outcome–input ratio to that of a comparison other (e.g., Deutsch, 1975). Application of an equality-based justice rule would suggest that everyone should receive equal outcomes, while a need-based justice rule would hold that individuals should receive outcomes in proportion to their individual needs (e.g., Deutsch, 1975).

Justice research then began examining procedural justice, or the fairness associated with the procedures used to allocate outcomes (e.g., Leventhal, 1980). Procedural justice generally relates to the structural elements of decision-making procedures, such as process control and opportunities for voice (e.g., Lind & Tyler, 1988). Subsequent research has identified at least six justice rules that are applied when assessing procedural fairness: accuracy, representativeness, bias suppression, consistency, ethicality, and correctability (e.g., Colquitt, 2001; Leventhal, 1980).

More recently, organizational justice research has expanded to incorporate the interpersonal aspects of fair treatment in organizations. Originally conceptualized as interactional justice (e.g., Bies & Moag, 1986), subsequent research has identified two subdimensions: informational justice, or the fairness perceptions associated with the information provided during the encounter, such as being given full disclosure and honest information; and interpersonal justice, or the fairness perceptions associated with the interpersonal treatment, such as being treated with dignity and respect (e.g., Colquitt, 2001; Greenberg, 1993).

Justice perceptions have been studied extensively over the past three decades, with several meta-analyses integrating findings across studies. Cohen-Charash and Spector (2001) examined antecedents of justice perceptions, focusing primarily on organizational outcomes, organizational practices, and characteristics of the perceiver, as well as consequences associated with fairness perceptions, including performance, extra-role and counterproductive behaviors, and attitudes and emotions. Similarly, Colquitt et al. (2001) examined justice consequences, but additionally examined the distinguishability of the different dimensions of justice perceptions. As was the case with LMX, justice has often been examined via a social exchange theory lens (e.g., Colquitt et al., 2013; Masterson et al., 2000).

As noted, LMX has been examined as both an antecedent (e.g., Dulebohn et al., 2012) and a consequence (e.g., Colquitt et al., 2013) of justice. While some LMX research has been conducted using the subdimensions of informational and interpersonal justice (e.g., Piccolo et al., 2008; Roch & Shanock, 2006; Walumbwa, Cropanzano, & Hartnell, 2009), most research to date examining the relationship has used the broader construct of interactional justice (e.g., Cropanzano et al., 2002; Masterson et al., 2000; Rupp & Cropanzano, 2002). Across the literature examining LMX and justice together, all three (or four, if interactional justice is broken into interpersonal and informational) dimensions of justice have been examined in relation to LMX, although individual studies tend to focus on a subset rather than incorporating all of them within a single study (for exceptions, see Burton, Sablynski, & Sekiguchi, 2008; Roch & Shanock, 2006; Wang, Liao, Xia, & Chang, 2010). Moreover, a few studies have examined perceptions of fairness in general (e.g., Deluga, 1994; Werbel & Henriques, 2009) or overall justice perceptions (e.g., Johnson, Truxillo, Erdogan, Bauer, & Hammer, 2009).

Beyond examining individual justice perceptions, justice researchers have also studied the extent to which workgroups and units develop shared cognitions regarding justice treatment, or justice climate (e.g., Naumann & Bennett, 2000; Whitman, Caleo, Carpenter, Horner, & Bernerth, 2012). Recent research examining the relationship between LMX and justice has integrated the concept of justice climate, particularly when examining LMX differentiation (e.g., Erdogan & Bauer, 2010).

The Multiple Conceptualizations of the LMX–Justice Relationship

There have been multiple attempts to jointly study LMX and justice over the years, including LMX as an antecedent of justice perceptions, LMX differentiation as an antecedent of justice

perceptions, justice as a moderator of the relationship between LMX and outcome variables, justice as an antecedent of LMX perceptions, and LMX as a moderator of the relationship between justice and outcome variables. We will review the literature on each of these characterizations of the relationship in turn.

LMX as an Antecedent of Justice Perceptions

Much of the work examining LMX as an antecedent to justice perceptions can be traced back to Scandura's (1999) conceptual article examining LMX from an organizational justice perspective. In her model, Scandura (1999) proposed that, as a leader and member begin to interact, a leader–member relationship emerges that takes the form of either an in-group or out-group type, causing members to feel more or less fairly treated in terms of distributive, procedural, and interactional justice. Scandura (1999) further noted that in-group members may be more likely to focus on procedural justice issues, due to their higher-quality relationship, while out-group members may be more likely to focus on distributive justice issues, given that their rewards are more based on economic exchange in the lower-quality LMX relationship. Overall, much of the underlying logic for justice perceptions as a consequence of LMX is that those in higher-quality relationships enjoy more favorable outcomes and treatment, leading to higher perceptions of fairness.

Pillai et al. (1999) tested a conceptual model in which LMX was hypothesized to be positively related to both distributive and procedural justice perceptions across five different samples representing the United States, Australia, India, Colombia, and the Middle East. The authors found support for LMX as an antecedent for both distributive justice and procedural justice in four of the samples (United States, Australia, Colombia, and Middle East), but for India, only the LMX–distributive justice relationship was significant. Pillai et al. (1999) suggested that the strong regard in the Indian culture for transformational leadership (which was included in the tested model) may weaken the LMX–procedural justice relationship.

Lee (2001) examined the relationship of LMX and justice within the context of cooperative communication, positing that LMX quality will be positively related to perceptions of distributive and procedural justice, which in turn will be positively related to cooperative communication among group members. All of the hypotheses were supported. In combination with Pillai et al.'s (1999) results, these findings provide consistent support for LMX as an antecedent of both distributive and procedural justice.

In 2006, Bhal proposed a model in which procedural and interactional, but not distributive, justice mediated the relationship between the perceived contribution dimension of LMX and organizational citizenship behavior (OCB). In other words, employees who perceive a higher-quality LMX relationship should perceive their procedural and interactional treatment to be more fair and thus be more inclined to perform OCB. The model was tested on a sample of IT professionals in India, and support was found for the expected mediating roles of procedural and interactional (but not distributive) justice. In a later study, Kim, Ok, and Lee (2009) tested the mediating roles of distributive and interactional justice between LMX dimensions and OCB toward the organization and supervisor, finding support for the mediating role of both forms of justice. Taken together, these studies show that all three dimensions of justice have been found to be mediators between LMX and OCB, again supporting the view of LMX as antecedent to justice perceptions.

Further studies have examined the role of justice perceptions as mediating between LMX (or dimensions of LMX) and outcomes including satisfaction (Bhal & Ansari, 2007), organizational commitment (Torka, Schyns, & Looise, 2010), and turnover intentions (Lee, Murrmann, Murrmann, & Kim, 2010), generally finding support for different dimensions of justice as a consequence of LMX and as a mediator of the relationship between LMX and the proposed variables. Moreover, justice climate has also been tested as a mediator between LMX and outcomes, such as the work by Ansari, Hung, and Aafaqi (2007), who found that procedural justice climate perceptions mediated between LMX and both organizational commitment and turnover intentions.

Two recent meta-analyses examined the findings across studies relating to LMX as an antecedent of justice. First, Dulebohn et al. (2012) treated justice as an outcome of LMX, stating that the LMX relationship forms quickly and is thus likely to precede justice perceptions and noting that more studies tend to model the relationship in this form. Results of the meta-analysis showed a significant relationship between LMX and both distributive justice (ρ = .44) and procedural justice (ρ = .55). In addition, LMX was found to partially mediate

the relationships between positive affectivity, contingent rewards, and leader trust with both distributive and procedural justice. In their meta-analysis, Rockstuhl, Dulebohn, Ang, and Shore (2012) focused on addressing the moderating effects of national culture on LMX and its antecedents and consequences. One of the relationships tested was the moderating effect of national culture on the relationship between LMX and justice perceptions. Specifically, the authors hypothesized that the positive relationships between LMX and distributive, procedural, and interactional justice dimensions would be stronger in individualistic countries than in collectivistic countries, because in collectivist cultures, the authority of a leader is unquestioned and thus how the leader treats a member is of minor consequence. The results of the meta-analysis, which included 253 studies in 23 countries, supported the proposed moderating effects of national culture on all three of the LMX to justice relationships.

LMX Differentiation as an Antecedent of Justice Perceptions

There have been several conceptual articles and empirical studies incorporating justice into the study of LMX differentiation. In their multilevel review of LMX differentiation, Henderson, Liden, Glibkowski, and Chaudhry (2009) argued that group members compare their own contributions and what they receive from leaders to the contributions and receipts of other group members, and that these comparisons serve to form members' procedural justice perceptions of the LMX relationship. Henderson et al. (2009) further argued that members' evaluations of the leader's bias and benevolence, along with the members' perceived standing within the group, would mediate between the LMX comparisons and the perceptions of procedural justice. The authors applied the group value model of procedural justice (e.g., Lind & Tyler, 1988), in which group members view fair treatment as a signal that they are valued and respected members of the group.

In an empirical study, Ma and Qu (2010) examined antecedents and consequences of LMX differentiation. The authors hypothesized that LMX differentiation would have a moderating effect on the relationship between LMX and members' interactional justice perceptions, in that the relationship would be stronger when LMX differentiation was high. Although an examination of the correlation matrix revealed a significant positive relationship between LMX and interactional justice (r = .44), no support for the moderation effect of

LMX differentiation was found. Ma and Qu (2010) posited that a low response rate among out-group members may have impacted their ability to find the moderation relationship.

Although not specifically dealing with LMX differentiation, Othman, Ee, and Shi (2010) outlined the potentially related concept of dysfunctional LMX. As defined by the authors, dysfunctional LMX occurs when a leader develops a high-quality LMX relationship with a member which is undeserved based on the member's contributions and performance. Othman et al. (2010) further proposed that other members will develop perceptions of unfairness, and thereby reduce their performance, citizenship behaviors, and commitment.

Justice as a Moderator of the Relationship between LMX and Outcome Variables

Several studies have tested whether justice climate perceptions may be a moderator of the relationship between LMX and outcome variables. Erdogan and Bauer (2010) proposed that both the distributive and procedural justice climate perceptions would moderate the relationship between LMX differentiation and outcome variables including job satisfaction, organizational commitment, coworker satisfaction, coworker helping behaviors, and withdrawal behaviors. The authors hypothesized that high LMX differentiation within a workgroup will make justice concerns more salient. Having a high distributive justice climate, meaning that most employees feel the distribution of outcomes is fair, or a high procedural justice climate, meaning that most workers believe that procedures adhere to principles of consistency, accuracy, bias suppression, representativeness, correctability, and ethicality, should lead employees to believe that LMX differentiation will not have harmful effects. Thus, Erdogan and Bauer (2010) hypothesized that LMX differentiation would be negatively related to outcome variables only when the justice climate was low. Their findings revealed that justice climate moderated the relationship between LMX differentiation and organizational commitment, satisfaction with coworkers, and withdrawal behaviors, as expected.

Hsiung (2012) proposed that the positive relationship between LMX and employee voice behavior would be moderated by procedural justice climate, such that the relationship would be stronger when procedural justice climate was high. The study found that work groups with high procedural justice climate scores had a stronger relationship between LMX and employee voice behavior. In another study involving procedural justice climate as a moderator, Sun, Chow, Chiu, and Pan (2013) tested the mediating role of outcome favorability between LMX and OCB, with the operationalization of outcome favorability including elements of fairness, while also proposing that the procedural justice climate would moderate the indirect relationship between LMX and OCB via outcome favorability. The authors proposed that when the procedural justice climate was high, employees would be even more likely to respond to high-quality LMX relationships and favorable outcomes with OCB. Results of the study supported the hypothesized relationship: high-quality LMX relationships were more positively related to OCB when employees reported higher procedural justice climate perceptions (Sun et al., 2013).

Justice as an Antecedent of LMX

Many of the studies modeling justice as an antecedent of LMX use social exchange theory as their underlying conceptual framework (e.g., Masterson et al., 2000; Rupp & Cropanzano, 2002). According to social exchange theory (Blau, 1964), individuals are likely to form social exchange relationships at work. These are generally long-term relationships characterized by one party providing a service, or something of value, to another party, causing the referent other to feel obligated to reciprocate the service at a later date. Thus, there is an exchange of services across time; however, social exchange relationships are different from those based on purely economic exchange, in that the obligations of each party to the other are generally unspecified, and there are often no clear standards for measuring each party's contributions (e.g., Liden, Sparrowe, & Wayne, 1997). Settoon, Bennett, and Liden (1996) noted that social exchange relationships might be described as "gestures of goodwill" that are reciprocated between the parties across time (p. 220).

Studies that model justice as an antecedent of LMX generally propose that a supervisor's fair treatment of an employee, whether through fair outcomes, the adoption and implementation of fair procedures, or fair interpersonal treatment and shared information, can be seen as discretionary behavior (Masterson et al., 2000). That is, supervisors often have the choice whether to enact higher or lower levels of fairness toward employees, and employees appear to consider whether actions are discretionary in holding others accountable for fairness-related actions (Folger & Cropanzano,

1998). In choosing to act fairly, employees may perceive that the supervisor is providing something of value to the employee, thereby enacting a higher-quality social exchange LMX relationship that the employee needs to reciprocate via behaviors and attitudes that benefit the supervisor and/or organization (e.g., Masterson et al., 2000). Thus, perceptions of fair treatment should be positively related to employees' LMX perceptions and subsequent behaviors and attitudes.

In an early study, Manogran, Stauffer, and Conlon (1994) proposed that employees' perceptions of interactional justice would influence their citizenship behaviors, job satisfaction, and organizational commitment by first influencing their perceptions of the quality of the LMX relationship with their supervisor. The study was conducted on hourly production employees in a manufacturing plant, and the results revealed that LMX mediated between interactional justice perceptions and citizenship behaviors, job satisfaction, and organizational commitment. Deluga (1994) was also an early tester of the justice to LMX relationship, using a more general supervisor fairness measure in his test. However, he did not find the hypothesized relationship, and posited that a restricted range in the fairness variable might have contributed to the lack of findings.

Masterson et al. (2000) relied heavily on social exchange theory to inform their study of the relationship between interactional justice perceptions and supervisor-related outcomes. Specifically, the authors proposed that the social exchange relationship of LMX mediates the relationship between interactional justice and supervisor-related outcomes, such as OCB directed at the supervisor, task performance, and job satisfaction. In essence, they argued that employees would see fair treatment by the supervisor (interactional justice) as a contribution to the social exchange relationship (LMX), and would attempt to reciprocate by increasing their behaviors and attitudes benefiting the supervisor (OCB-supervisor, task performance, and job satisfaction). The study's findings confirmed LMX as a mediator between interactional justice and all three supervisor-directed behaviors (Masterson et al., 2000).

Cropanzano et al. (2002) conducted a study to extend Masterson et al.'s (2000) findings, proposing that LMX would mediate the relationship between interactional justice and both supervisory satisfaction and job performance, and the results supported the hypothesized relationships. Another study, by Wayne, Shore, Bommer, and Tetrick (2002), examined whether LMX would mediate the relationship between distributive justice perceptions and OCB and performance, but the results did not support the hypotheses: distributive justice was not significantly related to LMX, so no mediation could occur. Murphy, Wayne, Liden, and Erdogan (2003) proposed that LMX would mediate both the interactional justice–social loafing and distributive justice–social loafing relationships. Their results indicated that LMX mediated the relationship between interactional justice and social loafing but that there was not a significant relationship between distributive justice and LMX, so no mediation could occur. Taken as a group, the research from this time period demonstrates support for the social exchange perspective: supervisory fair treatment, most often measured as interactional justice, appears to be viewed by employees as a contribution to the social exchange relationship, leading to higher-quality LMX perceptions and higher attempts to reciprocate with behaviors and attitudes likely to be appreciated by the supervisor.

In 2006, Roch and Shanock simultaneously examined the relationship between five dimensions of organizational justice (distributive, procedural, interactional, informational, and interpersonal) as they related to the dependent variables of LMX, POS, and pay satisfaction, in an effort to identify unique associations between the justice and outcome variables. Again, their results support the idea that supervisory fair treatment in the form of interactional justice, informational justice, and interpersonal justice were related to LMX.

In another line of research building on Masterson et al.'s (2000) findings, Rupp and Cropanzano (2002) developed a multifoci model of justice, suggesting that each of the justice dimensions (distributive, procedural, and interactional) could be associated with a specific source (e.g., supervisor or organization). They proposed that supervisory procedural justice and supervisory interactional justice should relate to supervisor-directed behaviors and attitudes via the social exchange relationship with the supervisor. Although they did not use LMX as their operationalization of the social exchange relationship with the supervisor, their theoretical arguments and overall results support the social exchange perspective of LMX as a mediator between justice perceptions and outcomes (Rupp & Cropanzano, 2002). Lavelle, Rupp, and Brockner (2007) further developed the multifoci approach in a conceptual paper, arguing that supervisory distributive, procedural, and interactional justice should work through supervisory social exchange relationships (i.e., LMX, perceived supervisor support, and supervisory trust) to influence supervisor commitment and identification with the supervisor, and ultimately citizenship behaviors toward the supervisor.

Over the ensuing years, there has been a host of research that has examined the relationship between justice perceptions, LMX, and other variables. One stream of research focused most closely on interactional justice in conjunction with LMX. Yagil (2006) proposed that interactional justice perceptions work through LMX to influence job satisfaction. This research is somewhat unique in that it included identical LMX measures from both the leader (SLMX; Erdogan & Bauer, 2013) and member (LMX) perspectives. Yagil (2006) found support for LMX mediating the relationship between interactional justice and job satisfaction. Interestingly, she also found support for interactional justice as a mediator in the relationship between SLMX and both LMX and procedural justice. Werbel and Henriques (2009) found no support for a relationship between distributive fairness and LMX, but did find that the "conditions of trust related to interactional justice" which were "availability, integrity, discreteness, and openness were significantly associated with LMX" (p. 791). Walumbwa et al. (2009) tested and found support for a model which had interpersonal and informational justice perceptions working through LMX to influence voluntary learning and, ultimately, job performance. El Akremi, Vandenberghe, and Camerman (2010) proposed and found support for a model in which informational and interpersonal justice worked through LMX to influence both supervisory and organizationally directed deviance behavior. In a recent study, Srikanth and Gurunathan (2013) found that interactional justice worked through LMX to influence job mobility preparedness. All of these studies point to the strong relationship between interactional justice and LMX, and find support for models in which interactional justice works through LMX to influence important organizational outcomes.

A different stream of research has focused on justice dimensions in addition to or beyond interactional justice. Sparr and Sonnentag (2008) hypothesized that overall fairness perceptions of feedback (operationalized with items representing all four dimensions of justice) would work through LMX to influence employees' reported job satisfaction

and perceived control at work. The model was supported, and the authors concluded: "This result suggests that fairness perceptions of feedback unfold their beneficial potential for job satisfaction and perceived control at work via the enhancement of LMX quality" (Sparr & Sonnentag, 2008, p. 218). Similarly, Oren, Tziner, Sharoni, Amor, and Alon (2012) tested the relationships between overall organizational justice perceptions, LMX, and OCB, finding support for both a direct effect and indirect effect through LMX of overall justice perceptions on OCB. Wang et al. (2010) found all three forms of justice to work through LMX to indirectly influence job dedication and interpersonal facilitation.

Erdogan, Liden, and Kraimer (2006) noted the importance of understanding whether the justice–LMX relationship holds across different organizations. To this end, they examined the extent to which different dimensions of organizational culture (respect for people, aggressiveness, and team orientation) moderated the relationship between interactional and distributive justice perceptions and LMX. Their results demonstrated that the relationship between interactional justice and LMX was stronger when the organization's culture was high in respect for people but less pronounced when team orientation was high. In addition, the relationship between procedural justice and LMX was stronger when the organization's culture was high in aggressiveness but less pronounced when team orientation was high (Erdogan et al., 2006). Thus, the results demonstrate that the organization's culture can have an important influence on the nature of the justice–LMX relationship.

Several meta-analyses have included the justice–LMX relationship in their analysis of the literature. Cohen-Charash and Spector (2001) conducted a meta-analysis of the justice literature and modeled LMX as a consequence of justice perceptions. They found four studies examining the distributive justice–LMX relationship (mean weighted $r = .27$); six studies examining the procedural justice–LMX relationship (mean weighted $r = .37$); and three studies examining the interactional justice–LMX relationship (mean weighted $r = .67$). Interestingly, the confidence interval for the interactional justice–LMX relationship (.60/.74) did not overlap with the confidence intervals for distributive justice–LMX (.20/.34) or procedural justice–LMX (.32/.42), suggesting that the interactional justice–LMX relationship is significantly stronger than that of the other two dimensions. More recently, Colquitt et al. (2013) conducted a meta-analytic test of justice via the social exchange perspective. Their results revealed corrected population coefficients for the justice dimensions and LMX as follows: distributive justice (r_c = .42); procedural justice (r_c = .50); informational justice (r_c = .53); and interpersonal justice (r_c = .57). Colquitt et al. (2013) used their meta-analytic results to test a structural equation model in which social exchange quality (including LMX) mediated between justice perceptions and performance, OCB, and counterproductive work behaviors, finding strong support for the proposed relationships. Overall, there is strong support across time and numerous studies for the social exchange view of justice perceptions influencing LMX, and working indirectly through LMX to influence other outcomes.

LMX as a Moderator of the Relationship between Justice and Outcome Variables

A final set of studies has examined the extent to which LMX is a moderator of the relationship between justice and outcome variables, such as OCB, performance, and withdrawal. There have been two theoretical lenses applied to this type of relationship. From the social exchange perspective, researchers have argued that the relationship between justice perceptions and outcome variables should be stronger when LMX is higher, because employees are not only responding positively to the fairness of the treatment, but they want to also benefit the supervisor with whom they have a high-quality social exchange relationship. Burton et al. (2008) tested this moderation model, and found that the relationships between both procedural and distributive justice perceptions and OCB were stronger when LMX quality was high. Interestingly, they also found that the relationship between interactional justice and both performance and OCB was mediated by LMX, as is also predicted by social exchange theory. They suggested that moderation was more appropriate for distributive and procedural justice because these perceptions deal more with organizational actions, while mediation was appropriate for interactional justice because the supervisor was the source of such fairness perceptions (Burton et al., 2008).

In a related study, Piccolo et al. (2008) found that LMX moderated the relationships between both interpersonal and procedural justice and the outcomes of felt obligations, OCB, and withdrawal, such that the relationships were stronger when LMX quality was high. Interestingly, Piccolo et al. (2008) tested alternative models whereby LMX

predicted justice and whereby LMX mediated the relationship between justice and the outcome variables, and neither fit as well as the hypothesized moderation model.

In contrast, fairness heuristic theory (Lind, 2001) predicts that individuals pay more attention to fairness cues when they do not have trust in an entity as a means of determining how to interact with that entity. Moreover, uncertainty management theory (Lind & van den Bos, 2002) suggests that individuals look to the social context (such as fairness cues) when faced with uncertainty and unpredictability in their environment. Together, these perspectives suggest that when LMX quality is low, employees will not have trust in the manager (Johnson et al., 2009) and will face more uncertainty due to not receiving as much information and support from their supervisor (Rosen et al., 2011), and thus justice cues will be more salient and stronger predictors of outcomes. In testing these models, Johnson et al. (2009) found that LMX moderated the relationship between overall departmental fairness perceptions and both task performance and OCB directed at the organization, such that the relationship was only significant when LMX was low; when LMX was high, the relationship between fairness perceptions and outcomes were nonsignificant, thus supporting the fairness heuristic theory perspective. Moreover, Rosen et al. (2011) tested the moderating relationship of LMX between both distributive and procedural justice perceptions and performance. Their results revealed support only for the role of LMX in moderating between distributive justice perceptions and performance, such that distributive justice was positively related to performance only when LMX quality was low, providing support for the uncertainty management theory perspective. Taken together, and in combination with the previous support of the social exchange theory (Burton et al., 2008; Piccolo et al., 2008), there is still much work to be done to understand the role of LMX in moderating justice-to-outcome relationships.

Proposed Model Integrating Justice and LMX

Having reviewed the literature that has examined justice and LMX simultaneously, we propose a model (Figure 5.1) as a starting point for future research. As indicated by the model, we suggest that employees are continually evaluating supervisor-enacted events in terms of fairness, and that those justice evaluations influence employees' perceptions

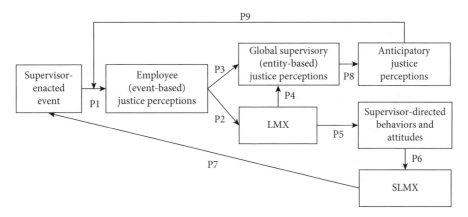

Fig. 5.1 A proposed model of the justice–LMX relationship.

of LMX and their global justice perceptions about the supervisor. Employee LMX perceptions will influence the employee's attitudes and behaviors directed toward the supervisor, influencing the supervisor's SLMX (i.e., the quality of the LMX from the supervisor's perspective), which will feed back to influence subsequent supervisor behavior toward the employee in the form of enacted events. At the same time, the employee's global justice perceptions about the supervisor will influence their expectations about the supervisor's fairness for the future (i.e., anticipatory justice), which have a feedback role in the evaluation of the fairness of future events. Below, we go through each stage of the model in turn.

Our model begins with the supervisor enacting an event, which the employee then evaluates in terms of fairness. Specifically, we propose that the employee forms an event-based justice perception, (Cropanzano, Byrne, Bobocel, & Rupp, 2001), a fairness perception associated with a specific workplace occurrence, such as a performance evaluation, pay raise, or work assignment. This can be differentiated from entity-based justice, which is a more global evaluation about the fairness associated with a unit that exists across time and events, such as a person (e.g., supervisor or coworker) or organization (Hollensbe, Khazanchi, & Masterson, 2008), and which is modeled as a consequence of LMX later in the proposed model.

The proposed relationship between a supervisor-enacted event and employee justice perceptions associated with that event has been well-researched in the justice literature. Findings support that employees evaluate the fairness of specific events such as performance appraisals (e.g., Taylor, Tracy, Renard, Harrison, & Carroll, 1995), pay decisions

(e.g., Folger & Konovsky, 1989), selection decisions (e.g., Gilliland, 1994), and layoff decisions (e.g., Skarlicki, Ellard, & Kelln, 1998), and that the evaluation can involve all four dimensions of organizational justice: distributive, procedural, informational, and interpersonal (e.g., Colquitt et al., 2001).

Thus, a specific event, enacted by the supervisor, provides a starting point into modeling the relationship between justice perceptions and LMX. Specifically, and in line with the findings of hundreds of studies in the justice field, we propose that:

Proposition 1: Employees form justice perceptions (distributive, procedural, informational, and interpersonal) of supervisor-enacted events.

We propose starting our model integrating justice and LMX with a supervisor-initiated event because of the current debate in the literature as to the proper form of the justice–LMX relationship. As revealed by the earlier literature review, to date there has been no definitive empirical finding establishing the directionality of these two constructs. Researchers have offered multiple theoretical arguments supporting the influence of LMX on justice perceptions, including the idea that employees in high-quality LMX relationships are more likely to perceive their treatment as fair than are employees in low-quality LMX relationships (e.g., Lee, 2001; Pillai et al., 1999; Sun et al., 2013) and that LMX forms so quickly that fairness perceptions must follow (e.g., Dulebohn et al., 2012). Other researchers have developed theoretical arguments proposing that justice perceptions influence LMX perceptions, with most relying on social exchange theory to propose that fair treatment is perceived as a voluntary contribution to the supervisor–subordinate relationship, thus influencing the subsequent evaluation of LMX quality (e.g., Colquitt et al., 2013; Lavelle et al., 2007; Masterson et al., 2000). Perhaps with a view to integrating these findings, several researchers have argued that justice perceptions influence LMX quality early in the supervisor–subordinate relationship, but that the directionality changes to LMX influencing justice perceptions after the relationship has been established (e.g., Ansari et al., 2007; Kim et al., 2009).

Given this ongoing debate, we choose to begin with a concrete event: the supervisor enacting a procedure or interacting with the employee. Doing so helps to step away from the "which came first" debate by focusing attention on a specific event to which the employee is responding and tracing through the potential effects of the employee's subsequent event-based justice perceptions to the more global constructs of LMX and entity-based supervisory justice perceptions. As Cropanzano et al., (2001) argued, *"events must first be evaluated before they can affect entity judgments of social actors"* (p. 191, italics in original). In essence, we propose that it does not matter whether a supervisor and employee are just beginning to work together or whether the dyad has multiple years of interaction experience; in either case, new events offer employees new information by which to (re-)evaluate the quality of the relationship and (re-)assess global evaluations of that supervisor. For example, an employee who is passed over for an expected promotion (event) is likely to evaluate the justice/injustice of that event. In turn, those justice perceptions may have an influence on the employee's evaluation of the quality of LMX with the supervisor as well as the global perceptions of the supervisor's fairness.

Thus, in modeling the justice–LMX relationship, we propose that event-based justice perceptions influence LMX. This proposition is consistent with the past research supporting the justice→LMX relationship via a social exchange lens (e.g., Burton et al., 2008; Cohen-Charash & Spector, 2001; Colquitt et al., 2013; Masterson et al., 2000; Murphy et al., 2003). According to the social exchange theory perspective, to the extent that supervisors enact fair events (as evaluated by distributive, procedural, informational and/or interpersonal justice perceptions), they are making positive contributions to the social exchange relationship with the employee, leading to higher evaluations of the quality of that relationship (e.g., LMX).

Proposition 2: Employees' event-based justice perceptions (distributive, procedural, informational, and interpersonal) influence their LMX perceptions.

Simultaneously, we propose that event-based justice perceptions influence employees' entity-based justice perceptions, and specifically the global perceptions of the supervisor's fairness. Again, this proposition is consistent with the integrative model of organizational justice outlined by Cropanzano et al. (2001) in which employees form event-based justice perceptions which then influence their entity-based justice perceptions of the party responsible for the event. This relationship is at least partially supported by the work of Hollensbe et al. (2008), who found that new entrants to organizations used some traditional elements of event-based justice in the formation of their entity-based justice perceptions of the organization and their supervisor.

Proposition 3: Employees' event-based justice perceptions (distributive, procedural, informational, and interpersonal) influence their entity-based global justice perceptions of the supervisor.

We model one additional relationship in this stage of the model, proposing that LMX influences employees' entity-based or global justice perceptions of their supervisor. We believe that this relationship is consistent with the many research studies that have found a positive relationship from LMX to justice (e.g., Dulebohn et al., 2012), and note that many of the studies that modeled this relationship used entity-based operationalizations of justice. For example, Sun et al. (2013) focused on the fairness of the supervisor's decisions in measuring outcome favorability, while many others (e.g., Bhal, 2006; Bhal & Ansari, 2007; Kim et al., 2009; Lee, 2001; Lee et al., 2010; Pillai et al., 1999) used the measures developed by Niehoff and Moorman (1993), which specifically focus on the general managers as the source of formal procedures and interactional justice-related behaviors, making these more representative of an entity-based justice perception (Cropanzano et al., 2001).

Proposition 4: Employees' LMX perceptions influence their (entity-based) global justice perceptions of the supervisor.

Thus, it may be that it is possible to remedy current competing theories about the directionality of the relationship between justice and LMX by specifying the type of justice perceptions to be studied. Support for propositions 2 and 4 would indicate that supervisory-related event-based justice perceptions influence LMX perceptions, which in turn influence employees' entity-based justice perceptions of the supervisor.

In the next stage of the model, we propose that employees' LMX perceptions influence their subsequent behaviors and attitudes toward the supervisor. This relationship is well-established in past research, and again is based on social exchange theory. To the extent that employees perceive that they have a high-quality exchange relationship with their supervisor, they feel obligated to reciprocate through adopting attitudes and enacting behaviors that benefit that supervisor (e.g., Masterson et al., 2000). Past research has found support for LMX as a predictor of supervisor-directed behaviors, including job performance, organizational citizenship behavior, and turnover, as well as supervisor-directed attitudes, such as commitment and job satisfaction (e.g., Dulebohn et al., 2012).

Proposition 5: Employees' LMX perceptions influence their supervisor-directed behaviors and attitudes.

We further propose that supervisors will note these employee behaviors and attitudes, and that will influence their perceptions of the quality of their exchange relationship with the employee (SLMX; Erdogan & Bauer, 2013) as well as their subsequent behaviors toward the employee. Again, we rely on social exchange theory for the development of this proposition. Proposition 5 states that employees engage in supervisor-directed behaviors and attitudes to reciprocate the supervisor's contributions to the relationship (i.e., past fair events and treatment). It thus seems likely that supervisors will, in turn, view these employee attitudes and behaviors as contributions to the social exchange relationship, thus influencing their SLMX perceptions and, ultimately, their future enactment of events relating to that employee.

Proposition 6: Employees' supervisor-directed behaviors and attitudes influence supervisors' SLMX perceptions.

Proposition 7: Supervisors' SLMX perceptions influence their enactment of employee-related events.

Returning to employees' entity-based justice perceptions of the supervisor's overall or global fairness (resulting from both their event-based justice perceptions [proposition 3] as well as their LMX perceptions [proposition 4]), we propose that, based on these entity-based justice perceptions, employees develop expectations of how fairly they will be treated in future events involving the supervisor. Researchers have referred to this as anticipatory justice (Shapiro & Kirkman, 2001). Anticipatory justice is a fairly new construct, and has not received much empirical attention to date, but we believe that this is a key variable that can help researchers better understand how entity-based justice perceptions are integrated into subsequent reactions to events.

In their original discussion of event- versus entity-based justice perceptions, Cropanzano et al. (2001) addressed the issue of possible reverse causality, or the case where entity-based justice perceptions could influence event-based justice perceptions. Specifically, they suggested that two supervisors who engage in the exact same behaviors might spark different reactions, depending upon their prior reputation for fairness (Cropanzano et al., 2001). Similarly, Degoey (2000), in his discussion of justice contagion, proposed that fairness reputation might have a subsequent impact on reactions to behavior. Several studies have supported these ideas. As Cropanzano et al. (2001) noted, research by van den Bos, Wilke, and Lind (1998) demonstrated that subjects who were primed to believe that the decision-maker would be fair were more likely to rate the decision-maker's actions as fair. Jones and Skarlicki (2005) found a similar effect, in a study in which subjects overheard two confederates talking about the experimenter's fairness in a previous encounter. That information had an incremental effect on subjects' justice ratings of the experimenter, beyond their own experiences (Jones & Skarlicki, 2005). Thus, it appears that perception of a person's fairness reputation may influence future perceptions of event-based justice.

Building off of work by Rodell and Colquitt (2009), we propose that the supervisor's justice reputation, as captured by the employee's entity-based justice perception of the supervisor, will influence the employee's expectations of supervisory fairness in the future, or anticipated justice. In a study conducted within the context of an organizational change, Rodell and Colquitt (2009) found global supervisory fairness perceptions significantly predicted employees' anticipatory justice, and that these two types of justice perceptions together predicted employees' reports of experienced justice during the organizational change.

Proposition 8: Employee perceptions of entity-based justice perceptions (e.g., global supervisory justice perceptions) influence their anticipatory justice perceptions (e.g., expected justice treatment in future encounters with the supervisor).

As noted above, the work of van den Bos et al. (1998), Jones and Skarlicki (2005), and Rodell and Colquitt (2009) generally demonstrate the potential effect of justice expectations on subsequent experiences of justice. We propose that anticipatory justice has a moderating effect on the relationship between the elements of the supervisor-enacted event and the employee's event-based justice perceptions. That is, we believe employees consider their expectations of fair treatment when assessing the fairness of a particular supervisor-enacted event. If the employee had high expectations of fair treatment that were not present in the enactment of the event, the subsequent evaluation of the event's distributive, procedural, informational, and interpersonal fairness might be lower than had the expectations of fair treatment not been as high. This is similar to Cropanzano et al.'s (2001) proposal that the exact same behaviors might be evaluated as more or less fair depending upon the actor's fairness reputation. It also is in line with previous findings that those with the highest levels of organizational commitment have the strongest reactions to perceived unfairness, given that it violates their expectations for the relationship (e.g., Brockner, Tyler, & Cooper-Schneider, 2002). Alternatively, it is possible that employees who have expectations for fairness will perceive what they anticipated to receive, a form of confirmation bias (e.g., Bell, Wiechmann, & Ryan, 2006). In either case, anticipatory justice perceptions will moderate the relationship between the event and justice perceptions. Thus, our final proposition is:

Proposition 9: Employee anticipatory justice perceptions moderate the relationship between the supervisor-enacted event and the employee's event-based justice perceptions.

Discussion and Future Directions for Research

In this chapter, we have reviewed the literature that has jointly examined LMX and justice and proposed a model of the LMX–justice relationship. We believe that this model addresses several issues that have been unresolved by research to date, although there are other issues that remain unaddressed and present interesting avenues for future research.

The Current State of Knowledge and the Proposed Model

While there has been substantial research which jointly studies LMX and justice, as our review reveals, there is no conclusive understanding of the relationships between these two important constructs. Various relational forms have been proposed, from direct causal relationships to mediating and moderating relationships, and support has been found for many of these proposed forms. Unfortunately, most of this research has collected data from a single source (e.g., employees), often within a single survey, resulting in an inability to tease apart the potential causal relationships among variables. As a result, we have good empirical evidence that LMX and justice are related, but we do not have a good understanding of the form of that relationship.

The proposed model builds off of past research findings and provides a path to reconciling the findings for various forms of the LMX–justice relationship through integrating both event- and entity-based justice perceptions as well as anticipatory justice. The model proposes that justice serves as both an antecedent and consequence of LMX, and that it is the type of justice perceptions that should dictate the form of the relationship. Specifically, we propose that employees assess the fairness of supervisor-enacted events (such as performance reviews, work assignments, or interpersonal encounters) and that their fairness perceptions (distributive, procedural, and/or interactional) of those events influence their perceptions of the quality of the LMX with that supervisor. Building off of social exchange theory (Blau, 1964) and past justice research (e.g., Masterson et al., 2000), we propose that supervisor-enacted events that are perceived to be fair will be viewed as discretionary and valuable contributions to the employee from the supervisor, thus increasing the perceived quality of the relationship (LMX) and leading to increased feelings of obligation to reciprocate in ways likely to be valued by the supervisor. In this way, event-based justice perceptions are antecedent to LMX.

However, this is only half of the story. We also propose that LMX is antecedent to entity-based justice perspective, specifically employees' global perceptions of supervisor fairness. Employees' perceptions of the quality of the leader–member exchange relationship with their supervisors will influence their perceptions of their supervisors' overall fairness; the higher quality the relationship, the more likely the supervisor is to be perceived as fair. This logic is consistent with the theoretical arguments offered by past researchers proposing the LMX–justice relationship (e.g., Dulebohn et al., 2012), and the relationship is supported by past research that has operationalized justice using scales referring to managers (i.e., entities) in the items (e.g., Lee et al., 2010; Pillai et al., 1999). In this way, the model potentially reconciles the two primary views of LMX as both antecedent and consequence of justice.

The proposed model also incorporates anticipatory justice perceptions, depicting them as both a consequence of global perceptions of supervisor fairness and as a moderator of the relationship between supervisor-enacted events and entity-based supervisory justice perceptions. Thus, as employees form global perceptions about their supervisor's fairness, at least partly based on LMX, they develop expectations about how fairly they will be treated in the future. These expectations come into play during the evaluation of the fairness of the next supervisor-enacted event. On the one hand, high expectations of fairness may moderate the relationship by causing employees to exhibit confirmatory bias (e.g., Bell et al., 2006), perceiving the fairness that they expect to see. On the other, high expectations of fairness may moderate the relationship by causing employees to perceive questionable events as more unfair than others who were not expecting high fairness, in line with the "higher they are, the harder they fall" logic formerly associated with organizational commitment (e.g., Brockner et al., 1992). Future research must test this moderation and perhaps identify the threshold at which anticipatory justice perceptions change from "rose colored glass" through which expectations are confirmed to "magnifying glass" through which unfairness is exaggerated.

Finally, the model incorporates both LMX and SLMX, demonstrating the interactive nature of employees' and supervisors' evaluations of their dyadic relationship. We propose that each party interprets the other party's behaviors as discretionary contributions to their social exchange relationship, influencing the perceived quality of the relationship and the resulting feelings of obligation to reciprocate in an appropriate way. The proposed relationship centered on LMX has already been demonstrated by some of the justice–LMX–outcomes research (e.g., Cropanzano et al., 2001; Masterson et al., 2000; Murphy et al., 2003); however, the SLMX relationship has not been as well researched, nor have the two been integrated together with justice as explicitly as is offered in the proposed model.

An empirical test of the model and its propositions will require longitudinal, multisource (employee and supervisor) data to fully capture the complexity of the supervisor–employee relationship and its changing nature via multiple interactions. In essence, we propose that employees and supervisors are continually monitoring the cues they receive about their relationships with one another, and that each new event provides an opportunity for reassessment and adjustment. To some degree, the model implies that, over time, dyads are likely to settle into a fairly stable pattern in which each interaction reinforces already held perceptions and beliefs. However, the model does allow for disruptions in this cycle; for example, supervisors perceiving high-quality SLMX could unintentionally enact events that employees perceive as unfair, either because supervisors view the event from a different perspective than the employees, or because the supervisors are compelled to act in accordance with organizational requirements (e.g., Scott, Colquitt, & Paddock, 2009). Future research will be needed to more fully identify the conditions under which the proposed justice–LMX relationship is likely to be stable as well as the circumstances that are likely to lead to disruptive changes.

LMX and Justice: Next Steps

Beyond the proposed model, there remains much work to be done at the intersection of LMX and justice, particularly involving two broad topics: the larger context in which LMX dyads are embedded, and dimensionality of LMX and justice. We first discuss potential next steps to advance learning around the effects of context, and we then conclude with avenues to incorporate dimensionality into the LMX–justice research.

As is highlighted in the LMX differentiation literature (e.g., Henderson et al., 2009), while supervisors have one-to-one relationships with each employee, these relationships exist within the context of all other dyadic relationships between the supervisor and other workgroup employees. Moreover, there is good evidence that individuals' justice perceptions are often influenced by the social context in which the individual is embedded (e.g., Masterson & Tong, in press). Thus, there is good reason to propose that research attempting to understand the LMX–justice relationship must consider the broader workgroup context in which the dyadic relationship is embedded.

The LMX differentiation literature addressed this issue by explicitly considering the quality of the supervisor's relationships with other employees in relation to the supervisor's relationship with the focal employee (e.g., Henderson et al., 2008). Studies examining justice climate also represent an attempt to explicitly consider the context in which leader–member relationships occur (e.g., Erdogan & Bauer, 2010). However, more work needs to be done to take the workgroup, and perhaps even larger organizational, context into account.

For example, it might be important to consider the larger social network in which an individual employee is embedded within his/her organization, and the LMX and justice comparison points that the individual is exposed to outside of his/her workgroup. LMX differentiation focuses on the differential relationships that leaders form with members within the workgroup, but it is likely that employees observe cues about LMX relationships between employees outside of their workgroup and their respective supervisors. Employees might routinely share such information as part of the "watercooler" talk within organizations. This kind of comparison information might lead employees to perceive higher- or lower-quality LMX with their own supervisors, depending on the information ("My supervisor really does support me, considering what Tom just went through with his supervisor" or "I'll bet my supervisor would never go to bat for me the way Karen's supervisor did for her").

Similarly, justice climate focuses on the shared fairness perceptions within a specified unit or workgroup (e.g., Naumann & Bennett, 2000), but employees have many other important relationships and sources of fairness-related information within their organizations. Several justice researchers have started taking a social networking perspective in attempting to better understand employee perceptions of fairness (e.g., Chia, Foo, & Fang, 2006; Umphress, Labianca, Brass, Kass, & Scholten, 2003). A better understanding of the LMX–justice relationship could be gained by incorporating employees' social networks as a potential source of information influencing both justice and LMX perceptions.

Another contextual issue that has received some attention but might require more is the organization as a relational partner and source of fairness perceptions. Several studies examining the LMX–justice relationship incorporated perceived organizational support (POS) as representing the quality of the social exchange relationship between the employee and the organization, and found that POS had a positive influence on LMX, while the relationship from LMX to POS was nonsignificant (Masterson et al., 2000; Wayne et al., 2002). This suggests that employees' perceptions of the quality of the relationship with their organization trickles down to influence LMX perceptions, although support was not found for the opposite effect. Moreover, with regard to entity-based justice perceptions, Hollensbe et al. (2008) found that employees reported using perceptions of supervisor fairness as an indicator of the organization's likely fairness, as well as perceptions of organizational fairness as an indicator of their supervisor's fairness. Taken together, these studies suggest that future research may need to more explicitly consider both POS and employees' global perceptions of organizational fairness as potentially influencing LMX and global perceptions of supervisor fairness, and thus their interrelationship.

Finally, while a few studies have examined and found varying impact of organizational (e.g., Erdogan et al., 2006) and national culture (e.g., Rockstuhl et al., 2012; Shao, Rupp, Skarlicki, & Jones, 2013), additional research is needed to check for how the relationship between LMX and justice may change depending upon the culture in which it is studied, whether organizational or national. Research in this area would require a thorough understanding of how dimensions of both LMX and justice may differ in various cultural contexts.

With regard to construct dimensionality, in our model, we have generally focused on justice and LMX as unidimensional. In terms of justice, we address different types of justice perceptions (event-based, entity-based, and anticipatory) but do not develop specific, differential propositions related to distributive, procedural, and interactional (informational/interpersonal). Partially, our decision was due to the fact that support can be found for each of the dimensions to be related to LMX, in different combinations, and in different contexts. Moreover, we believe that a key advancement might be in considering the different types of fairness (event-based, entity-based, and anticipatory) in conjunction with LMX as opposed to focusing on differential relationships among the justice dimensions and LMX. Similarly, although a few researchers who have examined the LMX–justice relationship operationalized and tested the underlying dimensions associated with LMX (e.g., contribution, respect, loyalty, and affect, Ansari et al., 2007; perceived contribution and affect; Bhal, 2006), we have chosen to focus on LMX as unidimensional, primarily due to its treatment as a single factor in much of the research.

However, future research may benefit from examining whether different dimensions of LMX are more or less related to justice perceptions. In particular, it may be interesting to consider whether event-based justice perceptions are more likely to impact particular LMX dimensions, as well as whether particular LMX dimensions are more related to entity-based perceptions of the supervisor's global fairness.

Conclusion

Years of research findings have demonstrated the importance of LMX and justice perceptions within organizations. To date, the LMX–justice relationship has been depicted in many different forms, ranging from LMX being antecedent to justice, to justice being antecedent to LMX, to various moderating and mediating relationships involving both LMX and justice. We have reviewed the extant literature examining the intersection between these two important constructs, and have proposed a model that integrates past research findings and attempts to identify a research agenda for moving the LMX–justice discussion forward. This model brings in different aspects of justice than have tended to be studied in conjunction with LMX, identifying event-based, entity-based, and anticipatory justice concepts as important with regard to LMX.

Future research must continue to refine our understanding of the relationship between LMX and justice through longitudinal, multisource data collection efforts that allow researchers to observe the interplay of these two variables and their relationship with other key variables influencing individual and organizational outcomes.

References

Adams, J. S. (1965). Inequity in social exchange. In L. Berkowitz (Ed.), *Advances in experimental social psychology* (Vol. 2, pp. 267–299). New York: Academic Press.

Anand, S., Hu, J., Liden, R. C., & Vidyarthi, P. R. (2011). Leader-member exchange: Recent research findings and prospects for the future. In A. Bryman, D. Collingson, K. Grint, B. Jackson, & M. Uhl-Bien (Eds.), *The Sage handbook of leadership* (pp. 311–325). Thousand Oaks, CA: Sage.

Ansari, M. A., Hung, D. K. M., & Aafaqi, R. (2007). Leader-member exchange and attitudinal outcomes: Role of procedural justice climate. *Leadership & Organization Development Journal, 28*, 690–709. doi: 10.1108/01437730710835443

Bell, B. S., Wiechmann, D., & Ryan, A. M. (2006). Consequences of organizational justice expectations in a selection system. *Journal of Applied Psychology, 91*(2), 455–466. doi: 10.1037/0021-9010.91.2.455

Bhal, K. T. (2006). LMX–citizenship behavior relationship: Justice as a mediator. *Leadership & Organization Development Journal, 26*, 106–117. doi: 10.1108/01437730610646615

Bhal, K. T., & Ansari, M. A. (2007). Leader-member exchange-subordinate outcomes relationship: Role of voice and justice. *Leadership & Organization Development Journal, 28*, 20–35. doi: 10.1108/01437730710718227

Bies, R. J., & Moag, J. S. (1986). Interactional justice: Communication criteria of fairness. *Research on Negotiation in Organizations, 1*, 43–55.

Blau, P. M. (1964). *Exchange and power in social life.* New York: John Wiley & Sons.

Brockner, J., Tyler, T. R., & Cooper-Schneider, R. (1992). The influence of prior commitment to an institution on reactions to perceived unfairness: The higher they are, the harder they fall. *Administrative Science Quarterly, 37*, 241–261.

Burton, J. P., Sablynski, C. J., & Sekiguchi, T. (2008). Linking justice, performance, and citizenship via leader-member exchange. *Journal of Business and Psychology, 23*, 51–61. doi: 10.1007/s10869-008-9075-z

Chia, H.-B., Foo, M.-D., & Fang, R. (2006). Workplaces as communities: The role of social networks in who seeks, gives, and accepts information on justice issues. *Journal of Community Psychology, 34*, 363–377. doi: 10.1002/jcop.20104

Cohen-Charash, Y., & Spector, P. E. (2001). The role of justice in organizations: A meta-analysis. *Organizational Behavior and Human Decision Processes, 86*, 278–321. doi: 10.1006/obhd.2001.2958

Colquitt, J. A. (2001). On the dimensionality of organizational justice: A construct validation of a measure. *Journal of Applied Psychology, 86*, 386–400. doi: 10.1037/0021-9010.86.3.386

Colquitt, J. A., Conlon, D. E., Wesson, M. J., Porter, C. O. L. H., & Ng, K. Y. (2001). Justice at the millennium: A meta-analytic review of 25 years of organizational justice research. *Journal of Applied Psychology, 86*, 425–445. doi: 10.1037/0021-9010.86.3.425

Colquitt, J. A., Scott, B. A., Rodell, J. B., Long, D. M., Zapata, C. P., Conlon, D. E., & Wesson, M. J. (2013). Justice at the millennium, a decade later: A meta-analytic test of social exchange and affect-based perspectives. *Journal of Applied Psychology, 98*, 199–236. doi: 10.1037/a0031757

Cropanzano, R., Byrne, Z. S., Bobocel, D. R., & Rupp, D. E. (2001). Moral virtues, fairness heuristics, social entities, and other denizens of organizational justice. *Journal of Vocational Behavior, 58*, 164–209. doi: 10.1006/jvbe.2001.1791

Cropanzano, R., & Mitchell, M. S. (2005). Social exchange theory: An interdisciplinary review. *Journal of Management, 31*, 874–900. doi: 10.1177/0149206305279602

Cropanzano, R., Prehar, C. A., & Chen, P. Y. (2002). Using social exchange theory to distinguish procedural from interactional justice. *Group & Organization Management, 27*, 324–351. doi: 10.1177/1059601102027003002

Degoey, P. (2000). Contagious justice: Exploring the social construction of justice in organizations. In B. M. Staw & R. I. Sutton (Eds.), *Research in organizational behavior* (Vol. 22, pp. 51–102). Greenwich, CT: JAI Press. doi: 10.1016/S0191-3085(00)22003-0

Deluga, R. J. (1994). Supervision trust building, leader-member exchange and organizational citizenship behaviour. *Journal of Occupational and Organizational Psychology, 67*, 315–326. doi: 10.1111/j.2044-8325.1994.tb00570.x

Deutsch, M. (1975). Equity, equality, and need: What determines which value will be used as the basis of distributive justice? *Journal of Social Issues, 31*, 137–149. doi: 10.1111/j.1540-4560.1975.tb01000.x

Dulebohn, J. H., Bommer, W. H., Liden, R. C., Brouer, R. L., & Ferris, G. R. (2012). A meta-analysis of antecedents and consequences of leader-member exchange: Integrating the past with an eye toward the future. *Journal of Management, 38*, 1715–1759. doi: 10.1177/0149206311415280

El Akremi, A., Vandenberghe, C., & Camerman, J. (2010). The role of justice and social exchange relationships in workplace deviance: Test of a mediated model. *Human Relations, 63*, 1687–1717. doi: 10.1177/0018726710364163

Erdogan, B., & Bauer, T. N. (2010). Differentiated leader-member exchanges: The buffering role of justice climate. *Journal of Applied Psychology, 95*, 1104–1120. doi: 10.1037/a0020578

Erdogan, B., & Bauer, T. N. (2013). Leader-member exchange (LMX) theory: The relational approach to leadership. *Oxford handbook of leadership and organizations*. Oxford University Press, Oxford.

Erdogan, B., & Liden, R. C. (2002). Social exchanges in the workplace: A review of recent developments and future research directions in leader-member exchange theory. In L. L. Neider & C. A. Schriesheim (Eds.), *Leadership* (pp. 65–114). Greenwich, CT: Information Age.

Erdogan, B., Liden, R. C., & Kraimer, M. L. (2006). Justice and leader-member exchange: The moderating role of organizational culture. *Academy of Management Journal, 49*, 395–406. doi: 10.5465/AMJ.2006.20786086

Folger, R., & Cropanzano, R. (1998). *Organizational justice and human resource management*. Thousand Oaks, CA: Sage.

Folger, R., & Konovsky, M. A. (1989). Effects of procedural and distributive justice on reactions to pay raise decisions. *Academy of Management Journal, 32*, 115–130. doi: 10.2307/256422

Gilliland, S. W. (1994). Effects of procedural and distributive justice on reactions to a selection system. *Journal of Applied Psychology, 79*, 691–701. doi: 10.1037/0021-9010.79.5.691

Greenberg, J. (1993). The social side of fairness: Interpersonal and informational classes of organizational justice. In R. Cropanzano (Ed.), *Justice in the workplace: Approaching fairness in human resource management* (pp. 79–103). Hillsdale, NJ: Erlbaum.

Henderson, D. J., Liden, R. C., Glibkowski, B. C., & Chaudhry, A. (2009). LMX differentiation: A multilevel review and examination of its antecedents and outcomes. *Leadership Quarterly, 20*, 517–534. doi: 10.1016/j.leaqua.2009.04.003

Henderson, D. J., Wayne, S. J., Bommer, W. H., Shore, L. M., & Tetrick, L. E. (2008). Leader-member exchange, differentiation, and psychological contract fulfillment: A multilevel examination. *Journal of Applied Psychology, 93*, 1208–1219. doi: 10.1037/a0012678

Hollensbe, E. C., Khazanchi, S., & Masterson, S. S. (2008). How do I assess if my supervisor and organization are fair? Identifying the rules underlying entity-based justice perceptions. *Academy of Management Journal, 51*, 1099–1116. doi: 10.5465/AMJ.2008.35732600

Hsiung, H.-H. (2012). Authentic leadership and employee voice behavior: A multi-level psychological process. *Journal of Business Ethics, 107*, 349–361. doi: 10.1007/s10551-011-1043-2

Johnson, J., Truxillo, D. M., Erdogan, B., Bauer, T. N., & Hammer, L. (2009). Perceptions of overall fairness: Are effects on job performance moderated by leader-member exchange? *Human Performance, 22*, 432–449. doi: 10.1080/08959280903248427

Jones, D. A., & Skarlicki, D. P. (2005). The effects of overhearing peers discuss an authority's fairness reputation on reactions to subsequent treatment. *Journal of Applied Psychology, 90*, 363–372. doi: 10.1037/0021-9010.90.2.363

Kim, W., Ok, C., & Lee, M. J. (2009). Antecedents of service employees' organizational citizenship behaviors in full-service restaurants in Korea. *Cornell Hospitality Quarterly, 50*, 180–197. doi: 10.1177/1938965509331922

Lavelle, J. J., Rupp, D. E., & Brockner, J. (2007). Taking a multifoci approach to the study of justice, social exchange, and citizenship behavior: The target similarity model. *Journal of Management, 33*, 841–866. doi: 10.1177/0149206307307635

Lee, J. (2001). Leader-member exchange, perceived organizational justice, and cooperative communication. *Management Communication Quarterly, 14*, 574–589. doi: 10.1177/0893318901144002

Lee, H.-R., Murrmann, S. K., Murrmann, K. F., & Kim, K. (2010). Organizational justice as a mediator of the relationships between leader-member exchange and employees' turnover intentions. *Journal of Hospitality Marketing & Management, 19*, 97–114. doi: 10.1080/19368620903455237

Leventhal, G. S. (1980). What should be done with equity theory? In K. J. Gergen, M. S. Greenberg, & R. H. Willis (Eds.), *Social exchange: Advances in theory and research* (pp. 27–55). New York: Plenum.

Liden, R. C., Sparrowe, R. T., & Wayne, S. J. (1997). Leader-member exchange theory: The past and potential for the future. In G. R. Ferris (Ed.), *Research in personnel and human resource management* (Vol 15, pp. 47–119). Greenwich, CT: JAI Press.

Lind, E. A. (2001). Fairness heuristic theory: Justice judgments as pivotal cognitions in organizational relations. In J. Greenberg & R. Cropanzano (Eds.), *Advances in organizational justice* (pp. 56–88). Stanford, CA: Stanford University Press.

Lind, E. A., & Tyler, T. R. (1988). *The social psychology of procedural justice*. New York: Plenum Press.

Lind, E. A., & van den Bos, K. (2002). When fairness works: Toward a general theory of uncertainty management. *Research in Organizational Behavior, 24*, 181–223.

Ma, L. & Qu, Q. (2010). Differentiation in leader–member exchange: A hierarchical linear modeling approach. *Leadership Quarterly, 21*, 733–744. doi: 10.1016/j.leaqua.2010.07.004

Manogran, P., Stauffer, J., & Conlon, E. J. (1994). Leader-member exchange as a key mediating variable between employees' perceptions of fairness and organizational citizenship behaviors. Paper presented at the national meeting of the Academy of Management, Dallas, TX.

Masterson, S. S., Lewis, K., Goldman, B. M., & Taylor, M. S. (2000). Integrating justice and social exchange: The differing effects of fair procedures and treatment on work relationships. *Academy of Management Journal, 43*, 738–748. doi: 10.2307/1556364

Masterson, S. S., & Tong, N. (in press). Justice perception formation in social settings. In R. Cropanzano & M. Ambrose (Eds.), *The Oxford handbook of justice in work organizations*. Oxford: Oxford University Press.

Moorman, R. H. (1991). Relationship between organizational justice and organizational citizenship behaviors: Do fairness perceptions influence employee citizenship? *Journal of Applied Psychology, 76*, 845–855. doi: 10.1037/0021-9010.76.6.845

Murphy, S. M., Wayne, S. J., Liden, R. C., & Erdogan, B. (2003). Understanding social loafing: The role of justice perceptions and exchange relationships. *Human Relations, 56*, 61–84. doi: 10.1177/0018726703056001450

Naumann, S. E., & Bennett, N. (2000). A case for procedural justice climate: Development and test of a multilevel model. *Academy of Management Journal, 43*, 881–889. doi: 10.2307/1556416

Niehoff, B. P., & Moorman, R. H. (1993). Justice as a mediator of the relationship between methods of monitoring and organizational citizenship behavior. *Academy of Management Journal, 36*, 527–556. doi: 10.2307/256591

Oren, L., Tziner, A., Sharoni, G., Amor, I., & Alon, P. (2012). Relations between leader-subordinate personality similarity and job attitudes. *Journal of Managerial Psychology, 27*, 479–496. doi: 10.1108/02683941211235391

Othman, R., Ee, F. F., & Shi, N. L. (2010). Understanding dysfunctional leader-member exchange: Antecedents and outcomes. *Leadership & Organization Development Journal, 31*, 337–350. doi: 10.1108/01437731011043357

Piccolo, R. F., Bardes, M., Mayer, D. M., & Judge, T. A. (2008). Does high quality leader-member exchange accentuate the effects of organizational justice? *European Journal of Work and Organizational Psychology, 17*, 273–298. doi: 10.1080/1359432070174517

Pillai, R., Scandura, T. A., & Williams, E. A. (1999). Leadership and organizational justice: Similarities and differences across cultures. *Journal of International Business Studies, 30*, 763–779.

Roch, S. G., & Shanock, L. R. (2006). Organizational justice in an exchange framework: Clarifying organizational justice distinctions. *Journal of Management, 32*, 299–322. doi: 10.1177/0149206305280115

Rockstuhl, T., Dulebohn, J. H., Ang, S., & Shore, L. M. (2012). Leader-member exchange (LMX) and culture: A Meta-analysis of correlates of LMX across 23 Countries. *Journal of Applied Psychology, 97*, 1097–1130. doi: 10.1037/a0029978

Rodell, J. B., & Colquitt, J. A. (2009). Looking ahead in times of uncertainty: The role of anticipatory justice in an organizational change context. *Journal of Applied Psychology, 94*, 989–1002. doi: 10.1037/a0015351

Rosen, C. C., Harris, K. J., & Kacmar, K. M. (2011). LMX, context perceptions, and performance: An uncertainty management perspective. *Journal of Management, 37*, 819–838. doi: 10.1177/0149206310365727

Rupp, D. E., & Cropanzano, R. (2002). The mediating effects of social exchange relationships in predicting workplace outcomes from multifoci organizational justice. *Organizational Behavior and Human Decision Processes, 89*, 925–946. doi: 10.1016/S0749-5978(02)00036-5

Scandura, T. A. (1999). Rethinking leader-member exchange: An organizational justice perspective. *Leadership Quarterly, 10*, 25–40. doi: 10.1016/S1048-9843(99)800007-1

Scott, B. A., Colquitt, J. A., & Paddock, E. L. (2009). An actor-focused model of justice rule adherence and violation: The role of managerial motives and discretion. *Journal of Applied Psychology, 94*, 756–769. doi: 10.1037/a0015712

Settoon, R. P., Bennett, N., & Liden, R. C. (1996). Social exchange in organizations: The differential effects of perceived organizational support and leader member exchange. *Journal of Applied Psychology, 81*, 219–227. doi: 10/1037/0021-9010.81.3.219

Shao, R., Rupp, D. E., Skarlicki, D. P., and Jones, K. S. (2013). Employee justice across cultures: A meta-analytic review. *Journal of Management, 39*, 263–301. doi: 10.1177/0149206311422447

Shapiro, D. L., & Kirkman, B. L. (2001). Anticipatory injustice: The consequences of expecting injustice in the workplace. In J. S. Greenberg & R. Cropanzano (Eds.), *Advances in organizational justice* (pp. 152–178). Stanford: Stanford University Press.

Shore, L. M., & Shore, T. H. (1995). Perceived organizational support and organizational justice. In R. Cropanzano & K. M. Kacmar (Eds.) Organizational politics, justice, and support: Managing the social climate of the workplace (pp. 149–164). Westport, CT: Quorum Books.

Skarlicki, D. P., Ellard, J. H., & Kelln, B. R. (1998). Third-party perceptions of a layoff: Procedural, derogation, and retributive aspects of justice. *Journal of Applied Psychology, 83*, 119–127. doi: 10.1037/0021-9010.83.1.119

Sparr, J. L., & Sonnentag, S. (2008). Fairness perceptions of supervisor feedback, LMX, and employee well-being at work. *European Journal of Work and Organizational Psychology, 17*, 198–225. doi: 10.1080/13594320701743590

Srikanth, P. B., & Gurunathan, L. (2013). Interactional justice and job mobility preparedness: Mediating role of leader-member exchange (LMX). *IUP Journal of Organizational Behavior 12*, 7–32.

Sun, L.-Y., Chow, I. H. S., Chiu, R. K., & Pan, W. (2013). Outcome favorability in the link between leader–member exchange and organizational citizenship behavior: Procedural fairness climate matters. *Leadership Quarterly, 24*, 215–226. doi: 10.1016/j.leaqua.2012.10.008

Taylor, M. S., Tracy, K. B., Renard, M. K., Harrison, J. K., & Carroll, S. J. (1995). Due process in performance appraisal: A quasi-experiment in procedural justice. *Administrative Science Quarterly, 95*, 495–523.

Torka, N., Schyns, B., & Looise, J. K. (2010). Direct participation quality and organisational commitment: The role of leader-member exchange. *Employee Relations, 32*, 418–434. doi: 10.1108/01425451011051622

Umphress, E. E., Labianca, G., Brass, D. J., Kass, E., & Scholten, L. (2003). The role of instrumental and expressive social ties in employees' perceptions of organizational justice. *Organization Science, 14*, 738–753. doi: 10.1287/orsc.14.6.738.24865

van den Bos, K., Wilke, H. A. M., & Lind, E. A. (1998). When do we need procedural fairness? The role of trust in authority. *Journal of Personality and Social Psychology, 75*, 1449–1458. doi: 10.1037/0022-3514.75.6.1449

Walumbwa, F. O., Cropanzano, R., & Hartnell, C. A. (2009). Organizational justice, voluntary learning behavior, and job performance: A test of the mediating effects of identification and leader-member exchange. *Journal of Organizational Behavior, 30*, 1103–1126. doi: 10.1002/job.611

Wang, X., Liao, J., Xia, D., & Chang, T. (2010). The impact of organizational justice on work performance: Mediating effects of organizational commitment and leader-member exchange. *International Journal of Manpower, 31*, 660–677. doi: 10.1108/01437721011073364

Wayne, S. J., Shore, L. M., Bommer, W. T., & Tetrick, L. E. (2002). The role of fair treatment and rewards in perceptions of organizational support and leader-member exchange. *Journal of Applied Psychology, 87*, 590–598. 10.1037//0021-9010.873.3.590

Werbel, J. D., & Henriques, P. L. (2009). Different views of trust and relational leadership: Supervisor and subordinate perspectives. *Journal of Managerial Psychology, 24,* 780–796. doi: 10.1108/02683940910996798

Whitman, D. S., Caleo, S., Carpenter, N. C., Horner, M. T., & Bernerth, J. B. (2012). Fairness at the collective level: A meta-analytic examination of the consequences and boundary conditions of organizational justice climate. *Journal of Applied Psychology, 97,* 776–791. doi: 10.1037/a0028021

Yagil, D. (2006). Perceptions of justice within leader-employee dyads. *International Journal of Organization Theory and Behavior, 9,* 291–306.

PART 2

Antecedents of LMX

How and Why High Leader–Member Exchange (LMX) Relationships Develop: Examining the Antecedents of LMX

Jennifer D. Nahrgang *and* Jungmin Jamie Seo

Abstract

In this chapter, the authors summarize the literature with regard to the development of LMX to answer the question "How and why do high LMX relationships develop?" They view LMX antecedents and their relationship with LMX development through the lens of role theory and assert that various antecedents are likely to influence different stages of the relationship as it proceeds through the role making process. Empirical evidence finds that LMX relationships develop quickly based on initial interactions between leaders and members and stabilize into either high-quality or low-quality relationships. Early in the relationship, similarity between leaders and members enhances the quality of the relationship as do components of the relationship such as expectations, liking, and trust. Over time, both members and leaders contribute positively to the relationship through their leadership behaviors, performance, effort, and delegation. Finally, various contextual variables also influence the development of the relationship.

Key Words: leader–member exchange, role theory, role making process, antecedents, LMX development, longitudinal

Introduction

From its inception as a theory, leader–member exchange (LMX) has staked its claim that unique relationships or exchanges exist between a leader and each of the leader's subordinates. Both theory and empirical data support the existence of high LMX relationships (in-groups) and low LMX relationships (out-groups) and the influence the relationships have on employee attitudes and performance (Dulebohn, Bommer, Liden, Brouer, & Ferris, 2012; Gerstner & Day, 1997; Ilies, Nahrgang, & Morgeson, 2007; Liden, Sparrowe, & Wayne, 1997). Much less research has examined the predictors of these starkly different types of relationships and the development of the relationship over time. Over 35 years ago, researchers noted "it is not clear what behaviors on the part of subordinates and on

the part of leaders result in the subordinates becoming members of each of these [exchange] groups" (House & Baertz, 1979, p. 410). Although models exist that theorize how or why the LMX relationship develops (i.e., Dienesch & Liden, 1986; Graen & Scandura, 1987), the empirical evidence for LMX development continues to be a critical area of investigation and one that promises to be a fruitful ground for future research.

The purpose of this chapter is to summarize the literature with regards to the development of LMX to answer the question "How and why do high LMX relationships develop?" This includes providing an understanding of the characteristics of the relationship over time and the antecedents to its development. Previous summaries of LMX development have primarily focused on member and leader characteristics, the interaction of those characteristics, as well as contextual characteristics (Liden et al., 1997). A recent meta-analysis of the LMX literature summarized similar antecedents (i.e., follower characteristics, leader behaviors and perceptions, and interpersonal relationship variables) and found that leader variables explained the most variance in LMX quality (Dulebohn et al., 2012). In this chapter, we view LMX antecedents and their relationship with LMX development through the lens of role theory (Kahn, Wolfe, Quinn, Snoek, & Rosenthal, 1964) and assert that various antecedents are likely to influence different stages of the relationship as it proceeds through the role development process (Dienesch & Liden, 1986; Graen & Scandura, 1987; Nahrgang, Morgeson, & Ilies, 2009). As with many chapters, our review includes boundary conditions. First, our review focuses on research in which the variables of interest were predicted in the study to be antecedents to LMX, rather than utilized as control variables. Second, although we recognize the importance of the Vertical Dyad Linkage (VDL) model of leadership (Dansereau, Graen & Haga, 1975; Graen & Cashman, 1975) in establishing LMX theory, our review focuses on studies which utilized LMX as their theoretical basis.

Development of LMX Over Time

When it comes to understanding how and why LMX relationships develop over time, a key foundational theory is that of role theory (Kahn et al., 1964). Role theory posits that members of an organization accomplish their work though roles, which are defined as a set of activities or behaviors. Role behaviors develop through a series of role episodes in which a member of the organization (i.e., role sender) who holds a set of role expectations, sends those expectations to another member of the organization (i.e., role receiver). The role receiver then responds to those expectations either though performance of role behaviors or through negotiating a different set of role expectations (see Figure 6.1). The theory suggests that personal characteristics influence role episodes by eliciting different role expectations and reactions to sent roles. Furthermore, the theory expects that aspects of interpersonal relationships such as power, affective bonds, dependence, and communication styles also influence role episodes (Kahn et al., 1964).

Researchers in LMX have used role theory to hypothesize about the development of LMX relationships through the role making process (Dienesch & Liden, 1986; Graen & Cashman, 1975; Graen & Scandura, 1987). Early work utilized role theory to propose that role making was a set of processes by which a dyad works through how each will behave in certain situations and agree upon the nature of their relationship (Graen, 1976; Graen & Cashman, 1975). Building from this, later theoretical work proposed that the relationship between a leader and a member develops through a sequence of three phases: role taking, role making, and role routinization (Graen & Scandura, 1987).

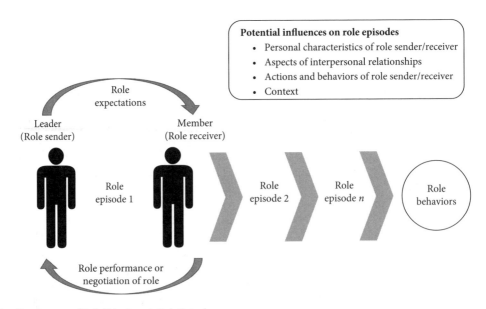

Fig. 6.1 Development of Role Behaviors via Role Episodes.

The first phase of role taking is a trial phase where the leader attempts to discover the relevant talents, motivations and limits of the member through a series of sent roles to the member and received responses by the member. This early phase is considered to be critical to the development of the relationship as the leader evaluates the member's performance and decides whether or not to initiate another sent role (Dansereau et al., 1975; Graen & Scandura, 1987). Furthermore, the phase includes the initial interaction between leader and member in which each member of the dyad brings unique characteristics, abilities, and attitudes to the interaction. This initial interaction is influenced by the socialization process as well as the characteristics of leaders and members, and is theorized to be an important determinant of the future state of the relationship (Dienesch & Liden, 1986; Dockery & Steiner, 1990; Graen & Cashman, 1975). The role taking phase is theorized to take a short amount of time, ranging from a few hours to a few months (Graen & Scandura, 1987).

Once the role taking phase is complete, the role making phase begins. In the role making phase, the leader and member begin to define the nature of their relationship and how each will behave in various situations (Graen & Cashman, 1975). One key difference from that of role theory (Kahn et al., 1964) is that in the role making phase, both leader and member can initiate a role episode. Within this phase various exchanges occur such as the exchange of information, support, latitude, and resources (Graen & Scandura, 1987). Over time, the exchanges in the role making phase develop into interlocking behaviors, which characterizes the last phase of role routinization. In the role routinization phase, the relationship is theorized to stabilize as leaders and members come to mutual expectations of behaviors. The dyadic relationship that develops from the interlocking of behaviors is characterized by relational dimensions such as trust, respect, loyalty, and liking (Graen & Scandura, 1987).

LMX theory posits that leaders will form unique dyadic relationships with each follower over time through the role making process. Although there have been a variety of studies examining antecedents to the relationship at particular stages in the role making process, very few empirical tests have examined the development of the relationship from the initial interaction through the role routinization phase. Empirical tests of LMX development are, however, generally supportive of the role-making theory of LMX development.

The role-making model of LMX development theorizes that LMX relationships develop quickly and then stabilize (Dienesch & Liden, 1986; Graen & Scandura, 1987). Longitudinal research examining LMX quality from the initial interaction to later stages of development have found that the quality of the relationship from both the leader's and follower's perspective, generally increases over time (Liden, Wayne, & Stilwell, 1993; Nahrgang et al., 2009). Furthermore, longitudinal research supports the idea that the relationship stabilizes rather quickly as assessments of LMX quality taken early in the relationship are strong predictors of LMX quality in later stages of the relationship. In particular, perceptions of LMX quality as early as 2 weeks into the relationship were significant predictors of the relationship at 6 weeks and, in turn, predictors of the relationship at 6 months (Liden et al., 1993). Bauer and Green (1996) also found that the quality of LMX 2 months into the relationship strongly predicted the quality of the relationship almost 6 months later. The most recent study of LMX development over time also supported the stabilization of LMX by finding that the relationship quality at the initial interaction predicted the quality of the relationship 8 weeks later and that both leader and member LMX followed a positive non-linear trajectory in which the relationship increased over time and then stabilized (Nahrgang et al., 2009).

Beyond understanding the nature of the LMX relationship, empirical research has supported basic tenets of the role making model of LMX development by finding that various antecedents predict LMX quality depending on the stage of the relationship (Graen & Scandura, 1987). Results have supported that LMX quality in the role taking phase is related to leader and member expectations, characteristics of leaders and followers, and similarity between leader and member. These longitudinal studies have also supported the fact that leader and member behaviors during the role episodes predict the quality of the relationship in later phases of the relationship (Bauer & Green, 1996; Liden et al., 1993; Nahrgang et al., 2009).

Antecedents to LMX

Based on the theorizing of the role making model and empirical evidence presented above, we proceed with our chapter by examining four categories of antecedents to the LMX relationship. As trust is one of the key components that distinguishes high and low LMX relationships, we utilize similar categories to those included in reviews of trust (Dirks & Ferrin,

2002). Specifically, we categorize antecedents into leader and member attributes, attributes of the relationship, leader and member actions and behaviors, and contextual characteristics. Tables 6.1 through 6.6 provide summaries of the studies included in each of these categories.

Leader and Member Attributes

Role theory suggests that personal characteristics are likely to influence role episodes due to the expectations that individuals form from these characteristics when initially interacting with their dyadic partner (Kahn et al., 1964). With that foundation, LMX researchers have examined a variety of personal characteristics as antecedents to LMX development. A key focus of the personal characteristics has been on the relationship between personality and LMX quality. Research has found that both leader and member personality characteristics such as extraversion and agreeableness (e.g., Nahrgang et al., 2009; Phillips & Bedeian, 1994), locus of control (e.g., Kinicki & Vecchio, 1994; Phillips & Bedeian, 1994), and positive and negative affectivity (Day & Crain, 1992; Engle & Lord, 1997) all relate to LMX quality. Due to the fact that the relationship between personality and LMX is reviewed more thoroughly in another chapter (see Chapter X), we chose to focus on other attributes of leaders and members, and in particular, similarity between leader and member attributes, which have been found to relate to the LMX relationship. See Tables 6.1 and 6.2 for a summary of studies investigating the relationship between leader and member attributes and similarity in attributes and LMX quality.

Competence and Ability. The role making process is predicated on the performance of role behaviors by the member and leader. Thus, one likely antecedent to LMX quality is the ability of the leader and member and principally at the initial interaction when neither leader nor member has performed role behaviors. Research has examined the relationship between ability or competence and the LMX relationship at the initial interaction. Dockery and Steiner (1990) found that one of the strongest predictors of leader LMX at the initial interaction was a member's ability. Although a member's perception of their own ability also positively related to member LMX, it was not significant when included with other predictors such as liking and upward influence tactics (Dockery & Steiner, 1990). Day and Crain (1992) supported this finding with results that found a significant relationship

between member's ability and leader's LMX quality at the initial interaction. The relationship between ability and competence and LMX quality likely extends beyond the initial interaction as well and in a field sample of sales managers, DelVecchio (1998) found that a leader's perception of a member's competence in skill and knowledge positively related to member LMX. In summarizing follower characteristics, meta-analytic evidence found a moderately positive relationship between follower competence and LMX quality ($\rho = .38$; Dulebohn et al., 2012).

Implicit Leadership Theory Characteristics. Implicit leadership theory (e.g., Lord, 1985) suggests that individuals hold cognitive schemas with regards to the characteristics of prototypical leaders. Work by Engle and Lord (1997) originally assessed the congruence between leader and member's implicit leadership theories and the role in the development of LMX, but did not find support for the relationship. More recent work by Epitropaki and Martin (2005) took a slightly different view of implicit leadership theory's role in the LMX relationship by asking employees to rate the extent to which their leader displayed prototypical and anti-prototypical leader characteristics. Results found that prototypical characteristics positively related to LMX quality, whereas antiprototypical characteristics negatively related to LMX quality. Furthermore, the extent to which their leader displayed characteristics that were congruent with their idea of a business leader also positively related to LMX quality (Epitropaki & Martin, 2005).

Similarity in Leader and Member Attributes

Although LMX research has investigated the extent to which attributes of the leader and member influence the LMX relationship, a substantial amount of research has examined similarity in attributes between the dyad partners and how similarity develops the relationship. Early work on LMX theory suggested that the degree of compatibility between leader and member would contribute to the type of relationship that forms between leaders and members (Dienesch & Liden, 1986; Graen & Cashman, 1975).

Demographic Similarity. A number of studies have examined the extent to which demographic characteristics such as age, gender, and education relate to the LMX relationship (e.g., Duchon, Green, & Taber, 1986; Green, Anderson, & Shivers, 1996; Maslyn & Uhl-Bien, 2001; Pelled & Xin, 2000; Phillips & Bedeian, 1994; Vecchio & Brazil, 2007) and found mixed results.

Table 6.1. Leader and Member Attributes (in chronological order).

Variable	Study	Direction and magnitude of relationship (* $p < .05$, ** $p < .01$)	Measurement of LMX (measure used)	Measurement of Attribute (measured used)	Study Sample & Context	Stage of Relationship (Relationship Tenure)
Competence & Ability	Dockery & Steiner, 1990	Member self-perceptions of ability – Member LMX $r = .24*$ Leader perceptions of member's ability–Leader LMX $r = .85*$	Member and leader LMX (Graen & Scandura, 1987)	Member ability (new)	188 undergraduate students participating in 47 groups in laboratory experiment	Role taking (initial interaction)
	Day & Crain, 1992	Member ability – Member LMX $r = -.10$ Member ability – Leader LMX B = $.10**$ Leader ability – Member LMX B = $-.09$ Leader ability – Leader LMX $r = -.15$	Member and leader LMX (Scandura & Graen, 1984)	Member and leader ability (attempts on Wonderlic Personnel Test; (Wonderlic & Associates, 1983))	75 members and 21 leaders 96 undergraduate students participating in groups in laboratory experiment	Role taking (initial interaction)
	DelVecchio, 1998	Member competence skill Member LMX $r = .19**$ Member competence knowledge Member LMX $r = .23**$	Member LMX (six sets of adjective pairs)	Leader perception of member competence in skill and knowledge (new)	155 employees and direct supervisors Business-to-business field sales people employed by manufacturing firms	Unknown stage
Implicit Leadership Theory Characteristics	Epitropaki & Martin, 2005	Prototypical leader characteristics – Member LMX $r = .70**$ Antiprototypical leader characteristics – Member LMX $r = -.29**$	Member LMX (Graen & Uhl-Bien, 1995)	Leader ILT (Epitropaki & Martin, 2004)	439 employees Six manufacturing and one services companies in the United Kingdom	Unknown stage

Table 6.2. Similarity in Leader and Member Attributes (in chronological order)

Variable	Study	Direction and magnitude of relationship (* $p < .05$, ** $p < .01$)	Measurement of LMX (measure used)	Study Sample & Context	Measurement of Attribute Similarity (measured used)	Stage of Relationship (Relationship Tenure)
Demographic	Liden, Wayne & Stilwell, 1993	Demographic similarity – Member LMX $r = 0.05, 0.08, -0.02$ Demographic similarity – Leader LMX $r = 0.16, 0.09, 0.16$	Member and leader LMX measured at 2 weeks, 6 weeks, 6 months (Scandura & Graen, 1984)	166 dyads of employees and direct supervisors Newly formed dyads Range of job types including secretary, electrician, librarian, admissions counselor, research scientist, and computer programmer	Similarity on gender, race, educational level, and age (Turban & Jones, 1988)	Role taking, Role Making, Role Routinization (initial interaction – 6 months)
	Green, Anderson & Shivers, 1996	Age similarity – Member LMX $r = 0.08$ Education similarity – Member LMX $r = -0.01$ Gender similarity – Member LMX $r = 0.20*$	Member LMX (Graen, Novak, & Sommerkamp, 1982)	208 employees from 31 public libraries	Similarity on age, education, gender (Tsui & O'Reilly, 1989; Wagner, Pfeffer, & O'Reilly, 1984)	Role Routinization (Average 3.2 years dyadic tenure)
	Bauer & Green, 1996	Gender similarity – Member LMX at time 1 $r = 0.07$ Gender similarity – Member LMX at time 2 $r = 0.00$	Member LMX measured at 14 and 34 weeks (Scandura & Graen, 1984; Liden et al., 1993)	311 employees and 165 direct supervisors Employees were recent college graduates working in new jobs Variety of college majors and industries	Similarity in gender (Liden et al., 1993; Turban & Jones, 1988)	Role taking/Role Making (12 and 34 weeks after job entry)
	Pelled & Xin, 2000	Study 1: Age similarity – Member LMX $r = .06$ Gender similarity – Member LMX $r = .24*$ Race similarity – Member LMX $r = 0.19$ Study 2: Age similarity – Member LMX $r = -0.05$ Gender similarity – Member LMX $r = 0.09$	Member LMX (Graen et al., 1982)	Study 1: 90 employees working in electronic production facility in US Study 2: 195 employees working in electronic production facility in Mexico	Similarity in age, gender, and race (Wayne & Liden, 1995; Green et al., 1996; Turban & Jones, 1988)	Study 1 and Study 2: Unknown stage

	Vecchio & Brazil, 2007	Significant leader gender x subordinate gender interaction F = 6.59**	Member LMX (Graen & Uhl-Bien, 1995; Scandura & Graen, 1984)	Similarity in Gender	1702 military cadets from 167 squads. Cadets in military field training	Role taking/Role Making (initial interaction – 4 weeks)
	Zhang, Wang & Shi, 2012	Age similarity –Member LMX r = – 0.08 Gender similarity – Member LMX r = – 0.04 Education similarity – Member LMX r = 0.00	Member LMX (Bauer & Green, 1996)	Similarity in age, gender, education (Bauer & Green, 1996)	165 employees and direct supervisors Credit card service branches in Chinese banking industry	Role making/Role routinization (average 1 year dyadic tenure)
Perceived similarity	Liden, Wayne & Stilwell, 1993	Member perceived similarity – Member LMX r = 0.70,* 0.56,* 0.35 Member perceived similarity – Leader LMX r = 0.23,* 0.21,* 0.24* Leader perceived similarity – Leader LMX r = 0.58,* 0.48,* 0.49* Leader perceived similarity – Member LMX r = 0.21,* 0.21,* - 0.03	Member and leader LMX measured at 2 weeks, 6 weeks, 6 months (Scandura & Graen, 1984)	Member and leader perceived similarity (Turban & Jones, 1988)	166 dyads of employees and direct supervisors Newly formed dyads Range of job types including secretary, electrician, librarian, admissions counselor, research scientist, and computer programmer	Role taking, Role Making, Role Routinization (initial interaction – 6 months)
	Phillips & Bedian, 1994	Leader perceived similarity – Member LMX r = 0.26*	Member LMX (Graen et al, 1982)	Leader perceived attitudinal similarity (new)	84 employees and 12 direct supervisors Registered nurses working in 12 work groups in large hospital	Role routinization (Average 1.9 years dyadic tenure)
	Engle & Lord, 1997	Member perceived similarity – Member LMX r = 0.64** Member perceived similarity – Leader LMX r = 0.24* Leader perceived similarity – Member LMX r = 0.28* Leader perceived similarity – Leader LMX r = 0.75**	Member and leader LMX (Scandura & Schriesheim, 1994)	Member and leader perceived similarity (Liden et al., 1993 and new items)	76 employees and 18 direct supervisors Marketing division of electric company	Role routinization (Average 2.3 years dyadic tenure)

(continued)

Table 6.2. Continued

Variable	Study	Direction and magnitude of relationship (* $p < .05$, ** $p < .01$)	Measurement of LMX (measure used)	Measurement of Attribute Similarity (measured used)	Study Sample & Context	Stage of Relationship (Relationship Tenure)
Personality similarity	Bauer & Green, 1996	Positive affectivity similarity – Member LMX at time 1 $r = 0.28$** Positive affectivity similarity – Member LMX at time 2 $r = 0.23$*	Member LMX measured at 14 and 34 weeks (Scandura & Graen, 1984; Liden et al., 1993)	Similarity in Positive affectivity (Watson et al., 1988)	311 employees and 165 direct supervisors Employees were recent college graduates working in new jobs Variety of college majors and industries	Role taking/Role Making (12 and 34 weeks after job entry)
	Zhang, Wang & Shi, 2012	Polynomial terms significant F = 9.4**	Member LMX (Bauer & Green, 1996)	Congruence in proactive personality (Seibert, Crant, & Kraimer, 1999)	165 employees and direct supervisors Credit card service branches in Chinese banking industry	Role making/Role routinization (average 1 year dyadic tenure)

Table 6.3. Attributes of Relationship (in chronological order)

Variable	Study	Direction and magnitude of relationship (* $p < .05$, ** $p < .01$)	Measurement of LMX (measure used)	Measurement of Relationship Attribute (measured used)	Study Sample & Context	Stage of Relationship (Relationship Tenure)
Expectations	Liden, Wayne & Stilwell, 1993	Member expectations of leader – Member LMX $r = 0.51,$* $0.55,$* 0.45* Leader expectations of member – Member LMX $r = 0.13, 0.21, 0.22$ Member expectations of leader – Leader LMX $r = 0.14, 0.09, 0.13$ Leader expectations of member – Leader LMX $r = 0.37,$* $0.52,$* 0.24	Member and leader LMX measured at 2 weeks, 6 weeks, 6 months (Scandura & Graen, 1984)	Expectations of member and leader measured at 0–5 days (new)	82 dyads of employees and direct supervisors Newly formed dyads Range of job types including secretary, electrician, librarian, admissions counselor, research scientist, and computer programmer	Role taking, Role Making, Role Routinization (initial interaction – 6 months)
	Wayne, Shore, & Liden, 1997	Leader expectations of member – Member LMX $r = 0.22,$** 0.25**	Member LMX (Scandura & Graen, 1984)	Expectations of member's pay grade (new)	252 dyads of employees and direct supervisors Random sample of salaried employees in large corporation	Role routinization (Average 3 years dyadic tenure)
Liking	Dockery & Steiner, 1990	Member liking of leader – Member LMX $r = 0.52$** Leader liking of member – Leader LMX $r = 0.66$**	Member and leader LMX (Graen & Scandura, 1987)	Member and leader liking (new)	188 undergraduate students participating in 47 groups in laboratory experiment	Role taking (initial interaction)
	Wayne & Ferris, 1990	Study 1: Leader liking of member – Leader LMX $r = 0.65$** Study 2: Leader liking of member – Leader LMX $r = 0.73$**	Study 1 and 2: Leader LMX (Scandura et al., 1986)	Study 1 and 2: Leader liking (new)	Study 1: 96 undergraduate students participating in laboratory experiment Study 2: 84 employees and 23 direct supervisors Various departments in banks (teller, book keeping, credit, etc.)	Study 1: Role taking (initial interaction) Study 2: Unknown stage

(continued)

Table 6.3. Continued

Variable	Study	Direction and magnitude of relationship (* $p < .05$, ** $p < .01$)	Measurement of LMX (measure used)	Measurement of Relationship Attribute (measured used)	Study Sample & Context	Stage of Relationship (Relationship Tenure)
	Liden, Wayne & Stilwell, 1993	Member liking of leader – Member LMX $r = 0.70,$* $0.59,$* 0.50* Leader liking of member – Member LMX $r = 0.31,$* $0.38,$* 0.16 Member liking of leader – Leader LMX $r = 0.17,$* 0.08, 0.20* Leader liking of member – Leader LMX $r = 0.41,$* $0.41,$* 0.41*	Member and leader LMX measured at 2 weeks, 6 weeks, 6 months (Scandura & Graen, 1984)	Member and leader liking measured at 2 weeks (Wayne & Ferris, 1990)	166 dyads of employees and direct supervisors Newly formed dyads Range of job types including secretary, electrician, librarian, admissions counselor, research scientist, and computer programmer	Role taking, Role Making, Role Routinization (initial interaction – 6 months)
	Engle & Lord, 1997	Member liking – Member LMX $r = 0.79$** Member liking – Leader LMX $r = 0.42$** Leader liking – Member LMX $r = 0.35$** Leader liking – Leader LMX $r = 0.88$**	Member and leader LMX (Scandura & Schriesheim, 1994)	Member and leader liking (Turban, Jones, & Rozelle, 1990; Wayne & Ferris 1990)	76 employees and 18 direct supervisors Marketing division of electric company	Role routinization (Average 2.3 years dyadic tenure)
	Wayne, Shore, & Liden, 1997	Liking of member by leader – Member LMX $r = 0.40$**	Member LMX (Scandura & Graen, 1984)	Liking (Wayne & Ferris, 1990)	252 dyads of employees and direct supervisors Random sample of salaried employees in large corporation	Role routinization (Average 3 years dyadic tenure)
Trust	Gomez & Rosen, 2001	Leader trust in member – Member LMX $r = 0.47$**	Member LMX (Kozlowski & Doherty, 1989)	Leader trust in member (Butler, 1990; Mishra, 1993)	128 dyads of employees and managers in 13 different organizations in diverse industries Half of managers focused on low-quality LMX while other half focused on high-quality LMX	Role making/Role routinization (67% working together 1–5 years)

Study	Findings	LMX measure	Trust measure	Sample	Outcome
Deluga, 1994	Trust building behavior (fairness) of leader – Member LMX r = 0.12	Member and leader LMX (Kozlowski & Doherty, 1989)	Member trust in the leader (Butler, 1991)	86 dyads of employees and direct supervisors Employees recruited from continuing education classes Diverse set of industries	Role routinization (Average 3.9 years dyadic tenure)
Scandura & Pellegrini, 2008	Member calculus-based trust – Member LMX r = 0.17* Member identification-based trust – Member LMX r = 0.29**	Member LMX (Scandura & Green, 1984)	Member trust in leader (Lewicki, Bunker & Stevenson (1997)	228 full time employees enrolled in Executive MBA Service, manufacturing, healthcare, and education industries	Role making/Role routinization (Average 1.5 year dyadic tenure)
Sue-Chan, Au, & Hackett 2012	Member trust in leader – Member LMX at Time 1 r = 0.69** Member trust in leader – Member LMX at Time 2 r = 0.64** Member trust in leader at Time 1 – Member LMX at Time 2 r = 0.39** Leader trust in member – Leader LMX at Time 1 r = 0.35*	Member LMX measured time 1 and time 2 and leader LMX measured time 1 (Graen & Uhl-Bien, 1995)	Member trust measured time 1 and time 2 and leader trust measured time 1 (Gabarro, 1978; Robinson, 1996)	158 employees and 53 supervisors Manufacturing facility in Malaysia	Role routinization (Average 2.7 years dyadic tenure)

Table 6.4. Leader Actions and Behaviors (in chronological order)

Variable	Study	Measurement of Leader Action/Behavior (measured used)	Measurement of LMX (measure used)	Direction and magnitude of relationship ($* p < .05$, $** p < .01$)	Study Sample & Context	Stage of Relationship (Relationship Tenure)
Initial Actions and Behaviors	Maslyn & Uhl-Bien, 2001	Member and leader effort (new)	Member and leader LMX (Graen & Uhl-Bien, 1995; Liden & Maslyn, 1998)	Member reported manager effort – Member LMX $r = 0.67**$, $0.55**$ Member reported manager effort – Leader LMX $r = 0.39**$	232 dyads of employees and direct supervisors Large, international service organization	Role making (Average .8 years dyadic tenure)
	Sluss & Thompson, 2012	Leader socialization tactics (Jones, 1986)	Member LMX (Schriesheim et al., 1992)	Socialization tactics – Member LMX $r = 0.49**$	213 employees New employees to 12 telemarking organizations	Role taking (new employees)
Delegation/ Latitude	Bauer & Green, 1996	Member perception of delegation (Yukl, 1990)	Member LMX measured at 14 and 34 weeks (Scandura & Graen, 1984; Liden et al., 1993)	Delegation – Member LMX at Time 1 $r = 0.36**$ Delegation –Member LMX at Time 2 $r = 0.38**$ Delegation at Time 1 – Member LMX at Time 2 $r = 0.18*$	311 employees and 165 direct supervisors Employees were recent college graduates working in new jobs Variety of college majors and industries	Role taking/Role Making (12 and 34 weeks after job entry)
	DelVecchio, 1998	Latitude given by leader to member (Liden & Graen, 1980)	Member LMX (six sets of adjective pairs)	Latitude – Member LMX $r = 0.65**$	155 employees and direct supervisors Business-to-business field sales people employed by manufacturing firms	Unknown stage
Leadership Behaviors	Kent & Chelladurai, 2001	Member ratings of transformational leadership of manager (Bass, 1985)	Member LMX (Graen et al., 1982)	Charismatic leadership – Member LMX $r = 0.24*$ Individualized consideration – Member LMX $r = 0.38**$ Intellectual stimulation – Member LMX $r = 0.19$	75 employees University athletic department	Unknown stage

Study	Relationship	LMX Measure	Leadership Measure	Sample	Stage
Wang, Law, Hackett, Wang & Chen, 2005	Transformational leadership – Member LMX r = 0.71**	Member LMX (Liden & Maslyn, 1998)	Transformational leadership (Chen & Farh, 1999)	162 employees and direct supervisors; Multiple organizations in China	Role routinization (Average 4 years dyadic tenure)
Barbuto, Wilmot, & Story, 2011	Member ratings of transformational leadership – Member LMX r = 0.41**; Leader ratings of transformational leadership – Member LMX r = 0.14*	Member LMX (Scandura & Graen, 1984)	Leader and member ratings of transformational leadership (Bass & Avolio, 1997)	83 elected community leaders and 391 administrative support staff; 93 county government offices	Unknown
Barbuto, Wilmot, Singh, & Story, 2012	Member ratings of Servant Leadership – Member LMX r = 0.77**; Leader ratings of servant leadership – Member LMX r = 0.12*	Member LMX (Scandura & Graen, 1984)	Leader and member ratings of servant leadership (Barbuto & Wheeler, 2006)	83 elected community leaders and 391 administrative support staff; 93 county government offices	Unknown
Chan & Mak, 2012	Benevolent leadership – Member LMX r = 0.41**	Member LMX (Scandura & Graen, 1984)	Member ratings of benevolent leadership (Cheng, Chou, & Farh, 2000)	223 dyads of leaders and direct supervisors; Members of non-profit organization in Hong Kong	Role routinization (average 4.2 year dyadic tenure)
Wayne, Shore, Bommer & Tetrick, 2002	Supervisor contingent rewards – LMX r = 0.77**; Noncontingent punishment – LMX r = -0.51**	Member LMX (Scandura & Graen, 1984)	Contingent rewards (Podsakoff, Todor, & Skov, 1982); Noncontingent punishment (Podsakoff, Todor, & Skov, 1982)	211 employees and 31 direct supervisors	Role making/Role routinization (average 1.5 year dyadic tenure)
Sahin, 2012	Theory X leadership style – Member LMX r = -0.30**; Theory Y leadership style – Member LMX r = 0.46**	Member LMX (Scandura & Graen, 1984)	Leader theory X and theory Y style (Kopelman, Prottas, & Davis, 2008)	173 employees and 56 direct supervisors; 16 mid-sized yacht building companies in Turkey	Unknown stage

(continued)

Table 6.4. Continued

Variable	Study	Measurement of LMX (measure used)	Measurement of Leader Action/ Behavior (measured used)	Direction and magnitude of relationship (* $p < .05$, ** $p < .01$)	Study Sample & Context	Stage of Relationship (Relationship Tenure)
	Aryee & Chen, 2006	Member LMX (Liden et al., 1993)	Supervisor control of awards (Podsakoff & MacKenzie, 1994)	Supervisor control of awards – Member LMX $r = 0.27**$	192 employees and 66 direct supervisors Household appliance manufacturer in China	Unknown stage
Performance	Deluga & Perry, 1991	Member LMX (Graen & Scandura, 1985)	Supervisor effectiveness (Bass, 1985)	Supervisor effectiveness – Member LMX $r = 0.65**$	376 individuals in graduate or continuing education courses Variety of occupations	Role routinization (average 3.4 years dyadic tenure)
	Nahrgang, Morgeson, & Ilies, 2009	Leader and member LMX (Graen & Uhl-Bien, 1995)	Leader and member performance (Liden et al., 1993)	Leader performance at time 3 – Member LMX at time 4 $r = 0.57**$ Leader performance at time 5 – Member LMX at time 6 $r = 0.58**$ Leader performance at time 7 – Member LMX at time 8 $r = 0.55**$	330 team members and 69 leaders Experiential class setting	Role taking – Role routinization (initial interaction – 8 weeks)

Table 6.5. Member Actions and Behaviors (in chronological order).

Variable	Study	Direction and magnitude of relationship (* p < .05, ** p < .01)	Measurement of LMX (measure used)	Measurement of Relationship Attribute (measured used)	Study Sample & Context	Stage of Relationship (Relationship Tenure)
Effort	Maslyn & Uhl-Bien, 2001	Member reported effort – Member LMX r = 0.38,** 29** Manager reported effort – Member LMX r = 0.36,** 0.28** Manager reported member effort – Member LMX r = 0.46,** 0.45** Member reported effort – Leader LMX r = 0.27** Manager reported effort – Leader LMX r = 0.48** Manager reported member effort – Leader LMX r = 0.68**	Member and leader LMX (Graen & Uhl-Bien, 1995; Liden & Maslyn, 1998)	Member and leader effort (new)	232 dyads of employees and direct supervisors Large, international service organization	Role making (average 0.8 years dyadic tenure)
Performance	Wayne & Ferris, 1990	Study 1: Member performance – Leader LMX r = 0.66** Study 2: Member performance – Leader LMX r = 0.54**	Study 1 and 2: Leader LMX (Scandura et al., 1986)	Study 1: Member impression management (manipulated) Study 2: Member impression management tactics (new)	Study 1: 96 undergraduate students participating in laboratory experiment Study 2: 84 employees and 23 direct supervisors Various departments in banks (teller; book keeping; credit, etc)	Study 1: Role taking (initial interaction) Study 2: Unknown stage
	Liden, Wayne & Stilwell, 1993	Performance of member –Member LMX r = 0.24,* 0.20,* –0.01 Performance of member –Leader LMX r = 0.54,* 0.42,* 0.36*	Member and leader LMX measured at 2 weeks, 6 weeks, 6 months (Scandura & Graen, 1984)	Performance of member (new)	166 dyads of employees and direct supervisors Newly formed dyads Range of job types including secretary, electrician, librarian, admissions counselor, research scientist, and computer programmer	Role taking, Role Making, Role Routinization (initial interaction – 6 months)

(*continued*)

Table 6.5. Continued

Variable	Study	Measurement of LMX (measure used)	Measurement of Relationship Attribute (measured used)	Study Sample & Context	Stage of Relationship (Relationship Tenure)	Direction and magnitude of relationship (* $p < .05$, ** $p < .01$)
	Deluga & Perry, 1994	Member LMX (Graen & Scandura, 1985)	Member Performance (Kipnis & Schmidt, 1988)	152 employees and direct supervisors. Employees in undergraduate or graduate courses. Variety of occupations	Role routinization (Average 2.1 years dyadic tenure)	Member performance – Member LMX $r = 0.35$** Member performance – Leader LMX $r = 0.71$**
	Bauer & Green, 1996	Member LMX measured at 14 and 34 weeks (Scandura & Graen, 1984; Liden et al., 1993)	Member performance (Katz, 1964)	311 employees and 165 direct supervisors. Employees were recent college graduates working in new jobs. Variety of college majors and industries	Role taking/Role Making (12 and 34 weeks after job entry)	Performance of Member – Member LMX at Time 1 $r = 0.48$** Performance of Member – Member LMX at Time 2 $r = 0.57$** Performance of Member Time 1 – Member LMX at Time 2 $r = 0.35$**
	Nahrgang, Morgeson, & Ilies, 2009	Leader and member LMX (Graen & Uhl-Bien, 1995)	Leader and member performance (Liden et al., 1993)	330 team members and 69 leaders. Experiential class setting	Role taking – role routinization (initial interaction – 8 weeks)	Member performance at time 3 – Leader LMX at time 4 $r = 0.46$** Member performance at time 5 – Leader LMX at time 6 $r = 0.45$** Member performance at time 7 – Leader LMX at time 8 $r = 0.54$**
Influence Behaviors	Dockery & Steiner, 1990	Member and leader LMX (Graen & Scandura, 1987)	Member upward influence tactics (Kipnis, Schmidt, & Wilkinson, 1980)	188 undergraduate students participating in 47 groups in laboratory experiment	Role taking (initial interaction)	Member self-perceptions of ingratiation – Member LMX $r = 0.48$** Member self-perceptions of assertiveness – Member LMX $r = -0.19$* Member self-perceptions of rationality – Member LMX $r = 0.33$** Leader perceptions of member's ingratiation – Leader LMX $r = 0.36$*

Findings	Study	Influence variable	LMX measure	Sample	Stage
Leader perceptions of member's assertiveness – Leader LMX $r = 0.00$ Leader perceptions of member's rationality – Leader LMX $r = 0.70^{**}$					
Study 1: Member impression management – Leader LMX $r = 0.63^{**}$ Study 2: Member job-focused tactics – Leader LMX $r = 0.15$ Member supervisor-focused tactics – Leader LMX $r = 0.18$ Member self-focused tactics – Leader LMX $r = 0.20$	Wayne & Ferris, 1990	Study 1: Member impression management (manipulated) Study 2: Member impression management tactics (new)	Study 1 and 2: Leader LMX (Scandura et al., 1986)	Study 1: 96 undergraduate students participating in laboratory experiment Study 2: 84 employees and 23 direct supervisors Various departments in banks (teller, book keeping, credit, etc)	Study 1: Role taking (initial interaction) Study 2: Unknown stage
Member upward friendliness – Member LMX $r = -0.02$ Member upward bargaining – Member LMX $r = -0.14^{**}$ Member upward reason – Member LMX $r = 0.05$ Member upward higher authority – Member LMX $r = -0.28^{**}$ Member upward coalition – Member LMX $r = -0.13^{*}$ Member upward assertiveness – Member LMX $r = -0.13^{**}$	Deluga & Perry, 1991	Member upward influence (Kipnis & Schmidt, 1982)	Member LMX (Graen & Scandura, 1985)	376 individuals in graduate or continuing education courses Variety of occupations	Role routinization (Average 3.4 years dyadic tenure)
Member self-perceptions of opinion conformity – Member LMX $r = 0.33^{**}$ Member self-perceptions of other enhancement – Member LMX $r = 0.26^{**}$ Member self-perceptions of self-presentation – Member LMX $r = 0.07$ Member self-perceptions of opinion conformity – Leader LMX $r = 0.25^{**}$	Deluga & Perry, 1994	Member upward influence (Kipnis & Schmidt, 1982; Pandey & Rastogi, 1979)	Member LMX (Graen & Scandura, 1985)	152 employees and direct supervisors Employees in undergraduate or graduate courses Variety of occupations	Role routinization (Average 2.1 years dyadic tenure)

(continued)

Table 6.5. Continued

Variable	Study	Direction and magnitude of relationship (* $p < .05$, ** $p < .01$)	Measurement of LMX (measure used)	Measurement of Relationship Attribute (measured used)	Study Sample & Context	Stage of Relationship (Relationship Tenure)
		Member self-perceptions of other enhancement – Leader LMX $r = 0.15$				
		Member self-perceptions of self-presentation – Leader LMX $r = 0.07$				
		Leader perceptions of opinion conformity – Member LMX $r = 0.15*$				
		Leader perceptions of other enhancement – Member LMX $r = 0.21**$				
		Leader perceptions of self-presentation – Member LMX $r = 0.16*$				
		Leader perceptions of opinion conformity – Leader LMX $r = 0.37**$				
		Leader perceptions of other enhancement – Leader LMX $r = 0.15*$				
		Leader perceptions of self-presentation – Leader LMX $r = 0.16*$				
	Schriesheim, Castro, & Yammarino, 2000	Member upward controllingness – Member LMX $r = 0.44**$, Member upward controllingness – Leader LMX $r = 0.34**$	Leader and member LMX (Scandura & Graen, 1984)	Member upward influence (Tepper, 1990)	75 banking managers and 150 direct subordinates Assessed both high and low performing subordinate	Role making/Role routinization (Average 1.4 years dyadic tenure)

Table 6.6. Contextual Characteristics (in chronological order)

Variable	Study	Direction and magnitude of relationship (* $p < .05$, ** $p < .01$)	Measurement of LMX (measure used)	Measurement of Contextual Characteristic (measured used)	Study Sample & Context	Stage of Relationship (Relationship Tenure)
Span of Supervision	Green, Anderson & Shivers, 1996	Unit size – Member LMX $r = -0.22$*	Member LMX (Graen et al., 1982)	Unit size (archival data)	208 employees from 31 public libraries	Role Routinization (Average 3.2 years dyadic tenure)
	Cogliser & Schriesheim, 2000	Unit size – Member LMX $r = -0.08$	Member LMX (Scandura & Graen, 1984)	Unit size (archival)	285 employees working in 65 work groups Large county library system	Role Routinization (Average 2.9 years dyadic tenure)
	Schriesheim, Castro, & Yammarino, 2000	Span of supervision – Member LMX $r = -0.32$** Span of supervision – Leader LMX $r = -0.13$	Leader and member LMX (Scandura & Graen, 1984)	Span of supervision (FTE employees)	75 banking managers and 150 direct subordinates Assessed both high and low performing subordinate	Role making/role routinization (Average 1.4 year dyadic tenure)
	Schyns, Paul, Mohr, Blank, 2005	Span of supervision – Member LMX $r = -0.14$*	Member LMX (Graen & Uhl-Bien, 1995)	Span of leadership	252 employees Working in Germany in variety of professions	Role routinization (Average 3.3 years dyadic tenure)
Climate	Wayne, Shore, & Liden, 1997	POS – Member LMX $r = 0.50$**	Member LMX (Scandura & Graen, 1984)	Perceived Organizational Support (Eisenberger, Huntington, Hutchison, & Sowa, 1986, Eisenberger, Fasolo, & Davislamastro, 1990)	252 dyads of employees and direct supervisors Random sample of salaried employees in large corporation	Role routinization (Average 3 years dyadic tenure)

(continued)

Table 6.6. Continued

Variable	Study	Measurement of LMX (measure used)	Measurement of Contextual Characteristic (measured used)	Study Sample & Context	Stage of Relationship (Relationship Tenure)
	Cogliser & Schriesheim, 2000	Member LMX (Scandura & Graen, 1984)	Work unit cohesiveness (Stogdill, 1965) Work unit climate (Pritchard & Karasick, 1973, Hackman & Oldham, 1980)	285 employees working in 65 work groups Large county library system	Role Routinization (Average 2.9 years dyadic tenure)
	Wayne, Shore, Bommer & Tetrick, 2002	Member LMX (Scandura & Graen, 1984)	Perceived Organizational Support (Eisenberger et al., 1986, 1990)	211 employees and 31 direct supervisors	Role making/Role routinization (average 1.5 years dyadic tenure)
	Kraimer & Wayne, 2004	Member LMX (Liden & Maslyn, 1998)	Perceived Organizational Support (new)	230 dyads of employees and direct supervisors Expatriates and supervisors in US based Fortune 500 companies	Unknown stage
	Aryee & Chen, 2006	Member LMX (Liden et al., 1993)	Work unit climate (Quinn & Spreitzer, 1991)	192 employees and 66 direct supervisors Household appliance manufacturer in China	Unknown stage
	Erdogan, Liden, & Kraimer, 2006	Member LMX (Liden & Maslyn, 1998)	Organizational culture (O'Reilly, Chatman, & Caldwell, 1991)	263 teachers and 253 randomly selected peers for culture measure 30 public school in Turkey	Unknown stage

Direction and magnitude of relationship (* p < .05, ** p < .01)

Cogliser & Schriesheim, 2000:
Work unit cohesiveness – Member LMX $r = 0.21^{**}$
Climate cooperativeness – Member LMX $r = 0.33^{**}$
Climate autonomy – Member LMX $r = 0.40^{**}$
Climate skill variety – Member LMX $r = 0.20^{**}$
Climate support – Member LMX $r = 0.42^{**}$
Climate social relations – Member LMX $r = 0.40^{**}$

Wayne, Shore, Bommer & Tetrick, 2002:
POS –Member LMX $r = 0.51^{**}$

Kraimer & Wayne, 2004:
Adjustment POS – Member LMX $r = 0.13^{*}$
Career POS – Member LMX $r = 0.14^{*}$
Financial POS – Member LMX $r = 0.04$
Global POS – Member LMX $r = 0.19^{**}$

Aryee & Chen, 2006:
Work unit climate – Member LMX $r = 0.53^{**}$

Erdogan, Liden, & Kraimer, 2006:
Respect for people – Member LMX $r = 0.24$
Aggressiveness – Member LMX $r = 0.26$
Team orientation – Member LMX $r = 0.20$

Thus, in line with work on relational demography which posits that at the dyadic level demographic similarity has a stronger impact on outcomes than individual level characteristics (Jackson et al., 1991; Tsui & O'Reilly, 1989; Turban & Jones, 1988), LMX researchers have also focused on demographic similarity between leader and member rather than just individual-level demographics of each partner (e.g., Dienesch & Liden, 1986; Duchon et al., 1986; Graen & Cashman, 1975).

Research studying demographic similarity as a predictor of LMX quality has produced mixed results. Liden and colleagues (1993) proposed that demographic similarity would have a positive influence on LMX from both the leader's and member's perspective. Results of the study did not support this hypothesis as demographic similarity positively, but not significantly, related to LMX quality at the beginning of the relationship. By the 6 month time frame of the relationship, demographic similarity had no bearing on the relationship. Later work by Green and colleagues (1996) found that of the three relational demography characteristics they studied, which included age, education, and gender, only gender similarity positively and significantly related to LMX quality as rated by the member. Research by Epitropaki and Martin (1999), however, did not find LMX quality to have a significant relationship with gender similarity nor with age or tenure similarity. In a field sample from the US, Pelled and Xin (2000) also examined age, gender and race similarity separately and found that only gender similarity positively related to the quality of the LMX relationship. In a separate field sample from Mexico, the researchers found that although gender similarity positively related to LMX quality, the relationship was not significant (Pelled & Xin, 2000). Bauer and Green (1996) also studied the influence of gender similarity on the development of the LMX relationship. Results from the study did not show that gender similarity had a significant relationship with LMX quality, nor did it have a significant relationship with delegation or performance as hypothesized in the study. Recent studies examining demographic similarity in LMX relationships have also found mixed results. In a field sample of military cadets, Vecchio and Brazil (2007) found that LMX was higher for subordinates who were of the same gender as their squad leader. Post hoc tests of mean differences found that LMX means for same gender male dyads were significantly higher than men working with female leaders and women working with male leaders. In a

study of individuals working in the Chinese banking industry, it was found that LMX quality did not differ based on age, gender, or education similarity (Zhang, Wang, & Shi, 2012).

Perceived Similarity. A more fruitful area of research on similarity has been work regarding the relationship between perceived similarity of leaders and members and the LMX relationship. As theories of interpersonal attraction would hypothesize, similarity between individuals with regards to attitudes and personality is related to interpersonal attraction and liking (Byrne, 1971). Thus, the extent to which leaders and members perceive each other to be similar, they will be more likely to like one another and the quality of the relationship will be enhanced (Liden et al., 1993). Empirical results support this assertion by finding that member perceived similarity is positively related not only to member LMX, but to leader LMX as well. Likewise, leader perceived similarity is also positively related to both leader and member LMX. Leaders and members demonstrated moderate agreement on perceived similarity ($r = 0.33$, $p < .05$) and not surprisingly, perceived similarity exhibited a stronger relationship with LMX at the beginning of the relationship, but dissipated over time (Liden et al., 1993). In a field sample of registered nurses and their immediate supervisors, Phillips and Bedian (1994) found that the leader's perception of similarity to the member in terms of attitudes on family, money, careers, goals, and education positively related to LMX quality. Likewise, in a field sample of employees working in an electric company, perceived similarity assessed from both leaders' and members' perspectives positively related to both leader and member LMX quality (Engle & Lord, 1997). Finally, meta-analytic evidence also found a positive relationship between perceived similarity and LMX quality ($\rho = .50$; Dulebohn et al., 2012).

Personality Similarity. One final category of similarity involves the extent to which leaders and members are similar with regards to personality. Bauer and Green (1996) found that positive affectivity similarity positively related to LMX quality, although this relationship was insignificant when performance was taken into account. Positive affectivity similarity positively related to performance, which led the authors to conclude that similarity indirectly related to LMX development. Recent work by Zhang and colleagues (2012) tested the congruence between a leader and follower's proactive personality. The study hypothesized that two equally proactive (or nonproactive) individuals were more likely to have a rewarding LMX relationship due to goal congruence and sharing similar perspectives regarding continuous improvement at work. Using polynomial regression, results of the study found that LMX was higher when a follower's proactive personality was in alignment with the leader's proactive personality and any deviation from the congruence line decreased LMX. Specifically, followers experienced lower-quality LMX and poorer work outcomes when their proactive personality was lower than their leader's personality rather than higher than their leader's personality (Zhang et al., 2012).

Attributes of the Relationship

As suggested by the role making model, the dyadic relationship that develops through the interlocking of behaviors contains numerous relational elements (Graen & Scandura, 1987). Attributes of the relationship not fully reviewed in this chapter include the perceived fairness or justice in the relationship (see Chapter X for a review of justice and LMX) and amount of interaction. Inherent in the development of LMX relationships are that the leader and member interact with one another over a period of time. Dyadic tenure has been found to positively relate to LMX (e.g., Maslyn & Uhl-Bien, 2001; Wayne, Shore, Bommer, & Tetrick, 2002) and to not relate to LMX (e.g., Scandura & Pellegrini, 2008; Schyns, Paul, Mohr, & Blank, 2005; Zhang et al., 2012). Research has found, however, that dyadic tenure, dyadic interaction and communication frequency increase the level agreement between leader and member, which is outside the focus of this chapter (Sin, Nahrgang, & Morgeson, 2009). Thus, we focus on three key attributes of the relationship: expectations, liking, and trust. Table 6.3 summarizes the studies examining the attributes of the relationship and LMX quality.

Expectations. A key component of role episodes are the role expectations each party has with regards to the relationship (Kahn et al., 1964). In the leadership literature, expectations of followers have been framed as a self-fulfilling prophecy, or Pygmalion effect, in which leaders' initial expectations of followers influence follower motivation and performance (Eden, 1990, 1992). In line with the Pygmalion effect, LMX researchers have theorized that both leaders and members form expectations of each other before, or early in, the role making phase and that these expectations significantly influence the development of LMX (Liden et al., 1993; Wayne, Shore, & Liden, 1997).

In their study of newly formed dyads, Liden and colleagues (1993) found expectations of future work competence assessed within the first few days of working together positively related to perceptions of LMX quality. Specifically, expectations that a member has of a leader's future work competence positively related to the quality of the LMX relationship (as rated by the member). These expectations continued to relate to the quality of the relationship as long as 6 months later. Likewise, the expectations that a leader has of a member's future work competence also positively related to the quality of the LMX relationship (as rated by the leader), although the effect seemed to dissipate over time. Expectations only impacted self-ratings of LMX quality, and did not impact the other partner's rating of LMX (Liden et al., 1993). In a subsequent study, researchers tested the hypothesis that high leader expectations would translate into challenging tasks, feedback, and training which in turn would influence the quality of LMX as rated by the member. Results of the study found that the expectations the leader had with regards to the member's future pay grade positively related to LMX quality (Wayne et al., 1997). The average tenure of the dyads in the study was 3 years, which suggests that leaders were likely to have formed accurate perceptions of the member but also demonstrates that expectations continue to influence the relationship past that of the role making phase. Meta-analytic evidence finds a positive relationship between leader's expectations of followers and LMX quality (ρ = .37; Dulebohn et al., 2012).

Liking. Theories of interpersonal attraction predict that the degree of similarity between partners relates to attraction and liking (Byrne, 1971). From this, LMX researchers have theorized that a key component to the development of LMX relationships is affect, or the degree of liking, between partners (Dienesch & Liden, 1986). Laboratory studies examining the initial interaction between leaders and members found that liking of the dyadic partner positively related to perceptions of LMX quality. Specifically, liking of the member by the leader positively related to the leader's perception of LMX quality. Likewise, liking of the leader by the member positively related to the member's perception of LMX quality (Dockery & Steiner, 1990). In both a laboratory experiment and field study, Wayne and Ferris (1990) found that liking of the member by the leader positively related to LMX quality as rated by the leader. In other field settings, liking of the dyadic partner has been found to be significantly related to LMX quality, regardless of whether the relationship is assessed from the leader or member perspective (Engle & Lord, 1997; Liden et al., 1993;). Although the relationship between liking and LMX quality was stronger when assessed from the same source, liking of the dyadic partner significantly related to LMX quality in 83% of the measurements and more importantly, continued to relate to LMX quality over a 6 month period (Liden et al., 1993). Another field study corroborates this evidence by finding the extent to which a leader likes a member is positively related to the member's perception of LMX quality (Wayne et al., 1997).

Trust. In their model of dyadic organizing, Graen and Scandura (1987) note that the quality of the dyadic interaction includes dyadic trust and high LMX relationships are often described as being characterized by mutual trust (Dienesch & Liden, 1986; Graen & Uhl-Bien, 1995; Schriesheim, Castro, & Cogliser, 1999). Thus, there is significant overlap between the two constructs although researchers have attempted to investigate how LMX and trust are differentiated and how they are similar (Brower, Schoorman, & Tan, 2000). Although some studies have examined trust as an outcome of LMX (Wat & Shaffer, 2005), in line with the purpose of this chapter, we examine trust as an antecedent to LMX relationships.

In their model integrating trust and LMX, Brower and colleagues (2000) assert that the LMX relationship develops as both the leader and member evaluate the trust of their dyadic partner. For example, a leader's trust in the member is built by assessing the member's ability, benevolence, and integrity. In addition, the propensity for the leader to relate also influences the trust in the member as this represents the propensity to trust in a hierarchical relationship such as with the member. The model then predicts that the leader's trust in the member will positively relate to risk taking behavior such as delegation of tasks to the member which indicates to the member how much the leader trusts him or her. Depending on the level of trust perceived by the member, the member responds with outcomes such as satisfaction, commitment, and citizenship behaviors (Brower et al., 2000).

Similar to the model proposed by Brower and colleagues (2000), one empirical study found that managerial trust, or the leader's trust in the member's competence, openness, consistency, and caring was found to be positively related to LMX quality as rated by the member. The study also found that LMX quality mediated the relationship between the leader's trust in the member and feelings of empowerment by the member (Gómez & Rosen, 2001). Recent empirical work also followed a similar line of inquiry by examining how both subordinates' trust in supervisor and supervisor's trust in subordinates related to LMX quality (Sue-Chan, Au, & Hackett, 2012). By utilizing path modeling, the study was able to test both trust in the partner predicting one's own LMX as well as trust in the partner predicting the other partner's LMX. Results of the study found that supervisor trust in the subordinate positively related to LMX quality as rated by the leader and subordinate trust in the supervisor also positively related to LMX quality as rated by the member. They did not find evidence for trust in the partner predicting the other partner's LMX. Furthermore, subordinate trust and LMX was measured at two different time periods and results revealed that subordinate trust in the supervisor at time 1 positively related to subordinate ratings of LMX at time 2 ($r = 0.39$, $p < .05$) but subordinate ratings of LMX at time 1 also positively related to subordinate trust in the supervisor at time 2 ($r = 0.41$, $p < .05$). Thus, it remains unclear as to whether trust serves as an antecedent or outcome to LMX. Trust building behavior on the part of the supervisor has also been investigated as an antecedent to LMX quality. Results of the study found that the extent to which leaders exhibited fairness to followers positively related to LMX quality as rated by the member, although the relationship was not significant (Deluga, 1994).

Scandura and Pellegrini (2008) took a slightly different look at trust by examining two types of trust operating in working relationships: calculus-based trust and identification-based trust. Calculus-based trust (CBT) is characterized by a transactional calculation that involves weighing the outcomes from sustaining the relationship relative to the costs of severing the relationship (Lewicki & Bunker, 1995), which is similar to the economic exchanges prevalent in low-quality LMX relationships. Thus, one would expect a negative relationship between CBT and LMX quality (Uhl-Bien, Graen, & Scandura, 2000). Empirical evidence found a non-linear relationship between CBT and LMX such that CBT was indeed low in high LMX relationships, but as CBT increased slightly, the quality of the LMX relationship increased as well. LMX quality decreased again after CBT reached its highest levels indicating that trust is not necessarily mutual and reciprocal and may be vulnerable in high LMX relationships as well (Scandura & Pellegrini, 2008).

In line with expectations that high LMX relationships are characterized by a high degree of trust, the study found that identification-based trust (IBT), demonstrated a positive linear relationship with LMX (Scandura & Pellegrini, 2008). IBT is characterized by a mutual understanding and appreciation of each other's needs in which leaders count on their followers for assistance and followers rely on their leaders for support and encouragement (Lewicki & Bunker, 1995). Although the study hypothesized trust as an antecedent to LMX, the design was cross sectional and thus does not help to tease apart the causality of the trust-LMX relationship (Scandura & Pellegrini, 2008). Overall, leader trust has been found to positively relate to the quality of LMX ($\rho = .73$, Dulebohn et al., 2012).

Leader and Member Actions and Behaviors

One of the principles of role making is the concept of interacts, or interlocked behavior (Graen & Scandura, 1987; Weick, 1979). In each role episode, once the role is sent, the dyadic partner can respond to the sent role in the form of specific behaviors (Kahn et al., 1964). In the following paragraphs, we focus on the actions and behaviors of leaders and followers, the results of which are summarized in Tables 6.4 and 6.5.

Leader Actions and Behaviors

Initial Interactions and Behaviors. For new employees, one way a leader can build relationships with members is through socialization. In a study of newcomers to organizations, Sluss and Thompson (2012) found that the extent to which leaders provided guidance, advice, and role modeling focused on the newcomer's job and organizational role help to develop more positive LMX relationships. Maslyn and Uhl-Bien (2001) also found that the extent to which a leader puts in effort towards the relationship positively related to LMX quality. If high effort on the part of the leader was reciprocated with lower effort on the part of the subordinate, then lower-quality LMX relationships developed.

Delegation or Latitude. In their study of LMX development, Bauer and Green (1996) proposed that delegation by the leader and performance by the member formed an interaction, which, in turn, would develop the LMX relationship. In terms of delegation, the study found that leader delegation positively related to member LMX. Although this was true within periods of time (i.e., Time 1 delegation–Time 1 LMX), the study also found that delegation by the leader positively related to

member LMX almost 5 months later. In the original VDL model of leadership (Dansereau et al., 1975; Graen & Cashman, 1975), negotiating latitude served as the core measure of the exchange quality between leader and member. DelVecchio (1998) modified this measure to study the extent to which a leader gave latitude or freedom and autonomy to the member. In the study, it was found that the quality of the relationship between salespersons and managers positively related to the latitude given to the member (DelVecchio, 1998).

Leadership Behaviors. Although LMX focuses on the unique relationships developed by each dyad, leaders also display leadership behaviors to all followers which may influence the development of the LMX relationship. One common leadership behavior is that of transformational leadership in which leaders articulate a vision to followers, provide individualized support and intellectual stimulation, and demonstrate charisma (Bass, 1985). High LMX relationships are characterized by social exchange and thus, researchers have proposed that transformational leadership behaviors on the part of leaders will positively relate to LMX quality because leaders build follower receptivity to social exchange (Wang, Law, Hackett, Wang, & Chen, 2005). Supporting this assertion, Wang and colleagues found that transformational leadership on the part of leaders positively related to member LMX. Furthermore, they found that LMX mediated the relationship between transformational leadership and member task performance and citizenship behaviors (Wang et al., 2005). Barbuto and colleagues (2011, 2012) utilized a sample of elected leaders and their support staff to assess the extent to which servant leadership and transformational leadership on the part of the leader related to LMX quality. Both servant and transformational leadership positively related to member LMX, regardless of whether the behavior of the leader was assessed by the leader or by the member. Kent and Chelladurai (2001) found a cascading effect for transformational leadership on LMX quality by examining three levels of followers, leaders, and leader's managers. Results of the study found that the extent to which a leader's manager displayed transformational leadership positively related to the quality of the LMX relationship between leaders and followers.

Others have also studied the transactional behaviors of leaders and their influence on LMX and found that contingent rewards positively related to LMX quality, whereas noncontingent punishment was negatively related to LMX (Wayne et al., 2002).

Aryee and Chen (2006) confirmed these results by finding that supervisor control of rewards also positively related to LMX quality. Meta-analytic evidence found a strong and positive relationship between transformational leadership and contingent reward behavior and LMX (ρ = .73 and ρ = .73, respectively; Dulebohn et al., 2012).

Other leadership styles expected to relate to LMX are that of benevolent leadership and theory X and theory Y. Benevolent leaders are particularly effective in building relationships due to their natural ability to demonstrate care and concern to followers. Recent research found a positive relationship between benevolent leadership style and LMX quality (Chan & Mak, 2012). Results of another empirical study found that theory Y leadership style positively related to LMX quality, whereas theory X negatively related to LMX quality. Although when placed in a regression equation together to predict LMX quality, only theory Y remained significantly related to LMX quality (Sahin, 2012).

Leader Performance. Finally, just like performance of a member on a sent role can influence the type of relationship that develops (Graen & Scandura, 1987), the performance of the leader influences the relationship as well. Early work by Deluga and Perry (1991) found that the perception of a supervisor's effectiveness positively related to LMX quality. In their longitudinal study examining the development of LMX over time, Nahrgang and colleagues (2009) found that leader performance measured 1 week prior to measuring LMX positively related to member LMX. Results of the study also found that leader performance positively related to changes in member LMX (Nahrgang et al., 2009).

Leader Actions and Behaviors

Member Performance. Just like that of leader performance, member performance is also theorized to relate to LMX quality. Early studies on the VDL model of leadership found that in-group status positively related to member performance (Liden & Graen, 1980; Vecchio & Gobdel, 1984). Further work in LMX theory found that a leader's ratings of member's performance positively related to both member and leader LMX (Liden et al., 1993). Bauer and Green's (1996) study of newcomers to the organization confirmed this with results indicating that member performance strongly related to member LMX and specifically found that member performance measured almost 5 months before member LMX positively related to LMX. Deluga and Perry

(1994) also found that member performance positively related to both member and leader LMX.

Wayne and Ferris (1990) examined the extent to which performance by a member related to LMX quality in both a laboratory and field study. Performance ratings were an important determinant of exchange quality in the laboratory experiment, but not in the field study. In the field study, performance ratings positively and significantly related to LMX quality, but the effect was not significant when tested in the full model. The most recent study investigating how member performance influences LMX quality studied the relationship over time. Performance and LMX were measured over an 8-week time interval and results found that performance measured 1 week prior to measuring LMX positively related to leader LMX. The study also found support for hypotheses which predicted that the trajectory of a leader's LMX quality over time was due to changes in member performance (Nahrgang et al., 2009)

Member Effort. Similar to that of performance, effort on the part of the member toward relationship development also positively influences LMX quality. In a field study, members who put forth effort built higher-quality LMX relationships with their managers. Furthermore, if higher effort on the part of the member were coupled with lower effort by the manager, this was associated with a lower-quality LMX relationship (Maslyn & Uhl-Bien, 2001).

Influence Behaviors. Finally, one way in which members may influence the quality of the LMX relationship is through exhibiting behaviors such as ingratiation, other enhancement, and self-presentation. Dockery and Steiner (1990) examined how a member's influence tactics at the initial interaction related to LMX quality. Results of the laboratory experiment found that use of ingratiation and rationality tactics by members positively related to leader LMX, although the results did not hold when included with liking and ability in a regression equation. As for member LMX, members who perceived themselves using ingratiation and rationality tactics also rated LMX quality higher. The use of assertiveness was seen by members as negatively relating to LMX quality, suggesting that at the initial interaction, members thought it was best to go with the leader's wishes rather than assert their own opinions. The negative relationship of assertiveness was confirmed in another field study by Deluga and Perry (1991) which found that influence tactics such as bargaining, assertiveness, cultivating backing by higher management, and forming coalitions all negatively related to member LMX.

In a similar study, ingratiation activity on the part of members including opinion conformity, other enhancement, and self-presentation positively related to both member and leader LMX. However, when performance by members was controlled for in the regression, other enhancement stood out as the ingratiation activity that most strongly predicted member LMX and opinion conformity most strongly predicted leader LMX (Deluga & Perry, 1994). Upward influence tactics on the part of members also positively related to both member and leader LMX in a working sample of bank managers and their subordinates (Schriesheim, Castro, & Yammarino, 2000). Wayne and Ferris (1990) examined similar behaviors on the part of members and hypothesized that these behaviors would have an indirect effect on LMX quality through liking and performance ratings. In a laboratory study in which they manipulated a member's impression management behaviors, they found the behaviors to develop the LMX relationship through positive relationships with leader liking for the subordinate and performance ratings. In the field setting, the behaviors positively related to supervisor liking which in turn related positively to LMX quality. Summaries of the effects of ingratiation and influence tactics on the LMX relationship find that influence tactics such as ingratiation and self-promotion positively relate to LMX quality (ρ ranges from 27 to 45), whereas assertiveness negatively relates to LMX quality ($\rho = -.12$; Dulebohn et al., 2012).

Contextual Characteristics

In their theory of LMX development, Dienesch and Liden (1986) noted that contextual factors such as work group composition, leader's power, and organizational policies and culture may influence the LMX process. Although some researchers have studied leader power (Cogliser & Schriesheim, 2000), research has primarily focused on work group composition in the form of work group size or span of supervision as well as the climate or support within the organization as contextual antecedents to the LMX relationship.

Span of Supervision. All leaders have constraints on their time and resources, and therefore it is difficult for leaders to form high-quality relationships with a large number of followers (Dansereau et al., 1975; Dienesch & Liden, 1986). Thus, the span of supervision, or the number of followers that are supervised by the leader, may negatively impact the quality of the LMX relationship. Several studies have supported the negative relationship between span of supervision and LMX. Both Green and colleagues and Schyns and colleagues found that the number of employees reporting to a supervisor was negatively related to the quality of LMX (Green et al., 1996; Schyns et al., 2005). Schriesheim and colleagues found that the span of supervision negatively related to leader LMX, although the effect was not significant. Span of supervision, however, was negatively related to member LMX (Schriesheim et al., 2000).

Work Climate. The climate surrounding the dyadic relationship in terms of cohesiveness and support are also likely to influence the LMX relationship. Research in this area has largely focused on perceived organizational support (POS) which can be categorized as another type of social exchange between the employee and the employing organization (Eisenberger, Huntington, Hutchison, & Sowa, 1986). Although research has found POS and LMX to have unique antecedents and consequences (Wayne et al., 1997), research has also found that the two positively relate to one another. Studies have found POS to have a moderately strong, positive relationship with LMX quality (Wayne et al., 1997; Wayne et al., 2002) and also found that for expatriates, POS also positively relates to LMX quality (Kraimer & Wayne, 2004). Other studies of work climate have focused on the extent to which the work unit emphasized human relations, teamwork and cohesion and have found that this type of climate positively relates to LMX quality (Aryee & Chen, 2006; Cogliser & Schriesheim, 2000).

Practical Implications and Future Directions

The research on LMX development points to several practical implications for employees and supervisors as they seek to develop their own dyadic relationship. First, as originally theorized, the early stages of the relationship, and in particular, the initial interaction, play a significant role in determining the future of the relationship (Bauer & Green, 1996; Liden et al., 1993; Nahrgang et al., 2009). Thus, leaders and followers should be aware that first impressions matter and in particular, that their characteristics and expectations influence assessments of the quality of the relationship. In particular, research demonstrates that similarity between the dyadic partners positively relates to LMX quality (e.g., Engle & Lord, 1997; Liden et al., 1993; Phillips & Bedian, 1994). Although this is not surprising given that we are often attracted to individuals similar to ourselves (Byrne, 1971), research demonstrates that the effect of similarity on the LMX relationship dissipates over time (Liden et al., 1993). Thus, leaders and members should not overemphasize similarity as finding a diverse set of employees enhances work group performance if properly managed (Harrison, Price, Gavin, & Florey, 2002).

A second practical implication is the interlocking that occurs from the behaviors of both member and leader and the LMX relationship. For leaders, at the beginning of the relationship, it is important for leaders to provide support to newcomers as well as show extra effort towards building the relationship (Sluss & Thompson, 2012; Maslyn & Uhl-Bien, 2001). Delegating tasks to the employee also helps to build the relationship (Bauer & Green, 1996) as does engaging in behaviors such as communicating a vision to the followers through transformational leadership and providing contingent rewards (Wang et al., 2005; Wayne et al., 2002). For followers to build a high-quality relationship with their leaders, they must perform the roles sent to them by the leaders (e.g., Liden et al., 1993; Nahrgang et al., 2009). Furthermore, ingratiation behaviors and self-promotion helps to build the relationship, but acting overly assertive can negatively impact the relationship (e.g., Dockery & Steiner, Schriesheim et al., 2000). Third, other than liking, trust holds one of the strongest relationships with LMX quality. For members, this means cultivating the leader's trust in their competence, openness, and consistency (Gómez & Rosen, 2001). Leaders can also engage in trust building behaviors such as exhibiting fairness to followers (Deluga, 1994).

The strong relationship with trust also points to areas of future research in the development of LMX, especially with regards to relationship repair. The LMX relationship has been found to be one of the most important relationships an employee has with regards to important outcomes such as job satisfaction, satisfaction with pay, and turnover intentions (Dulebohn et al., 2012). Thus a breach in the LMX relationship could have devastating consequences, and like trust, may be extremely difficult to repair (Lount, Zhong, Sivanathan, & Murnighan, 2008). Although research in trust suggests employees often experience a violation of trust by their leader (Conway & Briner, 2002; Robinson & Rousseau, 1994), research in LMX has yet to examine breaches of the social exchanges that take place within a high LMX relationship. One of the first steps for future research would be to understand how violations,

such as a member not meeting expectations or a leader failing to provide resources, impact the LMX relationship. As has been theorized by LMX researchers, members and leaders provide numerous resources to the relationship such as affiliation, status, service, information, money and goods (Wilson, Sin, & Conlon, 2010). Thus, future research should explore whether or not the failure to provide one of these resources constitutes an LMX violation and therefore, reduces the quality of the relationship (Chen, Tsui, & Zhong, 2008).

Another area of investigation for LMX researchers would be in understanding how LMX violations can be repaired. Research in trust has investigated numerous responses to violations of trust ranging from apology, denial and reticence (e.g., Ferrin, Kim, Cooper, & Dirks, 2007; Kim, Ferrin, Cooper, & Dirks, 2004), and has found that some responses are more effective than others depending on the type of violation or the context of the violation (e.g., Dirks, Kim, Ferrin, & Cooper, 2011; Kim, Cooper, Dirks, & Ferrin, 2013; Kim, Dirks, Cooper, & Ferrin, 2006). For LMX researchers, an area of fruitful research would be to understand what responses help repair the LMX relationship, and whether responses are successful or not successful depending on the stage of the relationship. As the early stages of the relationship have shown to be especially critical to the development of the relationship, one would expect that LMX violations in early stages have significantly different effects and are less likely to be repaired than if the violations occur in later stages of the relationship.

Beyond that of relationship repair, another area of future research would be to explore the long-term benefits of high-quality LMX relationships beyond just the current working relationship. Research in LMX has extended the effects of exchange relationships beyond that of the dyad by investigating how a supervisor's relationship with his or her boss (i.e., leader–leader exchange [LLX]) influence LMX (Tangirala, Green, & Ramanujam, 2007). Other areas of investigation would be in understanding how a member's relationship with their supervisor helps to determine the types of relationships members developed in the future with their own subordinates, or how impactful the first LMX relationship to a newcomer is to long-term organizational success.

Conclusion

As highlighted in this chapter, the development of high LMX relationships continues to be a fruitful area of research. Using role theory as our guide (Kahn et al., 1964), we asserted that the antecedents likely to influence the development of the relationship depend on whether the relationship is in the role taking, role making, or role routinization phase (Graen & Scandura, 1987). Empirical evidence of the role making process has found that LMX relationships tend to develop quickly based on initial interactions between leaders and members and stabilize into either a high-quality or low-quality relationship (Bauer & Green, 1996; Liden et al., 1993; Nahrgang et al., 2009). Early in the relationship, similarity between leaders and members tends to be one of the strongest predictors of LMX quality such that similarity enhances the quality of the relationship (see Table 6.2). Components of the relationship such as expectations, liking, and trust also contribute positively to developing high-quality LMX (see Table 6.3). Once past the beginning stages of the relationship, the actions of both members and leaders, such as leadership behaviors, performance, effort and delegation contribute positively to the relationship (see Tables 6.4 and 6.5). Finally, all LMX relationships exist with the organizational context, and thus, various contextual variables also influence the development of the relationship (see Table 6.6).

References

Aryee, S., & Chen, Z. X. (2006). Leader–member exchange in a chinese context: Antecedents, the mediating role of psychological empowerment and outcomes. *Journal of Business Research, 59*(7), 793–801.

Barbuto, J. E., & Wheeler, D. W. (2006). Scale development and construct clarification of servant leadership. *Group & Organization Management, 31*(3), 300–326.

Barbuto, J. E., Jr., Wilmot, M. P., Singh, M., & Story, J. S. P. (2012). Self-other rating agreement and leader-member exchange (LMX): A quasi-replication. *Perceptual and Motor Skills, 114*(2), 479–484.

Barbuto, J. E., Jr., Wilmot, M. P., & Story, J. S. (2011). Self-other rating agreement and leader-member exchange (LMX). *Perceptual and Motor Skills, 113*(3), 875–880.

Bass, B. M. (1985). *Leadership and performance beyond expectations* New York: Free Press.

Bass, B. M., & Avolio, B. J. (1997) *Full range leadership development: manual for the Multifactor Leadership Questionnaire.* Palo Alto, CA: Mind Garden.

Bauer, T. N., & Green, S. G. (1996). Development of leader-member exchange: A longitudinal test. *Academy of Management Journal, 39*(6), 1538–1567.

Brower, H. H., Schoorman, F. D., & Tan, H. H. (2000). A model of relational leadership: The integration of trust and leader–member exchange. *The Leadership Quarterly, 11*(2), 227–250.

Butler, J. K. (1991). Toward understanding and measuring conditions of trust—evolution of a conditions of trust inventory. *Journal of Management, 17*(3), 643–663.

Byrne, D. (1971). *The attraction paradigm.* New York: Academic Press.

Chan, S. C. H., & Mak, W. M. (2012). Benevolent leadership and follower performance: The mediating role of leader-member exchange (LMX). *Asia Pacific Journal of Management, 29*(2), 285–301.

Chen, X., & Farh, J. L. (1999, August). *The effectiveness of trans actional and transformational leader behaviors in Chinese organizations: Evidence from Taiwan.* Paper presented at the annual meeting of the Academy of Management, Chicago.

Chen, Z. X., Tsui, A. S., & Zhong, L. (2008). Reactions to psychological contract breach: a dual pesepctive. *Journal of Organizational Behavior, 29*(5), 527–548.

Cheng, B. S., Chou, L. F., & Farh, J. L. (2000). Paternalistic leadership scale: Construction and measurement of triad model. *Indigenous Psychological Research in Chinese Societies. 14*, 3–64.

Cogliser, C. C., & Schriesheim, C. A. (2000). Exploring work unit context and leader-member exchange: A multi-level perspective. *Journal of Organizational Behavior, 21*(5), 487–511.

Conway, N., & Briner, R. B. (2002). A daily diary study of affective responses to psychological contract breach and exceeded promises. *Journal of Organizational Behavior, 23*(3), 287–302.

Dansereau, F., Graen, G., & Haga, W. J. (1975). A vertical dyad linkage approach to leadership within formal organizations: A longitudinal investigation of the role making process. *Organizational Behavior and Human Performance, 13*(1), 46–78.

Day, D. V., & Crain, E. C. (1992). The role of affect and ability in initial exchange quality perceptions. *Group & Organization Management, 17*(4), 380–397.

Deluga, R. J. (1994). Supervisor trust building, leader-member exchange and organizational citizenship behaviour. *Journal of Occupational and Organizational Psychology, 67*(4), 315–326.

Deluga, R. J., & Perry, J. T. (1991). The relationship of subordinate upward influencing behaviour, satisfaction and perceived superior effectiveness with leader—member exchanges. *Journal of Occupational Psychology, 64*(3), 239–252.

Deluga, R. J., & Perry, J. T. (1994). The role of subordinate performance and ingratiation in leader-member exchanges. *Group & Organization Management, 19*(1), 67–86.

DelVecchio, S. K. (1998). The quality of salesperson-manager relationship: The effect of latitude, loyalty and competence. *The Journal of Personal Selling and Sales Management, 18*(1), 31–47.

Dienesch, R. M., & Liden, R. C. (1986). Leader-member exchange model of leadership: A critique and further development. *Academy of Management Journal, 11*, 618–634.

Dirks, K. T., & Ferrin, D. L. (2002). Trust in leadership: Meta-analytic findings and implications for research and practice. *Journal of Applied Psychology, 87*(4), 611.

Dirks, K. T., Kim, P. H., Ferrin, D. L., & Cooper, C. D. (2011). Understanding the effects of substantive responses on trust following a transgression. *Organizational Behavior and Human Decision Processes, 114*(2), 87–103.

Dockery, T. M., & Steiner, D. D. (1990). The role of the initial interaction in leader-member exchange. *Group & Organization Management, 15*(4), 395–413.

Duchon, D., Green, S. G., & Taber, T. D. (1986). Vertical dyad linkage: A longitudinal assessment of antecedents, measures, and consequences. *Journal of Applied Psychology, 71*(1), 56–60.

Dulebohn, J. H., Bommer, W. H., Liden, R. C., Brouer, R. L., & Ferris, G. R. (2012). A meta-analysis of antecedents and consequences of leader-member exchange: Integrating the past with an eye toward the future. *Journal of Management, 38*(6), 1715–1759.

Eden, D. (1990). *Pygmalion in management: Productivity as a self-fulfilling prophecy.* Lexington, MA: Lexington Books.

Eden, D. (1992). Leadership and expectations: Pygmalion effects and other self-fulfilling prophecies in organizations. *Leadership Quarterly, 3*(4), 271–305.

Eisenberger, R., Fasolo, P., & Davislamastro, V. (1990). Perceived organizational support and employee diligence, commitment, and innovation. *Journal of Applied Psychology, 75*(1), 51–59.

Eisenberger, R., Huntington, R., Hutchison, S., & Sowa, D. (1986). Perceived organizational support. *Journal of Applied Psychology, 71*(3), 500–507.

Engle, E. M., & Lord, R. G. (1997). Implicit theories, self-schemas, and leader-member exchange. *Academy of Management Journal, 40*(4), 988–1010.

Epitropaki, O., & Martin, R. (1999). The impact of relational demography on the quality of leader-member exchanges and employees' work attitudes and well-being. *Journal of Occupational and Organizational Psychology, 72,* 237–240.

Epitropaki, O., & Martin, R. (2004). Implicit leadership theories in applied settings: Factor structure, generalizability, and stability over time. *Journal of Applied Psychology, 89*(2), 293–310.

Epitropaki, O., & Martin, R. (2005). From ideal to real: A longitudinal study of the role of implicit leadership theories on leader-member exchanges and employee outcomes. *Journal of Applied Psychology, 90*(4), 659–676.

Ferrin, D. L., Kim, P. H., Cooper, C. D., & Dirks, K. T. (2007). Silence speaks volumes: The effectiveness of reticence in comparison to apology and denial for responding to integrity- and competence-based trust violations. *Journal of Applied Psychology, 92*(4), 893–908.

Gabarro, J. J. (1978). The development of trust influence and expectations. In A. G. Athos & J. J. Gabarro (Eds.), *Interpersonal behavior: Communication and understanding in relationships* (pp. 290–303). Englewood Cliffs, NJ: Prentice-Hall.

Gerstner, C. R., & Day, D. V. (1997). Meta-analytic review of leader-member exchange theory: Correlates and construct issues. *Journal of Applied Psychology, 82*(6), 827–844.

Gómez, C., & Rosen, B. (2001). The leader-member exchange as a link between managerial trust and employee empowerment. *Group & Organization Management, 26*(1), 53–69.

Graen, G. B. (1976). Role-making processes within complex organizations. *Handbook of industrial and organizational psychology.* Chicago: Rand McNally, 1245.

Graen, G. B., & Cashman, J. F. (1975). A role making model of leadership in formal organizations: A developmental approach. In J. G. Hunt & L. L. Larsons (Eds.), *Leadership frontiers* (pp. 143–165). Kent, OH: Kent State University Press.

Graen, G., Novak, M. A., & Sommerkamp, P. (1982). The effects of leader-member exchange and job design on productivity and satisfaction—testing a dual attachment model. *Organizational Behavior and Human Performance, 30*(1), 109–131.

Graen, G., & Scandura, T. A. (1985). *Leader-member exchange scale-17.* Cincinnati, OH: University of Cincinnati.

Graen, G. B., & Scandura, T. A. (1987). Toward a psychology of dyadic organizing. *Research in Organizational Behavior, 9,* 175–208.

Graen, G. B., & Uhl-Bien, M. (1995). Relationship-based approach to leadership—development of leader-member exchange (LMX) theory of leadership over 25 years—applying a multilevel multidomain perspective. *Leadership Quarterly, 6*(2), 219–247.

Green, S. G., Anderson, S. E., & Shivers, S. L. (1996). Demographic and organizational influences on leader–member exchange and related work attitudes. *Organizational Behavior and Human Decision Processes, 66*(2), 203–214.

Hackman, J. R., & Oldham, G. R. (1980). *Work Redsign.* Addison-Wesley: Reading, MA.

Harrison, D. A., Price, K. H., Gavin, J. H., & Florey, A. T. (2002). Time, teams, and task performance: Changing effects of surface- and deep-level diversity on group functioning. *Academy of Management Journal, 45*(5), 1029–1045.

House, R. J., & Baertz, M. L. (1979). Leadership: Some empirical generalizations and new research directions. *Research in Organizational Behavior, 1,* 341–424.

Ilies, R., Nahrgang, J. D., & Morgeson, F. P. (2007). Leader-member exchange and citizenship behaviors: A meta-analysis. *Journal of Applied Psychology, 92*(1), 269–277.

Jackson, S. E., Brett, J. F., Sessa, V. I., Cooper, D. M., Julin, J. A., & Peyronnin, K. (1991). Some differences make a difference—individual dissimilarity and group heterogeneity as correlates of recruitment, promotions, and turnover. *Journal of Applied Psychology, 76*(5), 675–689.

Jones, G. R. (1986). Socialization tactics, self-efficacy, and newcomers adjustments to organizations. *Academy of Management Journal, 29*(2), 262–279.

Kahn, R. L., Wolfe, D. M., Quinn, R. P., Snoek, J. D., & Rosenthal, R. A. (1964). *Organizational stress: Studies in role conflict and ambiguity.* Oxford, England: John Wiley.

Katz, D. (1964). The motivational basis of organizational-behavior. *Behavioral Science, 9*(2), 131–146.

Kent, A., & Chelladurai, P. (2001). Perceived transformational leadership, organizational commitment, and citizenship behavior: A case study in intercollegiate athletics. *Journal of Sport Management, 15*(2), 135–159.

Kim, P. H., Cooper, C. D., Dirks, K. T., & Ferrin, D. L. (2013). Repairing trust with individuals vs. Groups. *Organizational Behavior and Human Decision Processes, 120*(1), 1–14.

Kim, P. H., Dirks, K. T., Cooper, C. D., & Ferrin, D. L. (2006). When more blame is better than less: The implications of internal vs. External attributions for the repair of trust after a competence- vs. Integrity-based trust violation. *Organizational Behavior and Human Decision Processes, 99*(1), 49–65.

Kim, P. H., Ferrin, D. L., Cooper, C. D., & Dirks, K. T. (2004). Removing the shadow of suspicion: The effects of apology versus denial for repairing competence- versus integrity-based trust violations. *Journal of applied psychology, 89*(1), 104–118.

Kinicki, A. J., & Vecchio, R. P. (1994). Influences on the quality of supervisor–subordinate relations: The role of time-pressure, organizational commitment, and locus of control. *Journal of Organizational Behavior, 15*(1), 75–82.

Kipnis, D. & Schmidt, S. M. (1982). *Profiles of Organizational Influence Strategies (Form M).* San Diego, CA: University Associates.

Kipnis, D., & Schmidt, S. M. (1988). Upward-influence styles—relationship with performance evaluations, salary, and stress. *Administrative Science Quarterly, 33*(4), 528–542.

Kipnis, D., Schmidt, S. M., & Wilkinson, I. (1980). Interorganizational influence tactics: Explorations in getting one's way. *Journal of Applied Psychology, 65*, 440–452.

Kopelman, R. E., Prottas, D. J., & Davis, A. L. (2008). Douglas McGregor's theory X and Y: Toward a construct-valid measure. *Journal of Managerial Issues, 20*(2), 255–271.

Kozlowski, S. W. J., & Doherty, M. L. (1989). Integration of climate and leadership—examination of a neglected issue. *Journal of Applied Psychology, 74*(4), 546–553.

Kraimer, M. L., & Wayne, S. J. (2004). An examination of perceived organizational support as a multidimensional construct in the context of an expatriate assignment. *Journal of Management, 30*(2), 209–237.

Lewicki, R. J., & Bunker, B. B. (1995). *Trust in relationships: A model of development and decline*. Jossey-Bass.

Lewicki, R. J., Bunker, B. B., & Stevenson, M. A. (1997). *The three components of interpersonal trust: Instrument development and differences across relationships*. Paper presented at the meeting of the International Association of Conflict Management, Germany.

Liden, R. C., & Graen, G. (1980). Generalizability of the vertical dyad linkage model of leadership. *Academy of Management Journal, 23*(3), 451–465.

Liden, R. C., & Maslyn, J. M. (1998). Multidimensionafity of leader-member exchange: An empirical assessment through scale development. *Journal of Management, 24*(1), 43–72.

Liden, R. C., Sparrowe, R. T., & Wayne, S. J. (1997). Leader-member exchange theory: The past and potential for the future. *Research in Personnel and Human Resource Management, 15*, 47–119.

Liden, R. C., Wayne, S. J., & Stilwell, D. (1993). A longitudinal study on the early development of leader-member exchanges. *Journal of Applied Psychology, 78*(4), 662–674.

Lord, R. G. (1985). An information processing approach to social perceptions, leadership perceptions and behavioral measurement in organizational settings. In B. M. Straw & L. L. Cummings (Eds.), *Research in organizational behavior* (Vol. 7, pp. 85–128). Greenwich, CT: JAI Press.

Lount, R. B., Jr., Zhong, C.-B., Sivanathan, N., & Murnighan, J. K. (2008). Getting off on the wrong foot: The timing of a breach and the restoration of trust. *Personality and Social Psychology Bulletin, 34*(12), 1601–1612.

Maslyn, J. M., & Uhl-Bien, M. (2001). Leader–member exchange and its dimensions: Effects of self-effort and other's effort on relationship quality. *Journal of Applied Psychology, 86*(4), 697–708.

Mishra, A. K. (1993, August). *Breaking down organizational boundaries during crisis: The role of mutual trust*. Paper presented at the Academy of Management Conference, Atlanta.

Nahrgang, J. D., Morgeson, F. P., & Ilies, R. (2009). The development of leader–member exchanges: Exploring how personality and performance influence leader and member relationships over time. *Organizational Behavior and Human Decision Processes, 108*(2), 256–266.

O'Reilly, C. A., Chatman, J., & Caldwell, D. F. (1991). People and organizational culture: A profile comparison approach to assessing person-organization fit. *Academy of Management Journal, 34*(3), 487–516.

Pandey, J., & Rastogi, R. (1979). Machiavellianism and ingratiation. *Journal of Social Psychology, 108*(2), 221–225.

Pelled, L. H., & Xin, K. R. (2000). Relational demography and relationship quality in two cultures. *Organization Studies, 21*(6), 1077–1094.

Phillips, A. S., & Bedeian, A. G. (1994). Leader-follower exchange quality: The role of personal and interpersonal attributes. *Academy of Management Journal, 37*(4), 990–1001.

Podsakoff, P. M., & Mackenzie, S. B. (1994). An examination of the psychometric properties and normological validity of some revised and reduced substitutes for leadership scales. *Journal of Applied Psychology, 79*(5), 702–713.

Podsakoff, P. M., Todor, W. D., & Skov, R. (1982). Effects of leader contingent and noncontingent reward and punishment behaviors on subordinate performance and satisfaction. *Academy of Management Journal, 25*(4), 810–821.

Pritchard, R. D., & Karasick, B. W. (1973). The efects of organizational climate on managerial job performance and job satisfaction. *Organizational Behavior and Human Performance, 9*, 126-146.

Quinn, R. E., & Spreitzer, G. M. (1991). The psychometrics of the competing values culture instrument and an analysis of the impact of organizational culture on quality of life. In R. W. Pasmore & W. A. Pasmore (Eds.), *Research in Organizational Change and Development* (Vol. 5, pp. 115–142). Greenwich, CT: JAI Press.

Robinson, S. L. (1996). Trust and breach of the psychological contract. *Administrative Science Quarterly, 41*(4), 574–599.

Robinson, S. L., & Rousseau, D. M. (1994). Violating the psychological contract: Not the exception but the norm. *Journal of Organizational Behavior, 15*(3), 245–259.

Sahin, F. (2012). The mediating effect of leader-member exchange on the relationship between theory x and y management styles and affective commitment: A multilevel analysis. *Journal of Management & Organization, 18*(2), 159–174.

Scandura, T. A., & Graen, G. B. (1984). Moderating effects of initial leader member exchange status on the effects of a leadership intervention. *Journal of Applied Psychology, 69*(3), 428–436.

Scandura, T. A., Graen, G. B., & Novak, M. A. (1986). When managers decide not to decide autocratically: An investigation of leader-member exchange and decision influence. *Journal of Applied Psychology, 71*, 579–584.

Scandura, T. A., & Pellegrini, E. K. (2008). Trust and leader—member exchange: A closer look at relational vulnerability. *Journal of Leadership & Organizational Studies, 15*(2), 101–110.

Scandura, T. A., & Schriesheim, C. A. (1994). Leader-member exchange and supervisor career mentoring as complementary constructs in leadership research. *Academy of Management Journal, 37*, 1588–1602.

Schriesheim, C. A., Castro, S. L., & Cogliser, C. C. (1999). Leader-member exchange (LMX) research: A comprehensive review of theory, measurement, and data-analytic practices. *Leadership Quarterly, 10*(1), 63–113.

Schriesheim, C. A., Castro, S. L., & Yammarino, F. J. (2000). Investigating contingencies: An examination of the impact of span of supervision and upward controllingness on leader-member exchange using traditional and multivariate within- and between-entities analysis. *Journal of Applied Psychology, 85*(5), 659–677.

Schriesheim, C. A., Scandura, T. A., Eisenbach, R. J., & Neider, L. L. (1992). Validation of a new leader–member exchange scale (LMX-6) using hierarchically-nested maximum likelihood confirmatory factor analysis. *Educational and Psychological Measurement, 52,* 983–992.

Schyns, B., Paul, T., Mohr, G., & Blank, H. (2005). Comparing antecedents and consequences of leader–member exchange in a german working context to findings in the us. *European Journal of Work and Organizational Psychology, 14*(1), 1–22.

Seibert, S. E., Crant, J. M., & Kraimer, M. L. (1999). Proactive personality and career success. *Journal of Applied Psychology, 84*(3), 416–427.

Sin, H. P., Nahrgang, J. D., & Morgeson, F. P. (2009). Understanding why they don't see eye to eye: An examination of leader–member exchange (LMX) agreement. *Journal of Applied Psychology, 94*(4), 1048.

Sluss, D. M., & Thompson, B. S. (2012). Socializing the newcomer: The mediating role of leader-member exchange. *Organizational Behavior and Human Decision Processes, 119*(1), 114–125.

Stogdill, R. M. (1965). *Work group descriptions manual.* Columbus: Ohio State University, Bureau of Business Research.

Sue-Chan, C., Au, A. K. C., & Hackett, R. D. (2012). Trust as a mediator of the relationship between leader/member behavior and leader-member-exchange quality. *Journal of World Business, 47*(3), 459–468.

Tangirala, S., Green, S. G., & Ramanujam, R. (2007). In the shadow of the boss's boss: Effects of supervisors' upward exchange relationships on employees. *Journal of Applied Psychology, 92*(2), 309–320.

Tepper, B. J. (1990). *Influence tactics employed in charismatic and noncharismatic leader-follower interactions.* Unpublished doctoral dissertation, Department of Psychology, University of Miami.

Tsui, A. S., & O'Reilly, C. A. (1989). Beyond simple demographic effects—the importance of relational demography in superior-subordinate dyads. *Academy of Management Journal, 32*(2), 402–423.

Turban, D. B., & Jones, A. P. (1988). Supervisor-subordinate similarity: Types, effects, and mechanisms. *Journal of Applied Psychology, 73*(2), 228.

Turban, D. B., Jones, A. P., & Rozelle, R. M. (1990). Influences of supervisor liking of a subordinate and the reward context on the treatment and evaluation of that subordinate. *Motivation and Emotion, 14*(3), 215–233.

Uhl-Bien, M., Graen, G. B., & Scandura, T. A. (2000). Implications of leader member exchange (LMX) for strategic human resource management systems: Relationships as social capital for competitive advantage. In G. Ferris (Ed.), *Research in personnel and human resource management* (Vol. 18, pp. 137–185). Greenwich, CT: JAI Press.

Vecchio, R. P., & Brazil, D. M. (2007). Leadership and sex-similarity: A comparison in a military setting. *Personnel Psychology, 60*(2), 303–335.

Vecchio, R. P., & Gobdel, B. C. (1984). The vertical dyad linkage model of leadership—problems and prospects. *Organizational Behavior and Human Performance, 34*(1), 5–20.

Wagner, W. G., Pfeffer, J., & O'Reilly, C. A. (1984). Organizational demography and turnover in top-management groups. *Adminstrative Science Quarterly, 29,* 74–92.

Wang, H., Law, K. S., Hackett, R. D., Wang, D., & Chen, Z. X. (2005). Leader-member exchange as a mediator of the relationship between transformational leadership and followers' performance and organizational citizenship behavior. *Academy of Management Journal, 48*(3), 420–432.

Wat, D., & Shaffer, M. A. (2005). Equity and relationship quality influences on organizational citizenship behaviors—the mediating role of trust in the supervisor and empowerment. *Personnel Review, 34*(4), 406–422.

Watson, D., Clark, L. A., & Tellegen, A. (1988). Development and validation of brief measures of positive and negative affect: The PANAS scales. *Journal of Personality and Social Psychology, 54,* 1063–1070.

Wayne, S. J., & Ferris, G. R. (1990). Influence tactics, affect, and exchange quality in supervisor subordinate interactions—a laboratory experiment and field-study. *Journal of Applied Psychology, 75*(5), 487–499.

Wayne, S. J., & Liden, R. C. (1995). Effects of impression management on performance ratings—a longitudinal-study. *Academy of Management Journal, 38*(1), 232–260.

Wayne, S. J., Shore, L. M., Bommer, W. H., & Tetrick, L. E. (2002). The role of fair treatment and rewards in perceptions of organizational support and leader-member exchange. *Journal of Applied Psychology, 87*(3), 590–598.

Wayne, S. J., Shore, L. M., & Liden, R. C. (1997). Perceived organizational support and leader-member exchange: A social exchange perspective. *Academy of Management Journal, 40*(1), 82–111.

Weick, K. (1979). *The social psychology of organizing.* Reading, MA: Addison-Wesley.

Wilson, K. S., Sin, H.-P., & Conlon, D. E. (2010). What about the leader in leader-member exchange? The impact of resource exchanges and substitutability on the leader. *Academy of Management Review, 35*(3), 358–372.

Wonderlic, & Associates. (1983). *Wonderlic personnel test manual.* Northfield, IL: E. F. Wonderlic & Associates.

Yukl, G. P. (1990). *Managerial Practices Survey.* Manus Associates.

Zhang, Z., Wang, M., & Shi, J. (2012). Leader-follower congruence in proactive personality and work outcomes: The mediating role of leader-member exchange. *Academy of Management Journal, 55*(1), 111–130.

Leader and Follower Personality and LMX

Birgit Schyns

Abstract

This chapter reviews the literature around leader and follower personality and how they are related to leader and follower ratings of Leader–Member Exchange (LMX). The majority of LMX research assesses LMX from a follower point of view, but some work is available on leader ratings of LMX. With regard to the Big Five, follower characteristics seem more relevant to LMX ratings than leader characteristics. Although a secure attachment style of both leader and follower seems to be conducive to LMX, there is some argument that combinations of attachment styles can be positive for LMX in the shorter or longer run. Future research into the negative characteristics of leaders and followers and their effect on LMX ratings is encouraged, as is research into the subdimensions of the concept.

Key Words: Leader–Member Exchange, personality, Big Five, Attachment style, toxic triangle, consensus, agreement

Introduction

One of the main characteristics of leader–member exchange (LMX), which differentiates this approach from other approaches, is its focus on both leaders and followers and their dyadic relationship. While LMX research has extensively focused on outcomes of this relationship, including several meta-analyses (Gerstner & Day, 1997; Ilies, Nahrgang, & Morgeson, 2007), less is known about how these relationships emerge (Nahrgang, Morgeson, & Ilies, 2009). However, given the positive results of LMX, it would be interesting to find out more about what contributes to a good relationship quality between a leader and a follower. Antecedents of LMX in general are addressed elsewhere in this book (see Nahrgang & Seo, this volume). The focus of this chapter is specifically on the personality of leaders and followers and the impact of this on LMX.

When thinking about LMX and personality, the first question is: *Whose LMX and whose personality?* In terms of LMX, one of the stable results found in the literature is that the agreement between

leader and follower perspectives on their mutual relationship is rather low (Gerstner & Day, 1997; Sin, Nahrgang, & Morgeson, 2009). Although it is beyond the scope of this chapter to investigate in detail the reasons for this lack of agreement, it is something to keep in mind when thinking about leader- and follower-related antecedents. That is, antecedents have the potential to influence each perspective on LMX differently and they can have different effects on a mutual perspective of LMX.

In the first part of this chapter, I will review LMX from an individual level point of view, that is, looking into how the personalities of leaders and followers are related to follower- or leader-rated LMX. Very often in LMX research, only the followers' views of LMX are taken into account. However, this is only part of the picture. Here, I want to explore how far personality is related to the perception of LMX from a follower's point of view and a leaders' point of view. Research into individualized leadership (Yammarino & Dansereau, 2002) argues that leaders and followers base their evaluations of their mutual relationship on different dimensions. This can also mean that those different evaluations of LMX can have different antecedents. In this review, I will look at the evidence and incorporate both perspectives. As LMX from a leader's point of view is less often researched, some of these considerations are suggestions for future research. In addition, a leader's or a follower's personality does not function in isolation of each other. Thus, similarity between leader and follower as well as interactions of leader and follower personality on LMX evaluations can be explored. In line with research into the effect of consensus among followers in their ratings of LMX (e.g., Liden, Erdogan, Wayne, & Sparrowe, 2006 and Schyns, 2006), I will also explore how follower consensus in personality can serve as an antecedent of LMX.

Thus, this chapter reviews and extends LMX work on agreement between leader and follower personality and similarity among followers' personality of the same leader (consensus). Research in this area is rather scarce but important given the lack of agreement in LMX perspective that is found in the literature (e.g., Gerstner & Day, 1997 and Sin, Nahrgang, & Morgeson, 2009) and the quest for LMX excellence (consensus among followers and agreement between leader and follower on a high-quality LMX relationship; Schyns & Day, 2010). Questions guiding this part include the following: How does similarity in personality or the interaction between personality characteristics among followers and between leaders and followers have an impact on LMX (and whose LMX, the leader's or the follower's)? Which (leader/follower) personality characteristics impact LMX agreement and consensus?

In this chapter, I also outline what we do not yet know in terms of personality and LMX. One gap that seems quite apparent when reading LMX research is that there is very little research into negative personality and LMX. Do leaders or followers manipulate LMX relationships based on their personality characteristics? This is interesting as LMX relationships have mainly been investigated from a positive point of view and that includes the research into antecedents of LMX. It is also interesting in light of different perspectives of LMX, as negative traits might aim to manipulate the *other's* perception of the LMX relationship, while one's own view of the relationship remains instrumental and negative. A further question here is: Can LMX relationships result from similarity in negative personality characteristics, such as Machiavellianism?

The chapter is organized along the lines of levels of personality, starting with leader personality, continuing with follower personality, and concluding with issues of agreement and consensus.

Individual Level: Leader Personality

The review of existing work starts with a look at leader personality. Here, I review which characteristics of leaders are deemed to be relevant for establishing and maintaining LMX relationships. Although LMX theory states that both partners contribute to the mutual relationship (Graen & Uhl-Bien, 1995), some scholars argue that leaders initiate the relationship (Graen, 2003; Graen & Scandura, 1987). As LMX development is reviewed in a different chapter (see Nahrgang & Seo, 2015), I will not focus specifically on how leader personality influences the development of relationships over time or how this might change in the course of cooperation. In terms of leader–follower relationships from a leader's point of view, two perspectives seem relevant: Which personality characteristics make it more likely to establish and maintain relationships with each follower (Schyns, Maslyn, & Veldhoven, 2012) and which ones help them to establish and maintain relationships with many followers (e.g., in the context of large spans of control; Schyns, 2012). Most research focuses on leader personality and follower-rated LMX (e.g., Schyns, Maslyn, & Veldhoven, 2012).

Big Five

The most researched personality characteristics in terms of their relationship to LMX are the Big Five: Neuroticism, Extraversion, Openness, Agreeableness, and Conscientiousness. Looking at leaders only and which types of individuals are more prone to having good relationships, it is not surprising that many researchers argue that leaders who are agreeable are most likely to build and maintain positive relationships with their followers (e.g., Sears & Hackett, 2011). At the same time, leaders who are high on some of the Big Five (and low on others) are regarded as more likely to establish and maintain good quality relationships with a larger number of followers or across social distances (Schyns, 2012; Schyns et al., 2012).

Agreeableness is one of the Big Five that seems particularly relevant in LMX relationships (Bernerth, Armenakis, Feild, Giles, & Walker, 2007a). Leaders high in agreeableness are more likely to establish and maintain good quality relationships with each follower (Bernerth et al., 2007a), but also are more likely to be able to sustain a larger number of relationships (Schyns et al., 2012). Indeed, recent empirical evidence supports this idea. Sears and Hackett (2011) found that leader agreeableness was significantly related to follower-rated LMX (see also Nahrgang, Morgeson, & Ilies, 2009). However, Schyns et al. (2012) found that leader agreeableness is related to the follower-rated LMX dimensions affect and respect (but not to loyalty and contribution) but did not positively moderate the relationship between span of control and LMX. Nahrgang (2009) found significant correlations between leader agreeableness and leader-rated LMX only at later stages of the relationship. Here, agreeable leaders might generally view relationships as more positive. The relationship between leader agreeableness and follower-rated LMX was not significant. Thus, leader agreeableness seems to be related to (some dimensions of) follower- and leader-rated LMX.

As Schyns et al. (2012) argue, leaders who are extraverted communicate more and thus should find it easier to have positive relationships with followers. However, they found that extraversion was related to only one LMX dimension, that is, loyalty. Nahrgang et al. (2009) also investigated the role of leader extraversion in LMX relationships. They found that leader extraversion was related to leader-rated LMX at all four measurement points. Conversely, it was related to follower-rated LMX only at measurement point 3 of 4. Bernerth et al. (2007a) found no relationship between supervisor extraversion and follower-rated LMX. Therefore, leader extraversion seems to be related to leader-rated LMX more than to follower-rated LMX. This is interesting as it might mean that extravert leaders overestimate the quality of relationships they have with their followers.

Bernerth et al. (2007a) assumed that leader neuroticism would be negatively related to follower-rated LMX due to the emotional instability that comes with it. However, they found no empirical support for this assumption. It is difficult to judge how leader neuroticism would be related to leader-rated LMX, but possibly it is negatively related due to the emotional instability that might lead to a more negative view of relationships. As a consequence, leader neuroticism seems to be unrelated to follower-rated LMX and we do not know anything about its relationship to leader-rated LMX. Potentially, therefore, this personality trait is less relevant for LMX relationships than theoretically assumed.

With respect to leader conscientiousness, Bernerth et al. (2007a) argue that conscientious leaders should be more likely to build good quality relationships (from a follower perspective) than their nonconscientious counterparts as their interest in performance will make them engage more with their followers. Their results support this notion. Schyns et al. (2012), however, found negative relationships between leader conscientiousness and the follower-rated LMX dimensions loyalty and contribution. This could be due to a perceived strong achievement motivation of those leaders that followers might rate negatively. We do not know empirically how leader conscientiousness is related to leader-rated LMX. Based on the arguments of Bernerth et al. (2007a), we could assume that at least for high-performing followers, conscientious leaders will rate LMX higher as they would contribute to the group performance, which conscientious leaders should rate positively. So far, the results for leader conscientiousness and LMX seem mixed. For leader-rated LMX, the relationship might depend on follower performance. Further research is needed to look into this relationship and the process through which it functions.

Bernerth et al. (2007a) argue that leaders who are more open to experience are more likely to see and accept followers' offers for relationship exchanges. Their results, however, do not support this assumption. Their argument would indicate that leaders high in openness to experience view their relationships as more positive, but we do not have any empirical evidence for that. Consequently, the results for leader openness to experience and LMX seem to suggest a lack of relationship (at least for the follower perspective), although a theoretical argument would support a positive relationship.

Finally, Goodwin, Bowler, and Whittington (2009) constructed a combined instrument of personality adding up five items to assess the Big Five. They found that leader personality was significantly related to follower-rated LMX but not to leader-rated LMX. Due to the nature of this research, it is not clear from which aspects of leader personality this positive relationship emerges.

Conclusions: Big Five personality of leaders and LMX ratings. In terms of leader personality, agreeableness seems to be the most relevant personality characteristic for both leader- and follower-rated LMX. Results for other Big Five dimensions are at best mixed, and often other personality characteristics were shown to be unrelated to LMX ratings.

Attachment Style

Attachment styles describe the way in which individuals are able to form relationships with significant others (Ainsworth, 1967; Mikulincer & Shaver, 2005). The research differentiates between secure attachment styles, in which individuals have few problems becoming close to others and are able to trust them in relationships, and insecure attachments styles. There are two different insecure attachment styles: avoidant, in which individuals cope with their insecurities by retreating emotionally from others (Mikulincer & Shaver, 2007), and anxious, in which individuals cope with their insecurity by being clingy (Mikulincer & Shaver, 2007). These attachment styles are grounded in childhood experience and go back to early experiences of reactions of parents toward the child's needs (Ainsworth, 1967; Bowlby, 1982). Attachment styles are still activated in other relationships in adulthood, including romantic relationships (Mikulincer & Shaver, 2005) and leader–follower relationships (Richards & Hackett, 2012). The latter has been regarded as important, as leaders are sometimes seen as similar to parent figures (Keller & Cacioppe, 2001). However, there is also an argument that attachment styles can differ over different types of relationships, including relationships at work, depending on the experiences with these particular types of relationships (Overall, Fletcher, & Friesen, 2003). In general, insecure attachments styles are negatively related to relationship satisfaction (Mikulincer & Shaver, 2007).

Schyns (2012) argues that insecure leaders will find it difficult to establish and maintain good quality LMX relationships with (many) followers. Avoidant leaders will not even strive to do so and will reject their followers' attempts to form relationships with them. This should lead to low ratings of LMX from both perspectives. According to Davidovitz, Mikulincer, Shaver, Izsak, and Popper (2007), avoidant leaders rate themselves low in emotional-focused leader self-efficacy and low in prosocial leader motives. Both are likely to negatively impact LMX ratings by followers and are conceptually close enough to LMX to lead to the assumption that avoidant leaders would also rate LMX lower. Since avoidant individuals prefer to work alone and to avoid social relationships as well as conflict, Richards and Hackett (2012) argue that leaders with an avoidant attachment style are less likely to build good quality relationships with their followers, due to their preference and also their behavior. This is likely to lead to lower leader-rated LMX (due to preferences) and lower follower-rated LMX (due to the related behavior). Empirically, however, they could not confirm this relationship.

Kafetsios, Athanasiadou, and Dimou (2013) investigated the role of leader and member attachment styles on emotion regulation and affective outcomes at work. Insecure leaders and followers report higher negative and lower positive affect as well as lower job satisfaction (although some of the coefficients were very low) than secure leaders. They were surprised to find that supervisor avoidance was positively related to positive affect and negatively related to negative affect for followers high in suppression. They argue that this could be due to the particular implicit leadership theories in the context they investigated. This could be an important point to take into account when investigating leader–member relationships, namely that context-specific implicit leadership theories can change the effects of attachment styles on LMX.

Anxious leaders are likely to try very hard to establish relationships but might at the same time not trust their followers (Keller & Cacioppe, 2001) and thus, in the long run, good quality relationships will not be likely, due to a frustration of the leader's attachment needs. This should again lead to lower LMX ratings from both perspectives, but likely not from the beginning of the relationship. Especially, anxious leaders are likely to positively evaluate the followers at first, due to their need to establish a relationship. Richards and Hackett (2012) argue that leaders with an anxious attachment style are less likely to trust their followers. Although they continue to argue from a followers' point of view, the mechanism of low trust and consequent behaviors that obstruct the development of LMX relationships, such as the likely resulting lack of delegation, will lead to low-quality LMX relationships rated from both perspectives if the leader is anxiously attached. Empirically, they did not find a relationship between leader anxiety and leader- or follower-rated LMX.

According to Davidovitz et al. (2007), anxious leaders rate themselves high in control and self-enhancing leader motives, which are unlikely to be conducive to LMX from their point of view. Followers rated their anxious leaders as more personalized; again this is unlikely to be conducive to LMX ratings this time from a follower's point of view. However, leader anxious attachment style was positively related to follower ratings of their own socioemotional functioning. The study by Davidovitz et al. (2007) seems to point into the direction of more negative effects of avoidant rather than anxious leaders.

Since secure attachment style is defined as a lack of insecurity, these issues should not play a role in secure leaders, so they should be able to form good relationships with their followers. In principle, this should be the case for LMX measured from both perspectives. However, as I discuss below, particular combinations of attachment style might affect the ratings from followers of secure leaders negatively.

Conclusions: Leaders' attachment style and LMX ratings. Theoretically and empirically, securely attached leaders are most likely to establish and maintain positive LMX relationships with their followers. For anxious leaders, LMX quality, as rated by themselves and their followers, is likely to deteriorate, even though it might be positive in the beginning of the relationship. Avoidant leaders are unlikely to build good quality relationships with their followers.

Self-Evaluations and Proactivity

Most research involving LMX and self-efficacy looks into follower self-efficacy as a result of LMX (e.g., Schyns, Paul, Mohr, & Blank, 2005). Schyns (2012, p. 145) argues, however, that "leaders who are more confident about their job—that is, those that have a higher occupational self-efficacy belief—will find it easier to uphold good LMX relationships." In her view, this is because of better communication due to more available resources for leaders high in self-efficacy (i.e., they do not have to worry as much about other aspects of their performance). Murphy and Ensher (1999) found indeed that (female) leaders' self-efficacy was related to follower- and leader-rated LMX. Similarly, Sears and Hackett (2011) found that leader core self-evaluations are related to follower-rated LMX. Zhang, Wang, and Shi (2012) found that leader proactivity was related to follower-rated LMX in a study of proactivity congruence.

Conclusions: Leaders' self-evaluations/proactivity and LMX ratings. Due to their positive nature in terms of being confident about their job, leaders' self-evaluations are likely to be positively related to both leader- and follower-rated LMX. Figure 7.1 summarizes the conclusions from this chapter.

The personality characteristics reviewed in the previous section are mainly positive characteristics. This reflects current research into LMX in its positive focus (similar to other leadership research, see Schyns & Schilling, 2013). Only a few studies have investigated negative characteristics and LMX and those that do seem to focus mainly on follower

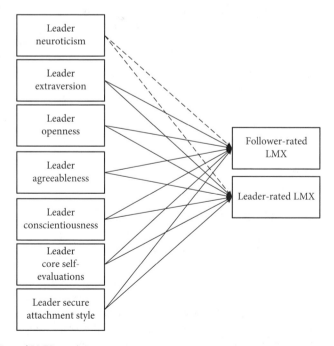

Fig. 7.1 Leader personality and LMX.

Note: Dotted lines denote a negative relationship and solid lines denote a positive relationship.

characteristics (Srivastava & Adams, 2011; Vecchio, 2005). This gap and its relevance are discussed further in the future research section.

Individual Level: Follower Personality

In LMX theory and research, the follower plays an important part in establishing and maintaining LMX relationships. Hence, it is important to investigate how followers' personality shapes LMX relationships. Even if leaders make the initial offer of a good quality relationship (Graen, 2003; Graen & Scandura, 1987), followers' different personality characteristics will make them more or less likely to buy into this relationship.

Big Five

Generally, agreeableness seems to be related to the ability to establish and maintain relationships (Asendorpf & Wilpers, 1998). We can assume that for followers high in agreeableness, it is easier to have a good relationship quality with their leader and that leaders find it easy to have a good relationship with agreeable followers. In that sense, we would assume that agreeableness is related to both follower- and leader-rated LMX. Empirical evidence is slightly mixed, although most results seem to support the notion that follower agreeableness is related to follower-rated LMX (Kamdar & Van Dyne, 2007; Sears & Hackett, 2011). However, Bernerth et al. (2007a) found that follower agreeableness was not significantly related to leader- or follower-rated LMX. In Nahrgang et al.'s (2009) study, only the relationship between follower agreeableness and follower-rated LMX at Time 1 was significant but not for other points in time. They could not find a relationship between follower agreeableness and leader-rated LMX. Hence, theoretical considerations and empirical evidence point toward a positive relationship between follower agreeableness and follower-rated LMX. There is little evidence for a relationship between follower agreeableness and leader-rated LMX, although theoretically we would assume this to be the case.

Follower extraversion should be related to LMX as extraverted followers should be more open to other people and find it easier to engage with them. Empirically, indeed, Nahrgang et al. (2009) found a positive correlation between follower extraversion and follower-rated LMX for several time points. The same was true for follower extraversion and leader-rated LMX, apart from Time 1. Bernerth et al. (2007a) also found a positive relationship between follower extraversion and follower-rated LMX. Therefore, theoretical considerations and empirical evidence point toward a positive relationship between follower extraversion and follower-rated LMX. The relationship between follower extraversion and leader-rated LMX is also positive, probably because extraverted followers find it easier to engage leaders in relationships, thus leading to higher leader-rated LMX.

As can be expected, Bernerth et al. (2007a) found a negative correlation between follower neuroticism and follower-rated LMX. We can assume that neurotic followers have a generally more negative view of relationships. Because neuroticism is connected to emotional instability, this trait is not conducive to forming relationships. Therefore, the same negative relationship between follower neuroticism and LMX should be found for leader-rated LMX. Thus, although there is little empirical evidence yet, follower neuroticism is likely to be negatively related to LMX from both perspectives.

With respect to conscientiousness, Kamdar and Van Dyne (2007) found a positive relationship between co-worker-rated conscientiousness and follower-rated LMX. The results are confirmed by Bernerth et al. (2007a) for both leader- and follower-rated LMX. This is likely due to the fact that conscientiousness is related to performance, which should be conducive to establishing leader–follower relationships. From the follower's point of view, a positive relationship with their leader will be part of their striving for positive achievement, and from the leader's point of view, conscientious followers tend to perform better and are thus likely to be regarded more positively. It therefore seems that LMX is positively related to follower conscientiousness from both perspectives.

Bernerth et al. (2007a) found that follower openness for experience is negatively related to follower-rated LMX. This was in contrast to the positive relationship they assumed based on the assumption that people who are open are also more open to relationships. They speculate that this could be due to those employees being seen as more creative and may be less reliable. However, it is necessary to keep in mind that this result refers to follower-rated LMX, not leader-rated LMX. Based on these assumptions, theoretically, a positive relationship between follower openness to experience and leader-rated LMX would be expected. Empirical evidence is still missing on this relationship. Why the relationship found between follower openness to experience and follower-rated LMX was negative is not quite clear. More research is needed to determine how and why openness to experience is related to LMX and how the mechanisms for this relationship might differ based on leader and follower perspectives.

Conclusions: Big Five personality of followers and LMX ratings. In comparison to leader personality, follower personality seems to be more relevant for LMX ratings, interestingly for both leader and follower ratings. Extraversion, conscientiousness, and neuroticism (negative) were all related to both LMX perspectives and agreeableness was related to follower-rated LMX. Only the results for openness were counterintuitive, as a negative relationship to follower-rated LMX was found.

Attachment Style

Attachment styles are not only relevant in leaders but also to followers, even when assuming that leaders initiate LMX. Arguably, secure followers should find it easy to accept a leader's offer for a good quality relationship as they tend to trust (significant) others and have no problems with closeness. Avoidant followers, on the other hand, are more likely to reject any offer to establish a relationship (but see below for interactions between attachment styles), leading to both leader and follower rating LMX as low quality. Anxious followers are likely to eagerly take up the offer for a good quality relationship initially, but are likely to be frustrated at a later stage when the leader cannot fulfill their attachment needs. Therefore, they might rate the LMX relationship lower in the long run. As the relationship is likely to actually deteriorate, it is likely that the same will be true for leader ratings in the longer run.

Although not in the context of LMX, Keller Hansbrough (2012) found that anxious participants of a video study perceived transformational leadership in nontransformational leaders, whereas avoidant participants did not. Staudigl and Schyns (2014) could replicate these results in a vignette study and in a field study (followers rating their own leaders), but only for avoidant participants. Similarly, we can assume that anxious followers "see" LMX, whether or not it is there, and avoidants do not, whether or not it is there.

Richards and Hackett (2012) argue that anxious followers do not (1) trust their leaders and (2) show behaviors such as a lack of independence that will deter leaders from building a high-quality LMX relationship with them (leader perspective). At the same time, this likely reactive withdrawal will confirm the follower's frustrated attachment needs

and lead to lower follower-rated LMX. Empirically, however, they did not find a relationship between follower anxiety and leader- or follower-rated LMX.

Similar to leader avoidance, follower avoidance is likely to lead to lower LMX ratings from both perspectives according to Richards and Hackett (2012). They found that this is indeed the case with follower avoidance being negatively related to both leader- and follower-rated LMX. Davidovitz et al. (2007) found that avoidant followers rate their leaders low in task- and emotion-related leadership self-efficacy, confirming the negative view avoidant individuals have of others, making it unlikely for them to rate their LMX with their leaders highly. Follower avoidance was also negatively related to their own socioemotional functioning, making it less likely that their leaders rate their LMX with them positively.

Conclusions: Followers' attachment style and LMX ratings. Although theoretically both insecure attachment styles should negatively impact LMX relationships, it seems that empirically, this is only the case for avoidant attachment style. Contrary to assumptions, anxious followers might "keep trying" with their leaders and thus rate LMX positively.

Self-Evaluations and Proactivity

Since self-evaluations are related to work-related performance (Judge & Bono, 2001), it is likely that followers' self-evaluations will at least be positively related to their leader's rating of LMX. According to Sears and Hackett (2011), follower core self-evaluations are related to follower-rated LMX because followers will be motivated and this will foster positive exchanges. They confirmed this assumption. Harris, Harris, and Eplion (2007) found a nonsignificant relationship between follower self-esteem and follower-rated LMX (but see Vecchio, 2005, for a positive relationship between follower self-esteem and follower-rated LMX), but a positive one for locus of control.

Follower proactivity should be positively related to leader-rated LMX as leaders are likely to see follower proactivity as a positive exchange unit. Zhang et al. (2012) confirmed this empirically. It should also be positively related to follower-rated LMX, but here it could actually be an outcome of a positive relationship, in so far as followers who trust their leaders more are more likely to show initiative. Li, Liang, and Crant (2010) indeed found a positive relationship between follower proactivity and follower-rated LMX (see also Joo & Ready, 2012, for a similar result).

Conclusions: Followers' self-evaluations/proactivity and LMX ratings. Both self-evaluations and proactivity are positively related to both perspectives of LMX. For leader-rated LMX, this could be due to higher follower performance, and for follower-rated LMX, it could be due to a generally higher motivation. Figure 7.2 summarizes the results for this section on follower personality.

Relationship Level: Similarity

Some of the research into leader–member similarity focuses on demographic similarity rather than personality (e.g., Bauer & Green, 1996 and Liden, Wayne, & Stilwell, 1993). There is little research yet into personality similarity and LMX relationship. Oren, Tziner, Sharoni, Amor, and Alon (2012) found that leader–follower similarity is negatively related to LMX as rated by followers. Zhang et al. (2012) found congruence effects for leader–follower proactivity on follower-rated LMX. However, with regard to the Big Five as well as core self-evaluations, it can be assumed that similarity in personality will enhance LMX relationships as seen from both perspectives. Neuroticism might be the one exception: When both supervisor and follower are emotionally unstable, it is unlikely that a good quality relationship can emerge (see Figure 7.3).

Relationship Level: Interaction of Leader and Follower Personality

The assumption about the effect of a relationship between similarity in personalities of leaders and followers and LMX ratings is based on similarity–attraction. However, for attachment styles, this assumption is not valid. This is easy to grasp when thinking about the LMX relationship between an avoidant follower and an avoidant leader, which is very unlikely to be positive or to even exist.

Attachment Styles

Research into romantic relationships has shown that there are interaction effects between the attachment styles of partners (Cohn, Silver, Cowan, Cowan, & Pearson, 1992, for insecure couples), although some argue that their own attachment style is more relevant for their own behavior than the combination of attachment styles of partners (Wampler, Shi, Nelson, & Kimball, 2003). For both partners to be secure seems an ideal combination, as in this case both partners have a positive view of self and others which is conducive to establishing and maintaining relationships (e.g., Senchak & Leonard, 1992). Both anxious and avoidant individuals are likely to benefit from relationships with secure partners. For anxious

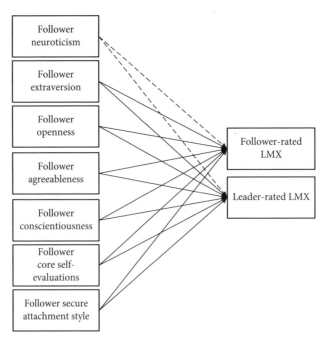

Fig. 7.2 Follower personality and LMX.

Note: Dotted lines denote a negative relationship and solid lines denote a positive relationship.

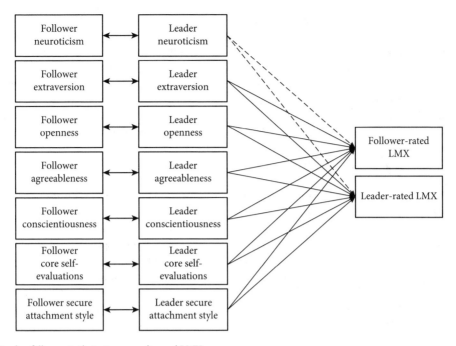

Fig. 7.3 Leader–follower similarity in personality and LMX.

Note: Dotted lines denote a negative relationship and solid lines denote a positive relationship.

individuals, the secure partner can make them feel more secure in their attachment needs. For avoidant individuals, a secure partner can become a safe haven for potentially being able to learn to trust more in relationships (see changes in attachment styles according to Kirkpatrick & Davis, 1994; see also Mikulincer & Shaver, 2007). A frequent combination of partners is anxious and avoidant (Kirkpatrick & Davis, 1994; but see Frazier, Byer, Fischer, Wright, & DeBord, 1996). However, this is a combination least likely to lead to a long-term satisfactory relationship, as the avoidant partner will not be able to meet the anxious partner's needs, who then in turn will become more "needy" and "clingy," leading to a further retreat from the avoidant partner (see Mikulincer & Shaver, 2007, for a summary). The combination of avoidant–avoidant seems very rare (Kirkpatrick & Davis, 1994), probably due to the fact that if both partners are not seeking out relationships, it is unlikely that a relationship develops. The same seems to be true for anxious–anxious combinations (Kirkpatrick & Davis, 1994). Insecure partners seem to violate the expectations of the other insecure partner (Kirkpatrick & Davis, 1994).

As I argued above, many researchers believe that attachment style research can be transferred to a leader–follower relationship (Thomas, Martin, Epitropaki, Guillaume, & Lee, 2013) as well as to many other types of relationships (Overall et al., 2003). It is therefore interesting to explore how this fundamental approach to relationships influences leader–follower dyadic interactions.

Thomas et al. (2013) argue that attachment incongruence between leaders and followers should lead to a lower LMX quality relationship. This is based on prior research into romantic relationships as outlined above. They, however, also refer to hierarchies of attachment representations (Overall et al., 2003). This means that there are "default heuristics," that is, a stable attachment style; "domain-specific attachment representations," which relate to different types of relationships; and "relationship-specific working models," which are models relating to individual-specific relationships with different people (Thomas et al., 2013, p. S66). In the context of leader–member relationships, this can be applied in such a way that those relationships will be influenced by a general attachment style, a learned attachment representation of leader–follower relationships, as well as models of the current leader–member relationship. Ideally, therefore, attachment congruence should be explored on different levels of attachment hierarchy. However, research to date has focused on general attachment styles, that is, how people have related to others in general, not on the relationship type or specific relationships.

Richards and Hackett (2012) argue that attachment styles can interact. Specifically, they argue that leaders and followers who are both anxious and, thus, looking for relationships might form a good quality LMX relationship after all. Their results supported this assumption. In contrast, because both parties are trying to avoid closeness, Richards and Hackett (2012) argue that when both leader and follower are avoidant, low LMX quality will result. However, empirically, they could not support this notion. However, it is necessary to keep in mind that Davidovitz et al. (2007) found that avoidant leaders have a negative effect on their followers' mental health, irrespective of followers' attachment style. This might give the leaders' attachment style more weight in LMX relationships and their outcomes, although negative interactions are likely.

Hinojosa, Davis McCauley, Randolph-Seng, and Gardner (2014) set up a number of propositions regarding leader and follower attachment styles and authentic leadership. They explicitly point out the similarities between authentic leadership and LMX with respect to trust, loyalty, and support. On the basis of the similarities between (secure) attachment style and what is needed to build an authentic (leadership) relationship, they argue that the best chances for an authentic leader–follower relationship are present when both parties have a secure attachment style. However, anxious followers might be helped by secure leaders to be able to establish such a bond. The leader–follower avoidant–avoidant combination is unlikely to develop an authentic relationship, although if just one party is avoidant, a relationship can develop over time and potentially with interventions. Hinojosa et al. (2014) also point out the importance of working attachment models, in the sense that attachment styles can be different for different types of relationships (e.g., leader–member

versus parent–child) depending on prior experiences and that attachment styles within a relationship can potentially change. As outlined previously, this is also important for LMX relationships in so far as attachment style specific for a working relationship might be a better concept and predictor for LMX and that longitudinal research could show whether or not or in how far, specific attachment working models can change in LMX relationships. It could be assumed that secure leaders might be able to make insecure followers more secure and thus develop better LMX relationships over time.

Conclusions: Interaction between leaders' and followers' attachment style on LMX ratings. In terms of achieving a good quality relationship, the most promising combination of attachment styles seems to be when both leader and follower are securely attached, specifically with respect to the specific relationship type of leader–follower relations. However, when the leader is secure, potentially anxious and avoidant followers can learn to trust and build a good quality LMX relationship with their leader (see Figure 7.4).

Group Level: Consensus in Follower Personality

Schyns and Day (2010) reviewed and discussed prior work on follower consensus regarding the LMX relationship with their supervisor. They argued that the best results for organizations can be achieved when all followers of one leader agree that they have a high-quality LMX relationship with their leader and their leader agrees with that (LMX excellence). Looking at it from the antecedents' point of view, however, the question is how far followers' similarity regarding personality characteristics can enhance or hinder LMX relationships. In line with prior research, I will focus on the Big Five, attachment styles, and self-evaluations in this section.

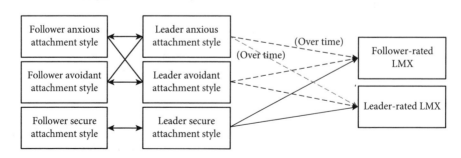

Fig. 7.4 Leader–follower attachment style and LMX.

Note: Dotted lines denote a negative relationship and solid lines denote a positive relationship.

Consensus and the Big Five Personality Characteristics

Agreeableness. Follower agreeableness has been shown to be positively related to dyadic LMX quality (e.g., Sears & Hackett, 2011). This is likely to be a trait that, if shared among followers of one leader, is unequivocally positive for LMX relationships, even at the extreme end.

Extraversion. While extraversion is positively related to individual-level dyadic LMX (Bernerth et al., 2007a; Nahrgang et al., 2009), it is not as clear if the same would be true for a whole group of extraverted followers. This is likely to depend on the context in which the work takes place, but it could be assumed that a leader might simply find that he or she does not have the resources to establish positive exchange relationships with a larger group of extraverted followers, as they might draw more on his or her time than introverted followers. Thus, there might be a cut off, where either too many or too extraverted followers lead to a decrease in the group LMX quality.

(Low) Neuroticism. As outlined above, theoretically, we could expect emotionally stable followers to be more likely to form individual dyadic relationships with their leaders (Bernerth et al., 2007a), and the empirical results support this notion (Bernerth et al., 2007a). It seems unlikely that a group of followers high in neuroticism would agree on their LMX relationships with their leader, thus creating a low consensus in LMX.

Conscientiousness. On an individual level, conscientiousness is likely to be positively related to LMX relationship quality (Kamdar & Van Dyne, 2007), although this might be questionable at the extremes (perfectionism). Conscientiousness is also related to performance (Barrick & Mount, 1991), which in turn is positively related to LMX ratings (Gerstner & Day, 1997). Hence, it is likely that consensus in conscientiousness is positive for group-level LMX, either directly or via enhanced group-level performance.

Openness. There does not seem to be much evidence that openness of individual followers is related to LMX quality (Bernerth et al., 2007a). Similarly, there is no real reason to assume that group-level openness would be beneficial or unfavorable for LMX relationships. However, it is possible to speculate that any similarity among followers regarding their personality might help them cooperate better and thus make LMX relationships with a larger group easier to achieve for a leader.

Consensus in Attachment Styles

Unless all followers share a secure attachment style, it is unrealistic to think that consensus in any of the insecure attachment styles could be positive for good quality exchange relationships. A group of anxiously attached followers would likely quickly exceed the resources of a leader due to their need for confirmation. Consensus in avoidant attachment style would, by definition, lead to low LMX quality exchange as followers would not strive to establish and maintain a relationship with their leader at all.

Consensus in Self-Evaluations

In general, based on individual-level results (see above), it could be assumed that self-esteem, self-efficacy, and core self-evaluations, when shared between followers, are positive for an LMX relationship. Those self-evaluations are linked to performance (Judge & Bono, 2001) and can thus be a positive contributor to LMX via this link. However, similar to the individual level, too high self-evaluations can turn negative (see Vancouver, Thompson, Tischner, & Putka, 2002), in the sense of overrating the self and thus might, in turn, become negative for LMX relationships when self-evaluations do not match actual performance.

Conclusions: Consensus in personality and LMX. Consensus in follower personality might be related to leader-rated LMX due to similarity, leading to better collaboration and better results, and due to similarity–attraction for follower-rated LMX (although only for agreeableness, conscientiousness, self-evaluations, and secure attachment style). Consensus in neuroticism is unlikely to be conducive to either perspective of LMX and so is consensus in insecure attachment style. For extraversion and openness, the effects of consensus are likely to be context specific.

Group Level: Leader Personality Characteristics Predicting Consensus in LMX

Schyns et al. (2012; see also Schyns, 2012, for a theoretical discussion) argued that some leaders are better able to establish and maintain good quality LMX relationships with a larger group of followers (in cases of large work groups/a large span of control). Generally, span of control and LMX seem to be negatively related to each other (Schyns & Blank, 2010). This makes sense, as establishing and maintaining good quality LMX relationships require effort and the resources of leaders are limited (Cogliser, Schriesheim, Scandura, & Gardner, 2009; Dansereau, Graen, & Haga, 1975; Schriesheim, Castro, & Yammarino, 2000). Since Schyns (2012) addresses this issue in more detail, I will just briefly summarize her results here. In terms of the Big Five, Schyns (2012; see also Schyns et al., 2012) argues that specifically, leaders' extraversion and agreeableness make them more likely to be able to establish and maintain a larger number of good quality LMX relationships; thus, leaders can potentially achieve a higher LMX consensus on a high level of LMX. She also argues that leaders high in occupational self-efficacy will be able (due to their higher perceived competence and thus less time dedicated to other tasks) to have more good quality relationships, leading to a higher follower LMX consensus. The same is true for leaders who possess a secure attachment style, as they have no problems with being close to others. Therefore, leaders' personality, ideally a combination of agreeableness, extraversion, occupational self-efficacy, and a secure attachment style, is likely to have an impact on the consensus of their followers regarding LMX ratings on a high level (LMX excellence sensu; Schyns & Day, 2010).

Future Directions

Developments in organizational methods such as multilevel modeling and the Actor–Partner Interdependence Model (APIM) can advance our knowledge about leader and follower personality as predictors of leader- and follower-rated LMX. This is true not only for similarity but also for differences/interaction effects of personality and could lead to a quest for finding ideal combinations of personalities to achieve LMX excellence.

Interaction Rather Than Similarity

Research investigating the agreement between leader and follower mainly focuses on similarity (but see, e.g., Richards & Hackett, 2012, on attachment style interactions). However, an interesting line for future research could involve examining the role of interactions between personality characteristics of leaders and followers and how they can affect LMX relationships. For example, how do leader introversion and follower extraversion interact regarding both leader- and follower-rated LMX? As Thomas et al. (2013) point out, recent methods such as APIM (Cook & Kenny, 2005) can help to disentangle effects of actor versus partner personality on the different relationship perspective ratings.

Patterns

Research into implicit leadership theories has started focusing on patterns of images of leaders and how they are related to leadership perceptions (Foti & Hauenstein, 2007). This approach could also be interesting for leader and follower personality and their perceptions of LMX. For example, apart from separate personality traits, is there a particular combination of traits that makes good quality LMX relationships more likely to develop?

Negative Traits

It is noticeable that most LMX research into the personality of leaders and followers focuses on positive characteristics (for an exception, see Vecchio, 2005). This is also in line with most research focusing on the positive side of LMX relationships (but see Lawrence & Kacmar, 2012, on stress and Mayer, 2004, for outgroup members). This is understandable in that positive relationships is something leaders (and followers) should strive for to achieve positive outcomes (see Schyns & Day, 2010). However, this focus leaves a gap and the question: What happens in leader–follower dyads when one partner or both partners possess negative characteristics? In the following, I develop theoretical considerations as to how negative personality characteristics along the dark triad of Machiavellianism, narcissism, and psychopathy of leaders, followers, or both are likely to affect LMX relationships.

THE DARK TRIAD: LEADERS

A first hunch regarding the effect of dark triad characteristics in leader on LMX relationships might be to say that they are likely to negatively affect the relationship quality. However, the picture might be more nuanced than that.

Leader Machiavellianism. Machiavellianistic leaders possess a manipulative personality (Kessler et al., 2010). In that sense, they might want a positive relationship with a particular follower if they find that they can manipulate this person to their own advantage, leading to a positive leader rating of LMX. However, it can be assumed that over time the follower will understand the underlying motivation of the leader or else the leader might not need the follower anymore and will then cut off the relationship, leading to a low-quality relationship from both perspectives. Therefore, the assumption would be that Machiavellianistic leaders might have good relationship with followers they can manipulate. However, in the longer run, the relationship will deteriorate.

Leader Narcissism. Grijalva, Harms, Newman, Gaddis, and Fraley (2015) point out that "future research should explore the different dyadic relationships that develop between narcissistic leaders and their subordinate" (p. 30). Narcissistic individuals have feelings of grandiosity, entitlement, dominance, and superiority (McFarlin & Sweeney, 2010). Holding a leader position is likely to feed into these feelings and confirm superiority to the individual leader. It seems unlikely that there are conditions under which this leader personality trait can lead to positive LMX relationships as the leader will not accept the follower's relevance and thus not seek out a positive relationship. The followers are also unlikely to seek out a positive relationship with such a leader as that would imply almost complete submission.

Leader Psychopathy. Subclinical levels of psychopathy are characterized by a lack of empathy and high impulsivity, among others. Although that seems to imply that there is little room for positive LMX relationships, the literature implies that psychopaths can be very charming at the beginning of relationships (Babiak & Hare, 2006) if and when it is to their advantage. The follower is unlikely to realize this charm as instrumental in the beginning, making it likely that a (seemingly) positive relationship can result—at least from the follower's point of view. The psychopathic leader himself or herself is less likely to report a positive relationship as relationships are not important to this type of personality. In the long run, when the follower has served his or her purpose, the leader is likely to cut off the relationship. Literature reports that the other party in the relationship is often completely surprised when this happens (Babiak & Hare, 2006). Thus, the positive view of the relationship from the follower's perspective is unlikely to persist for a longer time period due to the expected behavior by the leader.

THE DARK TRIAD: FOLLOWERS

As previously outlined, although some of the LMX literature emphasizes that leaders initiate the LMX relationship (Graen, 2003), the role of the follower in forming and maintaining LMX relationships is widely acknowledged (Graen & Uhl-Bien, 1995). It is therefore interesting to also look further into the dark triad in followers and see how those characteristics contribute to LMX relationships—or hinder them.

Follower Machiavellianism. Similar to Machiavellianistic leaders, Machiavellianistic followers can try to manipulate leaders to their advantage. That means that they would be willing to invest in fostering a positive LMX relationship as long as it is to their advantage. Whether or not the relationship between them and their leader can be positive depends on how successful they are in this manipulation. It can be assumed that leaders might have less to gain from LMX relationships and might be less likely to be manipulated by their followers. However, this is a matter of empirical investigation, probably in line with research into upward influence (e.g., Ansari & Kapoor, 1987).

Follower Narcissism. The traits associated with narcissism make it very unlikely that followers would succeed in having or even aim to have a positive LMX relationship with their leader. The feeling of superiority means that they would not accept the other person as their leader and the leader would be unlikely to accept their needs for superiority.

Follower Psychopathy. Again, the important point to keep in mind about psychopaths is their initial charm. Thus, leaders might be tempted to fall for this charm and assume they have a positive LMX relationship with their psychopathic follower. However, as psychopaths only use other people to progress, the leaders will likely find themselves "dumped" as soon as somebody more important (such as a higher up leader) has been accessed by the charm of the psychopathic follower.

THE DARK TRIAD: SIMILARITY

In a way, looking at leader and follower dark triad personality characteristics as they interact with each other is a very theoretical exercise as these characteristics are rare and, thus, it might be rather unlikely that both the leader and follower possess them. However, we are talking about subclinical levels of these characteristics, which means that they are less rare than clinical levels. Also, they are on a scale, meaning that leaders and followers can have a lower to higher level of these traits. What is perhaps even more important is the potential destructive power that a combination of leader and follower dark triad characteristics has for an organization, making it important to spot the issue even if it is a rare phenomenon.

Leader and Follower Machiavellianism. What happens if both leaders and followers show signs of a manipulative personality? The best answer to this might be that it depends. If they try to manipulate each other, given that they both know what to look out for, the likeliest outcome is a poor LMX relationship quality. However, if they decide to join forces and manipulate others toward joint goals, the relationship quality might actually be quite positive (though likely not in the long run when individual goals became more important again), to the detriment of other members of the organization and the organization as a whole.

Leader and Follower Narcissism. Given the feelings of superiority and the dominance that comes with narcissism, it is unlikely that leaders and followers who both share this personality trait would be able (or even willing) to engage in a positive LMX relationship quality.

Leader and Follower Psychopathy. This may be the most interesting interaction to explore as it is so difficult to predict the effects of shared psychopathy between leaders and followers and, at the same time, the potential explosive nature of two psychopaths in one organization. For initial relationships, the question is whether or not psychopaths detect the superficial charm in others or whether or not they actually care. Given their lack of interest in others, both parties might actually report a low relationship quality, even if their objective is to get along and work in a similar (destructive) direction. Figure 7.5 summarizes this section on the dark triad.

Outlook: Dimensions of Leader–Member Exchange

In this chapter, I have focused on leader and follower personality as antecedents of LMX. However, this review has mainly concentrated on LMX as a general, one-dimensional variable. Not all researchers agree with this approach to conceptualizing LMX. Dienesch and Liden (1986) and Liden and Maslyn (1998) have developed a four-dimensional instrument to assess LMX, consisting of affect, loyalty, professional respect, and contribution. Bernerth, Armenakis, Feild, Giles, and Walker (2007b) have developed an instrument

on Leader–Member Social Exchange which stresses the exchange nature of the relationship more than the relationship quality. Kuvaas, Buch, Dysvik, and Haerem (2012) developed an instrument that differentiates between economic and social leader–member exchange relationships. Looking at the personality characteristics reviewed here, it is possible that different results would emerge for different dimensions (some consideration has been given to this idea in Schyns et al., 2012), so that, for example, agreeableness might be more relevant to social than to economic exchange and so forth. Future research should differentiate between dimensions, where a more accurate picture of what is predictive of which LMX aspect is relevant.

General Conclusions

While we have a good knowledge about outcomes of LMX, including an increasing body of research taking into account multilevel issues such as how consensus in follower LMX is related to outcomes (Liden et al., 2006), or how agreement between leaders and followers on LMX affects outcomes (Cogliser et al., 2009), we still know very little about the antecedents of LMX. In this chapter, I reviewed the body of evidence regarding leader and follower personality and their interaction, and how they are related to LMX. What has become clear in this review is that we need much more research into leaders' and followers' personalities and their effects on LMX. Particularly interesting is the current focus on a rather narrow range of personality characteristics, mainly the Big Five. When research outside the Big Five has been conducted, it still remained focused on positive characteristics, such as self-evaluations or secure attachment styles. This is in line with the general, mainly positive focus of LMX (although there is more research now into stress as an outcome of LMX, Lawrence & Kacmar, 2012, or the effects on outgroup members, Mayer,

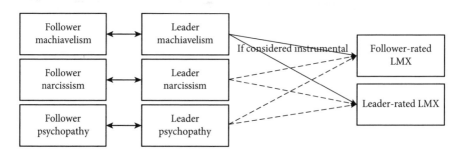

Fig. 6.5 Leader–follower toxic triangle and LMX.

Note: Dotted lines denote a negative relationship and solid lines denote a positive relationship.

2004). This chapter has outlined gaps in the literature and areas for future research. LMX continues to interest researchers and practitioners. It is high time that we find out more about how leaders' and followers' personalities influence the building and maintaining of good relationships.

Acknowledgments

I would like to thank Lena Staudigl for her help with the reference list.

References

Ainsworth, M. D. S. (1967). *Infancy in Uganda: Infant care and the growth of love.* Baltimore, MD: Johns Hopkins University Press.

Ansari, M., & Kapoor, A. (1987). Organizational context and upward influence tactics. *Organizational Behavior and Human Decision Processes, 40,* 39–49.

Asendorpf, J. B., & Wilpers, S. (1998). Personality effects on social relationships. *Journal of Personality and Social Psychology, 74,* 1531–1544. doi: 10.1037/0022-3514.74.6.1531.

Babiak, P., & Hare, R. D. (2006). *Snakes in suits: When psychopaths go to work.* New York: Harper Collins.

Barrick, M. R., & Mount, M. K. (1991). The Big Five personality dimensions and job performance: A meta-analysis. *Personnel Psychology, 44,* 1–26. doi: 10.1111/j.1744-6570.1991.tb00688.x.

Bauer, T., & Green, S. G. (1996). Development of a leader-member exchange: A longitudinal test. *Academy of Management Journal, 39,* 1538–1567. doi: 10.2307/257068.

Bernerth, J. B., Armenakis, A., Feild, H. S., Giles, W. F., & Walker, H. J. (2007a). Is personality associated with perceptions of LMX? An empirical study. *Leadership & Organization Development Journal, 28,* 613–631. doi: 10.1108/01437730710823879.

Bernerth, J. B., Armenakis, A., Feild, H. S., Giles, W. F., & Walker, H. J. (2007b). Leader-member social exchange (LMSX): Development and validation of a scale. *Journal of Organizational Behavior, 28,* 979–1003. doi: 10.1002/job.

Bowlby, J. (1982). *Attachment and loss: Vol. 1. Attachment* (2nd ed.). New York: Basic Books.

Cogliser, C. C., Schriesheim, C. A., Scandura, T. A., & Gardner, W. L. (2009). Balance in leader and follower perceptions of leader-member exchange: Relationships with performance and work attitudes. *Leadership Quarterly, 20,* 452–465.

Cohn, D. A., Silver, D. H., Cowan, C. P., Cowan, P. A., & Pearson, J. (1992). Working models of childhood attachment and couple relationships. *Journal of Family Issues, 13,* 432–449. doi: 10.1177/019251392013004003.

Cook, W., & Kenny, D. (2005). The actor-partner interdependence model: A model of bidirectional effects in developmental studies. *International Journal of Behavioral Development, 29,* 101–109. doi: 10.1080/01650250444000405.

Dansereau, F., Graen, G., & Haga, W. J. (1975). A vertical dyad linkage approach to leadership within formal organizations: A longitudinal investigation of the role making process. *Organizational Behavior and Human Performance, 13,* 46–78. doi: 10.1016/0030-5073(75)90005-7.

Davidovitz, R., Mikulincer, M., Shaver, P. R., Izsak, R., & Popper, M. (2007). Leaders as attachment figures: Leaders' attachment orientations predict leadership-related mental representations and followers' performance and mental health.

Journal of Personality and Social Psychology, 93, 632–650. doi : 10.1037/0022-3514.93.4.632.

Dienesch, R. M., & Liden, R. C. (1986). Leader-member exchange model of leadership: A critique and further development. *Academy of Management Review, 11,* 618–634. doi: 10.2307/258314.

Foti, R. J., & Hauenstein, N. M. A. (2007). Pattern and variable approaches in leadership emergence and effectiveness. *Journal of Applied Psychology, 92,* 347–355. doi: 10.1037/0 021-9010.92.2.347.

Frazier, P. A., Byer, A. L., Fischer, A. R., Wright, D. M., & DeBord, K. A. (1996). Adult attachment style and partner choice: Correlational and experimental findings. *Personal Relationships, 3,* 117–136. doi: 10.1111/j.1475-6811.1996.tb00107.x.

Gerstner, C. R., & Day, D. V. (1997). Meta-analytic review of leader-member exchange theory: Correlates and construct issues. *Journal of Applied Psychology, 82,* 827–844. doi: 10.10 37//0021-9010.82.6.827.

Goodwin, V. L., Bowler, W. M., & Whittington, J. L. (2009). A social network perspective on LMX relationships: Accounting for the instrumental value of leader and follower networks. *Journal of Management, 35,* 954–980. doi: 10.1177/0149206308321555.

Graen, G. (2003). Interpersonal workplace theory at the crossroads: LMX and transformational theory as special case of role making in work organizations. In G. B. Graen (Ed.), *LMX leadership: The series. Vol. 1: Dealing with diversity* (pp. 145–182). Greenwich, CT: Information Age.

Graen, G., & Scandura, T. A. (1987). Toward a psychology of dyadic organizing. *Research in Organizational Behavior, 9,* 175–208.

Graen, G., & Uhl-Bien, M. (1995). Relationship-based approach to leadership: Development of leader-member exchange (LMX) theory of leadership over 25 years: Applying a multi-level multi-domain. *Leadership Quarterly, 6,* 219–247.

Grijalva, E., Harms, P. D., Newman, D., Gaddis, B., & Fraley, R. C. (2015). Narcissism and leadership: A meta-analytic review of linear and nonlinear relationships. *Personnel Psychology 68,* 1–47.

Harris, K., Harris, R., & Eplion, D. (2007). Personality, leader-member exchanges, and work outcomes. *Journal of Behavioral & Applied Management, 8,* 92–107.

Hinojosa, A. S., Davis McCauley, K., Randolph-Seng, B., & Gardner, W. L. (2014). Leader and follower attachment styles: implications for authentic leader–follower relationships. *Leadership Quarterly, 25,* 595–610. doi: 10.1016/j.leaqua.2013.12.002.

Ilies, R., Nahrgang, J. D., & Morgeson, F. P. (2007). Leader-member exchange and citizenship behaviors: A meta-analysis. *Journal of Applied Psychology, 92,* 269–277. doi: 10.1037/0021-9010.92.1.269.

Joo, B.-K. (Brian) & Ready, K. J. (2012). Career satisfaction: The influences of proactive personality, performance goal orientation, organizational learning culture, and leader-member exchange quality. *Career Development International, 17,* 276–295. doi: 10.1108/13620431211241090.

Judge, T. A., & Bono, J. E. (2001). Relationship of core self-evaluations traits—self-esteem, generalized self-efficacy, locus of control, and emotional stability—with job satisfaction and job performance: A meta-analysis. *Journal of Applied Psychology, 86,* 80–92. doi: 10.1037/0021-9010.86.1.80.

Kafetsios, K., Athanasiadou, M., & Dimou, N. (2013). Leaders' and subordinates' attachment orientations, emotion regulation capabilities and affect at work: A multilevel analysis. *Leadership Quarterly, 25*, 512–527. doi: 10.1016/j.leaqua.2013.11.010.

Kamdar, D., & Van Dyne, L. (2007). The joint effects of personality and workplace social exchange relationships in predicting task performance and citizenship performance. *Journal of Applied Psychology, 92*, 1286–1298. doi: 10.1037/0021-9010.92.5.1286.

Keller Hansbrough, T. (2012). The construction of a transformational leader: Follower attachment and leadership perceptions. *Journal of Applied Social Psychology, 42*, 1533–1549. doi: 10.1111/j.1559-1816.2012.00913.x.

Keller, T., & Cacioppe, R. (2001). Leader-follower attachments: Understanding parental images at work. *Leadership & Organization Development Journal, 22*, 70–75.

Kessler, S. R., Bandelli, A. C., Spector, P. E., Borman, W. C., Nelson, C. E., & Penney, L. M. (2010). Re-examining Machiavelli: A three-dimensional model of Machiavellianism in the workplace. *Journal of Applied Social Psychology, 40*, 1868–1896. doi: 10.1111/j.1559-1816.2010.00643.x.

Kirkpatrick, L. A., & Davis, K. E. (1994). Attachment style, gender, and relationship stability: A longitudinal analysis. *Journal of Personality and Social Psychology, 66*, 502–512.

Kuvaas, B., Buch, R., Dysvik, A., & Haerem, T. (2012). Economic and social leader-member exchange relationships and follower performance. *Leadership Quarterly, 23*, 756 765.

Lawrence, E. R., & Kacmar, K. M. (2012). Leader-member exchange and stress: The mediating role of job involvement and role conflict. *Journal of Behavioral & Applied Management, 14*, 39–53.

Li, N., Liang, J., & Crant, J. M. (2010). The role of proactive personality in job satisfaction and organizational citizenship behavior: A relational perspective. *Journal of Applied Psychology, 95*, 395–404. doi: 10.1037/a0018079.

Liden, R. C., & Maslyn, J. M. (1998). Multidimensionality of leader-member exchange: An empirical assessment through scale development. *Journal of Management, 24*, 43–72. doi: 10.1177/014920639802400105.

Liden, R. C., Erdogan, B., Wayne, S. J., & Sparrowe, R. T. (2006). Leader-member exchange, differentiation, and task interdependence: Implications for individual and group performance. *Journal of Organizational Behavior, 27*, 723–746. doi: 10.1002/job.409.

Liden, R. C., Wayne, S. J., & Stilwell, D. (1993). A longitudinal study on the early development of leader-member exchanges. *Journal of Applied Psychology, 78*, 662–674. doi: 10.1037//0021-9010.78.4.662.

Mayer, D. M. (2004). *Are you in or out? A group-level examination of the effects of LMX on justice and customer satisfaction.* Doctoral dissertation, University of Maryland, College Park.

McFarlin, D. & Sweeney, P. D., (2010). The corporate reflecting pool: Antecedents and consequences of narcissism in executives. In T. Hansbrough & B. Schyns (Eds.), *When leadership goes wrong: Destructive leadership, mistakes and ethical failures* (p. 247–303). Charlotte, NC: Information Age Publishing.

Mikulincer, M., & Shaver, P. R. (2003). The attachment behavioral system in adulthood: Activation, psychodynamics, and interpersonal processes. In M. P. Zanna (Ed.), *Advances in experimental social psychology* (Vol. 35, pp. 53–152). New York: Academic Press.

Mikulincer, M., & Shaver, P. R. (2005). Attachment theory and emotions in close relationships: Exploring the attachment-related dynamics of emotional reactions to relational events. *Personal Relationships, 12*, 149–168. doi: 10.1111/j.1350-4126.2005.00108.x.

Mikulincer, M., & Shaver, P. R. (2007). *Attachment in adulthood: Structure, dynamics, and change.* New York: Guilford Press.

Murphy, S., & Ensher, E. (1999). The effects of leader and subordinate characteristics in the development of leader–member exchange quality. *Journal of Applied Social Psychology, 29*, 1371–1394. doi: 10.1111/j.1559-1816.1999.tb00144.x.

Nahrgang, J. D., Morgeson, F. P., & Ilies, R. (2009). The development of leader-member exchanges: Exploring how personality and performance influence leader and member relationships over time. *Organizational Behavior and Human Decision Processes, 108*, 256–266.

Oren, L., Tziner, A., Sharoni, G., Amor, I., & Alon, P. (2012). Relations between leader-subordinate personality similarity and job attitudes. *Journal of Managerial Psychology, 27*, 479–496. doi: 10.1108/02683941211235391.

Overall, N. C., Fletcher, G. J. O., & Friesen, M. D. (2003). Mapping the intimate relationship mind: Comparisons between three models of attachment representations. *Personality and Social Psychology Bulletin, 29*, 1479–1493. doi: 10.1177/0146167203251519.

Richards, D. A., & Hackett, R. D. (2012). Attachment and emotion regulation: Compensatory interactions and leader–member exchange. *Leadership Quarterly, 23*, 686–701. doi: 10.1016/j.leaqua.2012.03.005.

Schriesheim, C. A., Castro, S. L., & Yammarino, F. J. (2000). Investigating contingencies: An examination of the impact of span of supervision and upward controllingness on leader-member exchange using traditional and multivariate within- and between-entities analysis. *Journal of Applied Psychology, 85*, 659–677.

Schyns, B. (2006). Are group consensus in LMX and shared work values related to organizational outcomes? *Small Group Research, 37*, 20–35.

Schyns, B. (2012). The role of distance in leader-member exchange (LMX). In M. C. Bligh & R. E. Riggio (Eds.), *Exploring distance in leader-follower relationships: When near is far and far is near* (pp. 136–154). New York: Routledge.

Schyns, B., & Blank, H. (2010). The limits of interactional leadership: The relationship between leader-member exchange and span of control. In T. Rigotti, S. Korek, & K. Otto (Eds.), *Gesund mit und ohne Arbeit* (pp. 305–314). Lengerich, Germany: Pabst Science Publishers.

Schyns, B., & Day, D. (2010). Critique and review of leader-member exchange theory: Issues of agreement, consensus, and excellence. *European Journal of Work and Organizational Psychology, 19*, 1–29. doi: 10.1080/13594320903024922.

Schyns, B., Maslyn, J. M., & Veldhoven, M. P. M. Van. (2012). Can some leaders have a good relationship with many followers? The role of personality in the relationship between leader-member exchange and span of control. *Leadership & Organization Development Journal, 33*, 594–606. doi: 10.1108/01437731211253046.

Schyns, B., Paul, T., Mohr, G., & Blank, H. (2005). Comparing antecedents and consequences of leader-member exchange and a German working context to findings in the US. *European Journal of Work and Organizational Psychology, 14*, 1–22.

Schyns, B., & Schilling, J. (2013). How bad are the effects of bad leaders? A meta-analysis of destructive leadership and its outcomes. *Leadership Quarterly, 24*, 138–158.

Sears, G. J., & Hackett, R. D. (2011). The influence of role definition and affect in LMX: A process perspective on the personality—LMX relationship. *Journal of Occupational and Organizational Psychology, 84*, 544–564. doi: 10.1348/096317910X492081.

Senchak, M., & Leonard, K. E. (1992). Attachment styles and marital adjustment among newlywed couples. *Journal of Social and Personal Relationships, 9*, 51–64. doi: 10.1177/0265407592091003.

Sin, H.-P., Nahrgang, J. D., & Morgeson, F. P. (2009). Understanding why they don't see eye to eye: An examination of leader-member exchange (LMX) agreement. *Journal of Applied Psychology, 94*, 1048–1057. doi: 10.1037/a0014827.

Srivastava, A., & Adams, J. W. (2011). Relationship between cynicism and job satisfaction: Exploration of mechanisms. *Psychological Reports, 108*, 27–42. doi: http://dx.doi.org.proxy2.lib.umanitoba.ca/10.2466/02.07.09.14.PR0.108.1.27-42.

Staudigl, L. F., & Schyns, B. (2014). Implicit leadership theories, attachment style and leader-member exchange. Paper presented at the meeting of the Society of Industrial and Organizational Psychology in Hawaii.

Thomas, G., Martin, R., Epitropaki, O., Guillaume, Y., & Lee, A. (2013). Social cognition in leader–follower relationships: Applying insights from relationship science to understanding relationship-based approaches to leadership. *Journal of Organizational Behavior, 34*, 63–81. doi: 10.1002/job.

Vancouver, J. B., Thompson, C. M., Tischner, E. C., & Putka, D. J. (2002). Two studies examining the negative effect of self-efficacy on performance. *Journal of Applied Psychology, 87*, 506–516. doi: 10.1037/0021-9010.87.3.506.

Vecchio, R. (2005). Explorations in employee envy: Feeling envious and feeling envied. *Cognition & Emotion, 19*, 69–81. doi: 10.1080/02699930441000148.

Wampler, K. S., Shi, L., Nelson, B. S., & Kimball, T. G. (2003). The adult attachment interview and observed couple interaction: Implications for an intergenerational perspective on couple therapy. *Family Process, 42*, 497–515.

Yammarino, F. J., & Dansereau, F. (2002). Individualized leadership. *Journal of Leadership and Organizational Studies, 9*, 1–11. doi: 10.1177/107179190200900107.

Zhang, Z., Wang, M., & Shi, J. (2012). Leader-follower congruence in proactive personality and work outcomes: The mediating role of leader-member exchange. *Academy of Management Journal, 55*, 111–130. doi: 10.5465/amj.2009.0865.

PART 3

Consequences of LMX

LMX and Work Attitudes: Is There Anything Left Unsaid or Unexamined?

Olga Epitropaki *and* Robin Martin

Abstract

The relationship between Leader–Member Exchange (LMX) and work attitudes has been the focus of numerous LMX studies and meta-analyses. This chapter attempts a closer look into the "black box" of the LMX–work attitudes relationships and reviews existing research focusing on both direct relationships and boundary conditions and explanatory mechanisms. It also includes a summary of existing theoretical perspectives on LMX and explicitly addresses level-of-analysis issues in the LMX and attitudes research. Future research suggestions and theoretical extensions are discussed.

Key Words: LMX, Work attitudes, Job satisfaction, Organizational commitment, Team-member exchange,

LMX and Work Attitudes

Forty years after its initial launch as Vertical Dyad Linkage (VDL) theory (Dansereau, Graen, & Haga, 1975; Graen & Cashman, 1975), Leader–Member Exchange (LMX) theory remains one of the most popular lines of leadership research. As Dihn et al. (2014) point out, LMX is ". . . the archetypal social exchange leader-follower dyadic approach" (p. 39) that focuses on the leader–follower relationship rather than individual leader or follower traits, styles, or behaviors as other leadership theories. The great majority of empirical research on LMX, especially during the initial period from 1975 to 1985— which even now remains dominant—focused on the outcomes or consequences of LMX (i.e., job attitudes, perceptions, and behaviors). The central theoretical premise behind relations between LMX and outcomes is that leader–follower roles based strictly on the employment contract will result in less positive consequences for followers than will roles that have developed beyond what is expected by the employment contract (Liden et al., 1997). Quite simply, followers who receive more information and support from their leader and who engage

in tasks that require challenge and responsibility are expected to have more positive work attitudes and engage in more positive work behaviors than followers whose support is limited to what is required by the employment contract.

A particularly popular strand of research on LMX and outcomes has been the one examining the impact of LMX on job attitudes such as job satisfaction and organizational commitment. Out of the 865 articles on LMX that can be found in PsycInfo in February 2014, 209 of them examine job satisfaction as an outcome and 127 focus on organizational commitment. Prior research has strongly supported the positive effects of LMX on follower job satisfaction (Aryee & Chen, 2006; Epitropaki & Martin, 2005; Lapierre & Hackett, 2007; Liden, Wayne, & Sparrowe, 2000; Major et al., 1995; Mardanov, Heischmidt, & Henson, 2008; Martin et al., 2005; Masterson, Lewis, Goldman, & Taylor, 2000; Murphy & Ensher, 1999) and organizational commitment (Epitropaki & Martin, 2005; Kacmar, Carlson, & Brymer, 1999; Liden et al., 2000; Major et al., 1995; Martin et al., 2005; Schyns et al., 2005; Wayne et al., 1997). Older (e.g., Gerstner & Day,

1997) and recent meta-analyses (Dulebohn et al., 2012; Rockstuhl, Dulebohn, Ang, & Shore, 2012) report similar findings regarding the strength of the relationship between LMX and attitudes. Thus, if the relationship between LMX and job attitudes has been so thoroughly examined in the past and the findings remain consistent over time, should we then consider it as a saturated line of research in the LMX field and move our research focus to different directions? Have we already said and examined everything worth examining about this specific relationship? Have we shed full light on the "black box" of the relationship between LMX and work attitudes? These are the questions, and related ones, that we will try to address in this chapter.

We will first review existing research on LMX and work attitudes and outline its main theoretical underpinnings. We will then highlight limitations of existing research, examine different levels of analysis, and offer suggestions for future work that can further open the black box of the link between LMX attitudes.

Review of Research on LMX and Work Attitudes
Direct Relationships

From the early stages of leadership theorizing and research, its impact on employee work attitudes has been recognized and repeatedly investigated. Although an important body of knowledge has been accumulated in this respect, the absence of solid conclusions and final answers keeps the research interest alive. As Judge and Kammeyer-Mueller (2012) stress, "… job attitudes matter because jobs matter—to people's identities, to their health and to their evaluations of their lives" (p. 344). The premise that attitudes lead to behavior is grounded in the social psychological literature (Fishbein, 1973; Fishbein & Ajzen, 1975). Recent meta-analyses (e.g., Harrison, Newman, & Roth, 2006) challenged prior findings of job attitudes predicting only 3–4% of performance variance (e.g., Locke & Latham, 1990) and have shown that job attitudes predict a higher order behavioral construct of desirable contributions made to one's work role ($r = .59$). Judge et al. (2001) also report a mean true correlation between overall job satisfaction and job performance of .30. Riketta (2008) reports a weak but significant effect of job attitudes on subsequent performance (with baseline performance controlled) of .06 and concludes that job attitudes are more likely to influence performance than vice versa. Further, macrolevel studies have

highlighted the importance of work attitudes not only for individual performance but for organizational performance as well. Specifically, Patterson, West, Lawthom, and Nickell (1997) found that 12% and 13% of the variation between companies in their profitability was explained by variations in job satisfaction and organizational commitment, respectively. Job satisfaction was also found to explain 25% of the variance in company productivity, whereas organizational commitment explained 17% of the variance. Even after controlling for the effects of prior profitability and productivity, work attitudes still had predictive utility regarding performance (in the range of explaining 5–16% of the variance). Schneider, Hanges, Smith, and Salvaggio (2003) also showed that aggregated attitudes were related to organizational performance and further uncovered reciprocal relationships between the two. As implications of work attitudes exceed the microorganizational level, a better understanding of their antecedents such as the leader–follower relationship quality becomes critical for organizational performance and survival in difficult economic conditions.

In this review we will adopt the definition of job attitudes proposed by Judge and Kammeyer-Mueller (2012) as "evaluations of one's job that express one's feelings toward, beliefs about, and attachment to one's job" (p. 344). In accordance with this definition, we will focus on constructs with an evaluative component such as job satisfaction and organizational commitment and will not examine perceptions (e.g., justice), intentions (e.g., turnover intentions), motivational constructs (e.g., work engagement and well-being), or mental well-being (e.g., strain) that will be discussed in other chapters of this handbook.

Job Satisfaction

Locke (1976) defined job satisfaction in a general sense as a "… pleasurable or positive emotional state resulting from the appraisal of one's job or job experiences" (p. 1300). As such, job satisfaction is presumed to be a global construct encompassing specific facets of satisfaction, such as satisfaction with work, pay, supervision, promotion opportunities, and working conditions. Clegg and Wall (1981) viewed job satisfaction as representing a positive affective orientation toward the job, or to intrinsic and extrinsic facets of the job. Job satisfaction has sometimes also been described as the degree to which individuals like their job (e.g., Agho, Price, & Mueller, 1992).

As far as research on leadership and job satisfaction is concerned, the relationship between the two is of continuing interest. Early studies assessed relationships between traditional leadership behaviors (e.g., initiating structure and consideration) and follower job satisfaction (Coltrin & Glueck, 1977; Griffin & Bateman, 1986; Petty & Bruning, 1980; Schriesheim & Murphy, 1976). Several studies also report a positive relationship between dominant leadership constructs such as transformational leadership and job satisfaction (e.g., Avolio & Howell, 1992; Bass, 1985; Braun et al., 2013; Hater & Bass, 1988; Seltzer & Bass, 1990; Seltzer et al., 1989).

Job satisfaction has been repeatedly investigated as a consequence of LMX (e.g., Danserau et al., 1975; Major et al., 1995; Schriesheim et al., 1992; Seers & Graen, 1984) and positive relations are reported. Gerstner and Day's (1997) meta-analysis reported an average correlation of .46 between LMX and job satisfaction. Similarly, Dulebohn et al.'s (2012) recent meta-analysis reports a significant relationship between LMX and job satisfaction ($\rho = .49$) as well as satisfaction with the supervisor ($\rho = .68$). They reviewed 88 studies that examined the relationship between LMX and overall job satisfaction (e.g., Aryee & Chen, 2006; Epitropaki & Martin, 2005; Erdogan & Enders, 2007; Lapierre & Hackett, 2007; Liden, Wayne, & Sparrowe, 2000; Major et al., 1995; Mardanov, Heischmidt, & Henson, 2008; Martin et al., 2005; Masterson et al., 2000; Murphy & Ensher, 1999), 32 studies that reported significant positive effects of LMX on satisfaction with supervisor (e.g., Graen & Novak, 1982), and eight studies that examined satisfaction with pay as an outcome of LMX (e.g., Sparrowe, 1994; Stepina, Perrewe, Hassell, Harris, & Mayfield, 1991). The direct relationship between LMX and job satisfaction has, thus, been well-established and has consistently been found to be positive.

Organizational Commitment

Organizational commitment has been viewed as having three major components: (1) a person's strong belief in and an acceptance of the organization's goals, (2) a person's willingness to exert considerable effort on behalf of the organization, and (3) a person's desire to maintain membership in the organization (Porter, Steers, Mowday, & Boulian, 1974). Organizational commitment research has been dominated by the Allen and Meyer (1997) model that distinguishes among affective, normative, and continuance organizational commitment.

Affective commitment taps upon the emotional ties the employee develops with the organization primarily via positive work experiences whereas normative commitment captures the perceived obligation the individual feels toward the organization. Finally, continuance commitment addresses the cost–benefit (both economic and social) analysis in which individuals engage before they decide to leave an organization. Mowday, Porter, and Steers (1982) have suggested that gaining a greater understanding of the processes related to organizational commitment has implications for both employees and organizations. On the one hand, employees' level of commitment to an organization may make them more eligible to receive various rewards (both extrinsic and intrinsic) associated with membership. On the other hand, organizations value commitment among their employees, since it is typically assumed to reduce withdrawal behaviors such as lateness and turnover. In addition, committed employees may be more likely to engage in "extrarole" behaviors, such as organizational citizenship behavior (OCB), creativity, or innovativeness that can increase the competitive advantage of the organization (Mathieu & Zajac, 1990). As an antecedent, organizational commitment has been studied as a determinant of variables such as turnover, absenteeism, and performance (Griffin & Bateman, 1986; Mathieu & Zajac, 1990). On the other hand, as a consequence, organizational commitment has been linked to several personal and organizational variables ranging from job characteristics to organizational structures. Leadership has also been studied as a determinant of organizational commitment and consistent support has been found for a positive association between LMX and organizational commitment (e.g., Duchon et al., 1986; Green et al., 1996; Kinicki & Vecchio, 1994; Major et al., 1995; Wayne et al., 2009).

Gerstner and Day's (1997) meta-analysis reported an average correlation of .35 between LMX and overall organizational commitment. Similarly, Dulebohn et al.'s (2012) recent meta-analysis reports a significant relation between LMX and overall organizational commitment ($\rho = .47$), $\rho = .41$ for affective commitment and $\rho = .33$ for normative commitment. They further highlighted two main reasons why LMX is positively related to commitment: (1) leaders' encouragement of commitment during the role-making process (Graen, 1976) and employees' attachment and loyalty to the leader that serves as a proxy for the organization, and (2) the leaders' assigning of challenging tasks and offering feedback to high LMX followers that results in a heightened sense of commitment to the organization. Prior research has, overall, lent strong support for a positive direct relationship between LMX and organizational commitment.

Opening the "Black Box" of the Relationship between LMX and Work Attitudes

When opening the "black box" of the relationship between LMX and job satisfaction and commitment, several variables (individual and organizational characteristics) have been examined as explanatory mechanisms. For example, Graen, Novak, and Sommerkamp (1982) examined employee growth need strength and showed its moderating effect on the relationship between LMX and satisfaction with the leader. Ozer (2008) examined locus of control as a moderator between LMX and satisfaction but his results did not provide support for this effect. Prior research has also examined the interactive effects of political skill with LMX and showed that employees high in political skill report lower job satisfaction when LMX is high (Harris et al., 2009). It is employees who lack political skill that rely mostly on their quality with the leader as a factor for their job satisfaction. More recently, Kimura (2013) reported that the negative effects on organizational commitment caused by perceptions of politics attenuate only when LMX and political skill are at a high degree, and not when only one of these is high.

When it comes to organizational variables, special attention has been paid to the role of perceived organizational support (POS) and research has provided evidence for the mediating role of POS in the relationships between LMX and job satisfaction (e.g., Andrews & Kacmar, 2001). Wayne, Shore, and Liden (1997) further showed that POS but not LMX was positively related to affective commitment. It therefore seems that in the case of organizational commitment, the exchanges that employees have with the organization (POS) are more powerful predictors than the exchanges with the direct manager (LMX). Supervisor POS has, however, been found to be an important moderator of the relationship between LMX and satisfaction. Erdogan and Enders (2007) found the positive relationship between LMX and satisfaction to be stronger when the supervisor had high POS. Furthermore, Aryee and Chen (2006), using a Chinese sample, found that psychological empowerment mediated the relationship between LMX and job satisfaction whereas in an earlier study Liden, Wayne, and Sparrowe

(2012) did not find support for the mediating role of empowerment in the relationships between LMX, Team–Member Exchange (TMX), and job satisfaction and commitment when controlling for job characteristics. Frequency of interaction between leader and follower has further been found to be an important boundary condition for the relationship between LMX and job satisfaction (Golden & Veiga, 2008; Mossholder, Niebuhr, & Norris, 1990). Particularly in the virtual context of limited face-to-face interaction, employees were found to rely more on LMX for their evaluation of job satisfaction and organizational commitment (Golden & Veiga, 2008). Ozer (2008) further found that the positive relationship between LMX and satisfaction was stronger when task autonomy was high.

In addition to individual and organizational variables, national cultural characteristics have been examined as possible boundaries of exchange processes between leaders and followers and the positive relationships between LMX and work attitudes have been found to be somewhat differential across cultures (although still significant). Rockstuhl et al. (2012), in a meta-analysis of the role of national culture in moderating relationships between LMX and outcomes, found a stronger effect of LMX on job satisfaction in horizontal-individualistic (e.g., Western) contexts than in vertical-collectivistic (e.g., Asian) contexts. As an explanation for this effect they argued that "even though members in both cultures are sensitive to leader treatment, members' responses in vertical-collectivistic cultures are more likely to be influenced by collective interests and role-based loyalty" (p. 1098). National culture did not, however, affect the relationship between LMX and organizational commitment. Figure 8.1 presents the set of mediators and moderators examined within the LMX–work attitudes context.

LMX as a Mediating or Moderating Mechanism

The importance of LMX as a powerful mediating mechanism has been documented by numerous studies. For example, Zhang, Wang, and Shi (2012) have recently examined LMX as a mediator in the relationship between leader–follower proactive personality congruence and follower job satisfaction and affective commitment. Epitropaki and Martin (2005) also reported that LMX mediated the relationship between Implicit–Explicit Leadership Theories congruence and work attitudes and Martin et al. (2005) found that it mediated the relationship between locus of control and intrinsic/extrinsic job

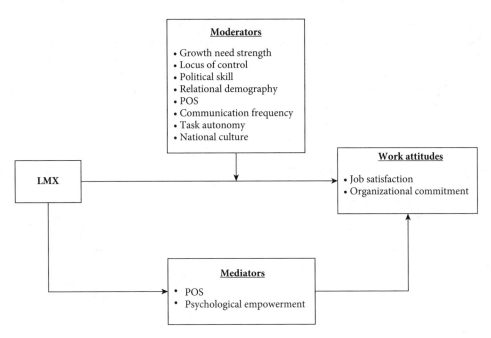

Fig. 8.1 Opening the "black box" of the LMX and attitudes relationship.

satisfaction and commitment. Green, Anderson, and Shivers (1996) focused on relational demography and found that LMX mediated the relationship between gender dissimilarity and job satisfaction and commitment. Janssen and Yperen (2004) found that it mediated the positive relationships between a mastery orientation and job satisfaction. Their findings suggested that employees focused on the development of competence through task mastery are more satisfied with their job because they tend to establish higher quality exchanges with their leaders.

Tekleab, Takeuchi, and Taylor (2005) examined the chain of relationships among organizational justice, social exchange variables, and work outcomes in a longitudinal study and found support for the mediating role of LMX in the relationship between interactional justice and job satisfaction. Conversely, POS and psychological contract violation were more powerful mediators of the relationship between procedural justice and job satisfaction. Masterson et al. (2000) had reached a similar conclusion regarding the differential mediating effects of LMX and POS in the relationships between interactional, procedural justice and job satisfaction and organizational commitment.

LMX has also frequently been examined as a moderator and boundary condition. Epitropaki and Martin (1999) examined LMX as a moderator of the relationship between relational demography and

work attitudes and found that age dissimilarity had a stronger negative effect for low LMX employees. Schriesheim, Neider, and Scandura (1998) found that LMX moderated the relationship between delegation and employee intrinsic and extrinsic satisfaction. Although originally hypothesized, their results did not support the moderating role of SLMX in the above relationship but documented its important role for the delegation–job performance relationship. Major et al. (1995) found that LMX moderated the relationship between newcomer expectations and job satisfaction 4 weeks after organizational entry. On the other hand, TMX was found to be a more powerful moderator of the relationship between newcomer expectations and organizational commitment.

Theoretical Underpinnings of the LMX–Attitudes Relationship

Social exchange. Social exchange theory (SET) (Blau, 1964) is arguably one of the fundamental conceptual paradigms underlying LMX. At the heart of social exchange theory are the concepts of equity and reciprocity. Individuals are more comfortable when they perceive that they are receiving benefits from the relationship equal to what they are putting into the relationship. They are also motivated to gain rewards or avoid costs in social exchanges (Homans, 1961). Gouldner (1960) further argued that the norm of reciprocity is universal and that people should return help received and avoid hurting the ones who have helped them. In the LMX context, SET suggests that leader–follower relationships develop from interactions between the two parties and are motivated by the mutual benefits derived from these exchanges (Blau, 1964; Brown & Trevino, 2006; Cropanzano & Mitchell, 2005; Erdogan & Bauer, in press). Early on in leader–member relationships, basic economic exchanges characterized by low trust are common, but over time, and as a result of matched behaviors on a *quid pro quo* (mutual reciprocity) basis and mutual risk taking (Brown & Mitchell, 2010; Brower, Schoorman, & Tan, 2000; Mayer et al., 1995), leader–follower relationships reach high levels of trust, lower levels of control, and long-term obligations.

Resources theory of social exchange. A theory that has been recently utilized in the LMX context is Foa and Foa's resource theory of social exchange (Wilson et al., 2010). Foa and Foa (1974) proposed that resources exchanged in relationships can be classified into one of six basic categories: money, goods, services, status, information, and love (affiliation/socioemotional resources). They further distinguished between two broad categories of resources: whether a resource is concrete or abstract and whether it is particular or universal. Concrete resources include tangible activities or products such as goods and services, whereas abstract resources are more symbolic, such as status and information. Particularistic resources are those in which the identity of the individual in the exchange relationship is important to the resource exchange, e.g., socioemotional resources (love). Universal resources are unaffected by who provides the resource, e.g., money. Wilson et al. (2010) applied this categorization to LMX and argued that leaders and members frequently exchange resources within and across these categories. Epitropaki and Martin (2013) also used this theoretical framework to explain differences in the upward influence tactics followers of high vs. low relative LMX used toward their transformational leaders.

Relative deprivation theory. Bolino and Turnley (2009) utilized relative deprivation theory, defined by Crosby (1976) as "... a tension state that exists in someone who perceives a discrepancy between the way things are and the way things ought to be" (p. 56), to explain consequences for the low-LMX groups. Rather than focusing on the benefits for people in high quality LMX relations—as most prior research did—Bolino and Turnley (2009) focused on employees in low-quality exchanges who experience deprivation in comparison to their co-workers and highlighted a series of possible responses to deprivation, both positive (e.g., engaging in self-improvement) and negative (e.g., counterproductive work behaviors). In relation to work attitudes, their model clearly predicted a negative effect of feelings of relative deprivation on job attitudes (e.g., reduced job satisfaction) but also stressed the importance of three moderators: (1) the degree of effort employees have made toward LMX development, (2) the extent to which leaders reevaluate their LMX relationships, and (3) employees' self-efficacy. Vidyarthi et al. (2014) utilized relative deprivation theory to examine the dynamics of LMX relationships in a dual leadership context and found that alignment of the two LMXs explained the variance in job satisfaction beyond that explained by both LMXs. They further reported a three-way interaction between the two LMXs and the frequency of communication with the agency leader on job satisfaction.

Levels of Analysis

The importance of explicitly addressing levels of analysis has been acknowledged in leadership research (see Dansereau & Yammarino, 1998; Yammarino & Dansereau, 2008). Levels of analysis are entities (in this case human beings) that are typically located in hierarchical order such that higher levels (e.g., work teams) include lower levels (e.g., followers). With respect to leadership research the key levels of analysis are the individuals or persons (independent subordinates, leader), dyads (leader–subordinate, follower–follower relationships), groups (work groups and teams), and organizations (collectives larger than groups and groups of groups). LMX has received substantial criticism regarding a lack of clarity on the levels of analysis incorporated in theory and research and in many cases a misalignment between the two (Dionne et al., 2014; Gooty & Yammarino, in press). Although LMX has been defined as the quality of the *dyadic relationship* between the leader and the follower and as a result the research unit should be the dyad, in reality the majority of studies have examined individual perceptions of the LMX quality, hence the misalignment between the basic premises of the theory and research application. Gooty et al. (2012) highlight three major challenges in LMX research: (1) the misalignment between theory/hypotheses and measurement/data analysis has worsened in the past few years (2005–2012) and roughly 50% of the articles specify it incorrectly or misalign levels; (2) lack of discussion on emergent processes that move LMX from the individual level to the dyadic and the group level; and (3) there are methodological challenges with the analysis of dyadic data that have prevented researchers from delving into that unit of measurement. The above challenges are also obvious in the LMX–work attitudes research as the majority of studies have adopted a member perspective and have looked at the link between LMX and attitudes on solely the individual level of analysis. However, the recent focus on group-level constructs such as LMX differentiation has reignited interest in attitudinal outcomes and has opened up new possibilities for LMX research. In this section, we will specifically address issues related to levels of analyses, review studies that have examined the effects of LMX on work attitudes at different levels, and offer suggestions for the future.

Individual level. The majority of the research presented above has focused on the individual level of analysis and has mainly examined the impact of member LMX on work attitudes (e.g., Aryee & Chen, 2006; Lapierre & Hackett, 2007; Liden et al., 2000; Major et al., 1995; Mardanov et al., 2008; Martin et al., 2005; Masterson et al., 2000; Murphy & Ensher, 1999; Wayne et al., 1997). It could be argued that this is the appropriate level of analysis as work attitudes represent individual evaluations of the job and the work environment. It is not uncommon, however, for these individual evaluations to be influenced by group-level constructs (such as justice climate) through social comparison processes (Vidyarthi et al., 2010, 2014) so it is important that we expand our lens. Even at this level there is further research to be conducted focusing on the leader's perspective that has previously been completely ignored. In addition to their managerial role, managers are also employees of an organization and as a result form their own evaluations about their job and their organizational environment. These evaluations are inevitably affected by critical relationships with their own superiors but also with their followers. It would thus be of interest to examine the effect of the quality of LMXs a leader has with his or her followers on his or her own work attitudes. Research could also examine the average type of relationships as well as variability of relationships as an antecedent of managerial work attitudes.

Three other LMX constructs have been operationalized at the individual level, although they refer

to group processes: *relative LMX* (Henderson et al., 2008; Epitropaki & Martin, 2013), *perceived LMX differentiation* (Hooper & Martin, 2008), and *TMX* (Seers, 1989; Seers, Petty, & Cashman, 1995). Relative LMX (RLMX) represents the degree to which an employee's LMX differs from average leader–subordinate LMX in the work group. Based on the norm of reciprocity, researchers have argued that employees with higher quality exchange relationships with their leaders than the group average will feel obligated to respond with behaviors that are valued by leaders (e.g., Henderson et al., 2008; Vidyarthi et al., 2010). Henderson et al. (2008) reported a positive relationship between RLMX and psychological contract fulfillment when controlling for individual LMX and recently Tse, Ashkanasy, and Dasborough (2012) found that RLMX was positively related to organizational identification. No prior study has explicitly addressed the role of RLMX in work attitudes.

Hooper and Martin (2008) conceptualized perceived LMX differentiation as "the amount of variability in LMX relationships perceived by team members (termed perceived LMX variability)" (p. 21). Across two samples, they found that perceived LMX variability accounted for additional variance in employee outcomes above that accounted for by personal LMX quality. They specifically found that perceived LMX variability was related to employee job satisfaction (global and extrinsic, but not intrinsic) and well-being and that this relationship was mediated by perceptions of relational team conflict. Perceived LMX differentiation is a promising construct that warrants further investigation as it captures members' perceptions of the shared reality of LMXs in their workgroups and engages them in an explicit social comparison process.

TMX is defined as an individual member's perceptions of his or her exchange relations within the group or team (Seers, 1989). It encompasses TMX contributions and TMX receipts (Ford & Seers, 2006). Contributions refer to actions in which a member engages to support work group members whereas receipts refer to the reciprocal opposites. Seers (1989) found longitudinally that TMX, above and beyond LMX, predicted job satisfaction. Major et al. (1995) found that new employees who had high perceived TMX experienced higher job satisfaction and commitment, and Liden, Wayne, and Sparrowe (2000) also reported a positive relationship between TMX and work satisfaction and commitment. On the other hand, Golden (2006) found the relationship between TMX and job satisfaction was more complicated and reported a curvilinear relationship such that job satisfaction increased as a function of TMX quality but decreased at higher levels. Witt et al. (1999) further found that TMX quality was positively related to individuals' commitment to teams, although this relationship was moderated by team identification. A recent meta-analysis (Banks et al., 2014) found that TMX showed incremental validity above and beyond LMX for work attitudes (organizational commitment and job satisfaction), but not for job performance and turnover intentions. Thus, perceptions of the horizontal relationships among team members (TMX) seem to play an important role for job attitudes over and above vertical exchanges (LMX).

Dyad level. Research that has truly focused on a dyad level has mainly examined leader–follower LMX agreement and its consequences through mainly polynomial regression procedures. A consistent finding is that leader and member views of the relationship often do not converge. Gerstner and Day (1997) reported a weighted sample correlation of .29 (.37 when corrected for measurement unreliability) and recently Sin, Nahrgang, and Morgeson (2009) in an analysis of 10,884 dyads found an overall agreement of $\rho = 37$. Zhou and Schriesheim (2010) also found strong support for a lack of convergence between the two perspectives and further indicated that leaders tended to focus more on task-oriented dimensions whereas followers were more oriented toward social aspects of the LMX relationship. Cogliser et al. (2009) using a sample of 285 matched pairs examined balance in perceptions and found that highly balanced–high LMX relationships were associated with high levels of job satisfaction and organizational commitment whereas highly balanced–low LMX relationships were related to low levels of attitudes. In unbalanced relationships results were generally intermediate. In relation to attitudes, their results showed that when followers overestimated the quality of the relationship they reported higher levels of job satisfaction and commitment. Recently, Gooty and Yammarino (2011) introduced the concept of *dyadic dispersion* to describe the degree to which leaders and followers do not share similar perceptions of LMX and talked about the lack of a *shared reality* within the dyad. They further developed a multisource, cross-level model examining dyadic dispersion of LMX as a moderator of the relationship between individual LMX and job performance. They do not, however,

formulate hypotheses for the role of dyadic dispersion in work attitudes.

Another construct that has been hypothesized to operate on a dyadic level is co-worker exchanges (CWXs). It captures the dyadic exchanges among co-workers who report to the same manager (Seers, 1989). Sherony and Green (2002) examined 110 co-worker dyads and found that greater diversity in a worker's CWX relationship, after controlling for LMX, was negatively related to his or her organizational commitment but not job satisfaction. They further reported that the quality of a worker's CWX did not moderate the relationship between CWX diversity and attitudes. Despite the initial promise of the construct, research has not taken off in the LMX field and as a result has been scarce. Recently, Tse, Lam, Lawrence, and Huang (2013), by adopting a balance theory and social comparison perspective, examined differences among co-workers' perceptions of the quality of LMX and their impact on contempt toward the co-worker and perceptions of help received from the co-worker. Results provided strong support for the moderating role of employees' social comparison orientation (SCO). Vidyarthi et al. (2014) added another dyadic component of interest, i.e., dual leadership exchanges in matrix organizational contexts. They found that the level of alignment or misalignment between the two relationships (LMX–client and LMX–agency) had an impact on employees' job satisfaction.

The need for an alignment of theory/hypotheses with measurement and data analyses in LMX research has been raised above. At the most basic level, LMX theory is located at the dyadic level with a focus on the relationship between a manager and each of his or her followers. Typically research examines LMX from the followers' perspective, and less frequently from the leaders', and correlates this with work attitudes. However, there are many potential benefits of examining LMX from both the follower and leader perspectives and how these might have an impact on work attitudes. Thus, a simple, but important research question is the following: which is the better predictor of follower work attitudes, follower LMX or leader LMX?

To enable an examination of both the follower and leader perspectives, Thomas et al. (2013) suggested that the dyadic methodology developed in research on interpersonal relations by Kenny and colleagues (Kenny, 1994; Kenny & Cook, 1999; Kenny, Kashy, & Cook, 2006) might be particularly useful. The essential aspect of this methodology is the collection of reciprocal data, i.e., data on the outcome variable (in this case LMX) from both members of a dyad (in this case leader and follower) on the dyadic variables of interest (in this case follower work attitudes). For instance, one might collect ratings of LMX from the follower and leader (and indeed, across many leader–follower dyads for the same manager) and relate these to work attitudes (such as followers' job satisfaction). These data structures, when subjected to the appropriate data analysis method, such as the Actor-Partner Interdependence Model (APIM; when leader and follower belong to only one dyad), the One-With-Many Model (OWM; when the leader has many followers), or the Social Relations Model (SRM; when the focus is on relationships between all team members including the leader, sometimes referred to as a "round robin" approach), make it possible to examine how both parties of a dyad contribute to a relationship or influence each other (for examples of these approaches in relation to LMX see Balkundi, Barsness, & Michael, 2009; LeDoux, Gorman, & Woehr, 2012; Richards & Hackett, 2012).

The OWM approach is particularly relevant in this context as it allows ratings of LMX to be collected from the "one" (in this case the leader) and from the "many" (in this case the followers) and thus allows the partition of variances into different aspects. For example, "actor" and "partner" effects reflect a person's general tendency to provide or elicit similar responses across partners whereas "relationship" effects reflect the unique relationships between two individuals (leader/follower) controlling for actor and partner effects. Thomas et al. (2013) provide an example of how the OWM approach might aid understanding of the relationship between LMX differentiation and work outcomes. As reviewed earlier, research has looked only at LMX differentiation, a follower's actual or perceived LMX quality variation on work outcomes. In the OWM method, the relationship effect captures similar variance, i.e., variation that is due to the unique relationship between a follower and a leader. Therefore, it is possible to include follower-, leader-, dyadic-, and group-level variables in these analyses to explain this variation and also to examine how the residuals of the relationship effect influence relevant work outcomes. The OWM approach enables researchers to examine relationship-based leadership phenomena in a more comprehensive way than traditional single-level models, and therefore can address theoretically interesting research questions concerning the relationship between LMX and work attitudes.

Group level. LMX differentiation has recently received substantial interest as a group-level construct of LMX. It is defined as the degree of within-group variation that exists when a leader forms different quality of relationships with different members (e.g., Erdogan & Bauer, 2010; Liden, Erdogan, Wayne, & Sparrowe, 2006; Martin et al., 2010). A high degree of variability creates conditions that promote competition and antagonism among team members, as individuals contest for a larger proportion of available attention and resources, whereas low levels of variability might enhance cooperation and social harmony in the group (Hooper & Martin, 2008). Researchers have further argued that variability is not necessarily a bad thing (e.g., Erdogan & Bauer, 2010; Erdogan & Liden, 2002) and that for some group members the presence of differentiation may be acceptable and even expected. Prior research has examined both perceived LMX differentiation (Hooper & Martin, 2008) as well as the actual level of differentiation (e.g., Erdogan & Bauer, 2010; LeBlanc & González-Romá, 2012), but the overall evidence regarding the role of LMX differentiation for individual outcomes remains inconclusive (e.g., Harris et al., 2014). Some researchers have advocated for the positive role of differentiation (e.g., Henderson et al., 2008; LeBlanc & González-Romá, 2012; Ma & Qu, 2010), whereas others supported the negative impact of LMX differentiation on work attitudes and its positive effect on work behaviors (e.g., Erdogan & Bauer, 2010; Hooper & Martin, 2008; Nishii & Mayer, 2009). Conversely, the role of mitigating factors such as organizational justice has been stressed unequivocally by most authors (e.g., Erdogan & Bauer, 2010; Scandura, 1999). In particular, work attitudes have been suggested to be highest when group members perceive that differentiated LMX relationships are fair (e.g., Liden et al., 2006). Clearly further research is needed to uncover the effects of LMX differentiation on work attitudes.

Figure 8.2 presents different levels of analysis in the context of LMX–work attitudes research.

Discussion
Future Theoretical Directions
We suggest that the following three theoretical streams could be utilized in the LMX context and help cast additional light on the LMX–work attitudes relationship: (1) social identity theory,

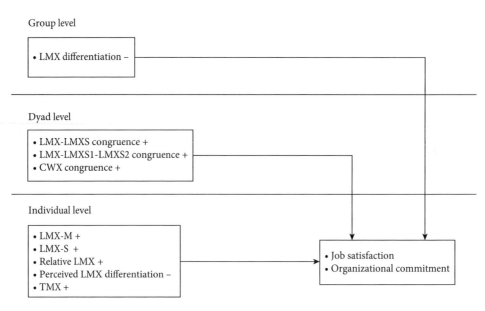

Fig. 8.2 Different levels of analysis in LMX–work attitudes research.

(2) intergroup leadership, and (3) relationship science and close relationships literature.

Social identity theory, SIT (Hogg, 2001; Tajfel & Turner, 1985). A recently developed approach to leadership based on the role of identification and how this develops between leaders and group members concerns the *social identity theory of leadership*, which has been developed principally by Hogg, van Knippenberg, and colleagues (Hogg, 2001; Hogg & van Knippenberg, 2003; Hogg, van Knippenberg, & Rast, 2012; for empirical overviews see Ellemers, de Gilder, & Haslam, 2004; Hogg et al., 2012; van Knippenberg, van Knippenberg, De Cremer, & Hogg, 2005). It proposes that effective leaders are highly group prototypical, i.e., they embody the desirable characteristics and behaviors of group members and therefore are in a position to influence group members.

The theory is based upon social identity theory (Tajfel & Turner, 1979) and social categorization theory (Turner, Hogg, Oakes, Reicher, & Wetherell, 1987). The premise of these approaches is that groups help to define and shape the thoughts, feelings, and behaviors of group members. Social identity refers to the part of a person's conception of their self that is based on their group memberships, which gives them a sense of "we." The more people identify with a particular social group, the more they see themselves as embodying the norms and values that are part of being in that group. People represent social groups in terms of prototypes that are "… context specific, multidimensional fuzzy

sets of attributes that define and prescribe attitudes, feelings, and behaviors that characterize one group and distinguish it from other groups" (Hogg, 2001, p. 187). A prototype, therefore, is a person's cognitive representation of what he or she believes to be the normative properties of the group. Prototypes in this approach are not anomalous to the concept of implicit leadership theories (ILTs; Epitropaki & Martin, 2004, 2005; Epitropaki et al., 2013; Lord et al., 1984). Whereas ILTs refer to a representation of a business leader (that might apply across many contexts), prototypes refer to what group members believe are the desirable ways to think, feel, and behave in *their* group and therefore set the norms for group behavior. Prototypical leaders are more central and important to self-definition than nonprototypical leaders because they embody group norms and are more likely to favor the ingroup and promote the well-being of the group. Numerous studies, across different occupations and cultures, have shown that prototypical leaders are perceived to be more desirable and effective than nonprototypical leaders (see Hogg et al., 2012, for a recent review). Social identity theory can open new horizons for LMX research. Some initial research has examined the conditions under which the social identity and LMX approaches predict effective leadership and impact work attitudes (Hogg & Martin, 2003; Hogg, Martin, Epitropaki, Mankad, Svenson, & Weeden, 2005). For example, Hogg et al. (2005) predicted that the effectiveness of a personalized style (treat people as individuals with their own needs, LMX approach) or a depersonalized style (treat the group as a whole, social identity approach) would depend on the group salience to the followers. They found that as group salience increased so did the effectiveness of the depersonalized leader. In other words, depersonalized leaders, who are group focused, were more effective when group salience is high. Future research could examine this more explicitly in relation to the leader–follower relationship with the expectation that group salience and identification should moderate when prototypical and nonprototypical leaders employing different leadership styles that emphasize them being group vs. individual orientated will be considered effective. Future research could also address implications for LMX differentiation. It could be assumed that in work groups with high group salience, highly prototypical leaders will engage in more or less uniform exchanges with members (low LMX differentiation), whereas groups with low group salience and low leader prototypicality will be characterized by highly differentiated exchanges.

Intergroup leadership. It is an increasingly common feature of the workplace that managers lead diverse groups from two or more distinct and self-contained groups that have their own individual identities. For example, in a manufacturing context, a site manager might lead several groups including a group of production managers and a group of quality controllers. Each group will be composed of people doing similar work and is likely to have its own specific group (or social) identity. This managerial situation is termed intergroup leadership and it is developing into a new research area. Much of the progress in this area builds upon the social identity approach to leadership described earlier (Hogg, van Knippenberg, & Rast, 2012; Platow, Reicher, & Haslam, 2009) and in political leadership (Pittinsky, 2010; Pittinsky & Simon, 2007). Although there have been calls to expand LMX research into the group level (Graen & Uhl-Bien, 1995), very little attention has focused on intergroup contexts.

One of the issues in intergroup leadership situations occurs when the leader is a member of one of the groups and therefore identifies more strongly with his or her own group (ingroup) than with alternative groups (outgroup). This might lead to intergroup competition and conflict that could be detrimental to performance. Research into intergroup relations shows that the categorization of people into different groups can lead to processes that promote intergroup conflict and prejudice.

For example, when people are categorized into two groups, especially ones in which membership of one's own group is psychologically important, it can lead to a cognitive process of minimizing the differences between members of one's own group ("we" are all similar) and maximizing the difference with members of the outgroup ("they" are very different from "us"). This can increase perceptions of "us" and "them," and although this might increase within-group cohesion it can lead to decreased cohesion between groups.

Of relevance to the theme of this chapter is the likely impact the above processes might have on perceptions of the LMX. As the relationship with the leader is likely to be important to followers' identity and group membership, there may be a tendency for perceptions of LMX to become more similar around an ingroup mean in highly cohesive groups and different from those in outgroups. In other words, perceptions of similar LMX among members of the same group come to reflect ingroup membership (we all like our manager) and as a way to differentiate from the members of the outgroup (they all dislike their manager). This leads to interesting research questions concerning the role of intergroup processes shaping LMX perceptions within and between groups and the consequence these processes might have on work attitudes.

Relationship science. In their recent review Thomas et al. (2013) proposed a cross-fertilization between close relationships literature and leadership processes with a special emphasis on the dyadic relationship between a leader and a follower. They specifically suggested that theories of close relationships such as attachment theory (see Hazan & Shaver, 1994; Mikulincer & Shaver, 2007, for a review) and relationship maintenance perspectives (e.g., Rusbult & Arriaga, 1997; Rusbult et al., 1991) can offer significant insights on the development of LMX relationships as well as their impact on work outcomes and attitudes. For example, it has been argued that the leader–follower relationship can also be conceptualized as an attachment relationship (see Game, 2011; Mayseless, 2010). According to this view, leaders are perceived as attachment figures because they perform two key care-giving functions: first, as a safe haven to provide support and comfort followers, especially in times of stress and uncertainty, and second, as a secure base to provide an opportunity to engage in creative exploration, skill acquisition, and self-development (Popper & Mayseless, 2003). By contrast, an insensitive and unresponsive leader is likely to produce insecurity and demoralization in followers (Davidovitz et al., 2007) as well as negative work attitudes.

Thomas et al. (2013) further argued that a cross-fertilization of relationship maintenance theoretical perspectives (see Berscheid, 1999) and leadership research might help address the frequent calls for LMX theory and research to go beyond the formative stages and explain the dynamics of how LMX develops over time (e.g., Martin et al., 2010; Nahrgang, Morgeson, & Ilies, 2009). Prior theoretical models (e.g., Graen & Uhl-Bien, 1991; Uhl-Bien & Graen, 1993) have focused on the early stages of LMX development and little is known about relationship development in mature LMX relationships as well as possible implications of relationship dynamics for job attitude change.

Suggestions for Future Research

We believe that it has become obvious from the above review that research on the relationship between LMX and work attitudes has not been saturated and there are several new avenues that future research can pursue. First, there is at the moment a lack of studies examining (or controlling for) the possible biasing effect of mood and emotions in the relation between LMX and attitudes, although recent evidence has indicated that job attitudes and mood/emotions covary (Judge & Kammeyer-Mueller, 2012). Future LMX research can thus incorporate affective processes when examining work attitudes and possibly utilize experience-sampling methodology (ESM) in which LMX, affect, and attitudes are measured once a day over a period of a few weeks. Such designs can cast additional light on the LMX development process and permit multilevel modeling of attitudes that allows for both within-individual (state) and between-individual (trait) effects (Judge & Kammeyer-Mueller, 2012). There is generally a very small number of longitudinal studies (e.g., Epitropaki & Martin, 2005) that have examined the possibility of reciprocal effects between LMX and attitudes as well as the temporal variations in job attitudes as a function of LMX development. Thus, the scope for longitudinal research is vast and, indeed crucial, to understanding the causal relationship between LMX and work attitudes.

Future research can also expand the lens to include broader concepts of satisfaction and "eudemonic" well-being (e.g., Ilies et al., 2005) or of good quality of life, i.e., *meaning in life* and *life satisfaction*. In the past decade, the construct of meaning in life has received renewed attention and legitimacy, in conjunction with a growing focus on positive psychology (Ryan & Deci, 2001; Seligman & Csikszentmihalyi, 2000). Life satisfaction has also been proposed as an important construct for organizational psychology by Erdogan, Bauer, Truxillo, and Mansfield (2012) who stated that "… management as a field has tended to define a 'happy worker' as someone satisfied with one's job but has paid scant attention to the more holistic concept of happiness in the form of life satisfaction" (p. 1039). In their comprehensive review they proposed that life satisfaction is a potential powerful mechanism through which people's work experiences are translated into desirable work behaviors and suggested that life satisfaction should be routinely included as an outcome together with job satisfaction in future research.

Research can also focus on other constructs alongside commitment that capture employees' attachment with the organization. Organizational identification, for example, is a construct that frequently has been confused with organizational commitment (Allen & Meyer, 1990; Mowday, Steers, & Porter, 1979), but research has shown that they are two separate constructs (e.g., Bergami & Bagozzi, 2000; Mael & Tetrick, 1992). According to Pratt (1998), the most salient distinction between the two is probably that identification explains the individual–organization relationship in terms of an individual's self-concept whereas commitment does not. Commitment refers to "acceptance" of organizational values. Identification goes beyond mere acceptance and is equated with "sharing" or "possessing" organizational values and beliefs. Ashforth and Mael (1989) have also proposed that the core difference between identification and commitment lies in the fact that identification is a cognitive/perceptual construct reflecting the extent to which the organization is incorporated in the self-concept, whereas commitment is more typically viewed as an attitude toward the organization. Van Knippenberg and Sleebos (2006) further concluded that identification reflects psychological oneness whereas commitment reflects a relationship between separate psychological entities. There has been one recent study that has examined the role of LMX in organizational identification. Specifically, Loi, Chen, and Lam (2014) in a two time-points investigation found a positive effect of LMX Time 1 on organizational identification Time 2 (after controlling for organizational identification Time 1). They also found that job security moderated the relationship between LMX and organizational identification. Employees with lower levels of job security were found to rely more on the relationship with the leader for crucial information regarding their job future and organizational membership. Organizational identification was further found to mediate the relationship between LMX Time 1 and job satisfaction Time 2. Organizational identification is thus a variable that holds promise for future LMX research. Tse, Ashkanasy, and Dasborough (2012) also found that relative LMX was positively related to social identification after controlling for individual LMX.

Another outcome of potential interest in the specific context is job embeddedness. Job embeddedness captures the extent to which individuals are enmeshed in their current jobs (Mitchell, Holtom, Lee, Sablynski, & Erez, 2001). Mitchell et al. (2001) defined job embeddedness as the combination of three organizational forces that keep people in their current jobs: (1) *Fit*, i.e., the extent to which a person's abilities and interests match organizational requirements and rewards, respectively; (2) *Links*, i.e., the number of ties people have with other employees and activities at work; and (3) *Sacrifice*, i.e., what people would have to give up if they had to leave the organization. In other words, highly embedded employees experience high fit with their current job, focus their energy on cultivating relationships within their current organization (rather than outside) and with their current leaders, and think they have a lot to lose if they lost their job. They, thus, have little desire to move elsewhere. Early studies have shown that job embeddedness has positive employee and organizational consequences such as performance and low turnover (e.g., Crossley, Bennett, Jex, & Burnfield, 2007; Halbesleben & Wheeler, 2008; Lee et al., 2004). Recent studies have, however, shown the "dark side" of job embeddedness and have found it to negatively affect individuals' career development behaviors (e.g., Ng & Feldman, 2010). Highly embedded employees have been found to engage less in activities to build social capital and networks that can help them find other employment. They have also been found to engage less in human capital development behaviors (e.g., attending training courses and engaging in job rotation). It will be of interest to explore the role of LMX in job embeddedness and the possible buffering role a good quality of relationship with the leader has on the possible negative effects of job embeddedness. It is possible that a high quality exchange with the leader and the increased access to resources and rewards that such a relationship entails shield employees from the possible negative effects of job embeddedness on career outcomes.

Conclusions

Although much is known about the direct relationships between LMX and work attitudes, we believe that this area of study is far from being extinct. In our review, we presented prior research and its theoretical underpinnings and, most importantly, offered new theoretical and empirical perspectives that can infuse new energy into this field of study.

References

Agho, A. O., Price, J. L., & Mueller, C. W. (1992). Discriminant validity of measures of job satisfaction, positive affectivity and negative affectivity. *Journal of Occupational and Organizational Psychology, 65*, 185–195.

Allen, N. J., & Meyer, N. J. (1990). Organizational socialization tactics: A longitudinal analysis of links to newcomers' commitment and role orientation. *Academy of Management Journal, 33*, 847–858.

Andrews, M. C., & Kacmar, K. M. (2001). Discriminating among organizational politics, justice, and support. *Journal of Organizational Behavior, 22*, 347–366.

Aryee, S., & Chen, Z. X. (2006). Leader-member exchange in a Chinese context: Antecedents, the mediating role of psychological empowerment and outcomes. *Journal of Business Research, 59*, 793–801.

Ashforth, B. E., & Mael, F. A. (1989). Social identity theory and the organization. *Academy of Management Review, 14*, 20–39.

Avolio, B. J., & Howell, J. M. (1992). *The effects of leadership behavior and leader-follower personality congruence on predicting follower satisfaction and consolidated business unit performance.* Center for Creative Leadership' Second Research Conference on Leadership, Colorado Springs, CO.

Balkundi, P., Barsness, Z., & Michael, J. H. (2009). Unlocking the influence of leadership network structures on team conflict and viability. *Small Group Research, 40*, 301–322.

Banks, G. C., Batchelor, J. H., Seers, A., O'Boyle, E. H., Pollack, J. M., & Gower, K. (2014). What does team–member exchange bring to the party? A meta-analytic review of team and leader social exchange. *Journal of Organizational Behavior, 35*, 273–295.

Bass, B. M. (1985). *Leadership and performance beyond expectations.* New York: Free Press.

Bauer, T. N., & Green, S. G. (1996). Development of leader-member exchange: A longitudinal test. *Academy of Management Journal, 39*, 1538–1567.

Bergami, M., & Bagozzi, R. P. (2000). Self-categorization, affective commitment and group self-esteem as distinct aspects of social identity in the organization. *British Journal of Social Psychology, 39*, 555–577.

Berscheid, E. (1999). The greening of relationship science. *American Psychologist, 54*, 260–266.

Blau, P. (1964). *Exchange and power in social life.* New York: Wiley.

Bolino, M. C., & Turnley, W. H. (2009). Relative deprivation among employees in lower-quality leader-member exchange relationships. *The Leadership Quarterly, 20*, 276–286.

Braun, S., Peus, C., Weisweiler, S., & Frey, D. (2013). Transformational leadership, job satisfaction, and team performance: A multilevel mediation model of trust. *The Leadership Quarterly, 24*, 270–283.

Brower, H. H., Schoorman, F. D., & Tan, H. H. (2000). A model of relational leadership: The integration of trust and leader-member exchange. *Leadership Quarterly, 11*, 227–250.

Brown, M. E., & Mitchell, M. S. (2010). Ethical and unethical leadership: Exploring new avenues for future research. *Business Ethics Quarterly, 20*, 583–616.

Brown, M. E., & Trevino, L. K. (2006). Ethical leadership: A review and future directions. *The Leadership Quarterly, 17*, 595-616.

Clegg, C. W., & Wall, T. D. (1981). A note on some new scales for measuring aspects of psychological well-being at work. *Journal of Occupational Psychology, 54*, 221–225.

Cogliser, C. C., Schriesheim, C. A., Scandura, T. A., & Gardner, W. L. (2009). Balance in leader and follower perceptions of leader-member exchange: Relationships with performance and work attitudes. *The Leadership Quarterly, 20*, 452–465.

Coltrin, S., & Glueck, W. F. (1977). The effect of leadership roles on the satisfaction and productivity of university research professors. *Academy of Management Journal, 20*, 101–116.

Crossley, C. D., Bennett, R. J., Jex, S. M., & Burnfield, J. L. (2007). Development of a global measure of job embeddedness and integration into a traditional model of voluntary turnover. *Journal of Applied Psychology, 92*, 1031–1042.

Dansereau, F., Graen, G. B., & Haga, W. (1975). A vertical dyad linkage approach to leadership in formal organizations. *Organizational Behavior and Human Performance, 13*, 46–78.

Dansereau, F., & Yammarino, F. J. (Eds.) (1998). Leadership: The multiple-level approaches (Part B: Contemporary and alternative). *Monographs in Organizational Behavior and Industrial Relations* (Vol. 24). Stamford, CT: JAI Press.

Davidovitz, R., Mikulincer, M., Shaver, P. R., Izsak, R., & Popper, M. (2007). Leaders as attachment figures: Leaders' attachment orientations predict leadership-related mental representations and followers' performance and mental health. *Journal of Personality and Social Psychology, 93*, 632–650.

Dihn, J., Lord, R. G., Gardner, W., Meuser J. D., Liden, R. C., & Hu, J. (2014). Leadership theory and research in the new millennium: Current theoretical trends and changing perspectives. *The Leadership Quarterly, 25*, 36–62.

Dionne, S. D., Gupta, A., Sotak, K. L., Shirreffs, K. A., Serban, A., Hao, C., Kim, D. H. & Yammarino, F. J. (2014). A 25-year perspective on levels of analysis in leadership research. *The Leadership Quarterly, 25*, 6-35.

Duchon, D., Green, S. G., & Taber, T. D. (1986). Vertical dyad linkage: A longitudinal assessment of antecedents, measures and consequences. *Journal of Applied Psychology, 71*, 56–60.

Dulebohn, J. H., Bommer, W. H., Liden, R. C., Brouer, R. L., & Ferris, G. R. (2012). A meta-analysis of antecedents and consequences of leader-member exchange: Integrating the past with an eye toward the future. *Journal of Management, 38*, 1715–1759.

Ellemers, N., De Gilder, D., & Haslam, S. A. (2004). Motivating individuals and groups at work: A social identity perspective on leadership and group performance. *Academy of Management Review, 29*, 459–478.

Epitropaki, O., & Martin, R. (1999). The impact of relational demography on the quality of leader-member exchanges (LMX) and employees' work attitudes and well being. *Journal of Occupational and Organizational Psychology, 72*, 237–240.

Epitropaki, O., & Martin, R. (2004). Implicit leadership theories in applied settings: Factor structure, generalizability and stability over time. *Journal of Applied Psychology, 89*, 293–310.

Epitropaki, O., & Martin, R. (2005). From ideal to real: A longitudinal study of the role of implicit leadership theories on leader-member exchanges and employee outcomes. *Journal of Applied Psychology, 90*, 659–676.

Epitropaki, O. & Martin, R. (2013). Transformational-transactional leadership and upward influence: The role of Relative Leader-Member Exchanges (RLMX) and Perceived Organizational Support (POS). *The Leadership Quarterly, 24*, 299-315.

Epitropaki, O., Sy, T., Martin, R., Tram-Quon, S., & Topakas, A. (2013). Implicit leadership and followership theories "in the wild": Taking stock of information-processing approaches to leadership and followership in organizational settings. *The Leadership Quarterly, 24*, 858–881.

Erdogan, B., & Bauer, T. N. (2010). Differentiated leader-member exchanges (LMX): The buffering role of justice climate. *Journal of Applied Psychology, 95*, 1104–1120.

Erdogan, B., & Bauer, T. N. (in press). Leader-member exchange (LMX) theory: The relational approach to leadership. In D. Day (Ed.), *Oxford handbook of leadership and organizations*. Oxford, UK: Oxford University Press.

Erdogan, B., Bauer, T. N., Truxillo, D. M., & Mansfield, L. (2012). Whistle while you work: A review of the life satisfaction literature. *Journal of Management, 38*, 1038–1083.

Erdogan, B., & Enders, J. (2007). Support from the top: Supervisors' perceived organizational support as a moderator of leader-member exchange to satisfaction and performance ratings. *Journal of Applied Psychology, 92*, 321–330.

Erdogan, B., & Liden, R. C. (2002). Social exchanges in the workplace: A review of recent developments and future research directions in Leader-Member Exchange theory. In L. L. Neider & C. A. Schriescheim (Eds.), *Leadership* (pp. 65–114). Greenwich, CT: Information Age Publishing.

Fishbein, M. A. (1973). The prediction of behavior from attitudinal variables. In C. D. Mortensen & K. Sereno (Eds.), *Advances in communication research* (pp. 3–31). New York: Harper & Row.

Fishbein, M., & Ajzen, I. (1975). *Belief, attitude, intention, and behavior: An introduction to theory and research*. Reading, MA: Addison-Wesley.

Foa, E. B., & Foa, U. G. (1974). *Societal structures of the mind*. Springfield, IL: Charles C. Thomas.

Ford, L. R., & Seers, A. (2006). Relational leadership and team climate: Pitting differentiation versus agreement. *Leadership Quarterly, 17*, 258–270.

Game, A. M. (2011). *Leadership and attachment theory: Understanding interpersonal dynamics in leader–follower relations* (p. 326). Thousand Oaks, CA: The SAGE Handbook of Leadership.

Gerstner, C. R., & Day, D. V. (1997). Meta-analytic review of leader-member exchange theory: Correlates and construct issues. *Journal of Applied Psychology, 82*, 827–844.

Golden, T. D. (2006). The role of relationships in understanding telecommuter satisfaction. *Journal of Organizational Behavior, 27,* 319–340.

Golden, T. D., & Veiga, J. F. (2008). The impact of superior-subordinate relationships on the commitment, job satisfaction, and performance of virtual workers. *Leadership Quarterly, 19,* 77–88.

Gooty, J., Serban, A., Thomas, J. S., Gavin, M. B., & Yammarino, F. J. (2012). Use and misuse of levels of analysis in leadership research: An illustrative review of leader-member exchange. *The Leadership Quarterly, 23,* 1080–1130.

Gooty, J. & Yammarino, F. J. (2011). Dyads in organizational research: Conceptual issues and multilevel analyses. *Organizational Research Methods, 14,* 456-483.

Gooty, J., & Yammarino, F. J. (in press). The leader-member exchange relationship: A multi-source, cross-level investigation. *Journal of Management.* doi: 10.1177/0149206313503009.

Gouldner, A. W. (1960). The norm of reciprocity: A preliminary statement. *American Sociological Review, 25,* 161–178.

Graen, G. B. (1976). Role-making processes within complex organizations. In M. D. Dunnette (Ed.), *Handbook of industrial and organizational psychology* (pp. 1201–1245). Chicago, IL: Rand McNally.

Graen, G. B., & Cashman, J. F. (1975). A role-making model of leadership in formal organisations: A developmental approach. In J. G. Hunt & L. L Larson (Eds.), *Leadership frontiers* (pp. 143–165). Kent, OH: Kent State University Press.

Graen, G. B., Novak, M. A., & Sommerkamp, P. (1982). The effects of leader-member exchange and job design on productivity and satisfaction: Testing a dual attachment model. *Organizational Behavior and Human Performance, 30,* 109–131.

Graen, G. B., & Uhl-Bien, M. (1995). Relationship-based approach to leadership: Development of leader-member exchange (LMX) theory of leadership over 25 years: Applying a multi-level multi-domain perspective. *Leadership Quarterly, 6,* 219–247.

Green, S. G., Anderson, S. E., & Shivers, S. L. (1996). Demographic and organizational influences on leader-member exchange and related work attitudes. *Organizational Behavior and Human Decision Processes, 66,* 203–214.

Griffin, R. W., & Bateman, T. S. (1986). Job satisfaction and organizational commitment. In C. L. Cooper & I. Robertson (Eds.), *International review of industrial and organizational psychology* (pp. 157–188). New York: Wiley.

Halbesleben, J. R. B., & Wheeler, A. R. (2008). The relative roles of engagement and embeddedness in predicting job performance and intention to leave. *Work and Stress, 22,* 242–256.

Harris, K. J., Harris, R. B., & Brouer, R. L. (2009). LMX and subordinate political skill: Direct and interactive effects on turnover intentions and job satisfaction. *Journal of Applied Social Psychology, 39,* 2373–2395.

Harris, T. B., Li, N., & Kirkman, B. L. (2014). Leader-member exchange (LMX) in context: How LMX differentiation and LMX relational separation attenuate LMX's influence on OCB and turnover intention. *The Leadership Quarterly, 25,* 314-328.

Harrison, D. A., Newman, D. A., & Roth, P. L. (2006). How important are job attitudes? Meta-analytic comparisons of integrative behavioral outcomes and time sequences. *Academy of Management Journal, 49,* 305–325.

Hater, J. J., & Bass, B. M. (1988). Superiors' evaluations and subordinates' perceptions of transformational and transactional leadership. *Journal of Applied Psychology, 73,* 695–702.

Hazan, C., & Shaver, P. R. (1994). Attachment as an organizational framework for research on close relationships. *Psychological Inquiry, 5,* 1–22.

Henderson, D. J., Liden, R. C., Glibkowski, B. C., & Chaudhry, A. (2009). LMX differentiation: A multilevel review and examination of its antecedents and outcomes. *Leadership Quarterly, 20,* 517–534.

Henderson, D. J., Wayne, S. J., Shore, L. M., Bommer, W. H., & Tetrick, L. E. (2008). Leader-member exchange, differentiation, and psychological contract fulfillment: A multilevel examination. *Journal of Applied Psychology, 93,* 1208–1219.

Hogg, M. A. (2001). A social identity theory of leadership. *Personality and Social Psychology Review, 5,* 184–200.

Hogg, M. A., Martin, R., Epitropaki, O., Mankad, A., Svensson, A., & Weeden, K. (2005). Effective leadership in salient groups: Revisiting leader-member exchange theory from the perspective of the social identity theory of leadership. *Personality and Social Psychology Bulletin, 31,* 991–1004.

Hogg, M. A., & van Knippenberg, D. (2003). Social identity and leadership processes in groups. In M. P. Zanna (Ed.), *Advances in experimental social psychology* (Vol. 35, pp. 1–52). San Diego, CA: Academic Press.

Hogg, M. A., van Knippenberg, D., & Rast, D. E. (2012). The social identity theory of leadership: Theoretical origins, research findings, and conceptual developments. *European Review of Social Psychology, 23,* 258–304.

Homans, G. (1961). *Social behavior.* New York: Harcourt, Brace & World.

Hooper, D., & Martin, R. (2008). Beyond personal leader-member exchange (LMX) quality: The effects of perceived LMX variability on employee reactions. *Leadership Quarterly, 19,* 20–30.

Janssen, O., & Van Yperen, N. W. (2004). Employees' goal orientations, the quality of leader-member exchange, and the outcomes of job performance and job satisfaction. *Academy of Management Journal, 47,* 368–384.

Judge, T. A., & Kammeyer-Mueller, J. D. (2012). Job attitudes. *Annual Review of Psychology, 63,* 341–367.

Judge, T. A., Thoresen, C. J., Bono, J. E., & Patton, G. K. (2001). The job satisfaction-job performance relationship: A qualitative and quantitative review. *Psychological Bulletin, 127,* 376–407.

Kacmar, K. M., Carlson, D. S., & Brymer, R. A. (1999). Antecedents and consequences of organizational commitment: A comparison of two scales. *Educational and Psychological Measurement, 59,* 976–994.

Kenny, D. A. (1994). *Interpersonal perception. A social relations analysis.* New York: Guilford Press.

Kenny, D. A., & Cook, W. L. (1999). Partner effects in relationship research: Conceptual issues, analytic difficulties, and illustrations. *Personal Relationships, 6,* 433–448.

Kenny, D. A., Kashy, D. A., & Cook, W. L. (2006). Dyadic data analysis. New York: Guilford Press.

Kimura, T. (2013). The moderating effects of political skill and leader-member exchange on the relationship between organizational politics and affective commitment. *Journal of Business Ethics, 116,* 587–599.

Kinicki, A. J., & Vecchio, R. P. (1994). Influences on the quality of supervisor-subordinate relations: The role of time-pressure, organizational commitment, and locus of control. *Journal of Organizational Behavior, 15*, 75–82.

Lapierre, L. M., & Hackett, R. D. (2007). Trait conscientiousness, leader-member exchange, job satisfaction and organizational citizenship behaviour: A test of an integrative model. *Journal of Occupational and Organizational Psychology, 80*, 539–554.

Le Blanc, P. M., & Gonzalez-Roma, V. (2012). A team level investigation of the relationship between leader–member exchange (LMX) differentiation, and commitment and performance. *The Leadership Quarterly, 23*, 534–544.

LeDoux, J., Gorman, C. A., & Woehr, D. J. (2012). The relative importance of dyadic relationships in predicting team process outcomes. *Small Group Research, 43*, 356–382.

Lee, T. W., Mitchell, T. R., Sablynski, C. J., Burton, J. P., & Holtom, B. C. (2004). The effects of job embeddedness on organizational citizenship, job performance, volitional absences, and voluntary turnover. *Academy of Management Journal, 47*, 711–722.

Liden, R. C., Erdogan, B., Wayne, S. J., & Sparrowe, R. T. (2006). Leader-member exchange, differentiation and task interdependence: Implications for individual and group performance. *Journal of Organizational Behavior, 27*, 723–746.

Liden, R. C., Sparrowe, R. T., & Wayne, S. J. (1997). Leader-member exchange theory: The past and potential for the future. *Research in Personnel and Human Resources Management, 15*, 47–119.

Liden, R. C., Wayne, S. J., & Sparrowe, R. T. (2000). An examination of the mediating role of psychological empowerment on the relations between the job, interpersonal relations, and work outcomes. *Journal of Applied Psychology, 85*, 407–416.

Liden, R. C., Wayne, S. J., & Stilwell, D. (1993). A longitudinal study on the early development of leader-member exchanges. *Journal of Applied Psychology, 78*, 662–674.

Locke, E. A. (1976). The nature and causes of job satisfaction. In M. D. Dunnette (Ed.), *Handbook of industrial and organizational psychology* (pp. 1297–1349). Chicago, IL: Rand McNally.

Locke, E. A., & Latham, G. P. (1990). *A theory of goal-setting and task performance.* Englewood Cliffs, NJ: Prentice Hall.

Loi, R., Chan, K. W., & Lam, L. W. (2014). Leader–member exchange, organizational identification, and job satisfaction: A social identity perspective. *Journal of Occupational and Organizational Psychology, 87*, 42–61.

Lord, R. G., Foti, R. J., & De Vader, C. L. (1984). A test of leadership categorization theory: Internal structure, information processing, and leadership perceptions. *Organizational Behavior and Human Performance, 34*, 343–378.

Mael, F. A., & Tetrick, L. E. (1992). Identifying organizational identification. *Educational & Psychological Measurement, 52*, 813–824.

Major, D. A., Kozlowski, S. W. J., Chao, G. T., & Gardner, P. D. (1995). A longitudinal investigation of newcomer expectations, early socialization outcomes, and the moderating effects of role development factors. *Journal of Applied Psychology, 80*, 418–431.

Mardanov, I. T., Heischmidt, K., & Henson, A. (2008). Leader-member exchange and job satisfaction bond and predicted employee turnover. *Journal of Leadership & Organizational Studies, 15*, 159–175.

Martin, R., & Epitropaki, O. (2001). Role of organizational identification, on implicit leadership theories (ILTs), transformational leadership and work attitudes. *Group Processes and Intergroup Relations, 4*, 247–262.

Martin, R., Epitropaki, O., Thomas, G., & Topakas, A. (2010). A review of Leader-Member Exchange (LMX) research: Future prospects and directions. *International Review of Industrial and Organizational Psychology, 25*, 35-88.

Martin, R., Thomas, G., Charles, K., Epitropaki, O., & McNamara, R. (2005). The role of leader-member exchanges in mediating the relationship between locus of control and work reactions. *Journal of Occupational and Organizational Psychology, 78*, 141–147.

Masterson, S. S., Lewis, K., Goldman, B. M., & Taylor, M. S. (2000). Integrating justice and social exchange: The differing effects of fair procedures and treatment on work relationships. *Academy of Management Journal, 43*, 738–748.

Mathieu, J. E., & Zajac, D. M. (1990). A review and meta-analysis of the antecedents and consequences of organizational commitment. *Psychological Bulletin, 108*, 171–194.

Mayer, R. C., Davis, J. H., & Schoorman, F. D. (1995). An integrative model of organizational trust. *Academy of Management Review, 20*, 709–734.

Mayseless, O. (2010). Attachment and the leader-follower relationship. *Journal of Social and Personal Relationships, 27*, 271–280.

Mikulincer, M., & Shaver, P. R. (2003). The attachment behavioral system in adulthood: Activation, psychodynamics, and interpersonal processes. *Advances in Experimental Social Psychology, 35*, 53–152.

Mitchell, T. R., Holtom, B. C., Lee, T. W., Sablynski, C. J., & Erez, M. (2001). Why people stay: Using organizational embeddedness to predict voluntary turnover. *Academy of Management Journal, 44*, 1102–1121.

Mossholder, K. W., Niebuhr, R. E., & Norris, D. R. (1990). Effects of dyadic duration on the relationship between leader behavior perceptions and follower outcomes. *Journal of Organizational Behavior, 11*, 379–388.

Mowday, R. T., Porter, L. W., & Steers, R. M. (1982). *Employee-organizational linkages.* New York: Academic Press.

Murphy, S. E., & Ensher, E. A. (1999). The effects of leader and subordinate characteristics in the development of leader-member exchange quality. *Journal of Applied Social Psychology, 29*, 1371–1394.

Ng, T. W. H., & Feldman, D. C. (2010). The effects of organizational embeddedness on development of social capital and human capital. *Journal of Applied Psychology, 95*, 696–712.

Ozer, M. (2008). Personal and task-related moderators of leader-member exchange among software developers. *Journal of Applied Psychology, 93*, 1174–1182.

Patterson, M., West, M., Lawthom, R., & Nickell, S. (1997). *Impact of people management practices on business performance.* London: Institute of Personnel and Development.

Petty, M. M., & Bruning, N. S. (1980). Relationships between employees' attitudes and error rates in public welfare programs. *Academy of Management Journal, 23*, 556–560.

Pittinsky, T. L. (2010). A two-dimensional model of intergroup leadership: The case of national diversity. *American Psychologist, 65*, 194–200.

Pittinsky, T. L., & Simon, S. (2007). Intergroup leadership. *The Leadership Quarterly, 18*, 586–605.

Popper, M., & Mayseless, O. (2003). Back to basics: Applying a parenting perspective to transformational leadership. *The Leadership Quarterly, 14*, 41-65.

Porter, L. W., Steers, R. M., Mowday, R. T., & Boulian, P. V. (1974). Organizational commitment, job satisfaction, and turnover among psychiatric technicians. *Journal of Applied Psychology, 59*, 603–609.

Pratt, M. G. (1998). To be or not to be: Central questions in organizational identification. In D. A. Whetten & P. C. Godfrey (Eds.), *Identity in organizations: Building theory through conversations* (pp. 171–208). Thousand Oaks, CA: Sage Publications.

Richards, D., & Hackett, R. D. (2012). Attachment and emotion regulation: Compensatory interactions and leader-member exchange. *Leadership Quarterly, 23*, 686–701.

Riketta, M. (2008). The causal relation between job attitudes and performance: A meta-analysis of panel studies. *Journal of Applied Psychology, 93*, 472–481.

Rockstuhl, T., Dulebohn, J. H., Ang, S., & Shore, L. M. (2012). Leader–member exchange (LMX) and culture: A meta-analysis of correlates of LMX across 23 countries. *Journal of Applied Psychology, 97*, 1097–1130.

Rusbult, C. E., & Arriaga, X. B. (1997). Interdependence theory. In S. Duck (Eds.), *Handbook of personal relationships: Theory, research, and interventions* (2nd ed., pp. 221–250). Chichester, England: Wiley.

Rusbult, C. E., Verette, J., Whitney, G. A., Slovik, L. F., & Lipkus, I. (1991). Accommodation processes in close relationships: Theory and preliminary empirical support. *Journal of Personality and Social Psychology, 60*, 53–78.

Ryan, R. M., & Deci, E. L. (2001). On happiness and human potentials: A review of research on hedonic and eudaimonic well-being. In S. Fiske (Ed.), *Annual review of psychology* (pp. 141–166). Palo Alto, CA: Annual Reviews, Inc.

Scandura, T. A. (1999). Rethinking leader-member exchange: An organizational justice perspective. *Leadership Quarterly, 10*, 25–40.

Schneider, B., Hanges, P. J., Smith, D. B., & Salvaggio, A. N. (2003). Which comes first: Employee attitudes or organizational financial and market performance? *Journal of Applied Psychology, 88*, 836–851.

Schriesheim, C. A., & Murphy, C. J. (1976). Relationship between leader behavior and subordinate satisfaction and performance: A test of some situational moderators. *Journal of Applied Psychology, 61*, 634–641.

Schriesheim, C. A., Neider, L. L., & Scandura, T. A. (1998). Delegation and leader-member exchange: Main effects, moderators, and measurement issues. *Academy of Management Journal, 41*, 298–318.

Schyns, B., Paul, T., Mohr, G., & Blank, H. (2005). Comparing antecedents and consequences of leader-member exchange in a German working context to findings in the US. *European Journal of Work and Organizational Psychology, 14*, 1–22.

Seers, A. (1989). Team-member exchange quality: A new construct for role-making research. *Organizational Behavior and Human Decision Processes, 43*, 118–135.

Seers, A., & Graen, G. B. (1984). The dual attachment concept: A longitudinal investigation of the combination of task characteristics and leader-member exchange. *Organizational Behavior and Human Performance, 33*, 283–306.

Seers, A., Petty, M. M., & Cashman, J. F. (1995). Team-member exchange under team and traditional management: A naturally occurring quasi-experiment. *Group & Organization Management, 20*, 18–38.

Seligman, M. E. P., & Csikszentmihalyi, M. (2000). Positive psychology: An introduction. *American Psychologist, 55*, 5–14.

Seltzer, J., & Bass, B. M. (1990). Transformational leadership: Beyond initiation and consideration. *Journal of Management, 16*, 693–703.

Seltzer, J., Nomerof, R. E., & Bass, B. M. (1989). Transformational leadership: Is it a source of more burnout and stress? *Journal of Health and Human Resource Administration, 12*, 174-185.

Sherony, K. M., & Green, S. G. (2002). Coworker exchange: Relationships between coworkers, leader-member exchange, and work attitudes. *Journal of Applied Psychology, 87*, 542–548.

Sin, H-P., Nahrgang, J. D., & Morgeson, F. O. (2009). Understanding why they don't see eye-to-eye: An examination of leader-member exchange (LMX) agreement. *Journal of Applied Psychology, 94*, 1048–1057.

Sparrowe, R. T. (1994). Empowerment in the hospitality industry: An exploration of antecedents and outcomes. *Journal of Hospitality & Tourism Research, 17*, 51-73.

Sparrowe, R. T., & Liden, R. C. (1997). Process and structure in leader-member exchange. *Academy of Management Review, 22*, 522–552.

Stepina, L., Perrewe, P. L., Hassell, B. L., Harris, J. R., & Mayfield, C. R. (1991). A comparative test of the independent effects of interpersonal, task, and reward domains on personal and organizational outcomes. *Journal of Social Behavior and Personality, 6*, 93–104.

Tajfel, H., & Turner, J. C. (1979). An integrative theory of intergroup conflict. In W. G. Austin & S. Worchel (Eds.), *The social psychology of intergroup relations* (pp. 33–47). Monterey, CA: Brooks/Cole.

Tajfel, H., & Turner, J. C. (1985). The social identity theory of intergroup behavior. In S. Worchel, & W. G. Austin (Eds.), *Psychology of intergroup relations*, (Vol. 2, pp. 7-24). Chicago: Nelson-Hall.

Tekleab, A. G., Takeuchi, R., & Taylor, M. S. (2005). Extending the chain of relationships among organizational justice, social exchange, and employee reactions: The role of contract violations. *Academy of Management Journal, 48*, 146–157.

Thomas, G., Martin, R., Epitropaki, O., Guillaume, Y., & Lee, A. (2013). Social cognition in leader-follower relationships: Applying insights from relationship science to understanding relationship-based approaches to leadership. *Journal of Organizational Behavior, 34*, S63–S81.

Tse, H. M., Ashkanasy, N. M., & Dasborough, M. T. (2012). Relative leader-member exchange, negative affectivity and social identification: A moderated-mediation examination. *Leadership Quarterly, 23*, 354–366.

Tse, H. M., Lam, C. K., Lawrence, S. A., & Huang, X. (2013). When my supervisor dislikes you more than me: The effect of dissimilarity in leader-member exchange on coworkers' interpersonal emotion and perceived help. *Journal of Applied Psychology, 98*, 974–988.

Turner, J. C., Hogg, M. A., Oakes, P. J., Reicher, S. D., & Wetherell, M. S. (1987). *Rediscovering the social group: A self-categorization theory.* Oxford, UK: Blackwell.

van Knippenberg, D., & Sleebos, E. (2006). Organizational identification versus organizational commitment: Self-definition, social exchange, and job attitudes. *Journal of Organizational Behavior, 27*, 571–584.

van Knippenberg, B., van Knippenberg, D., De Cremer, D., & Hogg, M. A. (2005). Research in leadership, self, and identity: A sample of the present and a glimpse of the future. *The Leadership Quarterly, 16*, 495–499.

Vidyarthi, P. R., Erdogan, B., Anand, S., Liden, R. C., & Chaudhry, A. (2014). One member, two leaders: Extending leader-member exchange theory to a dual leadership context. *Journal of Applied Psychology, 29*, 246–265.

Vidyarthi, P. R., Liden, R. C., Anand, S., Erdogan, B., & Ghosh, S. (2010). Where do I stand? Examining the effects of leader-member exchange social comparison on employee work behaviors. *Journal of Applied Psychology, 95*, 849–861.

Wayne, S. J., Coyle-Shapiro, J. A., Eisenberger, R., Liden, R. C., Rousseau, D. M., & Shore, L. M. (2009). Social influences. In H. J. Klein, T. E. Becker, & J. P. Meyer (Eds.), *Commitment in organizations: Accumulated wisdom and new directions* (pp. 253-284). Mahwah, NJ: Lawrence Erlbaum.

Wayne, S. J., Shore, L. M., Bommer, W. H., & Tetrick, L. E. (2002). The role of fair treatment and rewards in perceptions of organizational support and leader-member exchange. *Journal of Applied Psychology, 87*, 590–598.

Wayne, S. J., Shore, L. M., & Liden, R. C. (1997). Perceived organizational support and leader-member exchange: A social exchange perspective. *Academy of Management Journal, 40*, 82–111.

Wilson, K., Sin, H., & Conlon, D. (2010). What about the leader in leader-member exchange? The impact of resource exchanges and substitutability on the leader. *Academy of Management Review, 35*, 358–372.

Witt, L. A., Hochwarter, W. A., Hilton, T. F., & Hillman, C. M. (1999). Team-member exchange and commitment to a matrix team. *Journal of Social Behavior and Personality, 14*, 63–74.

Yammarino, F. J., & Dansereau, F. (2008). Multi-level nature of and multi-level approaches to leadership. *The Leadership Quarterly, 19*, 135–141.

Zhang, Z., Wang, M., & Shi, J. (2012). "Why (not) change?" effects of leader-follower congruence in proactive personality on LMX and work outcomes. *Academy of Management Journal, 55*, 111–130.

Zhou, X., & Schriesheim, C. A. (2010). Quantitative and qualitative examination of propositions concerning supervisor-subordinate convergence in descriptions of leader-member exchange (LMX) quality. *The Leadership Quarterly, 21*, 826–843.

Leader–Member Exchange and Performance: Where We Are and Where We Go From Here

Fadel K. Matta *and* Linn Van Dyne

Abstract

This chapter provides a critical and integrative review of leader–member exchange (LMX) as a predictor of four similar but different performance outcomes: task performance, affiliative extra-role behavior, change-oriented extra-role behavior, and adaptive performance. Looking to the past, the authors review this existing literature with a particular emphasis on identifying both mechanisms and boundaries to these relationships. This review suggests that high-quality LMX relationships are generally beneficial to performance whereas low-quality LMX relationships are generally detrimental to performance. Looking to the future, the authors propose that researchers can contribute to the LMX-to-performance literature by focusing on the boundaries of this relationship. Specifically, the authors recommend examining both the conditions under which high LMX may harm performance, as well as the conditions under which low LMX may not harm performance. The authors further consider the topics of supervisor-employee LMX congruence, time, and individual differences in altering the LMX-to-performance relationship.

Key Words: leader-member exchange, performance, task performance, organizational citizenship behavior, extra-role behavior, affiliative behavior, change-oriented behavior, voice, contextual performance, adaptive performance

Introduction

The leader–member exchange (LMX)-to-performance link is critically important to the LMX domain due to the implications that performance has for employees, leaders, and organizations. "Job performance is the most widely studied criterion variable in the organizational behavior and human resource management literatures" (Bommer, Johnson, Rich, Podsakoff, & Mackenzie, 1995, p. 587), and the relationship between LMX and performance is one of the most heavily researched topics in the LMX literature—as evidenced by the number of independent samples for performance variables included in LMX meta-analyses (Dulebohn, Bommer, Liden, Brouer, & Ferris, 2012; Gerstner & Day, 1997).

Despite the importance of the LMX-to-performance link, there has been no systematic review of the LMX-to-performance literature. This is problematic because a single meta-analytic effect size cannot capture the complexity of a literature (Aguinis, Pierce, Bosco, Dalton, & Dalton, 2011). Further, the LMX-to-performance link is particularly complex because job performance is a multidimensional construct (Campbell, 1990) that has continued to evolve with the changing demands of the workplace (Ilgen & Pulakos, 1999). Thus, the goals of this manuscript are to provide a systematic and critical review of the LMX-to-performance literature and to make recommendations for future research based on our analysis of the literature.

We begin by defining performance and comparing four similar but different types of performance: task performance, affiliative extra-role behavior, change-oriented extra-role behavior, and adaptive performance. We then review the LMX literature predicting each type of performance. Specifically, we review the literature that establishes the baseline LMX-to-performance relationships, the literature that elucidates why LMX affects performance by considering mediators of the linkage, and we discuss the roles of employee, leader, and contextual boundary conditions by discussing moderators of the linkage. After our review, we briefly discuss patterns in prior research and recommend the value of future research in five specific areas.

Defining Performance

The conceptualization of performance and how it is studied has evolved dramatically over the past half century. Traditionally, performance was understood and assessed in terms of task proficiency—performance on tasks specified in the job description. However, advances over the past 50 years have provided a more comprehensive view of the performance phenomenon by identifying a range of behaviors that contribute to organizational effectiveness but are not captured by task performance (Campbell, McCloy, Oppler, & Sager, 1993). Examples of new performance constructs include organizational citizenship behavior (Organ, 1988; Smith, Organ, & Near, 1983), extra-role behavior (Van Dyne, Cummings, & McLean Parks, 1995), contextual performance (Borman & Motowidlo, 1993), adaptive performance (Pulakos, Arad, Donovan, & Plamondon, 2000), prosocial organizational behavior (Brief & Motowidlo, 1986), voice (Van Dyne & LePine, 1998), whistle-blowing (Miceli & Near, 1984), and proactive behavior (Crant, 2000).

As described by Rotundo and Sackett (2002) as well as Griffin, Neal, and Parker (2007), there is partial overlap among many of these constructs, and therefore it is important to describe the theoretical basis for differentiating and integrating the various constructs that make up performance. Given that we are providing an integrative review of the LMX-to-performance relationship and performance is a multidimensional construct (Campbell, 1990), we first provide an organizing framework of four similar but distinct types of performance that we will use to organize our review of existing literature on the LMX-to-performance link (see Figure 9.1). This framework is adapted from the performance frameworks introduced by Johnson (2003), Griffin and colleagues (2007), and Van Dyne and colleagues (1995).

The first type of performance included in our framework linking LMX to performance is task

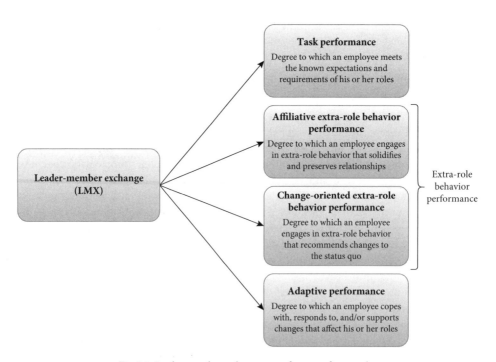

Fig. 9.1 Leader–member exchange-to-performance framework.

performance. Task performance is the degree to which an employee meets the known expectations and requirements of the role (Campbell et al., 1993). We include task performance as one of the four key performance outcomes because (a) it is the traditional focus of research on performance (Griffin et al., 2007), (b) it is the primary focus of research on LMX and performance (e.g., Dansereau, Graen, & Haga, 1975; Graen, Novak, & Sommerkamp, 1982; Liden & Graen, 1980; Vecchio & Gobdel, 1984), and (c) it is one of the most heavily researched behavioral outcomes in the LMX literature (Dulebohn et al., 2012; Gerstner & Day, 1997).

The second type of performance included in our framework that links LMX to performance is affiliative extra-role behavior. Affiliative extra-role behavior is the degree to which an employee engages in discretionary behaviors that go beyond delineated role expectations and aim to solidify and preserve relationships as well as benefit the organization (Van Dyne et al., 1995). Affiliative extra-role behaviors are important to our review because many of the core behavioral outcomes in the LMX literature involve solidifying and preserving relationships. This includes the relationships of LMX with organizational citizenship behavior (e.g., Ilies, Nahrgang, & Morgeson, 2007), helping (e.g., Van Dyne, Kamdar, & Joireman, 2008), altruism (e.g., Wayne & Green, 1993), contextual performance (e.g., Kraimer, Wayne, & Jaworski, 2001), safety-related citizenship (e.g., Hofmann, Morgeson, & Gerras, 2003), prosocial behavior (e.g., Pearson & Marler, 2010), and stewardship behavior (e.g., Kulkarni & Ramamoorthy, 2011).

The third type of performance included in our framework is change-oriented extra-role behavior. Change-oriented extra-role behavior is the degree to which an employee engages in discretionary behaviors that recommend changes to the status quo, go beyond delineated role expectations, and aim to benefit the organization (Van Dyne et al., 1995). We distinguish change-oriented extra-role behavior from affiliative extra-role behavior in our review because research has demonstrated differential relations for LMX with these two forms of extra-role behavior (Van Dyne et al., 2008). Examples of research on LMX and change-oriented behavior include the relationships between LMX and constructive deviance (e.g., Vadera, Pratt, & Mishra, 2013), voice (e.g., Burris, Detert, & Chiaburu, 2008), change-oriented behavior (e.g., Vigoda-Gadot & Beeri, 2012), whistle blowing

(e.g., Bhal & Dadhich, 2011), and employee resistance (e.g., Tepper et al., 2006).

The fourth and final type of performance in our framework linking LMX to performance is adaptive performance. Adaptive performance is the degree to which an employee copes with, responds to, and/or supports changes that affect their roles (Pulakos et al., 2000). We include adaptive performance based on the growing need for adaptivity in the changing and dynamic environments facing today's organizations (Ilgen & Pulakos, 1999). Our review of the literature focused on the eight dimensions of adaptive performance discussed by Pulakos and colleagues (2000): handling emergencies, handling work stress, creativity, dealing with uncertain situations, learning, interpersonal adaptability, cultural adaptability, and physical adaptability. Examples in the LMX literature include the relationships of LMX with expatriate performance (e.g., Pattie, Benson, Casper, & McMahan, 2013), expatriate success (e.g., Benson & Pattie, 2009), adaptive selling behaviors (e.g., Paparoidamis & Guenzi, 2009), creative performance (e.g., Tierney, Farmer, & Graen, 1999), innovative behavior (e.g., Scott & Bruce, 1994), and voluntary learning behavior (Walumbwa, Cropanzano, & Hartnell, 2009).

Now that we have defined these four types of performance, we review the literature on LMX and each type of performance in more detail. We start with task performance.

LMX and Task Performance
Establishing the Relationship

Early research in the organizational sciences focused on task performance instead of the broader conceptualizations of performance that are widely accepted today. Similarly, the LMX literature initially focused on task performance (i.e., task proficiency). The first two studies to demonstrate a relationship between LMX and performance were those of Dansereau and colleagues (1975) and Liden and Graen (1980). In each of these studies, results demonstrated that LMX was positively associated with supervisor-appraised performance (i.e., subjective performance) for leader–member dyads in university service departments. This initial evidence, however, operationalized performance from the leader's point of view, indicating the need to consider other operationalizations of performance (Dienesch & Liden, 1986).

Going beyond these initial studies, Graen and colleagues (1982) established the positive association between LMX and objective performance, measured by collecting weekly output records, in a field experiment involving administrative employees in a public service organization. Vecchio and Gobdel (1984) demonstrated a positive relationship between LMX and subjective as well as objective performance in a medium-sized, multiple-branch bank. Deluga (1998) further extended the LMX-performance link beyond subordinate performance and demonstrated a positive relationship between LMX and supervisor effectiveness (i.e., supervisor performance) using a sample of employees across a diverse array of organizational settings. In sum, the positive association of LMX with both subjective and objective task performance is well established and also substantiated by meta-analytic estimates (Dulebohn et al., 2012; Gerstner & Day, 1997).

Researchers have also examined more complex relationships and have considered the relative effects of different leadership approaches simultaneously. For example, Howell and Hall-Merenda (1999) simultaneously considered the effects of transformational leadership, contingent reward leadership, active management by exception, passive management by exception, and LMX on subordinate performance. Results showed that, when considered simultaneously, only active management by exception and LMX were positively associated with subordinate performance. Surprisingly, transformational leadership was not associated with subordinate performance after accounting for the effects of the other leadership approaches. Furthermore, results demonstrated that LMX was the only leadership approach that was not moderated by physical distance, further confirming the power of LMX as a predictor of task performance.

Researchers have also considered the relative effects of LMX in comparison with other forms of social exchange such as perceived organizational support. For example, Settoon, Bennett, and Liden (1996) demonstrated that LMX was a stronger predictor of task performance and organizational citizenship behavior (OCB), while perceived organizational support was a stronger predictor of organizational commitment. Wayne, Shore, and Liden (1997) demonstrated that LMX was related to leader-related outcomes (performance, doing favors, and OCB that benefits leaders), whereas perceived organizational support predicted organization-related outcomes (affective commitment, intentions to quit, and OCB that benefits the organization). In sum, evidence comparing social exchange mechanisms suggests that LMX is a key driver of task performance.

Finally, research also shows that LMX mediates the effects of more distal predictors on task performance. For example, Masterson, Lewis, Goldman, and Taylor (2000) showed that *interactional justice* influenced supervisor-rated task performance via LMX, using a sample of university employees. Janssen and Van Yperen (2004) demonstrated that LMX mediated the relationships of *mastery orientation* with leader-rated performance and innovative performance in a Dutch energy supplier. Wang, Law, Hackett, Wang, and Chen (2005) showed that LMX mediated the positive effect of *transformational leadership* on task performance across multiple organizations in China. Xu, Huang, Lam, and Miao (2012) demonstrated that LMX mediated the negative relationship between *abusive supervision* and task performance in a Fortune 500 telecommunications firm in China. Finally, Zhang, Wang, and Shi (2012) showed that LMX mediated the effect of *proactive personality congruence* (between employees and leaders) on performance for service employees in a Chinese bank.

Having described these LMX-to-task performance relationships, we now focus on reasons why LMX positively influences task performance. The next section reviews mediators that help to explain the LMX-to-task performance relationship.

Key Mediators of the LMX-to-Task Performance Relationship

First, we consider studies that predicted and demonstrated mediating effects for single mediators: supervisor liking, employee empowerment, and negative feedback seeking. Then we describe a study that tested three mediators (commitment to the supervisor, self-efficacy, and means efficacy) based on social exchange and efficacy theories.

Supervisor Liking. Judge and Ferris (1993) posited that "supervisors who have a close working relationship with certain subordinates in terms of the frequency and quality of their day-to-day interactions will be more likely to like those subordinates than others" (p. 87). Thus, high-quality supervisor–subordinate relationships cause supervisors to like some subordinates more than others, with subsequent effects on supervisor ratings of employee performance. Results in a sample of nurses supported these arguments and established *supervisor liking* as a mediator that links LMX with supervisor-appraised performance (i.e., subjective performance).

Empowerment. Shifting from a supervisor-focused mediator to an employee-focused mediator,

G. Chen, Kirkman, Kanfer, Allen, and Rosen (2007) argued that "employees who develop better relationships with their leader (i.e., higher LMX) feel more empowered and, in turn, are more motivated to perform effectively" (p. 333). Results in stores of a Fortune 500 home improvement company supported their prediction and showed that *empowerment* mediated the LMX-to-individual performance relationship.

Negative Feedback-Seeking. Z. Chen, Lam, and Zhong (2007) drew on social exchange theory to argue that high LMX would predict task performance because of its effect on *negative feedback seeking*. This is because high-quality relationships involve trust and make it easier for employees to approach their supervisors with questions about their roles. Thus, they should have greater role clarity. Specifically, "[s]ubordinates who seek negative feedback can avoid the detrimental consequences of poor performance as well as misunderstandings with their supervisors because they have a better understanding of, and control over, their working behavior" (p. 204). Examination of this hypothesis with data from Chinese corporations supported the prediction and showed that negative feedback-seeking mediated the relationship between LMX and performance.

Multiple Mediators. The final study that we discuss links LMX to task performance via three mediators: *commitment to the supervisor, self-efficacy*, and *means efficacy*. Walumbwa, Cropanzano, and Goldman (2011) drew on social exchange theory (for a review of social exchange theory and LMX, see Liden, Sparrowe, & Wayne, 1997) and efficacy theory (Bandura, 1977) to predict multiple mediating mechanisms as links between LMX and performance. Results in a sample of nurses in the southwestern United States demonstrated that commitment to the supervisor, self-efficacy, and means efficacy each partially mediated the effects of LMX on performance. More importantly, they showed that commitment to the supervisor, self-efficacy, and means efficacy together fully mediated the positive effect of LMX on performance. In sum, using multiple theoretical perspectives and mediators, Walumbwa and colleagues (2011) provided a more complete model of multiple mechanisms that help to explain why LMX predicts task performance.

As demonstrated by the above summary, a large amount of research links LMX to task performance, and a number of studies have supported mediators that help to explain this relationship. In the next section, we discuss processes that account for

boundary conditions that qualify the LMX-to-task performance relationships.

Key Moderators of the LMX-to-Task Performance Relationship

We organize this section into three topics. First, we discuss employee characteristics, followed by leader characteristics, and then contextual characteristics.

Employee Characteristics. Employee factors play an important role in changing the nature of the LMX-to-task performance relationship. Graen and colleagues (1982) proposed and demonstrated that *employee growth need strength* moderated the link between LMX and task performance, such that the effect was stronger for those with high growth need strength in comparison to those with low growth need strength. In contrast, Bauer, Erdogan, Liden, and Wayne (2006) showed that *extraversion* buffered the relationship between LMX and task performance in a sample of executives at a Fortune 500 pharmaceutical organization. LMX was not related to performance for those high in extraversion but was positively related to performance for those low in extraversion. Finally, Sekiguchi, Burton, and Sablynski's (2008) study of employees in a Fortune 100 telecommunications company and employees from a large, international manufacturing company demonstrated that *job embeddedness* moderated the relationship between LMX and task performance. Results showed that the positive relationship was stronger when job embeddedness was high and weaker when job embeddedness was low.

Leader Characteristics. Leader factors also play an important role in changing the nature of the LMX-to-task performance relationship. For example, G. Chen and colleagues (2007) demonstrated that *leadership climate* moderated the positive influence of LMX on individual empowerment and ultimately task performance, such that the influence of LMX was stronger when leadership climate was more positive. Erdogan and Enders (2007) drew on social exchange theory to posit that supervisor exchanges with the organization and supervisor exchanges with subordinates are interconnected. Analysis of data from six stores in a grocery chain in the northwestern United States established that *supervisor perceived organizational support* enhanced the relationship between LMX and subordinate job performance. The relationship was positive when supervisor perceived organizational support was high and buffered when supervisor perceived organizational support was low. Finally, Chang and

Johnson (2010) demonstrated that *leader relational identity* buffered the relationship between LMX and subordinate task performance in a sample across a diverse array of organizations and occupations. The relationship was positive when leader relational identity was low and buffered when relational identity was high.

Contextual Factors. Contextual factors are the most frequently studied moderators of the LMX-to-task performance relationship. Dunegan, Duchon, and Uhl-Bien (1992) demonstrated in a sample of pathology and lab employees from a university medical center that LMX and task performance were significantly related when *task challenge* was either very high or very low but not when task challenge was moderate. Integrating social comparison, social influence, and social exchange perspectives, Takeuchi, Yun, and Wong (2011) showed that *coworker exchange ideology* moderated the LMX-to-task performance relationship, such that the positive relationship was weaker when coworkers had a strong exchange ideology and stronger when exchange ideology was weak across a diverse array of organizations and occupations. Finally, research also shows that the *duration of dyadic relationships* (Duarte, Goodson, & Klich, 1994) and *frequency of communication* (Kacmar, Witt, Zivnuska, & Gully, 2003) moderated the LMX-to-task performance link.

Now that we have reviewed studies of LMX and performance of in-role work behaviors, we consider the second most commonly researched performance outcome in the LMX domain. The next section describes research on LMX as a predictor of affiliative extra-role behavior.

LMX and Affiliative Extra-Role Behavior
Establishing the Relationship

Affiliative extra-role behavior includes helping, organizational citizenship behavior, prosocial behavior, altruism, contextual performance, stewardship behavior, and safety citizenship. Wayne and Green (1993) conducted one of the first studies to tie LMX with affiliative extra-role behavior by showing a positive association between LMX and altruism using data from three hospitals and a large medical clinic in the Midwest. Basu and Green (1995) extended this finding by showing that LMX predicted organizational citizenship behavior targeted at individuals as well as organizational citizenship behavior targeted at organizations with data from a manufacturing plant of a Fortune 500 printing company. Similarly, Kraimer

and colleagues (2001) showed that LMX had positive effects on contextual performance in a sample of expatriates and supervisors from three US-based Fortune 500 companies. Further, Settoon and colleagues (1996) demonstrated that LMX is key social exchange mechanism driving OCB by establishing that LMX is a better predictor of organizational citizenship behavior whereas perceived organizational support is a better predictor of organizational commitment. In sum, the positive relationship between LMX and affiliative extra-role behavior is well established in the literature and is also substantiated by meta-analytic estimates (Dulebohn et al., 2012; Ilies et al., 2007).

Research also demonstrates that LMX mediates the effects of more distal predictors on affiliative extra-role behavior. For example, Hui, Law, and Chen (1999) demonstrated that LMX mediated the effect of *negative affectivity* on organizational citizenship behavior using a field sample in a Chinese joint venture. Masterson and colleagues (2000) showed that *interactional justice* influenced organizational citizenship behavior via LMX, with data from employees at a large public university. Wang and colleagues (2005) showed that LMX mediated the effect of *transformational leadership* on organizational citizenship behavior using data from multiple organizations in China. Karriker and Williams (2009) demonstrated that *agent-referenced distributive and procedural justice* influenced supervisor-targeted organizational citizenship behavior via LMX in a variety of occupations and organizations. Finally, Xu and colleagues (2012) showed that LMX mediated the effects of *abusive supervision* on organizational citizenship behavior toward the organization and organizational citizenship behavior toward individuals using data from a Fortune 500 telecommunications firm in China.

Although these studies strengthen the evidence that LMX predicts affiliative citizenship, they do not explain why LMX affects affiliative extra-role behavior. Thus, we next review research on key mediators that tie LMX to affiliative extra-role behavior.

Mediators of the LMX-to-Affiliative Extra-Role Behavior Relationship

Costs of Seeking Help and Help-Seeking Behavior. Anderson and Williams (1996) noted "[a]lthough few organizational studies of helping behavior have specifically examined how the nature of the relationship between individuals is associated with helping, studies have demonstrated that several leader behaviors (supportive, participative, and contingent reward behavior) are related to subordinate helping" (p. 283). Thus, they examined underlying mechanisms linking LMX with helping. Specifically, they posited that LMX would be associated with perceptions of the *costs of seeking help, help seeking behavior*, and helping behavior because "one would expect that high-quality working relationships would be characterized by a mutual sense of concern for each other and a sense of responsibility for providing help when needed, and, as a result, they would provide a basis for the expectation of receiving help in return for help provided. From an exchange perspective, helping would likely be perceived as an expected part of high-quality relationships" (p. 284). Results of their study supported the perceived costs of seeking help and help seeking behavior as mediators that linked LMX and helping in a sample of nursing staff at Midwestern hospitals.

Commitment and Trust. Walumbwa and colleagues (2011) used social exchange theory and the target similarity model to posit that *commitment to the supervisor* would mediate the relationship of LMX with organizational citizenship targeted toward the organization and citizenship targeted toward the supervisor. Results in a sample of nurses in the southwestern United States supported these predictions. Wat and Shaffer (2005) demonstrated that *trust in the supervisor* mediated the relationship between LMX and citizenship in a sample of Hong Kong investment banking personnel. Similarly, Tierney, Bauer, and Potter (2002) demonstrated that *organizational commitment* mediated the effect of LMX on affiliative extra-role behavior in a sample of Mexican white-collar workers.

Outcome Favorability and Justice. Sun, Chow, Chiu, and Pan (2013) suggested that "[t]he social exchange process in the current literature is overwhelmingly articulated as exchange of social-emotional resources, overlooking similarly important and paralleling exchange of economic and social resources" (p. 216). Empirical results showed that *outcome favorability* mediated the LMX-to-organizational citizenship behavior relationship in Chinese manufacturing firms. Bhal (2006) demonstrated that other forms of justice, including *procedural and interactional justice* mediated the effects of two dimensions of LMX—contribution and affect—on citizenship behavior using data collected from software organizations in India.

Now that we have summarized key studies that shed light on why LMX predicts affiliative extra-role behavior, we now consider moderators of the LMX—affiliative extra-role behavior relationship. Specifically, we review employee-related, leader-related, and contextual boundary conditions that buffer or enhance the effects of LMX on affiliative extra-role behavior.

Moderators of the LMX-to-Affiliative Extra-Role Behavior Relationship

Employee Characteristics. Although some studies have demonstrated moderators of the LMX-to-affiliative extra-role behavior linkage, this research is much less abundant than that on the LMX-to-task performance linkage. Sekiguchi and colleagues (2008) demonstrated that *job embeddedness* moderated the relationship between LMX and organizational citizenship behavior, such that the relationship was stronger when job embeddedness was high and weaker when embeddedness was low, in a sample from a Fortune 100 telecommunications company and a large, international manufacturing company. Van Dyne and colleagues (2008) demonstrated that *role perceptions*—whether helping is viewed as in-role or extra-role—changed the relationship between LMX and helping. Across two international samples, results showed that viewing helping as in-role buffered the negative effect of low-quality LMX on helping. Kamdar and Van Dyne (2007) demonstrated that *personality* (i.e., *agreeableness and conscientiousness*) interacted with LMX to predict helping targeted at the supervisor. In this study of engineers in an MNC, LMX weakened the relationships between personality and helping such that high LMX buffered the detrimental effects of personality when personality was less favorable.

Leader Characteristics. There also is less research on moderators of the LMX-to-affiliative extra-role behavior linkage compared with research on LMX-to-task performance linkage. Chang and Johnson (2010) demonstrated that *leader relational identity* moderated the relationship between LMX and organizational citizenship behavior, such that it was stronger when subordinates had supervisors with weak relational identities. Sparrowe, Soetjipto, and Kraimer (2006) demonstrated that the effect of *leader downward influence tactics* on member's helping behavior depended on LMX quality. Downward influence tactics predicted helping behavior when LMX was high and negatively impacted helping behavior when member LMX was low, in a sample from a Midwest distribution company.

Contextual Factors. Research on contextual factors that moderate the LMX-to-affiliative extra-role behavior linkage has grown over the past decade.

For example, Li, Liang, and Crant (2010) showed that *procedural justice climate* strengthened the indirect relationship between proactive personality and organizational citizenship behavior via LMX, in a sample from state-owned companies in China. Sun and colleagues (2013) demonstrated that *procedural justice climate* strengthened the indirect relationship between outcome favorability and organizational citizenship behavior via LMX, in a sample of manufacturing firms in China. Hofmann and colleagues (2003) demonstrated that the relationship between LMX and safety citizenship was moderated by *safety climate*, such that the relationship was stronger when there was a positive safety climate and weaker in negative safety climates, in a military sample. Finally, two meta-analyses demonstrated support for contextual moderators. Ilies and colleagues (2007) showed that LMX more strongly predicted *individually targeted citizenship* in comparison to *organizationally targeted citizenship*. Rockstuhl, Dulebohn, Ang, and Shore (2012) showed that the relationship between LMX and organizational citizenship behavior was stronger in *horizontal-individualistic* (e.g., Western) *contexts* in comparison to *vertical-collectivistic* (e.g., Asian) *contexts*.

Now that we have reviewed research on the relationship between LMX and performance of discretionary behavior that strengthens relationships and aims to benefit the organization, we move to a much less researched outcome of LMX. Next, we focus on LMX as a predictor of change-oriented extra-role behavior.

LMX and Change-Oriented Extra-Role Behavior
Establishing the Relationship

Change-oriented extra-role behavior includes change-oriented citizenship, voice behavior, constructive deviance, whistle-blowing, and employee resistance. Bettencourt (2004) drew on social exchange arguments to propose a positive link between LMX and change-oriented citizenship behavior. He posited that the "additional support, autonomy, information, and resources derived from such relationships stimulate risk-taking and a willingness to exceed the scope of one's formal job description" (p. 169). Results in a sample of retail associates supported this prediction. Elicker, Levy, and Hall (2006) demonstrated a positive relationship between LMX and voice within performance appraisal contexts using employees at a large petrochemical company. Tepper and colleagues (2006) linked LMX with employee resistance behaviors in two field samples and showed that

that refusing vs. negotiating depended on LMX. Finally, Botero and Van Dyne (2009) demonstrated that LMX was positively related to voice in the US and in Colombia.

We now move beyond main effects. In the next section, we consider research on why LMX affects change-oriented extra-role behavior and review key mediators that have been established in the literature.

Mediators of the LMX-to-Change-Oriented Extra-Role Behavior Relationship

Psychological Detachment. Burris and colleagues (2008) argued that "[h]igh-quality LMX relationships are associated with a variety of subordinate outcomes (e.g., performance, satisfaction, role clarity, and enlargement; Gerstner & Day, 1997) that can mitigate withdrawal and detachment cognitions . . . Because these withdrawal cognitions likely in turn reduce the extent to which employees give discretionary effort on the organization's behalf (for the reasons argued above), we predict a relationship between LMX and the level of voice that is mediated by subordinate psychological detachment" (p. 915). Results in a sample of restaurants in the United States demonstrated that *psychological detachment* mediated the LMX-to-voice relationship. Interestingly, psychological attachment did not predict voice or mediate the effects of LMX on voice.

Work-to-Family Spillover. Liu, Kwan, and Mao (2012) drew on social exchange theory to argue that positive affect and satisfaction from LMX would spillover into the family domain and lead to reciprocation via voice behavior. Results in a sample of blue-collar manufacturing employees in China supported the mediating role of *work-to-family spillover* on the LMX-to-voice relationship.

Felt Obligations. Vadera and colleagues (2013) reviewed the constructive deviance literature and posited that *felt obligations* should mediate the effects of LMX on constructive deviance (e.g., taking charge, voice, whistle-blowing, etc.). "The logic behind a felt obligation mechanism can be found in social exchange theory (Blau, 1964). This theory suggests that a reciprocal obligation is likely to develop between two (or more) parties through a series of mutual, although not necessarily simultaneous, exchanges. One party makes some form of contribution to the other party, and in doing so, develops an expectation of a return at a future time. The other party, having received something, develops a sense of obligation to reciprocate" (Vadera et al., 2013, p. 1252).

This summarizes key research on why LMX affects change-oriented extra-role behavior. Next, we discuss boundary conditions established in the literature that buffer or enhance the effects of LMX on change-oriented extra-role behavior.

Moderators of the LMX-to-Change-Oriented Extra-Role Behavior Relationship

Employee Characteristics. To our knowledge, only one study has considered employee or leader characteristics as moderators of the LMX-to-change-oriented extra-role behavior relationship. Van Dyne and colleagues (2008) demonstrated that the relationship between LMX and voice depended on *role perceptions*. Results across two international samples showed that viewing voice as in-role strengthened the relationship between LMX and voice.

Contextual Factors. In comparison to person-based moderators, there is more research on contextual influences that qualify the LMX-to-change-oriented extra-role behavior relationship. Bhal and Dadhich (2011) showed that the LMX-to-whistle-blowing relationship was strengthened when *moral intensity* was high, across three lab studies in India. Hsiung (2012) demonstrated second stage moderated mediation of the relationship between authentic leadership and voice via LMX. In a sample of real estate sales personnel, the link was enhanced by *procedural justice climate*. Finally, Vigoda-Gadot and Beeri (2012) showed that *perceptions of organizational politics* moderated the relationship between LMX and change-oriented citizenship. The relationship was stronger when perceptions of organizational politics were high and weaker when low.

Now that we have described the research on LMX as a predictor of discretionary behavior that aims to improve upon and change the status quo in ways that will benefit the organization, we shift our focus to the fourth type of performance predicted by LMX. This final behavior is adaptive performance.

LMX and Adaptive Performance
Establishing the Relationship

Adaptive performance includes a range of behaviors that represent actions that support or respond to changing contextual factors. Consistent with the conceptualization of adaptive performance advanced by Pulakos and colleagues (2000), we include both creative performance and expatriate performance as types of adaptive performance. This is because one aspect of adaptive performance requires "the individual to bring complex matters or situations to their desired end or develop creative solutions to novel, difficult problems" (p. 613) and because another aspect of adaptive performance "involves successfully integrating into a new culture or environment by fully understanding and willingly behaving in accordance with the accepted customs, values, rules, and structures operating within it" (p. 614). However, because Tierney (this volume) is dedicated to LMX and creativity, we only touch briefly on the literature covering the LMX-to-creative performance link.

Scott and Bruce (1994) first established the relationship between LMX and creativity, and a large number of studies have confirmed this finding (e.g., Basu & Green, 1997; Khazanchi & Masterson, 2011; Liao, Liu, & Loi, 2010; Olsson, Hemlin, & Pousette, 2012; Tierney et al., 1999; Van Dyne, Jehn, & Cummings, 2002; Yuan & Woodman, 2010). Kraimer and colleagues (2001) demonstrated a relationship between LMX and expatriate performance in a sample from three US-based Fortune 500 companies. Pattie and colleagues (2013) extended this work and showed that LMX mediated the effects of goal congruence on objective expatriate performance using survey and archival data from a large international consulting firm. Walumbwa and colleagues (2009) showed that LMX mediated the positive effect of interpersonal and informational justice on voluntary learning behaviors in a sample from a large automotive dealership in the southwestern United States. Finally, Paparoidamis and Guenzi (2009) demonstrated that LMX was positively associated with adaptive selling behaviors of field sales representatives in France.

Next, we provide more clarity as to why LMX affects adaptive performance by reviewing mediators that tie LMX to adaptive performance. We also discuss boundary conditions to the LMX-to-adaptive performance link.

Mediators of the LMX-to-Adaptive Performance Relationship

Our review identified a variety of mediators that help explain the LMX-to-creative performance or innovative performance relationships. These include *support, resource supply* (Scott & Bruce, 1994), *self-efficacy* (Liao et al., 2010), *expected image gains, expected positive performance outcomes* (Yuan & Woodman, 2010), *information sharing*

(Khazanchi & Masterson, 2011), *work engagement* (Agarwal, Datta, Blake-Beard, & Bhargava, 2012), *psychological empowerment,* and *felt obligations* (Pan, Sun, & Chow, 2012). We are not aware of other studies exploring mediators of adaptive behaviors.

Moderators of the LMX-to-Adaptive Performance Relationship

Very few studies have established moderators of the LMX-to-adaptive performance relationship—including studies of creative performance. One exception is Benson and Pattie's (2009) study of expatriate performance. Their results demonstrated that LMX *relationships with home* versus *host supervisors* had differential effects on expatriate outcomes. LMX with host country supervisors was more closely aligned with short-term outcomes and LMX with home country supervisors was more closely aligned with long-term outcomes in an international professional services firm. Moderators of the LMX-to-creative performance and innovative behavior relationships include *LMX differentiation* (Liao et al., 2010) and *organic vs. mechanistic work-unit structure* (Pan et al., 2012).

This summary of the linkage between LMX and positively intended adaptive behaviors that respond to changing contextual conditions concludes our review of the literature that examines LMX and four different performance outcomes. We next suggest directions for future research based on our review. Specifically, we focus on under-researched topics that have the potential to advance our understanding of LMX-to-performance relationships.

Suggestion for Future Research "New Moderators of the LMX-to-Performance Link"

The above review of the literature highlights six key conclusions: (a) LMX is a strong predictor of different types of performance, (b) social exchange theory is the predominant conceptual framework used to explain the LMX-to-performance relationship across the four performance categories, (c) social exchange is also most frequently used to justify mediators that link LMX with performance across the four types of performance, (d) contextual moderators have received more research attention than employee or leader characteristics across the four outcomes, (e) research attention has slowly shifted to a broader range of performance outcomes (e.g., task performance, then affiliative extra-role

behavior, then change-oriented extra-role behavior, and finally adaptive performance), and, finally, (f) the relationships between LMX and each of the four types of performance are overwhelmingly positive.

These six patterns identified in our review suggest new opportunities for research. Specifically, we recommend future research on under-researched aspects of LMX-to-performance relationships. For example, using a broader range of theoretical frameworks and going beyond social exchange, as illustrated by Walumbwa and colleagues (2011), is promising. Researchers can also contribute to the LMX domain by focusing on the less commonly researched domain of adaptive performance. This is especially critical given the importance of adaptability in the dynamic environments facing today's organizations (Ilgen & Pulakos, 1999; Pulakos et al., 2000). Researchers can also add to our understanding of LMX relationships by considering additional leader characteristics as moderators of the LMX-to-performance relationship (for an example, see Erdogan & Enders, 2007).

Going beyond these overall observations, we recommend five new approaches to thinking about moderators of the LMX-to-performance link (see Figure 9.2). The first is more nuanced consideration of crossed interactions because this would provide balance to the current emphasis on positive effects of LMX on performance. The second is research on buffering factors that mitigate the detrimental effects of low LMX on performance because this would have important practical implications for managers. The third is research on performance consequences of congruence between supervisor and employee ratings of LMX because this has received almost no empirical attention. The fourth is consideration of the role of time in influencing the LMX-to-performance link, which is also under-studied. Finally, the fifth recommendation is for research that examines individual differences as moderators of the relationships between LMX and all four types of performance because high LMX should have differential performance implications depending on dispositional characteristics.

Under What Conditions is LMX Negatively Related to Performance (Crossed Interactions)?

As documented by this review, LMX clearly has positive implications for performance. Researchers, however, should challenge the implicit assumption

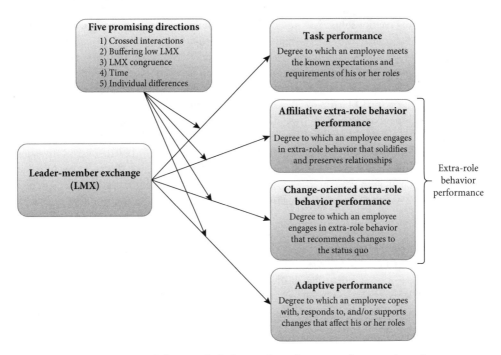

Fig. 9.2 Future research directions for leader–member exchange-to-performance relationships.

that LMX always positively predicts performance by theorizing and testing crossed interactions, which show both positive and negative relationships. As examples, we describe three studies that have demonstrated or suggested crossed interactions.

Erdogan and Enders (2007) provide one of the few studies we located that showed a crossed interaction. Specifically, they demonstrated that supervisor's perceived organizational support moderated the relationship between LMX and performance, with both positive and negative effects in their illustration of the interaction. LMX had a positive relationship when supervisor's perceived organizational support was high and a negative relationship when perceived organizational support was low. Although they did not report simple slopes, their results indicate the value of considering social exchange of supervisors (e.g., supervisor perceived organizational support) and employees (e.g., employee LMX) as a basis for predicting other crossed interactions.

Sekiguchi and colleagues (2008) demonstrated a three-way interaction between LMX, job embeddedness, and organization-based self-esteem that has implications for research targeting crossed interactions. Specifically, this study demonstrated that organization-based self-esteem moderated the LMX-to-performance relationship for employees high in embeddedness. LMX was negatively related to performance when organization-based self-esteem

was high and positively related to performance when organization-based self-esteem was low. This suggests that high-quality supervisor–subordinate relationships may detract from performance of employees who are highly embedded in their jobs and are also high in organization-based self-esteem. Perhaps the combination of embeddedness and organization-based self-esteem functions as a substitute for leadership, making high LMX dysfunctional. Based on this finding, we recommend research on other situations (e.g., high performers with significant tenure in their roles) where other self-concept constructs (e.g., strong identity or high independent identity) could cause crossed interactions where LMX is both positively and negatively related to performance.

Sparrowe and colleagues (2006) demonstrated that LMX interacts with leader downward influence tactics. By repositioning the interaction, with LMX as the independent variable and downward influence tactics as the moderator, LMX would be positively related to performance when downward influence tactics are high and negatively related when downward influence tactics are low—for two of the three downward influence tactics—inspirational appeals and consultation. This suggests that LMX may have negative implications for performance when supervisors do not engage in downward influence tactics. Reworded, if leaders with high-quality supervisor–subordinate relationships fail to use inspirational appeals and consultation, performance of high LMX subordinates may suffer. Accordingly, we recommend future research on other management tactics and types of leadership that may detract from the performance of employees with high-quality relationships. For example, LMX may be negatively related to employee performance if leaders use a laissez-faire style of management, fail to set clear and challenging goals for subordinates, or if they allow personal liking to interfere with their managerial role and do not provide corrective performance feedback.

What Buffering Factors Mitigate the Negative Effects of Low LMX?

Although some research has identified buffering factors that mitigate the negative effects of low LMX, additional studies are needed because of the practical implications for managers. As our review of the literature has shown, high LMX is beneficial for performance. On the other hand, this also means that low LMX is detrimental to performance. Finding ways to avoid the negative implications of low LMX is critically important because it should facilitate more effective utilization of leader resources. It is not practical for leaders to develop high-quality LMX relationships with all employees, but they may be able to use other management techniques to buffer the role of low LMX, and some employees may be less influenced by low LMX.

Several studies, for example, demonstrate that employee factors can mitigate the detrimental effects of low LMX, and this research sheds light on promising topics for future research. For example, Van Dyne and colleagues (2008) demonstrated that viewing helping as in-role (as opposed to extra-role) buffered the negative effect of low quality LMX on affiliative extra-role behavior (helping). Bauer and colleagues (2006) demonstrated that high extraversion (as opposed to low extraversion) buffered the negative effect of low LMX on performance. Other types of employee characteristics have the potential to buffer the negative effects of low LMX on performance because research shows that agreeableness and conscientiousness interact with LMX to predict performance (Kamdar & Van Dyne, 2007). For example, by repositioning the interactions in the Kamdar and Van Dyne study, with LMX as the independent variable and personality (i.e., agreeableness and conscientiousness) as the moderator, personality (i.e., agreeableness and

conscientiousness) buffers the detrimental effects of low LMX on performance.

Leader characteristics are also promising as mitigators of the negative effects of low LMX. Chang and Johnson (2010) demonstrated that the negative effects of low LMX on performance and organizational citizenship behavior were weakened when supervisors had strong relational identities. Anand, Vidyarthi, Liden, and Rousseau (2010) showed that special deals between leaders and followers buffered the detrimental effects of low LMX. In other words, idiosyncratic deals (i-deals) can substitute for LMX.

Finally, Bolino and Turnley (2009) developed the theoretical argument that low LMX influences organizational outcomes based on relative deprivation of low LMX employees and proposed potential moderators (buffers and enhancers) of the indirect relationship. The moderators suggested are wanting LMX (e.g., supervisor power, relationship costs, and availability of LMX substitutes), entitlement for LMX (e.g., subordinate effort), other's LMX status (e.g., LMX proportion and friend's LMX), self-blame for LMX status (e.g., LMX influenced by impression management), feasibility of changes to LMX status (e.g., temporary LMX status and previous high-quality LMX), and ability to change LMX status (e.g., previous employee effort, LMX re-evaluation, and self-efficacy). In sum, the existing research on employee, supervisor, and situational factors that may buffer the negative effects of low LMX and substitute for high LMX is promising and suggests the value of future research on other substitutes. This could include role perceptions, personality, self-efficacy, self-concept, and social comparison processes.

What Role Does LMX Congruence Play Relative to Performance Outcomes?

LMX is a unique leadership theory because it focuses on dyadic relationships rather than on leader traits and behaviors (Dulebohn et al., 2012). Nevertheless, LMX has traditionally been assessed from the leader's perspective *or* from the member's perspective even though meta-analytic evidence demonstrates that LMX agreement between leaders and subordinates is only moderate. For example, Gerstner and Day (1997) and Sin, Nahrgang, and Morgeson (2009) demonstrated a population estimate of the correlation (corrected for unreliability) of 0.37.

To date, few studies have considered the effects of LMX congruence on performance. Cogliser, Schriesheim, Scandura, and Gardner (2009), however, showed that balanced high LMX relationships predicted high performance, balanced low relationships predicted low performance, and incongruent relationships predicted intermediate levels of performance. However, this study artificially dichotomized the sample to test for agreement, and this approach has empirical limitations (see MacCallum, Zhang, Preacher, & Rucker, 2002). Markham, Yammarino, Murry, and Palanski (2010) also tested LMX congruence effects on performance but also dichotomized the sample.

Other theoretical perspectives may help to shed light on incongruence in LMX perceptions and performance. For example, self-verification theory (Swann, 1983) and cognitive dissonance theory (Festinger, 1957) emphasize the value of congruence for stability and predictability and position incongruence as a source of imbalance that leads to change. We recommend more nuanced theory building on the role of congruence between employee and manager perceptions of LMX and recommend future research on when and why congruence is meaningful to performance. We also recommend more robust analytical techniques such as polynomial regression and response surface methodology (Edwards, 2002) for analyzing the effects of congruence and incongruence.

What Role Does Time Play Relative to the LMX-to-Performance Link?

Time is another factor that is important to LMX and the LMX-to-performance relationship. As has been established in this review, LMX is positively related to performance, and longitudinal studies demonstrate that LMX predicts performance when measured at different times (e.g., Liden & Graen, 1980). Additionally, research has demonstrated that performance predicts LMX. For example, Liden, Wayne, and Stilwell (1993) demonstrated that performance predicted supervisor-rated LMX over time in a sample of new hires. Bauer and Green (1996) demonstrated that performance predicted LMX and change in LMX over time in a longitudinal study of graduates over the first 34 weeks in new jobs. Finally, Nahrgang, Morgeson, and Ilies (2009) demonstrated that employee extraversion and leader agreeableness influenced initial ratings of LMX, but performance influenced development of LMX over time using a longitudinal design and latent growth curve modeling.

Since LMX is an established predictor of performance, and performance is an established predictor of LMX, it seems reasonable to expect a reciprocal relationship between LMX and performance over time. Yet, to our knowledge no research has examined the reciprocal effects of LMX and performance over time. Furthermore, no empirical work has assessed when and why the reciprocal relationship tapers off or stabilizes. This is an important gap because theory on role taking, role making, and role routinization (e.g., Graen & Scandura, 1987) provides a theoretical framework to explore these relationships. In sum, we view longitudinal research on reciprocal relationships between LMX and performance over time and growth trajectory research as especially promising. Additionally, we recommend future research on potential boundary conditions that buffer or enhance these relationships over time.

How Do Individual Differences Change the Effects of High LMX on Performance?

Although research shows that LMX is positively related to task performance, affiliative extra-role behavior, change-oriented extra role behavior, and adaptive performance, it is unlikely that LMX is associated with all types of performance at all times. Instead, individual differences most likely influence which types of performance will be more strongly related to LMX at any point in time. Future research could integrate trait activation theory (Tett & Burnett, 2003; Tett & Guterman, 2000) and resource allocation theory (Kanfer & Ackerman, 1989) to consider specific individual differences that enhance the relationship between LMX and different types of performance while simultaneously weakening the effects of LMX on other types of performance. For example, trait activation theory arguments suggest that the relationship between LMX and change-oriented extra-role behavior might be positive and especially strong for those high in proactive personality, but resource allocation theory arguments suggest that this may divert resources away from task performance or away from affiliative extra-role behavior. Consistent with this idea, LePine and Van Dyne (2001) demonstrated that the personality trait of agreeableness was positively related to affiliative behavior and negatively related to change-oriented behavior. Thus, it would be useful for future research to consider trade-offs between LMX and types of performance as a function of individual differences.

Conclusion

The LMX-to-performance relationship is one of the most heavily researched in the LMX literature. As documented by this review, we know a substantial amount about leader-subordinate relations and their effects on performance based on the past 40 years of research. Researchers, however, have predominantly used social exchange theory frameworks and social exchange–based mediators, with an emphasis on contextual moderators and positive relationships across all four types of performance. Although this approach has allowed researchers to build consensus on many of these relationships, our review highlights promising future research opportunities. We hope our identification of under-researched topics triggers LMX research in new and novel directions and further deepens our understanding of the LMX-to-performance relationship.

References

Agarwal, U. A., Datta, S., Blake-Beard, S., & Bhargava, S. (2012). Linking LMX, innovative work behaviour and turnover intentions the mediating role of work engagement. *Career Development International, 17*, 208–230.

Aguinis, H., Pierce, C. A., Bosco, F. A., Dalton, D. R., & Dalton, C. M. (2011). Debunking myths and urban legends about meta-analysis. *Organizational Research Methods, 14*, 306–331.

Anand, S., Vidyarthi, P. R., Liden, R. C., & Rousseau, D. M. (2010). Good citizens in poor-quality relationships: Idiosyncratic deals as a substitute for relationship quality. *Academy of Management Journal, 53*, 970–988.

Anderson, S. E., & Williams, L. J. (1996). Interpersonal, job, and individual factors related to helping processes at work. *Journal of Applied Psychology, 81*, 282–296.

Bandura, A. (1977). Self-efficacy: Toward a unifying theory of behavioral change. *Psychological Review, 84*, 191–215.

Basu, R., & Green, S. G. (1995). Subordinate performance, leader-subordinate compatibility, and exchange quality in leader-member dyads—a field-study. *Journal of Applied Social Psychology, 25*, 77–92.

Basu, R., & Green, S. G. (1997). Leader-member exchange and transformational leadership: An empirical examination of innovative behaviors in leader-member dyads. *Journal of Applied Social Psychology, 27*, 477–499.

Bauer, T. N., Erdogan, B., Liden, R. C., & Wayne, S. J. (2006). A longitudinal study of the moderating role of extraversion: Leader-member exchange, performance, and turnover during new executive development. *Journal of Applied Psychology, 91*, 298–310.

Bauer, T. N., & Green, S. G. (1996). Development of leader-member exchange: A longitudinal test. *Academy of Management Journal, 39*, 1538–1567.

Benson, G. S., & Pattie, M. (2009). The comparative roles of home and host supervisors in the expatriate experience. *Human Resource Management, 48*, 49–68.

Bettencourt, L. A. (2004). Change-oriented organizational citizenship behaviors: The direct and moderating influence of goal orientation. *Journal of Retailing, 80*, 165–180.

Bhal, K. T. (2006). LMX-citizenship behavior relationship: Justice as a mediator. *Leadership & Organization Development Journal, 27*, 106–117.

Bhal, K. T., & Dadhich, A. (2011). Impact of ethical leadership and leader-member exchange on whistle blowing: The moderating impact of the moral intensity of the issue. *Journal of Business Ethics, 103*, 485–496.

Blau, P. M. (1964). *Exchange and power in social life.* New York: Wiley.

Bolino, M. C., & Turnley, W. H. (2009). Relative deprivation among employees in lower-quality leader-member exchange relationships. *The Leadership Quarterly, 20*, 276–286.

Bommer, W. H., Johnson, J. L., Rich, G. A., Podsakoff, P. M., & Mackenzie, S. B. (1995). On the interchangeability of objective and subjective measures of employee performance—a metaanalysis. *Personnel Psychology, 48*, 587–605.

Borman, W. C., & Motowidlo, S. J. (1993). Expanding the criterion domain to include elements of contextual performance. In N. Schmitt, W. C. Borman & Associates (Eds.), *Personnel selection in organizations* (pp. 71–98). San Francisco: Jossey-Bass.

Botero, I. C., & Van Dyne, L. (2009). Employee voice behavior interactive effects of LMX and power distance in the united states and colombia. *Management Communication Quarterly, 23*, 84–104.

Brief, A. P., & Motowidlo, S. J. (1986). Pro-social organizational behaviors. *Academy of Management Review, 11*, 710–725.

Burris, E. R., Detert, J. R., & Chiaburu, D. S. (2008). Quitting before leaving: The mediating effects of psychological attachment and detachment on voice. *Journal of Applied Psychology, 93*, 912–922.

Campbell, J. P. (1990). Modelling the performance prediction problem in industrial and organizational psychology. In M. D. Dunnette & L. M. Hough (Eds.), *Handbook of industrial and organizational psychology* (2nd ed., Vol. 1, pp. 678–732). Palo Alto, CA: Consulting Psychologist Press.

Campbell, J. P., McCloy, R. A., Oppler, S. H., & Sager, C. E. (1993). A theory of performance. In N. Schmitt, W. C. Borman & Associates (Eds.), *Personnel selection in organizations* (pp. 35–69). San Francisco: Jossey-Bass.

Chang, C. H., & Johnson, R. E. (2010). Not all leader-member exchanges are created equal: Importance of leader relational identity. *Leadership Quarterly, 21*, 796–808.

Chen, G., Kirkman, B. L., Kanfer, R., Allen, D., & Rosen, B. (2007). A multilevel study of leadership, empowerment, and performance in teams. *Journal of Applied Psychology, 92*, 331–346.

Chen, Z., Lam, W., & Zhong, J. A. (2007). Leader-member exchange and member performance: A new look at individual-level negative feedback-seeking behavior and team-level empowerment climate. *Journal of Applied Psychology, 92*, 202–212.

Cogliser, C. C., Schriesheim, C. A., Scandura, T. A., & Gardner, W. L. (2009). Balance in leader and follower perceptions of leader-member exchange: Relationships with performance and work attitudes. *Leadership Quarterly, 20*, 452–465.

Crant, J. M. (2000). Proactive behavior in organizations. *Journal of Management, 26*, 435–462.

Dansereau, F., Graen, G. B., & Haga, W. J. (1975). A vertical dyad linkage approach to leadership within formal organizations: A longitudinal investigation of the role making process. *Organizational Behavior and Human Decision Processes, 13*, 46–78.

Deluga, R. J. (1998). Leader-member exchange quality and effectiveness ratings: The role of subordinate-supervisor conscientiousness similarity. *Group and Organization Management, 23*, 189–216.

Dienesch, R. M., & Liden, R. C. (1986). Leader-member exchange model of leadership: A critique and further development. *Academy of Management Review, 11*, 618–634.

Duarte, N. T., Goodson, J. R., & Klich, N. R. (1994). Effects of dyadic quality and duration on performance-appraisal. *Academy of Management Journal, 37*, 499–521.

Dulebohn, J. H., Bommer, W. H., Liden, R. C., Brouer, R. L., & Ferris, G. R. (2012). A meta-analysis of antecedents and consequences of leader-member exchange: Integrating the past with an eye toward the future. *Journal of Management, 38*, 1715–1759.

Dunegan, K. J., Duchon, D., & Uhl-Bien, M. (1992). Examining the link between leader-member exchange and subordinate performance—the role of task analyzability and variety as moderators. *Journal of Management, 18*, 59–76.

Edwards, J. R. (2002). Alternatives to difference scores: Polynomial regression analysis and response surface methodology. In F. Drasgow & N. W. Schmitt (Eds.), *Advances in measurement and data analysis* (pp. 350–400). San Francisco: Jossey-Bass.

Elicker, J. D., Levy, P. E., & Hall, R. J. (2006). The role of leader-member exchange in the performance appraisal process. *Journal of Management, 32*, 531–551.

Erdogan, B., & Enders, J. (2007). Support from the top: Supervisors' perceived organizational support as a moderator of leader-member exchange to satisfaction and performance relationships. *Journal of Applied Psychology, 92*, 321–330.

Festinger, L. (1957). *A theory of cognitive dissonance.* Stanford, CA: Stanford University Press.

Gerstner, C. R., & Day, D. V. (1997). Meta-analytic review of leader-member exchange theory: Correlates and construct issues. *Journal of Applied Psychology, 82*, 827–844.

Graen, G. B., Novak, M. A., & Sommerkamp, P. (1982). The effects of leader—member exchange and job design on productivity and satisfaction: Testing a dual attachment model. *Organizational Behavior and Human Performance, 30*, 109–131.

Graen, G. B., & Scandura, T. A. (1987). Toward a psychology of dyadic organizing. *Research in Organizational Behavior, 9*, 175–208.

Griffin, M. A., Neal, A., & Parker, S. K. (2007). A new model of work role performance: Positive behavior in uncertain and interdependent contexts. *Academy of Management Journal, 50*, 327–347.

Hofmann, D. A., Morgeson, F. P., & Gerras, S. J. (2003). Climate as a moderator of the relationship between leader-member exchange and content specific citizenship: Safety climate as an exemplar. *Journal of Applied Psychology, 88*, 170–178.

Howell, J. M., & Hall-Merenda, K. E. (1999). The ties that bind: The impact of leader-member exchange, transformational and transactional leadership, and distance on predicting follower performance. *Journal of Applied Psychology, 84*, 680–694.

Hsiung, H. H. (2012). Authentic leadership and employee voice behavior: A multi-level psychological process. *Journal of Business Ethics, 107*, 349–361.

Hui, C., Law, K. S., & Chen, Z. X. (1999). A structural equation model of the effects of negative affectivity, leader-member exchange, and perceived job mobility on in-role and extra-role performance: A chinese case. *Organizational Behavior and Human Decision Processes, 77*, 3–21.

Ilgen, D. R., & Pulakos, E. D. (1999). Employee performance in today's organizations. In D. R. Ilgen & E. D. Pulakos (Eds.), *The changing nature of performance: Implications for staffing, motivation, and development* (pp. 21–55). San Francisco: Jossey-Bass.

Ilies, R., Nahrgang, J. D., & Morgeson, F. P. (2007). Leader-member exchange and citizenship behaviors: A meta-analysis. *Journal of Applied Psychology, 92*, 269–277.

Janssen, O., & Van Yperen, N. W. (2004). Employees' goal orientations, the quality of leader-member exchange, and the outcomes of job performance and job satisfaction. *Academy of Management Journal, 47*, 368–384.

Johnson, J. W. (2003). Toward a better understanding of the relationship between personality and individual job performance. In M. R. Barrick & A. M. Ryan (Eds.), *Personality and work* (pp. 83–120). San Francisco: Jossey-Bass.

Judge, T. A., & Ferris, G. R. (1993). Social-context of performance evaluation decisions. *Academy of Management Journal, 36*, 80–105.

Kacmar, K. M., Witt, L. A., Zivnuska, S., & Gully, S. M. (2003). The interactive effect of leader-member exchange and communication frequency on performance ratings. *Journal of Applied Psychology, 88*, 764–772.

Kamdar, D., & Van Dyne, L. (2007). The joint effects of personality and workplace social exchange relationships in predicting task performance and citizenship performance. *Journal of Applied Psychology, 92*, 1286–1298.

Kanfer, R., & Ackerman, P. L. (1989). Motivation and cognitive abilities: An integrative/aptitude-treatment interaction approach to skill acquisition. *Journal of Applied Psychology, 74*, 657–690.

Karriker, J. H., & Williams, M. L. (2009). Organizational justice and organizational citizenship behavior: A mediated multifoci model. *Journal of Management, 35*, 112–135.

Khazanchi, S., & Masterson, S. S. (2011). Who and what is fair matters: A multi-foci social exchange model of creativity. *Journal of Organizational Behavior, 32*, 86–106.

Kraimer, M. L., Wayne, S. J., & Jaworski, R. A. (2001). Sources of support and expatriate performance: The mediating role of expatriate adjustment. *Personnel Psychology, 54*, 71–99.

Kulkarni, S., & Ramamoorthy, N. (2011). Leader-member exchange, subordinate stewardship, and hierarchical governance. *International Journal of Human Resource Management, 22*, 2770–2793.

LePine, J. A., & Van Dyne, L. (2001). Voice and cooperative behavior as contrasting forms of contextual performance: Evidence of differential relationships with big five personality characteristics and cognitive ability. *Journal of Applied Psychology, 86*, 326–336.

Li, N., Liang, J., & Crant, J. M. (2010). The role of proactive personality in job satisfaction and organizational citizenship behavior: A relational perspective. *Journal of Applied Psychology, 95*, 395–404.

Liao, H., Liu, D., & Loi, R. (2010). Looking at both sides of the social exchange coin: A social cognitive perspective on the joint effects of relationship quality and differentiation on creativity. *Academy of Management Journal, 53*, 1090–1109.

Liden, R. C., & Graen, G. B. (1980). Generalizability of the vertical dyad linkage model of leadership. *Academy of Management Journal, 23*, 451–465.

Liden, R. C., Sparrowe, R. T., & Wayne, S. J. (1997). Leader–member exchange theory: The past and potential for the future. In G. R. Ferris (Ed.), *Research in personnel and human resources management* (pp. 47–119). Oxford, England: Elsevier Science.

Liden, R. C., Wayne, S. J., & Stilwell, D. (1993). A longitudinal study on the early development of leader-member exchanges. *Journal of Applied Psychology, 78*, 662–674.

Liu, J., Kwan, H. K., & Mao, Y. (2012). Mentorship quality and proteges work-to-family positive spillover, career satisfaction and voice behavior in china. *International Journal of Human Resource Management, 23*, 4110–4128.

MacCallum, R. C., Zhang, S. B., Preacher, K. J., & Rucker, D. D. (2002). On the practice of dichotomization of quantitative variables. *Psychological Methods, 7*, 19–40.

Markham, S. E., Yammarino, F. J., Murry, W. D., & Palanski, M. E. (2010). Leader–member exchange, shared values, and performance: Agreement and levels of analysis do matter. *The Leadership Quarterly, 21*, 469–480.

Masterson, S. S., Lewis, K., Goldman, B. M., & Taylor, M. S. (2000). Integrating justice and social exchange: The differing effects of fair procedures and treatment on work relationships. *Academy of Management Journal, 43*, 738–748.

Miceli, M. P., & Near, J. P. (1984). The relationships among beliefs, organizational position, and whistle-blowing status—a discriminant-analysis. *Academy of Management Journal, 27*, 687–705.

Nahrgang, J. D., Morgeson, F. P., & Ilies, R. (2009). The development of leader member exchanges: Exploring how personality and performance influence leader and member relationships over time. *Organizational Behavior and Human Decision Processes, 108*, 256–266.

Olsson, L., Hemlin, S., & Pousette, A. (2012). A multi-level analysis of leader-member exchange and creative performance in research groups. *Leadership Quarterly, 23*, 604–619.

Organ, D. W. (1988). *Organizational citizenship behavior: The good soldier syndrome.* Lexington, MA: Lexington books.

Pan, W., Sun, L. Y., & Chow, I. H. S. (2012). Leader-member exchange and employee creativity: Test of a multilevel moderated mediation model. *Human performance, 25*, 432–451.

Paparoidamis, N. G., & Guenzi, P. (2009). An empirical investigation into the impact of relationship selling and LMX on salespeople's behaviours and sales effectiveness. *European Journal of Marketing, 43*, 1053–1075.

Pattie, M. W., Benson, G., Casper, W., & McMahan, G. C. (2013). Goal congruence: Fitting international assignment into employee careers. *International Journal of Human Resource Management, 24*, 2554–2570.

Pearson, A. W., & Marler, L. E. (2010). A leadership perspective of reciprocal stewardship in family firms. *Entrepreneurship Theory and Practice, 34*, 1117–1124.

Pulakos, E. D., Arad, S., Donovan, M. A., & Plamondon, K. E. (2000). Adaptability in the workplace: Development of a taxonomy of adaptive performance. *Journal of Applied Psychology, 85*, 612–624.

Rockstuhl, T., Dulebohn, J. H., Ang, S., & Shore, L. M. (2012). Leader-member exchange (LMX) and culture: A meta-analysis of correlates of LMX across 23 countries. *Journal of Applied Psychology, 97*, 1097–1130.

Rotundo, M., & Sackett, P. R. (2002). The relative importance of task, citizenship, and counterproductive performance to global ratings of job performance: A policy-capturing approach. *Journal of Applied Psychology, 87*, 66–80.

Scott, S. G., & Bruce, R. A. (1994). Determinants of innovative behavior—a path model of individual innovation in the workplace. *Academy of Management Journal, 37*, 580–607.

Sekiguchi, T., Burton, J. P., & Sablynski, C. J. (2008). The role of job embeddedness on employee performance: The interactive effects with leader-member exchange and organization-based self-esteem. *Personnel Psychology, 61*, 761–792.

Settoon, R. P., Bennett, N., & Liden, R. C. (1996). Social exchange in organizations: Perceived organizational support, leader-member exchange, and employee reciprocity. *Journal of Applied Psychology, 81*, 219–227.

Sin, H. P., Nahrgang, J. D., & Morgeson, F. P. (2009). Understanding why they don't see eye to eye: An examination of leader-member exchange (LMX) agreement. *Journal of Applied Psychology, 94*, 1048–1057.

Smith, C. A., Organ, D. W., & Near, J. P. (1983). Organizational citizenship behavior—its nature and antecedents. *Journal of Applied Psychology, 68*, 653–663.

Sparrowe, R. T., Soetjipto, B. W., & Kraimer, M. L. (2006). Do leaders' influence tactics relate to members' helping behavior? It depends on the quality of the relationship. *Academy of Management Journal, 49*, 1194–1208.

Sun, L. Y., Chow, I. H. S., Chiu, R. K., & Pan, W. (2013). Outcome favorability in the link between leader-member exchange and organizational citizenship behavior: Procedural fairness climate matters. *Leadership Quarterly, 24*, 215–226.

Swann, W. B. (1983). Self-verification: Bringing social reality into harmony with the self. In J. Suls & A. G. Greenwald (Eds.), *Psychological perspectives on the self* (Vol. 2, pp. 33–66). Hillsdale, NJ: Erlbaum.

Takeuchi, R., Yun, S., & Wong, K. F. E. (2011). Social influence of a coworker: A test of the effect of employee and coworker exchange ideologies on employees' exchange qualities. *Organizational Behavior and Human Decision Processes, 115*, 226–237.

Tepper, B. J., Uhl-Bien, M., Kohut, G. F., Rogelberg, S. G., Lockhart, D. E., & Ensley, M. D. (2006). Subordinates' resistance and managers' evaluations of subordinates' performance. *Journal of Management, 32*, 185–209.

Tett, R. P., & Burnett, D. D. (2003). A personality trait-based interactionist model of job performance. *Journal of Applied Psychology, 88*, 500–517.

Tett, R. P., & Guterman, H. A. (2000). Situation trait relevance, trait expression, and cross-situational consistency: Testing a principle of trait activation. *Journal of Research in Personality, 34*, 397–423.

Tierney, P., Bauer, T. N., & Potter, R. E. (2002). Extra-role behavior among mexican employees: The impact of LMX, group acceptance, and job attitudes. *International Journal of Selection and Assessment, 10*, 292–303.

Tierney, P., Farmer, S. M., & Graen, G. B. (1999). An examination of leadership and employee creativity: The relevance of traits and relationships. *Personnel Psychology, 52*, 591–620.

Vadera, A. K., Pratt, M. G., & Mishra, P. (2013). Constructive deviance in organizations: Integrating and moving forward. *Journal of Management, 39*, 1221–1276.

Van Dyne, L., Cummings, L. L., & McLean Parks, J. (1995). Extra-role behaviors: In pursuit of construct and definitional clarity (a bridge over muddied waters). *Research in organizational behavior, 17*, 215–285.

Van Dyne, L., Jehn, K. A., & Cummings, A. (2002). Differential effects of strain on two forms of work performance: Individual employee sales and creativity. *Journal of Organizational Behavior, 23*, 57–74.

Van Dyne, L., Kamdar, D., & Joireman, J. (2008). In-role perceptions buffer the negative impact of low LMX on helping and enhance the positive impact of high LMX on voice. *Journal of Applied Psychology, 93*, 1195–1207.

Van Dyne, L., & LePine, J. A. (1998). Helping and voice extra-role behaviors: Evidence of construct and predictive validity. *Academy of Management Journal, 41*, 108–119.

Vecchio, R. P., & Gobdel, B. C. (1984). The vertical dyad linkage model of leadership: Problems and prospects. *Organizational Behavior and Human Performance, 34*, 5–20.

Vigoda-Gadot, E., & Beeri, I. (2012). Change-oriented organizational citizenship behavior in public administration: The power of leadership and the cost of organizational politics. *Journal of Public Administration Research and Theory, 22*, 573–596.

Walumbwa, F. O., Cropanzano, R., & Goldman, B. M. (2011). How leader-member exchange influences effective work behaviors: Social exchange and internal-external efficacy perspectives. *Personnel Psychology, 64*, 739–770.

Walumbwa, F. O., Cropanzano, R., & Hartnell, C. A. (2009). Organizational justice, voluntary learning behavior, and job performance: A test of the mediating effects of identification and leader-member exchange. *Journal of Organizational Behavior, 30*, 1103–1126.

Wang, H., Law, K. S., Hackett, R. D., Wang, D. X., & Chen, Z. X. (2005). Leader-member exchange as a mediator of the relationship between transformational leadership and followers' performance and organizational citizenship behavior. *Academy of Management Journal, 48*, 420–432.

Wat, D., & Shaffer, M. A. (2005). Equity and relationship quality influences on organizational citizenship behaviors—the mediating role of trust in the supervisor and empowerment. *Personnel Review, 34*, 406–422.

Wayne, S. J., & Green, S. A. (1993). The effects of leader-member exchange on employee citizenship and impression management behavior. *Human Relations, 46*, 1431–1440.

Wayne, S. J., Shore, L. M., & Liden, R. C. (1997). Perceived organizational support and leader-member exchange: A social exchange perspective. *Academy of Management Journal, 40*, 82–111.

Xu, E., Huang, X., Lam, C. K., & Miao, Q. (2012). Abusive supervision and work behaviors: The mediating role of LMX. *Journal of Organizational Behavior, 33*, 531–543.

Yuan, F. R., & Woodman, R. W. (2010). Innovative behavior in the workplace: The role of performance and image outcome expectations. *Academy of Management Journal, 53*, 323–342.

Zhang, Z., Wang, M., & Shi, J. Q. (2012). Leader-follower congruence in proactive personality and work outcomes: The mediating role of leader-member exchange. *Academy of Management Journal, 55*, 111–130.

LMX and Creativity

Pamela Tierney

Abstract

The purpose of this chapter is to provide an extended consideration regarding the connection between Leader–Member Exchange (LMX) and employee creativity. Given that it is a relational-based mode of leadership, the LMX perspective should allow for the more dynamic social aspects surrounding the emergence of workplace creativity. The chapter explores some of the deeper issues as they relate to the LMX creativity connection including potential mediators (self-efficacy, identity, motivation, sensemaking, and justice) by which LMX could shape creative engagement, when LMX may matter the most for creative efforts, how creativity may be relevant for LMX development, implications of LMX embeddedness for creativity, as well as ways in which LMX may be detrimental to employee creativity. Suggestions for future research are also provided.

Key Words: LMX, Creativity, relations, self-efficacy, creativity motivation, identity, justice, sensemaking, LMX development, LMX embeddedness

Introduction

There is an increasing awareness that leadership represents a significant mechanism for fostering employee creative performance (Tierney, 2008). Although a number of perspectives can be invoked to explore leadership's creativity influence, the Leader–Member Exchange (LMX) perspective is particularly useful because it embeds the role of leaders within the social relations framework, which has been tied to the emergence of creativity in the workplace (cf. Perry-Smith & Shalley, 2003). LMX stands apart from other forms of leadership that have been examined in relation to creative engagement (e.g., transformational leadership) in that its links to such activity rest solely on the facets of the interpersonal relationship shared between the leader and employee, the role behaviors they define as the basis of their connection, and how the resulting dynamics play out for employees' inclination to create as part of their work role. Although a growing number of studies have examined employee creativity using

LMX theory, there is still much to be investigated in this realm. The overall purpose of this chapter is to explore some of the complex dynamics that surround LMX relationships and employee creative performance, with a particular focus on the intrapersonal and interpersonal phenomena that LMX may evoke for employee creativity. The chapter will delve into a number of "deeper" issues as they relate to LMX and creativity that should facilitate our thinking about the connection between the two in more nuanced ways with an eye toward future inquiry.

LMX: A Natural Catalyst for Creativity

Numerous studies have sought to understand the emergence of employee creativity within a "relational" framework (see Perry-Smith, 2006). A subset of such studies has applied the concept of LMX in an attempt to understand how work-based social relations may shape employees' propensity to be creative at work. These studies have explored the role of LMX for creativity in a variety of ways. Some have considered the main effects of LMX on employee creative performance (e.g., Basu & Green, 1997; Joo, Yang, & McLean, 2013; Tierney, Farmer, & Graen, 1999), whereas others have examined LMX in an interactive manner with variables such as job autonomy (Volmer, Spurk, & Niessen, 2012), employee intrinsic motivation and cognitive style (Tierney et al., 1999, and stress (Van Dyne, Jehn, & Cummings, 2002). One study investigated the interactive effect of LMX and creativity on employee sales effectiveness (Martinaityte & Sacramento, 2013). Other studies have considered mediators for the LMX–creativity association including innovation climate perceptions (Dunegan, Tierney, & Duchon, 1992; Scott & Bruce, 1994), employee self-efficacy (Liao, Liu, & Loi, 2010), and the extent to which employees had "image gains" and expectation of positive outcomes from their efforts (Yuan & Woodman, 2010). Finally, one creativity study examined LMX as an outcome of employee's mastery orientation and the extent to which it led to employee creativity (Janssen & van Yperen, 2004).

LMX has been presented as a natural catalyst for fostering employee creativity (Tierney, 2008) and creative behavior identified as an inherent part of the LMX dyadic "coupling" process (Graen & Scandura, 1987). LMX has been acknowledged as a proximal determinant of employee performance (Chen & Kanfer, 2006). Within the landscape of contextual variables, factors proximal to employees have the greatest impact on creative performance (Shalley, Gilson, & Blum, 2000). In discussions of why context influences employee creativity, terms such as "motivating" and "enabling" often emerge (cf. Amabile, 1988). Examination reveals both creativity motivating and enabling elements endemic to the nature of LMX and the experiences high LMX employees have as part of their relationship with the leader (Tierney et al., 1999).

Motivating

The tendency to go "above and beyond" is a noted attribute of high LMX employees (Graen & Scandura, 1987). Research on organizational citizenship behavior (e.g., Illies, Nahrgang, & Morgeson, 2007) shows that employees engaged in high LMX dyads exhibit a drive toward behaviors that extend beyond the routine, and tend to define the parameters of their jobs as including a greater set of behaviors and responsibilities

as in-role (Hsiung & Tsai, 2011). In addition, research indicates that high LMX employees report engaging in more challenging and relevant tasks than their low LMX peers (Liden & Graen, 1980). The concept of challenge has been linked to the notion of goals as well as creative performance (Shalley, 1995). Employees perceiving a certain level of difficulty, meaning, and sense of achievement associated with their work will likely augment the level of effort extended toward that task necessary for creativity (Amabile, 1988). Thus, it may be expected that high LMX employees will tend to be goal oriented toward creativity. High levels of support for risk taking, and the provision of resources, rewards, and encouragement in the work context signal a support and receptiveness for creativity (Ford, 1996). All of these factors are common to high LMX dyads (Graen & Scandura, 1987; Graen & Uhl-Bien, 1995). Indeed, previous research (e.g., Dunegan, Tierney, & Duchon, 1992; Scott & Bruce, 1994) indicates that high LMX employees believe that they operate in a context that is supportive of innovative work. In addition, the enhanced levels of trust, advocacy, and interpersonal support high LMX employees experience (Duchon, Green, & Taber, 1986) may prompt them to produce creative outcomes. Finally, the expectation of high LMX employees to take risks and seek new challenges is a "green light" for creative engagement.

Enabling

The high-quality LMX should serve the creative efforts of its employees in a number of ways. Creativity is a time-consuming and resource-intensive endeavor. Employees who are to successfully engage in creativity need to be provided a certain amount of discretionary time and the latitude to contemplate, play around with new ideas, and engage in trial and error (Amabile, 1988). In addition, creative efforts entail adequate provision of raw materials and other elements that are to be the building blocks for their creative ideas (Amabile, 1988). As a means of facilitating the high LMX employees' success, their leaders ensure that they are equipped with both tangible (e.g., raw materials, equipment) and intangible (e.g., time) resources (Sparrowe & Liden, 2005). High LMX employees are also privy to greater amounts and frequencies of pertinent information (Sparrowe & Liden, 2005), including information that has broad implications for the employees and the organization as a whole (cf. van Dam, Oreg, & Schyns, 2008). Armed with critical information, employees can more effectively formulate new ideas and target their creative efforts in directions in which they are most needed and are likely to be well received.

Deeper Issues to Consider
When Does LMX Matter the Most for Creativity?

When an employee experiencing creativity-conducive conditions (either personal or contextual) is involved in a high LMX relationship, a natural assumption is that the creativity-enriching aspects of the dyad should augment the effect of the existing conditions, resulting in substantially higher levels of creativity. An interesting pattern has emerged, however, in a small number of creativity studies that have examined LMX in this regard. The pattern suggests that although, in general, LMX is conducive to creativity, it may be more relevant under certain conditions and for certain types of employees.

For example, studies have suggested that for employees with an "innovator" orientation (Tierney et al., 1999) or a strong creative self-efficacy (Tierney, 2010), the nature of their LMX dyad has no influence on their creative performance. These employees consistently produce creative work regardless of the quality of their relationship with their supervisor. A very different pattern was evidenced for "adaptor" employees or those with low creative self-efficacy, both of whom are naturally less inclined to be creative in their work. When adaptor and low creative self-efficacy employees experienced a high LMX dyad, they produced high levels of creative output commensurate with that of their innovator and high creative self-efficacy peers. When the LMX relationship was weak, creative performance between the adaptor and low creative self-efficacy employees was quite low. The authors surmised that involvement in the dyad provided these employees with the emotional and material support as well as a sense of obligation to push themselves in creative directions despite their predisposition against such activities.

Preliminary results from other studies support a similar pattern. For example, individuals depicting a highly agreeable personality tend to be quite conforming and are, therefore, less inclined to be innovative in their work. Yet a recent study (Erdogan, Enders, & Bauer, 2011) found that despite this tendency, employees characterized by high agreeableness did engage in high levels of creative performance when they were part of a high LMX relationship. The authors noted that engagement in a high LMX dyad may dampen natural tendencies that work against creative engagement, such as tendency to avoid risk and to conform as a means of being agreeable, thereby permitting employees to operate in a manner consistent with creativity. Another study (Van Dyne, Jehn, & Cummings, 2002) found that highly strained employees were more resilient in performing creatively when they were involved in a high LMX relationship.

These patterns indicate that LMX may be a contextual factor that lends itself to certain person–context interactional configurations suggested by Zhou and Hoever (2014). They suggest that some contextual factors that are normally creativity conducive (such as LMX) will exhibit "synergistic diminishing gains" when they are experienced by employees who naturally possess traits aligned with creative performance. In such scenarios, the potentially added benefit to creativity of being involved in a high LMX relationship is not realized because the employees have key personal resources (innovator orientation, high creative self-efficacy) that permit them to be highly creative already. In these scenarios, there is a limit or boundary condition around how influential LMX can be for creativity. In contrast, an "inhibitory-remedial" pattern (Zhou & Hoever, 2014) is suggested for high LMX employees characterized by personal traits that would tend to inhibit creative performance. The creative effort of these high LMX employees is most likely quite dependent on the relationship to provide a buffer or compensate for their traits that would otherwise be detrimental to creativity. In this regard, LMX leaders seem to enable employees who would be less inclined to be creative. For example, employees with an adaptor orientation or who are highly agreeable have a strong tendency toward conforming to the status quo—a pattern antithetical to creativity. Employees lacking in creative self-efficacy are hesitant to take risks in trying out new ideas because they don't believe in their ability to do so successfully. Stressed employees may experience levels of insecurity and cognitive distractions that hinder any possible creative efforts. Being immersed in a high LMX relationship is likely to provide such low creativity-potential employees with the stability, support, and encouragement they need to venture from the norm and experiment in doing things differently.

Extant models of creativity, as well as subsequent studies, have also pointed to the necessity of certain task or work attributes for creativity to take place among employees. A consistent theme among these works is that employees must experience operational autonomy, flexibility, and control in their work in order to be creative (e.g., Shalley & Gilson, 2004). Such freedom permits employees to experiment and to develop a sense of ownership of their work that is conducive to generating new ideas and creative problem solving (Amabile, 1988). Employees are also more likely to engage in creativity if their job is positively challenging, meaningful, and has impact (Amabile, 1988; Grant & Berry, 2011). The reality is that there are many jobs that are designed in ways that do not permit much latitude and do not readily provide employees with an immediate sense of meaning, impact, or challenge. To date, few studies (e.g., Joo, Yang, & McLean, 2013) have explicitly looked at the codetermining effect of LMX and job attributes on creative performance. We can speculate, however, that the same patterns of synergistic diminishing gains and inhibitory remediation may apply to the influence of LMX under conditions of different job attributes as well. If a job was characterized by an inherently low level of autonomy and control, the incremental latitude high LMX provides might be particularly central for the employee's creative attempts. Because of a high LMX leader's tendency to enhance the dyad member's sense of importance, and provide the opportunity to challenge in ways that go beyond the basic job, an employee may experience these task attributes conducive to creativity within the context of a high LMX relationship. If the employee conducted a job that was already designed in such a way as to provide latitude, challenge, and a sense of meaning, the LMX relation may have less of an effect on the employee's creative performance.

Beyond the nature of the work itself, the occupational context in which the job is conducted can also have a significant influence on employee performance (Morgeson & Campion, 2003; Morgeson, Dierdorff, & Hmurovic, 2010), including creative performance. It has been suggested that creativity is of increasing relevance across a number of occupational contexts and domains, including those that we typically consider to be incompatible with creativity (Tierney & Farmer, 2002). Of relevance for creativity is the notion that contexts can "amplify the adverse effects of poor work design" (Morgeson & Campion, 2003, p. 352). Factors such as "appropriate" work roles, norms, and opportunities for employees to pursue new ideas or creatively solve problems can be dictated by the type of occupational context in which the employee

resides. Engagement in a high LMX relationship in a context that in many ways is antithetical to creative activity may likely provide employees with a sense of support and encouragement, and redefine behavioral norms and role-appropriate behavior consistent with creativity, despite the broader context. A recent study (Volmer, Spurk, & Niessen, 2012) found that employees were most productive for creativity when they experienced a high level of job autonomy and LMX, a finding that contradicts the "inhibitory-remedial" pattern suggested above. Interestingly though, the employees were from manufacturing. It is reasonable that in a manufacturing context, engaging in exploration, experimenting with new ideas, and taking time to develop creative ideas may not be the norm, nor considered part of the employees' work role. It is possible that although job autonomy enhanced the likelihood that these employees would engage creatively, the numerous facets inherent in the particular occupational setting required the additional augmentation a high LMX relationship would bring in order for creativity to come to fruition.

What Are the Mediating Mechanisms at Play for LMX and Creativity?

A leader's influence on employee creativity can be manifest in numerous and complex ways (Shin, in press; Tierney, 2008). In general, leadership can potentially shape employee's creativity-related cognitions, motivation, and capacity (Amabile, 1988, 1996; Ford, 1996; Tierney, 2008), leading to enhanced creative performance. LMX has been linked to general employee outcomes through a variety of mediating mechanisms (cf. Chen, Kirkman, Kanfer, Allen, & Rosen, 2007; Liden, Wayne, & Sparrowe, 2000), so it is logical to assume that it may also link to creative performance through key mediators as well. These mediators are summarized in Figure 10.1.

Employee Self-Efficacy

Extant models of creativity (Amabile, 1988; Ford, 1996; Woodman et al., 1993) cite employee's sense of capacity as a necessary building block on which creative efforts are established. Research suggests that both more general job self-efficacy and creative self-efficacy are linked to creative performance (Tierney & Farmer, 2002). Studies suggest that leaders may play a role in influencing employee creativity by fostering both a sense of job efficacy (Liao, Liu, & Loi, 2010) and creative self-efficacy (Tierney & Farmer, 2002, 2004) in their employees. According

Fig. 10.1 Summary of potential mediators of the LMX to creative performance relationship reviewed.

to recent research (Walumbwa, Cropanzano, & Goldman, 2011), high-quality LMX relations shape employee performance through the development of employee self-efficacy and "means efficacy" (Eden, 2001). LMX can operate on such employee capability self-views in numerous ways (Schyns, 2004). The variety of tangible and intangible resources LMX employees receive, as well as the challenging task opportunities they are afforded (Graen & Scandura, 1987; Liden & Graen, 1980), should lead to more successful and meaningful efforts, providing employees with a sense of mastery (Bandura, 1986). Possessing performance-relevant resources also provides high LMX employees with a basis for assessing a sense of means efficacy—confidence that one has the external resources to adequately perform (Eden, 2011).

High LMX leaders also play an active coaching and mentoring or model role as part of their dyadic exchange (Kraimer, Seibert, Wayne, Liden, & Bravo, 2011) and provide constructive task feedback (Harris, Marris, & Eplion, 2007). Both mentoring and task feedback have been linked to an enhanced level of confidence in personal capacity for creative task activity (Zhou, 2008). High LMX dyadic exchanges are characterized by their learning and growth opportunities for employees (Erdogan & Bauer, 2014)—elements also central to efficacy building (Bandura, 1986). For example, high LMX employees are entrusted with integral duties that the leader would normally fulfill (Bauer & Green, 1996; Liden & Graen, 1980) and are afforded select opportunities to which their low LMX peers are not privy (Duchon et al., 1986; Law, Wong, Wang, & Wang, 2000). Such opportunities may include the chance to try new tasks, take on new risks and challenges, leeway to approach one's work in a new and different manner, and experiment with new approaches—all of which have also been linked to enhanced efficacy-building and creative productivity (Amabile, 1988; Tierney & Farmer, 2002).

Finally, the high-quality dyadic context is emotionally supportive with the leader actively encouraging employees and working to bolster their sense of confidence (Schyns, 2004). Such an environment permits the employee a sense of security from which to ask questions, take risks, fail and improve, and subsequently build a sense of efficacy. One study (Tierney & Farmer, 2004) found that leaders displaying a set of behaviors consistent with high LMX relationships (advocacy, provision of resource and personal support, recognition) resulted in employees reporting higher levels of confidence in their capacity to be creative. As such, high LMX involvement is likely to induce an elevated sense of efficacy in employees that they need to tackle creative endeavors.

Employee Sensemaking

Employee sensemaking is central to creativity in a number of ways (Drazin, Glynn, & Kazanjian, 1999). For example, in formulating a decision on whether or not to engage in creativity, employees may seek to understand whether creativity is an expected and legitimate behavior for them in their job (Ford, 1996). Employees look to their work context for informational cues as to appropriate behavior, and leaders are a prime source of such cues (Gioia & Poole, 1984). The description of LMX development (e.g., Graen & Uhl-Bien, 1995) reflects a sensemaking process on the part of both dyad members. Early work on LMX describes the phenomenon as a "role making process" (Graen & Scandura, 1987). As the quality of the exchange enhances, both the leader and the employee come to an understanding of roles commensurate with their relationship. As noted by Gioia and Poole (1984), the concept of roles is central to the sensemaking process in that ". . . when roles completely define relationships, role-specified scripts are evoked." Thus, LMX is a mechanism for providing high LMX employees with a script for behavior "appropriate" for their status. The fact that high LMX employees are provided with creativity-conducive resources and are encouraged to take risks, seek challenges, engage in nonroutine behaviors, and "go above and beyond" in their work makes it more likely that they will reach the conclusion that creativity is an acceptable and expected aspect of their work role. Previous work indicates that being part of a high LMX relationship is associated with employee perceptions that their work context supports creative efforts (Scott & Bruce, 1994) and values such work (Dunegan, Tierney, & Duchon, 1992). As such, the nature of the LMX relationship employees experience may shape perceptions they develop that are basic to their decision to pursue creative activity in their work.

Employee Motivation

Despite the fact that individual motivation is positioned as one of the most important factors for employee creativity, to date we lack much empirical evidence shedding light on how and why employees are motivated to be creative in their work (Shalley, Zhou, & Oldham, 2004). LMX might be useful in this regard, in that high LMX engagement is considered to elicit strong levels of work motivation among its employee dyad members (Erdogan & Bauer, 2014). Whereas intrinsic motivation stems from the inherent interest and enjoyment one derives from employment in a certain activity, extrinsic motivation arises from contextual factors and may take on a variety of forms (Gagne & Deci, 2005). Employees may come to the dyadic relationship with an intrinsic motivation for creativity intact, but it is worthwhile to consider the type of motivation LMX may trigger in employees when it is not already present, and why it concludes in creative effort.

An argument could be made that because a high LMX relationship affords employees the opportunity to be creative, exposure to such activity may foster the sense of enjoyment for creative efforts basic to intrinsic motivation. However, it may be more feasible that a prime driver of creative engagement among high LMX employees is the external expectation or sense of obligation stemming from their relationship. Employees with a strong relational orientation may be motivated to create because they feel obligated and believe it is necessary for the good of their LMX relationship (Tierney, in press). Therefore, the value the high LMX employee places on creativity may not be inherent to the activity itself, but instrumental in the sense that it helps address the needs of, or preserves, the dyad (Tierney, in press). In this regard, the motivation pattern exhibited would be extrinsic. This latter mode of creativity motivation among high LMX

employees may also be considered through the lens of prosocial motivation (Grant, 2008), which has been linked to creative behavior (Grant & Berry, 2011). As suggested above, if employees seek out creative engagement solely because they wish to contribute to the welfare of the dyad or leader, and wish to make a positive difference in this regard, their creativity may be considered prosocially motivated by LMX.

Employee Identity

Leadership is a natural catalyst for identity formulation (Lord, Brown, & Freiberg, 1999) and a number of studies have linked leadership with various identity types (e.g., Wang & Howell, 2012). A sense of identity also provides a natural framework for understanding creative action at work (Drazin, Glynn, & Kazanjian, 1999). As such, a number of studies have explored the possible connection between employee identity and creativity (e.g., Carmeli & Schaubroeck, 2007; Farmer, Tierney, & Kung-McIntyre, 2003; Hirst, van Dick, & van Knippenberg, 2009; Jaussi, Randel, & Dionne, 2007; Tierney & Farmer, 2011). Only a few studies have linked leadership with creativity via identity means (cf. Wang & Zhu, 2011), and none of these has explored the LMX mode of leadership in this regard. However, the leader–follower relationship has been theorized to have strong implications for employee identity formulation (Lord et al., 1999) and various forms of identity exist that present possible ways in which LMX may link to employee creativity.

In general, identity constructions are strongly influenced by social relations (Riley & Burke, 1995). For example, role identities are shaped via internalized role expectations from important members of the individual's social sphere. Creative role identity, defined as self-identification with playing the role of a creator (Farmer et al., 2003), is positively influenced when relevant members of the immediate work context convey expectations for the employee's creative engagement (Carmeli & Schaubroeck, 2007; Farmer et al., 2003). Given that LMX is a role-based relationship characterized by negotiated role expectations for the dyad incumbents (Graen & Scandura, 1987), combined with the fact that high LMX employees are provided the resources to be creative and are expected to "go above and beyond," it is plausible that such employees may internalize role expectations for being a creative employee as part of their identity. As such, LMX may lead to creative performance via an employee's sense of creative role identity. Leaders in a high-quality exchange relationship also have the potential to shape the employee's sense of "possible self" (Lord et al., 1999), a future, aspirational identity that the employee sees as feasibly attained. The dynamics of the high LMX relationship may also provide a setting whereby the employee can envision becoming a creative employee over time.

A second form of identity is relational identity, a dyadic identity in which sense of self is defined in terms of the relational partner (Brewer & Gardner, 1996). In the job context, sense of relational identity often entails identity with the immediate supervisor (Sluss & Ashforth, 2007). It has been suggested (Tierney, in press) that creative activity on the part of high LMX employees may be a function of relational identity with the LMX leader. Because strong relational identity tends to prompt actions that will meet the needs and expectations of the relational partner (Brewer & Gardner, 1996), it is likely that if dyad employees perceive that their leader needs employees to be creative, the employees will be creatively engaged. One study (Tierney, 2005) found that high LMX employees report both a strong creative role identity and a relational identity with their dyad leader. Both identity types were positively related to creative performance levels, providing preliminary support for the notion that LMX may influence employee creativity through the types of identities they develop when engaged in a high LMX relation.

Interpersonal Justice

The construct of justice has been tied to LMX and social exchange (Masterson, Lewis, Goldman, & Taylor, 2000; Wayne, Shore, Bommer, & Tetrick, 2002) and is increasingly examined as a contextual factor influential for a myriad of employee-related outcomes (Colquitt et al., 2013). Justice has also been recognized as an important contextual element for creative performance (Shalley & Gilson, 2004). Research shows that employees are more likely to engage in extrarole types of behavior when they believe that they have been treated fairly at work (e.g., Fahr, Early, & Linn, 1997). For many jobs, willingness to attack work-related problems with the intent to creatively solve them, and generating novel ideas for use of existing technology and creative alternatives to standard procedures, would all represent behavior that goes beyond the formal job description. Although the connection between justice and creativity seems intuitive, only a handful of studies have examined their association. (cf.

Clark & James, 1999; George & Zhou, 2007; Janssen, 2004; Schepers & van den Ber, 2007). It has been suggested that justice is critical for creativity attempts because employees need to feel that they are respected and are operating in a psychologically safe environment to be creatively engaged (George & Zhou, 2007).

Only one study (Khazanchi & Masterson, 2011) has explicitly examined justice and creativity in an LMX context, finding that LMX was an outcome of both interpersonal and informational justice. However, research reporting perceived fairness (e.g., Erdogan, Liden, & Kraimer, 2006) and leader integrity (Bauer & Green, 1996) as part of the LMX process suggests the feasibility of it also serving as a potential mediator of LMX and creativity. Consistent with the LMX model, over time and interacts, the high LMX employee should experience feelings of respect, advocacy, and security. In addition, due to the social exchange nature of the LMX relationship, a high LMX leader takes efforts to ensure that the investments the dyad employee makes are adequately rewarded and reciprocated (Graen & Uhl-Bien, 1995). Because a sense of security, feeling supported, and acknowledgment are antecedents of creative efforts, we might anticipate that high LMX employees holding strong justice perceptions would be more inclined to be innovative in their work as a means of repaying the leader.

Is Creativity Relevant for LMX Development?

Given the impact LMX relationships can have, researchers have been drawn to the issue of how such relationships develop. Although earlier conceptualizations of LMX provided a basic depiction of the steps that employees and leaders go through in becoming dyad partners, later work focused on more nuanced aspects of the development process (e.g., Bauer & Green, 1996; Dienesch & Liden, 1986; Graen & Uhl-Bien, 1995) including factors that define and influence the various stages of the relationship's evolution.

In the initial stage of LMX development, the basis for relational consideration revolves more around the characteristics of the leader and employee and the degree to which such traits are found appealing by the two individuals (Bauer & Green, 1996; Dienesch & Liden, 1986; Nahrgang et al., 2009). Which key characteristics are found to be attractive will depend for the most part on the nature of the dyad members. Such characteristics could include personality aspects, values, and competencies. One dynamic that appears to be relevant in this early stage is "similarity," whereby the potential dyad members are drawn to one another if they possess similar characteristics (Liden, Wayne, & Stilwell, 1993). Individuals hold personal profiles that will increase the likelihood that they will be creative in their work (Woodman et al., 1993). Multiple aspects comprise such a profile but common facets include a creative personality that often corresponds to attributes such as risk-taking propensity, extraversion, and innovative cognitive style (Shalley et al., 2004). In addition, someone with a creative profile conveys certain self-concepts tied to creative engagement such as creative self-efficacy and creative role identity (Tierney & Farmer, 2011). They also tend to hold a core value for creativity and possess an intrinsic motivation for creative work. As such, if a leader and employee both possess creativity-related characteristics, these may represent a basis for considering the further development of a high LMX relationship. On the other hand, if one of the individuals depicts characteristics that are antithetical to creativity, the more creativity-prone individual may find the notion of developing a strong relationship far less appealing.

The first stage of LMX development has been referred to as a "role taking" phase, an exploratory time in which the leader initially tests the employee's potential. The process involves the leader providing a "sent role" in the way of a performance request, and is usually accompanied with a certain level of delegation to the employee. If the employee accepts the role, and attempts to perform accordingly, the leader has a basis on which to determine whether the employee is worth investing in further. Individuals who possess creative profiles are likely to engage in creative behavior as a means of making themselves more attractive to potential dyad partners (Tierney, in press). The inclination and ability to bring creativity to the LMX performance-testing phase may result in successful and impressive outcomes that help the employee "stand out" from other employees, and ensure that he or she will be considered further for an LMX relationship.

The second stage of LMX development is the "role making" phase in which the dyad members determine the roles that will characterize their relationship. What is relevant from a creativity perspective is that this stage entails the leader and employee collaborating on unstructured tasks and problem solving (Graen & Scandura, 1987). Hence, application of creativity skills and joint creative engagement are important aspects of this critical LMX development phase. Because this phase entails the identification of valued roles, if the dyad members determine that creative action is critical to their success, one outcome of the leader–employee collaborative efforts might be that creative engagement becomes an ongoing part of the relationship. Given the risky nature of creativity, employees may tend to avoid such action unless they believe that it is viewed as legitimate by relevant members of their work context (Ford, 1996). Hence, the role-making phase may represent a process through which creative engagement becomes legitimized for employees. The final phase of LMX development is the "role routinization" stage. At this point, the negotiated roles from the previous phase have become "institutionalized" (Graen & Scandura, 1987) and second nature to the dyad members. Mature LMX relationships for which creativity has become a valued and normalized component at this stage could therefore be fertile settings for a consistent pattern of employee creative performance.

How Might the Embeddedness of LMX Influence Creativity?

Efforts to lead do not take place in a vacuum, and to truly understand the impact of leadership on employee performance, we must consider the impact of the leader's embeddedness within the larger system (Sparrowe & Liden, 1997). Two aspects of LMX embeddedness need to be considered in terms of their possible implications for employee creativity: LLX and LMX differentiation. LLX denotes the quality of the relationship an LMX leader experiences with his or her leader (Tangirala, Green, & Ramanujam, 2007). Early work (Graen, Cashman, Ginsburgh, & Schiemann, 1977) referred to the concept as the "linking pin" effect with an initial focus on how LMX leaders' upper relationships could shape the type of relationships they could have with their own employees. Although the topic has not garnered much research attention, recent studies (e.g., Erdogan & Enders, 2007; Tangirala et al., 2007) have suggested that a high-quality LLX is associated with higher levels of employee performance, sometimes through mechanisms such as employee empowerment (Zhou, Wang, Chen, & Shi, 2012).

It seems that the nature of the LLX relationship could definitely have implications for whether employees will be creative in their work from a number of perspectives. First, the LLX quality could serve as either an impediment or facilitating factor in the LMX leader's efforts to foster creativity among employees. As noted earlier, creativity requires a fair amount of job latitude, time, and resources. By definition, a low-quality LLX would fail to provide the LMX leader with these elements. If this were the case, it would be difficult for the leader to, in turn, provide the high LMX employees with the basics they needed to be creative in their work. At a more rudimentary level, without access to these elements to provide as contributions to the dyad, the LMX leader would have more difficulty even establishing the type of high-quality relationships that prompt employees to take risks and "go above and beyond" in ways necessary for creative performance. Another creativity-relevant factor is the manner in which the LLX may shape the LMX leader's attitudes and values toward creative work. In high-quality dyads, the members come to share perceptions and values (Scandura, Graen, & Novak, 1986). If LLX leaders do not value creative action, and believe it is an inappropriate mode of employee behavior, they may put pressure on their direct reports to encourage their employees to be more conservative in their work or follow standard operating procedures that are antithetical to creative action.

LMX differentiation addresses the reality that not all leader–employee relationships will be of equal quality within a work group. According to the LMX model, leaders may choose to develop high-quality relations with some employees, but not with others. Studies addressing the differentiation issue (e.g., Erdogan & Bauer, 2014; Erdogan & Liden, 2002) have shown that employees are adept at recognizing LMX differentiation within their work unit and respond to such variability. The pattern of results provided by these studies is mixed, and it is difficult to ascertain with certainty whether differentiation, overall, is positive or negative for employee performance (Erdogan & Bauer, 2014). Only one study to date (Liao, Liu, & Loi, 2010) has examined LMX differentiation as it relates to creative performance. The authors posited that LMX would lead to employees having a greater sense of efficaciousness (which subsequently led to creativity) if the employee experienced a differentiated dyadic exchange with the leader that was of high quality. The premise was that being singled out for a high LMX, in a context in which other employees did not share this type of leader relationship, would result in the employee feeling more respected and valued, which should boost his or her sense of competence. Contrary to what was expected, the self-efficacy of high LMX employees was highest when there was low LMX differentiation among

their team members. The interpretation for this unexpected finding was that high LMX employees in the high differentiation scenario might be concerned about injustice within the group, which detracted from the positive influence LMX could have had on their sense of efficacy. The growing interest in studying creativity in teams stems in part from the recognition that creative efforts and success are likely to require input from team members, and are influenced by the dynamics among these members (Shalley, Zhou, & Oldham, 2004). Research reporting heightened levels of creative performance in teams in which there is collaboration and cohesion among team members (Chen, Fahr, Campbell-Bush, & Wu, 2013) suggests that negative intrateam dynamics set off by high LMX differentiation could nullify any possible advantages for creativity that being distinguished as high LMX employees might provide.

Could LMX Be Destructive for Creativity?

Although we often view leadership as an inherently "good" phenomenon, a fair amount of attention has turned to the potential destructive aspects that leadership can bring (Schyns & Schilling, 2013). As such, recent work has focused on the "dark side" of leadership for employee engagement (see Liu, Liao, & Loi, 2012). Consistent with the substantive body of research suggesting the positive impact of LMX on performance (see Gerstner & Day, 1997), this chapter has provided an overall argument for LMX as a generative force for employee creative performance. However, given the strong influence LMX leaders are likely to have, there are certainly scenarios in which the LMX form of leadership could work against creativity. For example, the values, norms, and expectations defining the relationship will determine whether creativity will be a behavioral pattern in which the dyad partners engage (Tierney, in press). It is possible that the leader with whom the employee has a high-quality relationship does not personally value creative work, considers it too high risk, or considers it as not fitting within the parameters of the employee's job scope. If any of these factors are present, chances are good that creativity will not be considered "role-scripted" (Graen & Scandura, 1987) behavior and the high LMX employee will avoid creative work.

Creative engagement can be risky for employees because it involves working outside the norm, deviating from the status quo, and doing things in different and unexplored ways. Although such actions might be encouraged by the high LMX leader, they may not be well received by other members of the work group and may result in negative repercussions from which their leader cannot protect them. It could also be the case that the leader strongly encourages the employees to focus on specific, targeted areas for creative attention. Because the employee would be strongly swayed by the high LMX leader's opinions and perspectives, the employee could follow lines of creative pursuit that are not acceptable or appreciated in the broader work context external to the dyad.

Finally, as noted earlier, the differentiated relationships existing within a work group could be detrimental to the creative performance of its employees. In a high differentiation scenario, a lack of equal resource allocation and leader support will result in some employees not having the basics they need to engage in creativity. It may also lead to co-worker conflict, thereby decreasing the intragroup collaboration and support that enable creative productivity by individual members (see Taggar, 2002). Sentiments of injustice may result in co-worker resentment and unwillingness to support peers in ways that are necessary for creative efforts. Low LMX employees in a highly differentiated group may also question their capability and value as the leader has chosen not to pursue them for a high-quality relationship. Such negative self-views would work against their creative tendencies.

Moving Forward

This chapter has addressed a number of factors that should lend themselves to areas of future inquiry regarding the LMX–creativity connection. For instance, studies could explore how the configurational interactive patterns suggested by Zhou and Hoevar (2014) might apply to LMX and creativity. It would be useful to understand the types of employees, jobs, and work contexts in which LMX may have the most creative impact. The corollary is that there needs to be greater understanding of the conditions in which the attributes of the high LMX relationship are redundant with the other factors and play no incremental role for creativity. Identification of factors on both ends could lead to the most effective application of LMX relationships for promoting creativity among employees. A variety of potential mediators have also been proposed here. Inquiry into elements such as employee self-efficacy, motivation, identity, and sensemaking, as well as interpersonal justice, could shed light into the effect LMX might have on intrapersonal and interpersonal creativity-relevant factors as well as the manner in which LMX plays out in terms of creative performance.

For example, does engagement in a high-quality relationship with one's leader cause employees to become more intrinsically motivated for creativity, or would the motivational mechanism be more extrinsic in nature, driven by the needs of the dyad? Furthermore, would the specific motivational form elicited by LMX matter for creativity? Perhaps within the LMX context, the link to creativity is as strong through extrinsic motivation as it is through intrinsic motivation. Unsworth (2001) has suggested a variety of creativity types, "expected," "responsive," "contributory," or "proactive," that may be manifest in organizations as a result of different types of contextual influences. It would be interesting to determine if LMX would tend to result in one of these modes of creativity over others. Another interesting issue is whether LMX is a means by which employee's job and creative self-efficacy can be enhanced for creative performance. It would also be useful to determine if the LMX relationship had more sway on employee efficacy views than other relational types (e.g., co-workers). As noted earlier, there is considerable interest in understanding factors that shape LMX development. Another useful topic for inquiry would be assessing how, and if, employee creativity plays a role in the development of LMX relationships at their different stages. Various forms of leadership such as benevolent (Wang & Cheng, 2009) and empowering (Zhang & Bartol, 2010) have also been associated with creative performance (Shin, in press). Transformational leadership, in particular, has been widely explored as a vehicle for the engagement of employees in creativity. It would be beneficial to consider these leadership forms vis-à-vis LMX to determine how the various types shape creativity and which are most effective in this regard. Studies examining multiple modes of leadership in relation to creativity are rare, but such studies (e.g., Basu & Green, 1997) seem vital to adequately unraveling the aspects of leadership that are germane to employee creativity.

Practical Implications and Conclusions

As suggested in this chapter, there are many arguments to be made for LMX as a tool that organizations can leverage to increase the creative productivity of their work force. From a practical standpoint, having employees willing and able to bring creative problem solving to their jobs and proactively generate novel and useful ideas for new products or processes can serve organizations in their efforts to be more competitive and effective in their operations. In addition to providing the resources and interpersonal support employees need to be successfully creative, LMX may prove to be an effective means for establishing norms, values, and performance expectations that are influential in shaping employees' inclination for creative work. Importantly, the fact that LMX relationships reside at all levels of the organization, across different functional areas and job types, suggests that the potential for creative engagement throughout the organization can be quite strong. Prior research bears out this assertion as LMX involvement has been connected with employee creativity at both low and high levels of the hierarchy, as well as in job types (e.g., technicians) in which creativity is not usually a formal part of the work role (cf. Tierney et al., 1999).

In this regard, it is important that leaders understand how their actions and decisions about engaging employees in high-quality relations may be critical to an organization's efforts to promote creativity among its ranks. The message for organizations is that they need to support their leaders in their efforts to develop high-quality relations with their employees. As has been suggested here, part of that support includes ensuring that leaders have the opportunity to experience high-quality relations with their leaders, which they need to be effective stewards of employee creativity. Another means of support would be providing leaders with the training and resources they need to enable their relationship-building efforts. If LMX is the vehicle for promoting creativity that is being suggested here, and we know that it is unlikely that leaders will have the wherewithal or motivation to engage all employees in high-quality relations, it is imperative that organizations provide other means of resources and social support low LMX employees will need to be creative as well. For example, in the absence of LMX engagement, the role of the team members in substituting for creativity support is likely to be paramount.

Conclusions

The purpose of this chapter was to provide an extended consideration regarding the connection between LMX relationships and the emergence of employee creativity in the work context. The overall conclusion is that the LMX model has much promise for helping us understand how, and why, leaders can shape employee creativity. From both a conceptual and empirical perspective, we have come to realize that much of the momentum around creative activity in organizations stems from the social context at work. Of all of the current leadership theories, LMX is clearly the most social based, with its essence consisting of the interpersonal relationship that resides between employee and leader. LMX theory has a rich history of promoting a multitude of employee outcomes that organizations seek (Gerstner & Day, 1997). Given the economic, global, and technological nature of contemporary business, we can anticipate that organizations will increasingly rely on more of a creativity-based employee performance to thrive. If this turns out to be the case, the LMX model of leadership should become fundamentally more critical to organizations as an instrument for driving innovation and democratizing creative engagement throughout the workplace.

References

Amabile, T. M. (1988). A model of creativity and innovation in organizations. In B. M. Straw & L. L. Cummings (Eds.), *Research in organizational behavior* (Vol. 10, pp. 123–167). Greenwich, CT: JAI Press.

Amabile, T. M. (1996). *Creativity in context.* Boulder, CO: Westview.

Bandura, A. (1986). *Social foundations of thought and action* (pp. 5–107). Englewood Cliffs, NJ: Prentice Hall.

Basu, R., & Green, S. G. (1997). Leader–member exchange and transformational leadership: An empirical examination of innovative behaviors in leader–member dyads. *Journal of Applied Social Psychology, 27,* 477–499.

Bauer, T. N., & Green, S. G. (1996). Development of leader–member exchange: A longitudinal test. *Academy of Management Journal, 39,* 1538–1567.

Brewer, M. B., & Gardner, W. (1996). Who is this "We"? Levels of collective identity and self representations. *Journal of Personality and Social Psychology, 71,* 83–93.

Carmeli, A., & Schaubroeck, J. (2007). The influence of leaders' and other referents' normative expectations on individual involvement in creative work. *The Leadership Quarterly, 18,* 35–48.

Chen, G., Campbell-Bush, E., Farh, J., Wu, Z., & Wu, X. (2013). Teams as innovative systems: Multilevel motivational antecedents of innovation in R&D teams. *Journal of Applied Psychology, 98,* 1018–1027.

Chen, G., & Kanfer, R. (2006). Towards a systems theory of motivated behavior in work teams. *Research in Organizational Behavior, 27,* 223–267.

Chen, G., Kirkman, B. L., Kanfer, R., Allen, D., & Rosen, B. (2007). A multilevel study of leadership, empowerment, and performance in teams. *Journal of Applied Psychology, 92,* 331–346.

Clark, K., & James, K. (1999). Justice and positive and negative creativity. *Creativity Research Journal, 12,* 311–320.

Colquitt, J. A., Scott, B. A., Rodell, J. B., Long, D. M., Zapata, C. P., Conlon, D. E., & Wesson, M. J. (2013). Justice at the millennium, a decade later: A meta-analytic test of social exchange and affect-based perspectives. *Journal of Applied Psychology, 98*, 199–236.

Dienesch, R. M., & Liden, R. C. (1986). Leader-member exchange model of leadership: A critique and further development. *Academy of Management Journal, 11*, 618–634.

Drazin, R., Glynn, M. A., & Kazanjian, R. K. (1999). Multilevel theorizing about creativity in organizations: A sensemaking perspective. *Academy of Management Review, 24*, 286–307.

Duchon, D., Green, S. G., & Taber, T. D. (1986). Vertical dyad linkage: A longitudinal assessment of antecedents, measures, and consequences. *Journal of Applied Psychology, 71*, 56–60.

Dunegan, K. J., Duchon, D., & Uhl-Bien, M. (1992). Examining the link between leader member exchange and subordinate performance: The role of task analyzability and variety as moderators. *Journal of Management, 18*, 59–76.

Dunegan, K. J., Tierney, P., & Duchon, D. (1992). Perceptions of an innovative climate: Examining the role of divisional affiliation, work group interaction, and leader/subordinate exchange. *IEEE Transactions on Engineering Management, 39*, 227–236.

Eden, D. (2001). Means efficacy: External sources of general and specific subjective efficacy. In M. Erez, U. Kleinbeck, & H. Thierry (Eds.), *Work motivation in the context of a globalizing economy* (pp. 73–86). Hillsdale, NJ: Lawrence Erlbaum.

Erdogan, B., & Bauer, T. N. (2010). Differentiated leader-member exchanges (LMX): The buffering role of justice climate. *Journal of Applied Psychology, 95*, 1104–1120.

Erdogan, B., & Bauer, T. (2014). Leader-membership exchange (LMX) theory: The relational approach to leadership. In D. Day (Ed.), *Oxford handbook of leadership and organizations*. New York: Oxford University Press.

Erdogan, B., & Enders, J. (2007). Support from the top: Supervisors' perceived organizational support as a moderator of leader-member exchange to satisfaction and performance relationships. *Journal of Applied Psychology, 92*, 321–330.

Erdogan, B., Enders, J., & Bauer, T. B. (2011). The moderating role of LMX on personality and creative behavior. Presented as part of the symposium "LMX Perspectives on Creativity" at the national meeting of the Academy of Management, Montreal, CA.

Erdogan, B., & Liden, R. C. (2002). Social exchanges in the workplace: A review of recent developments and future research directions in leader-member exchange theory. In L. L. Neider & C. A. Schriesheim (Eds.), *Leadership* (pp. 65–114). Greenwich, CT: Information Age Press.

Erdogan, B., Liden, R. C., & Kraimer, M. L. (2006). Justice and leader-member exchange: The moderating role of organizational culture. *Academy of Management Journal, 49*, 395–406.

Fahr, J. L., Early, P. C., & Linn, S. C. (1997). Impetus for action: A cultural analysis of justice and organizational citizenship behavior in Chinese society. *Administrative Science Quarterly, 42*, 421–444.

Farmer, S. M., Tierney, P., & Kung-McIntyre, K. (2003). Employee creativity in Taiwan: An application of role identity theory. *Academy of Management Journal, 46*, 618–630.

Ford, C. M. (1996). A theory of individual creative action in multiple social domains. *Academy of Management Review, 21*, 1112–1142.

Gagne, M., & Deci, E. L. (2005). Self-determination theory and work motivation. *Journal of Organizational Behavior, 26*, 331–362.

Gerstner, C. R., & Day, D. V. (1997). Meta-analytic review of leader-member exchange theory: Correlates and construct issues. *Journal of Applied Psychology, 82*, 827–844.

Gioia, D. A., & Chittipeddi, K. (1991). Sensemaking and sensegiving in strategic change initiation. *Strategic Change Management, 12*, 433–448.

Gioia, D. A., & Poole, P. P. (1984). Scripts in organizational behavior. *The Academy of Management Review, 9*, 449–459.

Graen, G., Cashman, J. F., Ginsburg, S., & Schiemann, W. (1977). Effects of linking-pin quality on the quality of working life of lower participants. *Administrative Science Quarterly, 22*, 491–504.

Graen, G., & Scandura, T. (1987). Toward a psychology of dyadic organizing. In B. M. Straw & L. L. Cummings (Eds.), *Research in organizational behavior* (Vol. 9, pp. 175–208). Greenwich, CT: JAI Press.

Graen, G., & Uhl-Bien, M. (1995). Relation-based approach to leadership: Development of leader-member exchange (LMX) theory of leadership over 25 years: Applying a multi-level multi-domain perspective. *Leadership Quarterly, 6*, 219–247.

Grant, A. M. (2008). Does intrinsic motivation fuel the prosocial fire? Motivational synergy in predicting persistence, performance, and productivity. *Journal of Applied Psychology, 93*, 48–58.

Grant, A. M., & Berry, J. W. (2011). The necessity of others is the mother of invention: Intrinsic and prosocial motivations, perspective taking, and creativity. *Academy of Management Journal, 54*, 73–96.

Harris, K. J., Harris, R. B., & Eplion, D. M. (2007). Personality, leader-member exchange and work outcomes. *Journal of Behavioral and Applied Management, 8*, 92–107.

Hirst, G., van Dick, R., & van Knippenberg, D. (2009). A social identity perspective on leadership and employee creativity. *Journal of Organizational Behavior, 30*, 963–982.

Hsiung, H. & Tsai, W. (2011). Job definition discrepancy between supervisors and subordinates: The antecedent role of LMX and outcomes. *Journal of Organizational and Occupational Psychology, 82*, 89–112.

Ilies, R., Nahrgang, J. D., & Morgeson, F. P. (2007). Leader-member exchange and citizenship behaviors: A meta-analysis. *Journal of Applied Psychology, 92*, 269–277.

Janssen, O. (2004). How fairness perceptions make innovative behavior more or less stressful. *Journal of Organizational Behavior, 25*, 201–215.

Janssen, O., & Van Yperen, N. W. (2004). Employees' goal orientations, the quality of leader-member exchange, and the outcomes of job performance and job satisfaction. *Academy of Management Journal, 47*, 368–384.

Jaussi, K. S., Randel, A. E., & Dionne, S. D. (2007). I am, I think I can, and I do: The role of personal identity, self-efficacy, and cross-application of experiences in creativity at work. *Creativity Research Journal, 19*, 247–258.

Joo, B., Yang, B., & McLean, G. N. (2013). Employee creativity: The effects of perceived learning culture, leader-member exchange quality, job autonomy, and proactivity. *Human Resource Development International, 12*, 390–421.

Khazanchi, S., & Masterson, S. S. (2011). Who and what is fair matters: A multi-foci social exchange model of creativity. *Journal of Organizational Behavior, 32*, 86–106.

Kraimer, M. L., Seibert, S. E., Wayne, S. J., Liden, R. C., & Bravo, J. (2011). Antecedents and outcomes of organizational support for development: The critical role of career opportunities. *Journal of Applied Psychology, 96*, 485–500.

Law, L. S., Wong, C., Wang, D., & Wang, L. (2000). Effect of supervisor-subordinate guanxi on supervisory decisions in China: An empirical investigation. *International Journal of Human Resource Management, 11*, 751–765.

Liao, H., Lui, D., & Loi, R. (2010). Looking at both sides of the social exchange coin: A social cognitive perspective on the joint effects of relationship and quality of differentiation on creativity. *Academy of Management Journal, 53*, 1090–1109.

Liden, R. C., & Graen, G. (1980). Generalizability of the vertical dyad linkage model of relationship. *Academy of Management Journal, 23*, 451–465.

Liden, R. C., Sparrowe, R. T., & Wayne, S. J. (1997). Leader-member exchange theory: The past and potential for the future. *Research in Personnel and Human Resources Management, 15*, 47–119.

Liden, R. C., Wayne, S. J., & Sparrowe, R. T. (2000). An examination of the mediating role of psychological empowerment on the relations between the job, interpersonal relationship, and work outcomes. *Journal of Applied Psychology, 85*, 407–416.

Liden, R. C., Wayne, S. J., & Stilwell, D. (1993). A longitudinal study on the early development of leader-member exchanges. *Journal of Applied Psychology, 78*, 662–674.

Liu, D., Liao, H., & Loi, R. (2012). The dark side of leadership: A three-level investigation of the cascading effect of abusive supervision on employee creativity. *Academy of Management Journal, 55*, 1187–1212.

Lord, R. G., Brown, D. J., & Freiberg, S. J. (1999). Understanding the dynamics of leadership: The role of follower self-concepts in the leader follower relationship. *Organizational Behavior and Human Decision Processes, 78*, 167–203.

Martinaityte, I., & Sacramento, C. A. (2013). When creativity enhances sales effectiveness: The moderating role of leader-member exchange. *Journal of Organizational Behavior, 34*, 974–994.

Masterson, S. S., Lewis, K., Goldman, B. M., & Taylor, M. S. (2000). Integrating justice and social exchange: The differing effects of fair procedures and treatment on work relationships. *Academy of Management Journal, 43*, 738–748.

Morgeson, F. P., & Campion, M. A. (2003). Work design. In W. C. Borman, D. R. Ilgen, & R. J. Klimoski (Eds.), *Handbook of psychology: Industrial and organizational psychology* (Vol. 12, pp. 423–452). Hoboken, NJ: John Wiley & Sons.

Morgeson, F. P., Dierdorff, E. C., & Hmurovic, J. L. (2010). Work design in situ: Understanding the role of occupational and organizational context. *Journal of Organizational Behavior, 31*, 351–360.

Nahrgang, J. D., Morgeson, F. P., & Ilies, R. (2009). The development of leader-member exchanges: Exploring how personality and performance influence leader and member relationship over time. *Organizational Behavior and Human Decision Processes, 108*, 256–266.

Perry-Smith, J. E. (2006). Social yet creative: The role of social relationships in facilitating individual creativity. *Academy of Management Journal, 49*, 85–101.

Perry-Smith, J., & Shalley, C. E. (2003). The social side of creativity: A static and dynamic social network perspective. *Academy of Management Review, 28*, 89–106.

Riley, A., & Burke, P. J. (1995). Identities and self-verification in the small group. *Social Psychology Quarterly, 58*, 61–73.

Scandura, T. A., Graen, G. B., & Novak, M. A. (1986). When managers decide not to decide autocratically: An investigation of leader-member exchange and decision influence. *Journal of Applied Psychology, 71*, 579–584.

Schepers, P., & van den Berg, P. T. (2007). Social factors of work-environment creativity. *Journal of Business and Psychology, 21*, 407–428.

Schyns, B. (2004). The influence of occupational self-efficacy on the relationship of leadership behavior and preparedness for occupational change. *Journal of Career Development, 30*, 247–261.

Schyns, B., & Schilling, J. (2013). How bad are the effects of bad leaders? A meta-analysis of destructive leadership and its outcomes. *Leadership Quarterly, 24*, 138–158.

Scott, S. G., & Bruce, R. A. (1994). Determinants of innovative behavior: A path model of individual innovation in the workplace. *Academy of Management Journal, 37*, 580–607.

Shalley, C. E. (1995). Effects of coaction, expected evaluation, and goal setting on creativity and productivity. *Academy of Management Journal, 43*, 215–223.

Shalley, C. E., & Gilson, L. L. (2004). What leaders need to know: A review of social and contextual factors that can foster or hinder creativity. *Leadership Quarterly, 15*, 33–53.

Shalley, C. E., & Gilson, L. L., & Blum, T. C. (2000). Matching creativity requirements and the work environment: Effects on satisfaction and intentions to leave. *Academy of Management Journal, 43*, 215-223.

Shalley, C. E., Zhou, J., & Oldham, G. R. (2004). The effects of personal and contextual characteristics on creativity: Where should we go from here? *Journal of Management, 30*, 933–958.

Shin, S. (in press). Leadership and creativity: The mechanism perspective. In C. E. Shalley, J. Zhou, & M. Hitt (Eds.), *Oxford handbook of organizational creativity, innovation, & entrepreneurship*. New York: Oxford University Press.

Sluss, D. M., & Ashforth, B. E. (2007). Relational identity and identification: Defining ourselves through work relationships. *Academy of Management Journal, 32*, 9–32.

Sparrowe, R. T., & Liden, R. C. (1997). Process and structure in leader-member exchange. *Academy of Management Review, 22*, 522–552.

Sparrowe, R. T., & Liden, R. C. (2005). Two routes to influence: Integrating leader-member exchange and network perspectives. *Administrative Science Quarterly, 50*, 505–535.

Taggar, S. (2002). Individual creativity and group ability to utilize individual creative resources: A multilevel model. *Academy of Management Journal, 45*, 315–330.

Tangirala, S., Green, S. G., & Ramanujam, R. (2007). In the shadow of the boss's boss: Effects of supervisors' upward exchange relationships on employees. *Journal of Applied Psychology, 92*, 309–320.

Tierney, P. (2005). Relationships at work and sense of self: Exploring the concept of LMX-role identity. Paper presented at the national meeting of the Academy of Management, Honolulu, HI.

Tierney, P. (2008). Leadership and employee creativity. In J. Zhou & C. E. Shalley (Eds.), *Handbook of organizational creativity* (pp. 125–147). New York: Lawrence Erlbaum Associates.

Tierney, P. (2010). When LMX really matters for creativity: The influence of role fit and creative self-efficacy. Paper presented as part of the symposium "Social Relationships and Creativity at Work: Creativity as an Interpersonal Social Process" at the national meeting of the Academy of Management, Montreal, QC.

Tierney, P. (in press). An identity perspective on creative action in organizations. In C. E. Shalley, J. Zhou, & M. Hitt (Eds.), *Oxford handbook of organizational creativity, innovation, & entrepreneurship*. New York: Oxford University Press.

Tierney, P., & Farmer, S. M. (2002). Creative self-efficacy: Potential antecedents and relationship to creative performance. *Academy of Management Journal, 45*, 1137–1148.

Tierney, P., & Farmer, S. M. (2004). The Pygmalion process and employee creativity. *Journal of Management, 30*, 413–432.

Tierney, P., & Farmer, S. M. (2011). Creative self-efficacy development and creative performance over time. *Journal of Applied Psychology, 92*, 277–293.

Tierney, P., Farmer, S. M., & Green, G. N. (1999). An examination of leadership and employee creativity: The relevance of traits and relationships. *Personnel Psychology, 52*, 591–620.

Unsworth, K. (2001). Unpacking creativity. *Academy of Management Review, 26*, 289–297.

van Dam, K., Oreg, S., & Schyns, B. (2008). Daily work contexts and resistance to organizational change: The role of leader-member exchange, development climate, and change process characteristics. *Applied Psychology: An International Review, 57*, 313–334.

Van Dyne, L., Jehn, K. A., & Cummings, A. (2002). Differential effects of strain on two forms of work performance: Individual employee sales and creativity. *Journal of Organizational Behavior, 23*, 57–74.

Volmer, J., Spurk, D., & Niessen, C. (2012). Leader-member exchange (LMX), job autonomy, and creative work involvement. *Leadership Quarterly, 23*, 456–465.

Walumbwa, F. O., Cropanzano, R., & Goldman, B. M. (2011). How leader-member exchange influences effective work behaviors: Social exchange and internal-external efficacy perspectives. *Personnel Psychology, 64*, 739–770.

Wang, A. C., & Cheng, B. S. (2009). When does benevolent leadership lead to creativity? The moderating role of creative role identity and job autonomy. *Journal of Organizational Behavior, 31*, 106–121.

Wang, P., & Zhu, W. (2011). Mediating role of creative identity in the influence of transformational leadership on creativity: Is there a multilevel effect? *Journal of Leadership & Organizational Studies, 18*, 25–39.

Wang, X. H., & Howell, J. M. (2012). A multilevel study of transformational leadership, identification and follower outcomes. *Leadership Quarterly, 23*, 775–790.

Wayne, S. J., Shore, L. M., Bommer, W. H., & Tetrick, L. E. (2002). The role of fair treatment and rewards in perceptions of organizational support and leader-member exchange. *Journal of Applied Psychology, 87*, 590–598.

Woodman, R. W., Sawyer, J. E., & Griffin, R. W. (1993). Toward a theory of organizational creativity. *Academy of Management Review, 18*, 293–321.

Yuan, F., & Woodman, R. W. (2010). Innovative behavior in the work place: The role performance and image outcome expectations. *Academy of Management Journal, 53*, 323–342.

Zhang, X., & Bartol, K. M. (2010). Linking empowering leadership and employee creativity: The influence of psychological empowerment, intrinsic motivation, and creative process engagement. *Academy of Management Journal, 53*, 107–128.

Zhou, J. (2003). When the presence of creative coworkers is related to creativity: Role of supervisor close monitoring, developmental feedback, and creative personality. *Journal of Applied Psychology, 88*, 413–422.

Zhou, J. (2007). Promoting creativity through feedback. In J. Zhou & C.E. Shalley (Eds.), *Handbook of organizational creativity* (pp. 25–147). New York: Lawrence Erlbaum Associates.

Zhou, J. (2008). Promoting creativity through feedback. In J. Zhou & C. E. Shalley (Eds.), *Handbook of organizational creativity* (pp. 125–146). New York: Lawrence Erlbaum Associates.

Zhou, J., & Hoever, I. J. (2014). Research on workplace creativity: A review and redirection. *Annual Review of Organizational Psychology and Organizational Behavior, 1*, 333–359.

Zhou, J., & Shalley, C. E. (2003). Research on employee creativity: A critical review and directions for future research. In J. Martocchio (Ed.), *Research in personnel and human resources management* (pp. 165–217). Oxford, UK: Elsevier.

Zhou, L., Wang, M., Chen, G., & Shi, J. (2012). Supervisors' upward exchange relationships and subordinate outcomes: Testing the multilevel mediation role of empowerment. *Journal of Applied Psychology, 97*, 668–680.

Leader–Member Exchange from a Job-Stress Perspective

Sabine Sonnentag *and* Alexander Pundt

Abstract

In this chapter, the authors review the literatures on leader–member exchange (LMX) and on constructs related to job stress (job stressors, well-being, work–family interface), and describe how LMX is associated with these job-stress constructs. They present an integrative framework that specifies bidirectional relationships between LMX and job-stress constructs and that proposes LMX as a moderator in the relationships between the job-stress constructs. They summarize empirical research on the relationships of LMX with job stressors, well-being, and work–family variables and conclude by suggesting directions for practice and future research emphasizing the need for more methodologically sound studies.

Key Words: Leader–Member Exchange, LMX, job stress, well-being, work-family interface

Introduction

Relationships in the workplace are of considerable interest in organizational psychology and organizational behavior (Eby & Allen, 2012). A high-quality relationship between employees and their supervisors is thereby of particular relevance because supervisors have the formal power to provide and withdraw resources such as financial rewards, interesting job tasks, and career opportunities (Bono & Yoon, 2012). Leader–member exchange (LMX) is one construct that captures the quality of the relationship between leaders and followers (Uhl-Bien, 2006). Research on LMX has shown that a high-quality exchange between leader and followers plays an important role for follower performance and job satisfaction (Dulebohn, Bommer, Liden, Brouer, & Ferris, 2012). In addition to these well-documented effects of LMX on performance and satisfaction, a high-quality exchange can also be relevant for other aspects of an employee's working life. In this chapter, we focus on the interplay between LMX and processes related to job stress. We take a broad perspective on job stress and address job stressors (i.e., features of the work situation), impaired well-being (i.e., individual reactions to job stressors), and the work–family interface.

After a brief introduction into the concept of LMX, we will describe the other core concepts to be addressed in this chapter (job stressors, well-being, and work–family interface) and will provide an integrative framework of how LMX may be related to these concepts. In the sections that follow, we review the empirical evidence on the relationship between LMX and job stressors, LMX and well-being, and LMX and the work–family interface. We conclude with implications for research and practice.

The Concept of LMX

The basic premise of LMX theory is that leaders enter into an individually negotiated relationship with each of their subordinates and, therefore, do not treat all employees equally (Dansereau, Graen, & Haga, 1975). While early work on LMX was drawing on role theory (e.g., Graen & Scandura, 1987), current work is more based on social exchange theory (cf. Dulebohn et al., 2012). Hence, LMX relationships of high quality are characterized by long-termed reciprocation and feelings of mutual obligation whereas low-quality relationships are characterized by economic, short-termed, and immediately reciprocal exchange of tangible resources (Graen & Uhl-Bien, 1995). After the delegation of a complex task (also-called "initial offer," cf. Graen & Uhl-Bien, 1995) and a satisfactory performance of the follower, a leader–follower relationship can develop from the low-quality exchange status to a high-quality relationship (Bauer & Green, 1996).

Initially, researchers have explicitly distinguished between in-group and out-group (e.g., Dansereau et al., 1975). Followers in the in-group are characterized by having high levels of LMX whereas followers in the out-group are characterized by having a low-quality LMX. In later research, this distinction has been given up in favor of a more dimensional view of LMX in terms of relationship quality (Graen & Uhl-Bien, 1995). Two major conceptualizations of LMX are guiding current research. Graen and Uhl-Bien (1995) refer to a one-dimensional construct of LMX that embraces facets such as trust, respect, and mutual obligation and that is usually measured by a seven-item measure capturing the overall quality of the relationship between leaders and followers. Advancing this perspective, Dienesch and Liden (1986) argued for a multidimensional concept of LMX to provide more definitional and theoretical clarity. Emphasizing the exchange character of the leader–follower relationship, these authors define LMX as a four dimensional construct (see also Liden & Maslyn, 1998). These dimensions are *contribution*, defined as the "perception of the amount, direction, and quality of work-oriented activity each member puts forth toward the mutual goals (explicit or implicit) of the dyad" (Dienesch & Liden, 1986, p. 624), *loyalty*, defined as the extent to which leader and follower "publicly support each other's actions and character" (Liden & Maslyn, 1998, p. 46), *affect*, defined as the amount of mutual liking for each other which is primarily based "on interpersonal attraction rather than work or professional values" (Dienesch & Liden, 1986, p. 625), and *professional respect*, defined as "the perception of the degree to which each member of the dyad had built a reputation, within and/or outside the organization, of excelling at his or her line of work" (Liden & Maslyn, 1998, p. 49).

While previous research has mainly focused on antecedents and consequences of the individual level of LMX rated by the individual follower (cf. Dulebohn et al., 2012 for a meta-analysis), more recent research additionally takes into account two basic assumptions of the LMX approach: First, LMX describes a *mutual* relationship between leaders and followers and, therefore, needs to be addressed as a dyadic phenomenon. Hence, both leader and follower have their own view on the quality of LMX characterizing their mutual relationship. Although there is only a medium-sized agreement between leaders and follower about the level of LMX (Sin, Nahrgang, & Morgeson, 2009), the amount of agreement itself embraces important information about the relationship quality and is used in empirical studies (Schyns & Day, 2010). Second, LMX quality can *vary within a work group* between single followers who report to the same leader. Recent research has taken this premise into account by considering the degree of differentiation (Liden, Erdogan, Wayne, & Sparrowe, 2006) and variability (Hooper & Martin, 2008) of LMX within a workgroup, the amount of consensus between the followers (Schyns, 2006), and the level of a follower's LMX relative to the level of LMX of all other followers within a workgroup (Tse, Ashkanasy, & Dasborough, 2012).

Job Stressors, Well-being, and the Work–Family Interface
Core Concepts

Research on job stress addresses the question if and when job stressors have an impact on employee well-being (and vice versa). During recent decades, researchers became increasingly aware that not only job stressors in themselves, but also processes at the work–family interface may have an effect on employee well-being. In this section, we start with introducing the core concepts that we will discuss in our chapter in relation to LMX: Job stressors, well-being, and the work–family interface. Then, we will briefly summarize empirical findings on job stressors, well-being, and the work–family interface.

Job Stressors

Job stressors are features of the work environment that potentially lead to strain reactions (Kahn & Byosiere, 1992). The stressor concept comprises both single major and minor events (e.g., a traumatic on-the-job experience or an interaction with an angry customer) as well as chronic conditions that persist over a longer period of time. Research has identified various stressor categories (Sonnentag & Frese, 2012), including physical stressors (e.g., noise, heat, safety hazards), task-related job stressors (e.g., time pressure, workload, situational constraints), role stressors, social stressors (e.g., interpersonal conflicts, harassment), career-related stressors (e.g., job insecurity, underemployment), traumatic events, and stressful change processes (e.g., due to down-sizing). Within research on LMX, role stressors received particular attention (Dulebohn et al., 2012; Gerstner & Day, 1997). Role theory (Kahn, Wolfe, Quinn, Snoek, & Rosenthal, 1964) differentiates between three types of role stressors: *role conflict* refers to incompatible role expectations, *role ambiguity* (or: lack of role clarity) refers to unclear and not well-defined role expectations, and *role overload* refers to role expectations that are difficult to meet within the time available.

Well-being

Well-being is a broad concept. When describing well-being, researchers have differentiated between a hedonic and a eudaimonic perspective (Ryan & Deci, 2001; Waterman, 1993). The hedonic perspective focuses on *subjective well-being* as a positive subjective experience and evaluation of one's life (Diener, 1984; Diener, Oishi, & Lucas, 2003). Core components of subjective well-being are positive (i.e., pleasant) affect, the absence of nega-tive (i.e., unpleasant) affect, and life satisfaction (Diener, Suh, Lucas, & Smith, 1999). The eudai-monic perspective emphasizes the realization of the "true self" (Waterman, 1993) as the core of *psychological well-being*. According to Ryff (1989), psychological well-being includes as core dimen-sions self-acceptance, positive relations with others, autonomy, environmental mastery, purpose in life, and personal growth.

In the organizational literature, the term *well-being* is predominantly used in the sense of Diener's subjective well-being (Daniels, 2000; Warr, 1990). Job-related affective well-being can be described on the two axes *anxiety–contentment* and *depression–enthusiasm*, reflecting the two affec-tive dimensions of pleasure and arousal (Warr, 1990). For a long time, measures of job-related well-being focused on the absence of unwell-being (e.g., exhaustion, depressive symptoms); in recent years, positive states of well-being (e.g., feel-ing vigorous) received more attention (Bakker & Oerlemans, 2012).

A specific (un-)well-being construct that is closely linked to the job domain is burnout. Burnout can be defined as "a prolonged response to chronic emotional and interpersonal stressors on the job" (Maslach, Schaufeli, & Leiter, 2001, p. 397). According to Maslach and Jackson (1981), the core symptoms of burnout are emotional exhaustion, depersonalization (or: cynicism, Maslach et al., 2001), and reduced personal accomplishment. More recently, Demerouti, Bakker, Nachreiner, and Schaufeli (2001) described exhaustion and disen-gagement as the core dimensions of burnout. A typ-ical indicator of positive job-related well-being is work engagement, defined "as a positive, fulfilling, work-related state of mind" (Schaufeli & Bakker, 2004, p. 295). It comprises vigor, dedication, and absorption.

Work–Family Interface

The work–family interface refers to the encounter of work-related and family-related events, experiences, and processes in people's lives. Typically, experiences in one domain (e.g., work) affect experiences in the other domain (e.g., family) and vice versa (Eby, Maher, & Butts, 2010). This interaction between work and family experiences can have both negative aspects (e.g., work–family conflict) as well as positive ones (e.g., work–family enrichment). Greenhaus and Beutell (1985) characterized work–family conflict as an interrole conflict where the demands from one domain make it difficult to meet the demands from the other domain. This work–family con-flict is conceptualized as bidirectional. Hence, demands from the work domain can interfere with family demands and demands from the family domain can interfere with work demands. A term often used interchangeably with work–family conflict is work–family interference (Carlson & Frone, 2003).

More recently, Greenhaus and Powell (2006) introduced the concept of work–family enrichment as a positive experience at the work–family inter-face. Work–family enrichment means that experi-ences in one domain have a positive impact on the other domain, for instance when positive affect experienced on the job improves a person's func-tioning at home. A related concept is work–family facilitation that targets positive system-level out-comes (i.e., outcomes at the family or workplace level; cf. Keeney & Ilies, 2012).

Summary

There is a long research tradition within orga-nizational (health) psychology, organizational

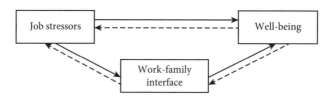

Fig. 11.1 Direct Relationships between job-stress constructs.

behavior, and related fields studying mutual relationships between job stressors, well-being, and features of the work–family interface. Figure 11.1 provides a simple conceptual model of these relationships. Numerous studies have demonstrated that job stressors are associated with poor individual well-being. For instance, employees who experience job stressors such as a high workload or situational constraints tend to report higher burnout scores (Crawford, LePine, & Rich, 2010) and more physical symptoms (Nixon, Mazzola, Bauer, Krueger, & Spector, 2011). Longitudinal studies have tried to shed light on the causal processes underlying these relationships between job stressors and poor well-being: although most theories argue for a causal effect of job stressors on poor well-being (Demerouti, et al., 2001; Karasek, 1979; Siegrist, 1996), it would be also plausible that poor well-being leads to a higher level of job stressors over time, for instance because employees with impaired well-being are less able to negotiate good working conditions. Sonnentag and Frese (2012) reviewed a total of 70 longitudinal studies on job stress and contrasted studies that provided evidence for a lagged relation from job stressors to a decrease in well-being with studies that provided evidence for a lagged relation from poor well-being to an increase in job stressors. More than half of the studies (58.6 percent) provided at least partial support for a lagged relation from stressors to a decrease in well-being, whereas 26.9 percent of the studies provided at least partial support for the reverse causal direction.

Beyond job stressors, aspects of the work–family interface are also relevant for employee well-being. Research has shown that work–family conflict is related to burnout, health problems, psychological strain, and poor life satisfaction (Amstad, Meier, Fasel, Elfering, & Semmer, 2011; Kossek & Ozeki, 1998). Work–family enrichment is positively related to physical and mental health as well as to life satisfaction (McNall, Nicklin, & Masuda, 2010). Findings from longitudinal studies are mixed and provide support for lagged relationships between

work–family conflict and poor well-being in some studies (Innstrand, Langballe, Espnes, Falkum, & Assland, 2008), but not in others (Hall, Dollard, Tuckey, Winefield, & Thompson, 2010; Kelloway, Gottlieb, & Barham, 1999). In addition, there is also some evidence for a reverse causation with poor well-being predicting an increase in work–family conflict over time (Britt & Dawson, 2005; Innstrand et al., 2008; Kelloway, et al., 1999).

Importantly, features of the work–family interface are not independent from job stressors. There is strong evidence that employees who report a high level of job stressors (e.g., role overload, role ambiguity) also experience a high level of work–family conflict (Byron, 2005; Ford, Heinen, & Langkamer, 2007). The underlying causal processes, however, remained largely unexplored (cf. Britt & Dawson, 2005, for an exception). With respect to work–family enrichment, the pattern of findings is inconsistent (Crain & Hammer, 2013) and it still remains unclear if job stressors hinder work–family enrichment.

The Interplay of LMX With Job Stressors, Well-being, and the Work–Family Interface: Organizing Framework

We propose that LMX is an important factor in the interplay between job stressors, well-being, and the work–family interface. Figure 11.2 displays the possible direct relationships between LMX and the other three construct domains. Figure 11.3 displays possible moderator effects of LMX.

With respect to direct relationships, LMX should be negatively associated with the experience of job stressors. One the one hand, LMX might lead to a reduction of job stressors. Within a high-quality exchange, it is more likely that leader and follower communicate about role requirements and clarify role expectations what should reduce role stressors. Furthermore, leaders might assign in-group members to less stressful work domains than out-group members. On the other hand, experiencing a high level of job stressors might lead to low-quality LMX because followers might

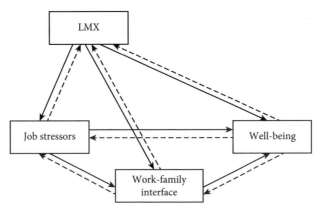

Fig. 11.2 Direct Relationships between LMX Job-stress constructs.

attribute a high stressor level to their leader's inability or unwillingness to provide a good work environment (cf. Davis & Gardner, 2004). In addition, having a low-quality LMX might be seen as a job stressor in itself. Moreover, LMX should be related to well-being. Experiencing a high-quality LMX should contribute to employee well-being, because having a high-quality LMX is a positive experience in itself and satisfies an employee's need to belong (Baumeister & Leary, 1995). Moreover, followers might experience a high-quality relationship with their leader as a resource (Bakker & Bal, 2010) that protects well-being. High levels of well-being might also improve LMX because positive affective states associated with well-being facilitate interpersonal trust (Lount, 2010) and social interaction processes (Barsade, 2002). Finally, LMX should be associated with processes at the work–family interface. For instance, a high-quality LMX may help clarify role expectations at the work–family interface which should reduce work–family conflict. Moreover, experiencing work–family conflict might stimulate

an employee to attribute the negative situation to the leader (cf. Shockley & Singla, 2011) which it turn will impair LMX.

LMX might not only be directly related to job stressors, well-being, and the work–family interface, but might also act as a moderator (cf. Figure 11.3). Specifically, it might moderate the relationship between job stressors and impaired well-being, the relationship between job stressors and the work–family interface, and the relationship between the work–family interface and well-being.

In the following sections of this chapter we will review empirical evidence both relationships of LMX with job stressors, well-being, and the work–family interface. Because empirical studies on the moderator effects of LMX are still rare, we will largely focus on direct relationships.

LMX and Job Stressors

A rather consistent stream of research has examined if and how LMX is related to followers' experience of job stressors (for an early field study, cf.

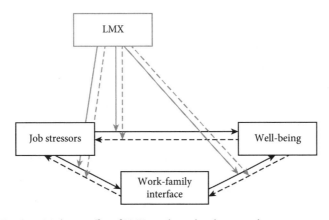

Fig. 11.3 Moderator effect of LMX on relationships between job-stress constructs.

Snyder & Bruning, 1985). Most of this research has focused on role stressors (mainly role conflict and role ambiguity), but also other stressors such as organizational politics or job demands have been addressed. In this section, we first review research on LMX and role stressors, and then turn to other types of stressors.

LMX and Role Stressors

A high LMX is characterized by a good relationship between leader and follower, implying trust, loyalty, and mutual support (Graen & Scandura, 1987). When having a high-quality exchange, leaders and followers engage in frequent communication (Gajendran & Joshi, 2012). Frequent communication provides the opportunity to clarify role expectations and to negotiate potentially conflicting or overtaxing role requirements. Therefore, it is reasonable to expect that LMX will be negatively related to role stressors. Indeed, many empirical studies have addressed the relationship between LMX and role stressors. The meta-analysis of Gerstner and Day (1997) included 12 effect sizes ($N = 3,728$) on the relationship between LMX and role conflict and 14 effect sizes ($N = 4,105$) on the relationship between LMX and role clarity (i.e., the opposite of role ambiguity). Correlations (corrected for unreliability of the LMX measure and of the role–stressor measure) were $r_c = -0.31$ for role conflict and $r_c = 0.43$ for role clarity. The more recent meta-analysis of Dulebohn et al. (2012) summarized findings from 14 studies ($N = 5,480$) on role conflict and from 18 studies ($N = 5,813$) on role ambiguity. Findings are consistent with those of Gerstner and Day's meta-analysis (rho = -0.33 for role conflict and rho = -0.42 for role ambiguity).

In addition to the negative linear relationship between LMX and role stressors, Jian (2014) examined a curvilinear relationship. Using data from a sample of 235 immigrant workers in the United States, Jian found evidence for the hypothesized inverted U-shaped relationship between LMX on the one hand and role conflict and role overload (but not role ambiguity) on the other hand: low and high levels of LMX were associated with low levels of role conflict and role overload, and a moderate level of LMX was associated with a relatively high level of role conflict and role overload. Thus, whereas at medium to high levels of LMX the relationship between LMX and role conflict and role overload mirrors the typical negative association as found when testing the linear relationship, the pattern is different at low to medium levels of LMX.

Possibly at low levels of LMX, leaders are reluctant to assign important and meaningful tasks to their followers, so that these followers' role conflict and role overload remains low.

Because of the cross-sectional design of most studies on the relationship between LMX and role stressors, causality remains unclear. A low stressor level could not only be seen as a consequence of a high-quality LMX, it could also be conceptualized as a predictor of LMX. For instance, by drawing on Graen and Scandura (1987), Sears and Hackett (2010) argued that role clarity predicts LMX: when leaders' and followers' role expectations converge and when no ambiguities about mutual roles remain, a high-quality LMX should develop. In a structural equation model, Sears and Hackett's (cross-sectional) data showed a significant path from role clarity to LMX in a sample of 161 managers and their supervisors.

To gain more insight into the causal processes between role stressors and LMX, longitudinal studies are highly needed. In a first attempt to understand the processes that might underlie the effect of LMX on role stressors, several studies tested mediator effects. For instance, Thomas and Lankau (2009) argued that organizational socialization, i.e., a process during which organizational members "are familiarized with expectations associated with their organizational role" (p. 421) acts as a mediator between LMX and role stressors (i.e., role conflict and role ambiguity). Empirical data from 422 employees in a US hospital provided evidence for a partial mediation: the better the LMX, the more followers felt that they were sufficiently familiarized with important aspects of organizational life (e.g., goals, history, language) what in turn was negatively related to role stressors.

Hornung, Rousseau, Glaser, Angerer, and Weigl (2010; Study 2) looked at task i-deals as another potential mediator between LMX and role stressors. Task i-deals are "individualized agreements between valued workers and their employers (as) the product of a negotiation" (Rousseau, 2001, p. 260). In a sample of 135 physicians from two German hospitals, Hornung et al. found a positive path from LMX to task i-deals that in turn were negatively related to role stressors (goal conflict, ambiguity, overload). When taking together the findings from Thomas and Lankau and from Hornung et al., it seems that the negative association between LMX and role stressors can be explained by two complementary adaptation processes: A high-quality LMX helps with an individual's adaptation to the organization during the socialization process and, in addition, it simulates or enables the adaptation of job features to the individual's preferences via the negotiation of task i-deals. Both adaptation processes in turn result in a work situation that is perceived to be less stressful.

Muldoon, Matthews, and Foley (2012) focused on empowerment as another mediator between LMX and role stressors. They argued that a high-quality LMX motivates employees to embrace their work roles and to experience meaning, competence, self-determination, and impact what in turn should give them the feeling that they are capable in dealing with the demands at work what should be reflected in a low degree of role stressors. The empirical study based on a sample of 226 US employees, mainly working in production, construction, and installation/maintenance jobs, showed a positive association between LMX and empowerment, and a negative association between empowerment and role stressors (role conflict, time pressure, qualitative overload). In addition, LMX had a negative direct relationship with role stressors. Overall, these studies addressing mediation processes suggest that LMX might enable employees to take a more active role on the job (negotiating task i-deals, feeling empowered) which in turn offers opportunities to experience less role stressors.

Although there is rather consistent evidence that LMX and role stressors are negatively related (Dulebohn et al., 2012; Gerstner & Day, 1997), the relationship between LMX and these stressors might not be equally strong under all circumstances. Tordera, González-Romá, and Peiró (2008) argued that psychological climate moderates the relationship between LMX and role overload. Specifically, they hypothesized that support climate will attenuate the association between LMX and role overload, whereas innovation climate, goal-orientation climate, and rules-orientation climate will exacerbate the association—mainly because these climates imply that employees will face higher work demands what makes a high-quality LMX more important. Using data from 282 employees working in health care centers, Tordera et al. found that innovation climate, goal-orientation climate, and rules-orientation climate moderated the association between LMX and role overload in the hypothesized direction. Support climate, however, did not turn out as a moderator, possibly because LMX and support climate were highly correlated. Overall, this study demonstrates that when working in a highly demanding environment, low-quality LMX and role overload become closely intertwined.

Kauppila (2014) also argued that organization-level variables might moderate the relationship between LMX and role stressors. Specifically, he argued that the relationship should be stronger when companies use a deliberate strategy-making pattern as opposed to a more emergent strategy-making pattern. Empirical data from 724 employees and 124 managers from Finnish organizations did not show the hypothesized interaction effect between LMX and business strategy on role clarity. At the individual level, LMX showed a correlation of $r = 0.30$ with role clarity—irrespective of the organization's strategy-making pattern.

LMX and Other Job Stressors

Research also examined if job stressors other than role stressors are associated with LMX. Specifically, studies addressed stressors such as organizational politics, workplace aggression, job demands, among others. Several studies examined the association between LMX and the perception of organizational politics. Perception of organizational politics refers to an employee's appraisal of specific influence processes within an organization such as favoritism or taking credit for another person's achievements (Ferris & Kacmar, 1992). Consistent across several studies, LMX showed a negative correlation (ranging between $r = -0.40$ and $r = -0.46$) with perception of politics (Andrews & Kacmar, 2001; Harris & Kacmar, 2005; Nelson, Basu, & Purdie, 1998), demonstrating that followers who experience a high-quality exchange with their leader experience less politics (or may be less inclined to attribute specific events to politics). Importantly, justice perceptions might play a fundamental role in the association between LMX and perceptions of politics: Andrews and Kacmar (2001) found that LMX was *positively* related to perceptions of organizational politics when controlling for distributive justice. It might be that in-group members with a high-quality LMX get a more detailed insider knowledge about organizational politics; differences in distributive justice between high-quality versus low-quality LMX members (cf. Dulebohn et al., 2012), however, might distort this association between LMX and perception of politics.

Research has identified workplace aggression as an important job stressor (Hershcovics & Reich, 2013). A study by Chang and Lyons (2012) has demonstrated that LMX might play a role in verbal aggression at work. Not surprisingly, these authors found a negative relationship between verbal aggression from the supervisor and LMX in their sample of 989 adults working in a diverse set of jobs. In addition, verbal aggression from co-workers and from customers was negatively associated with LMX—albeit to a lesser degree. Possibly, a high-quality LMX plays a protective role against co-worker and customer aggression and employees with a relatively low-quality LMX are more likely to become victims of verbal aggression from co-workers and customers. However, because of the cross-sectional design, we cannot rule out that experiencing verbal aggression at work might even threaten the exchange relationship between leader and follower because employees who experience aggression from third parties might feel that their supervisors do not do enough to protect them from these aggressive acts.

Jiang, Law, and Sun (2014) examined the relationship between LMX and five different types of job demands (physical workload, time pressure, demanding contacts with customers or clients, an unfavorable shiftwork schedule, a demanding physical environment) in a sample of 218 Chinese bank employees. These authors found a positive association between LMX and job demands. Leader moral integrity moderated this association: LMX was more strongly related to high demands when leaders' moral integrity was low than when it was high. Although causality remains unexplored also in this study, this finding may suggest that particularly leaders who lack moral integrity may assign demanding tasks, schedules, and environments to followers from their in-group because they expect that these followers perform well even under such demanding conditions.

A study by Walumbwa, Cropanzano, and Goldman (2011) offers indirect information on the association between LMX and job stressors. These authors examined the relationship between LMX and means efficacy (i.e., the "belief in the utility of the tools available for task performance," Eden, Ganzach, Flumin-Granat, & Zigman, 2010, p. 687). Low levels of means efficacy correspond closely to high levels of situational constraints (Peters & O'Connor, 1980)—as a typical workplace stressor. Empirically, Walumbwa et al. found a significant positive regression weight when predicting means efficacy from LMX. This finding implies that when LMX is high, employees believe that they have the tools to perform well, whereas when LMX quality is low they believe that they lack the appropriate tools, which can be seen as a typical job stressor.

Whereas the studies reviewed so far have addressed the question how LMX relates to stressors in followers' work situation, Kinicki and Vecchio (1994) have adopted a different approach. They examined how leaders' time-based stress (e.g., working with too tight deadlines) is associated with mean LMX and variance of LMX (i.e., LMX differentiation) within the leaders' units. Kinicki and Vecchio surveyed 138 employees and 24 branch managers working in a large bank. The analyses showed that managers who had a higher level of time-based stress had a higher level of LMX (as reported by their followers). In addition, when managers experienced a high level of time-based stress, LMX differentiation within their units was low—possibly because managers with high levels of time-based stress tried to develop good trusted relationships with many of their followers. This study on leaders' job stressors illustrates a highly interesting aspect of the association between LMX and job stressors that did not receive sufficient research attention after Kinicki and Vecchio's pioneering study.

Summary

Taken together, research on the association between LMX and job stressors has shown that a high-quality exchange between leader and follower is negatively related to a variety of job stressors, including role conflict, role ambiguity, role overload, but also perceptions of politics and workplace aggression (Chang & Lyons; 2012; Dulebohn et al., 2012; Harris & Kacmar, 2005). Studies have uncovered possible mediators in the relationship between LMX and role stressors, including socialization, empowerment, and i-deals (Hornung et al., 2010; Muldoon et al., 2012; Thomas & Lankau, 2009). However, strictly speaking, causality underlying the relationship between LMX and job stressors remains unclear. Although most of the studies used a framework in which LMX was conceptualized as a negative predictor of job stressors, the reverse causality cannot be ruled out. For instance, the point has been made that job stressors impede job performance (Gilboa, Shirom, Fried, & Cooper, 2008). A longitudinal study by Bauer and Green (1996) has shown that a follower's performance level in turn predicts a change in leader's delegation. Moreover, the possibility that the association between LMX and a low level of job stressors is caused by third variables should not be discarded prematurely (cf. Andrews & Kacmar, 2001).

LMX and Well-being

The relationship between leaders and followers has been regarded as one of the most important relationships individuals have in the workplace. A positive relationship with the leader contributes to followers' well-being and thriving, because it (1) contributes to the creation of physical, psychological, and social resources, (2) fosters generalized reciprocity, and (3) helps satisfy the employees' need to belong (Bono & Yoon, 2012). The particular importance of this leader–follower relationship can be traced to the formal power of the leader who has the power to provide rewards and resources such as attractive tasks or career opportunities. Empirical studies on the relationship between LMX and employee well-being used positive as well as negative indicators of well-being and investigated the relationship between LMX and well-being on different levels of analysis—the individual level, the within-person level, and the group level. In the following part of this chapter, we will provide an overview of empirical studies that investigated the relationship between LMX and well-being. First, we review studies using positive indicators of well-being, followed by a review of studies using negative indicators of well-being. Third, we consider nonlinear relationships between LMX and well-being. Finally, we take a closer look at the role of LMX differentiation within a work group.

LMX and Positive Indicators of Well-being

Starting with positive indicators of well-being, Atwater and Carmeli (2009) investigated the relationship between LMX and the employees' feelings of energy in a study of 193 employees from Israeli industrial and service organizations. In their two-wave survey with a time lag of two weeks, Atwater and Carmeli found a positive relationship between LMX and feelings of energy. Feelings of energy, in turn, mediated the relationship between LMX and creative work involvement.

Graves and Luciano (2013) investigated the role of self-determination in the relationship between LMX and employee vitality. In their study of 283 alumni and working students of a graduate business school in the United States, these authors found LMX to be associated with high levels of subjective vitality. Moreover, they found this relationship to be mediated via two basic needs that are relevant for self-determination (Gagné & Deci, 2005): The feeling of competence and the feeling of autonomy. In other words: A high quality LMX relationship seems to induce feelings of competence and

autonomy which in turn foster subjective vitality. Although Graves and Luciano (2013) tried to rule out reversed causal orderings by additionally testing alternative structural models, the findings regarding the mediating mechanisms have to be interpreted with care.

Well-being is a variable that fluctuates substantially within employees (Sonnentag, Dormann, & Demerouti, 2010). Thus, it also makes sense to investigate the relationship between LMX and well-being on a *within-person* level. Some researchers have conducted studies to address this issue. For example, Bakker and Bal (2010) investigated the relationship between LMX and work engagement on a weekly basis. In their study, they asked 115 primary school teachers in the Netherlands who had just started their job about LMX and their work engagement during the past week. Data collection took place every Friday during a time period of five consecutive workweeks. Bakker and Bal (2010) found weekly LMX to be positively related to weekly work engagement. Weekly work engagement, in turn, mediated the relationship between LMX and performance of the teachers. Following a similar approach in two daily-survey studies, Xanthopoulou and her co-workers conceptualized high-quality exchange between leader and followers as a job resource. They found that job resources predicted work engagement and positive emotions at the day level (Xanthopoulou, Bakker, Demerouti, & Schaufeli, 2009; 2012).

LMX and Negative Indicators of Well-being

The relationship between LMX and negative well-being indicators such as emotional exhaustion or other burnout symptoms has also been investigated in several studies. In their study of 91 US firefighters, Becker, Halbesleben, and O'Hair (2005) found high-quality LMX to be associated with low levels of emotional exhaustion and cynicism. Moreover, LMX mediated the relationship between defensive communication in an appraisal interview and burnout. This means that defensive communication in an appraisal interview is associated with low-quality LMX which in turn is related to a higher risk of burnout.

In the above-mentioned study of 422 employees of a US hospital, Thomas and Lankau (2009) found LMX to be negatively related employee burnout. In a structural equation model, they additionally found role stressors to mediate the relationship between LMX and burnout.

Huang, Chan, Lam, and Nan (2010) investigated the relationship between LMX and employee burnout in a study of 493 leader–member dyads from a call center in northern China. They also found a negative relationship between LMX and burnout. Moreover, one dimension of emotional intelligence—self-emotion appraisal—moderated this relationship. The relationship between LMX and burnout was stronger for employees with low levels of emotional intelligence while LMX was not related to burnout for employees with high levels of emotional intelligence. Moreover, these employees generally had lower levels of burnout. Thus, the employees' ability to understand and express their own emotions may substitute a high-quality LMX relationship.

Two studies point at a potential downside of LMX in predicting employee well-being: Brouer and Harris (2007), for example, investigated the relationship between LMX and work tension—a specific type of employee strain—depending on the followers' positive and negative affectivity as well as on the frequency of interaction between leader and follower. In their study of 539 employees from various organizations, these authors found a two-way interaction between LMX and negative affectivity. Hence, LMX was positively related to perceived work tension when followers' negative affectivity was high whereas LMX was negatively related to work tension when negative affectivity was low. Maybe, followers high in negative affectivity focus on the duties and expectations that are associated with high levels of LMX and fear to disappoint the leader and to risk their good relationship with the leader when they do not perform well. Moreover, Brouer and Harris (2007) found an interaction effect between LMX and frequency of leader–follower interactions. Hence, LMX was positively related to work tension when interaction frequency was low while LMX was negatively related to work tension when interaction frequency was high. Maybe, LMX combined with infrequent interaction leads to followers' unclear or overestimated role expectations which, in turn, increase the perception of work tension.

The above-mentioned study of Jiang et al. (2014) investigated the relationship between LMX and employee burnout in a sample of 218 employees working in a Chinese bank. Generally, these authors found a negative relationship between LMX and both emotional exhaustion and cynicism. Moreover, Jiang et al. found a *positive* indirect effect for LMX on emotional exhaustion via job demands and a negative indirect effect of LMX on cynicism via job

resources. Hence, this study provides evidence for a potential downside of LMX, because employees with high-quality LMX seem to perceive higher levels of job demands than those with low-quality LMX. Additionally, Jiang et al. found the positive indirect effect of LMX on emotional exhaustion via job demands to be moderated by leader moral integrity. For leaders with high levels of moral integrity, the indirect effect was weaker than for leaders with low levels of moral integrity.

Nonlinear Relationships between LMX and Well-being

Although these studies suggest that LMX has a rather positive impact on employee well-being, some authors argued that an extremely high level of LMX may lead to a decrease in well-being. For example, Harris and Kacmar (2006) suggested that a particularly high level of LMX might be associated with high expectations from the leader and strong feelings of obligation. Hence, followers with a high-quality LMX may perceive higher levels of stress than followers with a comparatively low-quality LMX because of these expectations and obligations. In two samples of 120 state-lottery employees and 418 water-management district employees, Harris and Kacmar (2006) investigated the relationship between LMX and job-induced tension. In both samples, they found a positive quadratic relationship between LMX and job-induced tension which resulted in a U-shape. Thus, employees with low-quality LMX perceived high levels of tension, employees with an average quality of LMX perceived low levels of tension, and employees with high-quality LMX perceived higher levels of tension again.

In their study of 182 police officers, Hochwarter and Byrne (2005) also found quadratic relationships between LMX and job tension which depended on employees' positive or negative affectivity. While these authors found an overall negative linear relationship between LMX and job tension, they found a U-shaped relationship between LMX and job tension for employees with high levels of positive affectivity—hence showing a pattern similar to the one found by Harris and Kacmar (2006). For employees with low levels of positive affectivity, the relationship between LMX and job tension showed the typical linear pattern. For employees with high levels of negative affectivity, Hochwarter and Byrne (2005) found a reversed U-shaped relationship between LMX and job tension. This means that people high in negative affectivity have the highest level of job tension when they are in medium-quality exchange relationship. However, they have lower levels of job tension when LMX quality is very high or very low. A possible explanation for this pattern may be as follows: Employees high in positive affectivity are highly enthusiastic (Watson, Clark, & Tellegen, 1988) and focus on the opportunities of a situation (Gormann et al., 2012). Very high levels of LMX may activate this promotion focus because it is associated with autonomy, competence, and obligation. Employees may feel inspired to work very hard, and, therefore, to perceive higher levels of work tension and exhaustion. Employees high in negative affectivity are rather nervous, distressed, and jittery (Watson et al., 1988), and tend to focus on dangers and potential losses that can arise from a situation (Gormann et al., 2012). These employees may interpret a medium level of LMX as an ambivalent and insecure relationship and work harder to avoid an impairment of their LMX relationship.

The Role of LMX Differentiation Within a Work Group

LMX theory has been built on the premise that leaders have unique relationships of different qualities with each of their followers (Graen & Uhl-Bien, 1995). The consequence of this premise would be that some followers within a work group have a high-quality relationship with their leader while others have a comparatively poor relationship with the same leader. Some researchers have considered this differentiation of LMX within a work group and started to investigate the consequences of differentiation (e.g., Le Blanc & González-Romá, 2012). The main focus of such research, however, has been on outcomes such as performance or work attitudes (Erdogan & Bauer, 2010; see Henderson, Liden, Glibkowski, & Chaudhry, 2009 for a review). Only a few studies have investigated the consequences of LMX differentiation within a work group for employee well-being. In their theoretical work, Bolino and Turnley (2009) argued that LMX differentiation leads to relative deprivation. Employees compare their own LMX relationship with their leader to the relationship others have which contributes to a *relative* LMX perception (Tse et al., 2012). Relatively low LMX will trigger the feeling of relative deprivation which means that the rewards an employee receives are less than the rewards others receive. Relative deprivation will lead to negative reactions such as stress or negative attitudes

and behaviors, but it can also lead to rather positive reactions such as self-improvement or constructive change. Bolino and Turnley (2009) suggested that the consequences of relative deprivation depend on followers' previous efforts and self-efficacy.

In an empirical study, Hooper and Martin (2008) investigated the consequences of LMX differentiation—measured as perceived variability of LMX—on employee well-being. In two distinct samples of 74 employees from various organizations and 357 Australian firefighters, they found LMX itself to be positively related to employee well-being whereas perceived LMX variability was negatively related to well-being. Furthermore, the authors showed that the relationship between LMX variability and well-being was mediated by team conflict. In other words: A high level of LMX variability may contribute to conflicts within a team which in turn lead to lower levels of well-being.

Summary

In conclusion, empirical evidence strongly suggests that LMX is positively related to employee well-being. The studies reviewed in this chapter show that LMX is related to positive indicators of well-being such as vitality, feelings of energy, or work engagement. Moreover, other studies have consistently shown a negative relationship between LMX and negative indicators of well-being such as job tension, strain, or burnout tendencies. Additionally, some studies showed curvilinear effects suggesting a drawback of a "too much" of LMX with regard to well-being at least under certain conditions. Overall, these findings underline the idea that the relationship between leader and follower plays an important role in explaining employee well-being.

It is important to note that while most studies proposed an effect of LMX on well-being, their cross-sectional designs do not allow conclusions about causality. The possibility of reversed causation has not yet received sufficient attention. Volmer, Niessen, Spurk, Linz, and Abele (2011) have provided evidence for a reversed causation in the relationship between job satisfaction and LMX. Hence, LMX may not only have an effect on job satisfaction, but also job satisfaction might have an effect on LMX. A similar pattern might occur when looking at the relationship between LMX and well-being: employees who feel well are better able to positively interact with their leader, perform better, and, thus, initiate and maintain a more positive relationship with their leader. By now, however, empirical evidence for such a reversed causation in the relationship between well-being and LMX is still missing.

LMX and the Work–Family Interface

In the previous sections of this paper, we have reviewed empirical research on how LMX relates to job stressors and employee well-being. For an increasing number of employees, not only experiences on the job, but also experiences at the work–family interface are a source of stress. For instance, the interference of job demands with responsibilities at home contributes to increased exhaustion over time (Innstrand et al., 2008). In the work–family literature, supervisor support has been shown to be associated with a low level of work–family conflict (Kossek, Pichler, Bodner, & Hammer, 2011) and a high level of work–family enrichment (Crain & Hammer, 2013). This finding suggests that leaders play an important role for employees' experiences of the work–family interface. Compared to the extensive literature on supervisor support, research on the relationship between LMX and the work–family interface is still in its infancy. In this section we will summarize this research.

LMX as a Predictor of Work–Family Variables

Several studies tested the relationship between LMX and work–family variables, mainly looking at work–family conflict or work–family interference. Overall, most studies found a negative relationship between LMX on the one hand and work–family conflict or work–family interference on the other hand (however, cf. Nelson et al., 1998 for a null finding). A classical study by Bernas and Major (2000) examined the relationship between LMX and work–family interference in a sample of 206 women who worked at least 30 hours per week outside the house. As expected, the bivariate relationship between LMX and work interference with family was negative. Path-modeling further showed that this negative relationship was partially mediated by reduced job stress (an overall measure comprising items assessing job stressors and strains).

Golden (2006) also found a negative relationship between LMX and work–family conflict in a sample of 294 telecommuters working in an US telecommunications organization. Major, Fletcher, Davis, and Germano (2008) used a multilevel design to investigate the relationship between LMX and employees' experience that work interferes with family. Data from 792 employees working in ten information technology companies showed that LMX indeed was negatively related to work–family interference. Brunetto, Farr-Wharton, Ramsay, and Shacklock (2010) studied the relationship between LMX and work–family conflict in a sample of 1,065 Australian nurses. Regression analysis showed that LMX was a negative predictor of work–family conflict. Using data from 334 Dutch midwives, Tummers and Bronkhorst (2014) tested how LMX was related to work–family interference. Structural equation modeling with cross-sectional data showed that LMX was negatively related to work–family interference, mediated by a reduced degree of work pressure.

Despite the overall negative relationship between LMX and work–family conflict or work–family interference, some caveats are necessary. For instance, Bernas and Major (2000) reported that the remaining direct effect of LMX on work–family interference was positive when including job stress as partial mediator between LMX and work–family conflict. This finding suggests that LMX might reduce job stressors and/or strains—and thereby it ameliorates work–family conflict. In addition, however, a high-quality LMX may increase work–family conflict by emphasizing the importance of the job. Bernas and Major concluded that "a good relationship with one's supervisor may represent a double-edged sword for working women" (p. 175). Brunetto et al. (2010) reported a positive relationship between LMX and work–family conflict in a sample of 180 Australian police officers. More than two thirds in this sample were male, questioning Bernas and Major's (2000) implicit conclusion that a positive relationship between LMX and work–family conflict might be gender-specific.

Culbertson, Huffman, and Alden-Anderson (2010) differentiated between the four components of LMX as proposed by Liden and Maslyn (1998; cf. Dienesch & Liden, 1986), namely contribution, loyalty, affect, and professional respect. Data collected from a sample of 179 persons employed in a broad range of jobs showed that the affect and loyalty dimensions—but neither contribution nor professional respect—predicted a low level of work–family conflict. Thus, it seems that there are some specific aspects of LMX that are particularly important for shaping followers' experience of the work–family interface.

Until now, only a few studies examined the relationship between LMX and work–family facilitation. The study by Tummers and Bronkhorst (2014) showed that LMX was positively related to work–family facilitation, mediated by a high degree of work meaningfulness. Similarly, Culbertson et al.'s (2010) study that differentiated between different components of LMX revealed that only the contribution dimension was positively related to work–family facilitation.

Taken together, most studies that examined the relationship between LMX and work–family conflict found a negative association; however, also positive associations have been detected in a minority of studies. Thus, although the overall association between LMX and work-family conflict seems to be negative, there appear to be specific instances when a high-quality LMX increases the pressure at the work–family interface, for instance when a high-quality LMX leads to increased responsibilities and commitment at work (e.g., Schyns, Paul, Mohr, & Blank, 2005) what in turn might interfere with family demands. Such interference might be particularly strong when having young children at home or when the partner is (also) employed full time.

Predicting LMX by Work–Family Variables

LMX can be seen not only as a predictor of a low level of work–family conflict and a high level of work–family facilitation. Work–family variables can also be regarded as a predictor of LMX: when followers experience that their work life interferes with their family life, they might attribute this role conflict to their leader, resulting in a low-quality LMX. Empirical studies started to address work–family variables as predictors of LMX.

In a sample of 236 Taiwanese employees working in the high-technology industry, Liao (2011) found work–family conflict to be a predictor of low-quality LMX. This author argued that possibly company-specific third variables such as a high workload and other high demands might cause work–family conflict in employees who then try to negotiate some relief with their leaders; in this specific industry, however, these leaders might have very limited discretion and therefore cannot grant a reduction of workload or provide sufficient support so that LMX deteriorates.

A high-quality LMX might not only result from an individual employee's experience of the work–family interface. Moreover, the way of how the organization as a whole addresses work–family issues might also influence LMX between leaders and individual followers. For instance, the study by Major et al. (2008) mentioned above showed a positive relationship between a well-developed work–family culture at the organization level (assessed by items such as "In this organization employees can easily balance their work and home lives," p. 886) and LMX.

Bagger and Li (2014) investigated how leader behavior towards work–family issues is associated with exchange quality between leader and follower. Specifically, these authors examined supervisory family support (i.e., "behavior exhibited by supervisors to their employees that will allow employees to achieve a balance between their responsibilities at home and at work," p. 1125). A first study based on a sample of 82 employees of a higher-education institution showed that supervisory family support (as perceived by the followers) was positively related to LMX (perceived by the followers) assessed two months later. A second study including data from 225 employees and their leaders again showed a strong bivariate relationship between supervisory family support and the exchange relationship with the leader. Family-friendly benefits provided *by the organization* did not predict a high-quality exchange between leader and follower, but did attenuate the relationship between supervisory family support and LMX. Thus, it seems that leader support for family issues is most important for LMX, but family-friendly benefits provided by the organization can attenuate the negative consequences when support from the leader is missing.

Most research on the work–family interface and LMX focused on the experience that work interferes with family life (work–family conflict). However, employees might also experience that family life interferes with work responsibilities (family–work conflict). Such family–work conflict might be particularly detrimental for LMX because it largely constrains the time and effort employees can contribute to the exchange relationship. A study by Lapierre, Hackett, and Taggar (2006) suggests that the association between family-work interference and LMX might be an indirect one. In a sample of 581 Canadian employees, these authors tested the interplay between family–work conflict, job enrichment (i.e., the experience that one's job offers skill variety, task significance, task identity, and autonomy; see Hackman & Oldham, 1976), and LMX. Cross-sectional analysis showed a negative association between family–work conflict and LMX which was mediated by job enrichment. This finding could imply that employees who experience that family issues interfere with their work role perceive less opportunities for job enrichment what might compromise their job performance, what in turn will negatively impact LMX (Bauer & Green, 1996). Overall, these studies on work–family variables as predictors of LMX demonstrate that LMX might not only influence employees' work–family interface, but that LMX in itself is embedded in complex processes operating at the organizational and the dyadic level.

Summary

Taken together, the studies summarized in this section have shown that LMX is related to followers' experience of the work–family interface. Most studies identified a negative relationship between LMX and work–family conflict and a positive relationship between LMX and work–family facilitation, with some evidence that this relationship might be mediated by reduced work pressure. In some instances, however, a high-quality LMX was associated with a high level of work–family conflict. Research on the curvilinear relationship between LMX and well-being (Harris & Kacmar, 2006) suggests that the relationship between LMX and the work–family interface might also be nonlinear: as LMX increases, work–family conflict decreases, but at extremely high levels of LMX, work–family conflict increases again.

Implications for Future Research and Practice

Although the relationship between LMX and job-stress constructs has not been the main focus of LMX research, the studies summarized in this chapter demonstrate close associations between LMX on the one hand and followers' job stressors, well-being, and experiences at the work–family interface on the other hand. The majority of the studies showed that a high-quality LMX is negatively related to role and other job stressors and positively related to well-being. Moreover, a high-quality LMX goes hand in hand with low levels of work–family conflict and high levels of work–family facilitation. Despite these rather consistent findings, a more nuanced picture is needed: First, some studies identified curvilinear relationships (Harris & Kacmar 2006) and moderator effects of organization-level variables (Bagger & Li, 2014; Todera et al., 2008), pointing at the need to specify more clearly when and how LMX and job-stress variables are related. Second, most of the studies reviewed here used relatively weak designs, following a cross-sectional approach and often relying on single-source data. To move research on the association between LMX and job-stress constructs forward, future studies need to use stronger research designs and to address unanswered research questions in a more systematic

way. In this final section of our chapter, we highlight some of the steps that need to be taken in future research and present implications for managerial practice.

Third Variables Should Be Taken into Consideration

Until now, research on LMX and job stress has often focused on zero-order correlations or has used LMX as the only predictor variable in a multiple-regression approach. Studies that did take third variables into account suggested that the relationship of LMX with job stressors, well-being, and the work–family interface might be influenced by third variables. For instance, Rousseau et al. (2008) found no relationship between LMX and health when controlling for work group integration. One reason for this finding might be a high interdependence between LMX and other social relationships at work. For example, work group integration might be a predictor of both well-being and LMX. Hence, future research should take social relationships with colleagues, customers, or even family members into account when investigating the role of the leader–follower relationship and consider the interplay between these different relationships for well-being (cf. Eby & Allen, 2012). Overall, future research should be more rigorous in ruling out common causes that might influence both LMX and variables referring to job stressors, well-being, and the work–family interface.

Longitudinal Research Is Highly Needed

Research on the association between LMX and job-stress constructs is largely based on cross-sectional study designs. In the majority of studies, LMX has been conceptualized as a predictor of job stressors, well-being, or work–family variables. However, some authors have argued that job stressors or work–family variables predict LMX (Sears & Hackett, 2010). Cross-sectional data do not allow for any clear conclusions about causality.

It is surprising that research on LMX and job stress has relied on relatively weak cross-sectional designs, particularly because research on the association between LMX and job performance or job satisfaction did use longitudinal designs (Bauer, Erdogan, Liden, & Wayne, 2006; Volmer et al., 2011) and because longitudinal studies have a long tradition in research on job stress (Ford, Matthews, Wooldridge, Mishra, Kakar, & Strahan, 2014; Sonnentag & Frese, 2012). Strictly speaking, also longitudinal designs cannot show causality, but they can come closer to insights about causal processes by testing for alternative causal pathways. However, these and other potential threats to making causal claims should be addressed in future studies (cf. Antonakis, Bendahan, Jacquart, & Lalive, 2010). Importantly, when designing longitudinal studies, attention must be paid to appropriate time lags between measurement points (Mitchell & James, 2001). For instance, the effect of LMX on job stressors could unfold rather quickly, whereas the effect of job stressors on LMX is a more delayed one.

More Attention Should Be Paid to Curvilinear Relationships

Some studies have examined curvilinear relationships. For instance, the studies by Harris and Kacmar (2006) and Hochwarter and Byrne (2005) showed a quadratic relationship between LMX and employee well-being, suggesting that there may be "too much of a good thing" (Harris & Kacmar, 2006) and a very high level of LMX might have a downside when it comes to employee well-being. Possibly, follower characteristics play a role here. The few studies that addressed curvilinear relationships underline the need to take the possibility of curvilinear effects into account when investigating the relationship between LMX and constructs related to job stress and well-being.

Conceptualize and Test LMX as a Moderator

The large majority of existing studies on LMX, job stressors, well-being, and the work–family interface looked at direct relationships between these constructs. As we have outlined in our organizing framework, LMX might also act as moderator in the relationships between job stressors, well-being, and the work–family interface. Most obviously, it might be seen as a resource that buffers the negative effects of job stressors on impaired well-being. Similarly, a high-quality LMX may attenuate the negative relationship between work–family conflict and poor well-being: employees who experience a high-quality LMX might more readily accept that the job interferes with their nonwork life, and as a consequence the negative impact of this interference on well-being might be reduced. Also "reverse" relationships between poor well-being and job stressors might be moderated by LMX. For instance, employees suffering from impaired well-being (e.g., a high level of exhaustion) might be less successful in negotiating a low-stressor job when they have a low-quality LMX; a high-quality LMX, however, may help in reducing job stressors when experiencing poor well-being.

Examine LMX Differentiation

The empirical evidence on the consequences of LMX differentiation within a work group for employee well-being is in a nascent stadium. Although initial findings suggest negative consequences of LMX differentiation for well-being (Hooper & Martin, 2008), potential moderators of this relationship remain to be explored. For instance, studies that addressed withdrawal behaviors and performance-related outcomes of LMX differentiation identified justice climate and employee negative affectivity as moderators (Erdogan & Bauer, 2010; Tse et al., 2012). To generate a more comprehensive picture of the role of LMX for employee well-being, future research may further investigate the relationship between LMX differentiation and well-being, by using multilevel designs and including moderator variables.

Look at Within-Person Relationships

During recent years, research on job stress has paid increasing attention to within-person processes and investigated how day-to-day fluctuations in job stressors are related to day-to-day fluctuations in well-being (Ilies, Dimotakis, & De Pater, 2010; Rodell & Judge, 2009). Similarly, studies examined exchange relationships at the day level (Xanthopoulou et al., 2009). These lines of research provide a new perspective in examining how job stress and leadership processes unfold at the day level. Future research might want to work towards an integration of day-level research on job stress and day-level research on LMX by examining how fluctuations in exchange relationships (or the perceptions thereof) impact on job stressors, well-being, and the experience of the work–family interface and how day-specific stressful events shape daily social exchange behaviors.

Pay More Attention to Leaders' Experience of Job Stress

When examining the relationship between LMX and job stress, the large majority of studies have looked at the followers' job stressors, well-being, and work–family interface. An exception is the classical study by Kinicki and Vecchio (1994) that addressed leaders' job stress. This study found that leaders' time-based stress is associated with mean levels of LMX and low levels of LMX differentiation. More research along these lines is needed. For instance,

Wilson, Sin, and Conlon (2010) have described that leaders can gain resources from their followers. These resources can include followers' commitment to the leader, effort invested by the followers, or information provided. Using this resource perspective for a stressor–strain framework, one could argue that resources can help leaders to deal with their job stressors, and thereby buffer the negative effects of job stressors on well-being. Possibly, resources can also be directly related to leader well-being (Bakker, Demerouti, & Sanz-Vergel, 2014). Moreover, LMX might not only impact leader well-being. Leader well-being might also contribute to a high-quality LMX, and a poor leader well-being might compromise it. For instance, leaders who suffer from a high level of exhaustion might be less motivated and less able to build high-quality relationships with their followers.

Implications for Practice

Our review of the literature on the role of LMX for job stressors, employee well-being, and the compatibility of work and family issues has shown that, despite of the relatively large number of studies, the issue of causality has rarely been addressed. Thus, the following practical recommendations have to be taken cautiously and with a large amount of care.

Given future research is able to establish the causal direction from LMX to job stressors, well-being, and work–family issues, training leaders in establishing as many high-quality LMX relationships as they can would be the most obvious practical implication (Major & Lauzun, 2010; Schyns, Maslyn, & van Veldhoven, 2012). Such training may include lectures and discussions on the LMX concept, individual reflections on the positive and negative components of the leaders' relationships with each of their followers, exercises in conversational techniques such as active listening, discussions on the leaders' expectations of the followers and the followers' needs and the resources that may be exchanged in a leader–follower relationship, and practices in one-on-one sessions (cf. Scandura & Graen, 1984). More specifically, such training should include a particular focus on the leaders' and followers' role expectations, attitudes, and resources needed with regard to job stressors, well-being, and the work–family interface (Major & Lauzun, 2010) and provide opportunities to learn how to negotiate and develop high-quality relationships characterized by clear role-expectations (in order to reduce job stressors), mutual trust and support (in order to foster well-being), and a certain degree of autonomy (in order to alleviate problems at the work–family interface).

However, if job stressors, well-being, or the compatibility of work–family issues would predict LMX, it would be necessary for leaders to develop some awareness of these relationships. Hence, leaders should be sensitized not to privilege those followers who already feel well, have low levels of job stress, and a high compatibility of work and family issues. Such sensitivity may be developed during LMX training when leaders reflect on the reasons for their tendency to differentiate between the followers their LMX relationships.

Additionally and based on recent research, LMX training should also cover the issue of LMX differentiation and provide an understanding of potential threats for employee well-being that are associated with too much differentiation. This aspect, however, should be combined with an awareness of the boundaries and limitations of the so-called LMX excellence (i.e., establishing as many high-quality relationships as possible; cf. Schyns & Day, 2010). For example, leaders with a large span of control may have more difficulties in establishing LMX relationships with all of their followers (Schyns et al., 2012). Moreover, leaders who are stressed themselves by increased time or performance pressure or by pursuing exceedingly difficult goals in a competitive environment may lack the capacities to establish high-quality relationships with all of their followers (e.g., Mawritz, Folger, & Latham, 2013). Although this is slightly beyond the scope of the present chapter, managerial action should also acknowledge organizational conditions that foster or hinder the negotiation and development of high-quality relationships.

References

Amstad, F. T., Meier, L. L., Fasel, U., Elfering, A., & Semmer, N. K. (2011). A meta-analysis of work-family conflict and various outcomes with a special emphasis on cross-domain verses matching-domain relations. *Journal of Occupational Health Psychology, 16,* 151–169.

Andrews, M. C., & Kacmar, K. M. (2001). Discriminating among organizational politics, justice, and support. *Journal of Organizational Behavior, 22,* 347–366.

Antonakis, J., Bendahan, S., Jacquart, P., & Lalive, R. (2010). On making causal claims: A review and recommendations. *Leadership Quarterly, 21,* 1086–1120.

Atwater, L. & Carmeli, A. (2009). Leader-member exchange, feelings of energy, and involvement in creative work. *Leadership Quarterly, 20,* 264–275.

Bagger, J., & Li, A. (2014). How does supervisory family support influence employees' attitudes and behaviors? A social exchange perspective. *Journal of Management, 40,* 1123–1150.

Bakker, A. B., & Bal, P. M. (2010). Weekly work engagement and performance: A study among starting teachers. *Journal of Occupational and Organizational Psychology, 83*, 189–206.

Bakker, A. B., Demerouti, E., & Sanz-Vergel, A. I. (2014). Burnout and work engagement: The JD-R approach. *Annual Review of Organizational Psychology and Organizational Behavior, 1*, 389–411.

Bakker, A. B., & Oerlemans, W. G. M. (2012). Subjective well-being in organizations. In K. S. Cameron & G. M. Spreitzer (Eds.), *The Oxford handbook of positive organizational scholarship* (pp. 178–189). New York: Oxford University Press.

Barsade, S. (2002). The ripple effect: Emotional contagion and its influence on group behavior. *Administrative Science Quarterly, 47*, 644–675.

Bauer, T. N., Erdogan, B., Liden, R. C., & Wayne, S. J. (2006). A longitudinal study of the moderating role of extraversion: Leader-member exchange, performance, and turnover during new executive development. *Journal of Applied Psychology, 91*, 298–310.

Bauer, T. N., & Green, S. G. (1996). Development of leader–member exchange: A longitudinal test. *Academy of Management Journal, 39*, 1538–1567.

Baumeister, R. F., & Leary, M. R. (1995). The need to belong: Desire for interpersonal attachments as a fundamental human motivation. *Psychological Bulletin, 117*, 497–529.

Becker, J. A. H., Halbesleben, J. R. B., & O'Hair, H. D. (2005). Defensive communication and burnout in the workplace. The mediating role of leader-member exchange. *Communication Research Reports, 22*, 143–150.

Bernas, K. H., & Major, D. A. (2000). Contributors to stress resistance: Testing a model of women's work-family conflict. *Psychology of Women Quarterly, 24*, 170–178.

Bolino, M. C., & Turnley, W. H. (2009). Relative deprivation among employees in lower-quality leader-member exchange relationships. *Leadership Quarterly, 20*, 276–286.

Bono, J. E., & Yoon, D. J. (2012). Positive supervisory relationships. In: T. D. Allen & L. T. Eby (Eds.), *Personal relationships: The effect on employee attitudes, behavior, and well-being* (pp. 43–66), New York, NY, US: Routledge.

Britt, T. W., & Dawson, C. R. (2005). Predicting work-family conflict from workload, job attitudes, group attributes, and health: A longitudinal study. *Military Psychology, 17*, 203–227.

Brouer, R., & Harris, K. (2007). Dispositional and situational moderators of the relationship between leader-member exchange and work tension. *Journal of Applied Social Psychology, 37*, 1418–1441.

Brunetto, Y., Farr-Wharton, R., Ramsay, S., & Shacklock, K. (2010). Supervisor relationships and perceptions of work-family conflict. *Asia Pacific Journal of Human Resources, 48*, 212–232.

Byron, K. (2005). A meta-analytic review of work-family conflict and its antecedents. *Journal of Vocational Behavior, 67*, 169–198.

Carlson, D. S., & Frone, M. (2003). Relation of behavioral and psychological involvement to a new four-factor conceptualization of work-family interference. *Journal of Business and Psychology, 17*, 515–535.

Chang, C.-H., & Lyons, B. J. (2012). Not all aggressions are created equal: A multifoci approach to workplace aggression. *Journal of Occupational Health Psychology, 17*, 79–92.

Crain, T. L., & Hammer, L. B. (2013). Work-family enrichment: A systematic review of antecedents, outcomes, and mechanisms. *Advances in Positive Organizational Psychology, 1*, 303–328.

Crawford, E. R., LePine, J. A., & Rich, B. L. (2010). Linking job demands and resources to employee engagement and burnout: A theoretical extension and meta-analytic test. *Journal of Applied Psychology, 95*, 834–848.

Culbertson, S. S., Huffman, A. H., & Alden-Anderson, R. (2010). Leader-member exchange and work-family interactions: The mediating role of self-reported challenge and hindrance-related stress. *The Journal of Psychology: Interdisciplinary and Applied, 144*, 15–36.

Daniels, K. (2000). Measures of five aspects of affective well-being at work. *Human Relations, 53*, 275–294.

Dansereau, F., Graen, G. B., & Haga, W. J. (1975). A vertical dyad linkage approach to leadership within formal organizations: A longitudinal investigation of the role making process. *Organizational Behavior and Human Performance, 13*, 46–78.

Davis, W. D., & Gardner, W. L. (2004). Perceptions of politics and organizational cynicism: An attributional and leader-member exchange perspective. *Leadership Quarterly, 15*, 439–465.

Demerouti, E., Bakker, A. B., Nachreiner, F., & Schaufeli, W. B. (2001). Job demands-resources model of burnout. *Journal of Applied Psychology, 86*, 499–512.

Diener, E. (1984). Subjective well-being. *Psychological Bulletin, 95*, 542–575.

Diener, E., Oishi, S., & Lucas, R. E. (2003). Personality, culture, and subjective well-being: Emotional and cognitive evaluations of life. *Annual Review of Psychology, 54*, 403–425.

Diener, E., Suh, E. M., Lucas, R. E., & Smith, H. L. (1999). Subjective well-being: Three decades of progress. *Psychological Bulletin, 125*, 276–302.

Dienesch, R. M., & Liden, R. C. (1986). Leader-member exchange model of leadership: A critique and further development. *Academy of Management Review, 11*, 618–634.

Dulebohn, J. H., Bommer, W. H., Liden, R. C., Brouer, R. L., & Ferris, G. R. (2012). A meta-analysis of antecedents and consequences of leader-member exchange: Integrating the past with an eye toward the future. *Journal of Management, 38*, 1715–1759.

Eby, L. T., & Allen, T. D. (2012). The study of interpersonal relationships: An introduction. In: T. D. Allen & L. T. Eby (eds.), *Personal relationships: The effect on employee attitudes, behavior, and well-being* (3–13), New York, NY, US: Routledge.

Eby, L. T., Maher, C. P., & Butts, M. M. (2010). The intersection of work and family life: The role of affect. *Annual Review of Psychology, 61*, 599–622.

Eden, D., Ganzach, Y., Flumin-Granat, R., & Zigman, T. (2010). Augmenting means efficacy to improve performance: Two field experiments. *Journal of Management, 36*, 687–713.

Erdogan, B., & Bauer, T. N. (2010). Differentiated leader–member exchanges: The buffering role of justice climate. *Journal of Applied Psychology, 95*, 1104–1120.

Ferris, D. L., & Kacmar, K. M. (1992). Perceptions of organizational politics. *Journal of Management, 18*, 93–116.

Ford, M. T., Heinen, B. A., & Langkamer, K. L. (2007). Work and family satisfaction and conflict: A meta-analysis of cross-domain relations. *Journal of Applied Psychology, 92*, 57–80.

Ford, M. T., Matthews, R. A., Wooldridge, J. D., Mishra, V., Kakar, U. M., & Strahan, S. R. (2014). How do occupational stressor-strain effects vary with time? A review and meta-analysis of the relevance of time lags in longitudinal studies. *Work & Stress*, 28, 9–30.

Gajendran, R. S., & Joshi, A. (2012). Innovation in globally distributed teams: The role of LMX, communication frequency, and member influence on team decisions. *Journal of Applied Psychology*, 97, 1252–1261.

Gagné, M. & Deci, E. L. (2005). Self-determination theory and work motivation. *Journal of Organizational Behavior*, 26, 331–362.

Gerstner, C. R., & Day, D. V. (1997). Meta-analytic review of leader-member exchange theory: Correlates and construct issues. *Journal of Applied Psychology*, 82, 827–844.

Gilboa, S., Shirom, A., Fried, Y., & Cooper, C. (2008). A meta-analysis of work demand stressors and job performance: Examining main and moderating effects. *Personnel Psychology*, 61, 227–271.

Golden, T. D. (2006). The role of relationships in understanding telecommuter satisfaction. *Journal of Organizational Behavior*, 27, 319–340.

Gorman, C. A., Meriac, J. P., Overstreet, B. L., Apodaca, S., McIntyre, A. L., Park, P., & Godbey, J. N. (2012). A meta-analysis of the regulatory focus nomological network: Work-related antecedents and consequences. *Journal of Vocational Behavior*, 80, 160–172.

Graen, G. B., & Scandura, T. A. (1987). Toward a psychology of dyadic organizing. *Research in Organizational Behavior*, 9, 175–208.

Graen, G. B., & Uhl-Bien, M. (1995). Relationship-based approach to leadership: Development of leader-member exchange (LMX) theory of leadership over 25 years: Applying a multi-level multi-domain perspective. *Leadership Quarterly*, 6, 219–247.

Graves, L. M., & Luciano, M. M. (2013). Self-determination at work: Understanding the role of leader-member exchange. *Motivation and Emotion*, 37, 518–536.

Greenhaus, J. H., & Beutell, N. J. (1985). Sources of conflict between work and family roles. *Academy of Management Review*, 10, 76–88.

Greenhaus, J. H., & Powell, G. N. (2006). When work and family are allies: A theory of work-family enrichment. *Academy of Management Journal*, 31, 72–92.

Hackman, J. R., & Oldham, G. R. (1976). Motivation through the design of work: Test of a theory. *Organizational Behavior and Human Performance*, 16, 250–279.

Hall, G. B., Dollard, M. F., Tuckey, M. R., Winefield, A. H., & Thompson, B. M. (2010). Job demands, work-family conflict, and emotional exhaustion in police officers: A longitudinal test of competing theories. *Journal of Occupational and Organizational Psychology*, 83, 237–250.

Harris, K. J., & Kacmar, K. M. (2005). Easing the strain: The buffer role of supervisors in the perceptions of politics-strain relationship. *Journal of Occupational and Organizational Psychology*, 78, 337–354.

Harris, K. J., & Kacmar, K. M. (2006). Too much of a good thing: The curvilinear effect of leader-member exchange on stress. *Journal of Social Psychology*, 146, 65–84.

Henderson, D. J., Liden, R. C., Glibkowski, B. C., & Chaudhry, A. (2009). LMX differentiation: A multilevel review and examination of its antecedents and outcomes. *Leadership Quarterly*, 20, 517–534.

Hershcovis, M. S., & Reich, T. C. (2013). Integrating workplace aggression research: Relational, contextual, and method considerations. *Journal of Organizational Behavior*, 34, S26–S42.

Hochwarter, W., & Byrne, Z. S. (2005). LMX and job tension: Linear and non-linear effects and affectivity. *Journal of Business and Psychology*, 19, 505–520.

Hooper, D. T., & Martin, R. (2008). Beyond personal leader-member exchange (LMX) quality: The effects of perceived LMX variability on employee reactions. *Leadership Quarterly*, 19, 20–30.

Hornung, S., Rousseau, D. M., Glaser, J., Angerer, P., & Weigl, M. (2010). Beyond top-down and bottom-up work redesign: Customizing job content through idiosyncratic deals. *Journal of Organizational Behavior*, 31, 187–215.

Huang, X., Chan, S. C. H., Lam, W., & Nan, X. (2010). The joint effect of leader-member exchange and emotional intelligence on burnout and work performance in call centers in China. *International Journal of Human Resource Management*, 21, 1124–1144.

Ilies, R., Dimotakis, N., & De Pater, I. E. (2010). Psychological and physiological reactions to high workloads: Implications for well-being. *Personnel Psychology*, 63, 407–436.

Innstrand, S. T., Langballe, E. M., Espnes, G. A., Falkum, E., & Assland, O. G. (2008). Positive and negative work-family interaction and burnout: A longitudinal study of reciprocal relations. *Work & Stress*, 22, 1–15.

Jian, G. (2014). Revisiting the association of LMX with perceived role stressors: Evidence for inverted U relationships among immigrant employees. *Communication Research*, 41, 52–73.

Jiang, J. Y., Law, K. S., & Sun, J. J. M. (2014). Leader-member relationship and burnout: The moderating role of leader integrity. *Management and Organization Review*, 14, 223–237.

Kahn, R. L., & Byosiere, P. (1992). Stress in organizations. In M. D. Dunnette & L. M. Hough (Eds.), *Handbook of industrial and organizational psychology* (2nd ed., Vol. 3, pp. 571–650). Palo Alto, CA: Consulting Psychologists Press.

Kahn, R. L., Wolfe, D. M., Quinn, R. P., Snoek, J. D., & Rosenthal, R. A. (1964). *Organizational stress: Studies in role conflict and ambiguity*. New York: Wiley.

Karasek, R. (1979). Job demands, job decision latitude, and mental strain: Implications for job redesign. *Administrative Science Quarterly*, 24, 285–306.

Kauppila, O.-P. (2014). So, what am I supposed to do? A multilevel examination of role clarity. *Journal of Management Studies*, 51, 737–763.

Keeney, J., & Ilies, R. (2012). Positive work-family dynamics. In K. S. Cameron & G. M. Spreitzer (Eds.), *The Oxford handbook of positive organizational scholarship* (pp. 601–614). New York: Oxford University Press.

Kelloway, E. K., Gottlieb, B. H., & Barham, L. (1999). The source, nature, and direction of work and family conflict: A longitudinal investigation. *Journal of Occupational Health Psychology*, 4, 337–346.

Kinicki, A. J., & Vecchio, R. P. (1994). Influences on the quality of supervisor-subordinate relations: The role of time-pressure, organizational commitment, and locus of control. *Journal of Organizational Behavior*, 15, 75–82.

Kossek, E. E., & Ozeki. (1998). Work-family conflict, policies, and the job-life satisfaction relationship: A review and directions for organizational behavior-human resources research. *Journal of Applied Psychology*, 83, 139–149.

Kossek, E. E., Pichler, S., Bodner, T., & Hammer, L. B. (2011). Workplace social support and work-family conflict: A meta-analysis clarifying the influence of general and work-family-specific supervisor and organizational support. *Personnel Psychology, 64*, 289–313.

Lapierre, L. M., Hackett, R. D., & Taggar, S. (2006). A test of the links between family interference with work, job enrichment and leader-member exchange. *Applied Psychology: An International Review, 55*, 489–511.

Le Blanc, P. M., & González-Romá, V. (2012). A team level investigation of the relationship between Leader–Member Exchange (LMX) differentiation, and commitment and performance. *Leadership Quarterly, 23*, 534–544.

Liao, P.-Y. (2011). Linking work-family conflict to job attitudes: the mediating role of social exchange relationships. *International Journal of Human Resource Management, 22*, 2965–2980.

Liden, R. C., Erdogan, B., Wayne, S. J., & Sparrowe, R. T. (2006). Leader-member exchange, differentiation, and task interdependence: Implications for individual and group performance. *Journal of Organizational Behavior, 27*, 723–746.

Liden, R. C., & Maslyn, J. M. (1998). Multidimensionality of leader-member exchange: An empirical assessment through scale development. *Journal of Management, 24*, 43–72.

Lount, R. B. Jr. (2010). The impact of positive mood on trust in interpersonal and intergroup interactions. *Journal of Personality and Social Psychology, 98*, 420–433.

Major, D. A., Fletcher, T. D., Davis, D. D., & Germano, L. M. (2008). The influence of work-family culture and workplace relationships on work interference with family: A multilevel model. *Journal of Organizational Behavior, 29*, 881–897.

Major, D. A. & Lauzun, H. M. (2010). Equipping managers to assist employees in addressing work-family conflict: Applying the research literature toward innovative practice. *The Psychologist-Manager Journal, 13*, 69–85.

Major, D. A., & Morganson, V. J. (2011). Coping with work-family conflict: A leader-member exchange perspective. *Journal of Occupational Health Psychology, 16*, 126–138.

Maslach, C., & Jackson, S. E. (1981). The measurement of experienced burnout. *Journal of Organizational Behavior, 2*, 99–113.

Maslach, C., Schaufeli, W. B., & Leiter, M. P. (2001). Job burnout. *Annual Review of Psychology, 52*, 397–422.

Mawritz, M. B., Folger, R., & Latham, G. P. (2013). Supervisors' exceedingly difficult goals and abusive supervision: The mediating effect of hindrance stress, anger, and anxiety. *Journal of Organizational Behavior, 35*, 358–372.

McNall, L. A., Nicklin, J. M., & Masuda, A. D. (2010). A meta-analytic review of the consequences associated with work-family enrichment. *Journal of Business and Psychology, 25*, 381–396.

Mitchell, T. R., & James, L. R. (2001). Building better theory: Time and the specification of when things happen. *Academy of Management Review, 26*, 530–547.

Muldoon, J., Matthews, R. A., & Foley, C. (2012). Mediated effects of physical risk factors, leader-member exchange and empowerment in predicting perceived injury risk. *Stress and Health, 28*, 149–162.

Nelson, D., Basu, R., & Purdie, R. (1998). An examination of exchange quality and work stressors in leader-follower dyads. *International Journal of Stress Management, 5*, 103–112.

Nixon, A. E., Mazzola, J. J., Bauer, J., Krueger, J. R., & Spector, P. E. (2011). Can work make you sick? A meta-analysis of the relationships between job stressors and physical symptoms. *Work & Stress, 25*, 1–22.

Peters, L. H., & O'Connor, E. J. (1980). Situational constraints and work outcomes: The influences of a frequently overlooked construct. *Academy of Management Review, 5*, 391–397.

Rodell, J. B., & Judge, T. A. (2009). Can "good" stressors spark "bad" behaviors? The mediating role of emotions in links of challenge and hindrance stressors with citizenship and counterproductive behaviors. *Journal of Applied Psychology, 94*, 1438–1451.

Rousseau, D. M. (2001). The idiosyncratic deal: Flexibility versus fairness. *Organizational Dynamics, 29*, 260–273.

Rousseau, V., Aubé, C., Chiocchio, F., Boudrias J.-S., & Morin, E. M. (2008) Social interactions at work and psychological health: The role of leader-member exchange and work group integration. *Journal of Applied Social Psychology, 38*, 1755–1777.

Ryan, R. M., & Deci, E. L. (2001). On happiness and human potentials: A review of research on hedonic and eudaimonic well-being. *Annual Review of Psychology, 52*, 141–166.

Ryff, C. D. (1989). Happiness is everything, or is it? Explorations on the meaning of psychological well-being. *Journal of Personality and Social Psychology, 57*, 1069–1081.

Scandura, T. A. & Graen, G. B. (1984). Moderating effects of initial leader-member exchange status on the effects of a leadership intervention. *Journal of Applied Psychology, 69*, 428–436.

Schyns, B., Maslyn, J. M., & van Veldhoven, M. P. M. (2012). Can some leaders have a good relationship with many followers? The role of personality in the relationship between leader-member exchange and span of control. *Leadership & Organization Development Journal, 33*, 594–606.

Schaufeli, W. B., & Bakker, A. B. (2004). Job demands, job resources, and their relationship with burnout and engagement: a multi-sample study. *Journal of Organizational Behavior, 25*, 293–315.

Schyns, B. (2006). Are group consensus in leader-member exchange (LMX) and shared work values related to organizational outcomes? *Small Group Research, 37*, 20–35.

Schyns, B., & Day, D. V. (2010). Critique and review of leader-member exchange theory: Issues of agreement, consensus, and excellence. *European Journal of Work and Organizational Psychology, 19*, 1–29.

Schyns, B., Maslyn, J. M., & van Veldhoven, M. P. M. (2012). Can some leaders have a good relationship with many followers? The role of personality in the relationship between leader-member exchange and span of control. *Leadership & Organization Development Journal, 33*, 594–606.

Schyns, B., Paul, T., Mohr, G., & Blank, H. (2005). Comparing antecedents and consequences of leader-member exchange in a German working context to findings in the US. *European Journal of Work and Organizational Psychology, 14*, 1–22.

Sears, G. J., & Hackett, R. D. (2010). The influence of role definition and affect in LMX: A process perspective on the personality - LMX relationship. *Journal of Occupational and Organizational Psychology, 84*, 544–564.

Shockley, K. M., & Singla, N. (2011). Reconsidering work-family interactions and satisfaction: A meta-analysis. *Journal of Management, 37*, 861–886.

Siegrist, J. (1996). Adverse health effects of high effort/low reward conditions. *Journal of Occupational Health Psychology, 1*, 27–41.

Sin, H.-P., Nahrgang, J. D., & Morgeson, F. P. (2009). Understanding why they don't see eye to eye: An examination of leader–member exchange (LMX) agreement. *Journal of Applied Psychology*, *94*, 1048–1057.

Snyder, R. A., & Bruning, N. S. (1985). Quality of vertical dyad linkages: Congruence of supervisor and subordinate competence and role stress as exploratory variables. *Group and Organization Studies*, *10*, 81–94.

Sonnentag, S., Dormann, C., & Demerouti, E. (2010). Not all days are created equal: The concept of state work engagement. In A. B. Bakker & M. P. Leiter (Eds.), *Work engagement: Recent developments in theory and research* (pp. 25–38). New York: Psychology Press.

Sonnentag, S., & Frese, M. (2012). Stress in organizations. In N. W. Schmitt & S. Highhouse (Eds.), *Handbook of Psychology. Volume 12: Industrial and Organizational Psychology* (Second ed., pp. 560–592). Hoboken: Wiley.

Thomas, C. H., & Lankau, M. J. (2009). Preventing burnout: The effects of LMX and mentoring on socialization, role stress, and burnout. *Human Resource Management*, *48*, 417–432.

Tordera, N., González-Romá, V., & Peiró, J. M. (2008). The moderator effect of psychological climate on the relationship between leader-member exchange (LMX) quality and role overload. *European Journal of Work and Organiszational Psychology*, *17*, 55–72.

Tse, H. H. M., Ashkanasy, N. M., & Dasborough, M. T. (2012). Relative leader–member exchange, negative affectivity and social identification: A moderated-mediation examination. *Leadership Quarterly*, *23*, 354–366.

Tummers, L. G., & Bronkhorst, B. A. C. (2014). The impact of leader-member exchange (LMX) on work-family interference and work-family facilitation. *Personnel Review*, *43*, 573–591.

Uhl-Bien, M. (2006). Relational leadership theory: Exploring the social processes of leadership and organizing. *Leadership Quarterly*, *17*, 654–676.

Volmer, J., Niessen, C., Spurk, D., Linz, A., & Abele, A. E. (2011). Reciprocal relationships between leader–member exchange (LMX) and job satisfaction: A cross-lagged analysis. *Applied Psychology: An International Review*, *60*, 522–545.

Walumbwa, F. O., Cropanzano, R., & Goldman, B. M. (2011). How leader-member exchange influences effective work behaviors: Social exchange and internal-external efficacy perspectives. *Personnel Psychology*, *64*, 739–770.

Warr, P. (1990). The measurement of well-being and other aspects of mental health. *Journal of Occupational Psychology*, *63*, 193–210.

Waterman, A. S. (1993). Two conceptions of happiness: Contrasts of personal expressiveness (eudaimonia) and hedonic enjoyment. *Journal of Personality and Social Psychology*, *64*, 678–691.

Watson, D., Clark, L. A., & Tellegen, A. (1988). Development and validation of brief measures of positive and negative affect: The PANAS scales. *Journal of Personality and Social Psychology*, *54*, 1063–1070.

Wilson, K. S., Sin, H.-P., & Conlon, D. E. (2010). What about the leader in leader-member exchange? The impact of resource exchange and the substitutability on the leader. *Academy of Management Review*, *35*, 358–372.

Xanthopoulou, D., Bakker, A. B., Demerouti, E., & Schaufeli, W. B. (2009). Work engagement and financial returns: A diary study on the role of job and personal resources. *Journal of Occupational and Organizational Psychology*, *82*, 183–200.

Xanthopoulou, D., Bakker, A. B., Demerouti, E., & Schaufeli, W. B. (2012). A diary study on the happy worker: How job resources relate to positive emotions and personal resources. *European Journal of Work and Organizational Psychology*, *21*, 489–517.

Leader–Member Exchange and Emotion in Organizations

Herman H. M. Tse, Ashlea C. Troth, *and* Neal M. Ashkanasy

Abstract

Although there is now an established literature to support the basic idea that emotions are inherent in social exchange processes between leaders and followers, research exploring the role of emotions in the formation and maintenance of leader–member exchange (LMX) relationships remains underdeveloped. In this essay, the authors begin by establishing the background and importance of this line of research. The essay then proceeds in three stages. In the first, the authors review the underlying theories used in the literature to study the implications of emotion-related constructs for LMX development. Second, they address three key areas important for improving understanding of the nexus of LMX and emotion: (1) LMX and emotional intelligence, (2) LMX and discrete emotions, and (3) LMX and emotional labor. Finally, they discuss the challenges of the extant research and identify avenues for future research.

Key Words: leader–member exchange, emotions, emotional intelligence, emotional labor

Introduction

It is now 15 years since Ashkanasy and his colleagues (Ashkanasy, Härtel, & Daus, 2002; Ashkanasy & Tse, 2000; Fisher & Ashkanasy, 2000) introduced the idea that interpersonal social exchanges between leaders and their followers involve emotions. In this instance, Katz and Kahn (1978) define social exchange as the joint activity of two or more individuals in a social relationship, where each individual has something the other party values and expects. Lawler (2001) subsequently set out an Affect Theory of Social Exchange, where exchange structures and processes produce a wide array of emotional responses. According to this theory, social interactions in workgroups can elicit and evoke different kinds of emotional experiences within individuals involved. In the specific context of leader–member exchange (LMX) relationships, this suggests that individuals with different emotions interact with their leader, and that this in turn triggers and transfers the emotions within interpersonal exchange processes (Barsade, 2002; Tse,

Dasborough, & Ashkanasy, 2005; Tse & Ashkanasy, 2008).

Referring specifically to LMX, scholars (e.g., Ashkanasy, 2003; Dasborough, 2006; Tse et al., 2005; Tse & Ashkanasy, 2008) argue that emotions play a critical role because of the physical proximity and frequency of interactions between leaders and followers in workgroups. Thus, if it is true that emotions are inherent in interpersonal interactions, it is axiomatic that the dynamic emotional process of LMX should also be studied to explain the structure and processes of supervisor–subordinate relationships (Tse et al., 2005; Tse & Ashkanasy, 2008). Surprisingly, however, and as Gooty, Connelly, Griffith, and Gupta (2010) point out, our understanding of the underlying role of emotions and other emotion-related constructs in social exchange processes between supervisors and subordinates in workgroups remains largely underdeveloped (Raja, Song, & Arvey, 2011).

This is despite the fact that the importance of emotion in LMX was raised 20 years ago by Graen and Uhl-Bien (1995), who suggested that LMX is a relationship-based approach to leadership that focuses on the unique dyadic relationships leaders form and maintain with their followers. More recently, Erdogan and Bauer (2014) echoed this idea by proposing that a fundamental basis of LMX is that the quality of the dyadic relationship between leaders and members is the key to understanding this phenomenon. Tse and his colleagues (Tse et al., 2005; Tse & Ashkanasy, 2008) have pointed out, moreover, that emotions can have important social functions and consequences in such exchange processes. These in turn can influence the behaviors and perceptions of both leaders and followers who experience the emotions. Emotions can also function as communication, conveying information about how both leaders and followers feel about things, social intentions, and their orientation toward each other in supervisor–subordinate relationships (van Kleef, 2009). As such, it is reasonable to conclude that emotions play a vital role in underlying and shaping the structure and process of LMX relationships formed in workgroups.

In fact, it has been a decade since Barsade, Brief, and Spataro (2003, p. 3) coined the term "affective revolution" (based on the increasing research attention directed to studying the role of emotions in organizational behavior). Since then, a considerable volume of research has been undertaken to attempt to understand the broader impacts and implications of emotions for organizational behavior. As a result, several distinct research streams (including positive and negative emotions, emotional intelligence, and emotional labor) have emerged, together with new theoretical frameworks such as affective events theory (AET), emotional contagion theory, and the appraisal theory of emotion. Each of these perspectives makes unique contributions to our knowledge of the role of these emotion-related constructs that can serve to shape the dynamic social exchange process between leaders and followers in workgroups.

In this essay, we therefore seek to contribute to the LMX and emotions literature in two important ways. First, our work responds to calls by Gooty et al. (2010) and Raja et al. (2011) to unify and to integrate the diverse research on emotions and leadership. Specifically, we seek to extend previous research on LMX by reviewing the role of discrete emotions, emotional intelligence, and emotional labor. As such, we hope to provide a more comprehensive understanding about the role of different aspects of emotion in leader–follower social exchange processes.

Second, by synthesizing the LMX and emotions literatures, we seek to identify underlying theories that have been used to understand the implications of different emotion-related constructs for LMX development. In particular, Gooty et al. (2010) and Raja et al. (2011) did not provide insights into the existing frameworks that are important and relevant for theoretical and practical development. We aim to rectify this shortcoming by identifying challenges and potential avenues for future research efforts as a means to stimulate more research interest in LMX and emotions.

In this essay we seek to accomplish these aims in three stages. In the first part of our essay, we review the underlying theories that have been applied to studying the role of different emotion-related constructs in the leader–member social exchange process within workgroups. In the second stage, we review existing research in three key areas of LMX and emotions: (1) LMX and emotional intelligence, (2) LMX and discrete emotions, and (3) LMX and emotional labor. Finally, we identify challenges and potential avenues for future research.

A Review of Three Underlying Theories

In this section, we review three key theories that have been used to understand relationships between LMX and emotions in workgroups. The theories include (1) Affective Events Theory, (2) Emotional Contagion Theory, and (3) the Appraisal Theory of Emotion. Each of these has its own premises, functions, and characteristics that can guide the development of major propositions and hypotheses in relation to the emotional process inherent in LMX relationships.

Theory 1: Affective Events

Affective Events Theory (AET: Weiss & Cropanzano, 1996) provides a useful framework for leadership researchers to understand the emotional experiences and subsequent emotional expressions and behaviors that arise as part of the leader–follower relationships (Ashkanasy, 2002; Dasborough, 2006; Gaddis, Connelly & Mumford, 2004; Gooty et al., 2010; Raja et al., 2011). According to AET, aspects of the organizational environment create positive and negative affective events (hassles and uplifts) for employees. The accumulation of these positive and negative affective events over time leads to positive or negative states in employees that, in turn, result in attitudinal states and behavioral responses

(Dasborough, 2006). Leaders are especially viewed as important organizational players who, via their behavior (e.g., giving feedback, allocating tasks etc.) and mood (e.g., enthusiastic, excited, angry, distressed), trigger affective events that have consequences for employees and teams (Dasborough, 2006; Gooty et al, 2010; Tse, Dasborough, & Ashkanasy, 2008). Ashkanasy and Daus (2002) for example, describe how an employee being hassled by a demanding boss (an affective event) becomes angry and disgruntled (an affective state), suffers job dissatisfaction (an attitudinal state), and consequently engages in deviant behavior (behavioral consequence).

In an empirical demonstration of this effect, Gaddis et al. (2004) investigated failure feedback by leaders as an affective event in the workplace. These authors found that subordinates' attitudes and performance are influenced by the nature of the feedback and the emotional response of the employee to the feedback. In essence, they confirmed AET predictions insofar as they found that the affective state evoked in an employee mediates the effect of the (affective) event on subsequent attitudes and behavior.

LMX AND EMOTIONS IN THE CONTEXT OF AET

In a recent review of leadership, affect, and emotions research, Gooty and her colleagues (2010) broadly classified leadership behaviors as favorable or unfavorable in terms of how such behaviors affect followers' moods at work. Unfavorable leader behaviors include abusive supervision, interpersonal injustice, and autocratic leader behaviors (Harvey, Stoner, Hochwater, & Kacmar, 2007; Hui, Law, & Chen, 1999) and are generally found to lead to negative follower affect and aversive outcomes. By contrast, favorable leader behaviors such as charismatic and supportive leadership usually evoke positive affect and behaviors in their followers. In this case, Erez et al. (2008) found that leader charisma typically induces positive affective expressions that lead to positive emotion in the followers.

While it is generally accepted that leadership behaviors and moods impact followers and the quality of the LMX relationship in the expected directions (as discussed), recent research highlights the role of an individual's own appraisals and interpretations of a particular event in determining her or his emotional reactions, subsequent actions and behaviors (Dasborough & Ashkanasy, 2002; Raja

et al., 2011). For example, emotional contagion susceptibility (one of the mechanisms thought to underlie the transfer of emotion process; see Johnson, 2008), emotional competencies (of the leader and the employee), as well as emotional regulation processes (Gross, 2013), all appear to have an impact on the variation and intensity of the resultant emotional experiences. As such, they also serve to shape subsequent attitudes and behaviors of the leader and employee as well as the quality of the LMX relationship (Raja et al., 2011).

Theory 2: Emotional Contagion

Emotional Contagion Theory (Hatfield, Cacioppo, & Rapson, 1992, 1994) postulates that individuals can "catch" the emotions of other members consciously or unconsciously. Moods and emotions can be spread implicitly through unconscious emotional contagion, vicarious affect, behavioral entrainment, and interaction synchrony (Kelly & Barsade, 2001). According to Hatfield and her associates (1992), emotional contagion is triggered via one or more of three mechanisms: (1) conscious cognitive processes, (2) conditioned or unconditioned emotional reactions, and (3) mimicry feedback. A conscious cognitive process results when an individual empathizes with another team member who is expressing an emotion, and tries to internalize and experience the displayed emotion (Davis, 1985). Transmission of emotion through this process varies depending on the personal factors of the sender and receiver of emotions. In a group setting, team members may empathize with an individual member experiencing and displaying emotions they cognitively interpret, and which are appropriate to their expectations within the context. By contrast, unconscious emotional contagion can result from either conditioned or unconditioned responses (based on biological instinct, upbringing, or prior experience). Finally, team members can be motivated to mimic the emotional displays of others in the team to appear to be a part of the workgroup (Hatfield et al., 1994). Irrespective of what mechanism is present, the implication of emotional contagion is that affect and its effects are almost always present within groups, and therefore inevitably impact team member interactions (Hatfield et al., 1994).

LMX AND EMOTIONS IN THE EMOTIONAL CONTAGION PROCESS

Although the theoretical basis of emotional contagion implies that emotional cognition processes occur among interpersonal team member interactions, Sy, Côté, and Saavedra (2005) empirically showed that it is also important during the social exchange process between leaders and followers. As such, LMX can be seen to play a vital role in facilitating the contagious process among members in workgroups. Given that all members are connected with each other and the leader through their LMX relationships, the differential qualities of the LMX become a major source to elicit an array of different emotional responses among members which may spread through the emotional contagion process (Barsade, 2002; Tee, Ashkanasy, & Paulsen, 2013; Tse & Ashkanasy, 2008).

For example, consider a team member who feels excited about a new assignment s/he just received from a leader; this level of excitement might then be picked up by other members through emotional contagion. In support of this, Tse and his colleagues (Tse & Troth, 2013; Tse et al., 2008) demonstrated that team members experience a wide range of emotional responses to the quality of relationships they have with their leader. These emotional responses in turn affect the overall team emotional experience. Along similar lines, De Dreu, West, Fischer, and MacCurtain (2001) proposed that group interaction is a type of "emotional incubator," where individual members' affective states combine to produce a collective emotional tenor that, in turn, influences individual team member attitudes and behaviors. Kelly and Barsade (2001) argue more specifically that teams embody a group mood, which can begin initially with the affective experiences of team members, then develops through a process of emotional contagion, including entrainment, modeling, and manipulation of affect (Barsade, 2002).

We argue on the basis of the foregoing evidence that leaders can convey their emotions (positive or negative) to team members through differential qualities of LMX relationships (Sy et al., 2005). Furthermore, the emotions experienced and displayed by different members through the emotional contagion process combine to create the group's affective tone. Interestingly, Tse et al. (2008) found that a positive affective climate facilitated the development of high-quality LMX, implying a virtuous cycle of positive affective tone and LMX relationship quality (Tee et al., 2013).

Theory 3 : Appraisal

The question that is yet to be answered at this point in our discussion however is: How do individuals respond to emotional cues in the first instance? The answer lies in the Appraisal Theory of Emotion, which Frijda (1986) defined as the process whereby actors appraise (evaluate) environmental cues and translate these into experienced emotional states (see also Moors, Ellsworth, Scherer, & Frijda, 2013, for the most up-to-date review). It is one of the oldest concepts in emotion theory, originating in the work of William James (1890), who also raised the issue of appraisal and causation, asking whether a person running from a bear experiences fear based on his or her perception of the bear or because s/he innately experiences fear in the presence of the bear. More recently, Lazarus and Folkman (1984) and Scherer (2001) expanded on appraisal theory, recognizing two sequential steps in the appraisal process: primary and secondary appraisal.

Primary appraisal involves the direct process of perceiving an environmental cue (e.g., a bear emerging from the woods), followed by a resulting physiological response (e.g., startle, sweating) and immediate behavioral responses (e.g., running away). Although earlier research (e.g., see Lazarus, 1991; Zajonc, 1985) debated the sequential order of cognitive vs. visceral appraisal (see Moors, 2013, for a recent review of the debates), most scholars now agree that emotions entail an interaction of both cognitive and noncognitive neural systems (Fischer, Shaver, & Carnochan, 1990; Moors et al., 2013). In this sense, Ashkanasy (2003, p. 11) concluded that, "emotion is . . . as an integration of innate, adaptive subsystems, derived from the evolutionary needs of survival (Tooby & Cosmides, 1990; LeDoux, 1995)."

Secondary appraisal follows immediately after primary appraisal, and refers to more considered behavioral approaches to the initial experience. Lazarus and Folkman (1984) argue in particular that secondary appraisal includes two distinct behavioral responses: emotion-focused and problem-focused. Emotion-focused responses involve attempts to deal directly with the experienced emotion. For example, on being accosted by a bear, a hunter might say to him- or herself "Don't panic. Calm down." Problem-focused coping involves behavioral actions intended to deal with the source of the emotional stimulus (e.g., running away from or shooting the bear). Although problem-focused coping is often cast as the more positive response, Gooty, Gavin, Ashkanasy, and Thomas (2014) found that emotion-focused coping can be a more appropriate response in particular work situations. Specifically, they found that emotionally intelligent police officers understood that they needed first to "cool" their emotions before engaging in behavior to deal with a difficult police enforcement situation.

LMX AND EMOTIONS IN THE CONTEXT OF APPRAISAL THEORY

Based on our earlier depiction of the LMX relationship as involving appraisal of emotional cues (Ashkanasy & Tse, 2000) combined with the view that appraisals are an essential component of the relationship development process (Smith & Kirby, 2009), it can be appreciated that the formation of LMX relationships must involve appraisal processes. In demonstration of this, Newcombe and Ashkanasy (2002) found that subordinates' LMX ratings flowed from their appraisal of a supervisor's emotional expression. Thus, a team member would be expected to engage in primary appraisal of a leader's behavior and affective expression, resulting in an immediate emotional reaction (Weiss & Cropanzano, 1996). The team member would then engage in secondary appraisal to decide on a behavioral response to the leader. This may be either emotion-focused, for example, attempts to regulate emotions including suppression of emotion or reappraisal of the situation (Gross, 1998); or it may be problem-focused, for example, agreeing to comply with a leader's work requests or refusing to comply. Dasborough and Ashkanasy (2002, 2005) argue further that the nature of the response depends on how the member attributes intention to the leader. If the leader is seen to be manipulative and insincere, the member is unlikely to be motivated to comply with the leader's influence attempts. If, on the other hand, the leader is seen to be sincere, then the member is more likely to comply. Dasborough and Ashkanasy (2005) also note that this is further reflected in the member's positive and/or negative responses to the leader's influence attempt.

Taken together, formation of high-quality LMX can be seen to be influenced by the member's appraisal of her or his leader's approach. The member's primary appraisal of the leader's approach results in an affective reaction which leads to secondary appraisal and an affective or behavioral response. Weiss and Cropanzano (1996) refer to this as emotion-driven versus judgment-driven behavior responses.

Understanding the Nexus of LMX and Emotion

In this second phase of this chapter, we move on to a discussion of how the foregoing theoretical perspectives can help us to understand the role emotions play in LMX relationships. In this regard, Ashkanasy (2003) argues that LMX quality essentially represents an emotional judgment that the leader makes (Ashkanasy & Tse, 2000). Factors contributing to LMX include similarity of attitudes (Phillips & Bedeian, 1994; Turban, Jones, & Rozelle, 1990), relationship satisfaction (McClane, 1991), psychological distance (Salzmann & Grasha, 1991), mentoring (Scandura & Schreisheim, 1994), and social discourse (Sias & Jablin, 1995). Recent research has demonstrated specifically that LMX is closely tied to emotional dimensions. In the experimental study we referred to earlier, Newcombe and Ashkanasy (2002) found that leaders who displayed positive emotions were judged to be expressing higher-quality LMX. This was true even when the leaders were delivering negative feedback. More recently, Jordan and Troth (2011) found in a longitudinal field study that LMX quality mediates the relationship between follower emotional intelligence and employee job satisfaction and turnover intention. These results confirm that the quality of the relationship between leader and follower is partially determined by the leader's ability to convey positive emotions to followers. In the following section, we particularly focus on three key areas: (1) LMX and emotional intelligence, (2) LMX and discrete emotions, and (3) LMX and emotional labor.

LMX and Emotional Intelligence

Over the last 15 years, researchers have begun to acknowledge the role of emotional intelligence in leader–follower relationships and subsequent outcomes. In this respect, Mayer and Salovey (1997) note that emotional intelligence abilities are principally concerned with managing interpersonal relations. In the specific instance of leadership, George (2000) argues that effective leaders make use of their emotional intelligence to develop high-quality relationships with followers. In this case, and based on the Mayer and Salovey (1997) definition of emotional intelligence, leaders use these skills to perceive, to assimilate, to understand, and ultimately to manage the emotions of their followers. In this instance, leaders who possess these abilities are more likely to be able to engage in both high-quality LMX relationships (which require a high level of trust that followers can perform their duties independently) and low-quality LMX relationships (which require a high level of management and control of followers).

Indeed, since the LMX relationship is also inherently a process of social interaction (Liden,

Wayne, & Stilwell, 1993), it is not surprising that emotional intelligence should come to be seen as having a role especially in interpersonal work situations where emotional feelings and displays are important (Jordan & Troth, 2011). While the construct of emotional intelligence has been controversial and variously described as a trait, an ability, and a process (Cherniss, 2010); the broadly accepted academic conceptualization of emotional intelligence is Mayer and Salovey's (1997) ability model, which involves the awareness of emotions, emotional knowledge, the use of emotions and emotion management (Ashkanasy & Daus, 2005). There is now significant evidence linking higher emotional intelligence to job performance (O'Boyle, Humphrey, Pollack, Hawver, & Story, 2011; Van Rooy & Viswesvaran, 2004), job satisfaction (Wong & Law, 2002), as well as to leadership emergence and transformational leadership (Côté, Lopes, Salovey & Miners, 2010; Humphrey, 2002).

As noted earlier, George (2000) was one of the first researchers to consider how emotional intelligence contributes to effective leadership in organizations. She reasoned that effective leaders possess certain emotional capabilities that enable them to influence and develop effective interpersonal relationships with their followers. While not specifically utilizing an LMX framework, George proposed that the four aspects of emotional intelligence contribute to effective leadership and transformational leadership in particular. Of particular relevance for LMX scholars is George's argument that leaders higher in emotional intelligence would be better able to promote trust and cooperation in their subordinates.

Building on this work, Dasborough and Ashkanasy (2002) highlight more specifically the central role emotional intelligence plays in the LMX relationship. Formulating a model of emotions and attribution of intentionality in LMX relationships, they argue that emotional intelligence plays an important moderating role in determining the likelihood of leaders engaging in both transformational and Machiavellianism behavior. The authors also propose that subordinates with higher emotional intelligence will more accurately perceive the intentionality of the leader's behaviors. This model makes two important contributions in terms of recognizing that high emotional intelligence has the potential to influence both transformational and "dark" leadership behaviors, as well as recognizing the role of both leader's and followers' emotional intelligence in the LMX relationship.

Despite conceptual work considering the place of emotional intelligence in the LMX relationship and despite evidence supporting the utility of emotional intelligence in predicting employee outcomes, very little empirical research has explored the impact of emotional intelligence on LMX development. In this small, albeit growing, body of research, some scholars have examined emotional intelligence as an antecedent of LMX (e.g., Jordan & Troth, 2011; Sears & Holmvall, 2010), while others have positioned emotional intelligence as a moderator in the LMX–outcome relationship (e.g., Huang, Chan, Lam, & Nan, 2010). Encouragingly, some empirical research is moving toward the dyadic level of analysis (e.g., Sears & Holmvall, 2010).

EMOTIONAL INTELLIGENCE AS AN ANTECEDENT TO LMX

George's (2000) theoretical work considering the effect of emotional intelligence on the LMX relationship has formed the basis of several empirical studies examining the effect of emotional intelligence on LMX and subsequent outcomes. At the individual level, Jordan and Troth (2011) showed the mediating effect of LMX (perceived by the follower) on the relationship between the follower's emotional intelligence, turnover intentions, and job satisfaction. Xiaqi, Kun, Chongsen, and Sufang (2012) also showed how the impact of leaders' emotional intelligence (measured using the WLEIS) on subordinates' trust is mediated by LMX and perceptions of abusive leadership. While these studies support the connection between emotional intelligence and LMX, there are weaknesses with both in terms of their self-report measures and, in the Xiaqi and colleagues' study, a cross-sectional design that makes it difficult to rule out common method variance and tease out the direction of the relationship between LMX and the outcome variables.

Moving beyond the individual level of analysis to examine the combined effect of leader and subordinate emotional intelligence on LMX quality, Sears and Holmvall (2010) conducted one of the first dyadic level studies to investigate the relationship between supervisor and subordinate levels of emotional intelligence on LMX quality (reported by the subordinate) for dyads in the public service. Sears and Holmvall drew on the Similarity-Attraction Paradigm (Byrne, 1971) to show that supervisor and subordinate emotional intelligence jointly contributes to LMX development such that the emotional intelligence similarity of the supervisor and subordinate is be significantly associated with

LMX quality. Controlling for conscientiousness and core self-evaluations, they found greater differences between supervisors and subordinates on emotional intelligence levels associated with lower LMX quality. There was also a significant effect of supervisor emotional intelligence at high levels of subordinate emotional intelligence. As expected, employees high in emotional intelligence reported significantly higher LMX quality when their supervisor was high in emotional intelligence.

Interestingly, and perhaps counterintuitively, there was also a significant effect of supervisor emotional intelligence at low subordinate emotional intelligence. Employees low in emotional intelligence reported higher LMX quality when their supervisor was lower in this intelligence. The practical implications drawn from this study were that HR initiatives designed to develop emotional intelligence need to target both employees and their managers to successfully promote LMX quality. The authors also concluded that their findings were consistent with the Similarity–Attraction Paradigm (Byrne, 1971) and Behavioral Integration Theory (Schaubroeck & Lam, 2002) and suggest that the emotional intelligence similarity between a leader and his or her subordinate may foster greater interpersonal attraction, communication, and behavioral coordination.

THE MODERATING EFFECT OF EMOTIONAL INTELLIGENCE ON LMX AND OUTCOMES

Another group of LMX researchers considered the moderating effect of emotional intelligence on the LMX–outcome relationship. For example, Huang et al. (2010) examined the joint effect of LMX and emotional intelligence on burnout and work performance in 493 leader–member dyads in the call centre of a large Chinese telecommunications organization. Rather than looking at the overall level of emotional intelligence, Huang and colleagues separately examined the four dimensions of emotional intelligence (self-emotion appraisal, other-emotion appraisal, use of emotion, and regulation of emotion: Wong & Law, 2002) and showed that LMX was more strongly associated with burnout and work performance for service workers with lower levels of self-emotion appraisal. On the other hand, and more surprisingly, the relationship between LMX and work performance was stronger for workers with higher levels of emotion use.

Again, and similar to Sears and Holmvall (2010), the Huang et al. (2010) study showed the usefulness of examining separate emotional intelligence dimensions insofar as they are not all necessarily salient and do not influence LMX in the same way. Indeed, Huang et al. concluded that their findings suggest that different dimensions of emotional intelligence may influence work outcomes to different degrees. Specifically, they found that, out of the four dimensions of emotional intelligence, use of emotion and regulation of emotion were related to burnout, while self-emotion appraisal and other-emotion appraisal were not. Regulation of emotion was the only dimension that was related to work performance. Likewise, the moderating effects of the emotional intelligence dimensions tend to differ as well. The most surprising finding, however, was that self-emotion appraisal moderates the LMX–performance link opposite to use of emotion. Thus, high-quality LMX is more likely to benefit subordinates with lower levels of self-emotion appraisal and subordinates with higher levels of use of emotion.

In summary, the Huang et al. (2010) study demonstrated that LMX is more strongly and positively related to work performance for service workers with a low level of self-emotion appraisal than service workers with a high level of self-emotion appraisal. In contrast, LMX appears to be more strongly and positively related to work performance for service workers with a high level of use of emotion than service workers with a low level of use of emotion. These results suggest that self-emotion appraisal and use of emotion may enact different psychological mechanisms to shape how LMX influences work performance. In essence, this work indicates that the four dimensions of emotional intelligence may not have uniformly direct and indirect effects on work attitudes and behaviors.

BOUNDARY CONDITIONS ON THE EMOTIONAL INTELLIGENCE–LMX RELATIONSHIP

A promising area of research looks at the contextual constraints of the emotional intelligence and LMX relationship. Under what conditions is the influence of emotional intelligence on leadership strongest (or weakest)? This avenue of research also enables managers to more finely target their interventions and training. In this regard, Vidyarthi, Anand, and Liden (2013) recently demonstrated how the effects of leaders' emotional intelligence (in this case, the specific dimension of emotional perceptions) on followers' behaviors vary in strength across two different conditions (within-group task interdependence; power distance between leader and follower). Integrating theory on emotional intelligence with social exchange theory, Vidyarthi and his colleagues explicitly built on George's (2000) proposal that a leader's ability to manage social relationships exerts a positive influence on employees' behaviors. Data were collected from a sample of 350 employees of a large Indian manufacturing organization nested within 74 workgroups. The authors showed that within-group task interdependence moderates the relationship between a leader's emotion perceptions and employees' job performance (the relationship is stronger when within-group task interdependence is high). Their results also showed that the influence of emotional intelligence, or the relationship between leaders' emotion perceptions and employees' performance, is weaker under conditions of high power distance. One of the practical implications of this study is that managers need to be aware that emotional perceptual skills are especially important in jobs requiring higher task interdependence (e.g., a project team requiring considerable interaction and coordination).

Vidyarthi et al. (2013) also argued that, since they controlled for the quality of LMX relationships between managers and employees, leaders' emotional intelligence can be effective even for those employees who may not share high-quality exchange relationships with their leaders. Thus, emotional competence provides an avenue through which leaders can motivate high performance from employees who are caught in lower-quality exchanges.

Taken together, the conceptual and empirical work on the impact of emotional intelligence on the LMX relationship work indicates four key conclusions: First, it is not simply a case of higher emotional intelligence being related to higher LMX (Dasborough & Ashkanasy, 2002; Sears & Holvall, 2010). Second, it is important to consider specific emotional intelligence abilities (e.g., Huang et al., 2010). Third, it is necessary to take a multilevel approach to the emotional intelligence and LMX relationship, especially given the evidence that emotional intelligence and LMX both concern interpersonal relationships (e.g., see George, 2000; Sears & Holvall, 2010; Vidyarthi et al., 2013). Fourth, it is essential to examine the potential mediating and moderating effects that influence the valence and nature of the emotional intelligence– LMX relationship (Vidyarthi et al., 2013).

LMX and Discrete Emotions

So far in this essay, our focus has been on how leaders and members perceive and interpret positive and negative emotions in their relationships with their followers. In this section we extend beyond the idea that leaders respond principally to positive and negative emotions, and consider specifically how they respond to discrete emotions. In this regard, Russell (1980) depicted affect in terms of a circumplex that embodies no less than 28 discrete emotions. We nonetheless focus specially on the basic emotions identified by Ekman (1999): anger, fear, disgust, sadness, surprise, and happiness; complemented by amusement, contempt, contentment, embarrassment, excitement, guilt, pride in achievement, relief, satisfaction, sensory pleasure, and shame.

The effect of discrete emotions can be shown in a situation where a leader is required to display positive emotions toward subordinates, despite negative feelings toward them. As Newcombe and Ashkanasy (2002) found, leaders who display positive emotion, even when delivering negative performance feedback, are associated with subordinate perceptions of high LMX. More recently, Humphrey and his colleagues (Ashkanasy & Humphrey, 2011a; Humphrey, 2008; Humphrey, Pollack, & Hawver, 2008) introduced the idea of "leading with emotional labor," where leaders manage their emotional expression to convey (mostly, but not always) emotional cues to their subordinates. Note, however, that the subordinate, especially if s/he has high emotional intelligence, may be able to detect the level of incongruity between the leader's felt and displayed emotions. In this regard, Ashkanasy and Humphrey (2011b) point out that leadership requires management of emotionally charged symbolism.

Consequently, if followers detect that a leader's influence attempt is insincere, then this might result in the leadership relationship breaking down, leading to cynicism and distrust (Kanter & Mirvis, 1989). Dasborough, Ashkanasy, Tee, and Tse (2009) argue that, once the leader picks up on this response, this is likely to lead to a vicious cycle of distrust and negative emotions, leading to further deterioration in LMX. In illustration of this, a combination of positive performance feedback and leader expression of negative emotion was found by Newcombe and Ashkanasy (2002) to result in the lowest ratings of leader LMX by subordinates. Therefore, it seems that a leader's insincere attempts to manipulate symbolism by displaying positive emotion results in subordinate cynicism, which is more likely than not to be counterproductive.

As we noted earlier, leader expressions of emotion are not limited to positive or negative affect; discrete emotions can have different effects, depending on different factors, including context and personality. For example, expressions of pride can reflect either authentic pride or hubristic pride (Tracey & Robbins, 2007). Hubristic pride is reflective of an exaggerated sense of self-worth, while authentic pride is an emotion associated with a genuine sense of achievement. Consequently, a leader expressing hubristic pride would be seen by subordinates to be expressing self-directed insincere emotions (Dasborough & Ashkanasy, 2002), resulting in the same kind of breakdown in symbolism discussed earlier.

Expression of negative emotions can similarly result in different responses depending on the particular discrete emotion being displayed, the circumstances of the display, and the personality of the leader. A considerable volume of research has examined the role of anger expression in work settings (e.g., see Geddes & Stickney, 2011, 2012) and noted that anger is an "approach" emotion very much in contrast to "avoidance" or negative emotions such as fear and sadness. A leader's expression of anger can result in negative consequences for subordinates, sometimes undermining LMX quality, although not always. As Newcombe and Ashkanasy (2002) found, when the target sees the anger as deserved, it is not necessarily regarded negatively.

Finally, the negative emotions of disgust and contempt have effects that can be especially deleterious to LMX relationships. Ekman (1999) commented that contempt was a particularly strong emotion because it implies derogation and power superiority. Thus, a supervisor who displays a contemptuous expression toward a subordinate is conveying a signal of total disrespect that is incompatible with high-quality LMX. Similarly, disgust implies disrespect and a poor-quality LMX. To explore the role of positive and negative emotions in LMX relationships further, Tse and Troth (2013) conducted a qualitative study interviewing 25 full-time employees working in a variety of team settings either within a large private health service provider or a medium-sized construction material company. Their interview findings demonstrated a variety of emotional responses in relation to the team members' experience of high-quality and low-quality LMX relationships. The most frequent emotions associated with high-quality LMX relationships were positive emotions, such as pleasant,

positive, and comfortable. Negative emotions were less frequently reported than positive emotions. The most frequent negative emotions discussed in relation to low-quality LMX relationships were stress, fear, and frustration. These findings suggest that subordinates are able to describe their specific emotional experiences in relation to high-quality and low-quality LMX relationships.

Clearly, the interpretation of specific discrete emotions by subordinates will depend on the specific context of the exchange, the nature of the existing relationship with the leader, and the personality fit with the leader. In particular, as implied in the opening discussion, emotional intelligence is likely to play a role, as individuals differ in their ability to differentiate emotions (i.e., emotional intelligence ability). Barrett, Gross, Christensen, and Benvenuto (2001) found that there is a relationship between an individual's capacity to regulate emotions and his or her ability to differentiate among discrete emotions. Hence, a subordinate who has trouble differentiating between a supervisor's expression of anger versus sadness is likely to have difficulty developing a high-quality LMX.

LMX and Emotional Labor
The final topic we address in this phase of our chapter is the role of emotional labor in the LMX relationship. Hochschild (1983, p. 7) characterized emotional labor as the "silent work of evoking and suppressing feelings in ourselves and in others" or the "management of feeling to create a publicly observable facial and bodily display." In her seminal work involving an ethnographic study of airline flight attendants, Hochschild (1983) proposed that organizations have rules that specify the emotions that employees should feel and express on the job (e.g., smiling). These organizational rules are now generally referred to as display rules (Ashforth & Humphrey, 1993; Rafaeli & Sutton, 1987). Hochschild identified two forms of emotional labor: Surface acting and deep acting. Surface acting occurs when employees change their outward emotional expressions but do not attempt to feel the emotions that they are displaying. Deep acting occurs when individuals attempt to actually feel the emotions they want to display. A third form, spontaneous or genuinely expressed emotion, is now also recognized (Ashforth & Humphrey, 1993; Diefendorff, Croyle, & Grosserand, 2005). Researchers have generally found that deep acting and genuine emotion are more effective forms of expression, while surface acting is more likely than the other forms to

lead to burnout (See Brotheridge & Grandey, 2002; Diefendorff et al., 2005).

Research into emotional labor has expanded rapidly over the last couple of decades (Humphrey, 2012), with more attention now paid to how leaders and managers use emotional labor to manage the moods, attitudes and performance of their followers (e.g., see Ashkanasy & Humphrey, 2011a; Brotheridge & Grandey, 2002; Humphrey et al., 2008). Relevant to this chapter, although empirical data are limited (e.g., Fisk & Friesen, 2012; Glasø & Einarsen, 2008), a small but growing group of scholars now considers the influence of emotional labor on the LMX relationship. This research typically draws on AET as an overarching framework to view affective events at work (e.g., demotivated workers; tight deadline; team conflict) as the initial trigger for leader emotional labor behaviors (Ashkanasy & Humphrey, 2011b). Attribution theory has also been used to consider how employees perceive their leaders' emotional labor behaviors and the subsequent outcomes for employees (e.g., job satisfaction; OCB) (Dasborough & Ashkanasy, 2002; Fisk & Friesen, 2012).

Emotional contagion is understood to be the primary mechanism through which leader emotional labor behavior influences subordinates (and thus the LMX relationship; see Ashkanasy & Humphrey, 2011a). As we discussed in the earlier (where we reviewed emotional contagion theory) emotional contagion is the reciprocal transfer of positive and negative emotions from one person to another, often when people mimic each other's emotional expressions, body language, and vocal tone (Hatfield et al., 1994). Hence, leaders express emotions to followers, and leaders in effect feed off the emotional reactions of followers (Raja et al., 2011).

Next, we examine in more detail the relationship between emotional labor and LMX and the move toward taking a dyadic approach to examining this connection. It is also important to consider the combined role of emotional intelligence and emotional labor on the quality of LMXs.

In terms of research that has directly looked at the LMX–emotional labor nexus, a small amount of research considers the role of emotional labor by leaders and the interplay between emotional labor processes and LMX quality. As the first to include a sample of managers in a study of emotional labor, Brotheridge and Grandey (2002) demonstrated how managers perform emotional labor as frequently as sales and customer service staff. Humphrey (2008) and his colleagues (e.g.,

Ashkanasy & Humphrey, 2011b; Humphrey et al., 2008) also outlined the process in which leaders engage in emotional labor to produce the right emotional expressions to motivate or influence their followers. Indeed, it is proposed that effective leaders engage in more sophisticated emotional labor judgments and behaviors in dealing with their subordinates compared to service workers who are faced with a more limited range of emotions appropriate to their occupation (Humphrey et al., 2008). Leaders need to display a variety of emotions, ranging from friendliness to sympathy to anger (in line with organizational display rules) when dealing with followers. Leaders must act cheerful and enthusiastic to encourage uninterested staff; express sympathy and support to frustrated subordinates; or show firm disapproval to disobedient subordinates (Ashkanasy & Humphrey, 2011b). In addition, leaders can use emotional labor processes to take control of the emotional contagion processes within the LMX relationship (Humphrey, 2008). By using deep or surface acting, leaders can gain control over their own emotions and use contagion to influence the emotions and moods of their followers. We argue that leaders' ability to do so effectively and appropriately has an important impact on the quality of LMX.

Researchers are increasingly taking a dyadic approach to understand more fully the implications of emotional labor for LMX quality (e.g., Ashkanasy & Humphrey, 2011a, b; Fisk & Friesen, 2012; Gardner, Fischer, & Hunt, 2009; Tse & Troth, 2013). For instance, Glasø and Einarsen (2008) investigated the extent to which leaders and followers express, suppress, or fake their emotions during interactions. Their results showed that emotional labor is a prominent feature of LMX and that both leaders and followers express their emotions to a higher degree than suppressing or faking them (both examples of surface acting) during exchanges. Leaders however reported expressing, suppressing and faking their emotions significantly more than their followers, which suggests that hierarchical level and societal norms also play a role.

In another empirical study, Fisk and Friesen (2012) showed how LMX quality influences follower reactions to the form of emotional labor engaged in by supervisors. Specifically, they found that deep acting is positively associated with job satisfaction for members with low-quality exchanges, while surface acting negatively affects participation in prosocial acts for individuals in high-quality exchanges. Thus, it seems followers react uniquely to different forms of leader emotional labor strategies, with such reactions depending partly on the quality of the LMX relationship.

COMBINING EMOTIONAL LABOR AND EMOTIONAL INTELLIGENCE

Researchers are also beginning to recognize the role of emotional intelligence in providing leaders the ability to perform emotional labor more effectively in the leader–follower relationship (Ashkanasy & Humphrey, 2011a, 2011b; Gardner et al., 2009; Humphrey et al., 2008). Drawing upon empirical work on leadership emergence in groups (Kellett, Humphrey, & Sleeth, 2002, 2006), Humphrey et al. (2008) asserts that the ability to recognize others' emotions should help leaders know when they need to perform emotional labor, for example, identifying when frustrated employees need sympathy. In addition, the ability to express their own emotions may help leaders to perform emotional labor. This is because emotional labor is only effective if the emotions are expressed in a way that has an effect on the follower. In essence, Humphrey and his associates postulate that leaders high in emotional intelligence are better at identifying emotions and knowing when situational demands call for them to engage in emotional labor. Leaders with a high ability to express their own emotions can therefore be expected to perform all three types of emotional labor better than their counterparts who are low in this ability.

Gardner et al. (2009) advanced a conceptual model depicting the influence of emotional intelligence on the relationship between emotional labor and the quality of LMX. They argued that the consistency of leader emotions with display rules, together with the type of display chosen (surface acting, deep acting or genuine emotion) combine to impact the leader's self reported authenticity, the favorability of follower impressions and the perceived authenticity of the leader by his or her followers (indicators of the LMX). Taking a multilevel approach, they proposed that individual emotional intelligence moderates leader emotional displays to affective events as well as follower reactions to such displays. Thus, it seems that emotional intelligence is a predictor of how situations are perceived (i.e., appraisal) by leaders (and likely followers), which then predicts the nature of the emotional labor performed. As we later suggest, an interesting area of future research is how both the emotional intelligence of leaders and followers jointly influence the emotional labor expressions of the leader and subsequent follower responses.

Future Research Directions

In this final section, we discuss and propose six emerging areas of research in LMX and emotions, and address a major challenge to this research. Emotional intelligence, emotional labor, and LMX constructs are all relationship-based and nested in interpersonal processes and functional systems at different organizational levels. As such, we organize our discussion of emerging areas for future research using a multilevel perspective which focuses on within-person, individual, interpersonal, and team levels of conceptualization in organizations (Ashkanasy, 2003).

Team Level

Owing to the rise of team-based structures in organizations, it is important that LMX researchers focus on the effect of dyadic LMX and its characteristics in a broader social context in which other exchange relationships are interconnected and embedded (Erdogan & Bauer, 2014; Tse et al., 2012; Vidyarthi, Liden, Anand, Erdogan, & Ghosh, 2010). The LMX and other interrelated relationships such as Coworker Exchange Relationships (CWX: Sherony & Green, 2002) serve as the basis to facilitate interpersonal interactions and emotional exchange processes (Tse et al., 2013). George (1996) suggests that individuals in workgroups tend to share similar levels of emotion. George (1990, p. 108) coined this phenomenon "Group Affective Tone," which is defined as "consistent or homogenous affective actions within a group." On this basis, it is arguable that members in high-quality LMX relationships are likely to experience similar positive emotions, whereas members in low-quality LMX relationships are likely to experience dissimilar negative emotions within the same workgroup (Collins, Lawrence, Troth, & Jordan, 2013). This sets up a situation whereby high- and low-LMX members are likely to have difficulty working together because they do not experience, nor display, the same (positive or negative) emotional states in their interactions within the workgroup. LMX researchers in future might do well to pursue this line of research to understand better how different qualities of LMX can create a healthy affective tone within a workgroup. Potential research questions include: (1) How can affective tone emerge from a set of different LMX relationships that members have developed and maintained with the leader in a workgroup? (2) How do social exchange processes shape shared perceptions or collective cognitions of affective activities and relationships within the workgroup? and (3) Is it possible for a highly respected and influential low-LMX member to spread positive or negative emotions more easily and quickly than the high-LMX members in a workgroup?

Dyadic Level

As suggested by Erdogan and Bauer (2014), and Vidyarthi and his colleagues, (2010) the different qualities of LMX relationships between leaders and followers should become a major source of social comparison because of the unequal resource and support distribution in a workgroup. Hence, subordinates constantly compare their own LMX with that of their coworkers to obtain information about their relative standing in a set of differentiated LMX relations. The perceptual differences of LMXs between subordinates will influence their emotional experience toward each other in coworker dyads (Vidyarthi et al., 2010). In this regard, Tse et al. (2013) conducted a field study by exploring whether the actual LMX (dis)similarity between two subordinates influences their interpersonal emotion exchanges toward each other in co-worker dyads. Their findings provide support for the hypothesis that LMX (dis)similarity between Coworker A (actor) and Coworker B (target) can influence an actor's experience of a disliking and hostile emotion for the target. However, what Tse et al. (2013) did not specifically explore is whether the LMX (dis) similarity between two coworkers can also lead to the actor experiencing a liking or positive emotion toward the target. For example, if LMX dissimilarity is high (i.e., actor's LMX is higher than target's LMX), an actor is likely to experience positive emotions such as pride, excitement, and contentment for the target, but the target is likely to experience negative emotions such as envy, anger and contempt for the actor. By studying more specific positive or negative emotions such as pride, excitement, anger, and contempt in the LMX (dis)similarity process, future research should be able to provide a complete understanding of the interpersonal dynamic in social relationships, capturing relevant emotions experienced and displayed by both parties toward each other in coworker dyads. This will potentially influence the overall interpersonal relationships needed for individual and team effectiveness (Tse et al., 2013).

A second research direction is suggested by Humphrey (2012). In a research incubator titled, "How do leaders use emotional labor?" Humphrey suggests that leader emotional labor is a specific set of behaviors that can be used by leaders to form high-quality LMX relationships. One important question confronting LMX and emotional labor researchers, therefore, is whether leaders' emotional labor is detrimental or beneficial to the development of LMX. The difficulty here, however, is how to manage followers' perceptions of surface and deep acting of emotional labor tactics that can positively or negatively affect the LMX relationship development. On the one hand, leaders who use deep acting and genuine emotional labor tactics are more likely to have better LMX relationships because they are also perceived as being authentic and honest (Gardner, Fischer, & Hunt, 2009). On the other hand, existing research also suggests that leaders' use of deep acting and genuine emotional labor tactics will raise the levels of expectation from their followers, and that leaders are likely to be judged as inauthentic and dishonest if they don't continue using the same tactics across different situations over time (Gardner et al., 2009).

In reality, it is very difficult for leaders to keep on using deep acting and genuine emotional labor tactics. An exhausted leader, for example, may express his or her negative emotions of frustration and irritation toward a subordinate in the situation of the subordinate underperforming (Humphrey, 2012). The use of deep acting instead of surface acting emotional labor tactics is likely to result in negative perceptions of leaders' emotional management that will further undermine the quality of their LMX relationships in this regard. To tackle this research problem, a series of lab and field studies can be undertaken to identify important boundary conditions and individual differences to explain how surface and deep acting emotional labor tactics can be effective in determining followers' perceptions of their leaders' emotions in managing difficult situations within LMX relationships.

Individual Level: Emotional Intelligence

Despite the focus on dyadic relationships, at the level of individual differences there are also exciting possibilities for research in the field of emotional intelligence and LMX. First, there is a necessity to move beyond self-reported emotional intelligence (especially WLEIS; Wong & Law, 2002). In this case, there is a need to consider ability measures such as the STEM (Situational Test of Emotional Management) and STEU (Situational Test of Emotional Understanding; MacCann & Roberts, 2008) or the MSCEIT (*Mayer Salovey Caruso Emotional Intelligence Test;* Mayer, 2003).

There is also value in collecting qualitative data to begin to understand better the thought processes leaders (and employees) experience when dealing with emotion eliciting events within the LMX relationship (see Tse & Troth, 2013, for an example of qualitative research).

Another emerging area is the pursuit of a more follower-centered approach. Indeed, George (2000) noted in her seminal paper that her focus was primarily on leaders but advocated more study of emotional intelligence in followers and its effects on the leadership process. In this vein, some exciting work has recently been published examining the influence of follower emotional intelligence on leader mood and task performance (Tee et al., 2013).

Last, Raja et al. (2011) noted that there has been little research explicitly addressing the effects of emotional intelligence on leadership effectiveness in the cross-cultural context. They cite work by Elfenbein and Ambady (2002) showing that emotion recognition is often more accurate in in-group settings where the emotion is expressed and recognized by someone of the same ethnic, national, and regional group. In line with Vidyarthi et al. (2013), Raja et al. (2011) notes that power distance in a society affects the preference for a certain type of leadership and that claims on the effectiveness of leaders high in emotional intelligence, for example, may not hold true universally.

Within-Person Level

As suggested by Fisher and To (2012) and Gooty, Gavin, and Ashkanasy (2009), utilizing the experience sample method (ESM) via dairies and smartphone technology may be a fruitful avenue in capturing the effect of emotional variations in LMX relationships. Given the frequency of interpersonal interactions between leaders and followers, it is important to understand whether both parties will experience similar or dissimilar emotions during the same interaction over a specific period of time (e.g., days and weeks). By using ESM, future research can help answer four important research questions: 1) Are leaders and followers in high-quality LMX relationships more likely to experience positive emotions over time than those in low-quality LMX relationships? 2) Are leaders and followers in low-quality LMX relationships more likely to experience negative emotions over time than those in high-quality LMX relationships? 3) Do leaders' positive emotions influence followers' negative emotional experiences over time? 4) How likely is it that the positive emotions of followers in high-quality

LMX relationships influence their leaders' negative emotions over time? The preliminary answers to these questions suggest that the differential qualities of LMX can predict the momentary variations of both positive and negative emotions experienced and displayed by leaders and followers in the same relationship. The emotional variations can further enable us to understand the emotional exchange process between leaders and followers within social and economic exchange relationships in workgroups (Fisher & To, 2012).

A Major Challenge: Misalignment of Theory, Measurement, and Analysis

Finally, it is important for us to mention a major challenge to existing LMX and emotions research, namely the misalignment of theory, measurement and analysis. In this regard, it is essential that theory is aligned with measurement and data analysis in the LMX and emotions research (e.g., Gooty, Serban, Thomas, Gavin, & Yammarino, 2012; Schriesheim, Castro, & Cogliser, 1999; Yammarino, Dionne, Chun, & Dansereau, 2005). Unfortunately, this has not been the case to date. In a recent review of the LMX literature, Gooty et al. (2012, p. 1095) concluded that "the misalignment between theory and measurement occurred in 68% of the 163 multilevel studies and that up to 86% of such misalignment occurred when the dyad level was the theoretical focus of the study."

Gooty and Yammarino (2013) conclude that most LMX studies do not conceptualize, measure, or analyze data at the dyadic level of analysis properly and have largely ignored the critical aspect of the dyadic nature of constructs. For example, existing LMX studies seldom collect reciprocal data from both members (i.e., leader and follower) of the dyad on the variables of interest (e.g., LMX, personality, or emotional experience in response to the LMX relationship, see Krasikova & LeBreton, 2012). Furthermore, the LMX literature to date has neglected the potential bias of data dependence. This is because a leader forms relationships with multiple followers in a workgroup, with each dyadic relationship (between a leader and a follower) never mutually exclusive or independent from other interrelated dyadic relationships (Kenny, Kashy, & Cook, 2006; Krasikova & LeBreton, 2012). Thus each leader is usually asked to rate his/her own emotional experience and emotional intelligence skills as well as emotional labor tactics used in LMX relationships with each of the followers in the same workgroup, resulting in a strong dependence effect that is likely to inflate hypothesized relationships between dyadic variables (Kenny et al., 2006).

To rectify the misalignment between theory and measurement in LMX and emotions research, it is important to conceptualize and measure LMX, discrete emotions, emotional intelligence, and emotional labor at the dyadic level using a round-robin peer-rating research design (Tse et al., 2013). Furthermore, a dyadic data analytical technique, the Social Relation Modeling (SRM) developed by Kenny, (1994) and Kenny and La Voie (1984) is specifically designed to capture and analyze relationship phenomena at the appropriate level of analysis (see Gooty & Yammarino, 2011). SRM can specify the nested structure of a data set by partitioning the variance of the behaviors into different components including individual, dyad and team (see Kenny, 1994). Thus, SRM is effective in overcoming the potential bias of data dependence in a peer-rated research design, which involves all followers providing survey responses for each other in a workgroup (Kenny & La Voie, 1984; Kenny et al., 2006). By together utilizing peer-rating research design and SRM with multilevel modeling, the possible dependency inherent to dyads within the same workgroup can be addressed, thereby facilitating a true understanding of the interpersonal dynamic of emotional process in the LMX research (Tse et al., 2013).

Conclusions

In summary, we proposed in this essay that LMX and emotions should be studied in an integrated context because emotions are inherent in social relationships. We identified three underlying theories that have been applied to study the relationships between LMX and other emotion-related constructs. We also presented a comprehensive review of three key emerging and fruitful areas of LMX and emotions research. We further proposed that future research should be directed to incorporating LMX, discrete emotions, emotional intelligence and emotional labor across within-person, individual, interpersonal, and team levels of conceptualization and analysis, and needs to address the issue of misalignment between theory, measurement, and analysis in LMX research.

References

Ashforth, B. E., & Humphrey, R. H. (1993). Emotional labor in service roles: The influence of identity. *Academy of Management Review, 18*, 88–115.

Ashkanasy, N. M. (2003). Emotions in organizations: A multi-level perspective. In F. Dansereau & F. J. Yammarino (Eds.), *Research in multilevel issues* (vol. 2, pp. 9–54). Oxford, UK: Elsevier Science.

Ashkanasy, N. M. (2002). Studies of cognition and emotion in organisations: Attribution, affective events, emotional intelligence and perception of emotion. *Australian Journal of Management, 27*, 11–20.

Ashkanasy, N. M., & Daus, C. S. (2002). Emotion in the workplace: The new challenge for managers. *Academy of Management Executive, 16*, 76–86.

Ashkanasy, N. M., & Daus, C. S. (2005). Rumors of the death of emotional intelligence in organizational behavior are vastly exaggerated. *Journal of Organizational Behavior, 26*, 441–452.

Ashkanasy, N. M., Härtel, C. E. J., & Daus, C. S. (2002). Diversity and emotion: The new frontiers in organizational behavior research. *Journal of Management, 28*, 307–338.

Ashkanasy, N. M., & Humphrey, R. H. (2011a). A multi-level view of leadership and emotions: Leading with emotional labor. In A. Bryman, D. Collinson, K. Grint, B. Jackson, & M. Uhl-Bien (Eds.), *Sage handbook of leadership* (pp. 363–377). London, UK: Sage.

Ashkanasy, N. M., & Humphrey, R. H. (2011b). Current research on emotion in organizations. *Emotion Review, 3*, 214–224.

Ashkanasy, N. M., & Tse, B. (2000). Transformational leadership as management of emotion: A conceptual review. In N. M. Ashkanasy, C. E. J. Härtel, & W. Zerbe (Eds.), *Emotions in the workplace: Research, theory, and practice* (([A-Z]).. 221–236). Westport, CT: Quorum Books.

Barrett, L. F., Gross, J., Christensen, T. C., & Benvenuto, M. (2001). Knowing what you're feeling and knowing what to do about it: Mapping the relation between emotion differentiation and emotion regulation. *Cognition and Emotion, 15*, 713–724.

Barsade, S. G. (2002). The ripple effect: Emotional contagion and its influence on group behavior. *Administrative Science Quarterly, 47*, 644–675.

Barsade, S. G., Brief, A. P., & Spataro, S. E. (2003). The affective revolution in organizational behavior: The emergence of a paradigm. In J. Greenberg (Eds.), *Organizational behavior: The state of the science* (pp. 3–52). Mahwah, NJ: Lawrence Erlbaum and Associates.

Brotheridge, C. M., & Grandey, A. A. (2002). Emotional labor and burnout: Comparing two perspectives of "people work." *Journal of Vocational Behavior, 60*, 17–39.

Byrne, D. (1971). *The attraction paradigm.* New York: Academic Press.

Cherniss, C. (2010). Emotional intelligence: Toward clarification of a concept. *Industrial and Organizational Psychology, 3*, 110–126.

Collins, A. L., Lawrence, S. A., Troth, A. C., & Jordan, P. J. (2013). Group affective tone: A review and future research directions. *Journal of Organizational Behavior, 34*, 43–62.

Côté, S., Lopes, P. N., Salovey, P., & Miners, C. T. (2010). Emotional intelligence and leadership emergence in small groups. *The Leadership Quarterly, 21*, 496–508.

Dasborough, M. (2006). Cognitive asymmetry in employee emotional reactions to leadership behaviors. *The Leadership Quarterly, 17*, 163–178.

Dasborough, M. T., & Ashkanasy, N. M. (2002). Emotion and attribution of intentionality in leader-member relationships. *The Leadership Quarterly, 13*, 615–634.

Dasborough, M. T., & Ashkanasy, N. M. (2005). Follower emotional reactions to authentic and inauthentic leadership influence. In W. L. Gardner, B. J. Avolio, & F. O. Walumbwa (Eds.), *Monographs in leadership and management* (vol. 3, pp. 281–300). Oxford, UK: Elsevier Science.

Dasborough, M. T., Ashkanasy, N. M., Tee, E. E. J., & Tse, H. H. M. (2009). What goes around comes around: How meso-level negative emotional contagion can ultimately determine organizational attitudes toward leaders. *The Leadership Quarterly, 20,* 571–585.

Davis, M. R. (1985). Perceptual and affective reverberation components. In A. B. Goldstein & G. Y. Michaels (Eds.), *Empathy: Development, training, and consequences* (pp. 62–108). Hillsdale, NJ: Lawrence Erlbaum & Associates.

De Dreu, C., West, M., Fischer, A., & MacCurtain, S. (2001). Origins and consequences of emotions in organizational teams. In R. L. Payne & C. L. Cooper (Eds.), *Emotions at work: Theory, research and applications for management* (pp. 199–217). Chichester, UK: Wiley.

Diefendorff, J. M., Croyle, M. H., & Gosserand, R. H. (2005). The dimensionality and antecedents of emotional labor strategies. *Journal of Vocational Behavior, 66,* 339–357.

Ekman, P. (1999). Basic Emotions. In T. Dalgleish & M. Power (Eds.), *Handbook of cognition and emotion* (pp. 45–60). Sussex, UK: Wiley.

Elfenbein, H. A., & Ambady, N. (2002). On the universality and cultural specificity of emotion recognition: A meta-analysis. *Psychological Bulletin, 128,* 203–235.

Erdogan, B., & Bauer, T. N. (2014). Leader-member exchange (LMX) theory: The relational approach to leadership. In D. Day (Ed.), *Oxford handbook of leadership and organizations* (pp. 407–433). New York: Oxford University Press.

Erez, A., Misangyi, V. F., Johnson, D. E., LePine, M. A., & Halverson, K. C. (2008). Stirring the hearts of followers: Charismatic leadership as the transferral of affect. *Journal of Applied Psychology, 93,* 602–616.

Fisher, C. D., & Ashkanasy, N. M. (2000). The emerging role of emotions in working life: An introduction. *Journal of Organizational Behavior, 21,* 123–129.

Fischer, K. W., Shaver, P. R., & Carnochan, P. (1990). How emotions develop and how they organise development. *Cognition and Emotion, 4,* 81–127.

Fisher, C. D., & To, M. L. (2012). Using experience sampling methodology in organizational behavior. *Journal of Organizational Behavior, 33,* 865–877.

Fisk, G. M., & Friesen, J. P. (2012). Perceptions of leader emotion regulation and LMX as predictors of followers' job satisfaction and organizational citizenship behaviors. *The Leadership Quarterly, 23,* 1–12.

Frijda, N. H. (1986). *The emotions.* New York: Cambridge University Press.

Gaddis, B., Connelly, S., & Mumford, M. D. (2004). Failure feedback as an affective event: Influences of leader affect on subordinate attitudes and performance. *The Leadership Quarterly, 15,* 663–686.

Gardner, W. L., Fischer, D., & Hunt, J. G. (2009). Emotional labor and leadership: A threat to authenticity? *The Leadership Quarterly, 20,* 466–482.

Geddes, D., & Stickney, L. T. (2012). Muted anger in the workplace: Changing the "Sound" of employee emotion through social sharing. In, N. M. Ashkanasy, C. E. J. Härtel, & W. J. Zerbe (Eds.), *Research on emotion in organizations* (vol. 8, pp. 85–103). Bingly, UK: Emerald Group Publishing.

Geddes, D., & Stickney, L. T. (2011). The trouble with sanctions: Organizational member responses to deviant anger displays at work. *Human Relations, 64,* 201–230.

George, J. M. (2000). Emotions and leadership: The role of emotional intelligence. *Human Relations, 53,* 1027–1055.

George, J. M. (1996). Group affective tone. In M. West (Eds.), *Handbook of work group psychology* (pp. 77–93). Chichester, UK: John Wiley & Sons.

George, J. M. (1990). Personality, affect, and behavior in groups. *Journal of Applied Psychology, 76,* 299–307.

Glasø, L., & Einarsen, S. (2008). Emotion regulation in leader–follower relationships. *European Journal of Work and Organizational Psychology, 17,* 482–500.

Gooty, J., Connelly, S., Griffith, J., & Gupta, A. (2010). Leadership, affect and emotions: A state of the science review. *The Leadership Quarterly, 21,* 979–1004.

Gooty, J., Gavin, M., & Ashkanasy, N. M (2009). Emotions research in OB: The challenges that lie ahead. *Journal of Organizational Behavior, 30,* 833–838.

Gooty, J., Gavin, M. B., Ashkanasy, N. M., & Thomas, J. S. (2014). The wisdom of letting go and performance: The moderating role of emotional intelligence and discrete emotions. *Journal of Occupational and Organizational Psychology, 87,* 392–413.

Gooty, J., Serban, A., Thomas, J. S., Gavin, M. B., & Yammarino, F. J. (2012). Use and misuse of levels of analysis in leadership research: An illustrative review of leader–member exchange. *The Leadership Quarterly, 23,* 1080–1103.

Gooty, J., & Yammarino, F. J. (2011). Dyads in organizational research: Conceptual issues and multi-level analyses. *Organizational Research Methods, 14,* 456–483.

Gooty, J., & Yammarino, F. J. (2013). The leader-member exchange relationships: A multisource and cross-level investigation. *Journal of Management* published online ahead of print, doi 10.1177/0149206313503009.

Graen, G. B., & Uhl-Bien, M. (1995). Relationship-based approach to leadership: Development of leader-member exchange (LMX) theory of leadership over 25 years: Applying a multi-level multi-domain perspective. *The Leadership Quarterly, 6,* 219–247.

Gross, J. J. (2013). Emotion regulation: Taking stock and moving forward. *Emotion, 13,* 359–365.

Gross, J. J. (1998). The emerging field of emotion regulation: An integrative review. *Review of General Psychology, 2,* 271–299.

Harvey, P., Stoner, J., Hochwarter, W., & Kacmar, C. (2007). Coping with abusive supervision: The neutralizing effects of ingratiation and positive affect on negative employee outcomes. *The Leadership Quarterly, 18,* 264–280.

Hatfield, E., Cacioppo, J., & Rapson, R. L. (1994). *Emotional contagion.* New York: Cambridge University Press.

Hatfield, E., Cacioppo, J., & Rapson, R. L. (1992). Primitive emotional contagion. *Review of Personality and Social Psychology, 14,* 151–177.

Hochschild, A, R. (1983). *The managed heart: Commercialization of human feeling.* Berkeley, CA: University of California Press.

Huang, X., Chan, S. C., Lam, W., & Nan, X. (2010). The joint effect of leader–member exchange and emotional intelligence on burnout and work performance in call centers in China. *The International Journal of Human Resource Management, 21,* 1124–1144.

Hui, C., Law, K. S., & Chen, Z. X. (1999). A structural equation model of the effects of negative affectivity, leader–member exchange, and perceived job mobility on in-role and extra-role performance: A Chinese case. *Organizational Behavior and Human Decision Processes, 77,* 3–21.

Humphrey, R. H. (2002). The many faces of emotional leadership. *The Leadership Quarterly, 13,* 493–504.

Humphrey, R. H. (2008). The right way to lead with emotional labor. In R. H. Humphrey (Eds.), *Affect and emotion: New* directions in management theory and research (pp. 1–17). Charlotte, NC: Information Age Publishing.

Humphrey, R. H. (2012). How do leaders use emotional labor? *Journal of Organizational Behavior, 33*, 740–744.

Humphrey, R. H., Pollack, J. M., & Hawver, T. H. (2008). Leading with emotional labor. *Journal of Managerial Psychology, 23*, 151–168.

James, W. (1890). *The principles of psychology.* New York: Dover.

Johnson, S. K. (2008). I second that emotion: Effects of emotional contagion and affect at work on leader and follower outcomes. *The Leadership Quarterly, 19*, 1–19.

Jordan, P. J., & Troth, A. (2011). Emotional intelligence and leader member exchange: The relationship with employee turnover intentions and job satisfaction. *Leadership & Organization Development Journal, 32*, 260–280.

Kanter, D. L., & Mirvis, P. H. (1989). *The cynical Americans: Living and working in an age of discontent and disillusion.* San Francisco, CA: Jossey-Bass.

Katz, D., & Kahn, R. L. (1978). *The social psychology of organizations.* Chichester, UK: Wiley.

Kellett, J. B., Humphrey, R. H., & Sleeth, R. G. (2002). Empathy and complex task performance: Two routes to leadership. *The Leadership Quarterly, 13*, 523–544.

Kellett, J. B., Humphrey, R. H., & Sleeth, R. G. (2006). Empathy and the emergence of task and relations leaders. *The Leadership Quarterly, 17*, 146–162.

Kelly, J. R., & Barsade, S. G. (2001). Mood and emotions in small groups and work teams. *Organizational Behavior and Human Decision Processes, 86*, 99–130.

Kenny, D. A. 1994. *Interpersonal perception: A social relations analysis.* New York: Guilford Press.

Kenny, D. A., Kashy, D. A., & Cook, W. L. (2006). *Dyadic data analysis.* New York: Guilford Press.

Kenny, D. A., & La Voie, L. (1984). The social relations model. In L. Berkowitz (Eds.), *Advances in experimental social psychology,* (pp. 142–182). Orlando, FL: Academic Press.

Krasikova, D. V., & LeBreton, J. M. (2012). Just the two of us: Misalignment of theory and methods in examining dyadic phenomena. *Journal of Applied Psychology, 97*, 739–757.

Lawler, E. J. (2001). An affect theory of social exchange. *American Journal of Sociology, 107*, 321–352.

Lazarus, R. S. (1991). *Emotion and adaptation.* New York: Oxford University Press.

Lazarus, R. S., & Folkman, S. (1984). *Stress, appraisal, and coping.* New York: Springer.

LeDoux, J. E. (1995). Emotion: Clues from the brain. *Annual Review of Psychology, 46*, 209–235.

Liden, R. C., Wayne, S. J., & Stilwell, D. (1993). A longitudinal study on the early development of leader-member exchanges. *Journal of applied psychology, 78*, 662–674.

Mayer, J. D. (2003). *Mayer Salovey Caruso Emotional Intelligence Test: MSCEIT.* MHS, Multi-Health Systems.

Mayer, J. D., & Salovey, P. (1997). What is Emotional Intelligence? In P. Salovey & D. J. Sluyter (Eds.), *Emotional development and emotional intelligence: Educational implications* (pp. 3–31). New York: Basic Books.

McClane, W. E. (1991). Implication of member role differentiation: Analysis of a key concept in the LMX model of leadership. *Group and Organization Studies, 16*, 102–113.

MacCann, C., & Roberts, R. D. (2008). New paradigms for assessing emotional intelligence: Theory and data. *Emotion, 8*, 540–551.

Moors, A. (2013). On the causal role of appraisal in emotion. *Emotion Review, 5*, 132–140.

Moors, A., Ellsworth, P. C., Scherer, K. R., & Frijda, N. H. (2013). Appraisal theories of emotion: State of the art and future development. *Emotion Review, 5*, 119–124.

Newcombe, M. J. & Ashkanasy, N. M. (2002). The role of affect and affective congruence in perceptions of leaders: An experimental study. *The Leadership Quarterly, 13*, 601–614.

O'Boyle, E. H., Humphrey, R. H., Pollack, J. M., Hawver, T. H., & Story, P. A. (2011). The relation between emotional intelligence and job performance: A meta-analysis. *Journal of Organizational Behavior, 32*, 788–818.

Phillips, A. S., & Bedeian, A. G. (1994). Leader-follower exchange quality: The role of personal and interpersonal attributes. *Academy of Management Journal, 37*, 990–1001.

Rafaeli, A., & Sutton, R. I. (1987). Expression of emotion as part of the work role. *Academy of Management Review, 12*, 23–37.

Raja, R., Song, Z., & Avery, R. D. (2011). Emotionality and leadership: Taking stock of the past decade of research. *The Leadership Quarterly, 22*, 1107–1119.

Russell. J. A. (1980). A circumplex model of affect. *Journal of Personality and Social Psychology, 39*, 1161–1178.

Salzmann, J., & Grasha, A. F. (1991). Psychological size and psychological distance in manager-subordinate relationships. *Journal of Social Psychology, 131*, 62–646.

Scandura, T. A., & Schreisheim, C. A. (1994). Leader-member exchange and supervisor career mentoring as complementary constructs in leadership research. *Academy of Management Journal, 37*, 1588–1602.

Schaubroeck, J., & Lam, S. S. (2002). How similarity to peers and supervisor influences organizational advancement in different cultures. *Academy of Management Journal, 45*, 1120–1136.

Scherer, K. R. (2001). Appraisal considered as a process of multilevel sequential checking. In K. R. Scherer, A. Schorr & T. Johnstone (Eds.), *Appraisal processes in emotion: theory, methods, research* (pp. 92–120). New York: Oxford University Press.

Schriesheim, C. A., Castro, S. L., & Cogliser, C. C. (1999). Leader–member exchange (LMX) research: A comprehensive review of theory, measurement, and data-analytic practices. *The Leadership Quarterly, 10*, 63–113.

Sears, G. J., & Holmvall, C. M. (2010). The joint influence of supervisor and subordinate emotional intelligence on leader–member exchange. *Journal of Business and Psychology, 25*, 593–605.

Sherony, K. M., & Green, S. G. (2002). Co-worker exchange: Relationships between co-workers, leader-member exchange, and work attitudes. *Journal of Applied Psychology, 87*, 542–548.

Sias, P. M., & Jablin, F. M. (1995). Differential superior-subordinate relations, perceptions of fairness, and coworker communication. *Human Communication Research, 22*, 5–38.

Smith, C. A., & Kirby, L. D. (2009). Putting appraisal in context: Toward a relational model of appraisal and emotion. *Cognition and Emotion, 23*, 1352–1372.

Sy, T., Côté, S., & Saavedra, R. (2005). The contagious leader: Impact of the leader's mood on the mood of group members, group affective tone, and group processes. *Journal of Applied Psychology, 90*, 295–305.

Tee, E. Y. J., Ashkanasy, N. M., & Paulsen, N. (2013). The influence of follower mood on leader mood and task performance: Evidence for an affective, follower-centric perspective of leadership. *The Leadership Quarterly*, *24*, 496–515.

Tracy J. L., & Robins, R. W. (2007). The psychological structure of pride: A tale of two facets. *Journal of Personality and Social Psychology*, *92*, 506–525.

Tooby, J., & Cosmides, L. (1990). The past explains the present: Emotional adaptations and the structure of ancestral environments. *Ethology and Sociobiology*, *11*, 375–424.

Tse, H. H. M., & Ashkanasy, N. M. (2008). The role of affect in vertical and lateral exchange work relationships in teams. In N. M. Ashkanasy & C. L. Cooper (Eds.), *Research companion to emotions in organizations* (pp. 499–512). Cheltenham, UK: Edwin Elgar.

Tse, H. H. M., Ashkanasy, N. M., & Dasborough, M. (2012). Relative leader-member exchange, negativity and social identification: A moderated-mediation examination. *The Leadership Quarterly*, *23*, 354–366.

Tse, H. H. M., Dasborough, M. T., & Ashkanasy, N. M. (2008). A multi-level analysis of team climate and interpersonal exchange relationships at work. *The Leadership Quarterly*, *19*, 195–211.

Tse, H. H. M., Dasborough, M. T., & Ashkanasy, N. M. (2005). The role of affect, fairness and social perception in team member exchange. In N. M. Ashkanasy, C. E. J. Härtel & W. J. Zerbe (Eds.), *Research on emotion in organizations* (vol. 1, pp. 143–171). Oxford, U.K: Elsevier Publication.

Tse, H. H. M., Lam, C. K., Lawrence, S. A., & Huang, X. (2013). When my supervisor dislikes you more than me: The effect of dissimilarity in leader-member exchange on coworkers' interpersonal emotion and perceived help. *Journal of Applied Psychology*, *98*, 974–988.

Tse, H. H. M., & Troth, A. C. (2013). Perceptions and emotional experiences in different supervisor-subordinate relationships. *Leadership and Organization Development Journal*, *34*, 271–280.

Turban, D. B., Jones, A. P., & Rozelle, R. M. (1990). Influences of supervisor liking of a subordinate and the reward context on the treatment and evaluation of that subordinate. *Motivation and Emotion*, *14*, 215–233.

Van Kleef, G. A. (2009). How emotions regulate social life: The emotions as social information (EASI) model. *Current Directions in Psychology*, *18*, 184–188.

Van Rooy, D. L., & Viswesvaran, C. (2004). Emotional intelligence: A meta-analytic investigation of predictive validity and nomological net. *Journal of Vocational Behavior*, *65*, 71–95.

Vidyarthi, P. R., Anand, S., & Liden, R. C. (2013). Do emotionally perceptive leaders motivate higher employee performance? The moderating role of task interdependence and power distance. *The Leadership Quarterly*, *25*, 232–244.

Vidyarthi, P. R., Liden, R. C., Anand, S., Erdogan, B., & Ghosh, S. (2010). Where do I stand? Examining the effects of leader-member exchange social comparison on employee work behaviors. *Journal of Applied Psychology*, *98*, 849–861.

Weiss, H. M., & Cropanzano, R. (1996). Affective events theory: A theoretical discussion of the structure, causes and consequences of affective experiences at work. In B. M. Staw & L. L. Cummings (Eds.), *Research in organizational behavior* (vol. 18, pp. 1–74). Westport, CT: JAI Press.

Wong, C. S., & Law, K. S. (2002). The effects of leader and follower emotional intelligence on performance and attitude: An exploratory study. *The Leadership Quarterly*, *13*, 243–274.

Xiaqi, D., Kun, T., Chongsen, Y., & Sufang, G. (2012). Abusive supervision and LMX: Leaders' emotional intelligence as antecedent variable and trust as consequence variable. *Chinese Management Studies*, *6*, 257–270.

Yammarino, F. J., Dionne, S. D., Chun, J. U., & Dansereau, F. (2005). Leadership and levels of analysis: A state-of-the-science review. *The Leadership Quarterly*, *16*, 879–919.

Zajonc, R. B. (1985). Emotion and facial difference: A theory reclaimed. *Science*, *228*, 15–21.

Leader–Member Exchange and Newcomer Adjustment

Le Zhou *and* Mo Wang

Abstract

Newcomer adjustment is the dynamic process through which new employees adapt to their new work environment and transition from organizational outsiders to insiders. Leader–member exchange (LMX) development is an important part of newcomer adjustment. This chapter aims to systematically examine the role of LMX in newcomer adjustment. In doing so, the authors hope to inspire new studies on this topic. They review and discuss previous research on (a) the antecedents of newcomer–supervisor LMX, (d) how LMX relates to newcomer adjustment outcomes, and (c) the role of LMX in expatriates and new manager adjustment. Their reviews on these three research areas summarize key theoretical arguments advanced by researchers and existing findings reported in empirical studies. Based on their qualitative review, they point out limitations in existing research on LMX and newcomer adjustment and suggest several future research directions.

Key Words: leader–member exchange, newcomer adjustment, socialization, leadership, expatriate adjustment

Introduction

Organizational socialization is the process through which new employees acquire the necessary knowledge, attitudes, and behaviors for participating as organizational members (Van Maanen & Schein, 1979). During the transition from organizational outsiders to insiders, *newcomer adjustment* manifests as changes in various indicators (Bauer, Bodner, Erdogan, Truxillo, & Tucker, 2007; Chao, O'Leary-Kelly, Wolf, Klein, & Gardner, 1994; Morrison, 1993; Wang, Zhan, McCune, & Truxillo, 2011). In the task aspect, newcomer adjustment includes understanding expectations for newcomers' positions (i.e., role clarity), learning the tasks of the job (i.e., task mastery), gaining confidence to achieve the task goal (i.e., self-efficacy), and acquiring knowledge about organizational policies, practices, norms, politics, etc. (i.e., organizational knowledge). In the social aspect, newcomers adjust by becoming liked and accepted by coworkers (i.e., social acceptance or social integration).

Meta-analytic research suggested that newcomer adjustment is related to individual job attitudes, task performance, and actual turnover (Bauer et al., 2007).

Organizational socialization research suggests that immediate supervisors of newcomers play an important role in the newcomer adjustment process (e.g., Bauer & Green, 1998; Jokisaari & Nurmi, 2009; Kammeyer-Mueller & Wanberg, 2003). One of the leadership constructs that have been repeatedly examined by socialization researchers is *leader–member exchange* (LMX). LMX refers to the quality of the exchange relationship between a supervisor–subordinate dyad (Graen & Uhl-Bien, 1995). Based on the linking-pin model (Likert, 1961) and the vertical dyadic linkage perspective on leadership (Dansereau, Graen, & Haga, 1975), LMX theory argues that supervisors develop differentiated relationships with their subordinates. High-quality LMX is characterized by mutual trust, respect, and obligation. When supervisors share high-quality

LMX with subordinates, their exchanges are beyond requirements specified in formal employment contracts (e.g., supervisors providing socioemotional support, subordinates performing extra-role behaviors). When supervisor–subordinate exchange relationship is of low quality, their exchanges are restricted to what are required to complete the job.

LMXs play important roles in newcomer adjustment. First, LMX can be viewed as a specific indicator of newcomer adjustment, considering that establishing high quality exchange relationships with supervisors is part of being assimilated by the work group (Harrison & Shaffer, 2005). In other words, LMX development is part of newcomers' transition from outsiders to insiders. Second, LMX can be influenced by and affect other indicators of newcomer adjustment. For example, LMX is correlated with newcomers' perceived empowerment (Chen & Klimoski, 2003). Third, LMX mediates the impact of antecedents of newcomer adjustment on more distal socialization outcomes (e.g., the indirect relationship between newcomer general self-efficacy and job performance; Chen & Klimoski, 2003). LMX can also attenuate or amplify the impact of antecedents of newcomer adjustment on individual outcomes (e.g., unmet expectations and job satisfaction; Major, Kozlowski, Chao, & Gardner, 1995). Finally, research taking a dynamic perspective suggests that in newcomer adjustment process, changes in LMX and individual outcomes, such as job

performance, are interwoven (e.g., Bauer & Green, 1996; Sparrowe & Liden, 1997).

Previous research on LMX and newcomer adjustment focused on answering two questions: (1) what the antecedents of newcomer–supervisor LMX are and how these antecedents influence LMX development, and (2) how LMX influences newcomer adjustment and distal outcomes. In addition, some studies have examined LMX in the adjustment processes of two special groups of newcomers: expatriates and new managers. We review research on these issues in the following three sections. In the last section of this chapter, we discuss limitations in existing studies and suggest some future research directions.

Antecedents of Newcomer–Supervisor LMX

As shown in Figure 13.1, newcomer adjustment is influenced by newcomer, supervisor, and organizational factors (Bauer et al., 2007; Fang, Duffy, & Shaw, 2011; Kammeyer-Mueller & Wanberg, 2003; Wang et al., 2011). These factors can have a unique or joint impact on adjustment indicators. Previous research has examined four forms of antecedents to supervisor–newcomer LMX: similarity between supervisor and newcomer in demographic characteristics and personality traits, expectations of supervisors and newcomers, supervisor socialization tactics, and network structures of supervisors and newcomers.

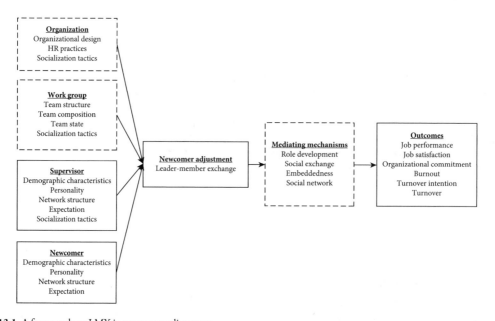

Fig. 13.1 A framework on LMX in newcomer adjustment.

Note. Solid boxes represent variables examined in previous empirical research. Dashed boxes represent variables proposed in this chapter.

Similarity

Some researchers propose that supervisor–subordinate similarity in demographic characteristics (e.g., gender) and deep-level characteristics (e.g., personality traits) influence LMX quality (Bauer & Green, 1996; Liden, Wayne, & Stilwell, 1993). Certain demographic characteristics (e.g., gender, race) are salient cues in social interactions when individuals first encounter each other, especially when additional information is limited (Hogg & Abrams, 1993; Tajfel & Turner, 1986). Over time, individuals' deep-level characteristics are also perceivable to others in social interactions (Harrison, Price, Gavin, & Florey, 2002). Social psychology research suggests that similarity is related to mutual attraction and liking between two parties (Byrne, 1971). In the organizational context, when supervisor–subordinate similarity is high, supervisors are more likely to hold positive feelings about the subordinates, and view subordinates as more trustworthy and competent for the task (e.g., Levin, Whitener, & Cross, 2006; Tsui & O'Reilly, 1989). Therefore, newcomers who are similar to supervisors are likely to receive more resources (e.g., job autonomy, socioemotional support) that are beneficial for task performance. Subordinates' improved job performance can in turn reinforce supervisors' positive evaluations of the subordinates and lead to more delegation to subordinates. Bauer and Green (1996) argue that through this ongoing positive association between supervisors' delegation and subordinates' job performance, high-quality LMX is developed from similarity. In addition, LMX quality can also be improved by the affective attraction associated with perceived similarity (Engle & Lord, 1997; Wayne & Ferris, 1990).

Empirical studies found that actual demographic similarity was not significantly related to LMX whereas perceived similarity and similarity in personality traits were significantly related to LMX. Specifically, Liden et al. (1993) measured similarity in gender, race, educational level, and age of newly formed supervisor–subordinate dyads. They found that the composite score of these four types of demographic similarity was not significantly related to LMX measured at two weeks, six weeks, and six months. However, supervisors' and subordinates' perceived similarity and liking of each other in the first five days of dyadic tenure were related to LMX measured at two weeks and six weeks. Similarly, Bauer and Green (1996) found that supervisor–subordinate gender similarity was not significantly related to supervisor delegation,

supervisor-rated performance, or LMX, whereas supervisor–subordinate similarity in positive affectivity was positively related to supervisor-rated performance, which was related to LMX. Zhang, Wang, and Shi (2012) found that supervisor–subordinate similarity in proactive personality was related to LMX.

Several reasons might explain why existing empirical studies failed to find support for the effect of demographic similarity on supervisor–newcomer LMX. First, it is possible that perceived similarity mediates the effect of actual demographic similarity on LMX. Harrison et al. (2002) found that perceived diversity of the work group mediates the effect of actual diversity on team social integration and team performance. Second, demographic characteristics might be more influential at the very beginning of relationship development process whereas over time deep-level similarity and actual resource exchanges become more influential in shaping LMX. In addition, the same demographic characteristic might have different psychological meanings in different contexts (Harrison & Klein, 2007). Different theoretical mechanisms underlying the effects of the same demographic variable might exist in different types of work groups. Finally, in terms of methodology, difference scores were used to capture similarity/dissimilarity in Liden et al. (1993) and Bauer and Green (1996). Considering the limitations of difference score approach to studying similarity (see Edwards, 1994 for detailed explanations), a response surface approach might reveal different results (e.g., Zhang et al., 2012).

Expectation

Newcomer research suggests that supervisors' expectations about newcomers, and newcomers' expectations about supervisors and themselves can influence supervisor–newcomer LMX (Chen & Klimoski, 2003; Liden et al., 1993). This idea about expectation–LMX relationship is consistent with the notion of self-fulfilling prophecy, or Pygmalion and Galatea effects in organizations (Eden 1990, 1992). Pygmalion effect happens when a subordinate acts in a way that is consistent with supervisor's expectations. Galatea effect happens when an employee acts in a way that is consistent with his/her own expectation.

Similar to the influence of expectation on action in other social contexts (Snyder & Stukas, 1999), expectation influences supervisor–newcomer LMX through a series of events. Supervisors' expectations about the newcomers and subordinates' expectations about the supervisors form quickly after newcomers enter the organization (Liden et al., 1993). Supervisors form expectations about subordinates based on available information, such as interview experiences, test scores, recommendations, and initial impressions. Supervisors tend to form higher expectations about newcomers with more overall work-related experience (Liden et al., 1993). Subordinates form expectations about the supervisors based on initial impressions or conversations with coworkers. Implicit leadership theory suggests that newcomers' expectations of supervisors might also be influenced by newcomers' experience with previous supervisors (Engle & Lord, 1997). For example, newcomers who have a new leader who is similar to a negatively perceived previous supervisor might hold low expectations about the supervisor and be less motivated to form a positive relationship with the new leader (Ritter & Lord, 2007). Newcomers' expectations of themselves are influenced by dispositional factors and personal history. Newcomers with higher general self-efficacy (i.e., "people's tendency to view themselves as capable of meeting task demands in a wide variety of situations", Chen, Gully, Whiteman, & Kilcullen, 2000, p. 838) and more work-related experience tend to form higher expectations about their own performance as a newcomer (Chen & Klimoski, 2003).

Guided by the expectations formed, newcomers and supervisors engage in social interactions (Chen & Klimoski, 2003; Liden et al., 1993). When supervisors form a positive expectation of the subordinate, supervisors are more likely to provide subordinates with constructive feedback, challenging tasks, desirable rewards, and training opportunities. Subordinates who form positive expectations about their supervisors are more likely to respond to supervisors' requests by performing better and becoming more committed to the job. When supervisors observe subordinates' satisfactory job performance, supervisors are likely to perceive that there is reciprocated social exchange between the two parties. Similarly, subordinates who obtain resources from supervisors are more likely to feel a sense of reciprocated social exchange. Supervisors' and subordinates' perceptions of positive social exchanges contribute to a high-quality exchange relationship (i.e., LMX). In addition, newcomers who hold higher expectations of themselves are likely to actually perform better, which is positively related to supervisor-rated performance and LMX (Bauer & Green, 1996).

Supervisor Socialization Tactics

Supervisor socialization tactics refer to supervisor behaviors that give newcomers advice and guidance according to newcomers' organizational roles (Bauer et al., 2007). Supervisor socialization tactics have various forms, such as explaining how to perform the task, providing task-related information, and acting as a role model to the newcomers (Jones, 1986; Van Maanen & Schein, 1979). Based on social exchange theory, supervisor socialization tactics are positively related to LMX. Supervisors provide resources to the newcomers through supervisor social tactics (Sluss & Thompson, 2012). These tangible (e.g., task-related materials) and intangible (e.g., emotional support) resources can assist newcomers to adjust to the new work environment. Continued resource exchanges from supervisors to newcomers may lead subordinates to perceive high-quality LMX. Improved task performance may lead supervisors to perceive high-quality LMX (Bauer & Green, 1996). Sluss and Thompson (2012) found that supervisor socialization tactics were related to newcomer-perceived LMX, which is in turn positively related to occupational identification and perceived person–organization fit.

Network Structure

Sparrowe and Liden (1997) proposed a structural model of LMX development taking the social network perspective. Sparrowe and Liden note that the social exchange relationship between a supervisor–subordinate dyad is embedded in and influenced by supervisor's and subordinate's relations with other actors in the organizational network (e.g., leaders' own supervisors, subordinates' contacts in other departments). These authors also challenge a core assumption of previous LMX research that subordinates mostly depend on immediate supervisors for critical resources (e.g., respect, loyalty, emotional support, and information) to survive in organizational life.

Sparrowe and Liden's (1997) model draws on Sahlins' (1972) work on reciprocity and research on social structures (Burt, 1992; Granovetter, 1973; Krackhardt, 1992, 1998). Sahlins (1972) proposes that there are three properties that define reciprocity: the immediacy of returns (ranging from instantaneous to an infinite period of time), equivalence of returns (ranging from comparable value to incomparable value), and interest of the two exchange parties (ranging from self-interest to concern for other). Based on these three properties, there are three types of reciprocity: generalized reciprocity (low equivalence, low immediacy, and concern for other), balanced reciprocity (high equivalence, high immediacy, and mutual interest), and negative reciprocity (high equivalence, high immediacy, and self-interest). Sparrowe and Liden argue that these three types of reciprocity characterize different levels of LMX.

Sparrowe and Liden's (1997) model is also influenced by research on strong vs. weak ties and structural holes. Built on Granovetter's (1973) argument of the strength of weak ties (i.e., distant and indirect social contacts), Burt (1992) examined the benefits of having structural holes in managers' social networks. A structural hole exists when there is no relationship between two contacts of a focal person. Burt argues that when a focal person's network is rich in structural holes, he/she is in an advantageous position to broker resources between the two unrelated contacts, to receive nonredundant information, and to play one contact against another in negotiation. When in competitive situations, individuals with networks rich in structural holes are more likely to obtain positive outcomes (e.g., early and faster promotion). However, in situations that are less competitive, strong ties (vs. weak ties) in a closely connected network may bring more positive outcomes to individuals (Krackhardt, 1992, 1998). According to Krackhardt (1998), "two people are Simmelian tied to one another if they are reciprocally and strongly tied to each other and if they are each reciprocally and strongly tied to at least one third party in common" (p. 24). Krackhardt (1998) suggests that strong ties like Simmelian ties may facilitate newcomers' socialization because such ties reduce individual actors' power and increase cohesion and group identity. Taken together, both structural holes and Simmelian ties in newcomers' social networks can potentially benefit newcomers.

Based on these two theoretical foundations, Sparrowe and Liden (1997) propose that LMX is influenced by supervisor's and newcomer's network structures. They argue that networks of strong ties are characterized by generalized reciprocity, networks with structural holes are characterized by balanced reciprocity, and networks of isolated actors are characterized by negative reciprocity. Sparrowe and Liden further delineate that in the initial relationship development stage, supervisors' and newcomers' network structures influence their expectations and perceived similarity of each other. If the supervisor and subordinate share a common contact, reciprocity formed with a third contact may influence early LMX quality. According to

balance theory (Heider, 1958), when both supervisors' and subordinates' relationships with the common contact are dominated by generalized reciprocity or negative reciprocity, they are also likely to develop generalized reciprocity. When supervisors' and subordinates' relationships with the common contact follow different reciprocity forms, supervisor–subordinate dyads are likely to develop balanced reciprocity or even negative reciprocity. In the next stage (i.e., sponsorship stage), early LMX quality influences how likely supervisors sponsor newcomers to join the supervisors' networks with managers outside the immediate work group. Newcomers' relationships with the new contacts are likely to imitate the leaders' relationships with those contacts. This way, subordinates' network structures match their supervisors' network structures (e.g., structural holes and Simmelian ties), which brings subordinates advantages and disadvantages associated with supervisors' network structures (Sparrowe & Liden, 2005). After newcomers develop new network contacts, newcomers and supervisors readjust their expectations, perceived similarity, and liking of each other, which influence subsequent LMX quality. Finally in the assimilation or termination stage, LMX quality influences the likelihood for subordinates to proactively share their networks with the supervisors, which in turn influences supervisors' outcomes. LMX quality also influences subordinates' outcomes. In the assimilation or termination stage, those subordinates who develop low-quality LMX might choose to leave the organization.

How LMX Influences Newcomer Adjustment

Empirical research found that supervisor–newcomer LMX is related to various outcomes of newcomer adjustment, including job performance, perceived person–organization fit (P-O fit), job satisfaction, organizational commitment, turnover intention, actual turnover, burnout, and occupational identification (Bauer, Erdogan, Liden, & Wayne, 2006; Chen & Klimoski, 2003; Jokisaari, 2013; Major et al., 1995; Sluss & Thompson, 2012; Thomas & Lankau, 2009). As illustrated in Figure 1, the mechanism underlying the influence of LMX on newcomer adjustment outcomes has been theorized from different theoretical perspectives.

Role Development
From the perspective of role theory (Katz & Kahn, 1978), a critical aspect of newcomer

adjustment is to understand and master the responsibilities of the newcomers' roles in the organization (Van Maanen & Schein, 1979). Socialization research suggests that newcomers' interaction with organizational "oldtimers" influences newcomers' role development processes and outcomes (Bauer & Green, 1998; Liu, Wang, Bamberger, Shi, & Bacharach, in press; Morrison, 1993; Ostroff & Kozlowski, 1992). Among the organizational oldtimers, newcomers' immediate supervisors are key players in newcomers' role-making process.

Graen and colleagues (e.g., Cashman, Dansereau, Graen, & Haga, 1976; Graen, Orris, & Johnson, 1973; Graen & Scandura, 1987) proposed a role-making model on newcomers' acquisition of their roles. According to this model, supervisors and newcomers reach role routinization stage after they define their exchange relationship (i.e., LMX) through the role-taking and role-making stages. In the role routinization stage, supervisors and subordinates have mutual expectations of each other's behaviors in day-to-day tasks. Either supervisors or subordinates may initiate an exchange. The other party receives the signal and acts according to the expectation based on their exchange relationship. When LMX is of high quality, supervisors tend to provide more resources beyond formal contract to subordinates when subordinates need support, and subordinates tend to put extra effort into task activities to reciprocate supervisors' support. When LMX is low, supervisors' and subordinates' role scripts are limited to requirements in formal employment contract. Therefore, subordinates in low-quality LMX receive relatively limited support from supervisors, which leads to lower job satisfaction and job performance.

In addition to directly influencing newcomer adjustment outcomes, LMX can also influence the effect of adjustment antecedents on adjustment outcomes. Major et al. (1995) argue that LMX can buffer the negative effect of newcomers' unmet expectations on newcomers' attitudinal outcomes (organizational commitment, job satisfaction, and turnover intention). This is because through role making, supervisors can redefine newcomers' role, which alleviates the negative effects of unmet expectations on newcomers' attitudes toward their jobs. In addition, high-quality LMX provides newcomers with psychological support from supervisors, which helps cope with the reality shock from unmet expectations and reduce role-related stress (Thomas & Lankau, 2009).

Social Exchange

Social exchange theory argues that social exchange relationship, e.g., LMX, develops from a series of social exchange episodes. Once social exchange relationship is formed, it is dominated by mutually agreed exchange terms (e.g., reciprocity). In addition, characteristics of exchange relationship influence future social exchanges, i.e., which resources are exchanged between the two parties (see Cropanzano & Mitchell, 2005 for a review). From the perspective of social exchange theory, two arguments have been advanced to explain how LMX influences newcomer adjustment outcomes.

First, high-quality LMX is characterized by mutual trust, respect, and obligation (Graen & Uhl-Bien, 1995). Therefore, newcomers' perceptions of high-quality LMX are associated with newcomers' perceived reciprocity and mutuality with their work context, and an overall positive attitude toward job (Sluss & Thompson, 2012). Specially, LMX is positively related to job satisfaction among newcomers, as the quality of social exchange relationship with the supervisor is part of the job experience. In other words, when LMX is of high quality, the overall job experience also becomes more satisfying. In addition, given that newcomers view supervisors as agents of organizations, LMX is also related to newcomers' perceptions about their relationships with the organization (cf. Eisenberger, Stinglhamber, Vandenberghe, Sucharski, & Rhoades, 2002). For example, newcomers' perceptions of LMX influence the extent to which newcomers perceive congruity between themselves and the organization (i.e., perceived P-O fit; Sluss & Thompson, 2012). Furthermore, LMX may induce a sense of obligation in the newcomers, thus reduce their turnover intention and prolong their organizational tenure (Bauer et al., 2006).

LMX theory also proposes that LMX influences the amount and quality of resources provided by supervisors to subordinates (Graen & Scandura, 1987; Graen & Uhl-Bien, 1995). These resources can be task-related information, developmental assignments, decision latitude, and socioemotional support, which can help newcomers accomplish task responsibilities. Thus, subordinates with high-quality LMX tend to perceive themselves as more empowered (Chen & Klimoski, 2003; Chen, Kirkman, Kanfer, Allen, & Rosen, 2007; Zhou, Wang, Chen, & Shi, 2012). Through providing resources to subordinates, LMX is positively related to job performance. Despite the popularity of the social exchange perspective on LMX and newcomer adjustment, no studies (to our knowledge) have empirically examined the role of resources (e.g., task assignments) or relationship characteristics (e.g., reciprocity) in the LMX–newcomer adjustment outcome relationship.

Embeddedness

On-the-job embeddedness refers to the situation where employees are well connected to social contacts at work, which drives the employees to stay within the organization due to the high cost of leaving the organization (Lee, Mitchell, Sablynski, Burton, & Holtom, 2004). Bauer et al. (2006) argue that LMX is an important component of newcomers' interpersonal connections at work. Therefore, high-quality LMX can increase on-the-job embeddedness and the sense of belongingness for the newcomers, which helps reduce newcomers' turnover intention and actual turnover (Bauer et al., 2006). There has been mixed findings regarding the relationship between LMX and actual turnover among employees of any length of organizational tenure. Meta-analysis by Gerstner and Day (1997) found that there was no significant relationship between LMX and actual turnover. There have been few studies that examined the LMX–turnover relationship in newcomers. In a sample of new executives, Bauer et al. (2006) found that LMX was related to turnover–hazard rate for introverted executives but LMX was not related to turnover–hazard rate for extraverted executives.

Social Network

Although Ronald Burt's research did not specifically focus on newcomers, his findings on the differential effect of social structures on career progression for higher-level managers vs. entry-level and women managers provide interesting insights on newcomer adjustment. Burt (1992) found that managers with structural holes (see definition above) in their social structures are promoted earlier and faster. However, the effect of structural holes on career progression is not consistent for all managers. Burt (1992) found that entry-level and female managers were more likely to be promoted early when they built a strong tie (see definition above) with members in their immediate work group and a higher-level manager whose network includes structural holes. Burt also noted that this beneficial effect of a hierarchical network goes away when entry-level and female managers share a strong tie with their immediate supervisor rather than with a higher-level manager. Burt (1992, 1998) argues that entry-level and female managers have low legitimacy and thus need sponsorship to take advantage of the benefits of structural holes. However, such sponsorship can only come from their strong ties with a higher-level (male) manager. Being in a clique with one's immediate supervisor provides little structural advantage for entry-level and female managers.

Morrison (2002) applied the social network perspective to examining how the pattern of newcomers' relations with more experienced organizational members influence newcomer adjustment. An important assumption of her study is that patterns of interpersonal ties among the focal newcomer and others have unique effect on newcomer adjustment, above and beyond the effect of individual attributes of newcomers and organizational insiders. Therefore, she argues that newcomers' relationships with supervisors should be viewed together with newcomers' relationships with peers. Morrison proposes that newcomers tend to have higher task mastery and role clarity when newcomers' informational network ties include supervisors as well as peers, because supervisors often have more job- and role-related experience. She also proposes the idea that newcomers have higher organizational commitment when newcomers' friendship network ties include supervisors in addition to peers, because a diverse set of contacts prevents newcomers from only establishing attachment to immediate supervisors without being attached to the organization. Empirical test results supported the positive relationship between hierarchical range of newcomers' informational and friendship ties and adjustment indicators and outcomes (i.e., organizational knowledge, task mastery, role clarity, social integration, and organizational commitment).

LMX and Specific Types of Newcomer Adjustment

LMX and Expatriate Adjustment

Expatriate research suggests that LMX helps expatriate buffer the negative impact of stressors on adjustment process and outcomes. Kraimer and Wayne (2004) proposed an integrated model on expatriate adjustment. The core idea of the model is that expatriate adjustment is under the joint influence of two types of factors: stressors (e.g., role stressor, situational stressor) that contribute to stress and support factors (e.g., perceived organizational support, spousal support, and LMX) that help cope with stress. Kraimer, Wayne, and Jaworski (2001) argue that LMX helps reduce stress in the expatriate adjustment process because LMX influences resources bestowed from supervisors to expatriates. Expatriates with high-quality LMX are more likely to receive additional information and assistance from supervisors to cope with the stress involved in adjusting to a different work environment. In addition, expatriates enjoying a high-quality LMX share mutual affective attraction and respect from supervisors, which helps reduce emotional reactions and facilitate adjustment. In addition, expatriates who share high-quality LMX with supervisors may want to repay the organization by staying with the organization longer after repatriation (Liu & Ipe, 2010).

Empirical studies reported mixed findings on the relationship between LMX and expatriate adjustment indicators. Kraimer et al. (2001) and Kraimer and Wayne (2004) found that LMX did not have significant effect on expatriate adjustment indicators (work, general, and interaction adjustment), although LMX was directly related to expatriate task performance and contextual performance. However, Harrison and Shaffer (2005) found that expatriates' work adjustment, interaction adjustment, and relationship building are positively associated with LMX.

Further, it is important to recognize that expatriates develop relationships with supervisors both in home and host countries. LMX with home and host country supervisors can influence expatriate adjustment in different ways. Benson and Pattie (2009) argue that host country supervisors are physically closer to the expatriates, which allows them to provide expatriates with knowledge about local living and business environment, immediate feedback, additional time off, flexible work schedule, and additional training and mentoring. Therefore, LMX with host country supervisors has a larger influence on expatriate adjustment and assignment accomplishment as compared to LMX with home country supervisors. Home country supervisors are in charge of selecting expatriates and assigning tasks after repatriation. Thus, expatriates with a high-quality LMX with home country supervisors are more likely be selected into positions that match the expatriates' skills and benefit their career interests. Given that host country supervisors have less authority on these matters, LMX with host country supervisors has a weaker influence on expatriates' perceived person–job fit and evaluations of their career prospect with the company. Supporting their expectation, Benson and Pattie (2009) found that high-quality LMX with host-country supervisors have a stronger impact on interaction and work adjustment to the host country and intentions to complete the overseas assignment, whereas high-quality LMX with home-country supervisors have a stronger impact on expatriates' perceived person–job fit and perception of whether they will reach their career goals in the current organization.

New Manager Adjustment

Although researchers have noted the importance of supervisors and networking on new manager development (e.g., Day, 2001; Dragoni, Park, Soltis, & Forte-Trammell, 2014), few studies have examined the role of LMX on new manager adjustment. New managers often need to transit from frontline employees to roles with more responsibilities and higher visibility, which requires them to establish social structures that facilitate them to change from being led to leading others (Burt, 1992). As reviewed earlier, Burt (1992) found that entry-level managers are likely to be promoted faster and earlier when they have a sponsor from upper-level managers. As for managers already in the upper level, building a network with structure holes is important for further promotion.

Bauer et al. (2006) argue that the beneficial effect of new managers' relationships with their own supervisors is contingent on new managers' personality. Specifically, Bauer et al. propose that LMX and extraversion complement each other in increasing new executives' job performance, turnover intention, and actual turnover (Bauer et al., 2006). This complementary effect is based on the assumption that even without high-quality LMX, extraverts are motivated to seek information, engage in social interactions, build connections, and pursue novel and challenging assignments. In contrast with extraverts, introverts tend to find it difficult to engage in social interactions and ask for information. Therefore, LMX has a stronger positive effect on job performance and turnover for introverts. Supporting Bauer et al.'s predictions, LMX was positively related to job performance and turnover–hazard rate, and negatively related to turnover intention only among individuals with low extraversion.

Limitations and Future Research Directions

Previous research on the role of LMX in newcomer adjustment has significantly advanced our understanding of organizational socialization. This body of research has also contributed to developing LMX theory and leadership theory in general. As Bauer and Green (1996) point out, newcomers are new both to their organization and their relationships with supervisors. Therefore, newcomer adjustment is a desirable setting for understanding LMX development and formation. Despite these contributions, studies on LMX and newcomer adjustment are not without limitations. In the following sections, we discuss several issues that we consider important to study in the future.

Dynamic Processes in LMX and Newcomer Adjustment

Literature suggests that newcomer adjustment involves the recursive influence between LMX and other adjustment indicators over time. For example, Bauer and Green (1996) describe a process in which supervisors' delegation and subordinates' performance influence each other over time. This ongoing mutual influence process shapes and defines LMX, which in turn influences subordinates' performance. Sparrowe and Liden (1997) argue that there is reciprocal influence among supervisors' and subordinates' social structures, expectations, perceived similarities, and LMX. Supervisors' and subordinates' social structures influence their expectations and perceived similarities of each other, which influence early LMX quality. Early LMX quality in turn influences the assimilation of supervisors' social structures to subordinates' social structure, and redefines supervisors' and subordinates' expectations, perceived similarities, and liking of each other. Through this dynamic process, subordinates' and supervisors' social networks are restructured, and LMX is developed.

Vancouver, Tamanini, and Yoder (2010) developed a computational model to formally account for the dynamic processes involved in organizational socialization (a simplified version is illustrated by solid lines in Figure 2). Based on self-regulation theory (see Vancouver, 2005 for a review) and the regulatory view on newcomer adjustment (e.g., Ashford & Tsui, 1991; Tsui & Ashford, 1994), Vancouver et al. (2010) argue that newcomers and supervisors follow discrepancy–reduction rule to strive toward ideal levels of role clarity and performance. In newcomers' self-regulation process, newcomers' perceived discrepancies in standard and current role clarity and competence levels direct newcomer information seeking. In the supervisors' other-regulation process, supervisors' perceived discrepancies in newcomers' role clarity and competence direct supervisors to engage in information giving. Information seeking and information giving together improve newcomers' current role clarity and competence levels. In addition, supervisors' perceptions of subordinates' adjustment state might be influenced by biases. The strength of the association between perceived discrepancies and actions might be influenced by dispositional characteristics.

One possible extension of Vancouver et al.'s (2010) model is to include LMX in the dynamic processes. As illustrated by the dashed lines in Figure 13.2, newcomer–leader similarity can influence leader perceived newcomer's task mastery and role clarity, and leader treatment of subordinates (Bauer & Green, 1996). Newcomer–leader similarity can also influence mutual liking and perceived

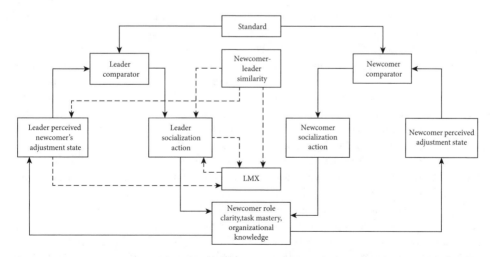

Fig. 13.2 A self-regulation model on the nonlinear relationship between LMX and newcomer adjustment.

Note. Solid lines represent relationships proposed by Vancouver, Tamanini, and Yoder (2010). Dashed lines represent relationships proposed in this chapter.

similarity of newcomers and leaders, which affects LMX directly (Sparrowe & Liden, 1997). Leader perceived newcomer's adjustment state and leader's action toward subordinates can influence LMX quality (Bauer & Green, 1996). According to social exchange theory, the relationship formed between supervisors and newcomers can in turn influence resources bestowed by supervisors to subordinates. From this dynamic perspective, changes in one indicator of newcomer adjustment (e.g., LMX, role clarity, socialization effort) influence changes in other adjustment indicators. These interwoven dynamic processes together form newcomer adjustment process. Future research can use computational modeling technique to develop theories on these nonlinear processes in newcomer adjustment.

Team Context

Socialization research has documented that peers in the same work group can influence newcomer adjustment (e.g., Kammeyer-Mueller & Wanberg, 2003). Specifically, Chen and Klimoski (2003) found that team members' expectations can significantly influence newcomer–supervisor LMX. In addition, a body of literature in small group research suggests that how teams react to newcomers (i.e., team receptivity) is related to team stability, functioning, and adaptation (see Rink, Kane, Ellemers, & Van Der Vegt, 2013, for a review). For example, the entry of newcomers to an existing group can increase the creativity of oldtimers and the overall creativity of the group (e.g., Choi & Thompson, 2005). Together, these two streams of research suggest that newcomer adjustment and team adjustment are closely related.

However, previous research has paid little attention to the role of interpersonal relationships, especially the relationship between newcomer and team leader, in newcomer adjustment in the team context. For example, it is not clear whether LMX can facilitate team receptivity to newcomers. Team reactivity research suggests that teams that have developed routines tend to be reluctant to socially accept newcomers and utilize newcomers' knowledge (Molleman & Van der Vegt, 2007; Moreland & Levine, 1982). If the team leader establishes LMX with the newcomers quickly, newcomers will be involved in decision making and be viewed as an in-group member to the team leader. In this situation, experienced team members might follow the leader to invite the newcomers to discuss work matters and accept the newcomers' opinions. In addition, there is limited research on whether newcomer–supervisor LMX development is influenced by teams' social structure upon newcomer entry. For example, when there is a faultline that separates the group by demographic characteristics and LMX, it is possible that newcomer–supervisor LMX forms faster and remains more stable than when there is no faultline. Furthermore, it is not clear whether newcomer–supervisor LMX development is influenced by team design characteristics (e.g., team size, team structure). For example, it is interesting to examine whether LMX development differs between traditional and virtual teams.

Organizational Context

Empirical evidence has consistently shown that organizations have significant impact on newcomers' transition to organizational insiders (Bauer et al., 2007). However, prior research has seldom examined the influence of organizational level factors on LMX and newcomer adjustment (Wang, Kammeyer-Mueller, Liu, & Li, in press). Contingency theories of leadership argue that the effectiveness of leadership on individual and collective outcomes depends on the situation (Vroom & Jago, 2007). Certain situational factors (e.g., task characteristics) can neutralize or substitute for leadership (Kerr & Jermier, 1978). Therefore, it is possible that formal human resource management policies and practices, e.g., organization socialization tactics, can substitute for the effect of supervisor socialization tactics on newcomer adjustment (cf. Henderson, Liden, Glibkowski, & Chaudhry, 2009). Given that supervisors' socialization tactics is one way through which supervisors exchange resources with newcomers (Sluss & Thompson, 2012), it is possible that LMX development follows different trajectories depending on the amount of organizational socialization tactics enacted.

In addition, organizational structure and design features might influence newcomer–supervisor LMX development as well. As compared to organizations that are highly bureaucratic and mechanic, organizations that are more organic have less clearly defined chain of command and task specialization (Burns & Stalker, 1961). In organizations with an organic design, exchange relationships with direct supervisors might be less critical than a social structure that includes a diverse set of contacts in the organization. Therefore, newcomers might develop LMX at different paces or to different levels depending on the organizational design. Furthermore, modern organizations use virtual teams, flexible work schedule, temporary contract workers, and computer-based orientation programs. It is not clear whether newcomer–supervisor exchange relationship still has the same impact on newcomer adjustment in these organizational settings that are less stable and involve less face-to-face interaction.

Conclusion

To conclude, previous research suggests that LMX development is part of newcomer adjustment. Both newcomers and supervisors can influence LMX, which in turn impacts newcomers' job attitudes, task performance, and likelihood to stay with the organization. However, most of previous socialization research has focused on distal adjustment outcomes (e.g., organizational commitment, turnover) and few studies have examined the adjustment process itself, including LMX development. In addition, the impact of the group and organization on newcomer–supervisor LMX development has not been fully investigated. Organizational socialization literature has embraced an interactionist perspective that examines the joint influence of organization and individual on newcomer adjustment (Bauer et al., 2007). Future studies should take an interactionist perspective to examine the joint influence of organizational situation, newcomer, and leader characteristics on LMX development.

Author Note

Le Zhou, Department of Work and Organizations, University of Minnesota. Mo Wang, Department of Management, University of Florida. Correspondence concerning this chapter should be addressed to Le Zhou, Department of Work and Organizations, University of Minnesota, Minneapolis, Minnesota 55455. Email: zhoul@umn.edu.

References

Ashford, S. J., & Tsui, A. S. (1991). Self-regulation for managerial effectiveness: The role of active feedback seeking. *Academy of Management Journal, 34*, 251–280.

Bauer, T. N., Bodner, T., Erdogan, B., Truxillo, D. M., & Tucker, J. S. (2007). Newcomer adjustment during organizational socialization: A meta-analytic review of antecedents, outcomes, and methods. *Journal of Applied Psychology, 92*, 707–721.

Bauer, T. N., Erdogan, B., Liden, R. C., & Wayne, S. J. (2006). A longitudinal study of the moderating role of extraversion: Leader-member exchange, performance, and turnover during new executive development. *Journal of Applied Psychology, 91*, 298–310.

Bauer, T. N., & Green, S. G. (1996). Development of leader-member exchange: A longitudinal test. *Academy of Management Journal, 39*, 1538–1567.

Bauer, T. N., & Green, S. G. (1998). Testing the combined effects of newcomer information seeking and manager behavior on socialization. *Journal of Applied Psychology, 83*, 72–83.

Benson, G. S., & Pattie, M. (2009). The comparative roles of home and host supervisors in the expatriate experience. *Human Resource Management, 48*, 49–68.

Burns, T. E., & Stalker, G. M. (1961). The management of innovation. University of Illinois at Urbana-Champaign's Academy for Entrepreneurial Leadership Historical Research Reference in Entrepreneurship.

Burt, R. S. (1992). *Structural holes: The social structure of competition*. Cambridge, MA: Harvard University Press.

Burt, R. S. (1998). The gender of social capital. *Rationality and Society, 10*, 5–46.

Byrne, D. (1971). *The attraction paradigm*. San Diego, CA: Academic Press.

Cashman, J., Dansereau, F., Jr., Graen, G., & Haga, W. J. (1976). Organizational understructure and leadership: A longitudinal investigation of the managerial role-making process. *Organizational Behavior and Human Performance, 15*, 278–296.

Chao, G. T., O'Leary-Kelly, A. M., Wolf, S., Klein, H. J., & Gardner, P. D. (1994). Organizational socialization: Its content and consequences. *Journal of Applied Psychology, 79*, 730–743.

Chen, G., Gully, S. M., Whiteman, J. A., & Kilcullen, R. N. (2000). Examination of relationships among trait-like individual differences, state-like individual differences, and learning performance. *Journal of Applied Psychology, 85*, 835–847.

Chen, G., Kirkman, B. L., Kanfer, R., Allen, D., & Rosen, B. (2007). A multilevel study of leadership, empowerment, and performance in teams. *Journal of Applied Psychology, 92*, 331–346.

Chen, G., & Klimoski, R. J. (2003). The impact of expectations on newcomer performance in teams as mediated by work characteristics, social exchanges, and empowerment. *Academy of Management Journal, 46*, 591–607.

Choi, H. S., & Thompson, L. (2005). Old wine in a new bottle: Impact of membership change on group creativity. *Organizational Behavior and Human Decision Processes, 98*, 121–132.

Cropanzano, R., & Mitchell, M. S. (2005). Social exchange theory: An interdisciplinary review. *Journal of Management, 31*, 874–900.

Dansereau, F., Graen, G., & Haga, W. J. (1975). A vertical dyad linkage approach to leadership within formal organizations: A longitudinal investigation of the role making process. *Organizational Behavior and Human Performance, 13*, 46–78.

Day, D. V. (2001). Leadership development: A review in context. *The Leadership Quarterly, 11*, 581–613.

Dragoni, L., Park, H., Soltis, J., & Forte-Trammell, S. (2014). Show and tell: How supervisors facilitate leader development among transitioning leaders. *Journal of Applied Psychology, 99*, 66–86.

Eden, D. (1992). Leadership and expectations: Pygmalion effects and other self-fulfilling prophecies in organization. *The Leadership Quarterly, 3*, 271–305.

Eden, D. (1990). *Pygmalion in management: Productivity as a self-fulfilling prophecy*. Lexington, MA: Lexington Books.

Edwards, J. R. (1994). The study of congruence in organizational behavior research: Critique and a proposed alternative.

Organizational Behavior and Human Decision Processes, 58, 51–100.

Eisenberger, R., Stinglhamber, F., Vandenberghe, C., Sucharski, I. L., & Rhoades, L. (2002). Perceived supervisor support: contributions to perceived organizational support and employee retention. *Journal of Applied Psychology, 87*, 565–573.

Engle, E. M., & Lord, R. G. (1997). Implicit theories, self-schemas, and leader-member exchange. *Academy of Management Journal, 40*, 988–1010.

Fang, R., Duffy, M. K., & Shaw, J. D. (2011). The organizational socialization process: Review and development of a social capital model. *Journal of Management, 37*, 127–152.

Gerstner, C. R., & Day, D. V. (1997). Meta-analytic review of leader–member exchange theory: Correlates and construct issues. *Journal of Applied Psychology, 82*, 827–844.

Graen, G., Orris, J. B., & Johnson, T. (1973). Role assimilation processes in a complex organization. *Journal of Vocational Behavior, 3*, 395–420.

Graen, G. B., & Scandura, T. A. (1987). Toward a psychology of dyadic organizing. In L. L. Cummings & B. M. Staw (Eds.), *Research in organizational behavior* (Vol. 9, pp. 175–208). Greenwich, CT: JAI Press.

Graen, G. B., & Uhl-Bien, M. (1995). Relationship-based approach to leadership: Development of leader-member exchange (LMX) theory of leadership over 25 years: Applying a multi-level multi-domain perspective. *The Leadership Quarterly, 6*, 219–247.

Granovetter, M. (1973). The strength of weak ties. *American Journal of Sociology, 78*, 1360–1380.

Harrison, D. A., & Klein, K. J. (2007). What's the difference? Diversity constructs as separation, variety, or disparity in organizations. *Academy of Management Review, 32*, 1199–1228.

Harrison, D. A., Price, K. H., Gavin, J. H., & Florey, A. T. (2002). Time, teams, and task performance: Changing effects of surface-and deep-level diversity on group functioning. *Academy of Management Journal, 45*, 1029–1045.

Harrison, D. A., & Shaffer, M. A. (2005). Mapping the criterion space for expatriate success: Task-and relationship-based performance, effort and adaptation. *International Journal of Human Resource Management, 16*, 1454–1474.

Heider, F. (1958). *The psychology of interpersonal relations.* New York: Wiley.

Henderson, D. J., Liden, R. C., Glibkowski, B. C., & Chaudhry, A. (2009). LMX differentiation: A multilevel review and examination of its antecedents and outcomes. *The Leadership Quarterly, 20*, 517–534.

Hogg, M. A., & Abrams, D. (1993). Towards a single process uncertainty-reduction model of social motivation in groups. In M. A. Hogg & D. Abrams (Eds.), *Group motivation: Social psychology perspectives* (pp. 173–190). London: Harvester-Wheatsheaf.

Jokisaari, M. (2013). The role of leader-member and social network relations in newcomers' role performance. *Journal of Vocational Behavior, 82*, 96–104.

Jokisaari, M., & Nurmi, J. E. (2009). Change in newcomers' supervisor support and socialization outcomes after organizational entry. *Academy of Management Journal, 52*, 527–544.

Jones, G. R. (1986). Socialization tactics, self-efficacy, and newcomers' adjustments to organizations. *Academy of Management journal, 29*, 262–279.

Katz, D., & Kahn, R. L. (1978). *The social psychology of organizations* (2nd ed.). New York: Wiley.

Kammeyer-Mueller, J. D., & Wanberg, C. R. (2003). Unwrapping the organizational entry process: Disentangling multiple antecedents and their pathways to adjustment. *Journal of Applied Psychology, 88*, 779–794.

Kerr, S., & Jermier, J. M. (1978). Substitutes for leadership: Their meaning and measurement. *Organizational Behavior and Human Performance, 22*, 375–403.

Krackhardt, D. (1998). Simmelian tie: Super strong and sticky. In R. M. Kramer & M. A. Neale (Eds.), *Power and influence in organizations* (pp. 21–38). Thousand Oaks, CA: Sage.

Krackhardt, D. (1992). The strength of strong ties: The importance of *philos* in organizations. In R. Eccles & N. Nohria (Eds.), *Networks and organizations: Structure, form, and action* (pp. 216–239). Cambridge, MA: Harvard Business School.

Kraimer, M. L., & Wayne, S. J. (2004). An examination of perceived organizational support as a multidimensional construct in the context of an expatriate assignment. *Journal of Management, 30*, 209–237.

Kraimer, M. L., Wayne, S. J., & Jaworski, R. A. A. (2001). Sources of support and expatriate performance: The mediating role of expatriate adjustment. *Personnel Psychology, 54*, 71–99.

Lee, T. W., Mitchell, T. R., Sablynski, C. J., Burton, J. P., & Holtom, B. C. (2004). The effects of job embeddedness on organizational citizenship, job performance, volitional absence, and voluntary turnover. *Academy of Management Journal, 47*, 711–722.

Levin, D. Z., Whitener, F. M., & Cross, R. (2006). Perceived trustworthiness of knowledge sources: the moderating impact of relationship length. *Journal of Applied Psychology, 91*, 1163–1171.

Liden, R. C., Wayne, S. J., & Stilwell, D. (1993). A longitudinal study on the early development of leader-member exchanges. *Journal of Applied Psychology, 78*, 662–674.

Likert, R. (1961). *New patters of management.* New York: McGraw-Hill.

Liu, S., Wang, M., Bamberger, P., Shi, J., & Bacharach, P. (in press). The dark side of socialization: A longitudinal investigation of newcomer alcohol use. *Academy of Management Journal.*

Liu, Y., & Ipe, M. (2010). The impact of organizational and leader–member support on expatriate commitment. *The International Journal of Human Resource Management, 21*, 1035–1048.

Major, D. A., Kozlowski, S. W. J., Chao, G. T., & Gardner, P. D. (1995). A longitudinal investigation of newcomer expectations, early socialization outcomes, and the moderating effects of role development factors. *Journal of Applied Psychology, 80*, 418–431.

Molleman, E., & Van der Vegt, G. S. (2007). The performance evaluation of novices: The importance of competence in specific work activity clusters. *Journal of Occupational and Organizational Psychology, 80*, 459–478.

Moreland, R. L., & Levine, J. M. (1982). Socialization in small groups: Temporal changes in individual-group relations. *Advances in experimental social psychology, 15*, 137–192.

Morrison, E. W. (1993). Longitudinal study of the effects of information seeking on newcomer socialization. *Journal of Applied Psychology, 78*, 173–183.

Morrison, E. W. (2002). Newcomers' relationships: The role of social network ties during socialization. *Academy of Management Journal, 45*, 1149–1160.

Ostroff, C., & Kozlowski, S. W. (1992). Organizational socialization as a learning process: The role of information acquisition. *Personnel Psychology*, *45*, 849–874.

Rink, F., Kane, A. A., Ellemers, N., & Van Der Vegt, G. (2013). Team receptivity to newcomers: Five decades of evidence and future research themes. *The Academy of Management Annals*, *7*, 247–293.

Ritter, B. A., & Lord, R. G. (2007). The impact of previous leaders on the evaluation of new leaders: an alternative to prototype matching. *Journal of Applied Psychology*, *92*, 1683–1695.

Sahlins, M. (1972). *Stone age economics*. New York: Aldine De Gruyter.

Sluss, D. M., & Thompson, B. S. (2012). Socializing the newcomer: The mediating role of leader–member exchange. *Organizational Behavior and Human Decision Processes*, *119*, 114–125.

Snyder, M., & Stukas, A. A., Jr. (1999). Interpersonal processes: The interplay of cognitive, motivational, and behavioral activities in social interaction. *Annual Review of Psychology*, *50*, 273–303.

Sparrowe, R. T., & Liden, R. C. (1997). Process and structure in leader-member exchange. *Academy of Management Review*, *22*, 522–552.

Sparrowe, R. T., & Liden, R. C. (2005). Two routes to influence: Integrating leader-member exchange and social network perspectives. *Administrative Science Quarterly*, *50*, 505–535.

Tajfel, H., & Turner, J. (1986). The social identity theory of intergroup behavior. In S. Worchel & W. Austin (Eds.), *Psychology of intergroup relations* (pp. 7–24). Chicago, IL: Nelson-Hall.

Thomas, C. H., & Lankau, M. J. (2009). Preventing burnout: The effects of LMX and mentoring on socialization, role stress, and burnout. *Human Resource Management*, *48*, 417–432.

Tsui, A. S., & Ashford, S. J. (1994). Adaptive self-regulation: A process view of managerial effectiveness. *Journal of Management*, *20*, 93–121.

Tsui, A. S., & O'reilly, C. A. (1989). Beyond simple demographic effects: The importance of relational demography in superior-subordinate dyads. *Academy of Management Journal*, *32*, 402–423.

Vancouver, J. B. (2005). The depth of history and explanation as benefit and bane for psychological control theories. *Journal of Applied Psychology*, *90*, 38–52.

Vancouver, J. B., Tamanini, K. B., & Yoder, R. J. (2010). Using dynamic computational models to reconnect theory and research: Socialization by the proactive newcomer as example. *Journal of Management*, *36*, 764–793.

Van Maanen, J., & Schein, E. H. (1979). Toward a theory of organizational socialization. *Research in Organizational Behavior*, *1*, 209–264.

Vroom, V. H., & Jago, A. G. (2007). The role of the situation in leadership. *American Psychologist*, *62*, 17–24.

Wang, M., Kammeyer-Mueller, J. D., Liu, Y., & Li, Y. (in press). Context, socialization, and newcomer learning. *Organizational Psychology Review*.

Wang, M., Zhan, Y., McCune, E., & Truxillo, D. (2011). Understanding newcomers' adaptability and work-related outcomes: Testing the mediating roles of perceived P-E fit variables. *Personnel Psychology*, *64*, 163–189.

Wayne, S. J., & Ferris, G. R. (1990). Influence tactics, affect, and exchange quality in supervisor-subordinate interactions: A laboratory experiment and field study. *Journal of Applied Psychology*, *75*, 487–499.

Zhang, Z., Wang, M., & Shi, J. (2012). Leader-follower congruence in proactive personality and work outcomes: The mediating role of leader-member exchange. *Academy of Management Journal*, *55*, 111–130.

Zhou, L., Wang, M., Chen, G., & Shi, J. (2012). Supervisors' upward exchange relationships and subordinate outcomes: Testing the multilevel mediation role of empowerment. *Journal of Applied Psychology*, *97*, 668–680.

Consequences of High LMX: Career Mobility and Success

Maria L. Kraimer, Scott E. Seibert, *and* Stacy L. Astrove

Abstract

This chapter provides a summary of the research linking leader–member exchange (LMX) to career success and mobility. Theoretical perspectives linking LMX to the different types of career success, including social exchange and tournament theories, are briefly reviewed. A typology of career success, built around the dimensions of extrinsic–intrinsic and subjective–objective indicators, is then introduced. This broad definition of career success includes traditional career outcomes such as promotions and turnover as well as skill development, perceived career opportunities, and career satisfaction. A narrative review of empirical research linking LMX to these career outcomes is then provided. The chapter concludes with suggestions for theoretically advancing this research stream and offers insights for individuals, leaders, and organizations managing career success.

Key Words: LMX, career success, turnover, career satisfaction, career mobility

Introduction

In this chapter, we focus on the career outcomes of high-quality leader–member exchange (LMX). We have four goals in this chapter. First, we review two key theories that have provided explanations for why LMX is related to career success and mobility. Second, we provide a theoretical framework for organizing the various indicators of career success. In doing so, we define career success in terms of multiple dimensions that unify the somewhat fragmented literature on career success. Third, we provide a narrative review of the research linking LMX to career success outcomes to bring readers up to date on the existing research. Finally, we offer future research directions to advance our theoretical understanding of how and why LMX can positively contribute to employees' career success.

Overview of Theoretical Perspectives Linking LMX to Career Success and Mobility

LMX theory traditionally assumes that through a role-making process (Graen & Uhl-Bien, 1995),

subordinates and supervisors develop unique relationships with each other. A high-quality exchange relationship is characterized by a high degree of mutual trust, respect, loyalty, and obligation (Graen & Uhl-Bien, 1995; Liden & Maslyn, 1998). Low-quality exchange relationships rarely develop beyond requirements in the basic employment contract. Social exchange theory (Blau, 1964) and tournament theory (Rosenbaum, 1984) provide theoretical foundations for linking LMX to career mobility and success.

Social Exchange Theory

When considering organizational turnover (i.e., mobility) and intrinsic career success (i.e., job satisfaction) as outcomes of LMX, researchers have most often relied on social exchange theory. The core tenet of social exchange theory is that individuals tend to form more trusting, long-term-oriented relationships with select others who can provide valued resources, such as support, information, and opportunities, and with whom a pattern of reciprocity has developed over time (Blau, 1964). Leader–member exchange relationships represent one such potential social exchange relationship; a high LMX relationship means that the leader and member have a high degree of mutual trust, loyalty, and obligation to reciprocate to each other (Liden & Maslyn, 1998). A low LMX relationship is more transactional in nature. Thus, LMX relationships vary in terms of the amount of resources, information, trust, and support exchanged between the leader and member. Resources and support from leader to member may include greater job challenge, career opportunities, and recommendations for promotions (Kraimer, Seibert, Wayne, Liden, & Bravo, 2011). Because of the greater resources and support being exchanged in high-quality leader–member relations, such members will be more satisfied with their jobs and more committed to the organization. As such, LMX is proposed to be negatively related to voluntary turnover and positively related to satisfaction with intrinsic aspects of the job.

Tournament Theory

When predicting objective career outcomes such as promotions and salary, tournament theory (Rosenbaum, 1979) provides a theoretical role for LMX. Rosenbaum (1979, 1984) coined the tournament metaphor to describe upward mobility patterns within organizations based on earlier research from Turner (1960). Turner (1960) identified two different systems of upward mobility originally based on observations of American and English educational systems: the American system based on a contest-mobility norm and the English system based on a sponsored-mobility norm. The contest-mobility norm represents a merit-based system in which upward mobility is a function of a person's abilities and hard work and is open to all qualified contenders. A sponsored-mobility norm represents a class-based system because those already possessing elite status select new entrants into their social circle based on class membership or other signals of social class. Those selected into the system are then provided with support and guidance. Rosenbaum (1984) applied this perspective to archival data on a cohort's upward movement through ranks within an organization over a 13-year period. He found that both contest-mobility norms and sponsored-mobility norms function within organizations, with the former dominating earlier in an employee's tenure and the latter dominating as the employee advances upward in the organization. Researchers have since applied the sponsored-mobility perspective to explain

why LMX positively relates to career success (e.g., Wayne, Liden, Kraimer, & Graf, 1999).

Specifically, the sponsored-mobility norm suggests that organizational leaders sponsor selected employees and not others based on attributes other than merit or performance. It is necessary for leaders to make this differentiation in sponsorship because it is not efficient for each individual leader to expend the time and resources needed to sponsor all subordinates, and the hierarchical structure of organizations means that not all individuals will be promoted (Rosenbaum, 1984). Thus, the sponsored-mobility norm and leader–member exchange theory share the assumption that it is not efficient or possible for leaders to develop high-quality relationships with all subordinates (Dansereau, Graen, & Haga, 1975; Wayne et al., 1999). Furthermore, a high-quality exchange relationship means that the supervisor provides sponsorship and support to that employee (Sparrowe & Liden, 1997). As such, an employee's LMX should be positively related to his or her career progression consistent with a sponsored-mobility norm of upward mobility. We recognize, however, that sponsorship through LMX may partly come about as a result of the member's high performance or merit (e.g., Liden, Wayne, & Stilwell, 1993); thus, LMX sponsorship does not entirely preclude the possibility that a contest-mobility norm is also in operation. We return to this point in future research directions.

Typology of Career Success

Historically, career success was defined in terms of a narrow range of extrinsic outcomes, such as salary, rank, or number of promotions (Heslin, 2005). Beginning in the mid-1980s, however, career researchers sought to expand the notion of career success to correspond to the increasingly "boundaryless" (Arthur, 1994) nature of work and the need for individuals to manage their own self-directed careers (Hall, 2002). Career scholars have since begun to use qualitative and quantitative methods to explore a fuller set of potential outcomes related to an individual's career. These efforts have resulted in a number of career success typologies.

The simplest typologies recognized the traditional extrinsic measures of career success mentioned above, but also included intrinsic constructs, such as satisfaction with the progress of your career (e.g., Boudreau, Boswell, & Judge, 2001; Judge, Cable, Boudreau, & Bretz, 1995). Intrinsic (also sometimes referred to as internal) career success is based on an individual's own personal standards regarding the meaning of success (Abele & Wiese, 2008). Other researchers have used a similar dichotomy, but one based on the nature of the measure, objective or subjective, rather than the motivational basis of the outcome, intrinsic or extrinsic (e.g., Breland, Treadway, Duke, & Adams, 2007; Ng, Eby, Sorensen, & Feldman, 2005). Dries and colleagues (2008) defined objective measures of career success as "observable, measurable, and verifiable attainments" (p. 254). Objective measures are typically the more traditional extrinsic indicators of career success such as salary or promotions (Abele & Wiese, 2008; Ng et al., 2005). In contrast, subjective career success is defined as individuals' subjective judgments about their career success, which is often measured in terms of career satisfaction (Ng et al., 2005). Previous researchers have sometimes used the terms extrinsic and objective as well as intrinsic and subjective interchangeably (Ng et al., 2005). However, this has created construct confusion as extrinsic indicators of success are not always objective (such as perceptions of promotability or employability) and intrinsic indicators are not always subjective (career satisfaction is based on objective, tangible criteria such as organizational rank and income). As such, there is a need to clarify and distinguish among these four dimensions of career success.

Due to the growing complexity of careers and the increased responsibility of employees to manage their own careers, Sturges (1999) sought to use qualitative methods to better understand the way employees understand their own career success. She found that employees think about both internal and external factors as well as objective versus subjective factors when discussing their own career success. She found that few of the individuals she interviewed considered all of the different possible career outcomes when thinking about their careers, but tended to use clusters of similar constructs. Thus, rather than identifying abstract dimensions that might underlie people's career success judgments, Sturges identified four *types of individuals* based on the criteria of career success they tended to use. Climbers defined career success in terms of external and objective criteria such as pay level, promotions, and hierarchical level. Influencers defined career success in terms of external and subjective criteria, such as having an impact on the business or leaving a mark. Experts were concerned with internal and objective criteria, including competence and recognition. Self-realizers were concerned with

the internal and subjective, defining career success according to their own standards. In comparison, Abele and Wiese (2008) attempted to define the dimensions of career success in terms of three categories: objective career success (pay, promotions, position, and performance), self-referent subjective career success (evaluation based on an internal self-set standard), and other-referent subjective career success (evaluation based on a significant other comparison). Dries et al. (2008) similarly identified four categories of career success: interpersonal achievement (objective performance, advancement, and factual contributions to organizations), intrapersonal achievement (self-development and creativity), interpersonal affect (receiving recognition, working well with others, and serving society in an ethical way), and intrapersonal affect (achieving financial and employment security as well as intrinsic satisfaction). Although there is considerable convergence across these three typologies, the literature can be critiqued as scholars continue to use the terms interchangeably and imprecisely (Seibert, Kraimer, Holtom, & Pierotti, 2013).

Building on these previous typologies and definitions in the career success literature as reviewed above, we propose that career success be defined in terms of two dimensions: intrinsic versus extrinsic criteria and subjective versus objective criteria (see Table 14.1). We define *intrinsic career success* as career achievements that are meaningful to the individual because they fulfill important psychological needs or end-state values held by the individual. These achievements are viewed by an individual as valuable ends in themselves and may directly affect feelings of well-being, self-worth, and self-identity. *Extrinsic career success* is defined as career outcomes that have instrumental value to the individual because they are likely to help the individual achieve further career or life goals. Extrinsic career achievements are therefore only indirectly related to the satisfaction of psychological needs and end-state values. The intrinsic–extrinsic is a distinction that has been central to many career theories including theories of the boundaryless career (Arthur, 1994), the Kaleidescope career (Mainiero & Sullivan, 2005), and other conceptualizations of career success (Abele & Wiese, 2008; Heslin, 2005; Sturges, 1999).

The second dimension that forms the basis of our typology is the subjective–objective distinction. This dimension recognizes that some career achievements are relatively objective, concrete, clearly observable, and verifiable whereas other career achievements

Table 14.1. Definition of career success.

Quadrant	Description
I. Extrinsic and Objective	This quadrant focuses on career outcomes that have external visibility, have instrumental value, and can be observed. This would include hierarchical rank, number of promotions, job changes, and salary. These types of outcomes can be instrumental in helping individuals achieve more career success or life goals.
II. Extrinsic and Subjective	This quadrant focuses on career outcomes that are externally visible and of instrumental value as judged by oneself or others. Example career outcomes include assessments of promotability and employability, perceived career opportunities, and satisfaction with pay and promotions.
III. Intrinsic and Objective	This quadrant focuses on personally meaningful assessments of career success based on observable or verifiable outcomes. Individuals are able to objectively monitor their career success and compare it to personal aspirations. Recognition, status, power, impact, and influence would be examples of career achievements that hold intrinsic value and can be objectively observed.
IV. Intrinsic and Subjective	This quadrant focuses on career outcomes that are personally meaningful, based on one's own judgments/perceptions. This would include job satisfaction, work–life balance satisfaction, and career satisfaction with job challenge and skill development.

are less easily observed and require subjective judgment regarding their existence, level, or value. The distinction between subjective and objective career success is consistent with other work-related outcomes such as job performance, which can be measured objectively through result-oriented metrics or subjectively by others' judgments/ratings (Aguinis, 2013). *Subjective career success* refers to career outcomes that require perceptions, judgments, or evaluations about your success; these may be your own judgments or the judgments of others, but refer to outcomes that involve inherent ambiguity or uncertainty regarding their value. *Objective career success* is defined as the observable or verifiable outcomes

an individual has achieved; others should be able to readily agree that the career outcome has been achieved and the relative level of the achievement is clear and unambiguous. By crossing the two dimensions, four types of career success outcomes can be identified. In Figure 14.1, we provide an example of career outcomes for each type of career success.

We do not mean to imply by the presentation of this typology that the career outcomes across the quadrants are independent of each other. Indeed, many theoretical perspectives recognize that objective career success positively impacts subjective career success (Gunz & Heslin, 2005) and research has demonstrated that the corrected correlations between salary and career satisfaction and promotion and career satisfaction were .30 and .22, respectively (Ng et al., 2005). For example, extrinsic outcomes such as salary can be used to meet basic physical needs, which in turn provide psychological satisfactions. The value of extrinsic outcomes can also be internalized by the individual (Deci & Ryan, 1985), impacting the individual's feeling of satisfaction or self-worth. Thus, we would expect the various career outcomes to be relayed along a continuous dimension rather than being purely typological, to vary in their placement somewhat across individuals, and to be correlated with each other in practice.

Review of Research on Leader–Member Exchange and Career Outcomes

In this section we review the research linking LMX to career success and mobility, organized in terms of our typology. Table 14.2 provides a summary of each article included in our review.

Extrinsic and Objective Career Outcomes

This quadrant captures observable outcomes that have extrinsic value. Our review includes the research linking LMX to salary, promotions, and turnover. We include turnover in this criterion space because interorganizational job changes usually come with pay increases (Gomez-Mejia & Balkin, 1992).

Tournament theory (Rosenbaum, 1979) and the role-making process of LMX theory (Graen & Uhl-Bien, 1995) have provided theoretical explanations for why LMX may positively relate to salary and promotions. As previously described from the tournament theory perspective, LMX is a form of sponsored-mobility in which leaders provide their high LMX members with support and guidance. Thus, followers with high-quality relationships

	Extrinsic	**Intrinsic**
Objective	• Salary • Promotions • Hierarchical level • Job changes (Turnover) I	• Recognition and Awards • Status and Reputation • Power and Impact III
Subjective	• Assessment of promotability • Career satisfaction–pay and advancement • Perceived career opportunities • Perceived employability II	• Career satisfaction–job challenge and skill development • Satisfaction with work-life balance • Job satisfaction IV

Fig. 14.1 Typology of career success outcomes.

with their supervisors will receive career benefits that help them obtain promotions and larger pay increases (Wayne et al., 1999). Scandura and Schriesheim (1994), however, argue LMX is more akin to a transactional exchange relationship and only if the leader provides career mentoring (i.e., visibility, exposure, and challenging assignments) will a follower obtain such benefits. Scandura and Schriesheim (1994) demonstrated that LMX and supervisor career mentoring are empirically distinct constructs. Consistent with their argument that LMX is a transactional relationship, they found that neither member-rated nor supervisor-rated LMX predicted salary growth rate or promotions, but supervisory career mentoring did predict both career outcomes. In their study, salary growth rate was measured as the employees' inflation-adjusted current salary minus starting salary divided by company tenure. In comparison, Wayne and colleagues (1999) found that member-rated LMX, but not supervisory mentoring, positively related to salary increases 18 months later among a sample of technical and professional staff in a U.S-based company. Yet, Byrne and colleagues (2008) found that neither LMX nor supervisor career mentoring predicted current salary (obtained from company records); Morrow and colleagues (2005) also found that LMX was not correlated with current pay in a sample of truck drivers. One possible explanation for the differing results is the time frame studied. Scandura and Schriesheim (1994) asked employees

to report current LMX and supervisory mentoring and used that to predict changes in salary since starting at the company. Byrne and colleagues (2008) similarly had cross-sectional data such that employees' current LMX and supervisory mentoring predicted current salary, not taking into account salary growth over time. Wayne and colleagues (1999) used current reports of LMX and supervisory career mentoring to predict *future* changes in salary over a short period of time. So, it is possible that career mentoring impacts changes in salary and promotion rates over a longer period of time, whereas the quality of the supervisory relationship impacts more short-term, immediate outcomes such as performance ratings and merit-based pay raises. A study (Schaubroeck & Lam, 2002) that specifically examined how LMX influenced future promotion decisions, which is presumably coupled with a pay raise, further supports this contention.

Specifically, with a sample of U.S. and Hong Kong bank tellers in the same multinational bank, Schaubroeck and Lam (2002) examined several factors, including LMX, to predict whether the bank teller was promoted to the next level 2 months later. Promotion decisions were made at the same time in all bank branches and considered all bank tellers who had been in that position for at least 2 years. Their results found that teller's reports of LMX positively related to whether the bank teller was promoted, controlling for supervisor–subordinate personality similarity and quality of communication with the

Table 14.2. Summary of Articles Examining LMX and Career Outcomes.

Citation	Career Outcome	LMX Source	Research Design	Theory/Perspective	Key Findings
Ballinger, G. A., Lehman, D. W., & Schoorman, F. D. (2010). Leader-member exchange and turnover before and after succession events. *Organizational Behavior and Human Decision Processes, 113,* 25–36.	Turnover	Member	Time-lagged (21 months)	LMX theory; job embeddedness theory	Following a succession event, individuals with high-quality LMX relationships with their former leaders were more likely to leave than individuals with low-quality LMX relationships with their former leaders. When there was no succession event, members with high-quality LMX relationships were less likely to turnover than individuals with low-quality LMX relationships.
Bauer, T. N., Erdogan, B., Liden, R. C., & Wayne, S. J. (2006). A longitudinal study of the moderating role of extraversion: Leader-member exchange, performance, and turnover during new executive development. *Journal of Applied Psychology, 91*(2), 298–310.	Turnover, status	Member	Time-lagged (3.5 months)	LMX theory; job embeddedness theory	LMX was negatively related to turnover when individuals were low in extraversion. When individuals were high in extraversion, LMX was not related to turnover.
Breland, J. W., Treadway, D. C., Duke, A. B., & Adams, G. L (2007). The interactive effect of leader-member exchange and political skill on subjective career success. *Journal of Leadership & Organizational Studies, 13*(3), 1–14.	Career satisfaction (subjective career success)	Member	Cross-sectional	LMX theory; social capital theory	LMX was positively related to subjective career success only when employees were low in political skill.
Byrne, Z. S., Dik, B. J., & Chiaburu, D. S. (2008). Alternatives to traditional mentoring in fostering career success. *Journal of Vocational Behavior, 72*(3), 429–442.	Salary, promotions, career satisfaction, perceived career opportunities (PCO; called organizational career satisfaction), peer respect, job satisfaction	Member	Cross-sectional	LMX theory	LMX was positively related to career satisfaction. Supervisory mentoring was positively related to PCO. LMX was positively related to self-reports of being respected by peers. LMX was more strongly related to career satisfaction when individuals were low in proactive personality.

Citation	Variables	Source	Study type	Theory	Findings
Carlson, D. S., & Perrewe, P. L. (1999). The role of social support in the stressor-strain relationship: An examination of work-family conflict. *Journal of Management, 25*(4), 513–540.	Assessment of promotability	Leader	Member and supervisor responses	Impression management social information processing theory	LMX was significantly positively correlated with assessment of promotability (not the primary focus of the study).
DeConinck, J. B. (2009). The effect of leader-member exchange on turnover among retail buyers. *Journal of Business Research, 62,* 1081–1086.	Turnover, career satisfaction—pay and advancement	Member	Time-lagged (1 year)	LMX theory; job characteristics model	Supervisor satisfaction, pay raise satisfaction, organizational commitment, and withdrawal cognitions mediated the negative relationship between LMX and turnover.
Dulebohn, J. H., Bommer, W. H., Liden, R. C., Brouer, R L., & Ferris, G. R. (2012). A meta-analysis of antecedents and consequences of leader-member exchange: Integrating the past with an eye toward the future. *Journal of Management, 38,* 1715–1759.	Turnover, career satisfaction—pay, psychological empowerment (related to power and impact) job satisfaction	Member	Meta-analysis	LMX theory	LMX had a significant negative relationship with turnover ($\rho = -.17$). LMX had a significant positive relationships with satisfaction with pay $\rho = .27$), empowerment ($\rho = .67$), and job satisfaction ($\rho = .49$).
Erdogan, B., Kraimer, M. L., & Liden, R. C. (2004). Work value congruence and intrinsic career success: The compensatory roles of leader-member exchange and perceived organizational support. *Personnel Psychology, 57,* 305–332.	Career satisfaction, job satisfaction	Member	Cross-sectional	LMX theory; "leader as substitute"	Employee–organization work value congruence was positively related to career satisfaction only when LMX was low. When LMX was high, career satisfaction was high regardless of the level of work value congruence.
Gerstner, C. R., & Day, D. V. (1997). Meta-analytic review of leader-member exchange theory correlates and construct issues. *Journal of Applied Psychology, 82*(6), 827–844.	Turnover, job satisfaction	Not specified in the turnover and job satisfaction analyses	Meta-analysis	LMX theory	LMX was not significantly related to turnover (corrected $r = -.04$). LMX was significantly related to job satisfaction (corrected $r = .50$).
Han, G. (2009). Trust and career satisfaction: The role of LMX. *Career Development International, 15*(5), 437–458.	Career satisfaction	Member	Cross-sectional	LMX theory; social capital theory	LMX mediated the positive relationship between trust in peers and career satisfaction.

(*continued*)

Table 14.2. Continued

Citation	Career Outcome	LMX Source	Research Design	Theory/Perspective	Key Findings
Harris, K. J., Kacmar, K. M., & Carlson, D. S. (2006). An examination of temporal variables and relationship quality on promotability ratings. *Group & Organization Management, 31*, 677–699.	Assessment of promotability	Member	Member and supervisor responses	Role-making theory; dyadic-exchange theory	Longer organizational and leader–follower tenure strengthened the relationship between LMX and assessments of promotability.
Harris, K. J., Wheeler, A. R, & Kacmar, K. M. (2011). The mediating role of organizational job embeddedness in the LMX- outcome relationships. *The Leadership Quarterly, 22*, 271–281.	Turnover	Member	Time-lagged (1 year)	Conservation of resources theory; LMX theory; job embeddedness theory	Job embeddedness mediated the negative relationship between LMX and turnover.
Joo, B., & Ready, K. J. (2012). Career satisfaction: The influences of proactive personality, performance goal orientation, organizational learning culture, and leader–member exchange quality. *Career Development International, 17*(3), 276–295.	Career satisfaction	Member	Cross-sectional	LMX theory; "leader as substitute"	Individual performance goal orientation was positively related to career satisfaction only among individuals who were low in LMX.
Kailasapathy, P., Kraimer, M. L., & Metz, L. (2014). The interactive effects of leader–member exchange, gender and spouse's gender role orientation on work interference with family conflict. *The International Journal of Human Resource Management, 25*(19), 2681–2701.	Work interference with family conflict	Member	Employee and spouse responses	Social support theory; gender role orientation theory; gender role theory; LMX theory	LMX was negatively related to work interference with family. When female employees had spouses with egalitarian gender role orientation, LMX had a positive relationship with work interference with family conflict.
Kraimer, M. L., Seibert, S. E., Wayne, S. J., Liden, R. C., & Bravo, J. (2011). Antecedents and outcomes of organizational support for development: The critical role of career opportunities *Journal of Applied Psychology, 96*(3), 485–500.	Turnover, perceived career opportunities, perceived employability, job satisfaction	Member	Time-lagged (1 year)	Career motivation theory; social exchange theory	LMX was positively related to PCO and job satisfaction (not the primary purpose of the study). LMX was not significantly related to perceived external job alternatives (also not a focus of the study).

Reference	Outcome	Source	Design	Theory	Findings
Law, K. S., Wong, C-S., Wang, D., & Wang, L. (2000). Effect of supervisor-subordinate guanxi on supervisory decisions in China: An empirical investigation. *International Journal of Human Resource Management, 11*(4), 751–765.	Assessment of promotability	Member	Member and supervisor responses	LMX theory; *guanxi*	LMX is distinct from leader–member *guanxi*. LMX did not relate to promotability when examining *guanxi* and LMX together. LMX was positively correlated with promotability.
Liao, S-H., Hu, D-C., & Chung, H-Y. (2009). The relationship between leader-member relations, job satisfaction and organizational commitment in international tourist hotels in Taiwan. *The International Journal of Human Resource Management, 20*(8), 1810–1826.	Career satisfaction—pay and advancement (called job satisfaction)	Member	Cross-sectional	Social exchange theory	LMX was positively related to satisfaction with pay and promotions.
Major, D. A., Fletcher, T. D., Davis, D. D., & Germano, L. M. (2008). The influence of work-family culture and workplace relationships on work interference with family: A multilevel model. *Journal of Organizational Behavior, 29*(7), 881–897.	Work interference with family conflict	Member	Cross-sectional	LMX theory	LMX was negatively related to work interference with family conflict. LMX mediated the relationship between work-family culture and work interference with family. Co-worker support also mediated the negative relationship between LMX and work interference with family.
Morrow, P. C., Suzuki, Y., Crum, M. R., Ruben, R., & Pautsch, G. (2005). The role of leader-member exchange in high turnover work environments. *Journal of Managerial Psychology, 20*(8), 681–693.	Salary, turnover	Member	Time-lagged (1 year)	LMX theory; job embeddedness theory	LMX was not correlated with pay. LMX had a nonlinear relationship with turnover. Turnover was lowest when LMX was moderate. Turnover was highest at lower and higher levels of LMX.
Nishii, L. H., & Mayer, D. M. (2009). Do inclusive leaders help to reduce turnover in diverse groups? The moderating role of leader-member exchange in the diversity to turnover relationship. *Journal of Applied Psychology, 94*(6), 1412–1426.	Group turnover	Member (aggregated to create group mean LMX)	Time-lagged (turnover rates were calculated each month for 7 months)	LMX theory; social categorization theory	When the group mean of LMX was high or the group differentiation on LMX was low, the relationships between group diversity and group turnover, as well as tenure diversity and group turnover, were attenuated.
Scandura, T. A., & Schriesheim, C. A. (1994). Leader-member exchange and supervisor career mentoring as complementary constructs in leadership research. *Academy of Management Journal, 37*(5), 1588–1602.	Salary; promotions	Member and leader	Member and supervisor responses	Social exchange theory	LMX and supervisory career mentoring are distinct constructs. Supervisory career mentoring accounted for significant variance beyond LMX for salary and promotion. LMX accounted for significant variance beyond supervisory career mentoring for performance.

(continued)

Table 14.2. Continued

Citation	Career Outcome	LMX Source	Research Design	Theory/Perspective	Key Findings
Schaubroeck, J., & Lam, S. S. K. (2002). How similarity to peers and supervisor influences organizational advancement in different cultures. *Academy of Management Journal, 45*(6), 1120–1136.	Promotions	Member	Time-lagged (2 months)	Social exchange theory	LMX was positively related to whether or not the bank teller was promoted. Supervisor's job performance ratings partially mediated the relationship between LMX and promotion decision. The relationship between LMX and promotion decision was similar in both Hong Kong (collectivistic culture) and U.S. (individualistic culture) samples.
Sherman, K. E., Kennedy, D. M., Woodard, M. S., & McComb, S. A. (2012). Examining the "exchange" in leader-member exchange. *Journal of Leadership & Organizational Studies, 19*, 407–423.	Turnover	Member and leader	Time-lagged (6 months)	LMX theory	When members perceived low LMX and leaders perceived high LMX, member and leader LMX perceptions were positively related to member turnover.
Sparrowe, R. T., & Liden, R. C. (2005). Two routes to influence: Integrating leader-member exchange and social network perspectives. *Administrative Science Quarterly, 50*, 505–535.	Power and impact (influence)	Member	Time-lagged (9 months at site 1; 7 months at site 2; 8 months at site 3)	LMX theory, social network perspective	LMX was positively related to other's ratings of the follower's influence. This relationship was stronger when the leader was highly central in his or her advice network.
Tekleab, A. G., Takeuchi, R., & Taylor, M. S. (2005). Extending the chain of relationships among organizational justice, social exchange, and employee reactions: the role of contract violations. *Academy of Management Journal, 48*(1), 146–157.	Turnover, job satisfaction	Member	Time-lagged (T2: 3 years; T3: additional 3 years)	Social exchange theory	Job satisfaction and turnover intentions mediated the negative relationship between LMX and turnover.
Wayne, S. J., Liden, R. C., Kraimer, M. L., & Graf, J. I. K. (1999). The role of human capital, motivation and supervisor sponsorship in predicting career success. *Journal of Organizational Behavior, 20*, 577–595.	Salary, promotions, career satisfaction	Member	Time-lagged (18 months)	Tournament theory	Limited support for the contest-mobility system and strong support for the sponsored-mobility system. LMX was positively related to salary progression, assessment of promotability, and career satisfaction. Supervisory career mentoring was positively related to promotability.

supervisor. The positive effect of LMX on promotion decisions was partially mediated by supervisors' job performance ratings. Furthermore, the effect of LMX on promotion decisions was equally strong in Hong Kong (collectivistic cultures) and the U.S. (individualistic cultures) work units. This study supports our above contention that LMX is more likely to impact immediate outcomes such as performance ratings in current job, merit-based pay raises, and promotions to the next job level. Unfortunately this study did not include supervisory career mentoring so the two constructs cannot be directly compared.

With regard to organizational changes, a number of studies have examined the relationship between LMX and turnover. Most of this research relies on social exchange theory and the contention that a high-quality LMX relationship will reduce employee turnover. The argument is that employees with high LMX are more likely to receive greater benefits and resources compared to low LMX employees, making it more likely that high LMX employees will stay in the organization due to the sacrifices they would make by leaving. Despite this logical argument, the empirical evidence is quite weak. Gerstner and Day's (1997) meta-analysis found that LMX and turnover are not significantly correlated (Gerstner & Day, 1997) and Dulebohn and colleagues (2012) found a small negative correlation (rho = −.17) based on only nine studies.

Given the weak correlation between LMX and turnover, many studies have investigated potential moderators and mediators. Bauer, Erdogan, Liden, and Wayne (2006) examined follower extraversion as a moderator and found that LMX was negatively related to turnover only among executives who are low in extraversion (i.e., introverted). They suggested that based on job embeddedness theory (Mitchell, Holtom, Lee, Sablynski, & Erez, 2001), introverts will be more dependent on their leaders to establish social relationships with the organization (i.e., "links" in the job embeddedness theory framework). Due to the embedding nature of social links, LMX is more important to turnover decisions for introverts than for extraverts.

Whereas Bauer and colleagues (2006) sought to explain when LMX reduces turnover, two other studies examined potential moderators that explain when LMX will *increase* turnover. Sherman and colleagues (2012) examined member and leader differences in LMX perception as a moderator of the LMX–turnover relationship. They found that when members perceived low LMX, but leaders perceived high LMX, both member's and leader's LMX

perceptions positively related to member's turnover. According to Sherman and colleagues (2012), this may reflect a situation in which the member, who perceives low LMX, is dissatisfied with the job and leader, whereas the leader, who considers the member to be part of his or her ingroup, is providing the member with more job responsibilities and opportunities that the member may not want. As a result, the incongruence in LMX perceptions may facilitate the member's departure from the organization. Ballinger, Lehman, and Schoorman (2010) examined whether leader succession (whether the leader departs the work unit) moderated the LMX–turnover relationship. In a sample of veterinarian workers in which they had access to employee's quit dates, they found that LMX increased the probability of member's turnover (measured 21 months later) by 39% in units in which the leader had departed, compared to when there was no change in leader.

Switching the role of LMX, Nishii and Mayer (2009) examined LMX at the group level as a moderator of demographic diversity and group turnover (the turnover rate within groups). In a sample of grocery store workers in which groups represented store departments, they found that the positive relationship between group diversity and turnover, as well as tenure diversity and turnover, is weaker when the group mean LMX is high. Theoretically, their findings suggest that leaders can help make diverse members feel included and identify with the group, thus reducing the effect of diversity on turnover.

In terms of potential mediators that explain why LMX decreases turnover, several theoretical explanations have been found. Based on job embeddedness theory, Harris and colleagues (2011) examined whether organizational embeddedness (defined in terms of links, sacrifices, and fit; Mitchell et al., 2001) mediated the negative relationship between LMX and turnover 1 year later with a sample of U.S. employees in an automotive dealership. In support of their hypothesis, organizational embeddedness fully mediated the negative relationship between LMX and turnover suggesting that LMX not only provides social links but also provides employees with benefits and resources that would have to be "sacrificed" upon leaving the organization. Based on LMX and social exchange theory, DeConinck (2009) found that LMX indirectly decreased turnover through LMX's positive relationship with pay raise satisfaction, supervisor satisfaction, and organizational commitment. Likewise,

Tekleab, Takeuchi, and Taylor (2005) found that LMX was indirectly related to turnover through its positive relationship with job satisfaction, which in turn was negatively related to turnover intentions and subsequent voluntary turnover.

Finally, Morrow and colleagues (2005), in a sample of truck drivers, examined the curvilinear relationship between LMX and voluntary turnover and found that turnover was lowest when LMX is moderate and turnover was higher when LMX was low or high (i.e., a U-curve relationship between LMX and turnover). This is consistent with findings that LMX sometimes reduces turnover and sometimes increases turnover. Morrow and colleagues (2005) explain this curvilinear effect in terms of push–pull dynamics: low LMX employees are "pushed" out of the organization and high LMX employees are "pulled" out by attractive external opportunities.

In sum, in cross-sectional studies empirical research has provided little support for the ability of LMX to predict the number of promotions in a person's career and current salary. However, the research does suggest that LMX predicts future promotions and pay raises measured at a later point in time. There is also evidence that LMX indirectly reduces turnover through embedding mechanisms and social exchanges. The direction of the relationship between LMX and turnover (positive or negative) also depends on situational factors and member characteristics.

Extrinsic and Subjective Career Outcomes

For this quadrant, we review the research linking LMX to career satisfaction, supervisor's assessments of promotability, and an employee's own perceptions of mobility and career opportunities within the organization. All of these outcomes represent subjective judgments of extrinsic career outcomes. We review career satisfaction under the extrinsic dimension because most studies have used the five-item scale developed by Greenhaus, Parasuraman, and Wormley (1990), which largely taps into extrinsic factors (income, career advancement, and overall "success"); only one item directly asks about an intrinsic factor (skill development). Tournament theory, social capital theory, and "leader as a substitute" perspectives have been explored as potential explanations for why LMX positively relates to career satisfaction.

Wayne and colleagues (1999) frame their study around Rosenbaum's (1984) contest and sponsored mobility model of tournament theory. They considered human capital and motivational variables as representative of the contest mobility system, whereas LMX and mentoring signified the sponsored mobility system. They found strong support for the sponsored mobility system, indicating that employees' relationship quality with supervisors was more important to career satisfaction than was employees' human capital and motivation.

Other authors have conceptualized the LMX–career satisfaction relationship using social capital theory (e.g., Breland et al., 2007; Byrne et al., 2008; Han, 2009). Because leaders are more likely to distribute their limited resources to members who have the strongest LMX relationship (Dansereau, Cashman, & Graen, 1973), high LMX followers will obtain actual and perceived advantages that can help individuals achieve their career goals. Byrne et al. (2008) found that LMX positively related to career satisfaction, controlling for supervisory career mentoring. The positive relationship between LMX and career satisfaction was stronger among employees low in proactive personality, suggesting that such individuals rely more on their leader for career-related resources and support. These findings mirror those reviewed above from Bauer et al. (2006) in which LMX reduced turnover only among introverted employees. Han (2009) examined the relationship between LMX and career satisfaction using a social capital lens. The study indicated that LMX was positively related to career satisfaction, suggesting that individuals in a high-quality exchange relationship will be more likely to gain resources and information from their supervisors that can facilitate the achievement of their career goals.

Breland and colleagues (2007), however, proposed that the social capital benefits of LMX may be less important for politically skilled individuals. Political skill is the ability to understand others and to use such knowledge to influence others to act in a way that enhances your own personal or organizational goals (Ahearn, Ferris, Hochwarter, Douglas, & Ammeter, 2004). Breland and colleagues (2007) argue that politically skilled individuals have larger social networks and thrive in social situations, thus, they have other means to accrue resources and advantages related to career success. As such, LMX will have a weaker relationship with career satisfaction when the follower has high, versus low, political skill. Indeed, Breland and colleagues (2007) found that LMX positively related to subjective career success (measured as a self-evaluation of the individual's career based on any dimensions important to the person) only among employees lower in political skill. This finding is also consistent with the findings of Bauer et al. (2006) and Byrne et al. (2008); LMX is more important to career outcomes among individuals lower in "social skills" such as political skill, extraversion, or proactivity.

From a "leader as substitute" perspective, we found two studies that examined LMX as a potential substitute for unfavorable situations or personal characteristics. Erdogan, Kraimer, and Liden (2004) hypothesized and found that LMX moderates the relationship between work value congruence and career satisfaction. Specifically, they found that employee–organization work value congruence positively related to career satisfaction only when LMX was low; when there was high-quality LMX, career satisfaction was high regardless of the level of work value congruence. Their findings thus suggest that LMX may be a substitute for low work value congruence as a high-quality LMX relationship may provide employees with support or resources even when employee values do not match the values of an organization. These findings are also consistent with the findings of Nishii and Mayer (2009) indicating that LMX moderated the relationship between group diversity and turnover, reviewed above. In terms of an individual characteristic, Joo and Ready (2012) found, in a sample of Korean workers, that LMX moderated the relationship between performance goal orientation and career satisfaction such that an individual's performance goal orientation positively related to career satisfaction only among individuals with low LMX. Individuals with a performance goal orientation are motivated to prove their ability or avoid negative judgments. Joo and Ready (2012) argue that performance goal-oriented individuals are likely to be more satisfied with their careers because they set lower career goals for themselves. However, another explanation may be that low LMX matches the employees' performance goal orientation. Thus, it is the congruence between the situation and the employees' performance-prove goal that leads to greater career satisfaction.

With regard to more specific aspects of career satisfaction, Dulebohn and colleagues (2012) argued that LMX should be positively related to pay satisfaction because high-quality LMX provides the member with more support, interaction, and rewards (e.g., sponsorship), which can translate into higher pay. Indeed, their meta-analysis of eight studies found a corrected correlation coefficient of .27 between LMX and pay satisfaction. Likewise, Liao, Hu, and Chung (2009) found that LMX positively related to satisfaction with pay and promotions in a sample of Taiwanese hotel workers.

Moving on to promotability, we found three studies that examined LMX and assessments of promotability. Based on the sponsored-mobility norm of tournament theory, Wayne and colleagues (1999) found that LMX was positively related to the supervisor's ratings of the follower's promotability, controlling for human capital (organization and job tenure, education, and training) and motivation variables (hours worked and desire for upward mobility) (Wayne et al., 1999). Harris, Kacmar, and Carlson (2006) extend this finding by demonstrating that organizational tenure and leader–follower relationship tenure moderate the LMX and promotability assessment relationship. Specifically, they found that this relationship is stronger when relationship tenure or organizational tenure is longer, compared to shorter tenures. Their findings point to the role of time in the leader–follower role-making process: the longer an individual is in a high-quality LMX relationship the more benefits she or he has received and thus the more likely she or he will be perceived as promotable. Lastly, in a sample of Chinese workers, Law, Wong, Wang, and Wang (2000) found that LMX was distinct from leader–member "*guanxi*" and that although LMX was positively correlated with the leader's ratings of the follower's promotability, LMX did not relate to promotability when examining *guanxi* and LMX simultaneously. Thus, the role of LMX in predicting promotability assessments may be culturally dependent.

Finally, two studies have examined the relationship between LMX and perceived career opportunities in the organization: Byrne and colleagues (2008) found that LMX did not predict satisfaction with career opportunities in the organization. However, Kraimer and colleagues (2011) found that LMX positively correlated with perceived career opportunities in the organization ($r = .20, p < .01$), although this relationship was not the focus of the study. The moderately weak relationship in the latter study combined with the nonsignificant relationship in the former study suggest that there may be moderators that enhance or attenuate whether LMX relates to followers' perceptions of career opportunities. Such moderators may include career self-management activities, mentoring received from other senior managers, and individual differences such as political skill or proactive personality.

Overall, the empirical evidence provides support for a positive relationship between LMX and career satisfaction, although the strength of this relationship may depend on an employee's personal characteristics. The research also supports a positive relationship between LMX and the leader's assessment of the member's promotability, although other leadership constructs may be more important than LMX in non-U.S. cultures. The two studies that examined employees' perceptions of career opportunities in relation to LMX provide initial support for examining moderators of this relationship.

Intrinsic and Objective Career Outcomes

In this quadrant we examine objectively observable career outcomes, but outcomes that have primarily intrinsic meaning and value to the individual. The outcomes categorized in this quadrant include informal status, reputation, perceived power, and impact. The sponsorship mobility norm provides a theoretical explanation for why employees in a high-quality LMX relationship may obtain greater status, reputation, and power. When a follower is a member of a strong LMX relationship and the leader sponsors the individual by introducing him or her to the leader's contacts or promoting him or her to others in the organization, then the follower will be perceived to have more influence and status. Empirically, we found only two studies that examined an outcome reflecting an individual's status. Byrne and colleagues (2008) found that followers' LMX quality was positively related to their self-report of being respected by peers, controlling for human capital variables (e.g., education, tenure, and training received) and the amount of supervisory mentoring received. These findings suggest that it is the quality of the relationship itself, and not just the leader's career support, that provides employees with perceived reputational advantages. Sparrowe and Liden (2005) propose that the quality of the relationship matters because of the high level of mutual dependence and power that emerges in high-quality leader–member relationships. In particular, followers with high LMX have greater influence over others because they actually have more access to valuable resources and are perceived by others to have greater access to the leader's expertise, influence, or power. Thus, high LMX followers can trade on these actual and perceived advantages. Using a social network approach, Sparrowe and Liden (2005) indeed found that LMX was positively related to other's ratings of the follower's influence, and that this relationship was stronger when the leader was highly central in his or her advice network.

Related to power and impact, a few studies have examined the correlation between LMX and psychological empowerment. Psychological empowerment is defined as employees' cognitions about the meaning of their work, their competence in performing the job, and the amount of self-determination and impact they have. The support, increased responsibility, decision-making input, and access to information that leaders provide to their high LMX followers should increase those followers' psychological empowerment. Indeed, Dulebohn and colleagues' (2012) meta-analysis of 11 studies found a corrected correlation coefficient of .67 between LMX and psychological empowerment.

Overall, initial evidence suggests that LMX quality provides followers with reputational advantages and influence. However, this is based on only two studies; more research is needed that examines when and how LMX relates to the follower's influence, status, or reputation. Although the positive relationship between psychological empowerment and LMX is well established, we do not know whether LMX relates to others' perceptions of the follower's power within the organization.

Intrinsic and Subjective Career Outcomes

This quadrant includes satisfaction with intrinsic factors such as your job, work–life balance, and skill development. Theoretically, we expect LMX to be positively associated with these intrinsic outcomes because members with high-quality LMX relationships are more likely to be assigned challenging tasks, receive performance feedback, and be provided with emotional and instrumental support (Dienesch & Liden, 1986; Liden, Sparrowe, & Wayne, 1997). More challenging jobs, social support, and feedback allow employees to develop more skills and have more enriched jobs, both of which are related to job satisfaction (Hackman & Oldham, 1980). Emotional and instrumental support from the leader can also help the employee better balance work and family demands (Carlson & Perrewe, 1999; Dienesch & Liden, 1986). Consistent with this theorizing, meta-analyses have demonstrated that LMX is positively associated with general job satisfaction (Dulebohn et al., 2012; Gerstner & Day, 1997). In particular, Dulebohn and colleagues (2012) reported a corrected correlation coefficient of .49 between LMX and job satisfaction in a meta-analysis of 88 studies, demonstrating the strong positive association between these two constructs.

The research relating LMX to work–family balance is much more limited. We found only two studies on this topic and both examined work–family conflict as the outcome, specifically work interference with family (WIF) conflict. In a sample of U.S. workers, Major and colleagues (2008) found that LMX negatively related to WIF conflict and Kailasapathy, Kraimer, and Metz (2014) replicated this negative correlation in a sample of Sri Lankan workers. However, this latter study also had a three-way interaction such that LMX *increased* WIF conflict for a subset of their sample: female employees who had spouses with an egalitarian gender role orientation (i.e., believe men and women should share work and household responsibilities) (Kailasapthy et al., 2014). They explain this nonintuitive finding by suggesting that women may feel obligated to reciprocate high-quality LMX by working more hours than they desire, and their spouses' nontraditional gender views facilitate this action because the spouse helps with house and child care duties. This may be especially true in a high power distance and masculine culture such as Sri Lanka in which female employees show respect and deference to their (male) supervisors. This study suggests the need to further examine LMX and work–family balance (conflict) across different cultures. We also refer the readers to the chapter in this handbook on LMX and work–life balance (Sonnentag, Chapter 11) for further insights into how LMX helps or hinders employees' work–life balance.

Finally, our review of the literature did not reveal any studies that specifically measure satisfaction with skill development as an outcome of LMX.

Future Research Directions and Practical Implications

A number of outstanding theoretical issues remain to be resolved regarding the relationship between LMX and career success and mobility. Our review identified a number of theoretical perspectives we encourage researchers to consider: tournament theory, job embeddedness theory, and conservation of resources theory. We then provide practical implications for individuals and leaders before concluding our chapter.

Theoretical Directions for Future Research

Tournament theory (Rosenbaum, 1984), although a convenient framework for understanding various factors related to career progress, does not neatly accommodate LMX. High-quality LMX relationships may be based upon similarity-liking and thus represent a kind of social sponsorship unrelated to merit, or it may arise from the leader's perception that the follower is a dependable, trustworthy, and high performing subordinate, reflecting merit (Liden et al., 1993). In this sense, it is not clear whether high LMX with your leaders better fits the sponsored-mobility or the contest-mobility norm described by Turner (1960). In addition, without considering the leaders' LMX with other members of the work group, it is not possible to determine whether a leader is truly sponsoring *select* members. Selected sponsorship is a primary assumption of the sponsored-mobility norm (Rosenbaum, 1984). Recent work focusing on relative LMX as a driver of employee attitudes and outcomes (Vidyarthi, Liden, Anand, Erdogan, & Ghosh, 2010) may be well suited for the examination of mobility contests or tournaments. This is because the relative standing of a follower within the group captures the type of competition for limited rewards such as pay and promotion that are the focus of tournament theory. We therefore encourage future researchers to examine member's relative LMX within the group, along with member's job performance, as predictors of career outcomes.

Job embeddedness (Mitchell et al., 2001) is another theory that offers promise for greater theoretical understanding of how LMX impacts members' turnover decisions. Theoretically and empirically, researchers have suggested that LMX creates social links that would be sacrificed should the follower leave the job or organization (Bauer et al., 2006; Harris et al., 2011), one of the dimensions of job embeddedness. If the loss of your current LMX relationship with your supervisor is viewed as a sacrifice, perceptions of the quality of future LMX relationships at a new job may be an important compensatory gain. In particular, LMX may be a weak embedding mechanism because it is probable that the leader may eventually leave that work group through either an internal promotion or organizational exit (e.g., Ballinger et al., 2010). It is also possible that followers who are seeking outside opportunities may develop expectations of how well they will work with the new leader and the opportunities that leader may provide them during the recruitment process. Thus, your current LMX may not be enough to retain an employee when that employee believes she or he will also have a high LMX at the next organization. Future research is needed to determine whether individuals consider potential LMX quality during the recruitment process and whether they compare potential LMX at another organization to their LMX in their current job as part of the turnover decision process.

Alternatively, LMX may embed followers by facilitating the creation of additional social links or social capital for them (Bauer et al., 2006; Sparrowe & Liden, 1997). Sparrowe and Liden (1997) provide the theoretical basis, explaining the association between LMX and follower social capital. According to Sparrowe and Liden (1997), a high-quality LMX relationship with your leader may prompt the leader to integrate a follower into his or her presumably more extensive network of relationships, facilitating a more extensive and influential network for the follower. Sparrowe and Liden (2005) provided empirical evidence supporting this perspective, showing that followers' networks lead them to have more influence in the organization when followers shared trust ties with their leader, but only when the leader was also central in the organization's network. Because the follower's social network is more likely to include senior colleagues when it is shared with their leader, we would argue that sponsorship networks of this type can also be viewed as a developmental network (Higgins & Kram, 2001). Developmental network characteristics have been associated with career advancement (Seibert, Kraimer, & Liden, 2001) and might be used as a mediator to explain why LMX should be associated with positive career outcomes. However, a moderating relationship also appears to be present in the literature. Consistent results suggest that LMX is a more important source of support or social capital among individuals lower in "social skills" or initiative such as political skill, extraversion, or proactivity (Bauer et al., 2006; Breland et al., 2007; Byrne et al., 2008). Thus, based on social network theories and the developmental network perspective (Higgins & Kram, 2001; Seibert et al., 2001), we encourage future researchers to examine the specific types of social links (or networks) that members gain through LMX relationships and when they may or may not lead to desirable career outcomes.

Building on the embeddedness perspective, recent developments in conservation of resources (COR) theory (Halbesleben, Neveu, Paustian-Underdahl, & Westman, 2014) might provide a useful lens for understanding when employees may see LMX as a valuable resource they wish to conserve. According to COR theory, LMX may be a social support type of resource in and of itself, if the high-quality supervisor relationship helps the member meet his or her own self-defined and self-set goals. In our context, career goals are the goals of interest. In addition, LMX may provide the means for an employee to gain other constructive resources, such as opportunities for professional development, which may help him or her achieve other career goals. Thus, employees with high LMX relationships may come to view that relationship as a valuable resource. From this perspective then, research is needed to examine which other types of resources or other organizational benefits may explain or compensate for the LMX resource or lack of resource. For example, perceived career opportunities may act as a mediator of the LMX–career outcome relationship, explaining why the loss of LMX may be viewed as a sacrifice (Mitchell et al., 2001, identified career opportunities as specific organizational sacrifice that embeds employees in the organization). Alternatively, perceived career opportunities could be a moderator of the LMX to turnover relationship, explaining when LMX will be more valued (e.g., Kraimer et al., 2011). Halbesleben and colleagues (2014) review a range of resources that could be integrated with LMX theory to better understand when and how LMX relates to the achievement of career goals.

In terms of the LMX construct itself, it seems necessary to conduct further research to distinguish LMX from other supervisor behaviors such as coaching or career mentoring. Scandura and Schriesheim (1994) found that supervisors distinguished between LMX and career mentoring toward a specific member, but members did *not* distinguish between their LMX quality and the career mentoring received from the supervisor. This means that leaders make a distinction between providing career advice, coaching, and personal career support to the employee (the career mentoring scale items in their study) and showing confidence in, trust in, and having a good working relationship with the employee (LMX scale items). Furthermore, it may be that leaders are selecting only certain employees to sponsor in terms of career mentoring; indeed, Scandura and Schriesheim (1994) had a much lower mean score for supervisor career mentoring than supervisor LMX. In addition, as their study demonstrated, it may be the career mentoring aspects of the relationship, and not necessarily the quality of the relationship itself, that accounts for members' enhanced career outcomes. Members, however, seem to consider the amount of career advice and sponsorship when evaluating the LMX quality; perhaps these career functions are captured in the trust and respect dimensions of LMX from a member's perspective. The fact that leaders differentiate career mentoring from LMX and members do not make this distinction may explain why leader ratings and member ratings of the same LMX relationship are only moderately correlated; meta-analyses have found a corrected correlation coefficient of .37 (Gerstner & Day, 1997). Research is clearly needed to further address why leaders and members do not necessarily agree on LMX and which other leader behaviors are captured by measures of LMX quality. Given that the large majority of studies in our review measured LMX from the member's perspective (see Table 14.2 for the source of LMX measure), it is possible that it is actually supervisor career mentoring and coaching behaviors that explain the relationships between LMX and the career outcomes included here.

In terms of specific career outcomes, from Table 14.2 we can see that there are many more studies examining LMX and extrinsic career outcomes than there are studies examining intrinsic career outcomes. For the most part, the studies in our review found that LMX positively relates to the followers' extrinsic outcomes of promotions, the supervisor's assessment of promotability, and career satisfaction with pay and advancement. With regard to the intrinsic career outcomes, the research evidence supports a strong positive relationship between LMX and psychological empowerment (Dulebohn et al., 2012). However, there are few studies linking LMX to power, status, recognition, satisfaction with skill development, and satisfaction with work–life balance. From a COR theory perspective, we suggest that the intrinsic, objective outcomes (e.g., recognition, status, and power) may provide theoretical explanations for why LMX relates to the extrinsic career outcomes. In turn, consistent with intrinsic motivation theories (Deci & Ryan, 1985), extrinsic career outcomes may impact intrinsic, subjective career outcomes (satisfaction with skill development and work–life balance). We encourage future research to test such mediated models with time-lagged data if possible.

Practical Implications

Based on our review, we offer a number of practical implications for individuals and leaders. For individuals, our review suggests that a high-quality LMX relationship can be one important resource for achieving intrinsic and extrinsic career goals, especially promotions and salary raises within the same job or organization. Thus, it is in individuals' career interest to form high-quality exchange relationships with their supervisors. Research on

antecedents to LMX suggests that individuals who fulfill role expectations through high job performance and are more similar to their supervisors are more likely to have high LMX (Liden et al., 1993). LMX quality was more important to several career outcomes among individuals low on extraversion, political skill, or proactivity. Thus, individuals who are uncomfortable in social situations might instead focus on forming a high-quality relationship with their immediate supervisor based on their performance and dependability. Leaders should in turn exert extra effort to form high-quality LMX relationships with such followers, incorporating them into their networks and embedding them into the organization. Indeed, it seems that a high-quality LMX relationship with a socially adepted follower is "wasted effort," at least in terms of producing improved career outcomes. But for less socially adepted followers, leaders can be an important social link to the other members of the organization that allow them to become more embedded.

Although LMX positively relates to employees' job and career satisfaction, our review suggests that leaders may not be the most effective embedding mechanism when retention is the primary concern. The relationship between LMX and followers' voluntary turnover is weak. Thus, when retention is the goal, organizations should focus on other embedding mechanisms such as creating opportunities for employees to develop broader social links beyond their immediate work group, and offering broader organizational sacrifices such as a work–life balance supportive culture or many career opportunities. Furthermore, research demonstrated that high LMX may actually prompt members to quit when their leaders leave the organization or work unit (Ballinger et al., 2010). Thus, whenever a manager with supervisory responsibilities leaves the work unit, organizations should meet with the members of that work group to discuss succession issues and show that the organization values those members. Such special attention and effort toward the work group members may help decrease their desire to leave as well.

Conclusions

In this chapter, we provided a review of the theory and research linking LMX to a range of career outcomes. In doing so, we offered a typology to clarify and distinguish the large number of career outcomes that have been examined in the careers literature. Overall, our review demonstrates that LMX positively relates to subjective measures of both intrinsic and extrinsic career success, but the results with respect to objective measures of intrinsic and extrinsic career success is less consistent, weaker, or more qualified by moderators. We hope that our suggestions for future research will prompt further investigations into the role of LMX in explaining career success and satisfaction.

References

Abele, A. E., & Wiese, B. (2008). The nomological network of self-management strategies and career success. *Journal of Occupational and Organizational Psychology, 73*, 490–497.

Aguinis, H. (2013). *Performance management* (3rd ed.). Upper Saddle River, NJ: Pearson Prentice Hall.

Ahearn, K. K., Ferris, G. R., Hochwarter, W. A., Douglas, C., & Ammeter, A. P. (2004). Leader political skill and team performance. *Journal of Management, 30*, 309–327.

Arthur, M. B. (1994). The boundaryless career: A new perspective for organizational inquiry. *Journal of Organizational Behavior, 15*, 295–306.

Ballinger, G. A., Lehman, D. W., & Schoorman, F. D. (2010). Leader-member exchange and turnover before and after succession events. *Organizational Behavior and Human Decision Processes, 113*, 25–36.

Bauer, T. N., Erdogan, B., Liden, R. C., & Wayne, S. J. (2006). A longitudinal study of the moderating role of extraversion: Leader-member exchange, performance, and turnover during new executive development. *Journal of Applied Psychology, 91*, 298–310.

Blau, P. M. (1964). *Exchange and power in social life.* New Brunswick, NJ: Transaction Publishers.

Boudreau, J. W., Boswell, W. R., & Judge, T. A. (2001). Effects of personality on executive career success in the United States and Europe. *Journal of Vocational Behavior, 58*, 53–81.

Breland, J. W., Treadway, D. C., Duke, A. B., & Adams, G. L. (2007). The interactive effect of leader-member exchange and political skill on subjective career success. *Journal of Leadership & Organizational Studies, 13*, 1–14.

Byrne, Z. S., Dik, B. J., & Chiaburu, D. S. (2008). Alternatives to traditional mentoring in fostering career success. *Journal of Vocational Behavior, 72*, 429–442.

Carlson, D. S., & Perrewe, P. L. (1999). The role of social support in the stressor-strain relationship: An examination of work-family conflict. *Journal of Management, 25*, 513–540.

Dansereau, F., Cashman, J., & Graen, G. (1973). Instrumentality theory and equity theory as complementary approaches in predicting the relationship of leadership and turnover among managers. *Organizational Behavior and Human Performance, 10*, 184–200.

Dansereau, F., Jr., Graen, G., & Haga, W. J. (1975). A vertical dyad linkage approach to leadership within formal organizations: A longitudinal investigation of the role making process. *Organizational Behavior and Human Performance, 13*, 46–78.

Deci, E. L., & Ryan, R. M. (1985). The general causality orientations scale: Self-determination in personality. *Journal of Research in Personality, 19*, 109–134.

DeConinck, J. B. (2009). The effect of leader-member exchange on turnover among retail buyers. *Journal of Business Research, 62*, 1081–1086.

Dienesch, R. M., & Liden, R. C. (1986). Leader-member exchange model of leadership: A critique and further development. *Academy of Management Review, 11*, 618–634.

Dries, N., Pepermans, R., & Carlier, O. (2008). Career success: Constructing a multidimensional model. *Journal of Vocational Behavior, 7*, 254–267.

Dulebohn, J. H., Bommer, W. H., Liden, R. C., Brouer, R. L., & Ferris, G. R. (2012). A meta-analysis of antecedents and consequences of leader-member exchange: Integrating the past with an eye toward the future. *Journal of Management, 38*, 1715–1759.

Erdogan, B., Kraimer, M. L., & Liden, R. C. (2004). Work value congruence and intrinsic career success: The compensatory roles of leader-member exchange and perceived organizational support. *Personnel Psychology, 57*, 305–332.

Gerstner, C. R., & Day, D. V. (1997). Meta-analytic review of leader-member exchange theory: Correlates and construct issues. *Journal of Applied Psychology, 82*, 827–844.

Gomez-Mejia, L. R., & Balkin, D. B. (1992). Determinants of faculty pay: An agency theory perspective. *Academy of Management Journal, 35*, 921–955.

Graen, G. B., & Scandura, T. A. (1987). Toward a psychology of dyadic organizing. In L. L. Cummings & B. M. Staw (Eds.), *Research in organizational behavior* (Vol. 9, pp. 175–208). Greenwich, CT: JAI Press.

Graen, G. B., & Uhl-Bien, M. (1995). Relationship-based approach to leadership: Development of leader-member exchange (LMX) theory of leadership over 25 years: Applying a multi-level multi-domain perspective. *Leadership Quarterly, 6*, 219–247.

Greenhaus, J. H., Parasuraman, S., & Wormley, W. M. (1990). Effects of race on organizational experiences, job performance evaluations, and career outcomes. *Academy of Management Journal, 33*, 64–86.

Gunz, H. P., & Heslin, P. A. (2005). Reconceptualizing career success. *Journal of Organizational Behavior, 26*, 105–111. doi: 10.1002/job.300

Hackman, J. R., & Oldham, G. R. (1980). *Work redesign.* Reading, MA: Addison-Wesley.

Halbesleben, J. R. B., Neveu, J-P., Paustian-Underdahl, S. C., & Westman, J. (2014). Getting to the "COR": Understanding the role of resources in conservation of resources theory. *Journal of Management, 40*, 1334–1364.

Hall, D. T. (2002). *Careers in and out of organizations.* Thousand Oaks, CA: Sage.

Han, G. (2009). Trust and career satisfaction: The role of LMX. *Career Development International, 15*, 437–458.

Harris, K. J., Kacmar, K. M., & Carlson, D. S. (2006). An examination of temporal variables and relationship quality on promotability ratings. *Group & Organization Management, 31*, 677–699.

Harris, K. J., Wheeler, A. R., & Kacmar, K. M. (2011). The mediating role of organizational job embeddedness in the LMX-outcome relationships. *The Leadership Quarterly, 22*, 271–281.

Heslin, P. A. (2005). Conceptualizing and evaluating career success. *Journal of Organizational Behavior, 26*, 113–136.

Higgins, M. C., & Kram, K. E. (2001). Reconceptualizing mentoring at work: A developmental network perspective. *Academy of Management Review, 26*, 264–268.

Joo, B., & Ready, K. J. (2012). Career satisfaction: The influences of proactive personality, performance goal orientation, organizational learning culture, and leader-member exchange quality. *Career Development International, 17*, 276–295.

Judge, T. A., Cable, D. M., Boudreau, J. W., & Bretz, R. D. (1995). An empirical investigation of the predictors of executive career success. *Personnel Psychology, 48*, 485–519.

Kailasapathy, P., Kraimer, M. L., & Metz, I. (2014). The interactive effects of leader–member exchange, gender and spouse's gender role orientation on work interference with family conflict. *The International Journal of Human Resource Management, 25*, 2681–2701.

Kraimer, M. L., Seibert, S. E., Wayne, S. J., Liden, R. C., & Bravo, J. (2011). Antecedents and outcomes of organizational support for development: The critical role of career opportunities. *Journal of Applied Psychology, 96*, 485–500.

Law, K. S., Wong, C-S., Wang, D., & Wang, L. (2000). Effect of supervisor-subordinate guanxi on supervisory decisions in China: An empirical investigation. *International Journal of Human Resource Management, 11*, 751–765.

Liao, S-H., Hu, D-C., & Chung, H-Y. (2009). The relationship between leader-member relations, job satisfaction and organizational commitment in international tourist hotels in Taiwan. *The International Journal of Human Resource Management, 20*, 1810–1826.

Liden, R. C., & Maslyn, J. M. (1998). Multidimensionality of leader-member exchange: An empirical assessment through scale development. *Journal of Management, 24*, 43–72.

Liden, R. C., Sparrowe, R. T., & Wayne, S. J. (1997). Leader-member exchange theory: The past and potential for the future. *Research in Personnel and Human Resources Management, 15*, 47–119.

Liden, R. C., Wayne, S. J., & Stilwell, D. (1993). A longitudinal study on the early development of leader-member exchanges. *Journal of Applied Psychology, 78*, 662–674.

Mainiero, L. A., & Sullivan, S. E. (2005). Kaleidoscope careers: An alternative explanation for the "opt-out" revolution. *Academy of Management Executive, 19*, 106–123.

Major, D. A., Fletcher, T. D., Davis, D. D., & Germano, L. M. (2008). The influence of work–family culture and workplace relationships on work interference with family: A multilevel model. *Journal of Organizational Behavior, 29*, 881–897.

Mitchell, T. R., Holtom, B. C., Lee, T. W., Sablynski, C. J., & Erez, M. (2001). Why people stay: Using job embeddedness to predict voluntary turnover. *Academy of Management Journal, 44*, 1102–1121.

Morrow, P. C., Suzuki, Y., Crum, M. R., Ruben, R., & Pautsch, G. (2005). The role of leader-member exchange in high turnover work environments. *Journal of Managerial Psychology, 20*, 681–693.

Ng, T. W. H., Eby, L. T., Sorensen, K. L., & Feldman, D. C. (2005). Predictors of objective and subjective career success: A meta-analysis. *Personnel Psychology, 58*, 367–408.

Nishii, L. H., & Mayer, D. M. (2009). Do inclusive leaders help to reduce turnover in diverse groups? The moderating role of leader-member exchange in the diversity to turnover relationship. *Journal of Applied Psychology, 94*, 1412–1426.

Rosenbaum, J. E. (1979). Tournament mobility: Career patterns in a corporation. *Administrative Science Quarterly, 24*, 220–241.

Rosenbaum, J. E. (1984). *Career mobility in a corporate hierarchy.* Orlando, FL: Academic Press.

Scandura, T. A., & Schriesheim, C. A. (1994). Leader-member exchange and supervisor career mentoring as complementary constructs in leadership research. *Academy of Management Journal, 37*, 1588–1602.

Schaubroeck, J., & Lam, S. S. K. (2002). How similarity to peers and supervisor influences organizational advancement in different cultures. *Academy of Management Journal, 45*, 1120–1136.

Seibert, S. E., Kraimer, M. L., Holtom, B. C., & Pierotti, A. J. (2013). Even the best laid plans sometimes go askew: Career self-management processes, career shocks, and the decision to pursue graduate education. *Journal of Applied Psychology, 98*, 169–182.

Seibert, S. E., Kraimer, M. L., & Liden, R. C. (2001). A social capital theory of career success. *Academy of Management Journal, 44*, 219–237.

Sherman, K. E., Kennedy, D. M., Woodard, M. S., & McComb, S. A. (2012). Examining the "exchange" in leader-member exchange. *Journal of Leadership & Organizational Studies, 19*, 407–423. doi: 10.1177/1548051812442963

Sparrowe, R. T., & Liden, R. C. (1997). Process and structure in leader-member exchange. *Academy of Management Review, 22*, 522–552.

Sparrowe, R. T., & Liden, R. C. (2005). Two routes to influence: Integrating leader-member exchange and social network perspectives. *Administrative Science Quarterly, 50*, 505–535.

Sturges, J. (1999). What it means to succeed: Personal conceptions of career success held by male and female managers at different ages. *British Journal of Management, 10*, 239–252.

Tekleab, A. G., Takeuchi, R., & Taylor, M. S. (2005). Extending the chain of relationships among organizational justice, social exchange, and employee reactions: The role of contract violations. *Academy of Management Journal, 48*, 146–157.

Turner, R. J. (1960). Sponsored and contest mobility and the school system. *American Sociological Review, 25*, 855–867.

Vidyarthi, P. R., Liden, R. C., Anand, S., Erdogan, B., & Ghosh, S. (2010). Where do I stand? Examining the effects of leader-member exchange social comparison on employee work behaviors. *Journal of Applied Psychology, 95*, 849–861.

Wayne, S. J., Liden, R. C., Kraimer, M. L., & Graf, I. K. (1999). The role of human capital, motivation and supervisor sponsorship in predicting career success. *Journal of Organizational Behavior, 20*, 577–595.

Wayne, S. J., Shore, L. M., & Liden, R. C. (1997). Perceived organizational support and leader-member exchange: A social exchange perspective. *Academy of Management Journal, 40*, 82–111.

PART 4

LMX Beyond the Dyad

LMX Differentiation: Understanding Relational Leadership at Individual and Group Levels

Smriti Anand, Prajya R. Vidyarthi, *and* Hae Sang Park

Abstract

We review research in the variability in leader–member exchange relationships (LMX), called LMX differentiation, since its conception in LMX research. We examine the relevant theories of social comparison, relative deprivation, and organizational justice to underpin the motives and consequences of LMX differentiation. We also outline the overlap and distinction between these competing theories. We provide a comprehensive narrative of extant theoretical and empirical research that has examined various facets of LMX differentiation. Our detailed review identifies antecedents, moderators, and consequences at the individual level, meso level, and group level of analysis. We also highlight gaps in research to outline criticisms of extant studies. Finally, we provide theoretical directions and ideas for empirical investigation in future research.

Key Words: leadership, LMX, LMX differentiation, individual and group level

Introduction

Leader–member exchange (LMX) theory is rooted in the principle that leaders differentiate between their followers (Liden & Graen, 1980). That is leaders establish high-quality relationships with a few and lower-quality relationships with the rest. Within a group each leader–follower dyad is therefore characterized by a unique quality of exchange such that the entire group covers the continuum from low-quality relationships limited to the terms of the employment contract to high-quality relationships characterized by affect and mutual influence (Gerstner & Day, 1997). It has been suggested by some LMX scholars that this differentiation allows leaders to make effective use of their time and limited resources (Henderson, Liden, Glibkowski, & Chaudhry, 2009; Liden, Erdogan, Wayne, & Sparrowe, 2006).

LMX is a unique theory of leadership in that in contrast to other theories it does not assume followers are passive recipients of leadership. LMX theory proposes that the relationship between a leader and a follower develops over three stages: role making, role taking, and role routinization (Bauer & Green, 1996). Both the leader and the follower actively shape the tenor of this relationship. At the beginning the leader assigns a role to the follower, which he or she chooses to accept or reject (i.e., complete the task well or not). Over a few repeated exchanges both parties adjust their expectations and the relationship quality starts to mature. This entire process happens within the first few days of interactions between a leader and a follower. High-quality exchanges develop with followers who fulfill their assigned roles. The LMX literature attests to the broad array of rewards associated with a high-quality relationship. Followers benefit through enhanced negotiation latitude, trust, respect, autonomy, challenging assignments, and satisfaction with job and manager, whereas the organization benefits through enhanced positive attitudes and behaviors such as organizational commitment, performance, and citizenship behaviors (Dulebohn, Bommer, Liden, Brouer, & Ferris, 2012).

Considering this process in the context of the workgroup, leaders assign challenging tasks to high LMX members because they are more likely to fulfill those duties (Dansereau, Graen, & Haga, 1975). Low LMX members, on the other hand, get more mundane tasks because that is what is expected from them. Differentiation thus may allow leaders to be more effective. Workgroup members are quite aware of the differences in LMX status (Duchon, Graen, & Taber, 1986) and therefore differentiation has significant effects on group dynamics and outcomes for both individual members and the group as a whole.

Though LMX theory has received continued attention from scholars for over 40 years, the bulk of this research has focused on individual follower's outcomes as if the relationship exists in a vacuum. Leadership scholars have noted this omission (e.g., Liden, Sparrowe, & Wayne, 1997) and now there is growing interest in understanding differentiation to explain outcomes of LMX for the individual followers and for the entire group. In this chapter, we review developments in LMX differentiation research since 1995, when the first influential qualitative study by Sias and Jablin appeared. Our review is based on studies cited in social sciences indexes since 1995. Our database searches between 1995 and 2014 showed 31 empirical and conceptual studies with an explicit focus on differentiation in LMX. We do not include any conference papers or unpublished manuscripts. Our review begins with a detailed discussion of primary theoretical perspectives used by scholars to understand differentiation. We focus on three theories: social comparison theory, relative deprivation theory, and organizational justice theory. Then we provide a detailed review of empirical studies exploring the various facets of differentiation. We conclude with a discussion of weaknesses in LMX differentiation research and make recommendations for future researchers. Figure 15.1 depicts the antecedents and consequences of LMX differentiation, and Figure 15.2 represents moderating effects of LMX differentiation.

Theoretical Underpinnings of LMX Differentiation
Social Comparison Theory

Festinger (1954) postulated that all human beings have an innate drive to evaluate themselves by comparing their opinions, abilities, and possessions with similar others. This is especially true in the absence of objective standards for measurement against which individuals can assess themselves. Notably, the fundamental concept of LMX differentiation is also founded on the notion that members compare their LMX with the LMXs of their workgroup peers and thus social comparison theory is the underlying motivation behind LMX differentiation. This is also because LMX is inherently a social exchange relationship, and thereby comparison between LMXs is tantamount to social comparison. Social comparison theory (Festinger, 1954; Wood 1996) also stipulates that individuals compare constantly, i.e., on a day-to-day basis, with relevant others (Goodman, 1977; Greenberg, Ashton-James, & Ashkanasy, 2007). Social comparison theorists maintain that social comparison is inevitable because information accrued from social comparison provides cognition of one's own abilities and skills (Festinger, 1954), possibility of performing tasks well (Goethals & Darley, 1977; Goodman, 1977), and acceptance and respect in the workgroup (Darley, 2004) (cf. Hu & Liden, 2013).

Social comparison includes both conscious effort and subconscious awareness of one's position relative to others. These conscious and subconscious processes are driven by innate biological needs and serve the purpose of evolutionary adaptation, otherwise one's status within a group would remain unknown and undesirable competition within the group would ensue (Beach & Tesser, 2000; Buunk & Mussweiler, 2001; Spence, Ferris, Brown, & Heller, 2011). LMX differentiation is inevitable in a workgroup because, on the one hand, social comparison is indispensable and, on the other hand, LMX is a subjective or perceptual measure of the quality of a relationship. Thus, members rely largely on social comparison for self-evaluation. Workgroup peers are likely referents for making comparisons because they report to the same supervisor, possess similar qualifications and experiences, and are the primary agents of interaction and interdependence (Henderson, Wayne, Shore, Bommer, & Tetrick, 2008; Hu & Liden, 2013; Tse, Ashkanasy, & Dasbrough, 2012). Vidyarthi, Liden, Anand, Erdogan, and Ghosh (2010) drew upon this notion of social comparison to propose LMX social comparison (i.e., LMXSC) as a direct and subjective measure, distinct from LMX and relative LMX (RLMX, defined as one's LMX in comparison to the average level of LMX in the workgroup), and empirically showed that LMXSC explained variance in outcomes beyond the effects of LMX and RLMX.

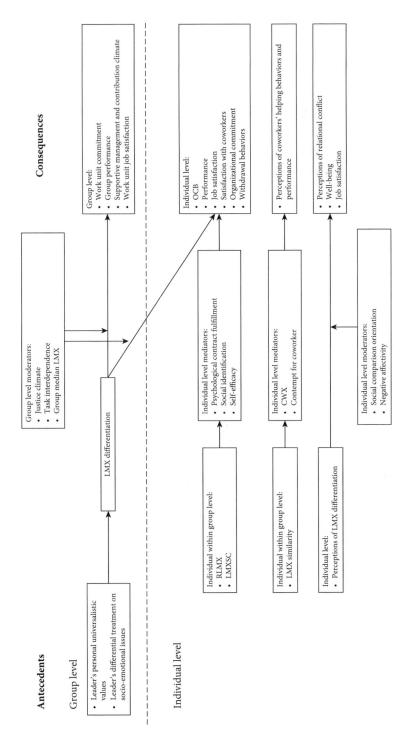

Fig. 15.1 Antecedents, mediators, consequences, and moderators.

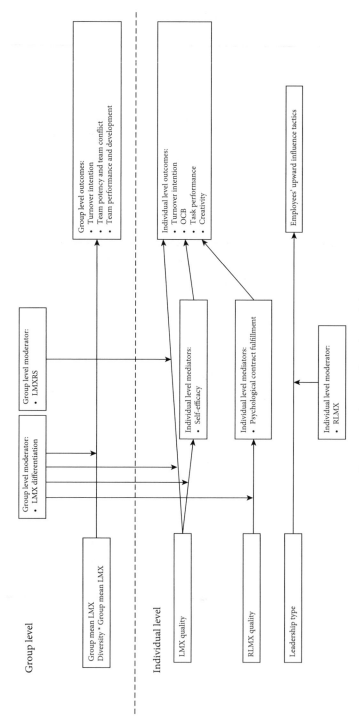

Fig. 15.2 Moderating effects of LMX differentiation.

Because of its wide prevalence social comparison can be viewed as the primary motive or explanatory force behind LMX differentiation in organizational settings. Once the process of social comparison sets in, outcomes may also depend on one's relative standing and fairness versus unfairness attributions. Thus, in addition to social comparison theory, theories of relative deprivation and organizational justice provide a comprehensive framework to explain the outcomes of LMX differentiation.

Relative Deprivation Theory

Relative deprivation is described as a state of tension arising from perceptions of discrepancy between the way things are and the way things ought to be (Crosby, 1976). An individual's judgment of relative deprivation is accompanied by feelings of anger and resentment (Smith, Pettigrew, Pippin, & Bialosiewicz, 2012), which become a conduit to negative individual and social outcomes. Smith et al. (2012) postulated a three-stage process of relative deprivation such that in the first stage a cognitive or social comparison ensues, which leads to the second stage of cognitive appraisal of disadvantage; in the final stage justice and fairness-related attribution is made.

Runciman (1966) outlined preconditions of relative deprivation as someone lacking something that others have and which she or he wants and believes to be attainable. All the preconditions of relative deprivation are likely to be met in a typical leader–member dyad embedded in a workgroup. This is because low LMX members lack high-quality relationships but desire those, for they see high LMX members obtaining greater social and economic rewards. Consequently, Bolino and Turnley (2009) reasoned that LMX differentiation has the downside of relegating low LMX members to develop perceptions of relative deprivation. Because LMX differentiation is a norm rather than an exception, many members may have a lower-quality LMX relationship compared to members on the positive end of LMX differentiation. Employees at the lower end of LMX differentiation thus may become envious of their peers. Low LMX members develop a perception of relative deprivation, which explains their lower attitudes and behaviors. This is consistent with Martin's (1981) postulation that relative deprivation could result in stress and negative attitudes.

Relative deprivation theory can also be used to understand the effects of changes in the nature of LMX over time. Bolino and Turnley (2009) argued that outcomes of relative deprivation may partly depend on employees' hopefulness or frustration regarding how their LMX status may change in the future. Finally, the overlap of relative deprivation theory with social comparison theory and organizational justice theory (described next) is noteworthy. Relative deprivation theory (Crosby, 1976; Martin, 1981; Walker & Smith, 2002) employed in LMX differentiation suggests that members compare their own LMX with those their referents have (i.e., social comparison) and they perceive that their LMX is less than they could or should have (i.e., equity theory). For example, many low LMX members are likely to perceive LMX differentiation as unfair (Lee, 2001; Sias & Jablin, 1995; Vecchio, Griffeth, & Hom, 1986). Similarly, Erdogan and Bauer (2010) extended relative deprivation theory to reason that the relationships between LMX differentiation and employee outcomes are dependent on the justice climate of the workgroup. Despite the similarities and overlaps between relative deprivation theory and theories of organizational justice and social comparison (Festinger, 1954; Greenberg, 1987), relative deprivation theory remains more suited to examine perspectives of low LMX members (Bolino & Turnley, 2009).

Organizational Justice Theory

Adams (1965) stated that individuals seek to maintain proportionality between their inputs and outcomes in reference to comparable others. The application and implication of this principle of justice in work settings is called organizational justice theory (Colquitt, Conlon, Wesson, Porter, & Ng, 2001; Cropanzano & Greenberg, 1997; Greenberg, 1987, 1990). The notion of LMX differentiation, if based on relevant criteria, follows the principle of equity and organizational justice and leads to commensurate outcomes at individual and group levels. Organizational justice theory suggests that members at the higher end of LMX differentiation develop positive attitudes and behaviors compared to their counterparts at the lower end of LMX differentiation. Although the theory of equity sufficiently explains individual-level outcomes, this principle alone may not fully account for relationships at the group level. Because LMX differentiation operates simultaneously at the individual level and the group level, this consideration is vitally important. At the group level, an unequal distribution of resources is likely to violate the norm of equality, even when it follows the principles of equity at the individual level. Although high differentiation may be equitable at the individual level, the same high differentiation may be perceived as unfair from a group perspective. Thus, the nature of the relationships between LMX differentiation and outcomes may differ across these two levels. At the group level, accounting for both equity and equality may be needed to avoid making erroneous propositions and drawing wrong conclusions. Indeed, LMX theorists have proposed that the nature of the relationship at the group level is different from that at the individual level (Boies & Howell, 2006; Henderson et al., 2009; Le Blanc & González-Romá, 2012; Liden et al., 2006).

Within-group variance in LMX quality, also a measure of group LMX differentiation, is an indicator of dispersion or distribution in LMX in the workgroup. This variance in LMX is an indicator of equity such that high variance suggests greater equity in the allocation of LMX resources because more deserving members develop high LMX relationships and unworthy members are relegated to low LMX relationships. On the other hand, low variance in LMX serves the purpose of equality because most members have nearly the same level of LMX. Although this duality may be adequate to explain LMX differentiation outcomes at the individual level, the average or median level of LMX is needed as an additional variable for theorizing group-level relationships. Within-group median LMX (Liden et al., 2006) is an indicator of the average level of LMX in a workgroup. Median and variance are distinct and both are essential to making group-level predictions. This is because even though differentiation in allocating time and energy and in economic and social resources is an effective approach at the individual level, this approach can lead to unintended consequences at the group level as it may defy the sense of equality. Figure 15.3 shows a conceptual mapping of high and low dispersion and group median LMX and their likely cognition at the group level. Indeed, Le Blanc and Gonzalez-Roma (2012) showed that the relationships between LMX differentiation and team outcomes are moderated by median LMX quality. Similarly, Erdogan and Bauer (2010) showed that justice climate buffered the relationship between LMX differentiation and outcomes such that differentiation led to negative outcomes when justice climate was low. Scandura (1999) asserted that LMX differentiation leading to the formation of ingroups and outgroups has implications for organizational justice, and Han and Bai (2012) provided empirical evidence of this effect.

Extant Research on LMX Differentiation

LMX scholars agree that leaders differentiate between their team members, and that members are aware of the extent of such differentiation. It is argued that differentiation allows leaders to create optimal fits between employees and their assignments leading to higher performance for the team (Dansereau et al., 1975). Furthermore, because LMX quality is based on efforts made by both the leader and the follower (Maslyn & Uhl-bien, 2001), differentiation may allow leaders to create equitable relationships with members in line with their investments. Leaders tend to trust high LMX followers, giving them more of a free hand with interesting and challenging tasks. Low LMX members, on the other hand, are likely to receive more specific directions pertaining to routine tasks. Social comparisons between group members can then create perceptions of unfairness, especially when it is not clear why the leader favors some members over others. The rewards innate to a high-quality relationship make the differentiation more salient to low LMX members and are likely to create perceptions of unfairness (Liden et al., 1997). Thus, it is possible

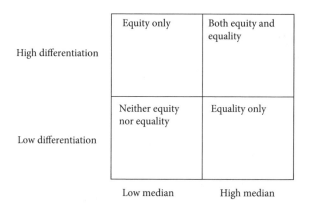

Fig. 15.3 Group level LMX differentiation and average LMX level.

for high LMX to benefit the focal individual, but hurt the overall group by violating the principles of equality (Scandura, 1999). Furthermore, because individuals wish to maintain a balance among their various relationships in the workgroup (Heider, 1958), high LMX individuals are likely to become attracted to each other and split the workgroup into an ingroup and outgroup consisting of those close to the leader (i.e., with similarly high LMX quality) and those remaining at the periphery (i.e., with similarly low LMX quality), respectively. This potential to either enhance team outcomes or to undermine group fairness and harmony makes it imperative that LMX researchers analyze the consequences of LMX differentiation.

For almost 30 years, LMX researchers have focused on individual group member's outcomes. However, as LMX theory matured, scholars began to realize that a lack of understanding of how the theory operates at multiple levels is limiting the theory's influence (House & Aditya, 1997). A number of LMX scholars made the call to conceptualize LMX at multiple levels of theory and analyze it accordingly (e.g., Schriesheim, Castro, & Cogliser, 1999). As a result, interest has grown among LMX researchers in exploring differentiation and understanding how it shapes outcomes for both the individual and the group. LMX differentiation has been studied in three distinct ways. First, differentiation is a within-group dispersion construct, so a number of scholars have operationalized it at the group level by assessing actual variability in LMX quality across workgroups (e.g., Liden et al., 2006). Several others have operationalized it at the individual level by seeking individual follower's perceptions of within-group variability (e.g., Van Breukelen, Konst, & Van Der Vlist, 2002). More recently, scholars have also explored LMX differentiation at the individual within-group level or meso level (Yammarino, Dionne, Chun, & Dansereau, 2005) to assess individuals' relative LMX standing and its consequences (e.g., Henderson et al., 2008). In the following sections we discuss findings from these three streams of LMX differentiation research.

LMX Differentiation at the Individual Level

In one of the earliest investigations of LMX differentiation, Sias and Jablin (1995) explored sensemaking processes and subgroup formation due to differential treatment from the leader. In detailed interviews, the authors found that unless clear evidence of competence is presented, employees considered a co-worker's favored status to be unfair and reduced communication with the favored person. On the other hand, when differentiation was considered to be fair, the favored person actually became a conduit of information between the leader and the rest of the group. Group members also distanced themselves from a disfavored co-worker if they felt that the adverse treatment was based on fair reasons. These findings provided support for earlier conjectures on the potential of differentiation to split the workgroup into an ingroup and an outgroup, which may lead to intragroup relational problems, such as mutual dislike and rejection that are detrimental to the overall group.

Van Breukelen et al. (2002) extended this line of research to a quantitative framework. They found attenuating effects of individual member perceptions of within-group LMX variability on the positive LMX to work unit commitment association, possibly because differential treatment from the leader may have created doubts about the fairness and integrity of the leader and therefore may have neutralized the positive effects of LMX. One drawback of this study is that leader differentiation among group members was assessed only in terms of friendliness and feedback, which means that the study cannot capture variability in other aspects of LMX such as the exchange of economic resources. Next, Hooper and Martin (2008) invoked the principles of equality and the consistency of justice theory to propose negative consequences of individual perceptions of LMX differentiation after controlling for individual LMX quality. They found that LMX differentiation created feelings of relational conflict and subsequently reduced employee well-being and job satisfaction. Finally, Van Breukelen, Van Der Leeden, Wesselius, and Hoes (2010) found that leader's differential treatment on socioemotional issues (e.g., sympathy) was negatively associated with member perceptions of LMX and team atmosphere, whereas differential treatment on task issues (e.g., influence on team strategy) was negatively associated with team performance. Personal LMX quality was positively related to both team atmosphere and team performance after controlling for differential treatment. In other words, members do notice differential treatment, but their own LMX quality is more influential in determining their perception of team performance and team atmosphere.

In summary, differentiation reduced employee satisfaction, distanced them from their groups, and created perceptions of lower team performance. Altogether, these studies suggest that employees prefer equality and consistency in their work unit to a strong degree of differentiation from the leader.

LMX Differentiation at the Meso level

Each LMX relationship exists in the context of all other LMXs in the group, and members compare their personal LMX with all the others to make sense of their own place in the group hierarchy. A number of scholars have taken this perspective and explored the outcomes of member's relative LMX standing. RLMX has been operationalized in multiple ways: Drawing on social comparison theory (Festinger, 1954) Henderson et al. (2008) calculated actual RLMX as the difference between personal LMX and group aggregate LMX; Vidyarthi and colleagues (2010) have operationalized RLMX as the divergence between personal LMX and group aggregate (more rigorous methodological approach; Edwards, 1994), and also coined a new measure to assess employees' subjective perceptions of their relative standing called LMX social comparison (LMXSC). Taking a different approach, Harris, Li, and Kirkman (2014) assessed actual relational separation between co-workers' LMX as the absolute distance between an individual's LMX quality and other members' LMX quality and named it LMXRS. Finally, Sherony and Green (2002) along with Tse, Lam, Lawrence, and Huan (2013) relied on balance theory and employed a social network-based approach to understanding how LMX differences between two co-workers influence their outcomes.

Balance theory (Heider, 1958) implies that when two co-workers develop different levels of LMX relationships with their leader, a triadic relational imbalance will arise among the three parties that may result in negative sentiments and poor social interactions among them. Consistent with balance theory, Sherony and Green (2002) found that co-workers with high LMX were likely to develop high-quality relationships with each other and low-quality relationships with colleagues in lower LMX relationships, thus effectively creating two subgroups. These findings were later replicated and extended by Tse and colleagues (2013), who found that (dis)similarity in LMX between pairs of co-workers increased perceptions of contempt, which in turn decreased perceptions of help received. Furthermore, these relationships held only for employees with a high social comparison orientation. By reducing perceptions of co-workers' helping behaviors LMX (dis)similarity has the potential to hurt individual member's performance. These findings thus emphasize

the detrimental effects of triadic imbalance on team dynamics and performance.

Henderson and his colleagues (2008) explored differentiation at both meso and group levels to find positive relationships between RLMX and performance and citizenship behaviors via psychological contract fulfillment, which became stronger as LMX differentiation (variability across the workgroup) increased. In other words, the advantages of a person's relative standing increased as groups became more differentiated. Vidyarthi and colleagues (2010) extended this line of inquiry by introducing a new construct called LMXSC, which referred to an individual's subjective perceptions of relative LMX standing with respect to the other LMXs in the workgroup. They argued that the extant practice of using the difference between individual LMX and group mean LMX to calculate an individual's actual LMX standing did not fully capture group members' perceptions of their relative LMX status. In line with these arguments, they found that LMXSC explained outcome variance beyond both personal LMX and RLMX (defined as the divergence between individual LMX and group aggregate LMX), and mediated the positive relationship between RLMX and performance and organizational citizenship behavior (OCB).

Hu and Liden (2013) applied the RLMX utilizing the divergence approach to understand the process through which meso level differences in LMX influence team members' attitudes and behaviors. Consistent with the tenets of social comparison theory, they found that RLMX determined employee self-efficacy and subsequent job satisfaction, performance, and OCB. These benefits of RLMX diminished when employees perceived a high level of team identification and other members' team supportive behaviors. This is because a positive team context (i.e., high identification and support) makes individuals focus on similarities rather than differences between self and the target of comparison. These findings emphasize the importance of team context in understanding the effects of LMX differentiation.

Similarly, Tse et al. (2012) applied a contingency approach to understand the outcomes of RLMX. They found that employees who feel accepted because of their high RLMX standing are more likely to identify with their workgroup and be high performers. However, this process does not apply equally to all employees; those low on negative affectivity are more likely to respond to positive evaluations of RLMX. Contingency approach was also employed by Epitropaki and Martin (2013) to explore the effect of RLMX on the relationship between leadership and employee upward influence tactics in the context of perceived organizational support (POS)—another harbinger of organizational resources parallel to LMX. They found positive associations between transformational leadership and soft influence tactics (e.g., ingratiation), whereas transactional leadership was positively related to the use of both soft and hard (e.g., assertiveness) influence tactics. Furthermore, employees perceive their environment to be resource constrained when both RLMX and POS are low, whereas high RLMX and high POS create perceptions of resource munificence. Under resource constrained rather than munificent conditions employees are more likely to use a higher degree of soft influence tactics with transformational managers and both soft and hard tactics with transactional managers. These findings demonstrate the contextual effects of exchange relationships in that employees are motivated by the quality of relationships to choose appropriate influence tactics.

Harris et al. (2014) explored LMXRS concomitant with group-level LMX differentiation, because both represent related yet independent differentiated leadership constructs that are part of the team context and provide fairness cues needed for group members' identity assessments. They found that employees engage in their groups only in the presence of high individual LMX and low differentiation (LMX differentiation and LMXRS), possibly because a high degree of differentiation undermines their perceptions of fairness and takes away from the positive effects of high-quality LMX.

In summary, studies of differentiation at the individual within-group level had in general positive outcomes for the individuals (see Harris et al., 2014, for an exception). Various aspects of the group context set boundaries for these effects. These findings closely follow those from LMX research. There is a strong need for consensus on operationalization of RLMX and analytical methods before firm conclusions can be made.

LMX Differentiation at the Group Level

Scholars agree that leaders vary in the extent to which they differentiate among their followers. Some leaders may establish high LMX with only a few followers, whereas others may establish high-quality exchange relationships with most group members. Many leaders might establish just low-quality exchange relationships with everyone. This differentiation within the group affects outcomes for the entire group, and has received attention from many LMX researchers. For example, Boies and Howell (2006) found that higher levels of mean LMX in the group were associated with higher group potency and lower group conflict. Furthermore, these relationships were stronger in groups with higher LMX differentiation, indicating that LMX differentiation was beneficial in the presence of high group mean LMX, and detrimental otherwise, possibly because followers perceive inequity and competition for the leader's attention in groups with high LMX differentiation and low mean LMX, whereas groups with high LMX differentiation and high mean LMX are characterized by a positive tone and peer influence (from high LMX members). In a similar line of inquiry, Ford and Seers (2006) found that group mean LMX was positively related, but LMX differentiation was negatively related, to within-group agreement on climate. Schyns (2006), on the other hand, explored the effect of group consensus on LMX (opposite of LMX differentiation) on team outcomes. Schyns found a positive association between group consensus and group mean level of job satisfaction. Furthermore, in the presence of high work values LMX consensus was positively related to group performance. These results imply that the impact of LMX differentiation depends on contextual factors such as member work values.

Next, Stewart and Johnson (2009) approached LMX differentiation from a diversity management perspective to argue that differentiation is more salient in diverse workgroups, which are already prone to have fault lines based on demographic differences. They found that in groups with a high LMX mean, as gender diversity increased LMX differentiation enhanced team performance, but this positive effect did not exist in relatively gender homogeneous groups. Overall, these results suggest that the combined effects of LMX differentiation and LMX mean are more relevant in diverse rather than homogeneous teams. These findings must be taken with some caution though, as this research included temporary groups in classroom settings, which may have artificially inflated the effects. Nishii and Mayer (2009) also explored the effects of aggregated LMX and LMX differentiation in demographically diverse teams. They argued that by having many high-quality LMXs in the team (i.e., high group mean LMX), a leader creates a psychologically safe environment and enhances the quality of interpersonal interactions between members. On the other hand, LMX differentiation can be seen as an exclusion, which can engender perceptions of unfairness and adversely affect the entire group. In addition, the presence of preexisting status and power differentials makes LMX differentiation and group mean more salient in diverse groups than in homogeneous groups. They found that the relationship between diversity and turnover was attenuated by LMX mean and strengthened by LMX differentiation. Furthermore, this relationship is (1) weakest when LMX mean is high and differentiation is low, and (2) strongest when LMX mean is high and differentiation is high. These findings suggest that leaders' exclusion of just a few from the ingroup (i.e., high LMX relationships) is particularly detrimental in diverse groups.

In contrast to these cross-sectional studies, Naidoo and her colleagues (2011) examined how LMX mean and differentiation impacted team performance over the team's life cycle. Considering that differentiated LMX relationships take time to develop, they argue that both the group mean of LMX and LMX differentiation are more strongly related to team performance in later rather than earlier stages. Their results showed that the positive impact of LMX quality on team performance is stronger as time goes by. LMX differentiation at later times was also positively related to team performance. Again, findings must be interpreted with caution because the teams were very small (two followers per team), which may have made individuals more sensitive to differentiation and inflated the effect of sizes. Finally, Le Blanc and Gonzalez-Roma (2012) employed a contingency perspective to understand the mixed findings of LMX differentiation research. They argued that when leaders have many high-quality LMXs (i.e., high LMX median), differentiation does not create much inequality in resource distribution and thus does not affect team outcomes. They also investigated team members' perceived dissimilarity regarding work values as a possible antecedent of LMX differentiation, because these differences make it more difficult for the leaders to give equal attention to all followers. They found that team members are likely to experience LMX differentiation when they perceive more dissimilarities in terms of work values. In addition, LMX differentiation is able to enhance team commitment and team performance only when the group median of LMX quality is low.

So far we have discussed studies looking only at group-level outcomes. A number of scholars have applied multilevel frameworks to explore outcomes of differentiation at both the individual and group level to reveal a more fine-grained picture of the effects of LMX differentiation. The first study in this stream was conducted by Liden and his colleagues (2006). These scholars employed a contingency perspective in multilevel framework. Invoking the tenets of role clarity, efficient distribution of tasks and resources, and equity they argued that the positive effects of differentiation surface only when followers perceive underlying bases to be fair. Results showed that in groups with a higher degree of differentiation low LMX members improve their performance so that their effort can eventually lead to better LMX. At the group level, LMX differentiation is positively associated with performance in workgroups with high levels of task interdependence or low median LMX. In a similar vein, Erdogan and Bauer (2010) contended that LMX differentiation creates within-group differences in terms of access to leader-granted socioemotional and economic resources, which makes workgroup justice concerns more salient. Therefore, the cross-level association between differentiation and employee outcomes is contingent upon the level of procedural and distributive justice climate in the workgroup. They found that the negative effects of LMX differentiation occurred only in a low justice climate. LMX differentiation was negatively related to employees' organizational commitment and satisfaction with co-worker relations, and positively related to employee withdrawal behaviors only in the presence of a low distributive or procedural justice climate. LMX differentiation also showed a positive association with helping behaviors directed to co-workers only when the distributive justice climate was high. These findings suggest that LMX differentiation may have positive effects in groups characterized by high justice climate; however, a lack of justice is likely to invoke negative effects of LMX differentiation.

Liao, Liu, and Loi (2010) investigated how two dominant forms of social exchange in organizations, namely LMX and team member exchange (TMX), function in each other's presence. Drawing on social cognitive theory and social comparison theory, they developed a cross-level contingent process model to explain the independent effects of LMX and TMX on employee creativity through self-efficacy. Using data gathered from steel manufacturing technicians at three different time points they found that both LMX and TMX had unique positive effects on employee self-efficacy, which in turn led to higher creativity. Furthermore, these indirect effects of LMX and TMX on employee creativity were moderated by LMX and TMX differentiation, respectively.

LMX was positively related to self-efficacy and creativity only when LMX differentiation was low. On the other hand, TMX was positively related to self-efficacy and creativity only when TMX differentiation was high. These findings show that LMX is not the only source of social exchange in workgroups; co-workers are another important party to social exchange. These two sources complement each other to provide resources and motivation for promoting self-efficacy beliefs and creativity. Furthermore, differentiation in LMX and differentiation in TMX work in opposite ways. This is because TMX is a horizontal exchange that provides socioemotional support, but LMX, being a vertical exchange, also involves economic resources. High LMX differentiation involving a favorable distribution of economic resources to a chosen few may create perceptions of unfairness and thus undermine the linkage between LMX and creativity.

Taking a different approach, Ma and Qu (2010) turned their attention to antecedents of LMX differentiation. They argued that leader's individual differences influence the development of LMX and thus the extent of LMX differentiation in a workgroup. They found a negative relationship between leaders' personal universalistic values (i.e., adherence to rule-based decision making without considering context or social relationships) and LMX differentiation. Next, they tested LMX scholars' (e.g., Gerstner & Day, 1997) argument that leaders' ratings reflect both objective performance and the closeness of their relationships to the followers. After controlling for objective performance, LMX indeed inflated leaders' subjective performance evaluations of the followers. In addition, this relationship was strengthened by LMX differentiation. In other words, in high LMX differentiation groups ingroup and outgroup distinction becomes prominent and leaders favor ingroup followers to a larger degree to evaluate their performance more positively.

Finally, Gooty and Yammarino (2014) drew on shared reality theory to define a new construct, dyadic dispersion LMX, which refers to the degree to which leaders and followers do not share similar perceptions of LMX quality. They argued that extant LMX research is based only on follower ratings of LMX and ignores the other party in the exchange. Results showed that a lack of shared reality of LMX within the dyad attenuates the positive individual LMX–performance association. This association is also weakened by group-level LMX differentiation possibly because followers perceive that norms of equality are being violated by within-group differences in LMX.

In summary, the multilevel studies in particular attest to the positive effects of differentiation and the associated boundary conditions (Table 15.1). Studying differentiation at only one level such as the individual level may falsely lead to the belief that differentiation is bad for the group (e.g., Hooper & Martin, 2008). Differentiation is not always good or bad; its effects depend on the group contexts.

Criticisms of LMX Differentiation Research and Directions for Future Research

Though LMX theory has been around for over 40 years and differentiation lies at the heart of this classic theory, research on differentiation is still at a nascent stage. LMX differentiation remains a critical issue in organizations because of its potential to affect the entire workgroup. Due to advances in I/O research methods, interest in differentiation research is now burgeoning. However, there remain a large number of issues to be resolved. These issues relate to the following broad categories: measurement and research methods used in differentiation research, evolution of differentiation over the team life cycle, boundary conditions for LMX differentiation, and the somewhat narrow focus of the theory.

Measurement and Research Methods Used in LMX Differentiation Research

Our review of extant research revealed that scholars are assessing differentiation in a number of ways, which poses difficulties for drawing meta-analytical conclusions needed for the advancement of the theory. For example, there is no clear consensus on the current group-level measure of differentiation. A number of studies have used standard deviation in LMX ratings across the group (e.g., Gooty & Yammarino, 2014), whereas others have used variance (e.g., Erdogan & Bauer, 2010), and yet others have used Rwg (e.g., Boies & Howell, 2006). Although LMX research is based on perceptual measures, its derivative differentiation research relies primarily on statistical measures geared to assess "actual" rather than "perceived" differentiation. Because perceptions are more powerful than reality (Kristof-Brown, Zimmerman, & Johnson, 2005), it behooves researchers to develop measures to assess perceived differentiation. Both Van Breukelen et al. (2002) and Vidyarthi et al. (2010) have proposed perceptual measures to assess individual perceptions of within-group differentiation; however there is no group level measure.

Table 15.1. Summary of LMX Differentiation Research.

Title and Author(s)	Research Design	Sample Industry	Sample Country	Demographic Details of Sample	Data Source	Levels of Analysis	Measure	Findings
Boies, K., & Howell, J. M. (2006). Leader–member exchange in teams: An examination of the interaction between relationship differentiation and mean LMX in explaining team-level outcomes. *Leadership Quarterly, 17*, 246–257.	Cross-sectional	Military	Canada	99% of participants were male	Group members only	Group level	LMX differentiation: Rwg index	(1) Group mean of LMX is positively related to team potency but negatively related to team conflict. (2) These relationships are stronger in groups with high LMX differentiation. In other words, LMX differentiation is beneficial when group mean LMX is high, and detrimental otherwise.
Bolino, M. C., & Turnley, W. H. (2009). Relative deprivation among employees in lower-quality leader-member exchange relationships. *Leadership Quarterly, 20*, 276–286.	Conceptual paper							Based on relative deprivation theory, the authors propose a theoretical model identifying when employees with relatively low-quality LMX are most likely to feel aggrieved. In addition, the factors that may determine how employees respond to feelings of relative deprivation arising from their LMX relationships are discussed.

Citation	Design	Sample/Industry	Country	Gender	Sample	Level of analysis	Measure	Findings
Dionne, S. D., Gupta, A., Sotak, K. L., Shirreffs, K. A., Serban, A., Hao, C., Kim, D. H., & Yammarino, F. J. (2014). A 25-year perspective on levels of analysis in leadership research. *Leadership Quarterly, 25*, 6–35.	Review paper				790 conceptual and empirical studies published in the *Leadership Quarterly*			Only 37% of conceptual and 33% of empirical papers published over the entire history of LQ explicitly specified the appropriate level of analysis. Multilevel data analysis techniques are used in less than one-fifth of all articles. The authors reiterate the need for appropriate levels-based measurement and alignment between theory and data.
Epitropaki, O., & Martin, R. (2013). Transformational–transactional leadership and upward influence: The role of Relative Leader–Member Exchanges (RLMX) and Perceived Organizational Support (POS). *Leadership Quarterly, 24*, 299–315.	Time lagged (1 year apart)	Manufacturing and service companies	Great Britain	Mostly male (78%)	Employees only	Individual level	RLMX: individual LMX minus the group mean for LMX	When employees perceive their managers as transformational leaders, they are likely to use soft upward tactics under resource-constrained conditions (i.e., low RLMX and low POS) than in resource-munificent conditions (i.e., high RLMX and high POS). Employees are also likely to employ higher levels of soft and hard tactics to influence a transactional manager in resource-constrained rather than in resource-munificent conditions.

(continued)

Table 15.1. Continued

Title and Author(s)	Research Design	Sample Industry	Sample Country	Demographic Details of Sample	Data Source	Levels of Analysis	Measure	Findings
Erdogan, B., & Bauer, T. N. (2010). Differentiated leader–member exchanges: The buffering role of justice climate. *Journal of Applied Psychology, 95*, 1104–1120.	Cross-sectional	Retail (clothing)	Turkey	Young (mean age 22 years) employees with about 1 year of job experience	Employees and managers	Cross-level (individual level outcomes and group level main effects)	LMX differentiation: within-group variance	(1) LMX differentiation is negatively related to employees' organizational commitment and satisfaction with co-worker relations only when the distributive or procedural justice climate is low. (2) LMX differentiation is positively related to employee withdrawal behaviors only when the distributive or procedural justice climate is low. (3) LMX differentiation is positively related to helping behaviors targeting co-workers only when the distributive justice climate is high.
Ford, L. R., & Seers, A. (2006). Relational leadership and team climates: Pitting differentiation versus agreement. *Leadership Quarterly, 17*, 258–270.	Cross-sectional	Manufacturing and graveyard facilities	Europe and United States	Mostly male (75%)	Employees only	Group level	LMX differentiation: standard deviation of LMX within group	(1) High group mean of LMX quality is predictive of within-group agreement on supportive management, challenge, and contribution climate. (2) LMX differentiation is negatively related to agreement on supportive management and contribution climate.

Reference	Design	Industry	Country	Sample	Level of analysis	LMX construct	Key findings
Gooty, J., & Yammarino, F. J. (2014). The leader-member exchange relationship: A multisource, cross-level investigation. *Journal of Management*.	Cross-sectional		United States	Employees and supervisors	Individual and group level	LMX differentiation: standard deviation of LMX within group	(1) Dyadic dispersion LMX (differences in follower and leader ratings of LMX) moderates the individual LMX–performance association such that the relationship is positive only when dyadic dispersion LMX is low. (2) LMX differentiation attenuates the individual LMX–performance association.
Gooty, J., Serban, A., Thomas, J. S., Gavin, M. B., & Yammarino, F. J. (2012). Use and misuse of levels of analysis in leadership research: An illustrative review of leader–member exchange. *Leadership Quarterly, 23*, 1080–1103.	Review paper			163 empirical studies published between 1972 and 2012			Interest in LMX research continues to grow, and the majority of multilevel studies cast theory and hypotheses at the same level. However, measurement and data analyses still need to improve.
Harris, T. B., Li, N., & Kirkman, B. L. (2014). Leader–member exchange (LMX) in context: How LMX differentiation and LMX relational separation attenuate LMX's influence on OCB and turnover intention. *Leadership Quarterly, 25*, 314–328.	Cross-sectional	Manufacturing, electronics, telecommunication and hotels	China	Employees and managers	Cross-level (individual-level outcomes, meso-level and group-level moderators)	LMX differentiation: within-group variance LMX; relational separation: the square root of the summed squared differences between an individual's LMX and other individual's LMX divided by the total number of respondents in the group.	LMX differentiation and LMXRS both attenuate the association between LMX and OCB and turnover intent.

(continued)

Table 15.1. Continued

Title and Author(s)	Research Design	Sample Industry	Sample Country	Demographic Details of Sample	Data Source	Levels of Analysis	Measure	Findings
Henderson, D. J., Wayne, S. J., Shore, L. M., Bommer, W. B., & Tetrick, L. E. (2008). Leader–member exchange, differentiation, and psychological contract fulfillment: A multilevel examination. *Journal of Applied Psychology, 93*, 1208–1219.	Cross-sectional	Manufacturing	United States	Mostly white male (97.5%)	Employees and managers	Cross-level and individual within-group level	RLMX (individual–group mean LMX) and LMX differentiation (within-group variance)	(1) PC fulfillment mediates the relationship between RLMX and performance and OCB.(2) The positive relationship between RLMX and PC fulfillment is strengthened by LMX differentiation.
Henderson, D. J., Liden, R.C., Glibkowski, B. C., & Chaudhry, A. (2009). LMX differentiation: A multilevel review and examination of its antecedents and outcomes. *Leadership Quarterly, 20*, 517–534.	Conceptual paper							The authors provide a theoretical framework identifying antecedents and outcomes of LMX differentiation.
Hooper, D. T., & Martin, R. (2008). Beyond personal leader–member exchange (LMX) quality: The effects of perceived LMX variability on employee reactions. *Leadership Quarterly, 19*, 20–30.	Cross-sectional	Customer service, sales, healthcare, administrative staff, firefighters	Australia	Mostly male (97%)	Employees only	Individual level	One-item measure of individual perception of LMX differentiation	Employee perceptions of LMX variability have a negative indirect effect on job satisfaction and well-being via relational team conflict.

Reference	Design	Industry	Sample	Country	Participants	Level	Definition	Findings
Hu, J., & Liden, R. C. (2012). Relative leader-member exchange within team contexts: How and when social comparison impacts individual effectiveness. *Personnel Psychology*, 65, 1–46	Cross-sectional	Beverage	All participants hold at least a college degree	China	Employees and managers	Cross-level and individual within-group level	RLMX: divergence between individual and group aggregate LMX	(1) RLMX is positively related to in-role performance, OCB, and job satisfaction via self-efficacy (2) Self-efficacy partially mediates the relationship between RLMX and in-role performance and job satisfaction, and fully mediates the relationship between RLMX and OCB. (3) Team identification (group level) attenuates RLMX's direct effect on self-efficacy, and indirect effects on in-role performance and OCB. (4) Team supportive behavior (individual level) attenuates RLMX's direct effect on self-efficacy and indirect effect on in-role performance.
Le Blanc, P. M., & Gonzalez-Roma, V. (2012). A team level investigation of the relationship between leader–member exchange (LMX) differentiation, and commitment and performance. *Leadership Quarterly*, 23, 534–544.	Cross-sectional	Education (secondary school level)	Autonomy was recently increased for the school teachers	Netherlands	School teachers and principals	Group level	LMX differentiation: standard deviation of LMX within group	(1) LMX differentiation is positively related to team commitment and team performance only when the group median of LMX quality is low. (2) Team members' perception of dissimilarities among members are positively related to LMX differentiation.

(*continued*)

Table 15.1. Continued

Title and Author(s)	Research Design	Sample Industry	Sample Country	Demographic Details of Sample	Data Source	Levels of Analysis	Measure	Findings
Liao, H., Liu, D., & Loi, R. (2010). Looking at both sides of the social exchange coin: A social cognitive perspective on the join effects of relationship quality and differentiation on creativity. *Academy of Management Journal*, 53, 1090–1109.	Time-lagged	Manufacturing	China		Employees and managers	Cross-level (individual-level outcomes and group-level moderators)	LMX differentiation: within-group variance	(1) LMX is positively related to employee creativity via self-efficacy. (2) LMX quality is positively related to self-efficacy and creativity when LMX differentiation is low.
Liden, R. C., Erdogan, B., Wayne, S. J., & Sparrowe, R. T. (2006). Leader-member exchange, differentiation, and task interdependence: Implications for individual and group performance. *Journal of Organizational Behavior*, 27, 723–746.	Cross-sectional	Manufacturing, distribution, telecommunication, education (university level)	United States		Employees and managers	Individual and group level (both individual-level and group-level outcomes and moderators)	LMX differentiation: within-group variance in individual-level LMX scores	(1) Increases in LMX differentiation are accompanied by increases in individual performance only for low LMX members. (2) The relation between LMX differentiation and group performance is strengthened by task interdependence. (3) LMX differentiation is positively related to group performance only in groups with a low LMX median.

Citation	Design	Industry	Country	Sample	Level	LMX differentiation	Findings
Ma, L., & Qu, Q. (2010). Differentiation in leader–member exchange: A hierarchical linear modeling approach. *Leadership Quarterly, 21,* 733–744.	Cross-sectional	High tech and mining	China	Employees and managers	Cross-level (individual-level outcomes and group-level moderator)	standard deviation of LMX within group	(1) Leaders' universal values are negatively associated with LMX differentiation. (2) LMX differentiation strengthens the relation between LMX and follower's subjective performance.
Maksom, H. H. B., & Winter, R. (2009). Leader-member exchange differentiation in the military platoon. *Leadership & Organization Development Journal, 30,* 696–708.	Cross sectional	Military	Singapore	Young participants with little job experience	Employees only	Group level	Group mean of LMX	Leaders (military platoon commanders) develop higher-quality LMX with higher ranking and permanent employees (NCOs) than with the lower ranking and temporary recruits.
McClane, W. E. (1991). Implications of member role differentiation: Analysis of a key concept in the LMX model of leadership. *Group & Organizational Studies, 16,* 102–113.	Cross- sectional	Education (university level)	United States	Students	Employees and managers	Group level	Group mean of LMX (operationalized as negotiating latitude) LMX differentiation: sum of the absolute value of the difference between each group member's LMX and the group mean LMX	(1) High group mean of LMX quality is associated with high levels of satisfaction with leader, task, and co-workers. (2) LMX differentiation is negatively related to satisfaction with task.

(continued)

Table 15.1. Continued

Title and Author(s)	Research Design	Sample Industry	Sample Country	Demographic Details of Sample	Data Source	Levels of Analysis	Measure	Findings
Naidoo, L. J., Scherbaum, C. A., Goldstein, H. W., & Graen, G. B. (2011). A longitudinal examination of the effects of LMX, ability, and differentiation on team performance. *Journal of Business and Psychology, 26,* 347–357.	Longitudinal	Education (university level)	United States	Students	Employees, managers, external raters	Group level	LMX differentiation: within-group varianceLeader-rated LMX was used	LMX differentiation is positively related to team performance, but not to team development.
Nishii, L. H., & Mayer, D. M. (2009). Do inclusive leaders help to reduce turnover in diverse groups? The moderating role of leader–member exchange in the diversity to turnover relationship. *Journal of Applied Psychology, 94,* 1412–1426.	Cross-sectional	Retail (superstore)	United States	Mostly white male (81%)	Employees and archival data	Group level	LMX differentiation: standard deviation of LMX within group	(1) The relationship between diversity and turnover is weaker under conditions of high LMX mean for both forms of diversity (i.e., demographic and tenure diversity). (2) High LMX differentiation exacerbates (or low LMX differentiation attenuates) the positive relationship between demographic diversity and turnover. (3) Tenure diversity is negatively associated with turnover only when LMX differentiation is low. (4) The interaction between demographic diversity and LMX differentiation is significant only when the LMX mean is high.

Citation	Design	Industry	Country	Participants	Level	LMX measure	Findings
Scandura, T. A. (1999). Rethinking leader–member exchange: An organizational justice perspective. *Leadership Quarterly, 10*, 25–40.	Conceptual paper						The author presents a theoretical framework of LMX development over time and suggests that LMX differentiation divides workgroups into ingroups and outgroups, which has implications for organizational justice.
Schyns, B. (2006). Group consensus in leader–member exchange (LMX) and shared work values related to organizational outcomes? *Small Group Research, 37*, 20–35.	Cross-sectional	Banking and insurance	Germany	Employees and managers	Group level	LMX differentiation: standard deviation of LMX	(1) LMX consensus (opposite of differentiation) is positively associated with group mean level of job satisfaction. (2) LMX consensus is positively related to group performance in the presence of high work values.
Sherony, K. M., & Green, S. G. (2002). Coworker exchange: Relationships between coworkers, leader–member exchange, and work attitudes. *Journal of Applied Psychology, 94*, 1412–1426.	Cross-sectional	Engineering and health services	United States	Employees only	Individual-level and individual within-group level (co-worker dyad)	Social network-based (dis)similarity between co-workers' LMX	Co-workers with high LMX are likely to develop high-quality relationships with each other and low-quality relationships with colleagues in lower LMX relationship.

(*continued*)

Table 15.1. Continued

Title and Author(s)	Research Design	Sample Industry	Sample Country	Demographic Details of Sample	Data Source	Levels of Analysis	Measure	Findings
Sias, P. M., & Jablin, F. M. (1995). Differential superior-subordinate relations, perceptions of fairness, and coworker communication. *Human Communication Research*, 22, 5–38	Cross-sectional	Multiple	United States		Employees only	Individual level	Qualitative study with detailed interviews	(1) Differential treatment changes the dynamics of communication among co-workers such that members perceived to receive favorable treatment unfairly tend to get isolated from the group communication network, whereas those perceived to be rewarded fairly play a central role. (2) Members perceived to be punished fairly tend to be isolated from the rest of the group, whereas those receiving punishment unfairly are drawn into the group communication network.
Stewart, M. M., & Johnson, O. E. (2009). Leader-member exchange as a moderator of the relationship between work group diversity and team performance. *Group & Organizational Studies*, 34, 507–535.	Cross sectional	Military	United States	Data were collected during 8-day interactive strategic crisis simulation Mostly male (83%)	Followers and external rating providers	Group level	Group mean of LMX and LMX differentiation (standard deviation)	When aggregated LMX (group mean of LMX) is high, LMX differentiation is positively associated with work group performance in more gender diverse groups.

Reference	Design	Industry	Country	Sample	Level	Variable	Findings
Tse, H. H. M., Ashkanasy, N. M., & Dasborough, M. T. (2012). Relative leader–member exchange, negative affectivity and social identification: A moderated-mediation examination. *Leadership Quarterly, 23*, 354–366.	Cross-sectional	Banking	Australia	Employees and managers	Individual within-group level	RLMX (individual–group mean LMX)	(1) After controlling for perceptions of LMX, social identification mediates the relationship between RLMX and job performance. (2) Negative affectivity (NA) attenuates the relationship between RLMX and social identification. (3) NA moderated the indirect effect of RLMX on job performance.
Tse, H. H. M., Lam, C. K., Lawrence, S. A., & Huan, X. (2013). When my supervisor dislikes you more than me: The effect of dissimilarity in leader–member exchange on coworkers' interpersonal emotion and perceived help. *Journal of Applied Psychology, 98*, 974–988.	Cross-sectional	Telecommunication and high tech	China	Employees and managers	Individual level and individual within-group level (co-worker dyad)	(Dis)similarity between individual LMX quality and co-workers' LMX quality	(1) (Dis)similarity in LMX between co-workers A and B increases Co-worker A's feelings of contempt for co-worker B and decreases co-worker A's perception of help received from co-worker B. (2) These relationships hold only for focals with high social comparison orientation (SCO). (3) Contempt is a crucial mediator that transmits the interactive effect of LMX (dis)similarity and SCO on perceptions of help received from co-workers. (4) Aggregate level of perceived help from co-workers is positively related to sales performance of individual employees.

(*continued*)

Table 15.1. Continued

Title and Author(s)	Research Design	Sample Industry	Sample Country	Demographic Details of Sample	Data Source	Levels of Analysis	Measure	Findings
Van Breukelen, W., Konst, D., & Van Der Vlist, R. (2002). Effects of LMX and differential treatment on work unit commitment. *Psychological Reports, 91*, 220–230.	Cross-sectional	Government	Netherlands	Mostly male (85%)	Employees only	Individual level	Individual perception of LMX differentiation	Perception of differential treatment weakens the positive relationship between LMX quality and work unit commitment.
Van Breukelen, W., Van Der Leeden, R., Wesselius, W., & Hoes, M. (2010). Differential treatment within sports teams, leader–member (coach–player) exchange quality, team atmosphere, and team performance. *Journal of Organizational Behavior, 33*, 43–63.	Cross-sectional	Amateur sports	Netherlands		Players and coaches	Individual level (with group-level control variables)	Individual perceptions of differential treatment within teams	(1) Social differential treatment is negatively associated with team atmosphere and LMX. (2) Task-related differential treatment (regarding influence on team composition and tactics) is negatively related to subjective team performance. (3) After controlling for differential treatment LMX quality is positively related to team atmosphere and subjective team performance.
Vidyarthi, P. R., Liden, R. C., Anand, S., Erdogan, B., & Gosh, S. (2010). Where do I stand? Examining the effects of leader–member exchange social comparison on employee work behaviors. *Journal of Applied Psychology, 98*, 974–988	Cross-sectional	Manufacturing	India		Employees and managers	Individual within-group level	RLMX (divergence between individual LMX and group mean LMX) and LMXSC (employees' subjective rating of RLMX)	(1) After controlling for LMX and RLMX, employee's perceptions of LMXSC are positively related to job performance and citizenship behaviors. (2) A significant part of the effects of RLMX on job performance and citizenship behaviors is mediated through LMXSC.

Use of the statistical measure of relative LMX standing also suffers from a methodological flaw. Despite several reminders from Edwards and colleagues (Edwards, 1994; Edwards & Parry, 1993) on the methodological problems related to the use of difference terms, researchers continue to operationalize RLMX as the difference between a person's individual LMX rating and the group aggregate, rather than using divergence or convergence between the two in a polynomial regression framework. These concerns also apply to the newly introduced difference-based measure of actual LMX relational separation (Harris et al., 2014).

Furthermore, differentiation is usually assessed from LMX ratings taken from the followers, which raises a number of questions: does differentiation exist only in the followers' minds? Does differentiation refer to leader's perceptions of within-group variability? This lack of precision in defining differentiation is lamentable (Gooty, Serban, Thomas, Gavin, & Yammarino, 2012) and certainly detrimental to the future development of the theory. Because the leader is the one differentiating between followers based on various characteristics such as ability, leader ratings of LMX (i.e., SLMX) might be a more proximal and superior indicator of LMX differentiation (for an example, see Naidoo, Scherbaum, Goldstein, & Graen, 2011).

Evolution of LMX Differentiation over the Team Life Cycle

Initial studies on LMX have asserted that the relationship develops in as little as 3 days (Liden, Wayne, & Stilwell, 1993) and the quality of the relationship remains stable from then on. In view of that it would be interesting to observe the temporal nature of within-group differences in LMX. However, there are very few longitudinal studies that have explored how the nature of LMX differentiation changes over time. Our review found two studies with a time-lagged design (Epitropaki & Martin, 2013; Liao et al., 2010) to avoid common source common method variance, and only one study with a longitudinal design to explore changes in LMX differentiation over time (Naidoo et al., 2011). However, this study was conducted with student teams in a classroom setting and findings need to be generalized in a real world organizational setting. Establishment of LMX involves a leader giving an assignment (i.e., role making), a follower choosing to perform the assignment well (i.e., role taking), and subsequent role routinization. Furthermore, LMX differentiation is a process of role differentiation

such that a leader assigns challenging tasks to capable followers (i.e., high LMX) who are most likely to successfully complete those and somewhat mundane tasks to all others (Dansereau et al., 1975). It is possible that at early stages of group development leaders do not fully understand all of their followers' abilities to effectively differentiate. Then, it makes sense that over time leader's comparative knowledge increases, LMX perceptions stabilize, and differentiation increases (Nahrgang, Morgeson, & Ilies, 2009). LMX scholars need to explore how LMX differentiation starts, how it changes over time, when it becomes stable, how it varies with team composition (i.e., a high or low LMX individual exits the group), etc.

Along with the process of LMX differentiation development and maintenance, hardly any attention has been paid to the drivers of LMX differentiation. LMX is a unique theory of leadership in that it does not assign a passive role to the followers. Followers choose to establish a high or low quality of LMX by accepting or rejecting the role given by the leader. However, few studies have explored what individual attributes of followers are likely to lead to differentiation. It is conceivable to think that homogeneity and diversity among members of the group may affect the acceptability of the level of differentiation leaders make among the followers. For example, Le Blanc and Gonzalez Roma (2012) found that work value dissimilarity among team members was instrumental in creating LMX differentiation, but these findings need to be tested over time. Along similar lines it is conceivable that leaders' personality and other characteristics may affect the degree of differentiation they make among their followers. For example, future research may explore whether personality factors such as openness to experience or self-monitoring or locus of control affect leaders' propensity to bestow more or less differentiation. Likewise, perceptual and cognitive characteristics such as equity sensitivity and prototypically of leaders' role may affect LMX differentiation. Finally, work characteristics such as span of control, complexity of tasks, and outcome interdependence may also affect LMX differentiation. Future research may explore these questions.

In addition, if there is evidence that leaders vary in the extent of differentiation (e.g., Liden et al., 2006), then what drives this difference between leaders? Ma and Qu (2010) assert that leaders who embrace universalistic rather than particularistic values are less likely to differentiate. Other individual attributes of leaders merit an inquiry from LMX researchers. A number of LMX scholars (e.g., Tangirala, Green, & Ramanujam, 2007) have looked at leader's vertical relationships with their leaders (i.e., leader–leader exchange—LLX) and the influence of this on followers. In line with this research one question is: Do leaders emulate their leaders in their behaviors pertaining to LMX differentiation? Drawing on social learning theory another related question is: Do leaders observe their colleagues and emulate their LMX differentiation patterns?

Boundary Conditions for LMX Differentiation

Findings on the effects of LMX differentiation have been mixed at best. For example, Liden et al. (2006) established that in highly task-interdependent groups, differentiation was beneficial to team performance. Similarly, Erdogan and Bauer (2010) established that differentiation was accepted in high justice climate. Clearly, this line of research needs to employ a contingency approach and understand the various contextual factors in the workgroup that can make outcomes of differentiation positive or negative. Factors that merit attention include the following: organizational culture, group power distance, and group collectivism. Future research may, for example, develop theory and empirically investigate if respect for people or team orientation positively or negatively moderates the relationship between LMX differentiation and individual level outcomes. Likewise, because ideas ingrained in LMX differentiation are the antithesis of collectivistic norms, research is needed to settle the question about how group collectivism has a direct or moderating effect on LMX differentiation and its correlates. Similarly, because power distance concerns the acceptability of the unequal distribution of power, leaders' prerogative to differentiate among followers may partly depend on the power distance climate of the group.

Another caveat to consider is that LMX relationships exist in the context of other social exchanges in the workgroup; exploring differentiation in isolation is likely to yield misleading findings. For example, Ford and Seers (2006) and Liao et al. (2010) also looked at TMX and TMX differentiation when studying the effects of LMX differentiation. By including another form of social exchange their models are more complete and their findings are more rigorous. Other forms of exchanges (e.g., POS) can certainly set boundaries on the effects of LMX differentiation and merit inclusion in future research models.

Narrow Focus of LMX Differentiation Theory

Most studies of differentiation have looked at a narrow range of outcomes, such as individual and team performance and helping behaviors. For advancement as well as continued practical relevance scholars need to explore other outcomes, such as how differentiation influences the social networks in the workgroup. In a qualitative study, Sias and Jablin (1995) found that differentiation shaped the workgroup communication networks such that both unfairly favored and fairly disfavored members were removed. Differentiation research needs to be integrated with social network theory to further our understanding of both phenomena.

Scholars also need to explore LMX differentiation in other contemporary organizational settings, such as a matrix organization. LMX theory assumes followers have only one leader in the workplace; however, employees increasingly report to multiple leaders and establish multiple LMXs simultaneously (Vidyarthi, Erdogan, Anand, Liden, & Chaudhry, 2014). In a sample of information technology consultants reporting to a permanent leader and a client leader, Vidyarthi and colleagues (2014) found that follower job satisfaction was diminished when the two LMXs were not aligned. Employees establish multiple LMXs and they all matter, so the next question is: How does differentiation work in this multileader context? Does one leader's differentiation influence employee outcomes coming from the other LMXs?

Another interesting avenue for future research is virtual teams. Employees understand LMX differentiation as part of the sensemaking process in workgroups (e.g., Sias & Jablin, 1995). That is, employees pay attention to how leader treats the other team members in order to make sense of their own situation and the team dynamics. Leader's smile and closeness, for example, provide cues about the favored status of a colleague. However, these physical cues do not exist in virtual teams, so how do employees perceive LMX differentiation in this context? Does LMX differentiation exist in this context? If yes, then is it still meaningful?

Finally, the bulk of the LMX differentiation research is limited to white collar samples, although hierarchy is more likely to matter in blue collar settings. It is conceivable that industry characteristics (i.e., services versus manufacturing or for-profit versus non-for-profit) may show a nuanced difference. This is because both the need for and acceptability of LMX differentiation may vary across different industries. Future research designed to measure this difference is needed. It would also be interesting to determine the pattern of LMX differentiation in a team with multiple hierarchical levels. For example, in military settings in which workgroups consist of employees at different hierarchical levels reporting to the same leader it has been found that leaders established better LMX with higher ranking and permanent employees than with lower ranking and temporary employees (Maksom & Winter, 2009). Researchers must explore differentiation in different industries and different levels of hierarchy.

Conclusions

LMX researchers have examined antecedents and consequences of dyadic relationship between leaders and members for over 40 years. Although inherent in the original conceptualization, LMX differentiation research has only burgeoned in recent years with the recognition that dyadic relationships are embedded in workgroups where other LMXs coexist and they impact one another. Our review outlined the major theoretical frameworks underlying LMX differentiation and their relationship with correlates at individual and group levels. We described what extant LMX differentiation research has explored and we extend the research by outlining what remains to be discovered in the future.

References

Adams, J. S. (1965). Inequity in social exchange. In L. Berkowitz (Ed.), *Advances in experimental psychology*. San Diego, CA: Academic Press.

Bauer, T. N., & Green, S. G. (1996). Development of leader-member exchange: A longitudinal test. *Academy of Management Journal, 39*, 1538–1567.

Beach, S. R., & Tesser, A. (2000). Self-evaluation maintenance and evolution: Some speculative notes. In L. Wheeler & J. Suls (Eds.), *Handbook of social comparison: Theory and research* (pp. 123–140). Dordrecht, Netherlands: Kluwer Academic Publishers.

Boies, K., & Howell, J. M. (2006). Leader–member exchange in teams: An examination of the interaction between relationship differentiation and mean LMX in explaining team-level outcomes. *Leadership Quarterly, 17*, 246–257.

Bolino, M. C., & Turnley, W. H. (2009). Relative deprivation among employees in lower-quality leader-member exchange relationships. *Leadership Quarterly, 20*, 276–286.

Buunk, B. P., & Mussweiler, T. (Eds.). (2001). New directions in social comparison research. *European Journal of Social Psychology, 31*, 467–607.

Colquitt, J. A., Conlon, D. E., Wesson, M. J., Porter, C. O., & Ng., K. Y. (2001). Justice at the millennium: A meta-analytic review of 25 years of organizational justice research. *Journal of Applied Psychology, 86*, 425–445.

Cropanzano, R., & Greenberg, J. (1997). Progress in organizational justice: Tunneling through the maze. In C. Cooper & I. Robertson (Eds.), *International review of industrial and organizational psychology* (pp. 317–372). New York: Wiley.

Crosby, F. (1976). A model of egoistical relative deprivation. *Psychological Review, 83*, 85–113.

Dansereau, F., Graen, G., & Haga, W. J. (1975). A vertical dyad linkage approach to leadership within formal organizations: A longitudinal investigation of the role making process. *Organizational Behavior and Human Performance, 13*, 46–78.

Darley, J. M. (2004). Social comparison motives in ongoing groups. In M. B. Brewer & M. Hewstone. (Eds.), *Emotion and motivation* (pp. 281–297). Oxford, UK: Blackwell.

Duchon, D., Green, S. G., & Taber, T. D. (1986). Vertical dyad linkage: A longitudinal assessment of antecedents, measures, and consequences. *Journal of Applied Psychology, 71*, 56–60.

Dulebohn, J. H., Bommer, W. H., Liden, R. C., Brouer, R, L., & Ferris, G. R. (2012). A meta-analysis of antecedents and consequences of leader-member exchange: Integrating the past with an eye toward the future. *Journal of Management, 38*, 1715–1759.

Edwards, J. R. (1994). The study of congruence in organizational behavior research: Critique and a proposed alternative. *Organizational Behavior and Human Decision Processes, 58*, 51–100.

Edwards, J. R, & Parry, M. E. (1993). On the use of polynomial regression equations as an alternative to difference scores in organizational research. *Academy of Management Journal, 36*, 1577–1613.

Epitropaki, O., & Martin, R. (2013). Transformational–transactional leadership and upward influence: The role of Relative Leader–Member Exchanges (RLMX) and Perceived Organizational Support (POS). *Leadership Quarterly, 24*, 299–315.

Erdogan, B., & Bauer, T. N. (2010). Differentiated leader–member exchanges: The buffering role of justice climate. *Journal of Applied Psychology, 95*, 1104–1120.

Festinger, L. (1954). A theory of social comparison processes. *Human Relations, 7*, 117–140.

Ford, L. R., & Seers, A. (2006). Relational leadership and team climates: Pitting differentiation versus agreement. *Leadership Quarterly, 17*, 258–270.

Gerstner, C. R., & Day, D. V. (1997). Meta-analytic review of leader–member exchange theory: Correlates and construct issues. *Journal of Applied Psychology, 82*, 827–844.

Goethals, G. R., & Darley, J. (1977). Social comparison theory: An attributional approach. In J. M. Suls & R. L. Miller (Eds.), *Social comparison processes: Theoretical and empirical perspectives* (pp. 259–278). Washington, DC: Halsted/Wiley.

Goodman, P. S. (1977). Social comparison process in organizations. In G. Salancik and B. Staw (Eds.), *New directions in organizational behavior*. Chicago: St. Clair Press.

Gooty, J., Serban, A., Thomas, J. S., Gavin, M. B., & Yammarino, F. J. (2012). Use and misuse of levels of analysis in leadership research: An illustrative review of leader–member exchange. *Leadership Quarterly, 23*, 1080–1103.

Gooty, J., & Yammarino, F. J. (2014). The leader-member exchange relationship: A multisource, cross-level investigation. *Journal of Management.*

Greenberg, J. (1987). A taxonomy of organizational justice theories. *Academy of Management Review, 12,* 9–22.

Greenberg, J. (1990). Organizational justice: Yesterday, today, and tomorrow. *Journal of Management, 16,* 399–432.

Greenberg, J., Ashton-James, C. E., & Ashkanasy, N. M. (2007). Social comparison process in organizations. *Organizational Behavior and Human Decision Processes, 102,* 22–41.

Han, H. G., & Bai, Y. (2012). In need of each other: The moderator of task interdependence between LMX variability and justice. *Journal of Nursing Management, 20,* 1–8.

Harris, T. B., Li, N., & Kirkman, B. L. (2014). Leader–member exchange (LMX) in context: How LMX differentiation and LMX relational separation attenuate LMX's influence on OCB and turnover intention. *Leadership Quarterly, 25,* 314–328.

Heider, F. (1958). *The psychology of interpersonal relations.* New York: John Wiley.

Henderson, D. J., Liden, R.C., Glibkowski, B. C., & Chaudhry, A. (2009). LMX differentiation: A multilevel review and examination of its antecedents and outcomes. *Leadership Quarterly, 20,* 517–534.

Henderson, D. J., Wayne, S. J., Shore, L. M., Bommer, W. B., & Tetrick, L. E. (2008). Leader-member exchange, differentiation, and psychological contract fulfillment: A multilevel examination. *Journal of Applied Psychology, 93,* 1208–1219.

Hooper, D. T., & Martin, R. (2008). Beyond personal leader-member exchange (LMX) quality: The effects of perceived LMX variability on employee reactions. *Leadership Quarterly, 19,* 20–30.

House, R. J., & Aditya, R. N. (1997). The social scientific study of leadership: Quo vadis? *Journal of Management, 23,* 409–473.

Hu, J., & Liden, R. C. (2013). Relative leader-member exchange within team contexts: How and when social comparison impacts individual effectiveness. *Personnel Psychology, 65,* 1–46.

Kristof-Brown, A. L., Zimmerman, R. D., & Johnson, E. C. (2005). Consequences of individuals' fit at work: A meta-analysis of person-job, person-organization, person-group, and person-supervisor fit. *Personnel Psychology, 58,* 281–342.

Le Blanc, P. M., & Gonzalez-Roma, V. (2012). A team level investigation of the relationship between leader-member exchange (LMX) differentiation, and commitment and performance. *Leadership Quarterly, 23,* 534–544.

Lee, J. (2001). Leader-member exchange, perceived organizational justice, and cooperative communication. *Management Communication Quarterly, 14,* 574–589.

Liao, H., Liu, D., & Loi, R. (2010). Looking at both sides of the social exchange coin: A social cognitive perspective on the joint effects of relationship quality and differentiation on creativity. *Academy of Management Journal, 53,* 1090–1109.

Liden, R. C., Erdogan, B., Wayne, S. J., & Sparrowe, R. T. (2006). Leader-member exchange, differentiation, and task interdependence: Implications for individual and group performance. *Journal of Organizational Behavior, 27,* 723–746.

Liden, R. C., & Graen, G. (1980). Generalizability of the vertical dyad linkage model of leadership. *Academy of Management Journal, 23,* 451–465.

Liden, R. C., Sparrowe, R. T., & Wayne, S. J. (1997). Leader-member exchange theory: The past and potential for the future. In G. R. Ferris (Ed.), *Research in personnel and human resources management* (Vol. 15, pp. 47–119). Greenwich, CT: JAI Press.

Liden, R. C., Wayne, S. J., & Stilwell, D. (1993). A longitudinal study on the early development of leader-member exchanges. *Journal of Applied Psychology, 78,* 662–674.

Ma, L., & Qu, Q. (2010). Differentiation in leader–member exchange: A hierarchical linear modeling approach. *Leadership Quarterly, 21,* 733–744.

Maksom, H. H. B., & Winter, R. (2009). Leader-member exchange differentiation in the military platoon. *Leadership & Organization Development Journal, 30,* 696–708.

Martin, J. (1981). Relative deprivation: A theory of distributive injustice for an era of shrinking resources. In B. M. Staw & L. L. Cummings (Eds.), *Research in organizational behavior* (Vol. 3, pp. 53–107). Greenwich, CT: JAI Press.

Maslyn, J. M., & Uhl-Bien, M. (2001) Leader–member exchange and its dimensions: Effects of self-effort and other's effort on relationship quality. *Journal of Applied Psychology, 86,* 697–708.

Nahrgang, J. D., Morgeson, F. P., & Ilies, R. (2009). The development of leader-member exchanges: Exploring how personality and performance influence leader and member relationships over time. *Organizational Behavior and Human Decision Processes, 108,* 256–266.

Naidoo, L. J., Scherbaum, C. A., Goldstein, H. W., & Graen, G. B. (2011). A longitudinal examination of the effects of LMX, ability, and differentiation on team performance. *Journal of Business Psychology, 26,* 347–357.

Nishii, L. H., & Mayer, D. M. (2009). Do inclusive leaders help to reduce turnover in diverse groups? The moderating role of leader–member exchange in the diversity to turnover relationship. *Journal of Applied Psychology, 94,* 1412–1426.

Runciman, W. G. (1966). *Relative deprivation and social justice.* Berkeley, CA: University of California Press.

Scandura, T. A. (1999). Rethinking leader–member exchange: An organizational justice perspective. *Leadership Quarterly, 10,* 25–40.

Schriesheim, C. A., Castro, S. L., & Cogliser, C. C. (1999). Leader–member exchange (LMX) research: A comprehensive review of theory, measurement, and data-analytic practices. *The Leadership Quarterly, 10,* 63–113.

Schyns, B. (2006). Group consensus in Leader-member exchange (LMX) and shared work values related to organizational outcomes? *Small Group Research, 37,* 20–35.

Sherony, K. M., & Green, S. G. (2002). Coworker exchange: Relationships between coworkers, leader–member exchange, and work attitudes. *Journal of Applied Psychology, 94,* 1412–1426.

Sias, P. M., & Jablin, F. M. (1995). Differential superior-subordinate relations, perceptions of fairness, and coworker communication. *Human Communication Research, 22,* 5–38.

Smith, H. J., Pettigrew, T. F., Pippin, G. M., & Bialosiewicz, S. (2012). Relative deprivation: A theoretical and meta-analytic review. *Personality and Social Psychology Review, 16,* 203–232.

Spence, J. R., Ferris, L., Brown, D. J., & Heller, D. (2011). Understanding daily citizenship behaviors: A social comparison perspective. *Journal of Organizational Behavior, 32,* 547–571.

Stewart, M. M., & Johnson, O. E. (2009). Leader-member exchange as a moderator of the relationship between work group diversity and team performance. *Group & Organizational Studies, 34,* 507–535.

Tangirala, S., Green, S. G., & Ramanujam, R. (2007). In the shadow of the boss's boss: Effects of supervisors' upward exchange relationships on employees. *Journal of Applied Psychology*, *92*, 309–320.

Tse, H. H. M., Ashkanasy, N. M., & Dasborough, M. T. (2012). Relative leader–member exchange, negative affectivity and social identification: A moderated-mediation examination. *Leadership Quarterly*, *23*, 354–366.

Tse, H. H. M., Lam, C. K., Lawrence, S. A., & Huan, X. (2013). When my supervisor dislikes you more than me: The effect of dissimilarity in leader-member exchange on coworkers' interpersonal emotion and perceived help. *Journal of Applied Psychology*, *98*, 974–988.

Van Breukelen, W., Konst, D., & Van Der Vlist, R. (2002). Effects of LMX and differential treatment on work unit commitment. *Psychological Reports*, *91*, 220–230.

Van Breukelen, W., Van Der Leeden, R., Wesselius, W., & Hoes, M. (2010). Differential treatment within sports teams, leader-member (coach-player) exchange quality, team atmosphere, and team performance. *Journal of Organizational Behavior*, *33*, 43–63.

Vecchio, R. P., Griffeth, R. W., & Horn, P. W. (1986). The predictive utility of the vertical dyad linkage approach. *Journal of Social Psychology*, *126*, 617–625.

Vidyarthi, P. R., Erdogan, B., Anand, S., Liden, R. C., & Chaudhry, A. (2014). One member, two leaders: Extending leader-member exchange theory to a dual leadership context. *Journal of Applied Psychology*, *99*, 468–483.

Vidyarthi, P. R., Liden, R. C., Anand, S., Erdogan, B., & Gosh, S. (2010). Where do I stand? Examining the effect of leader-member exchange social comparison on employee work behaviors. *Journal of Applied Psychology*, *95*, 849–861.

Walker, I., & Smith, H. J. (2002). Fifty years of relative deprivation research. In I. Walker & H. J. Smith (Eds.), *Relative deprivation: Specification, development, and integration* (pp. 1–9). Cambridge: Cambridge University Press.

Wood, J. V. (1996). What is social comparison and how should we study it? *Personality and Social Psychology Bulletin*, *22*, 520–537.

Yammarino, F. J., Dionne, S. D., Chun, J. A., & Dansereau, F. (2005). Leadership and levels of analysis: A state-of-the-science review. *Leadership Quarterly*, *16*, 879–919.

Tracing Structure, Tie Strength, and Cognitive Networks in LMX Theory and Research

Raymond T. Sparrowe *and* Cécile Emery

Abstract

This chapter reflects on the growing relationship between Leader–Member Exchange (LMX) theory and research and social network analysis. We first discuss the themes of structure and tie strength in relation to several of the theoretical formulations of LMX theory that have served as the foundation for subsequent research. This section proceeds chronologically, beginning with the earliest work on the Vertical Dyad Linkage (as the LMX perspective was initially known) and concluding with recent empirical research integrating LMX and social networks. Our goal is to provide a narrative review of the development of the themes of structure and tie strength within the LMX literature. We then turn to recent developments in the field in which LMX differentiation figures prominently both theoretically and empirically, and engage in a close critical reading of this work from the perspective of cognitive social networks. We conclude by summarizing the opportunities for future research that emerge from our narrative and conceptual analysis.

Key Words: leader–member exchange, vertical dyad linkage, social networks, cognitive networks

Introduction

This chapter offers a discussion of Leader–Member Exchange (LMX) theory in relation to three themes that are central to social network analysis: the importance of informal social structure, the nature and dimensionality of dyadic relationships ("tie strength"), and mental representations of social structure (cognitive social networks).

The structural theme identifies the importance of the configuration of relationships within which nodes (individuals, groups, and/or organizations) are embedded. Borgatti, Mehra, Brass, and Labianca (2009) nicely summarize this theme: "Whereas traditional social research explained an individual's outcomes or characteristics as a function of other characteristics of the same individual" (p. 894), in social network analysis "a node's outcomes and future characteristics depend in part on its position in the network structure" (p. 893). Hence

there is the prevalence of centrality in its various forms in many applications of network theory to leadership research (e.g., Balkundi, Kilduff, & Harrison, 2011; Goodwin, Bowler, & Whittington, 2009; Mehra, Dixon, Brass, & Robertson, 2006; Sparrowe & Liden, 2005; Venkataramani, Green, & Schleicher, 2010).

Tie strength refers to the quality of the relationship between two contacts and, as such, is a dyadic-level construct. Granovetter's (1973) preliminary definition of tie strength is "a (probably) linear combination of the amount of time, the emotional intensity, the intimacy (mutual confiding), and the reciprocal services which characterize the tie" (p. 1361). His counterintuitive hypothesis was that weak rather than strong ties are important for outcomes—for example, in finding a job (Granovetter, 1974). Strong ties, in contrast to weak ties, are associated with the formation and maintenance of trust, loyalty, and interpersonal support between leaders and members (Brass & Krackhardt, 1999). This is not to say, however, that tie strength is wholly independent of informal social structure. As Granovetter has pointed out, it is weak ties—not strong ties—that bridge to distant social locales. Or, in Burt's (1992) unique terminology, "the causal agent in the phenomenon is not the weakness of a tie but the structural hole it spans" (p. 27).

That tie strength and LMX are both dyadic level constructs brings them readily into partial alignment with one another, even though the primary conceptualization of LMX—be it unidimensional (negotiating latitude, as in Dansereau, Graen, & Haga, 1975) or multidimensional (contribution, loyalty, respect, and liking, as in Liden & Maslyn, 1998)—differs from the dimensions specified by Granovetter (1973). The fundamental question that we wish to explore is whether to conceptualize LMX relationship quality within a nomological network of hierarchical relations, or to find an alternative conceptualization that is not hierarchy specific. Why? Because a hierarchy-free conceptualization makes the leader–member dyad commensurate in its dimensions to nonhierarchical dyads, as found in much social network research.

Less well developed is the relationship between the structural theme of network theory and LMX research, in part because much of LMX research has focused on the antecedents and outcomes of dyadic relationship quality independent of the networks in which those dyads are embedded. Although scholars (Sparrowe & Liden, 1997, 2005) have noted how early expressions of LMX theory implied an appreciation for how resources flow through the formal organizational structure (e.g., Graen, Cashman, Ginsburg, & Schiemann, 1977), we will demonstrate in this review that several of the major expressions of LMX theory over the past four decades touch on this theme.

Our third theme, cognitive networks, is gathering growing interest in applications of social network theories to organizational phenomena (see Brands, 2013, for a review of this work). Cognitive networks are mental representations of individuals' social networks in which there are actors ("nodes") and the relationships among them ("ties"). In contrast to "actual" networks in which each actor ("ego") reports his or her relationship with other actors ("alters"), in cognitive networks those ties among alters' contacts are as perceived by ego. A cognitive social structure, then, combines actual relations

with perceived relations into a three-dimensional network (Krackhardt, 1987). Whether the network as perceived by ego (the cognitive network) accurately reflects what his or her alters themselves report (the "actual" network) becomes a matter of theoretical and empirical interest. Cognitive networks have not been explored previously in LMX research, but we suggest that leaders' and members' cognitions about the quality of their own dyadic relationships, as well as how they mentally represent "ingroups" and "outgroups," are cognitive social structures. Thus—to anticipate what follows—at the group level, the mental representations of LMX differentiation offer a touchstone for dialogue with the theory underpinning cognitive social networks.

We begin with an analysis of the themes of structure and tie strength in relation to several of the theoretical formulations of LMX theory that have served as the foundation for subsequent research. This material proceeds chronologically, beginning with the earliest work on the Vertical Dyad Linkage (as the LMX perspective was initially known) and concluding with recent empirical research integrating LMX and social networks. Our goal is to provide a narrative review of the development of the themes of structure and tie strength within the LMX literature. We then turn to recent developments in the field in which LMX differentiation figures prominently both theoretically and empirically, and engage in a close critical reading of this work from the perspective of cognitive social networks. We conclude by summarizing the opportunities for future research that emerge from our narrative and conceptual analysis.

Uncovering Tie Strength and Informal Structure in LMX Research

The LMX perspective is represented by an extensive stream of research over the past decades. Much of that research is empirical, but there have been a number of theoretical articles that both summarize what has been done in the past and break new ground for work in the future. We rely primarily on several of these comprehensive theoretical formulations of LMX in tracing our themes of informal structure and tie strength. In understanding the initial formulations of LMX theory (then, the Vertical Dyad Linkage) we draw from two sources: Graen et al. (1977) and Cashman, Dansereau, Graen, and Haga (1976). Reflecting on a decade of research, Dienesch and Liden (1986) sought to reconceptualize the nature and dimensionality of the dyadic relationship and, in 1987, Graen and Scandura imagined dyadic relationships beyond the vertical dyad, thus introducing the concept of a "dyadic network." Graen and Uhl-Bien (1995) developed this concept in greater detail in "Stage 4" of their model of relationship-based leadership, explicitly linking dyadic relationship quality among individuals to the network of task interdependencies through which they perform the work. Shortly thereafter, Sparrowe and Liden (1997) put forward a model specifying how LMX and social networks jointly contribute to member assimilation in organizations. These theoretical formulations have been followed in the past decade by several noteworthy empirical efforts linking LMX and social networks.

Structure and Tie Strength in the Vertical Dyad Linkage: Graen et al. (1977) and Cashman et al. (1976)

The historical basis for exploring the relationship between LMX and social network analysis can be located in the early expressions of the predecessor to LMX, the "Vertical Dyad Linkage" (VDL) model of leadership. The notion of the "Vertical Dyad," borrowed from Likert (1961), refers to a "linking pin" in a vertical chain of relationships spanning members, their leaders, their leaders' leaders ("bosses"), and so forth on up to the top that define the hierarchy of an organization. Likert had suggested that effective leaders display both effective upward

influence with their bosses and a supportive downward leadership style with their members (as cited in House, Filley, & Gujarati, 1971, p. 422). When discussing the results of their study of members, leaders, and bosses in a university setting, Graen et al. (1977) conclude as follows: "Thus, leaders in higher-quality linking pins, having established *strong ties* with their bosses, are in better positions to facilitate the accomplishments of their members" (p. 503, emphasis ours).

In Cashman et al. (1976) this "linking pin" framework was joined to the distinctive insight of VDL research, namely, that leaders differentiate based on the quality of the relationships they form with their members, ingroups and outgroups. These differentiated VDLs, when organized hierarchically, map the "organizational understructure" through which resources flow. Thus, "[m]embers whose superior can command greater resources are likely to experience fewer organizational problems and thereby report greater satisfaction with their work situation than members who are not as fortunate [. . .] The chief assumption here is that responsibility and authority flow more readily through In-group VDLs than through Out-group VDLs" (pp. 282–283). Figure 16.1 represents a network of vertical dyads as imagined by Cashman et al. (1976).

From a network perspective, it is interesting to note several features of this network. First, it is

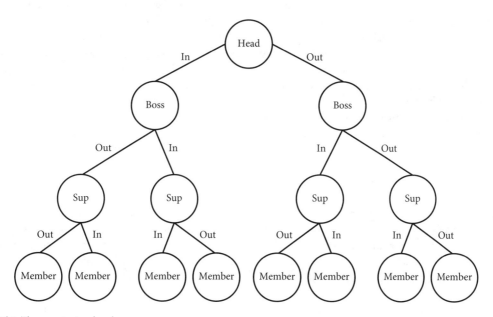

Fig. 16.1 The organizational understructure.

obviously "vertical" in the sense that the important ties follow the formal organizational hierarchy. (With apologies to Krackhardt and Hanson, 1993, this is not the "company behind the chart"; it *is* the chart!) The absence of horizontal ties from boss to boss, supervisor to supervisor, and member to member makes it apparent that the linkages in the organizational understructure are organized hierarchically into a network. Furthermore, applying the logic of dyadic relationship quality—the benefits of "in" dyads versus the costs of "out" dyads—it appears that the third member from the left is in a terrific position whereas the member farthest to the right is in desperate straits (!). And that is precisely the point: even in its earliest formulation, LMX theory recognized the significance of not only the immediate vertical dyad, but also those once, twice, or three times removed for member outcomes.

With few exceptions, this point seems to have been quickly forgotten. Much of the empirical research that followed within the VDL and, subsequently, LMX perspectives has engaged in uncovering the antecedents and outcomes of the quality of the relationship between leaders and members within dyads and not in relation to entire chains of linkages. This emphasis can easily be seen by looking forward to the comprehensive review of LMX research by Liden, Sparrowe, and Wayne (1997) and the meta-analysis of Gerstner and Day (1997); although both mention an emerging interest in the potential interplay between LMX and social networks, the preponderance of the empirical research reviewed in these articles takes the leader–member dyad as its primary unit of analysis. But this is not to say that the network orientation was completely lost in the theoretical developments within the LMX domain. It reemerges in the work of Graen and Scandura (1987), to which we will turn after examining the next chronological development in LMX theory.

Refining the LMX Relationship: Dienesch and Liden (1986)

The emphasis in Dienesch and Liden (1986) is on two concerns: reenvisioning the nature of the LMX relationship from a unidimensional to a multidimensional construct and offering a model of the process through which LMX develops. Although the core linking pin idea whereby relations beyond the immediate dyad matter is given passing notice—"it has been shown that leaders who do not have a good relationship with their immediate superior tend to have less to offer subordinates than leaders who

have cultivated good relationships with their immediate superiors" (p. 630)—the possibility that other dyads, indeed entire networks, might be important is not addressed. The focus is not on the structure of dyadic relationships, but on the dimensionality (nature and strength of ties) of leader–member relationships.

What Dienesch and Liden (1986) contribute in terms of tie strength is potentially significant for relating LMX and network perspectives. Previous work conceptualized the dyadic relationship in relation to the "negotiating latitude" (e.g., Dansereau et al., 1975) accorded to members by their leaders; Dienesch and Liden (1986) proposed that the relationship be conceptualized in terms of three related dimensions, loyalty, contribution, and affect (liking). In a subsequent effort to develop a measure of multidimensional LMX, Liden and Maslyn (1998) added a fourth dimension, professional respect. What is interesting about this development for our theme of tie strength is this: whereas "negotiating latitude" is intrinsically hierarchical in concept (what the leader grants to the member), the multidimensional construct taps relationship quality in more general terms. We can easily imagine co-worker relationship quality being understood in relation to the contribution offered by each partner, the loyalty each shows toward the other, the extent to which each respects the other, and the degree to which each likes the other. The multidimensional model thus applies equally well to horizontal as to vertical relationships, and so offers a single operationalization of tie strength that could be applied to both vertical and horizontal relationships in explaining the relative impact of various forms of ties on outcomes. We return to this opportunity in our conclusion as an occasion for future research.

Dyadic Networks and Relationship Quality in Graen and Scandura (1987)

Graen and Scandura (1987) present a constructive formulation of a theory of "dyadic organizing" that brings into an integrated conceptual framework the key ideas of VDL and LMX research. The "building blocks" of interlocking dyads remain, but they are placed within the context of "unstructured problems" whereby organizational members exchange their cooperation—for example, "contributions"—in solving such problems for discretionary resources—"inducements"—offered by their managers (pp. 177–179). This interplay of inducements and contributions is the process whereby differentiated roles emerge within groups. When leaders have discretionary resources to offer as inducements, and members possess the capabilities and motivation necessary to "collaborate successfully on an unstructured task," the two exchange partners are likely to engage in role negotiation. Absent managers' discretionary resources, and/or members' ability and willingness to cooperate, "little role emergence can take place" (p. 186).

The "dyadic structure" that emerges from role-making processes is conceptualized by Graen and Scandura (1987) as two dimensional: relationship *quality* and *coupling* (see Figure 16.2).

LMX *quality* includes the extent to which leaders and members show loyalty, support, and trust toward each other. LMX *coupling*—as in "loosely" versus "closely" coupled—reflects the extent to which leaders delegate to members, granting them "a great deal of latitude" (Graen & Scandura, 1987, p. 192) in how they accomplish their work. LMX develops through a role-making process in which leaders offer discretionary inducements and members reciprocate with contributions. As the member demonstrates greater contributions, the leader grants increasing latitude, until the mature phase of the LMX relationship when the role-making process has reached the routinization stage and becomes

loosely coupled; that is, "[t]he member needs less direction ("initiation of structure") to complete the assignment than at earlier phases" (p. 192).

Graen and Scandura's (1987) two-dimensional formulation bears reflection in light of the contemporaneous developments concerning the nature and dimensionality of LMX (e.g., Dienesch & Liden, 1986). Graen and Scandura (1987) emphasize that the relationship quality emerging from the "coupling" during the role-making process precedes and so is the foundation for relationship quality. LMX development is not simply a process of acquaintance and growing familiarity; rather, trust and loyalty follow from role taking (leaders 'sampling' members' responses to inducements), role development, and role routinization. Furthermore, and in opposition to Dienesch and Liden (1986), the one relational attribute that Graen and Scandura (1987, p. 191) expressly exclude is affect; high-quality LMX might be a "strong tie" (Graen et al., 1977, p. 503) but high-quality LMXs are not friendship ties.

With respect to structure, Graen and Scandura's (1987) formulation of the nature and development of LMX initiates a modest revision of the close alignment of the organizational understructure and the formal organizational hierarchy characteristic

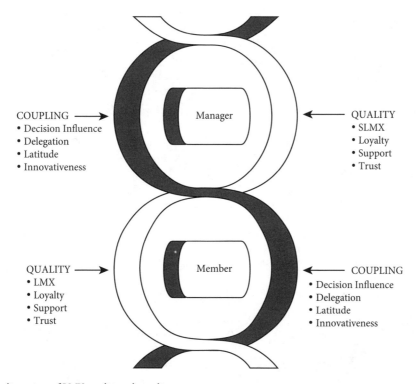

Fig. 16.2 Two dimensions of LMX, quality and coupling.

Reprinted from Graen, G. B., & Scandura, T. A. (1987). Toward a psychology of dyadic organizing. *Organizational Behavior, 9*, 192. ©1987, with permission from Elsevier.

of the Vertical Dyad Linkage approach (Cashman et al., 1976). Modest is the appropriate adjective because Graen and Scandura (1987) are definitive in their claim that "[c]learly, dyadic organizing is a within-unit phenomenon" (p. 197). They also affirm the importance of vertical dyads: "In terms of resource dependency, the quality at the linking pin between upper and lower dyads in the management hierarchy appears to be critical" (p. 199). But there is also a point at which Graen and Scandura (1987) sever the bonds between the "organizational understructure" and the hierarchy represented in the formal organizational chart and this development occurs in their discussion of dyadic networks:

> It should be noted that any focal actor can share a large number of different dyads. Each engages only a part of the focal actor's personality and comprises only a part of his or her environment. The total set of all relevant dyads for a focal actor within an organization is conceptualized as a dyadic network. Such a network may include dyads to which the focal actor is not a member (e.g., the one immediately above in the hierarchy). The referent is clearly the individual's and not the organization's dyadic network. (pp. 202–203)

This assembly of dyadic relations is now understood by Graen and Scandura (1987) to encompass not only a member's formal (hierarchical) relations but also—at least potentially—those relations that are informal as well. Furthermore, these relations can be "mapped conceptually and empirically [. . . so

that. . .] an understructure can be made visible and analyzable. This understructure represents a hidden face of social organization" (p. 202), and is illustrated in Figure 16.3.

The relations on the left show the focal individual (focal), his or her superior (boss), and several members (M1–M3). The relations on the right represent those individuals not vertically connected to the focal individuals, but with whom he or she interacts. They include a person at the same level in the hierarchy (peer), the peer's boss (shared with the focal), another contact higher in the hierarchy (Z), and several of the peer's subordinates (M4–M5). Graen and Scandura's (1987) interpretation of this network holds that the relationships with Peer and M3 are the most relevant because they are "sharing dyads with multiple connecting dyads," whereas person Z is least relevant because he or she is "distantly connected with only a single connection" (p. 202).

From the network analysis perspective, the idea that the structure and quality of informal relationships beyond the vertical dyad matter for outcomes is hardly novel. Within the LMX literature, however, it represents a distinctively different take on the way the original insight about linking pin relationships is understood. This insight is reflected in Scandura's (1988) dissertation research in which managerial outcomes are related not only to LMX and mentoring relationships, but also to what she terms "professional networking" relationships that include peers, subordinates, and other ties within and beyond the organization. Measures included

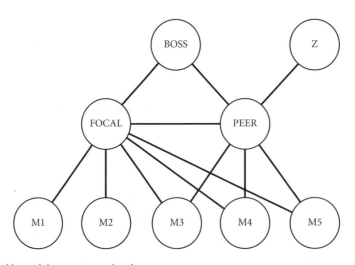

Fig. 16.3 Dyadic assemblies and the organizational understructure.

Adapted from Graen, G. B., & Scandura, T. A. (1987). Toward a psychology of dyadic organizing. *Organizational Behavior, 9*, 192. ©1987, with permission from Elsevier.

both networking behavior (a 12-item self-report measure) as well as an ego-network measure tabulating both the number and strength of ties. Although the empirical results were mixed, it is clear that the theory and empirical tests relating networks and LMX to managerial performance and career outcomes in Scandura's dissertation represents a significant (and under-recognized) advance in integrating the two perspectives.

Aligning Networks with Task Interdependencies: Graen and Uhl-Bien (1995)

The next significant development in the formulation of LMX theory is that of Graen and Uhl-Bien (1995), who organized the history of LMX research into four stages: "Stage 1 is the discovery of differentiated dyads; Stage 2 is the investigation of characteristics of LMX relationships and their organizational implications (e.g., outcomes of LMX); Stage 3 is the description of dyadic partnership building; and Stage 4 is the aggregation of differentiated dyadic relationships to group and network levels" (p. 225). It is Stage 4 that is of interest here.

Building on the idea of "network assemblies" in Graen and Scandura (1987), Graen and Uhl-Bien (1995) describe how these networks emerge from differentiated dyadic relationships as follows: "The leadership structure [. . .] emerges from the enactment of formally defined roles by organizational members [. . .] who develop a network of relationships based on mutual dependencies" (p. 234). Key here is to realize that the dependency in question is task related; the leadership structure is "mapped" onto the task structure of the organization: "Stage 4 involves investigating patterns of relationship quality within the leadership structure, taking into consideration the criticality of relationships for task performance, as well as the effects of differentiated relationships on each other and on the entire structure" (p. 234). At the group level of analysis, relating dyadic relationship quality and task interdependence involves understanding the antecedents and outcomes of differentiation; that is, "how higher-quality and lower-quality exchanges are aggregated within a single work unit and what their combined effect is on group-level work processes and outcomes" (p. 234). Extending beyond the group level to the organizational level, the central question becomes "What are the critical task networks and what kinds of relationships are necessary for effective enactment of these networks?" (p. 235). Finally, at the level of multiple organizations, the central question

posed at Stage 4 of the Graen and Uhl-Bien (1995) framework is: "Are individuals who are effectively positioned within the organizational structure (e.g., who have high-quality relationships with critical others) more effective in external relationships, in what way, and how does this affect organizational performance?" (p. 235).

The core idea of Graen and Uhl-Bien's (1995) "Stage 4" is that dyadic ties are important for group and organizational outcomes to the extent that they link individuals who are critical in the network of task interdependencies. This idea is novel in that it no longer takes for granted the importance of the vertical (leader–member) dyad and, instead, brings task interdependence and criticality into the picture. It also has considerable intuitive appeal because separating task-relevant ties from other ties would seem to be important in modeling how networks shape performance. Nevertheless, it has not been the subject of empirical work with the LMX literature—perhaps because of methodological limitations in modeling relationships between networks with the techniques traditionally used in LMX research. Network analysis, however, has well-established theory and methods for such analyses (Krackhardt & Carley, 1998). We sketch the implications of this idea for future research in our conclusion.

Tie strength is not addressed in depth in the Graen and Uhl-Bien (1995) formulation of LMX at "Stage 4," but it is a primary focus in Stages 1 and 2 where differentiated relationship quality and its outcomes are emphasized. Nevertheless, it plays an important role. If the dyadic ties linking individuals together reflect high-quality relationships ("strong ties") then the work will flow effortlessly through the network of task interdependencies.

Locating the "Exchange" in LMX and Extending the Domain beyond the Dyad: Sparrowe and Liden (1997)

Sparrowe and Liden (1997) bring LMX and social network theory together under a larger narrative, adapted from early LMX theory (Cashman et al., 1976), that recounts how members enter an organization, are "sponsored" by their leaders, and subsequently are "assimilated"—that is, gain legitimacy as influential "players" (Burt, 1997) or withdraw. What social network theory contributes to this narrative is as follows: During the "Initial Relationship Development" phase, contacts shared by the leader and new member may function as a "cue that anchors perceptions of similarity and frames expectations about future exchange" (Sparrowe & Liden, 1997, p. 534), thereby affecting the initial development of LMX quality. Subsequently, during the "Sponsorship" phase, leaders incorporate members into their networks of trusted relationships—and the extent to which a given member is incorporated is a function of the exchange quality she or he enjoys with the leader. Sponsorship grants members the legitimacy through which they develop their own networks beyond those shared with their leaders. Finally, during the "Assimilation" phase, members reciprocate by incorporating their leaders into their own networks, such that "leaders can be expected to benefit from the social resources and relationships derived from members' networks, just as members benefited from their leaders' networks under sponsorship" (p. 542).

Sparrowe and Liden's (1997) model of the interplay of LMX and social network during the dynamics of the assimilation process draws primarily on the structural theme in social network theory. They do, however, address the nature of the dyadic relationship by portraying it in relation to reciprocity; specifically, to Sahlins's (1972) reciprocity continuum. The conceptual logic relating exchange theories and various conceptualizations of LMX is developed in detail in Liden et al. (1997). What is important for our purposes is to grasp the implication of this approach; the advantage Sparrowe and Liden (1997) claim is that, unlike other conceptualizations that are somewhat specific to the vertical dyad, the reciprocity continuum can be applied to "the entire domain of exchange relationships in which LMX relationships are embedded" (p. 526). Although not explicitly stated as such, this advantage suggests that exchange quality in leader–member dyads and tie strength in larger informal networks could share a common operationalization in reciprocity. Empirical research (Uhl-Bien & Maslyn, 2003) has confirmed that the dimensions of reciprocity identified by Sahlins cluster in ways that are consistent with LMX theory.

Structure and Tie Strength: Recent Empirical Research

In the past decade there have been a number of empirical explorations of how social network theories and methods enable the understanding of LMX, its antecedents, and its outcomes in ways that move "beyond the dyad" and in ways presaged by earlier theoretical work. We next identify the central empirical contributions of this work.

Sparrowe and Liden (2005) offer empirical support for several of the central propositions of their earlier theorizing. Members, they find, gain influence not only because they enjoy high-quality LMX relationships but also through their central positions in the advice network. The relationship between centrality and influence, in turn, depends on sponsorship: the extent to which a member is part of his or her leader's inner circle of trusted contacts. Furthermore, the outcome of sponsorship depends on the leader's own advice network centrality. Where leaders are high in advice centrality, sponsorship enhances the relationship between members' own centrality and influence. However, when leaders are low in advice centrality, sponsorship is detrimental: being in these leaders' inner circles decreases the relationship between a member's own advice centrality and his or her influence.

If relationship quality is shaped by the social context beyond the dyad, then this would imply that the antecedents of LMX established in previous research should be examined in light of leaders' and members' social networks. Goodwin et al. (2009) explore how antecedents of LMX quality are shaped by network centrality. With respect to members, they show that the relationship between the leader's frequency of interaction and the member's perceptions of LMX is moderated by the leader's centrality. With respect to leaders, they show that the relationship between the similarity a leader has with a member and the leader's perceptions of LMX quality is moderated by the member's centrality.

Venkataramani et al. (2010) offer three contributions to understanding how LMX should be understood as extending beyond the dyad. The first involves elaborating the mediating role played by members' perceptions of their leaders' status. Leaders who are central in peer networks and who enjoy high-quality vertical relationships are accorded greater status by their members and establish higher quality relationships with them. Second, the mediating role of status perceptions (and LMX) extends to members' discretionary attitudes and behaviors, supporting the idea that "leader's perceived status and member's LMX [. . . are. . .] the intervening variables that transmitted the effects of leader's social ties onto member outcomes" (p. 1079). Third, these perceptions of status are especially important to members who themselves are low in centrality within the group in forming LMX quality: "when members are well-connected within their own peer network, they have alternative sources of some valued resources, such as social support, information, and informal status within the group" (p. 1080).

These three studies can be seen as empirical elaborations of ideas either implicit or explicit in the earlier theoretical formulations of LMX theory; Venkataramani et al. (2010) echoes Graen et al. (1977) by building on the importance of networks that surround leaders for members; Goodwin et al. (2009) demonstrates that leaders' and members' network centrality shape the exchange processes that lie at the core of LMX; and Sparrowe and Liden (2005) tease out the interplay of LMX and networks in the emergence of influence through sponsorship.

Social Networks and LMX Differentiation

Within the LMX perspective, research in the past decade has begun to move beyond its prior emphasis on the dyad. This work is motivated in part by the nature of LMX itself: just as differentiation has important implications for member outcomes at the dyadic level, so also should it have important implications at the group level. Recent research thus has begun to examine LMX differentiation, operationalized as the mean and/or variability in LMX, as a group level construct affecting team outcomes (e.g., Boies & Howell, 2006; Liden, Erdogan, Wayne, & Sparrowe, 2006) as well as a contextual factor that impacts member outcomes (e.g., Erdogan & Bauer, 2010; Henderson, Wayne, Shore, Bommer, & Tetrick, 2008; Liao, Liu, & Loi, 2010; Tse, Ashkanasy, & Dasborough, 2012). Moving from the dyadic to the group level of analysis affords a novel opportunity for dialogue with social network analysis because differentiated LMX relationships can be understood as a hub-and-spoke network structure with ties of varying strength. This is a dialogue still in its infancy, and so much of what follows is intended to build a foundation for future research at the intersection of LMX and social network theories.

An initial expression of this dialogue (Sparrowe, 2014) has pointed out that LMX differentiation research, by focusing on the hub-and-spoke network of dyadic relations with the leader, overlooks ties among members. From the social network perspective, this is a critical omission because the ties among members are important for understanding the informal social structure of the group. Evenly distributed ties among members would describe a cohesive informal structure, whereas clustered ties would suggest cliques or even opposing subgroups.

Focusing only on group mean and variance is likely to mask these important differences and their potential impact on individual and group outcomes. An important exception to this approach is that of Li and Liao (2014), who modeled four configurations of LMX differentiation: shared, bimodal, minority, and fragmented—each affecting performance through its effects on coordination. Although this study suggests that there are traces of different informal structures in dyadic ties, focusing solely on leader–member relations cannot capture the informal social structure with the same breadth as social network approaches.

Variations in the Psychological Experience of LMX Differentiation

In furthering this dialogue between LMX and social network theory our interest lies in the psychological processes whereby differentiation affects individual (and group) outcomes. We first take up the question of members' experience of differentiation as it has been formulated in the literature in four ways: (1) Perceived LMX Differentiation (PLMXD), which refers to a member's perceptions of the distribution of LMX relationships within the group (Hooper & Martin, 2008; Swaab, Emery, & Booth, 2014); (2) Relative LMX (RLMX), which refers to a member's position relative to other members of the group (Henderson et al., 2008; Hu & Liden, 2013); (3) LMX Social Comparison (LMXSC), which refers to the subjective ratings by individuals of their LMX compared to the LMXs of co-workers and distinct from "actual" differentiation (Vidyarthi, Liden, Anand, Erdogan, & Ghosh, 2010); and (4) LMX Relational Separation (LMXRS), which reflects a member's disparity from others in the group (Harris, Li, & Kirkman, 2014). After introducing these variations in LMX differentiation we consider their implications from the perspective of social networks.

PLMXD, RLMX, and LMXSC derive their theoretical foundations from social comparison theory. In the case of PLMXD, Hooper and Martin (2008) hold that differentiation engenders social comparison, which results in perceptions of unfairness. They demonstrate empirically that members' perceptions of differentiation have negative effects on satisfaction and well-being, even as individual LMX is positively related to these outcomes. Similarly, proponents of RLMX hold that LMX differentiation "creates a psychological boundary for interpersonal comparison that may lead each employee to be aware of her or his relative standing in a workgroup.

Thus, an employees' relative standing of her or his LMX relationship (RLMX; defined as an employee's LMX quality relative to the average LMX quality of others within a workgroup) may also influence her or his work attitudes and behaviors" (Tse et al., 2012, p. 354).

Empirically, RLMX has been shown to be related to in-role and extra-role performance through self-efficacy[1] (Hu & Liden, 2013), to job performance through social identification with the group (Tse et al., 2012), as well as to in-role performance and to the sportsmanship—but not helping—dimensions of citizenship behaviors through psychological contract fulfillment (Henderson et al., 2008). LMXSC was introduced as the psychological representation of RLMX: "we argue that actual differences in LMX between a focal individual and coworkers (RLMX) influence focal employees' subjective perceptions of these differences in LMX (LMXSC)" (Vidyarthi et al., 2010, p. 850) and thus are expected to mediate the relationships between RLMX and outcomes. This expectation finds significant empirical support: LMXSC fully mediates the relationship between RLMX and Organizational Citizenship Behaviors (OCBs), and partially mediates the relationship between RLMX and in-role performance (Vidyarthi et al., 2010).

Where PLMXD, RLMX, and LMXSC differ lies in their respective operationalization and measurement. PLMXD requires respondents to count the number of group members who have LMX quality ranging in five steps from very poor to very good (Hooper & Martin, 2008). Based on the assumption that members seek objective information in forming social comparisons (Hu & Liden, 2013), RLMX was operationalized as the difference between a member's score and the average LMX for the group. In Henderson et al. (2008), RLMX was computed as the difference between the member's LMX and the group mean, whereas Hu and Liden (2013) employed response surface modeling to tease out the effects of the components of RLMX simultaneously. Consistent with the psychological nature of the LMXSC construct, Vidyarthi et al. (2010) developed and validated a six-item scale in which respondents compare themselves to other members; for example, "I have a better relationship with my manager than most others in my work group" (p. 853).

LMXRS, in contrast to the other three variations on LMX differentiation, draws from the group engagement model (Tyler & Blader, 2000, 2003). This view holds that leaders, through the differentiated relationship they form with members, foster relative standing within the group (Harris et al., 2014). In contrast to RLMX, what matters is not the sign or direction of the difference but the absolute value, because, following a distinction made by Harrison and Klein (2007), LMXRS is a measure of separation rather than disparity (Harris et al., 2014). This distinction becomes clearer when the computation of LMXRS is understood: the formula, derived from Tsui, Egan, and O'Reilly (1992), takes the difference between one member's LMX score and every other member's LMX score, squares each of those scores, sums them, and then takes the square root of the sum and divides it by the number of members in the group. In the model of Harris et al. (2014), LMXRS moderated the relationships between LMX and performance and turnover intentions at the individual level, and LMX differentiation moderated the relationships between LMX and performance and LMX and turnover intentions.

The empirical support for these elaborations on LMX differentiation offers impressive empirical evidence for the value of moving beyond the individual leader–member dyad and modeling the larger context of leader–member relations within the group. That these constructs are closely related conceptually, but independently explain incremental variance in outcomes—as in Harris et al. (2014), is especially interesting. What is distinctive about these constructs is how each seeks to illuminate the psychological or cognitive processes underlying the effects of LMX differentiation, be it through social comparison or assessments of relative standing and the group engagement model. Both psychological processes, we would point out, require members to form mental representations of the quality of the relationships other members enjoy with the leader, and it is those representations that serve as the reference point for determining an individual's position relative to others. The question then becomes one of where these representations of the relationships other members form with the leader stand with respect to structure. Are they social networks? And, if so, how might social network theory inform and illuminate our understanding of LMX differentiation and its role as a contextual factor?

Mental Representations of LMX Differentiation as Cognitive Networks

In the most basic sense these representations are networks insofar as they have the requisite features of nodes (the leader and the members of the group) and ties (the dyadic relationships linking members to the leader). Because the ties between other members and the leader are as perceived by the focal member ("ego" in social network parlance), these are cognitive networks (Krackhardt, 1987) as opposed to "actual" networks in which ties are reported by the other members themselves. The difference between cognitive networks and "actual" networks is a topic of emerging interest in social network research, especially in relation to the possibility that cognitive networks often do not perfectly represent actual ties or the strength of ties (Brands, 2013). An individual might perceive a tie where one does not exist, or fail to recognize an existing tie. Some scholars have attributed inaccuracy in network perceptions to the workings of systematic biases, such as a propensity to see balance in relations among friends (Krackhardt & Kilduff, 1999) and to group contacts into clusters ("small worlds") to a greater degree than what is actual (Kilduff, Crossland, Tsai, & Krackhardt, 2008).

In addition to the emphasis on accuracy, a second important development in the understanding of cognitive networks is the realization that they are *activated* representations of social structure. The distinctions among the potential, activated, and mobilized networks are helpful here. The potential network includes "full set of contacts people have at their disposal"; the activated network includes "the subset of the potential network that actually comes to mind in a given situation"; and the mobilized network "is the subset of the activated network that people actually solicit resources from" (Smith, Menon, & Thompson, 2012, p. 68). Following the logic of Smith et al. (2012), the activated network includes who "comes to mind" when individuals mentally represent a subset of their full set of contacts. Furthermore, the potential network lies largely beneath conscious awareness, but can be made accessible through priming. The "name generator" items on social network surveys that invite respondents to identify their friends, neighbors, or contacts "with whom you have discussed important matters" are examples. But networks are activated "in the wild" as well as in response to threats, such as the imminent loss of one's job (Smith et al., 2012) or impending organizational restructuring (Srivastava, 2014). A clear implication for understanding network accuracy is that virtually all activated networks are inaccurate in the sense that they are incomplete representations of the potential network. But that is only part of the story. Other factors may shape activated network representations in systematic ways;

for example, when facing a job threat, high-status individuals activated larger networks than low-status individuals (Smith et al., 2012).

As Brands (2013) points out, "[i]mplicit in the work on systematic bias in network perceptions is the assumption that accurate perceptions of networks are somehow advantageous" (p. S93). In part, this assumption reflects a necessary condition if individuals are to reap benefits from their brokerage networks: "those who have an accurate understanding of the relationships around them are better equipped to deploy social strategies that involve, for example, playing one individual off against another" (p. S93). There is empirical evidence supporting this assumption. Krackhardt (1990) has demonstrated that organizational members whose perceptions of advice networks are accurate are seen as more powerful than their peers. The converse also finds empirical support: individuals can benefit from the inaccuracy in the network perceptions of others; Kilduff and Krackhardt (1994) have shown that being perceived as having highly placed friends enhances one's reputation for performance, whether or not one actually has those friends.

Evaluating Variations from the Cognitive Network Perspective

Thus, given this background, we suggest that when a member mentally represents the leader–member relations within the group, this is an activated cognitive network. The strength of each tie in this activated network—that is, the LMX quality—is what she or he perceives and may or may not reflect what either the leader or member would themselves report. Furthermore, it is a subset of the potential group network because it omits ties among members. With these ideas in mind, we return to each of the variations in LMX differentiation.

PLMXD. The primary feature of note about PLMXD is that it is based on the focal member's activated network of leader–member relations rather than other members' self-reports of LMX quality. The measure itself, in which respondents identify how many members fall into one of five categories of relationship quality, is not particularly fine-grained. Even so, it could be used to estimate the mean and variation in LMX for each member and those values could be evaluated for consistency or agreement. If members' own self-reports of LMX quality also were available, it would be possible to create an "actual" network of LMX relations to which each member's cognitive network could be compared. Perhaps accuracy would be related to individual outcomes, or perhaps the overall accuracy within the group would be related to group-level outcomes.

RLMX. Research modeling LMX differentiation by means of RLMX follows its original formulation in Graen, Liden, and Hoel (1982) in which a focal member's own LMX score is subtracted from the mean value of LMX in the group (as in Henderson et al., 2008; Hu & Liden, 2013; Tse et al., 2012). The resulting RLMX value serves as a proxy for the member's own assessment of her or his relative standing with the leader through social comparison. Several questions about the formulation of RLMX can be raised from the cognitive network perspective introduced above. The first concerns the assumption that the social comparison process engaged by the focal member is based on accurate information about the dyadic relationship quality of others. Given the growing evidence of bias in the perceptions of networks—and here, differences in tie strength—whether this assumption holds is an empirical question that deserves exploration.

The second question concerns the referent of social comparison, the average LMX for the group. Even if it were assumed that members' cognitive network perceptions accurately reflect actuality, how the "average" is represented by the focal member needs clarification. Is this a matter of explicit mental arithmetic, or is there a more intuitive process at play? This question goes unanswered in Tse et al. (2012) and Henderson et al. (2008); only Hu and Liden (2013) attempt an answer: "people tend to choose the 'average' or the whole team as the referent point and evaluate whether they are better than or worse than average" (p. 132). If there is low LMX differentiation in the group then perhaps the focal member would easily estimate the average because the group to which she or he belongs can be perceived in its entirety and mentally represented as a whole. But if there is high differentiation, would that also be the case? Under high differentiation, there is no "actual" or "objective" average afforded to the perception of the focal member; at best, she or he would have to serially represent the relationship quality of each dyad and then estimate the average.

Furthermore, Hu and Liden (2013) state that this evaluation of relative standing can occur unconsciously as when "seeing other teammates laughing and happily talking with the leader may send subliminal signals of the quality of others' relationships with the leader and implicitly affect the focal employee's evaluation of the self" (p. 133).

This assertion does not sound like explicit mental arithmetic performed upon accurate perceptions of actual dyadic relations. It suggests instead the activation of cognitive networks in which the focal member's relative status within the informal hierarchy of differentiated LMX relationships is already represented.

If it is difficult to imagine members computing the group LMX means through mental arithmetic to arrive at their RLMX, then it is even more difficult to imagine how they determine their LMXRS. Clearly, LMXRS is intended to serve as a proxy for a psychological process through which a sense for one's relational separation is determined. Harris et al. (2014) interpret this process in relation to the group engagement model, such that what matters is not the degree of disparity in social comparison but the degree of separation from the group with which a member would identify. In terms of operationalization, however, the crucial difference between RLMX and LMXRS can be illustrated with a figure representing two networks of LMX relationships.

In Figure 16.4a, Member 3 (M3) has an LMX score of six, well above the other members all of whom have LMX scores of two. In Figure 4b the situation is reversed; M3 has an LMX score of two whereas the other members have LMX scores of six. The interesting question then becomes how is the psychological response of Member 3 in these two conditions to be interpreted? In Figure 4b, M3 has the lowest RLMX score (−3.20) and the highest LMXRS score (1.60); both scores would suggest lower performance and higher turnover intentions relative to other members of the group. But in Figure 16.4a, Member 3 has the identical LMXRS score (1.60) and yet the highest RLMX score (+3.20), and there the predictions diverge completely. Although Harris et al. (2014) conducted supplementary analyses in which LMXRS explained variance in outcomes when controlling for RLMX, it remains difficult to sort out these differences at the conceptual or theoretical level.

The cognitive social network perspective may shed some light on these questions. In network terms, the psychological experience of LMXRS is that of being a social isolate—that is, having substantially fewer ties or no ties at all within a salient social group—and the outcomes of such isolation. Consistent with the interpretation of the group engagement model by Harris et al. (2014), being an isolate reflects social distance regardless of the direction (positive or negative). Being granted high standing relative to other members through the

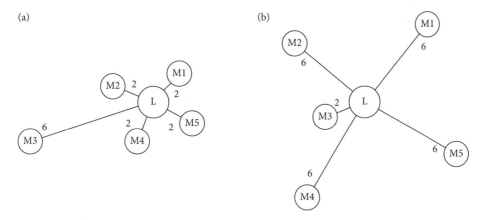

Fig. 16.4 Contrasting RLMX and LMXRS, two cases.

quality of the relationship with the leader may be of marginal value if it isolates the member from the all the other members. Even if the other members all have low LMXs, it is an ingroup of one. However, more so that in the case of RLMX, the absence of any mention of the structure of the ties among members makes this interpretation more speculative than it needs to be. Although the leader can affect standing through the quality of relationships she or he fosters with members, the group engagement model is about identification and cooperation with the group. Knowing what the ties are among members is crucial for understanding the informal structure of identification. Figure 16.5 is intended to clarify the importance of ties among members in understanding social isolation. Figures 16.5a and 16.5b represent the same hypothetical group as in Figure 16.4a; differentiation is relatively low (four of the five members have LMX scores of 2.0), and the fifth member has a high LMX score that makes her a social isolate in the network of leader–member relations. Figures 16.5a and 16.5b add possible ties among the members of the group. For the sake of discussion, assume that these ties reflect high-quality social exchange relationships (e.g., trust or friendship).

In Figure 16.5a, representing M3's activated network of her group, she finds herself to be an isolate over against a clique within the group—and this is in spite of the fact that she enjoys a high LMX relationship. She is in the leader's "in-group" but is not in the group, and so, following the logic of Harris et al. (2014), would be unlikely to engage in discretionary cooperation (i.e., OCBs) with other members. Now consider Figure 16.5b, which in terms of leader–member relations is identical to Figure 16.5a; as a result, the values of RLMX and

LMXRS for every member are identical in each. But M3 is clearly in a different situation. She may be an isolate in Figure 16.5a, but she certainly is not in Figure 16.5b where she is not confronting a clique.

The same overall pattern holds when M3 has a low LMX but all her peers have high-quality relationships; Figures 16.5c and 16.5d add ties among members to Figure 16.4b. In Figure 16.5c, M3 finds herself in the midst of a cohesive group in spite of her low LMX score. Another member, M5, is the social isolate. And in Figure 16.5d, M3 is truly among the "outs"—both vis-à-vis the leader network and among the other members of her group. LMXRS alone cannot account for these differences; nor, for that matter, can RLMX. The scores on those constructs are identical for every member in each of the hypothetical groups in Figure 16.5.

LMXSC. The approach to LMX Differentiation as a context factor taken by Vidyarthi et al. (2010) initially appears to resolve the problematic relationship between actual relations, as reflected in RLMX, and the psychological evaluation of one's standing vis-à-vis the leader relative to others in the group. It achieves this by modeling LMXSC—intended to be a psychological evaluative state—as a mediator; that is, as the outcome of social comparison processes. The wording of five of the six items in the LMXSC scale explicitly requires the respondent to engage in comparison; for example, "I have a better relationship with my manager than most others in my work group" and "Relative to the others in my work group, I receive more support from my manager" (p. 853).

The fact that LMXSC fully mediated the relationship between RLMX and OCBs certainly speaks favorably for this approach. However, some

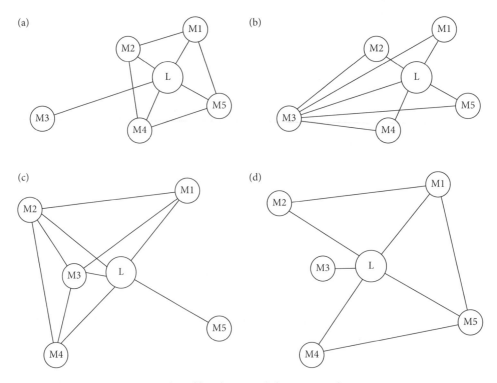

Fig. 16.5 Adding the missing links among members.

issues related to RLMX and social comparison deserve further reflection. For RLMX to serve as the exogenous factor in a causal sequence it is necessary to assume that members activate an accurate mental representation of the dyadic relationship quality of others. As we have discussed, that assumption is open to empirical verification. Second, to answer scale items "relative to others" in the group need not require mental arithmetic to compute a mean, but it does involve calling up a mental representation of one's place vis-à-vis the leader relative to other members. We speculate here, but it seems plausible that the cognitive network activated in responding to the scale items itself bears information about the focal member's status. No explicit calculation would be required; status shapes the form and structure of cognitive networks when activated (Smith et al., 2012). This possibility deserves empirical examination. Insofar as the network correlates of status include in-degree (prestige) and betweenness centrality (brokerage), it would be important to model the network within the group in its entirety.

Conclusions and Directions for Future Research

By tracing the themes of tie strength and structure in the primary expressions of LMX theory as well as

related empirical work we believe we have brought the two perspectives into greater alignment. Our close reading of recent work on LMX differentiation from the perspective of cognitive social networks finds areas of both agreement and disagreement. Four different opportunities for further research have emerged; we briefly summarize each below.

Hierarchy-Free Conceptualization of Tie Strength

Although there are important conceptual similarities between LMX quality and tie strength, the two are operationalized differently. In social network analysis, tie strength is often measured with a single item tapping one of the dimensions identified by Granovetter in his seminal work (Granovetter, 1973). LMX, in contrast, is typically measured by a multi-item scale. LMX-7 (Graen & Uhl-Bien, 1995), one of the more frequently used scales, has items that are specific to the hierarchical leader–member relationship. The LMX-MDM scale (Liden & Maslyn, 1998) is not hierarchical in nature, but consists of 12 items. Although it is feasible to design a study with both LMX and social network data, each must be operationalized using its native measure as in Venkataramani et al. (2010) or Goodwin et al. (2009). A full integration of

LMX and network approaches would be enhanced by the genuine commensurability of their respective measures. It may be feasible to develop an abbreviated measure of relationship quality that correlates highly with the LMX-7 and LMX-MDM as well as with the dimensions of tie strength identified by Granovetter (1973).

Not Just Actors and Ties, but Multiple Networks

The idea developed by Graen and Uhl-Bien (1995), whereby dyadic networks develop in concert with task interdependencies, parallels work by Krackhardt and Carley (1998) in which networks are specified to reflect not only relations among individuals but also among tasks and knowledge. There are thus actor-by-actor networks, task-by-task networks (task interdependence), and knowledge-by-knowledge networks (knowledge interdependence). More interesting still, there are actor-by-knowledge networks (who knows what) and actor-by-task networks (who does what), as well as task-by-knowledge networks (what must be known to perform a task). Using meta-matrix techniques implemented in the Organizational Risk Analyzer software package (Carley, Pfeffer, Reminga, Storrick, & Columbus, 2013), these multiple networks can be evaluated simultaneously to produce a large number of social network indices and statistics. This approach is well suited for testing the implications of the interplay between dyadic relationship quality and task criticality identified by Graen and Uhl-Bien (1995).

Theorizing about and Modeling Entire Networks

Our close reading of the research on RLMX and LMXRS points to the importance of theoretical development and empirical tests that take into account the full context of social relations among members, and not just those ties vis-à-vis the leader. This is not meant to imply that activated cognitive networks with only leader–member ties are uninformative! The empirical support found for understanding important member outcomes through modeling RLMX (Henderson et al., 2008; Hu & Liden, 2013; Tse et al., 2012) and LMXRS (Harris et al., 2014) clearly indicates that these constructs illuminate the effects of LMX differentiation. Activated cognitive networks of leader–member relations show evidence of being highly salient. At the same time, however, the perspective taken by social network theory would be skeptical of the claim that the structure and strength of the ties

between the leader and members fully capture the social context. And although the leader-centric view represented in RLMX and LMXRS is consistent with early formulations of the Vertical Dyad Linkage (Cashman et al., 1976; Graen et al., 1977), subsequent developments in LMX theory by Graen and Scandura (1987) and Graen and Uhl-Bien (1995) recognize the importance of understanding "horizontal" and other ties within and beyond the immediate group. Similarly, empirical work, such as that of Venkataramani et al. (2010), Goodwin et al. (2009), and Sparrowe and Liden (2005), points to the value of looking beyond the leader–member dyad in order to illuminate member outcomes.

Cognitive Networks and Accuracy

Using the average of other group members' own self-reports of LMX quality as a proxy for the focal member's referent in social comparison processes is not an unreasonable approach in light of the practical difficulties involved in gathering cognitive network data. But, in the case of RLMX research, it makes sense to argue that perception is reality—or at least the reality that matters for understanding the member's own social comparison processes. As we have discussed in the foregoing, research (Brands, 2013) has demonstrated that activated cognitive networks display systematic biases. Our suggestion is not that accuracy become the gold standard. Rather, what would be helpful in future research is a more complete understanding of the nature of mental representations of social networks as well as greater insight into the nature and origins of biased perceptions. To what extent are these "biases" actually heuristics that evolved for navigating complex social relations, in the same way that many cognitive "biases" actually are evolved heuristics designed to facilitate "fast and frugal" decision making (Gigerenzer & Goldstein, 1996)? Modeling the activated cognitive networks, rather than relying on "actual" relations as proxies for members' own mental representations, would bring our empirical work closer to the phenomenon we are attempting to understand.

Note

1. In Hu and Liden (2013), self-efficacy partially mediated the relationship between RLMX and in-role performance, but fully mediated the relationship between RLMX and OCBs.

References

Balkundi, P., Kilduff, M., & Harrison, D. A. (2011). Centrality and charisma: Comparing how leader networks and attributions affect team performance. *Journal of Applied Psychology*, 96(6), 1209–1222.

Boies, K., & Howell, J. M. (2006). Leader-member exchange in teams: An examination of the interaction between relationship differentiation and mean LMX in explaining team-level outcomes. *Leadership Quarterly*, 17(3), 246–257.

Borgatti, S. P., Mehra, A., Brass, D. J., & Labianca, G. (2009). Network analysis in the social sciences. *Science*, 323(5916), 892–895.

Brands, R. A. (2013). Cognitive social structures in social network research: A review. *Journal of Organizational Behavior*, 34, S82–S103.

Brass, D. J., & Krackhardt, D. (1999). The social capital of twenty-first-century leaders. In J. G. Hunt, G. E. Dodge, & L. Wong (Eds.), *Out-of-the-box leadership: Transforming the twenty-first-century army and other top-performing organizations* (pp. 179–194). Greenwich, CT: Elsevier Science/ JAI Press.

Burt, R. S. (1992). *Structural Holes: The social structure of competition*. Cambridge, MA: Harvard University Press.

Burt, R. S. (1997). The contingent value of social capital. *Administrative Science Quarterly*, 42(2), 339–365.

Carley, K. M., Pfeffer, J., Reminga, J., Storrick, J., & Columbus, D. *ORA user's guide 2013*. Pittsburgh, PA: Institute for Software Research, Carnegie Mellon University.

Cashman, J., Dansereau, F., Graen, G., & Haga, W. J. (1976). Organizational understructure and leadership: A longitudinal investigation of the managerial role-making process. *Organizational Behavior & Human Performance*, 15(2), 278–296.

Dansereau, F., Graen, G., & Haga, W. J. (1975). A vertical dyad linkage approach to leadership within formal organizations: A longitudinal investigation of the role making process. *Organizational Behavior & Human Performance*, 13(1), 46–78.

Dienesch, R. M., & Liden, R. C. (1986). Leader-member exchange model of leadership: A critique and further development. *Academy of Management Review*, 11(3), 618–634.

Erdogan, B., & Bauer, T. N. (2010). Differentiated leader–member exchanges: The buffering role of justice climate. *Journal of Applied Psychology*, 95(6), 1104–1120.

Gerstner, C. R., & Day, D. V. (1997). Meta-analytic review of leader–member exchange theory: Correlates and construct issues. *Journal of Applied Psychology*, 82(6), 827–844.

Gigerenzer, G., & Goldstein, D. G. (1996). Reasoning the fast and frugal way: Models of bounded rationality. *Psychological Review*, 103(4), 650–669.

Goodwin, V. L., Bowler, W. M., & Whittington, J. L. (2009). A social network perspective on LMX relationships: Accounting for the instrumental value of leader and follower networks. *Journal of Management*, 35(4), 954–980.

Graen, G., Cashman, J. F., Ginsburg, S., & Schiemann, W. (1977). Effects of linking-pin quality on the quality of working life of lower participants. *Administrative Science Quarterly*, 22(3), 491–504.

Graen, G. B., Liden, R. C., & Hoel, W. (1982). Role of leadership in the employee withdrawal process. *Journal of Applied Psychology*, 67(6), 868–872.

Graen, G. B., & Scandura, T. A. (1987). Toward a psychology of dyadic organizing. *Research in Organizational Behavior*, 9, 175–208.

Graen, G. B., & Uhl-Bien, M. (1995). Relationship-based approach to leadership: Development of leader-member

exchange (LMX) theory of leadership over 25 years: Applying a multi-level multi-domain perspective. *The Leadership Quarterly*, 6(2), 219–247.

Granovetter, M. (1973). The strength of weak ties. *American Journal of Sociology*, 78, 1360–1380.

Granovetter, M. (1974). *Getting a job: A study of contacts and careers*. Cambridge, MA: Harvard University Press.

Harris, T. B., Li, N., & Kirkman, B. L. (2014). Leader-member exchange (LMX) in context: How LMX differentiation and LMX relational separation attenuate LMX's influence on OCB and turnover intention. *Leadership Quarterly*, 25(2), 314–328.

Harrison, D. A., & Klein, K. J. (2007). What's the difference? Diversity constructs as separation, variety, or disparity in organizations. *Academy of Management Review*, 32(4), 1199–1228.

Henderson, D. J., Wayne, S. J., Shore, L. M., Bommer, W. H., & Tetrick, L. E. (2008). Leader-member exchange, differentiation, and psychological contract fulfillment: A multilevel examination. *Journal of Applied Psychology*, 93(6), 1208–1219.

Hooper, D. T., & Martin, R. (2008). Beyond personal leader–member exchange (LMX) quality: The effects of perceived LMX variability on employee reactions. *The Leadership Quarterly*, 19(1), 20–30.

House, R. J., Filley, A. C., & Gujarati, D. N. (1971). Leadership style, hierarchical influence, and the satisfaction of subordinate role expectations: A test of Likert's influence proposition. *Journal of Applied Psychology*, 55(5), 422–432.

Hu, J., & Liden, R. (2013). Relative leader-member exchange within team contexts: How and when social comparison impacts individual effectiveness. *Personnel Psychology*, 66(1), 127–172.

Kilduff, M., Crossland, C., Tsai, W., & Krackhardt, D. (2008). Organizational network perceptions versus reality: A small world after all? *Organizational Behavior and Human Decision Processes*, 107(1), 15–28.

Kilduff, M., & Krackhardt, D. (1994). Bringing the individual back in: A structural analysis of the internal market for reputation in organizations. *Academy of Management Journal*, 37(1), 87–108.

Krackhardt, D. (1987). Cognitive social structures. *Social Networks*, 9(2), 109–134.

Krackhardt, D. (1990). Assessing the political landscape: Structure, cognition, and power in organizations. *Administrative Science Quarterly*, 35(2), 342–369.

Krackhardt, D., & Carley, K. (1998). *A PCANS Model of Structure in Organizations*. Proceedings from the International Symposium on Command and Control Research and Technology, Monterey, CA.

Krackhardt, D., & Hanson, J. R. (1993). Informal networks: The company behind the charts. *Harvard Business Review*, 71(4), 104–111.

Krackhardt, D., & Kilduff, M. (1999). Whether close or far: Social distance effects on perceived balance in friendship networks. *Journal of Personality and Social Psychology*, 76(5), 770–782.

Li, A. N., & Liao, H. (2014). How do leader-member exchange quality and differentiation affect performance in teams? An integrated multilevel dual process model. *Journal of Applied Psychology*, 99(5), 847–866.

Liao, H., Liu, D., & Loi, R. (2010). Looking at both sides of the social exchange coin: A social cognitive perspective on the joint effects of relationship quality and differentiation on creativity. *Academy of Management Journal*, 53(5), 1090–1109.

Liden, R. C., Erdogan, B., Wayne, S. J., & Sparrowe, R. T. (2006). Leader-member exchange, differentiation, and task interdependence: Implications for individual and group performance. *Journal of Organizational Behavior*, 27(6), 723–746.

Liden, R. C., & Maslyn, J. M. (1998). Multidimensionality of leader-member exchange: An empirical assessment through scale development. *Journal of Management*, 24(1), 43–72.

Liden, R. C., Sparrowe, R. T., & Wayne, S. J. (1997). Leader-member exchange theory: The past and potential for the future. In G. R. Ferris (Ed.), *Research in personnel and human resources management* (Vol. 15, pp. 47–119). Greenwich, CT: Elsevier Science/JAI Press.

Likert, R. (1961). *New patterns of management*. New York, NY: McGraw-Hill.

Mehra, A., Dixon, A. L., Brass, D. J., & Robertson, B. (2006). The social network ties of group leaders: Implications for group performance and leader reputation. *Organization Science*, 17(1), 64–79.

Sahlins, M. (1972). *Stone age economics*. New York, NY: Aldine de Gruyter.

Scandura, T. (1988). *Beyond the dyad: Interdependence in management networks*. (Doctoral dissertation). Retrieved from UMI Dissertation Services. (Order Number 8822804).

Smith, E. B., Menon, T., & Thompson, L. (2012). Status differences in the cognitive activation of social networks. *Organization Science*, 23(1), 67–82.

Sparrowe, R. T. (2014). Leadership and social networks: Initiating a different dialog. In D. Day (Ed.), *Oxford handbook of leadership and organizations* (pp. 434–454). New York, NY: Oxford University Press.

Sparrowe, R. T., & Liden, R. C. (1997). Process and structure in leader-member exchange. *Academy of Management Review*, 22(2), 522–552.

Sparrowe, R. T., & Liden, R. C. (2005). Two routes to influence: Integrating leader-member exchange and social network perspectives. *Administrative Science Quarterly*, 50(4), 505–535.

Srivastava, S. B. (2014). *Sidewalks and tracks in the grass: The interplay of formal, semiformal and informal networks in organizational restructuring*. Working Paper, University of California, Berkeley.

Swaab, A., Emery, C., & Booth, J. E. (2014). *Dissecting perceived LMX differentiation: An exploration of antecedents and a moderator*. Presented at the Academy of Management Conference in Philadelphia, PA.

Tse, H. H., Ashkanasy, N. M., & Dasborough, M. T. (2012). Relative leader-member exchange, negative affectivity and social identification: A moderated-mediation examination. *The Leadership Quarterly*, 23(3), 354–366.

Tsui, A. S., Egan, T. D., & O'Reilly, C. A. (1992). Being different: Relational demography and organizational attachment. *Administrative Science Quarterly*, 37(4), 549–579.

Tyler, T. R., & Blader, S. L. (2000). *Cooperation in groups: Procedural justice, social identity, and behavioral engagement*. New York, NY: Psychology Press.

Tyler, T. R., & Blader, S. L. (2003). The group engagement model: Procedural justice, social identity, and cooperative behavior. *Personality and Social Psychology Review*, 7(4), 349–361.

Uhl-Bien, M., & Maslyn, J. (2003). Reciprocity in manager-subordinate relationships: Components, configurations, and outcomes. *Journal of Management*, 29(4), 511–532.

Venkataramani, V., Green, S. G., & Schleicher, D. J. (2010). Well-connected leaders: The impact of leaders' social network ties on LMX and members' work attitudes. *Journal of Applied Psychology*, 95(6), 1071–1084.

Vidyarthi, P., Liden, R., Anand, S., Erdogan, B., & Ghosh, S. (2010). Where do I stand? Examining the effects of leader-member exchange social comparison on employee work behaviors. *Journal of Applied Psychology*, 95(5), 849–861.

Leader–Member Exchange and Organizational Culture and Climate

Vicente González-Romá

Abstract

This chapter reviews the literature on the relationships among organizational culture, leader–member exchange quality, and climate. It summarizes the knowledge accumulated to date, points out the limitations of the studies conducted, and suggests themes and questions for future research. Finally, a heuristic model is proposed that integrates the three constructs.

Key Words: LMX quality, LMX differentiation, organizational culture, organizational climate, psychological climate,

Introduction

Founding leaders establish the values and assumptions upon which an organization's culture is initially built (Schein, 1985). These values and assumptions inspire and help define the Human Resources Management (HRM) policies, procedures and practices that translate the organization's espoused values into enacted ones (see Ford et al., 2008, for an example). Leadership processes, styles and behaviors can be considered a subset of these HRM practices. Once implemented, these HRM policies, procedures and practices and the organizational environment they contribute to shaping are the targets of climate perceptions (Kopelman, Brief, & Guzzo, 1990; Ostroff, Kinicki, & Tamkins, 2003). Therefore, leadership, organizational culture and organizational climate are three interrelated constructs. The general goal of the present chapter is to examine the relationships between leader–member exchange (LMX) quality and organizational culture and climate. Thus, we will review the studies focused on these relationships, summarizing the knowledge accumulated up to now, identifying limitations and gaps in the literature, and suggesting issues for future research.

The chapter is organized in four main sections. First, we briefly define the three constructs involved. Second, we review the studies involving LMX quality and organizational culture. Third, we focus on the studies addressing the relationships between LMX quality and organizational climate. And fourth, we provide a heuristic model integrating the examined and suggested relationships among the three constructs.

Constructs Defined

Organizational culture refers to a set of shared values, normative beliefs, and underlying assumptions that characterize organizations and shape the way of doing things inside them (Schein, 1985; Verbeke, Volgering, & Hessels, 1998). Because cultural elements (i.e., values, normative beliefs, and underlying assumptions) are shared among organizational members, organizational culture is an organizational property, that is, a collective or higher-level construct. However, as we will see later, in most empirical studies organizational culture has been operationalized at the individual level of analysis as employee perceptions of organizational culture.

Organizational climate refers to employees' shared perceptions of the policies, procedures and practices that are rewarded, supported and expected in a given organizational environment (Rousseau, 1988; Schneider, 1990). As mentioned above, because organizational climate involves shared perceptions, it is also a higher-level construct. Depending on the work-unit whose climate is being studied (i.e., the whole organization, a department, a work team), climate can be operationalized at different higher levels of analysis (e.g., organization, department, team) by aggregating the corresponding employees' climate scores (provided that a sufficient level of within-unit agreement is shown). In these cases, the aggregated scores obtained are indicators of the *aggregate climate* of the particular work-unit. The employees' climate scores represent the meaning that single employees assign to a specific work-unit, and these scores are indicators of *psychological climate*.

LMX theory posits that leaders develop differential types of relationships with each of their work-unit members through a series of work-related exchanges (Graen & Cashman, 1975; Graen & Scandura, 1987). The quality of these relationships reflects the extent to which a leader and his/her work-unit members mutually exchange resources and support. Whereas low-quality LMX relationships are based on exchanges directly specified by the employment contract, high-quality LMX relationships include exchanges of both material and nonmaterial resources beyond what is required by the formal employment contract. In high-quality LMX relationships, leaders and work-unit members generally show high levels of mutual respect, trust, affection and obligation (Dansereau, Graen, & Haga, 1975; Graen, 1976; Graen & Schiemann, 1978; Graen & Uhl-Bien, 1995; Liden, Wayne, & Stilwell, 1993). The development of differential relationships between leaders and their work-unit members is referred to as *LMX differentiation* (Liden, Erdogan, Wayne, & Sparrowe, 2006; Henderson, Liden, Glibowski, & Chaudhry, 2009).

As in the cases of organizational culture and climate, LMX theory also involves constructs located at different levels of analysis. LMX is a dyadic phenomenon that has most frequently been measured from the perspective of work-unit members (Hiller, DeChurch, Murase, & Doty, 2011), with LMX quality operationalized at the individual level. LMX differentiation is a higher-level dispersion construct that is operationalized at the work-unit level by means of variability statistics. Thus, LMX differentiation indicators show the degree of within-unit variation in members' reports of LMX quality. Finally, in the past few years researchers have begun to examine the work-unit level relationships of LMX (e.g., Liden et al., 2006; Boies & Howell, 2006; Le Blanc & González-Romá, 2012). To do so, work-unit members' LMX scores are aggregated at the work-unit level by means of central tendency statistics.

The first paragraph of this chapter suggests that organizational culture contributes to modeling leadership behaviors, which in turn help to shape climate perceptions. Frequently, the empirical studies reviewed address either the relationship between organizational culture and LMX quality, or the relationship between the latter and climate. Following this trend in the literature, next we review the studies on organizational culture and LMX quality, and then those involving LMX quality and climate.

LMX and Organizational Culture

The relationship between organizational culture and LMX quality was suggested early in the history of LMX theory. Dienesch and Liden (1986) proposed that organizational culture was one of the contextual factors that could influence LMX development. The basic idea underlying this relationship is that the shared values, normative beliefs and assumptions of certain organizational cultures promote leadership behaviors and leader–member relationships that fit the characteristics of high-quality LMX (Erdogan, Liden, & Kraimer, 2006; Graen, 2003; Major, Fletcher, Davis, & Germano, 2008). These cultures stress the importance of friendly and supportive relationships, cooperation and trust among organizational members, teamwork and concern about employee welfare (Aryee & Chen, 2006; Erdogan et al., 2006; Major et al., 2008; Pearson & Maler, 2010). These cultures stimulate the development of value-congruent behaviors and relationships by leaders and work-unit members, thus fostering high-quality LMXs. Interestingly, the values of these cultures fit the characteristics of one of the organizational culture types proposed by Quinn and colleagues within their Competing Values Model: the group or clan culture (Cameron & Quinn, 2006; Quinn & Rohrbaugh, 1983; Quinn & Spreitzer, 1991). Thus, it is plausible to assume that group organizational cultures will foster high-quality LMXs. The empirical evidence accumulated up to now seems to support this idea (see Table 17.1).

Table 17.1. Empirical studies on the relationship between organizational culture and LMX quality.

	Sample	Design	Level[a]	Main findings
Organizational culture as antecedent				
Major, Fletcher, Davis and Germano (2008)	792 from 10 US organizations	Cross-sectional	Cross-level	Organizations' work-family culture had a positive relationship with employees' reports of LMX quality
Erdogan, Liden and Kraimer (2006)	516 teachers from 30 high schools in Turkey	Cross-sectional	Cross-level	Schools' team orientation culture had a positive cross-level relationship with teachers' reports of LMX quality
Aryee and Chen (2006)	192 employees of a Chinese manufacturing firm	Cross-sectional	Individual	Work-unit's group culture was positively related to LMX quality
Herrera, Duncan and Lee (2013)	300 US working adults	Cross-sectional	Individual	Collectivism was positively related to total LMX quality and LMX dimensions
Joo (2010)	516 Korean employees	Cross-sectional	Individual	Organizational learning culture was positively related to LMX quality
Islam, Khan, Ahmad and Ahmed (2013)	415 employees of Malaysian banks	Cross-sectional	Individual	Organizational learning culture was positively related to LMX quality
Organizational culture as a moderator				
Erdogan, Liden and Kraimer (2006)	516 teachers from 30 high schools in Turkey	Cross-sectional	Cross-level	The organizational culture dimensions of respect for people, aggressiveness, and team orientation moderated the individual-level relationships between justice perceptions and LMX quality
Liu, Cai, Li, Shi and Fang (2013)	190 employees from Chinese firms	Cross-sectional	Individual	Collectivism-oriented Human Resource Management moderated the relationship between LMX quality and organizational identification
LMX quality as a moderator				
Erdogan, Kraimer and Liden (2004)	516 teachers from 30 high schools in Turkey	Cross-sectional	Individual	LMX quality moderated the relationship between value congruence (the correlation between teachers' personal value profiles and schools' value profiles) and career satisfaction
Vukonjanski, Nikoli, Hadži, Terek and Nedeljkovi (2012)	256 Serbian middle managers	Cross-sectional	Individual	LMX quality moderated the relationship between organizational culture dimensions and job satisfaction facets

[a] Level at which the relationship between organizational culture and LMX quality was investigated.

Note. The order of the studies in the table follows the order in which they are reviewed in the text.

Organizational Culture as an Antecedent of LMX Quality

Based on the rationale described above, most of the empirical studies examining the relationship between organizational culture and LMX quality have considered the former as a hypothetical antecedent of the latter. Only two studies have conceptualized *and* operationalized culture at the organizational level of analysis. In a cross-sectional study, Major and colleagues (2008) investigated the relationships between work–family organizational culture and LMX quality. They analyzed a sample of 792 information technology employees from 10 US organizations. Work–family organizational culture was defined as "the shared assumptions, beliefs, and values regarding the extent to which an organization supports and values the integration of employees' work and family lives" (p. 882). The results obtained with hierarchical linear modeling showed that work–family culture (an organizational-level variable) had a positive cross-level relationship with organizational members' reports of LMX quality (an individual-level variable). These results supported their idea that high-quality relationships between leaders and work-unit members "are more likely to emerge when they are consistent with the organization's culture" (Major et al., 2008, p. 883).

Erdogan and colleagues (2006) examined, in a cross-sectional study, the relationships among organizational culture, justice perceptions and LMX quality. The study sample was composed of 516 teachers from 30 high schools in Turkey. In an effort to reduce same-source bias, LMX and justice data were collected from a subsample of focal teachers, whereas data on organizational culture were provided by a distinct subsample of peers. It is interesting to note that, using hierarchical linear modeling methods, Erdogan and colleagues observed that one of the organizational culture dimensions considered (team orientation) had a positive cross-level relationship with teachers' reports of LMX quality. They concluded that members of an organization with a culture that emphasizes collaborative behavior and cooperation, interdependence, getting along with others, friendship and harmonious relationships are more motivated to form high-quality leader–member relationships.

Other studies addressing the relationship between organizational culture and LMX quality operationalized the former at the individual level of analysis. Thus, these studies investigated the relationship between employees' perceptions of organizational culture and individual reports of LMX quality. In a cross-sectional study with 192 employees of a Chinese manufacturing firm, Aryee and Chen (2006)[1] investigated the relationship between perceptions of work-unit's group culture (Quinn & Spreitzer, 1991) and LMX quality. They observed a positive relationship between the two variables and suggested that a group culture "(with its emphasis on consensus decision-making, cooperation,

warmth and friendliness) provides a less threatening context that facilitates initiation of relationship building and the subsequent role-making process between a supervisor and his/her subordinate" (Aryee & Chen, 2006, p. 799).

Herrera, Duncan, and Ree (2013) examined, in a cross-sectional study, the relationships between three dimensions of organizational culture (individualism, collectivism, and gender egalitarianism; House et al., 2004) and four dimensions of LMX quality (contribution, loyalty, affect, and professional respect; Liden and Maslyn, 1998). Individualism was defined as "the degree to which individuals express pride, loyalty, and cohesiveness in their organizations" (Herrera et al., 2013, p. 55). Collectivism was defined as the degree to which organizational practices "encourage and reward collective distribution of resources and collective action" (p. 55). Finally, gender egalitarianism was conceptualized as the extent to which an organization "minimizes gender-role differences while promoting gender equality" (p. 55). The study sample was composed of 300 US working adults from different organizations. Employees' total scores on LMX quality and in the four LMX dimensions were regressed on the three culture dimensions in separate regression analyses. The results obtained showed that collectivism was the only culture dimension that showed a significant positive relationship with total LMX quality and with each of the LMX dimensions. Regarding the other two culture dimensions, only gender egalitarianism showed a significant positive relationship with LMX loyalty. Herrera and colleagues (2013) concluded that collectivism was the driving factor in the relationship between the respondents' perceptions of organizational culture and LMX quality.

Joo (2010) investigated the relationship between perceived organizational learning culture and LMX quality in a cross-sectional study with 516 Korean employees working in organizations from different industrial sectors. An organizational learning culture is characterized by encouraging dialogue, collaboration and team learning, empowering organizational members to have a collective vision, and using leaders to model and support learning. As expected, Joo reported a statistically significant, positive correlation between organizational learning culture and LMX quality. Recently, Islam, Khan, Ahmad and Ahmed (2013) replicated Joo's study in a sample of 415 employees of Malaysian banks and found the same result.

Organizational Culture as a Moderator

A few studies have considered organizational culture as a moderator of the relationships between LMX quality and other hypothetical correlates. The rationale underlying the role of organizational culture as a moderator variable can be based on two general arguments. First, as mentioned above, organizational culture is a contextual variable that sets constraints and boundary conditions for organizational phenomena. Second, organizational members are more sensitive and responsive to the presence and absence of stimuli and behaviors that are indicators of their organization's core values (Erdogan et al., 2006). Thus, in cultures with values that promote the development of high-quality relationships among employees, LMX quality will flourish, and its associations with potential functional correlates will be enhanced. In cultures whose values do not stress the development of high-quality relationships, supportive LMXs may find obstacles, and the associations between LMX quality and functional correlates will be weakened. Nevertheless, the specific moderation effect will depend on the variables under investigation.

Erdogan and colleagues (2006), in the sample of Turkish teachers and schools mentioned above, examined whether three dimensions of organizational culture (respect for people, aggressiveness, and team orientation) moderated the relationships between individual perceptions of interactional and distributive justice (the predictor variables), on the one hand, and LMX quality (the criterion), on the other. Respect for people refers to "the extent to which fairness, tolerance, and respect for individual rights are core values" (p. 397). Aggressiveness refers to "the degree to which competitiveness and taking quick advantage of opportunities are shared values" (p. 397). Finally, team orientation was defined as "the degree to which collaborative behavior is valued" (p. 397). The authors found that school-level respect for people moderated the individual-level relationship between interactional justice perceptions and LMX quality, so that when respect for people was high, the relationship was enhanced (a synergistic cross-level interaction). Similarly, schools' aggressiveness moderated the individual-level relationship between distributive justice perceptions and LMX quality, so that when schools' aggressiveness was high, the relationship was enhanced. Finally, schools' team orientation moderated the relationship between interactional and distributive justice perceptions, on the one hand, and LMX quality, on the other, so that when team orientation was high, the two relationships were weakened (antagonistic cross-level interactions). Erdogan and colleagues (2006) pointed out that in schools with a culture high in respect for people, characteristics such as the level of kindness and sensitivity in communications became salient for LMX, which enhanced the relationship between interactional justice and LMX. Similarly, in schools with a culture high in aggressiveness, more tangible aspects, such as whether the reward distribution was equitable, became more salient, which enhanced the relationship between distributive justice and LMX quality. However, in schools with a high team orientation, the existing kind, supportive and collaborative environment, made teachers not base their evaluations of LMX on justice perceptions. Thus, although organizational culture moderated the relationship between justice perceptions and LMX, the specific moderation effect depended on the culture dimension considered.

Liu, Cai, Li, Shi, and Fang (2013) investigated whether employees' perceptions of collectivism-oriented Human Resource Management (C-HRM) moderated the relationship between LMX quality and organizational identification. C-HRM was defined as a set of HRM practices that emphasize maintaining harmonious relationships in the organization, and collective interests, goals, and norms. Because the HRM practices implemented in a given organization are based on its values, we infer that an organization in which C-HRM is practiced to a great extent will have collectivist values. In their cross-sectional, individual-level study, Liu and colleagues (2013) analyzed a sample of 190 leader–follower dyads from electronic firms in two Chinese cities. Data on LMX quality were provided by the surveyed leaders, whereas data on C-HRM and organizational identification were collected from followers. The results obtained showed that C-HRM moderated the positive relationship between LMX quality and organizational identification, so that the relationship was stronger when C-HRM was high than when it was low.

LMX Quality as a Moderator

In two studies involving organizational culture and LMX quality, the latter was considered as a moderator. Using the sample of teachers and schools mentioned above (Erdogan et al., 2006), Erdogan and colleagues (2004) investigated whether LMX quality moderated the relationship between value congruence and job and career satisfaction. Value congruence was operationalized by computing the correlation between teachers' personal value profiles and schools' value profiles. They found some empirical support for the compensatory role of LMX quality. Erdogan and colleagues argued that when value congruence is low, employees have to behave in ways that are congruent with the organization's values but inconsistent with their own values. This dissonance produces dissatisfaction. Under these circumstances, "high LMX relationships may provide employees with the affective and resource-based support to deal with the potential negative effects of low value congruence" (Erdogan et al., 2004, p. 311). These authors observed that LMX quality only moderated the relationship between value congruence and career satisfaction (but not job satisfaction). The interaction "effect" was as expected: value congruence was positively related to career satisfaction when LMX was low, but not when it was high.

Finally, Vukonjanski, Nikoli, Hadži, Terek, and Nedeljkovi (2012) examined, in a cross-sectional study, whether the relationships between nine organizational culture dimensions and nine facets of job satisfaction were moderated by LMX quality. They analyzed a sample of 256 Serbian middle managers working in different organizations. Although they found some empirical support for the moderation hypothesis, they did not provide any theoretical rationale for it. Moreover, the large number of statistical tests involved in the analyses they conducted implied a high risk of capitalization on chance and a high probability of Type I error (a risk that was not corrected).

Studies on LMX Quality and Organizational Culture: Conclusions, Limitations, and Future Research

The number of studies carried out is still insufficient to draw solid conclusions about the relationship between organizational culture and LMX quality. Most of the studies (six out of nine) examined the direct relationship between the two constructs. In this regard, the empirical evidence accumulated up to now seems to suggest that organizational cultures that emphasize the importance of supportive and harmonious relationships, interest in employees, collaboration and cooperation, and teamwork foster the development of high-quality LMX. As mentioned above, the characteristics of these cultures fit the group or clan

organizational culture type proposed by Quinn and colleagues within their Competing Values Model (Cameron & Quinn, 2006; Quinn & Rohrbaugh, 1983; Quinn & Spreitzer, 1991).

Interestingly, the association between group-like *organizational* cultures and LMX quality has been observed across six studies conducted in five different countries (US, Turkey, China, Korea, and Malaysia), even though these countries represent different *national* cultures in terms of horizontal individualism vs. vertical collectivism (Triandis, 1995; Triandis & Gelfand, 1998), which might mean that the relationship between group-like organizational cultures and LMX quality can be generalized to distinct national cultures. This idea should be tested by future studies. In any case, the tentative conclusions presented above have to be interpreted with caution, taking into account the limitations shown by the reviewed studies, which we discuss next.

The first limitation has to do with the studies' design. All the reviewed studies were cross-sectional. Therefore, the information they provide about causality between the involved variables is rather limited. We need studies in which at least the key variables are measured following a time order that is congruent with the hypothetical causal sequence. Second, although organizational culture is a higher-level construct, most studies operationalized it at the individual level. This practice involves some conceptual misspecification and produces ambiguity about the estimates of the investigated relationships, since the relationships that a given variable shows with other variables can change across levels. Future studies examining the relationship between organizational culture and LMX quality should operationalize organizational culture at higher levels of analysis (e.g., organizational or work-unit level,[2] as in Erdogan et al. (2006) and Major et al. (2008)). Finally, in most of the studies, LMX quality and organizational culture data were obtained from the same source (the employees). Along with the fact that analyses were frequently carried out at the individual level, this concern can increase same-source bias, yielding values for correlation and regression coefficients that overestimate the relationships between variables. In order to prevent this problem, LMX and organizational culture data should be obtained from different subsamples of employees (see Erdogan et al., 2006).

Future research addressing the relationship between LMX quality and organizational culture should consider the role of culture strength.

Culture strength has been defined as the degree of within-unit agreement about culture elements (e.g., values and normative beliefs) (González-Romá & Peiró, 2014). Recent research on organizational culture suggests that the influence of organizational culture is enhanced when work-unit culture strength is high (González-Romá & Peiró, 2014). This means that the influence of a unit's group culture on LMX quality should be strengthened by culture strength in the particular culture dimension. Moreover, at the work-unit level of analysis, the combination of high intensity in group culture (i.e., a high aggregate score) and high culture strength should lead to a high work-unit score on LMX quality and low LMX differentiation. If in a given work-unit the values of a group culture are intense and shared by all its members, all of them will be actively involved in the development of high-quality LMXs, which will increase aggregate LMX and reduce LMX differentiation. These ideas should be tested by future studies.

Considering that HRM practices can be used to reinforce and shape specific values (Ngo & Loi, 2008), future research should investigate to what extent LMX can be used to establish and promote the values of a group culture. This idea is congruent with the assumption that organizational culture and HRM practices are reciprocally related (Bowen & Ostroff, 2004; Yeung, Brockbank, & Ulrich, 1991). Finally, we need more empirical investigations on the moderator influence of organizational culture on relationships involving LMX quality. In this regard, it is worth mentioning that no studies have examined the moderator influence of higher-level organizational culture on the relationship between LMX quality and its hypothetical outcomes.

LMX and Climate

The influence of leadership on group climate was documented by the classic studies by Lewin, Lippit, and White (1939) on "Patterns of aggressive behavior in experimentally created 'social climates'". In these studies, three different leadership styles (i.e., authoritarian, democratic, and laissez faire) were manipulated to create three distinct types of "social atmosphere" in groups of children. Later, Litwin and Stringer (1968) also documented leadership's influence on climate in a study with three simulated organizations whose leaders showed different leadership styles. From then until now, the cumulative empirical evidence has shown that leaders have an important influence on climate formation (González-Romá & Peiró, 2014). Leaders provide

unit members with information about organizational policies, procedures and practices, and other work-unit–related issues (González-Romá, Peiró, & Tordera, 2002). They act as interpretative filters of relevant events and facts (Kozlowski & Doherty, 1989), contributing to shaping unit members' perceptions of the work-unit. Moreover, work-unit leaders' behavior is relatively easy to observe, so that leaders are proximal agents to model work-unit members' behavior and inform them about the behaviors that are expected, rewarded and supported. Therefore, it is not surprising that leaders have been described as "climate engineers" (Naumann & Bennett, 2000).

In some of the studies addressing the relationships between leadership and climate, LMX was the leadership model involved. Next, we review these studies (see Table 17.2).

LMX Quality as an Antecedent of Climate

The rationale underlying the influence of LMX quality on work-unit climate perceptions posits that because leaders are the most salient representatives of the organization's policies, procedures and practices, employees will tend to generalize their perceptions of leaders to their work environment (Kozlowski & Doherty, 1989; Scott & Bruce, 1994). Therefore, work-unit members with high-quality LMXs with their leaders will have more functional and positive climate perceptions than members with low-quality LMXs. The results reported by the empirical studies conducted at the individual level of analysis support this trend.

INDIVIDUAL-LEVEL STUDIES

Kozlowski and Doherty (1989), using a US sample composed of 16 supervisors and their 165 subordinates from a manufacturing organization, conducted the first study about the relationships between LMX and climate perceptions. In their cross-sectional study, they found positive correlations between LMX quality and employees' scores on seven (out of eight) organizational climate subscales. Cogliser and Schriesheim (2000) examined, in a cross-sectional study, the individual-level relationships between LMX quality and five climate dimensions (conflict, autonomy, skill variety, support, and social relations). Using a sample of 285 US employees of a library system who worked in 65 work groups, they decomposed each correlation into its between (group level) and within (individual level) components by means of within and between analysis (WABA). They found that four

Table 17.2. Empirical studies on the relationship between LMX quality and climate.

	Sample	Design	Level[a]	Main findings
LMX quality as antecedent				
Kozlowski and Doherty (1989)	165 subordinates from a US manufacturing organization	Cross-sectional	Individual	LMX quality was positively correlated with employees' scores on seven (out of eight) organizational climate facets
Cogliser and Schriesheim (2000)	285 US employees of a library system who worked in 65 work groups	Cross-sectional	Individual	LMX quality was positively correlated with employees' scores on four (out of five) climate facets
Tordera, González-Romá, and Peiró (2008)	383 Spanish health care employees	Cross-sectional	Individual	LMX quality was positively related to psychological climate of support
de la Rosa-Navarro and Carmona-Lavado (2010)	909 Spanish bank employees	Cross-sectional	Individual	LMX quality was positively related to two psychological climate facets (communication and employee welfare)
Ansari, Hung, and Aafaqui (2007)	224 Malaysian managers	Cross-sectional	Individual	LMX contribution, loyalty, affect and professional respect were positively correlated with procedural justice climate, but only respect showed a significant regression coefficient
Dunegan, Tierney, and Duchon (1992)	198 employees of an international chemical company	Cross-sectional	Individual	LMX and CWX quality, and their interaction, were related to climate innovation-related facets
Scott and Bruce (1994)	172 employees of a US industrial corporation	Cross-sectional	Individual	LMX quality had a significant positive relationship with the climate facets of support for innovation and resource supply; CWX quality did not
Tierney (1999)	157 employee-leader dyads from a US organization	Cross-sectional	Individual	LMX quality and inter-member relational quality were positively related to psychological climate for change; employees' reports of LMX quality interacted with supervisors' psychological climate for change
Cogliser and Schriesheim (2000)	285 US employees of a library system who worked in 65 work groups	Cross-sectional	Work-unit	LMX quality was positively correlated with work-unit climate on four (out of five) climate facets
Thomson and colleagues (2011)	711 nursing staff working in 34 US inpatient units of an academic medial center	Cross-sectional	Work-unit	LMX quality was positively related to five (out of eight) safety climate facets

(*continued*)

Table 17.2. Continued

	Sample	Design	Level[a]	Main findings
Tordera and González-Romá (2013)	413 Spanish employees working in 24 health care units	Longitudinal	Work-unit	LMX differentiation moderated the relationship between LMX quality and innovation climate
Kozlowski and Doherty (1989)	165 subordinates from a US manufacturing organization	Cross-sectional	In-group *vs* out-group	Employees with high LMX quality scores showed less variability in climate perceptions than employees with low LMX quality scores. Employees with high quality LMX had climate scores more similar to their supervisors' climate scores
Ford and Seers (2006)	276 employees members of 51 work-units from 4 US companies	Cross-sectional	Work-unit	LMX quality, CWX quality and within-unit variability in CWX quality were related to climate strength

Climate as antecedent

Erdogan, Liden, and Kraimer (2006)	516 teachers from 30 high schools in Turkey	Cross-sectional	Individual	Interactional justice climate was positively related to LMX quality; distributive justice was not
Erdogan and Liden (2006)	100 Turkish employees of two manufacturing plants	Cross-sectional	Individual	Interactional justice climate was positively related to LMX quality; distributive justice was not
Fein, Tziner, Lusky, and Palachy (2013)	105 employees of an Israeli telephone company	Cross-sectional	Individual	Interactional justice climate and ethical climate were positively related to LMX quality; distributive and procedural justice were not
Ishaq, Hussain, Nawaz, Asim, and Cheema (2012)	452 Pakistanis faculty members	Cross-sectional	Individual	Procedural justice perceptions were positively related to LMX quality, and the latter fully mediated the procedural justice-OCB relationship

Climate as a moderator

Tordera, González-Romá, and Peiró (2008)	383 Spanish health care employees	Cross-sectional	Individual	The negative relationship between LMX quality and role overload was moderated by psychological climate facets (innovation, and goals and rules orientation)
Hsiung (2012)	404 Taiwanese salespersons from 70 work-units	Cross-sectional	Cross-level	The positive individual-level relationship between LMX quality and voice behavior was moderated by work-units' procedural justice climate
Sun, Chow, Chiu, and Pan (2013)	238 employees from 42 work-units of 6 Chinese manufacturing firms	Longitudinal	Cross-level	The indirect, individual-level lagged effect of LMX quality on OCB was moderated by units' procedural justice climate

(continued)

Table 17.2. Continued

	Sample	Design	Level[a]	Main findings
Hofmann, Morgeson, and Gerras (2003)	94 subjects from 25 US Army teams	Cross-sectional	Cross-level	Work-units' safety climate moderated the individual-level relationship between LMX quality and safety OCB
Tse, Dasborough, and Ashkanasy (2008)	215 employees of 36 Australian bank branches	Cross-sectional	Cross-level	The individual-level relationship between LMX quality and workplace friendship was moderated by work-units' affective climate
Chen, Kirkman, Kanfer, and Allen (2007)	445 members from 62 teams of a US company	Cross-sectional	Cross-level	The individual-level relationship between LMX quality and individual empowerment was moderated by leadership climate
Erdogan and Bauer (2010)	276 Turkish employees working in 25 work-units	Cross-sectional	Cross-level	Work-units' procedural and distributive justice climate moderated the cross-level relationship between LMX differentiation and individual outcomes
Chen, Lam, and Zhong (2007)	238 Chinese employees working in 45 teams	Cross-sectional	Cross-level	Teams' empowerment climate was positively related to employees' sense of empowerment, which in turn moderated the individual-level relationship between LMX quality and negative feedback-seeking behavior
Zhong, Lam, and Chen (2011)	238 Chinese employees working in 45 teams	Cross-sectional	Cross-level	Teams' empowerment climate was positively related to employees' sense of empowerment, which in turn moderated the individual-level relationship between LMX quality and OCB

[a] Level at which the relationship between LMX quality and climate was investigated.

Note. The order of the studies in the table follows the order in which they are reviewed in the text.

out of the five individual-level correlations computed were positive and statistically significant. The next three studies were conducted outside the US. In a cross-sectional study with 383 Spanish health care employees, Tordera, González-Romá, and Peiró (2008) observed a positive relationship between LMX quality and a psychological climate of support. In another cross-sectional study conducted in Spain, de la Rosa-Navarro and Carmona-Lavado (2010) found, in a sample of 909 bank employees, that LMX quality was positively related to two psychological climate facets (communication and employee welfare). Finally, Ansari, Hung, and Aafaqui (2007), in a cross-sectional study with 224 Malaysian managers from distinct multinational companies, examined the relationships between each of the four dimensions of LMX quality defined by Liden and Maslyn (1998; contribution,

loyalty, affect and professional respect) and procedural justice climate. Ansari and colleagues found that the four LMX dimensions showed significant positive correlations with procedural justice climate. However, when the four LMX dimensions were considered together as predictors of the latter variable, only LMX respect showed a significant positive relationship.

In addition to the LMX quality–psychological climate relationship, several individual-level studies also analyzed the relationship between coworker exchange (CWX) quality[3] and climate perceptions. When a unit member holds high-quality CWXs, his/her relationships with the other work-unit members are characterized by mutual trust, respect, and cooperation (Seers, 1989). Social interaction is one of the bases for climate formation (Ashforth, 1985; Moran & Volkwein, 1992; Schneider & Reichers,

1983). Through social interaction, coworkers communicate to a given focal unit member their interpretations and attributed meanings about the events that occur in their work-unit, contributing to shaping the focal unit member's climate perceptions. Focusing on CWX quality, its relationship with climate perceptions can be based on the fact that coworkers are a key element of employees' psychosocial work environment. Thus, the quality of the relationships that a focal unit member has with his/her coworkers has a relevant impact on his/her perceptions of the entire work environment. Therefore, work-unit members with high-quality CWXs are expected to have more functional and positive climate perceptions than members with low-quality CWXs.

Dunegan, Tierney, and Duchon (1992) investigated whether LMX and CWX quality were related to six climate facets that were supposed to foster innovative activities. In their cross-sectional study, they analyzed a sample composed of 198 employees of an international chemical company. After controlling for employees' division, CWX quality explained significant and unique variance in all climate facets. Once division and CWX quality were controlled for, LMX quality accounted for significant and unique variance in five of the six climate facets. Interestingly, the interaction between CWX and LMX quality was statistically significant in all cases, so that the most desirable climate scores were reported when both CWX and LMX quality were high. In a cross-sectional study on the determinants of innovative behavior, Scott and Bruce (1994) analyzed a sample of 172 employees of a US industrial corporation. They examined whether LMX and CWX quality were related to two dimensions of a climate supportive of innovation (support for innovation and resource supply). The results obtained by means of structural equations modeling (SEM) techniques pointed out that, whereas LMX quality had a significant positive relationship with the two climate facets, CWX quality did not show any significant relationships. Finally, Tierney (1999) investigated whether LMX quality and intermember relational quality were related to psychological climate for change. Her sample was composed of 157 dyads (from a U.S. organization) in which both the employee and the supervisor responded. The results obtained from this cross-sectional study showed that LMX quality and intermember relational quality were positively related to psychological climate for change. In addition, Tierney found an interaction between LMX quality and supervisors'

psychological climate for change. For employees with medium- and high-quality LMX, their climate perceptions became higher as their supervisors' psychological climate for change increased. However, for employees with low-quality LMX, the observed trend was the opposite: their climate perceptions became lower as their supervisors' psychological climate for change increased. These findings suggest that "employees may not only reject social cues regarding change climate from their low LMX supervisor, but the lower quality of their interactions may have a detrimentally confounding effect resulting in the employee having lower climate perceptions than they might otherwise have" (Tierney, 1999, p. 130).

HIGHER-LEVEL STUDIES

Some empirical studies investigated the relationship between LMX quality and climate perceptions at higher levels of analysis. As suggested above, through communication and modeling behavior, leaders can contribute to shaping work-units' shared climate perceptions (González-Romá & Peiró, 2014). Focusing on LMX, by maintaining high-quality relationships with most work-unit members, leaders can improve their work-units' climate. This assertion assumes that the relationship between LMX quality and climate also occurs at the work-unit level of analysis. The available empirical evidence seems to support this assumption. As mentioned, Cogliser and Schriesheim (2000) decomposed the correlations between LMX quality and five climate dimensions into between (group level) and within (individual level) components by means of WABA. They found that in four out of the five correlations considered, both the within and between components were positive and statistically significant. Therefore, they concluded that the LMX quality–climate relationship occurred both within and between groups. Taking these results into account, future examination of this relationship at higher levels of analyses was theoretically and empirically justified.

Thompson and colleagues (2011) investigated the relationship between LMX quality and eight dimensions of safety climate in a sample of 711 nursing staff working in 34 US inpatient units of an academic medical center. After aggregating the LMX quality and safety climate scores at the unit level, the 34 units were divided into 3 groups (tertiles) based on the distribution of the aggregate LMX scores. Then, a MANOVA and a series of planned comparisons between groups (tertiles) were conducted to ascertain whether differences in aggregate LMX quality were associated with differences in aggregate safety climate. The results obtained in their cross-sectional study showed significant differences among the three LMX groups in five of the eight safety climate facets considered. In all cases, the differences were as expected: the higher the aggregate LMX quality, the higher the aggregate safety climate. Interestingly, different types of patient care units (e.g., critical care, medical-surgical, specialty) were included in each of the three groups compared. Thomson and colleagues (2011) interpreted this finding as suggesting that unit climate was "more directly influenced by leadership behavior than the type of patient care provided" (p. 484). This conclusion is congruent with research on climate formation: whereas the influence of leadership is well-documented, the influence of work-units' structural characteristics is less clear (González-Romá & Peiró, 2014).

In a recent longitudinal study, Tordera and González-Romá (2013) examined whether the relationship between work-unit LMX quality and innovation climate was moderated by LMX differentiation. The moderation hypothesis was based on Mischel's (1973) concept of situational strength. When LMX differentiation is low (a strong situation), work-unit members interpret LMXs in a similar way, which fosters similar climate perceptions within the unit. When LMX differentiation is high (a weak situation), work-unit members interpret LMXs in very different ways, which yields very dissimilar climate perceptions. These situations affect the predictability of work-unit climate: the relationship between aggregate LMX quality and unit climate will be greater when LMX differentiation is low rather than when it is high. The authors tested this hypothesis in a Spanish sample of 413 employees working in 24 health care units. Measures were gathered at two time points separated by one year. The results obtained showed that after controlling for innovation climate at Time 1, aggregate LMX quality at Time 1 did not predict innovation climate at Time 2. However, the interaction term formed by Time 1 aggregate LMX quality and Time 1 LMX differentiation did predict it. Tordera and González-Romá (2013) observed that the relationship between aggregate LMX quality at Time 1 and innovation climate at Time 2 was stronger when LMX differentiation was low than when it was high. These results supported the moderator role of LMX differentiation in the relationship between LMX quality and innovation climate at the work-unit level.

In the studies presented above, aggregate unit climate (operationalized as the average of unit members' climate scores) was considered as the criterion variable. Unit climate can be described on the basis of aggregate climate and climate strength (namely, the degree of within-unit agreement in climate perceptions). Recent empirical research has shown that climate strength plays a relevant moderator role in the relationships between work-unit climate and outcomes (for a review see González-Romá & Peiró, 2014). Two studies investigated the relationships between LMX quality and indicators of climate strength. A pioneer investigation in this regard was the aforementioned study conducted by Kozlowski and Doherty (1989). They posited that given the characteristics of high-quality LMXs, where communication is frequent, and trust, loyalty and mutual support are exchange currencies, leaders have many opportunities to model the climate perceptions of the employees involved in these relationships. Thus, the authors hypothesized that subordinates with high-quality LMX would show greater consensus on climate perceptions than subordinates with low-quality LMX. Additionally, they also hypothesized that subordinates with high-quality LMX would show greater agreement with their supervisors' climate perceptions than subordinates with low-quality LMX. Kozlowski and Doherty (1989) divided their sample into two subgroups corresponding to employees above and below the sample median in LMX quality. Then, they compared the variance in the climate scales shown by the two groups. As expected, they observed that employees with high LMX quality scores tended to exhibit less variability in their climate perceptions than employees with low LMX quality scores. Moreover, they also observed that the climate scores of employees with high-quality LMX were significantly more similar to their supervisors' climate scores than the climate scores of employees with low-quality LMX. Although Kozlowski and Doherty (1989) did not directly examine work-units' climate strength, their findings suggested that LMX quality could be one of its antecedents. This idea was investigated in the following study.

Ford and Seers (2006) examined, in a cross-sectional study, the relationships between aggregate LMX quality and LMX differentiation, on the one hand, and climate strength in five climate facets, on the other. Their sample was composed of 276 employees who were members of

51 work-units from 4 different companies located in the US. They found that aggregate LMX quality was positively related to climate strength in two out of the five climate facets considered. However, LMX differentiation did not show any significant relationships. They also investigated the relationships that aggregate CWX quality and within-unit variability in CWX quality had with climate strength. They observed that aggregate CWX quality was positively related to climate strength in one of the climate facets examined, whereas within-unit variability in CWX quality was related to climate strength in two of the climate facets examined. Together, these results suggest that aggregate and dispersion indicators of the quality of the exchanges within work-units can contribute to promoting climate strength.

Climate as an Antecedent of LMX Quality

Although most studies addressing the relationship between LMX quality and climate considered the former variable to be an antecedent of the latter, a few studies assumed that the relationship was in the opposite direction. It has been suggested that climate may impact the initial interaction between leaders and members (Cogliser & Schriesheim, 2000). For instance, if a new work-unit member perceives a hostile and dysfunctional climate in his/her work-unit, he/she may be reluctant to dedicate time, effort and emotional resources to developing high-quality relationships with his/her supervisor due to the possibility that in this unit climate, the investment will not pay off.

Interestingly, in the four empirical studies in which climate was considered an antecedent of LMX quality, the climate facets involved were distinct dimensions of justice climate. In this case, the climate–LMX quality relationship can be explained as follows: when unit members perceive that they are treated fairly by their leader (and consequently, perceive high levels of justice climate), they infer that their leader is committed to them. Based on the norm of reciprocity, unit members want to reciprocate the source of perceived justice, and will contribute to developing high-quality relationships with their leader (Erdogan et al., 2006; Erdogan & Liden, 2006).

The four empirical studies were cross-sectional, and the relationship between justice climate and LMX quality was examined at the individual level of analysis. In the study with Turkish teachers mentioned above, Erdogan and colleagues (2006) found that interactional justice was significantly and positively related to LMX quality; however, distributive justice was not. Similar results were obtained by Erdogan and Liden (2006) with a sample of 100 employees working in two manufacturing plants in Turkey. They found that whereas employee perceptions of interactional justice were significantly and positively related to LMX quality, perceptions of distributive justice were not. More recently, Fein, Tziner, Lusky, and Palachy (2013) examined the relationships that three dimensions of justice perceptions (interactional, procedural, and distributive) and ethical climate had with LMX quality. Their sample was composed of 105 employees of an Israeli telephone company. They found that only interactional justice and ethical climate showed a significant positive relationship with LMX quality. Finally, Ishaq, Hussain, Nawaz, Asim, and Cheema (2012) investigated whether LMX quality mediated the relationship between procedural justice perceptions and organizational citizenship behavior (OCB) in a sample of 452 faculty members working in higher education organizations located in Pakistan. The results obtained showed that procedural justice perceptions were positively related to LMX quality, and the latter fully mediated the procedural justice–OCB relationship. Therefore, the results of these four studies are congruent with the idea that psychological justice climate is related to LMX quality.

Climate as a Moderator

Climate refers to perceptions of the organizational and work environment (Rousseau, 1988). The characteristics of this environment affect the relationships that develop within it. Thus, some studies have investigated the moderator role of climate in the relationships between LMX quality and its hypothetical correlates. The rationale underlying this moderation is based on two general arguments. First, climate signals the kind of responses that can be enacted to reciprocate high-quality LMXs (Hofmann, Morgeson, & Gerras, 2003). For instance, in a work-unit with a high safety climate, behaviors strengthening safe performance in the work-unit (e.g., following safety procedures, and showing and teaching safety procedures to new unit members) are highly valued. Therefore, in these units these behaviors will frequently be used to reciprocate high-quality LMXs (Hofmann et al., 2003). Second, certain climate facets can enhance or decrease the importance of LMX for the well-being and performance of work-unit members. For instance, in a work-unit with a high innovation climate, members will have additional work demands related to the implementation of new ideas. In this context, the relevance of LMX quality as a means to provide unit members with additional resources for handling the increased workload is greater than in a work-unit with a low innovation climate (Tordera et al., 2008). Consequently, the impact of LMX quality should be greater.

In one of the studies where climate was considered as a moderator, it was operationalized at the individual level (that is, as psychological climate). In a cross-sectional study mentioned, Tordera and colleagues (2008) investigated whether four facets of psychological climate (support, innovation, goals orientation, and rules orientation) moderated the relationship between work-unit members' reports of LMX quality and members' role overload. The moderation hypothesis was supported for three of the four climate facets (except support). As expected, the negative relationship between LMX quality and role overload was stronger when psychological climate was high than when it was low.

Other studies conceptualized climate as a shared perception and operationalized it at higher levels of analysis. Two studies investigated whether work-units' procedural justice climate moderated individual-level relationships involving LMX quality. In a cross-sectional study, Hsiung (2012) examined whether work-units' procedural justice climate moderated the individual-level relationship between LMX quality and employee voice behavior. The study sample was composed of 70 units with 404 Taiwanese salespersons. Hsiung found empirical support for the hypothesized cross-level interaction: the positive relationship between LMX quality and employee voice behavior was stronger in work-units with high procedural justice climate than in those with low procedural justice climate. Sun, Chow, Chiu, and Pan (2013) investigated whether the indirect, individual-level effect of LMX quality on OCB (through outcome favorability)[4] was moderated by units' procedural justice climate. The study sample was composed of 238 employees from 42 work-units of 6 Chinese manufacturing firms. Data were collected at three different time points and from two different sources (Time 1 = employees' LMX quality reports and climate perceptions; Time 2 = employees' outcome favorability data; Time 3 = employee OCB rated by supervisors). The results obtained showed that the indirect lagged effect of LMX quality on OCB was moderated by units' procedural justice climate, so that the indirect relationship was statistically significant (and

positive) when procedural justice climate was high, but not when it was low.

Other studies involved other climate facets. Hofmann and colleagues (2003), in a cross-sectional study, tested whether work-units' safety climate moderated the individual-level relationship between LMX quality and safety OCB. Their sample was composed of 94 subjects from the US Army working in 25 teams. They found that the expected cross-level interaction was significant: the relationship between LMX quality and safety OCB was positive and statistically significant when teams' safety climate was high, but not when it was low. Tse, Dasborough, and Ashkanasy (2008) investigated whether work-units' affective climate (i.e., the extent to which interactions within the team are characterized by warmth, support, acceptance, sincerity, and enthusiasm) moderated the individual-level relationship between LMX quality and workplace friendship. They tested the hypothesized cross-level interaction in a cross-sectional study involving 215 employees of 36 Australian bank branches. The results obtained supported the interaction: the relationship between employees' reports of LMX quality and workplace friendship was positive and significant when work-units' affective climate was high, but the relationship was nonsignificant when work-units' affective climate was low. Finally, Chen, Kirkman, Kanfer, Allen, and Rosen (2007) examined the moderator role of work-units' leadership climate (i.e., the extent to which the leader enacts empowering behaviors, such as "encouraging the team to set its own goals and self-manage its tasks and involving the team in decisions that affect members"; Chen et al., 2007, p. 333) in the relationship between LMX quality and unit members' empowerment. Chen and colleagues analyzed a sample of 445 members of 62 teams from a US company. The results reported in their cross-sectional study supported the hypothesized cross-level interaction: the positive relationship between LMX quality and individual empowerment was stronger when leadership climate was high than when it was low.

In the studies presented in the last paragraph, LMX quality was operationalized at the individual level of analysis and climate at the work-unit level. Erdogan and Bauer (2010) conducted a study in which both LMX and climate indicators were operationalized at the work-unit level of analysis. Specifically, they investigated whether procedural and distributive justice climate moderated the cross-level relationship between LMX differentiation and five individual level outcomes (job satisfaction,

satisfaction with coworkers, organizational commitment, helping behaviors, and withdrawal behavior). In their cross-sectional study, Erdogan and Bauer analyzed a sample of 276 Turkish employees working in 25 work-units. Employees reported data on LMX, climate, commitment and satisfaction indicators; helping behavior data were collected from supervisors, and withdrawal behavior information was obtained from company records. Erdogan and Bauer (2010) obtained ample empirical support for the moderation hypothesis: although none of the climate facets moderated the relationship between LMX differentiation and job satisfaction, they moderated the relationships with the other individual criteria. According to their hypotheses, distinct moderation patterns appeared: LMX differentiation was (negatively) related to organizational commitment and satisfaction with coworkers only when work justice climate facets were low; it was (positively) related to helping behaviors only when distributive justice was high; and it was (positively) related to withdrawal behavior only when justice climate dimensions were low.

In ending this section, we review two related cross-sectional studies conducted by Chen and colleagues (Chen, Lam, & Zhong, 2007; Zhong, Lam, & Chen, 2011), in which work-unit empowerment climate (i.e., "the extent to which a group makes use of structures, policies, and practices to support employees' access to power"; Chen et al., 2007, p. 205) was considered an "indirect moderator" of relationships involving LMX quality. The two studies analyzed a sample composed of 238 Chinese employees working in 45 teams. In the first study, Chen and colleagues (2007) examined whether teams' empowerment climate was positively related to employees' sense of empowerment (a cross-level effect), which in turn moderated the individual-level relationship between LMX quality and negative feedback-seeking behavior (an individual-level interaction). In the second study, the involved cross-level effect was the same, but the individual-level relationship addressed was between LMX quality and OCB. The results obtained in the two studies showed that teams' empowerment climate was positively related to employees' sense of empowerment, which in turn moderated the relationship between LMX quality and the two criteria considered. When negative feedback-seeking behavior was the criterion, LMX quality was more strongly (and positively) related to it for employees with a lower sense of empowerment. When OCB was the criterion, LMX quality was more strongly

(and positively) related to it for employees with a higher sense of empowerment. Thus, through its direct relationship with individual empowerment, empowerment climate affected the relationships between LMX quality and the two considered outcomes.

Studies on LMX Quality and Climate: Conclusions, Limitations, and Future Research

The results of the studies conducted on the relationships between LMX quality and climate suggest a number of conclusions. First, at the individual level of analysis, work-unit members' reports of LMX quality are positively related to distinct facets of psychological climate (e.g., support, communication, welfare, responsibility, teamwork, innovation, justice, conflict). Thus, regarding the content of the climate facets involved, we can say that the LMX quality–psychological climate relationship is a broad-range relationship. Second, although the number of studies investigating how LMX *and* CWX quality relate to psychological climate is small, the available empirical evidence suggests that the two exchange constructs are important in shaping work-unit members' climate perceptions. This idea is congruent with research on climate formation, which points out that social interaction between leaders and their work-unit members, and among the latter, are the two most important factors (González-Romá & Peiró, 2014). Third, the relationship between LMX quality and climate occurs at the individual and work-unit levels of analysis (Cogliser & Schriesheim, 2000). Moreover, the scarce available empirical evidence suggests that, at the work-unit level of analysis, LMX, CWX and climate dispersion constructs (e.g., LMX differentiation and climate strength) deserve more attention. For instance, LMX differentiation seems to moderate the relationship between LMX and climate (Tordera & González-Romá, 2013), and within-unit variability in CWX quality is related to climate strength (Ford & Seers, 2006). Fourth, work-unit aggregate climate is a higher-level moderator of the individual level relationships between LMX quality and distinct correlates. This means that the role of work-unit climate as a contextual variable that affects the consequences of LMX quality within a given environment is empirically supported. And fifth, although approximately 50% of the reviewed studies were conducted in the US, the relationship between LMX quality and climate has been observed in different countries.[5] This evidence suggests that this relationship might be generalizable across country borders. The results of a recent meta-analysis on the correlates of LMX quality across 23 countries classified in two cultural groups (horizontal-individualistic vs. vertical-collectivistic) seem to support this idea, although at the same time they provide some nuances. In this meta-analysis, Rockstuhl, Dulebohn, Ang, and Shore (2012) obtained statistically significant mean correlations corrected for measurement error (ρ) between LMX quality and perceptions of distributive, procedural and interactional justice, in samples from both horizontal-individualistic *and* vertical-collectivistic countries. However, the correlations in countries with horizontal-individualistic cultures tended to be greater than the correlations in countries with vertical-collectivistic cultures. In horizontal-individualistic cultures, "personal relationships and liking are more likely to influence how an individual reacts to people in authority", whereas in vertical-collectivistic cultures, there is a stronger respect for authority figures, and responses to them are "based on not only personal relationships or liking but also role-based obligations" (Rockstuhl et al., 2012, p. 1098). Future research should address the generalizability of the LMX quality–climate relationship across national cultures involving other climate facets.

The empirical studies addressing the relationship between LMX quality and climate present some limitations. First, all but two studies (Sun et al., 2013; Tordera & González-Romá, 2013) were cross-sectional. Thus, they offer very limited information about causality relationships. This limitation is especially relevant because different causal orderings have been proposed (e.g., LMX quality → climate, and climate → LMX quality), and in order to test them we need longitudinal studies. Second, LMX quality and climate data were provided by the same source (the employees), which can inflate correlation and regression coefficients estimating the relationship between these two constructs. Although this problem is difficult to avoid in individual-level studies, it can be handled in investigations involving work-unit aggregate climate and in which the size of the sampled units is large enough: one half of the work-unit members could provide data on work-unit climate, and the other half on LMX quality. Finally, some studies did not clearly indicate the level of analysis involved in their constructs, theoretical assumptions and hypotheses; aggregation of individual-level variables was not justified, and the analyses were conducted at levels that surpassed the

appropriate level (e.g., Thomson et al., 2011). These concerns are especially important in this area of inquiry because LMX and climate variables can be conceptualized and operationalized at distinct levels of analysis, and their relationships can be observed at different levels and across levels. Thus, researchers should be very precise and rigorous in specifying these aspects.

Future studies should take these limitations into account. Moreover, future research on the relationship between LMX quality and climate should address the following issues. First, given that distinct causal orderings have been assumed for the LMX quality–climate relationship, future studies should examine whether the two constructs are reciprocally related, and if this is the case, estimate the relative strength of the two causal paths. To do so, these studies will have to implement longitudinal designs in which LMX quality and climate are measured at a minimum of two time points.

Second, and related to the previous point, some scholars who posited that climate affects the development of LMX have suggested that climate's impact is especially relevant during the initial stage of the leader–member interaction (Cogliser & Schriesheim, 2000). To determine whether this is the case, future studies should sample new work-unit members and focus on how the climate of their new work-unit influences the trajectory of LMX–quality development over time. This can be accomplished by means of longitudinal designs in which LMX quality is measured several times over time, together with growth modeling models in which work-unit climate is considered a predictor of these trajectories' slope and intercept.

Third, Kozlowski and Doherty (1989) reported that employees with high quality LMX had greater agreement with their supervisors' climate perceptions than subordinates with low quality LMX. However, because the number of work-units in their sample was very small, they could not test this relationship at the work-unit level, which would represent a more rigorous test of the respective hypothesis (Kozlowski & Doherty, 1989). Moreover, they used difference scores as indicators of agreement, which are known to have important problems (see Edwards, 2001). Recent research using the polynomial regression and response surface techniques proposed by Edwards (1994, 1995, 2001, 2002) has shown that disagreement between team members' and team leaders' climate perceptions can have important dysfunctional consequences for team functioning (Bashshur,

Hernández, & González-Romá, 2011). Thus, it is important to examine, at the appropriate level and using adequate methods, whether LMX quality is a relevant predictor of leader–team disagreement on climate perceptions. This research could highlight a new virtue of LMX quality. To do so, we suggest using the strategies suggested by Edwards (1995) to investigate the antecedents of congruence.

Finally, the presence of dispersion constructs in the empirical literature on the relationship between LMX quality and climate is still scarce. However, the few studies that considered these constructs report important findings that suggest interesting questions for future development in the field. For instance, Tordera and González-Romá (2013) found that LMX differentiation moderated the relationship between aggregate LMX and work-unit innovation climate. Is this moderator effect generalizable to other climate facets? As mentioned above, some scholars suggest that the influence of work-unit climate on LMX development is especially important at the initial stages of the relationship. Can a work-unit climate of support among unit members be contagious for a new leader so that this climate stimulates the leader's supportive behaviors? Is this influence of work-unit climate on LMX development moderated by climate strength? Is the impact of work-unit climate more intense when there is high climate strength? LMX differentiation has shown cross-level "effects" on individual outcomes under certain levels of justice climate (Erdogan & Bauer, 2010). We suggest that LMX differentiation can also have "effects" at the work-unit level on climate dimensions whose content refers to support, cooperation and collaboration among unit members. LMX differentiation creates status differences within the work team based on the quality of leader–member relationships (Liden et al., 2006). Based on the similarity–attraction paradigm (Byrne, 1971; Berscheid & Walster, 1978; Green, Anderson, & Shivers, 1996), we posit that as LMX differentiation increases, team members' attraction to other team members (with distinct LMX relationships with their leader) will decrease, inhibiting behaviors of interest and concern for other team members, and cooperation with them.

Integrating LMX Quality, Organizational Culture, and Climate

The literature on organizational culture, leadership and climate suggests that organizational culture contributes to modeling leadership behaviors, which in turn help to shape climate perceptions. An important gap in the LMX literature we reviewed is that there is no study in which this causal sequence has been tested. In fact, studies examining the relationships among organizational culture, LMX quality and climate are scarce (see Erdogan et al., 2006, for an exception). With the intention of stimulating research involving the three constructs, we have elaborated the heuristic model shown below (see Figure 17.1). This model displays most of the research findings and shows some of the suggested relationships that could be addressed by future studies.

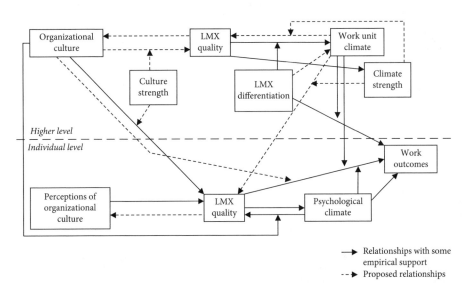

Fig. 17.1 Heuristic model integrating LMX quality, organizational culture and climate.

We want to highlight some characteristics of the model. First, it is congruent with the 'organizational culture–LMX quality–climate' sequence mentioned above, but it also considers the existence of reciprocal relationships between them. These reciprocal relationships have not been tested yet, but in some cases there is empirical evidence supporting one (e.g., aggregate LMX quality–work-unit climate) or both paths involved (e.g., LMX quality and psychological climate). Second, the model assumes that organizational culture, LMX quality, and climate can be operationalized at different levels. Thus, their relationships can be displayed at the individual and higher levels, and across levels. And third, at the work-unit level distinct aspects of the three constructs can be operationalized as aggregate and dispersion variables. This element, together with the multilevel nature of the relationships concerned, means this area of research has good prospects for future development.

Conclusion

Research on organizational culture, LMX quality, and climate has a long road ahead. The empirical findings accumulated up to now are promising, but there is room for improvement and development. Improvement has to be materialized mainly in the design of future studies: we need longitudinal studies that address the issues of causality and the impact of organizational culture and climate on LMX development. Development in the field can be fostered, we think, by answering the research questions formulated in this chapter.

Acknowledgment

The elaboration of this chapter was supported by Research Grant PSI2010-21746 from the Spanish Ministry of Science and Innovation.

Notes

1. In their empirical study, Aryee & Chen (2006) referred to work-unit climate instead of work-unit culture. However, the 5-item scale they used to measure work-unit climate was derived from the group culture scale of the Competing Values Model of organizational culture (Quinn and Spreitzer, 1991). In fact, the only two items that Aryee and Chen (2006) provided as examples ("My work-unit emphasizes human relations, team work and cohesion" and "My work-unit emphasizes assessment of employee concerns and ideas", overlap with two of the items on Quinn and Spreitzer's (1991) group culture scale ("Assessing employee concern and ideas" and "Human relations, teamwork, cohesion"). Because of this, I concluded that what Aryee and Chen (2006) really measured was employees' perceptions of work-unit culture.

2. A substantial degree of differentiation in culture values may exist within organizations (Martin, 1992, 1995). This differentiation may be rooted in the distinct roles employees perform, structural variables (e.g., hierarchical level, department membership) or social interaction cliques, and it may be the basis for the existence of subcultures within organizations (see Jermier, Slocum, & Gaines, 1991).

3. CWX quality has also been labeled team-member exchange quality (Seers, 1989) and quality of work group exchanges (Dunegan, Tierney, & Duchon, 1992).

4. Outcome favorability refers to "the perceived benefits and costs of a decisional resource allocation outcome where the greater the difference between the benefits and costs of a decisional outcome, the higher the probability of the allocation outcome will be considered favorable" (Sun et al., 2013, p. 216).

5. Specifically, the LMX quality-psychological climate relationship has been observed in samples from the US, Spain, and Malaysia; the psychological climate-LMX quality relationship has been reported in studies conducted with Turkish, Israeli and Pakistanis samples; the relationship between LMX quality and climate at the work-unit level has been documented in samples from the US and Spain; and the moderator role of climate in the relationships between LMX quality and its correlates has been observed in samples form the US, Spain, Taiwan, China, Australia and Turkey.

References

Ansari, M. A., Hung, D. K. M., & Aafaqi, R. (2007). Leader-member exchange and attitudinal outcomes: Role of procedural justice climate. *Leadership and Organization Development Journal*, 28, 690–709.

Aryee, S., & Chen, Z. X. (2006). Leader-member exchange in a Chinese context: Antecedents, the mediating role of psychological empowerment and outcomes. *Journal of Business Research*, 59, 793–801.

Ashforth, B. E. (1985). Climate formation: Issues and extension. *Academy of Management Review*, 4, 837–847.

Bashshur, M. R., Hernández, A., & González-Romá, V. (2011). When managers and their teams disagree: A longitudinal look at the consequences of differences in perceptions of organizational support. *Journal of Applied Psychology*, 96, 558–573.

Berscheid, E., & Walster, E. H. (1978). *Interpersonal attraction.* 2nd ed. Reading, MA: Addison-Wesley.

Boies, K., & Howell, J. M. (2006). Leader- member exchange in teams: An examination of the interaction between relationship differentiation and mean LMX in team-level outcomes. *Leadership Quarterly*, 17, 246–257.

Bowen, D. E., & Ostroff, C. (2004). Understanding HRM-firm performance linkages: The role of the "strength" of the HRM system. *Academy of Management Review*, 29, 203–221.

Byrne, D. (1971). The ubiquitous relationship: Attitude similarity and attraction: A cross-cultural study. *Human Relations*, 24, 201–207.

Cameron, K. S. & Quinn, R. E. (2006). *Diagnosing and changing organizational culture: Based on the competing values framework.* San Francisco: Jossey-Bass.

Chen, G., Kirkman, B. L., Kanfer, R., Allen, D., & Rosen, B. (2007). A multilevel study of leadership, empowerment, and performance in teams. *Journal of Applied Psychology*, 92, 331–346.

Chen, Z. G., Lam, W., & Zhong, J. A. (2007). Leader-member exchange and member performance: A new look at individual-level negative feedback-seeking behavior and team-level empowerment climate. *Journal of Applied Psychology*, 92, 202–212.

Cogliser, C. C., & Schriesheim, C. A. (2000). Exploring work-unit context and leader-member exchange: A multi-level perspective. *Journal of Organizational Behavior*, 21, 487–511.

Dansereau, F. Graen, G., & Haga, W. (1975). A vertical dyad linkage approach to leadership within formal organizations: A longitudinal investigation of the role-making process. *Organizational Behavior and Human Performance*, 13, 46–78.

de la Rosa-Navarro, M. D., & Carmona-Lavado, A. (2010). The influence of leader member exchange on the employee's commitment. *Universia Business Review*, 26, 112–133.

Dienesch, R. M., & Liden, R. C. (1986). Leader-member exchange model of leadership: A critique and further development. *Academy of Management Journal*, 11, 618–634.

Dunegan, K. J., Tierney, P., & Duchon, D. (1992). Perceptions of an innovative climate: Examining the role of divisional affiliation, work group interaction, and leader/subordinate exchange. *IEEE Transactions on Engineering Management*, 39, 227–236.

Edwards, J. R. (1995). Alternatives to difference scores as dependent variables in the study of congruence in organizational research. *Organizational Behavior & Human Decision Processes*, 64, 307–324.

Edwards, J. R (2002). Alternatives to difference scores: Polynomial regression analysis and response surface methodology. In F. Drasgow & N. Schmitt (Eds), *Measuring and Analyzing behavior in organizations: Advances in measurement and data analysis* (pp. 350–400). San Francisco, CA: Jossey-Bass.

Edwards, J. R. (1994). The study of congruence in organizational behavior research: Critique and a proposed alternative. *Organizational Behavior & Human Decision Processes*, 58, 51–100.

Edwards, J. R. (2001). Ten difference score myths. *Organizational Research Methods*, 4, 265–287.

Erdogan, B., & Bauer, T. N. (2010). Differentiated leader-member exchanges: the buffering role of justice climate. *Journal of Applied Psychology*, 95, 1104–1120.

Erdogan, B., Kraimer, M. L., & Liden, R. C. (2004). Work value congruence and intrinsic career success: The compensatory roles of leader-member exchange and perceived organizational support. *Personnel Psychology*, 57, 305–332.

Erdogan, B., & Liden, R. C. (2006). Collectivism as a moderator of responses to organizational justice: Implications for leader-member exchange and ingratiation. *Journal of Organizational Behavior*, 27, 1–17.

Erdogan, B., Liden, R. C., & Kraimer, M. L. (2006). Justice and leader-member exchange: The moderating role of organizational culture. *Academy of Management Journal*, 49, 395–406.

Fein, E. C., Tziner, A., Lusky, L., & Palachy, O. (2013). Relationships between ethical climate, justice perceptions, and LMX. *Leadership & Organization Development Journal*, 34, 147–163.

Ford, L. R., & Seers, A. (2006). Relational and team climates: pitting differentiation versus agreement. *Leadership Quarterly*, 17. 258–270.

Ford, R. C., Wilderom, C. P. M., & Caparella, J. (2008). Strategically crafting a customer-focused culture: an inductive case study. *Journal of Strategy and Management*, 1, 143–167.

González-Romá, V., & Peiró, J. M. (2014). Climate and culture strength. In B. Schneider & K. Barbera (Eds.), *The Oxford Handbook of Organizational Climate and Culture* (pp. 496–531). New York: Oxford University Press.

González-Romá, V., Peiró, J. M., & Tordera, N. (2002). An examination of the antecedents and moderator influences of climate strength. *Journal of Applied Psychology*, 87, 465–473.

Graen, G. B. (1976). Role-making processes within complex organizations. In: M. D. Dunette (Ed.), *Handbook of Industrial and Organizational Psychology* (pp. 1201–1245). Chicago: Rand McNally.

Graen, G. B. (2003). Interpersonal workplace theory at the crossroads: LMX and transformational theory as special cases of role making in work organizations. In G. B. Graen (Ed.), *Dealing with diversity* (pp. 145–182). Greenwich: Information Age Publishing.

Graen, G. B., & Cashman, J. F. (1975). A role-making model in formal organizations: A developmental approach. In J. G. Hunt & L. L. Larson (Eds.), *Leadership frontiers* (pp. 143–165). Kent, OH: Kent State Press.

Graen, G. B., & Scandura, T. A. (1987). Toward a psychology of dyadic organizing. In L. L. Cummings & B. M. Staw (Eds.), *Research in organizational behaviour* (Vol. 9, pp. 175–208). The Netherlands: JAI Press.

Graen, G. B., & Schiemann, W. (1978). Leader-member agreement: A vertical dyad linkage approach. *Journal of Applied Psychology*, 63, 206–212.

Graen, G. B., & Uhl-Bien, M. (1995). Development of Leader-Member exchange theory of leadership over 25 years: Applying a multi-domain perspective. *Leadership Quarterly*, 6, 219–247.

Green, S. G., Anderson, S. E., & Shivers, S. L. (1996). Demographic and organizational influences on leader-member exchange and related work attitudes. *Organizational Behavior and Human Decision Processes*, 66, 203–214.

Henderson, D. J., Liden, R. C., Glibowski, B. C., & Chaudhry, A. (2009). LMX differentiation: A multilevel review and examination of its antecedents and outcomes. *Leadership Quarterly*, 20, 517–534.

Herrera, R., Duncan, P., & Ree, M. (2013). Aligning organizational culture with leader-member exchange. *Global Business and Organizational Excellence*, 32, 53–65.

Hiller, N. J., DeChurch, L. A., Murase, T., & Doty, D. (2011). Searching for outcomes of leadership: A 25-year review. *Journal of Management*, 37, 1137–1177.

Hofmann, D. A., Morgeson, F. P. & Gerras, S. J. (2003). Climate as a moderator of the relationship between leader-member exchange and content specific citizenship: Safety climate as an exemplar. *Journal of Applied Psychology*, 88, 170–178.

House, R., Hanges, P., Javidan, M., Dorfman, P., & Gupta, V. (2004). *Culture, leadership, and organizations: The GLOBE study of 62 societies*. London, UK: Sage.

Hsiung, H. H. (2012). Authentic leadership and employee voice behavior: A multi-level psychological process. *Journal of Business Ethics*, 107, 349–361.

Ishaq, M. I., Hussain, N. M., Nawaz, M. M., Asim, A. I., & Cheema, L. J. (2012). Assessment of LMX as mediator in procedural justice—organizational citizenship behavior relationship. *New Educational Review*, 29, 202–211.

Islam, T., Khan, S. R., Ahmad, U. N. U., & Ahmed, I. (2013). Organizational learning culture and leader-member exchange quality. The way to enhance organizational commitment and reduce turnover intentions. *The Learning Organization, 20*, 322–337.

Jermier, N. J., Slocum, J. W., Jr., Fry, L. W., & Gaines, J. (1991). Organizational subcultures in a soft bureaucracy. *Organization Science, 2*, 170–194.

Joo, B. K. (2010). Organizational commitment for knowledge workers: the roles of perceived organizational learning culture, leader-member exchange quality, and turnover intention. *Human Resource Development Quarterly, 21*, 69–85.

Kopelman, R. E., Brief, A. P., & Guzzo, R. A. (1990). The role of climate and culture in productivity. In B. Schneider (Ed.), *Organizational climate and culture* (pp. 282–318). San Francisco, CA: Jossey-Bass.

Kozlowski, S. W. J., & Doherty, M. L. (1989). Integration of climate and leadership: examination of a neglected issue. *Journal of Applied Psychology, 74*, 546–553.

Le Blanc, P. M., & González-Romá, V. (2012). A team level investigation of the relationship between Leader–Member Exchange (LMX) differentiation, and commitment and performance. *Leadership Quarterly, 23*, 534–544.

Lewin, K., Lippitt, R., & White, R. K. (1939). Patterns of aggressive behavior in experimentally created "social climates." *Journal of Social Psychology, 10*, 271–299.

Liden, R. C., Erdogan, B., Wayne, S. J., & Sparrowe, R. T. (2006). Leader-member exchange, differentiation, and task interdependence: Implications for individual and group performance. *Journal of Organizational Behavior, 27*, 723–746.

Liden, R. C., & Maslyn, J. M. (1998). Multidimensionality of leader-member exchange: An empirical assessment through scale development. *Journal of Management, 24*, 43–72.

Liden, R. C., Wayne, S. J., & Stilwell, D. (1993). A longitudinal study on the early development of leader-member exchanges. *Journal of Applied Psychology, 78*, 662–674.

Litwin, G. H., & Stringer, R. A., Jr. (1968). *Motivation and organizational climate*. Boston: Harvard University, Graduate School of Business Administration.

Liu, Z. Q., Cai, Z. Y., Li, J., Shi, S. P., & Fang, Y. Q. (2013). Leadership style and employee turnover intentions: a social identity perspective. *Career Development International, 18*, 305–324.

Major, D. A., Fletcher, T. D., Davis, D. D., & Germano, L. M. (2008). The influence of work-family culture and workplace relationships on work interference with family: a multilevel model. *Journal of Organizational Behavior, 29*, 881–897.

Martin, J. (1992). *Cultures in organizations: Three perspectives*. New York: Oxford University Press.

Martin, J. (1995). Organizational culture. In N. Nicholson (Ed.), *The Blackwell encyclopedic dictionary of organizational behavior* (pp. 376–382). Cambridge, MA: Blackwell.

Mischel, W. (1973). Toward a cognitive social learning reconceptualization of personality. *Psychological Review, 80*, 252–283.

Moran, E. T., & Volkwein, J. F. (1992). The cultural approach to the formation of organizational climate. *Human Relations, 45*, 19–47.

Naumann, S. E., & Bennett, N. (2000). A case for procedural justice: development and test of a multilevel model. *Academy of Management Journal, 43*, 881–889.

Ngo, H.-Y., & Loi, R. (2008): Human resource flexibility, organizational culture and firm performance: an investigation of multinational firms in Hong Kong. *The International Journal of Human Resource Management, 19*, 1654–1666.

Ostroff, C., Kinicki, A. J., & Tamkins, M. M. (2003). Organizational culture and climate. In W. C. Borman, D. I. Ilgen & R. J. Klimoski (Eds), *Handbook of psychology, Volume 12, Industrial and organizational psychology* (pp. 565–594). Hoboken, NJ: John Wiley & Sons.

Pearson, A. W., & Marler, L. E. (2010). A leadership perspective of reciprocal Stewardship in Family Firms. *Entrepreneurship Theory and Practice, 6*, 1117–1124.

Quinn, R. E., & Rohrbaugh, J. (1983). A spatial model of effectiveness criteria: towards a competing values approach to organizational analysis. *Management Science, 29*, 363–377.

Quinn, R. E., & Spreitzer, G. M. (1991). The psychometrics of the competing values culture instrument and an analysis of the impact of organizational culture on quality of life. *Research in Organizational Change and Development, 5*, 115–142.

Rockstuhl, T., Dulebohn, J. H., Ang, S., & Shore, L. M. (2012). Leader–member exchange (LMX) and culture: a meta-analysis of correlates of LMX across 23 countries. *Journal of Applied Psychology, 97*, 1097–1130.

Rousseau, D. M. (1988). The construction of climate in organizational research. In C. L. Cooper & I. Robertson (Eds.), *International Review of Industrial and Organizational Psychology* (pp. 137–158). London: John Wiley & Sons.

Schein, E. (1985). *Organizational culture and leadership*. San Francisco: Jossey-Bass.

Schneider, B. (1990). The climate for service: An application of the climate construct. In B. Schneider (Ed.), *Organizational climate and culture* (pp. 383–412). San Francisco, CA: Jossey-Bass.

Schneider, B. & Reichers, A. (1983). On the etiology of climates. *Personnel Psychology, 36*, 19–40.

Scott, S. G., & Bruce, R. A. (1994). Determinants of innovative behavior: A path model of individual innovation in the workplace. *Academy of Management Journal, 37*, 580–607.

Seers, A. (1989). Team-member exchange quality: A new construct for role-making research. *Organizational Behavior and Human Decision Processes, 43*, 118–135.

Sun, L. Y., Chow, I. H. S., Chiu, R. K., & Pan, W. (2013). Outcome favorability in the link between leader-member exchange and organizational citizenship behavior: Procedural fairness climate matters. *Leadership Quarterly, 24*, 215–226.

Thompson, D. N., Hoffman, L. A., Sereika, S. M., Lorenz, H. L., Wolf, G. A., Burns, H. K., Minnier, T. E., & Ramanujam, R. (2011). A relational leadership perspective on unit-level safety climate. *Journal of Nursing Administration, 41*, 479–487.

Tierney, P. (1999). Work relations as a precursor to a psychological climate for change: The role of work group supervisors and peers. *Journal of Organizational Change Management, 12*, 120–133.

Tordera, N., & González-Romá, V. (2013). Leader-member exchange (LMX) and innovation climate: The role of LMX differentiation. *The Spanish Journal of Psychology, 16*, 1–8.

Tordera, N., González-Romá, V., & Peiró, J. M. (2008). The moderator effect of psychological climate on the relationship between leader–member exchange (LMX) quality and role overload. *European Journal of Work and Organizational Psychology, 17*, 55–72.

Triandis, H. C. (1995). *Individualism and collectivism*. Boulder, CO: Westview Press.

Triandis, H. C., & Gelfand, M. J. (1998). Converging measurement of horizontal and vertical individualism and collectivism. *Journal of Personality and Social Psychology*, *74*, 118–128.

Tse, H. H. M., Dasborough, M. T., & Ashkanasy, N. M. (2008). A multi-level analysis of team climate and interpersonal exchange relationships at work. *Leadership Quarterly*, *17*, 55–72.

Verbeke, W., Volgering, M., & Hessels, M. (1998). Exploring the conceptual expansion within the field of organizational behavior: Organizational climate and organizational culture. *Journal of Management Studies*, *35*, 303–329.

Vukonjanski, J., Nikolic, M., Hadzic, O., Terek, E., & Nedeljkovic, M. (2012). Relationship between GLOBE organizational culture dimensions, job satisfaction and leader-member exchange in Serbian organizations. *Journal for East European Management Studies*, *17*, 333–368.

Yeung, K. O., Brockbank, J. W., & Ulrich, D. O. (1991). Organizational culture and human resources practices: An empirical assessment. *Research in Organizational Change and Development*, *5*, 59–81.

Zhong, J. A., Lam, W., & Chen, Z. G. (2011). Relationship between leader-member exchange and organizational citizenship behaviors: Examining the moderating role of empowerment. *Asia Pacific Journal of Management*, *28*, 609–626.

PART 5

Issues in LMX

"Good" Leadership: Using Corporate Social Responsibility to Enhance Leader–Member Exchange

Drew B. Mallory *and* Deborah E. Rupp

Abstract

This chapter explores how leader–member exchange (LMX) may be affected by the targeted implementation of leader-driven corporate social responsibility (CSR). Building from contemporary social exchange conceptualizations, in which LMX is enveloped, the authors argue that leader-driven CSR is positioned to act as an antecedent to strong LMX formation and an amplifier postdevelopment. As a special form of third-party justice, leader-driven CSR offers employees a unique opportunity to witness and interact with leaders in a way that may enhance leader-directed justice perspectives, further impacting employee LMX perceptions and exaggerating typical CSR effects. In addition, CSR may engender *parasocial LMX,* or perceived and indirect LMX relationships employees can develop with leaders at multiple levels in the organizational hierarchy. A number of moderating factors that may affect LMX quality in either direction are introduced, including employee awareness and participation, employee justice perceptions, and individual differences.

Key Words: LMX, leadership, leader–member exchange, corporate social responsibility

Introduction

In a discourse on leader–member exchange (LMX), we may wonder who invited corporate social responsibility (CSR) to the party. After all, what does Starbucks feeding orphans in Qatar (Starbucks Corporation, 2011) or Ford increasing fuel economy (Ford Motor Company, 2012) have to do with exchange relationships between leaders and subordinates?

Forbes Magazine recently spoke to this issue in their annual count of companies with the best CSR reputations:

> "CSR speaks to who the company is, what it believes in and how it is doing business," says Kasper Ulf Nielsen, executive partner at Reputation Institute. "It's a core element of reputation and can be used to help establish trust and goodwill amongst stakeholders . . . [CSR] is a key tool for companies to use to improve support from stakeholders like consumers, regulators, financial community, *and employees* [emphasis added]." (Smith, 2013)

Purveyors of the relational literature will note the similarities between this description of CSR's strategic potential and what has been evidenced about the power of social exchange. Social exchange theory speaks of differential, dyadic, trust-based relationships, which develop out of accumulating evidence of perceived costs and benefits associated with interaction. It has been posited that CSR, or any organizational effort aimed at positively impacting society or the environment, grants corporate stakeholders of all kinds this very opportunity (Balmer, Fukukawa, & Gray, 2007).

Yet although CSR has traditionally been examined for its reputational sway over *external* stakeholders (shareholders, consumers, etc.), it is increasingly proposed as a way by which *internal* stakeholders (employees, as is noted above) may also receive information regarding company past, present, and future behavior. It is from this position that we will explore the ways in which CSR, when leader driven, can serve as a driver of the social exchange processes inherent to LMX, resulting in higher LMX perceptions, lower LMX differentiation, and a greater impact of CSR efforts.

Background: CSR and LMX

In recent years, CSR scholars have explored the role that CSR can play in the development of social exchange processes in the workplace (Aguilera, Rupp, Williams, & Ganapathi, 2007; Jones, 2010; Rupp, Ganapathi, Aguilera, & Williams, 2006; Skarlicki & Kulik, 2004). The bulk of this research has focused on social exchange between employees and the organization as a whole. This chapter will extend this work by drawing the focus to the dyadic level—specifically by illustrating some of the mechanisms by which this occurs not only between employees and their direct supervisors, but also between employees and leaders at increasingly higher levels in the organizational hierarchy. In this discussion, we will take an interactionist perspective as we introduce a range of contextual and individual difference variables (e.g., justice perceptions, cultural values, moral identity) as boundary conditions on the relationships between leader-driven CSR, employee perceptions of leader-driven CSR, LMX, and employee attitudes and behaviors. Our broad, theoretical model is illustrated in Figure 18.1.

With this orientation in mind, we begin our discussion with a review of the most salient elements from the LMX and CSR literatures.

Leader–Member Exchange

Although LMX has been thoroughly discussed throughout this volume, we provide a very brief review here in order to frame our theoretical position. We defer to other sources for a complete critique of the research, however, as our intent is mainly to highlight the aspects of LMX theory and research pertinent to and overlapping CSR scholarship.

The supervisor–subordinate relationship has been a focus of organizational research for nearly 40 years (Scandura, 1999). Pioneering work explored the process of relational development, resulting in the discovery that supervisors allocate differential attention to some reports over others (Dansereau, Graen, & Haga, 1975). Through this uneven allocation of psychological resources, certain employees were seen to develop trust-based relationships with supervisors whereas others have not (Liden & Graen, 1980). From these early findings arose LMX theory, which focuses on the antecedents and consequences of varying leader–member relational quality across leader–member dyads, referred to as *LMX differentiation* (Graen & Scandura, 1987; Graen & Uhl-Bien, 1995).

Within an LMX perspective, relational quality is argued to develop primarily as a leader and follower engage in specific types of interactions. "High-quality" LMX emerges out of relationships adhering to social exchange patterns, which are built on the mutual exchange of valued tangible and nontangible resources (Graen & Scandura, 1987, p. 181; Martin, Epitropaki, Thomas, & Topakas, 2010, p. 37). In the presence of high-quality LMX, this resource exchange often transcends the direct requirements of the job and engenders voluntary and reciprocal obligation between the leader

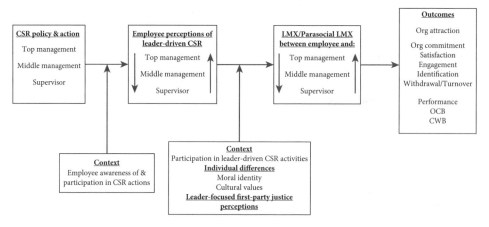

Fig. 18.1 Theoretical Model.

and follower (Henderson, Liden, Glibkowski, & Chaudhry, 2009). Relationships that remain distant and largely contractual, functioning as transactional, *quid pro quo*, mostly economic exchanges, engender "low-quality" LMX.

Meta-analytic reviews have evidenced strong connections between the quality of LMX and an array of employee perceptions, attitudes, and behaviors (Dulebohn, Bommer, Liden, Brouer, & Ferris, 2012; Gerstner & Day, 1997; Ilies, Nahrgang, & Morgeson, 2007). Outcomes linked to high-quality LMX include employee job satisfaction, organizational commitment, and organizational citizenship behaviors (Henderson et al., 2009; Masterson, Lewis, Goldman, & Taylor, 2000). Conversely, low-quality LMX has been tied to employee turnover (Gerstner & Day, 1997), role conflict, and a host of withdrawal-related attitudes and behaviors (Dulebohn et al., 2012). At the highest levels, organizations benefit from employees with high-quality LMX through cost savings associated with lower turnover and increased productivity (Henderson et al., 2009). Numerous antecedents to LMX quality and differentiation have been identified (Dulebohn et al., 2012; Erdogan, Liden, & Kraimer, 2006; Gerstner & Day, 1997), though we note only one set here in particular. Although both leader and member qualities contribute to the development of LMX, a recent meta-analysis evidenced that expectations of follower success, contingent reward behavior, and transformational leadership accounted for the most variance in LMX quality. Specific leader traits (such as perceived extraversion and agreeableness) and interpersonal predictors (such as follower liking of the leader and mutually perceived similarity) also played a significant role. Collectively these findings suggest that whatever influence employees have on leader–member relationships, *LMX is most strongly influenced by leaders* (rather than followers; Dulebohn et al., 2012). In our subsequent discussion on CSR's potential impact on LMX, we weigh this conclusion heavily as we pay particular attention to the role that leaders have in fostering positive exchange relationships.

Although the basic tenets of LMX have garnished considerable evidentiary support, emerging perspectives continue to provide room for growth and expansion. In recent years, some aspects of the traditionally accepted premises of LMX have come under scrutiny. We now introduce three such developments that serve as the backdrop for our subsequent discussion. First, as previously observed, LMX has typically been conceptualized as forming primarily within the supervisor–subordinate dyad. Recently, however, social exchange scholars have examined work relationships at multiple levels within the organizational hierarchy (Henderson, Wayne, Shore, Bommer, & Tetrick, 2008), moving beyond the supervisor–subordinate dyad to include other related members (e.g., Seers, 1989). Drawing from multilevel theory, Henderson et al. (2009) predicted that, particularly as firm members across hierarchical levels interact more closely, top-level organizational norms would affect values, attitudes, and behaviors operating at the work-unit level. Specifically, they proposed that organizational-level cultural standards, specifically norms regarding respect, team orientation, and aggressiveness, consequently play a significant role in LMX differentiation patterns (p. 524). As we will subsequently discuss, CSR, when enacted and performed by firm leaders, offers a potent opportunity for such norms to crystalize and propagate.

Second, LMX has been argued to develop early and to remain relatively stable, once formed, over time (Liden, Wayne, & Stilwell, 1993). However, Bolino and Turnley (2009) took issue with this belief and articulated arguments for research into the fluidity of LMX throughout an employee's career. We will contend that there is reason to expect that under certain circumstances, CSR may engender greater fluidity of employee-perceived LMX.

Finally, whereas LMX is usually accepted as an independent workplace experience, conceptually different from other constructs pertaining to the employee's social milieu, Cropanzano and Byrne (2000) have pointed out that many of the relational constructs explored in the literature (e.g., LMX, commitment, trust, support, psychological contracts) are all (imperfect) operationalizations of social exchange. As such, whereas our model pulls primarily from the LMX literature, we also acknowledge that a broader and more unified foundation in social exchange is best for exploring how CSR engenders relational capital between leaders and followers (see also Cropanzano & Mitchell, 2005).

Collectively, the above contributions have highlighted the rich complexity of relational networks that exists both within and between individuals at all levels of the organization. LMX can no longer be seen as merely the dyadic relationship between supervisor and subordinate, and must be examined within the contexts wherein those relationships lie, and where employees perceive leadership to exist. Accordingly, an employee may now be conceived to be engaged in multiple, nested exchange relationships, including those with other employees, supervisors, higher-level managers, and the organization itself (Henderson et al., 2008; Lavelle, Rupp, & Brockner, 2007; Lavelle, Rupp, Manegold, & Thornton, 2015). Of course, this makes precisely observing, measuring, and identifying the source(s) of the full LMX experience a complex endeavor.

In fact, despite the hardy empirical support offered for LMX theory, there are recognized needs for greater articulation surrounding the "how" and "why" of LMX. Walumbwa, Cropanzano, and Goldman (2011) called for attention toward the intervening processes between LMX and employee outcomes. We agree with this recommendation, but add that identifying further antecedents to LMX is equally essential. Understanding the requisite workplace contexts and behavioral patterns (of both leaders and employees) for LMX formation not only strengthens the theoretical foundation of LMX, but assists both scholars and practitioners by shedding light on how associated outcomes may be most fully recognized. As will become increasingly apparent, as both a cross-level and organizational-level set of value-laden norms and behaviors, CSR is well poised, if appropriately utilized, to act as an antecedent to LMX development.

Corporate Social Responsibility

Historical foundations. To understand the claims we have introduced regarding CSR's influence on social exchange, a brief summary of the CSR literature (alongside some history of the CSR "movement" in the global world of business) is in order. Across the world, CSR is now considered a requisite business practice (Creyer, 1997; Guler, Guillén, & Macpherson, 2002; Matten & Moon, 2008; Sen & Bhattacharya, 2001). Modern firms feel ever increasing pressure from stakeholders, both internal (e.g., top management teams, executive boards) and external (e.g., shareholders, advocacy groups), to act in ways that are perceived of as socially and environmentally responsible (Aguilera et al., 2007). Organized consumer activism, such as the grassroots-led Nike boycotts of the 1990s (Knight & Greenberg, 2002), places additional checks on corporate ethical behavior (Kozinets & Handelman, 2004). Indeed, today's modern businesses are recognized and rewarded not only for doing well financially, but also for "doing good" societally (i.e., contributing to

societal and environmental well-being; Sen & Bhattacharya, 2001).

Fundamentally, as we introduced before, CSR may be thought of as any efforts on behalf of an organization that are targeted on making a positive social or environmental impact (Davis, 1973; Waddock & Bodwell, 2004; Wood, 1991). These efforts take many forms. Waddock and Graves (1997) separated CSR into three categories: internal behaviors and processes, inputs, and outputs. Both internal behaviors and processes and inputs entail strategies and actions taken within the organization, whereas outputs focus on behaviors seen and experienced by outside stakeholders. Internal behaviors and processes involve how an organization treats its employees and customers, extending even so far as to encompass the types of products or services a firm produces or provides, respectively. Inputs include internally directed, and often high-level, CSR efforts and policies, such as financial investments in environmentally sustainable operations or vetting the responsible practices of contractors. Outputs represent the category most often associated with CSR, as they are external stakeholder focused and visible to the public (e.g., shareholders and consumers). They include activities such as employee volunteerism programs, corporate philanthropy, and community relations. Over the course of this chapter, we will reexamine these definitions from the perspective of employees.

Despite the fervor with which CSR proponents have typically preached corporate social and environmental engagement, there has historically been little consensus that businesses do—or even *should*—have a responsibility to society at all. In fact, CSR has often been positioned as a direct opposition to the thesis of work. Famed economist Milton Friedman presented a frequently referenced (and more frequently misunderstood) typification of this perspective with his declaration that "there is only one social responsibility of business—to use its resources and engage in activities designed to increase its profits so long as it . . . engages in open and free competition without deception and fraud" (Friedman, 1962, p. 59).[1]

Consequentially, for many years a great deal of sociological, economic, and strategic management research was generated aimed at evidencing how firm-level actions impact firm-level outcomes. A particular focus of this research was on evidencing the connection between CSR indicators and organizational economic performance. To that end, scholars made many advances in demonstrating that what is good for society can indeed be good for business. Most recently, however, where the debate seems to have settled (through multiple meta-analytic investigations), is that whereas there does seem to be a positive relationship between social/environmental actions and financial performance (Margolis, Elfenbein, & Walsh, 2009; Orlitzky, Schmidt, & Rynes, 2003), the effect size is not large enough to suggest that CSR, as it stands, is best utilized *only* as a fiscally strategic endeavor (Olson-Buchanan, Bryan, & Thompson, 2013). Instead, it is now clear that research is needed to understand the *other* ways in which CSR creates value for a full range of stakeholders, including employees and the intended beneficiaries of CSR outside of the organization (see Margolis & Walsh, 2003).

A new era with new questions. Within organizational psychology and "micro"-organizational behavior research, CSR is a topic still emerging from its nascence. Indeed, with some important exceptions (Greening & Turban, 2000; Jones, Willness, & Macneil, 2009; Turban & Greening, 1997), it is only recently that CSR has been taken on directly as a truly *psychological* topic of inquiry. That is to say, psychologists have only now begun to utilize the microlens of investigation in examining the motivations of and effects on the individual employee and manager alike, as they comply with, advocate for, and participate in organizationally sanctioned socially responsible activities (Rupp, Skarlicki, & Shao, 2013).

As CSR research has progressed, a variety of employee-level organizational outcomes associated with CSR have been identified. These outcomes will not be unfamiliar to social exchange scholars. They include reduced employee turnover intentions (Jones, 2010), improved employee relations (Agle, Mitchell, & Sonnenfeld, 1999; Glavas & Piderit, 2009), improved affective commitment (Carmeli, Gilat, & Waldman, 2007), increased organizational citizenship behaviors (OCBs; Jones, 2010; Lin, Lyau, Tsai, Chen, & Chiu, 2010; Rupp, Shao, Thornton, & Skarlicki, 2013; Sully de Luque, Washburn, Waldman, & House, 2008), and reduced counterproductive work behaviors (CWBs; Viswesvaran, Deshpande, & Milman, 1998).

These recent advances notwithstanding, the need for elaboration on the means by which CSR affects organizational members remains great. At the highest level, such a line of inquiry speaks to the call for more person-centric research within organizational science. Attempting to understand how socially (ir)responsible firm actions are perceived, interpreted, and responded to by employees, and how they can engender social exchange as experienced by employees, will provide necessary insight into the *experience* of CSR from the perspective of employees (Ryan & Ford, 2010; Weiss & Rupp, 2011; Rupp & Mallory, 2015), and thus afford a better understanding of the experience of work in general. The direct practical implications for such a line of research are equally compelling. Understanding what motivates individuals within organizations to make socially conscious decisions on behalf of the firm adds to our ability to more clearly define how capitalism and compassion, as well as self-interest and ethicality, can intersect within and between organizations and individuals (George, 2013). It stands to contribute to the resolution of perceived tensions between CSR's ultimate purpose of decreasing human suffering and the traditional corporative drive toward profit (Margolis & Walsh, 2003). By substantiating the connections between organizational CSR behaviors and individual-level stakeholder responses, the efficacy of CSR initiatives for positively impacting the "triple bottom line" of economic, social, and environmental performance (Elkington, 2004) may be better realized, leading to more effective programs, and ultimately greater organizational—and societal—outcomes.

CSR as a special form of organizational justice. It is been long established that social exchange emerges as employees experience justice from their leaders (Cropanzano & Mitchell, 2005; Erdogan, 2002; Mansour-Cole & Scott, 1998; Masterson et al., 2000; Scandura, 1999). Traditionally, this "justice" refers to how employees believe that they themselves have been treated by those with authority over them. Rupp (2011) has coined this type of justice as "looking in." However, advances in the justice literature have documented that not only do employees make differentiated judgments about how fairly multiple parties within the organizational hierarchy (e.g., direct supervisors as well as upper management) treat *them personally* (Lavelle et al., 2015; Rupp, Shao, Jones, & Liao, 2014), but they also form judgments about how these various parties treat *others*. Rupp (2011) refers to these sort of perceptions as "looking around," and research has documented strong effects for both third-party (e.g., co-worker; Skarlicki & Kulik, 2004) justice perceptions and justice climate (i.e., how an entire group of employees is treated by an authority member; Rupp & Thornton, 2014).

By extension, if we are to study CSR from the employee's perspective, it has been argued that CSR perceptions should be considered a special

Table 18.1. Crossing the Sources of Justice Information (Rupp, 2011) with the Categories of CSR Behaviors (Waddock & Graves, 1997) to Distinguish between Employee CSR and Justice Perceptions

	Internal Behaviors and Processes	Inputs	Outputs
Looking in	First-party justice perceptions, e.g., *"how fairly am I treated by my supervisor and others?"*		
Looking around	Third-party justice perceptions and justice climate, e.g., *"how fairly are my co-workers treated?/ how fairly is my team treated?"*		
Looking out		CSR perceptions (traditionally attributed to the organization*)	
		e.g., *perceptions of the CSR of the firm's financial investments; perceptions of the environmental sustainability of the firm's operations*	e.g., *perceptions of the firm's corporate volunteerism programs, philanthropic efforts, or community activism*

* This article will extend this idea to consider how CSR perceptions can be attributed to leaders through leader-driven CSR.
Note: This table depicts the many different parties that may be perceived of as *targets* of (in)justice (i.e., the self, co-workers, external stakeholders). Note that for each of these perceptions, there may also be multiple *sources* (i.e., different parties held accountable/responsible for the actions seen as fair or unfair, such as leaders, the organization as a whole, and other parties).

case of third-party justice perceptions, in that employees consider how socially responsible (or just) organizational leadership has been toward various stakeholder groups (most notably society and the environment). Rupp (2011) refers to these sorts of perceptions as "looking out," as they form from employees witnessing the treatment of stakeholders outside of the organization, the intended beneficiaries of CSR. By overlaying this perspective (i.e., looking in, looking over, and looking out) with the three "types" of CSR proposed by Waddock and Graves (1997) and described above (i.e., internal processes and behaviors, inputs, and outputs), we can map the perceptual landscape of employees' justice and CSR perceptions (which we have depicted in Table 18.1). As is shown, when appraising organizational justice, employees do not only evaluate and react to how they, their co-workers, and their teams are treated by organizational authorities (which we cast as employee justice perceptions), but they also consider the social responsibility these authorities show through their actions toward both internal and external stakeholder groups (which we cast as employee CSR perceptions).

Shifting the Focus of CSR Perceptions

The target similarity framework (Lavelle et al., 2007) adds further context to Table 18.1 and illustrates the key difference between conventional and leader-driven CSR. The framework integrates research on justice as it pertains to the varied social exchange relationships that can occur between employees and actors at all rungs of the organizational hierarchy. Recognizing that employees make justice judgments about multiple sources, the model asserts that these source-specific observations engender source-specific social exchange relationships, which lead to responses "targeted" at the original source of the felt (in)justice, with a certain amount of crossover occurring across sources and resultant effects. A recent review of the model depicts evidence for such effects across a range of contexts (Lavelle et al., 2015). Accordingly, for justice perceptions to affect social exchange between leaders and employees (LMX), these perceptions must be associated with the leaders themselves (Cropanzano, Prehar, & Chen, 2002; Masterson et al., 2000). However, information conveyed by CSR perceptions often comes exclusively from organization-level sources, such as HR or appointed CSR representatives. As such, when CSR is delivered through conventional routes, resultant third-party justice perceptions are likely to be attributed to the organization [which might explain the many organizationally directed exchange-based outcomes employee CSR perceptions have been shown to effect (e.g., organizational commitment, organizational attraction, organization identification)].

We posit (as supported by the literature reviewed above), that although it is clear that multiple sources of justice exist within an organization, organizational leadership has the potential to hold a great deal of accountability with regard to CSR, and thus leaders, at multiple points in the organizational hierarchy, can stand to influence LMX quality through their CSR-related actions. Consequentially, as we will discuss below, when leaders are positioned as the focal drivers of CSR initiatives and messages, resultant CSR perceptions will not only be attributed to the organization, but will also be attributed to the leader. Expanding the source of CSR perceptions from organizations only to specific leaders offers employees increased access to information that can subsequently feed the growth of social exchange (with the leader). Each opportunity that employees have to engage with leaders (at any level) in the delivery of CSR provides a possibility not only for the formation of leader-specific CSR perceptions, but also for the engenderment of direct social exchange with those leaders. As CSR norms (policies and behaviors) form in a top-down fashion in most firms, we will accordingly examine how top-level support for CSR can create a chain reaction of justice and social exchange that reverberates in all levels of the organization.

Integrating CSR and LMX
Leadership as a Driver of CSR

In a survey of 400 companies participating in the U.N. Global Compact, Bhattacharya, Sen, and Korschun (2008) found that 71% of CSR programs were initiated by the CEO, 57% by the Board of Directors, and 56% by senior management. Whereas the top-down development of CSR strategy can engender employee dissatisfaction if CSR activities do not match well with individual interests or expectations, it also gives top management the unique opportunity to express its values in a way that may be felt throughout the organization and subsequently influence associated social exchange relationships. Here we identify two ways in which this may occur. First, by creating a culture of CSR within the organization, an environment of social justice is created, which influences the development of supportive leadership behaviors and, consequently, LMX. Second, employee knowledge of upper management's engagement with CSR creates the potential for employees hierarchically "disconnected" from particular management levels the opportunity to form unique, one-way LMX relationships with leaders at those level (*parasocial LMX*). We further discuss each of these two phenomenon below.

The trickling-down of CSR culture. The essential role of top management on company-wide program adoption and the establishment of normative behaviors has been well documented across many areas (Rodgers, Hunter, & Rogers, 1993), including in the acceptance of technology-assisted support systems (Neumann & Hadass, 1980), energy management (Bohlander & Kinicki, 1988), safety policies (Minter, 1991), and organization-wide cultural shift (Myerson & Hamilton, 1986). Leadership backing for organizational activities and change is crucial to establishing company-wide support. Similar arguments have been made for both LMX (Henderson et al., 2009) and CSR (Aguilera et al., 2007; Grant, 2012; Reed, Aquino, & Levy, 2007). From this, we expect that that top-level CSR-related leader behaviors would not only influence company-wide adoption of CSR practices, but that it would also influence the CSR-related actions of top management's immediate subordinates (e.g., middle management, supervisors). Ultimately, we predict that this tickle-down effect will reach leaders most proximal to the focal employee, at which point the most likely LMX effects may be seen (see Figure 18.1). However, this trickle-down effect may also engender a unique type of social exchange development we call *parasocial LMX,* which we shall subsequently discuss.

Despite most frequently evidencing social exchange at the organizational level in research, CSR naturally appeals to many facets of social exchange critical to LMX formation. In particular, it has the potential to affect perceptions of similarity and value congruence (Dulebohn et al., 2012; Liden et al., 1993) and, consequently, liking (Wayne, Shore, & Liden, 1997), which we have noted are key antecedents to high-quality LMX. Whereas actual similarity and value congruence between leaders and followers have shown only limited association with LMX and follower liking, follower perceptions of similarity (including values) are highly predictive of perceived exchange (Brouer, Duke, Treadway, & Ferris, 2009; Goodwin, Bowler, & Whittington, 2009; Hayibor, Agle, Sears, Sonnenfeld, & Ward, 2011). CSR programs and policies have previously been demonstrated to increase organizational attractiveness and perceived similarity between the organization's values and those of both prospective and current employees (Jones, 2010; Jones, Willness, & Madey, 2013). When individual leaders are seen to personally embody CSR (and accordingly, drive CSR actions on behalf of the firm) through both delivering CSR messages and leading CSR efforts, we expect employees susceptible to CSR messages to perceive these values and sense increased congruence and liking with these leaders.

Of course, given that employees often have the most exposure to their direct supervisor, we might expect that the direct supervisor's CSR-related actions would have the strongest effect on LMX (compared to the CSR-related behaviors of more distal managers and executives). This need not negate the potential for employees' perceptions of highly visible CSR-related actions from middle managers and executives to engender perceived social exchange with these high-level leaders. As such, we propose a cascading of perceived LMX with (and between) leaders at multiple levels of the management hierarchy, driven by the CSR-related actions at each subsequent level (as is depicted in Figure 18.1). In this way, highly visible CSR values and actions among an organization's top leadership may set in place a chain reaction of social exchange that may strengthen employees' perceived ties to leaders at multiple organizational levels.

Parasocial LMX. Present conceptualizations of LMX would not predict that an employee would perceive an LMX relationship at all with a leader with whom they do not interact. Indeed, the frequency of leader–follower interaction is a known moderator of follower-rated LMX (Goodwin et al., 2009). Accordingly, highly removed leaders, such as the CEO, may be expected to have zero LMX with nondirect employees. However, LMX scholars who have taken a multilevel perspective have both predicted and shown that as organizational members interact more frequently, opportunities for the transference of values, norms, and behaviors increase (Cogliser & Schriesheim, 2000; Henderson et al., 2009). We expand this perspective by predicting that in certain situations one-way, or *parasocial* exchange relationships between employees and higher-level leaders, may develop—even when followers have little or no direct interaction with such individuals.

Though originating in the communications literature, the concept of parasocial relationships has long been recognized in psychology as a unique type of relationship between individuals and highly visible public figures, both real and fictional (Horton & Wohl, 1956). Despite their necessarily one-directional nature, parasocial relationships have been shown to have profound effects on individuals, often leading to attitudinal or behavioral changes consistent with those elicited from direct interpersonal interactions, including increased

feelings of belongingness (Derrick, Gabriel, & Hugenberg, 2009), higher levels of acceptance of outgroups (Schiappa, Gregg, & Hewes, 2005), and increased self-esteem (Derrick, Gabriel, & Tippin, 2008). Treadway, Adams, Ranft, and Ferris (2009) explored a similar phenomenon in their study of the known and probable effects of "celebrity" CEOs on various stakeholders, including managers and employees. In their discussion of proposed firm-level outcomes, they suggest that as these leaders participate in interactions that promote loyalty and trust, employees will begin to associate the leader with their own identities and ingroup membership. Citing social exchange theory, they predicted the resultant development of LMX relationships between affected employees and the CEO. We echo and expand this proposition, positing CSR as a prime mechanism by which higher-level leaders may engender leader-specific trust and loyalty in nondirect followers at all levels of the organizational hierarchy, and suggest that this effect will be most potent when CSR adoption is actively embraced by leaders at multiple levels. Indeed, we expect parasocial LMX to be possible from any "higher-level" leader or leader team whose influence on CSR is widely visible (e.g., the CEO, a particular VP, or the top management team as a group).

Strengthening LMX Formation and Reducing Differentiation

The existence of both parasocial LMX via CSR and CSR-enhanced LMX with direct supervisors may have further consequences in the case of LMX differentiation. Recent meta-analytic findings have shown that leaders, rather than followers, are responsible for much of what is required to develop high-quality LMX (Dulebohn et al., 2012). As leaders form relationships with new reports, differentiation, or the variability in relational quality between a leader and his or her members, unavoidably occurs. Although those employees benefiting from differentiation in the form of higher LMX quality enjoy increased individual outcomes, low-quality LMX employees suffer from increased risks of turnover and lower levels of overall satisfaction.

There are two issues regarding LMX differentiation that leader-driven CSR can address. The first is simply a function of the limitations placed on leader resources. Because high-quality LMX relationships require both social and transactional exchanges (Dulebohn et al., 2012), limited resources (e.g., time, tangible resources, social abilities) sharply curtail the ability of leaders to create universally high-quality LMX (Gerstner & Day, 1997; Graen, 1976; Graen, Cashman, Ginsburg, & Schiemann, 1977). Commensurately, regardless of leader-specific traits (e.g., transformational leadership), differentiation will emerge. The second issue pertains to the justice perceptions employees form when viewing discrepant leader–member interactions. In an early study on this, Sias and Jablin (1995) reported that the inevitable varying treatment among employees underlying differentiated LMX may often be accompanied by perceptions of unfairness. These findings have since been verified on a larger scale (Omilion-Hodges & Baker, 2013), and have further emphasized the contextual nature of social exchange perception formation, which is not limited to dyadic leader–subordinate interaction.

When leaders across the organization are given both the authority and opportunity to engage in high-visibility CSR behaviors, CSR stands to become an additional resource on which managers can rely in influencing and empowering their reports, whether directly or indirectly. Even when leaders are still constrained to prioritize resource distribution, greater emphasis on CSR can provide employees with increased opportunities to assay the qualities of their leaders, the chance to survey the ways in which their leaders value others (e.g., third-party justice perceptions), and additional direct opportunities for social exchange formation when participation in CSR activities is offered. When leaders drive CSR within the firm, the strong signals CSR communicates pertaining to organizational similarity, attractiveness, and support may translate into leader–member perceptions of similarity, liking, and support.

The effects of leader-driven CSR would be strongest, of course, early in the employee's tenure with the organization, as perceptions of LMX and other workplace-related perceptions are still forming (Erdogan, Kraimer, & Liden, 2004; Liden et al., 1993). However, regardless of the extant level of LMX, highly visible leader-driven CSR may increase the potential for high-quality LMX formation (or reformation) in a more evenly distributed way across employees (i.e., reducing differentiation).

Boundary Conditions

Our goal thus far has been to argue that employees can make distinct judgments about the CSR behaviors carried out not only by leaders who have direct authority over them, but also by leaders in higher levels in the organizational hierarchy. Furthermore, we have sought to articulate how these multifoci CSR perceptions can influence LMX and parasocial LMX quality (and lower differentiation) with these various authority figures, thus serving to affect the many outcomes of LMX documented across the literature (see Figure 18.1). Until this point, we have alluded only to a number of boundary conditions to which our propositions are confined, but have not explored them in full. Below we present more fully a series of variables predicted to moderate these effects.

Employee Awareness of and Participation in CSR Actions

Awareness. Of all potential moderators, visibility (e.g., the extent to which employees are aware of leader-driven CSR policies and actions) and proximity (e.g., the degree to which employees are able to participate in CSR activities) have been the most evidenced in previous research. For example, after conducting a series of focus groups, a global survey, and multiple online surveys, Bhattacharya et al. (2008) showed that the benefits of CSR to employee well-being are dependent on the employees' awareness and involvement in CSR. Consistent with the claims of other CSR scholars (Jones, 2010; Rupp et al., 2006) they found that 90% of surveyed employees (*n* = 10,000) believed businesses should participate in CSR; however, only 37% were aware of their respective company's CSR policies and activities. They blamed this lack of awareness on poor strategic implementation of managers, who, they claimed, showed a lack of understanding on how to capitalize on the positive effects of CSR within their companies. Naturally, when employees are kept in a state of ignorance (and, by extension, noninvolvement), it would be difficult to imagine how CSR could engender LMX. As such, we would not expect LMX relationships to be significantly impacted by CSR in organizations that disseminate CSR information only via external foundations or the human resources department (Bhattacharya et al., 2008; Reed et al., 2007). However, there are myriad ways in which individual leaders (or leadership teams) may be positioned as stewards of CSR and agents of change, with varying degrees of employee awareness. The more aware employees are of both their leaders' actions pertaining to CSR and the firm's overall CSR efforts, the more employees will have the opportunity to sense the aligned values, stakeholder support, and trust that can further fuel social exchange.

Participation. As implied above and depicted in Figure 18.1, we also expect the relationship between leader-driven CSR and LMX to be further strengthened when employees have the opportunity to participate directly in leader-driven CSR initiatives. First, through involvement in CSR, employees are afforded the opportunity to become more aware of leader-driven CSR activities. Second, participation not only provides employees more exposure to leaders with whom they might otherwise have limited access, it also exposes them to the leaders' social values and stakeholder concern, which may further allow for the trust-building inherent in social exchange processes.

Research has documented a number of pro-social benefits of CSR participation, including increased citizenship behaviors (Grant & Mayer, 2009) and a variety of positive firm-directed attitudes and behaviors (De Gilder, Schuyt, & Breedijk, 2005). Whereas no studies have directly examined the specific proposition posed here, research on related topics is beginning to emerge. For example, Jones (2010) showed that employees with a dispositional orientation toward repaying social "debts" (e.g., strong exchange ideology; Eisenberger, Huntington, Hutchison, & Sowa, 1986) who participated in a corporate volunteer program showed higher supervisor-reported OCBs measured six months later. Jones also hypothesized that in addition to the more existential benefits to employees engaged in "doing good," CSR activities also offer opportunities for socialization, creativity, and skillbuilding. Leaders who effectively harness these opportunities that CSR participation allows will simultaneously harness the potential of CSR for building LMX (and the corresponding benefits of doing so).

Employee Justice Perceptions

As we articulated earlier, employee perceptions of leader-driven CSR actions and policies are just one piece of a multifoci and multitarget justice-related perceptual landscape. As shown in Table 18.1, employees also consider their own experienced justice, as well as the treatment of other individuals and groups with whom they work (Rupp, 2011). These perceptions are expected to interact with CSR perceptions in complex ways.

Rupp, Shao, et al. (2013) found that prospective employees' first-party distributive justice perceptions moderated the effect of CSR perceptions for both job intention pursuits and OCBs. Although both groups were positively affected by

a potential employer's CSR activities, participants experiencing a low first-party distributive justice condition were more impacted by a firm's CSR activities than their peers. They speculated that employees experiencing greater injustice may be primed to be more sensitive toward the injustice of others, and thus respond more positively to a firm's attempts to assist others.

Research has also shown the importance employees place on the consistency of treatment. This refers not only to leaders applying policies and procedures consistently across employees (i.e., procedural justice; Leventhal, 1980[2]), but also to individuals perceiving a consistent level of fair treatment by different parties with whom they interact. Research has shown that when employees feel inconsistently treated by multiple parties, the response can be as severe as when they are treated consistently unfairly (Rupp, Bashshur, & Liao, 2007).

Finally, research has explored self–other social comparisons with regard to fair treatment. This refers not only to classic formulations of equity and distributive justice (Adams, 1965), but also to social interactions and the application of policies (Colquitt, 2004; DeCremer & Hiel, 2006; Kray & Allan Lind, 2002; Spencer & Rupp, 2009; Van den Bos & Lind, 2002). Indeed, it is difficult to draw firm conclusions from this literature, given the tension that has been documented between employee motives that are more instrumental than moral in nature. There are documented instances in which employees seek to protect their own self-interest as well as situations in which they show a willingness to sacrifice their own resources in order to restore justice (Kahneman, Knetsch, & Thaler, 1986; Turillo, Folger, Lavelle, Umphress, & Gee, 2002).

This brings us back to the potential interaction of employee first-party (self-focused) justice perceptions with their perceptions of leader-driven CSR in influencing LMX. In light of the complexities articulated above, great precision is needed in order to offer any specific propositions. That is, to make theory-based predictions about this potential moderating effect, we must be very specific about the source and target attributed to both justice and CSR (Lavelle et al., 2015). Here we are referring specifically to the joint effects of (1) how fairly an employee feels he or she is treated by a leader, and (2) the employee's CSR perceptions *attributed to that same leader* on the employee's subsequently perceived LMX (again, with this same leader). In particular, we expect that the power of leader-driven

CSR to positively influence LMX will be enhanced when first-party justice is similarly high. This not only signals leader consistency and integrity, but it also shows an expanded circle of moral regard on behalf of the leader (Reed & Aquino, 2003). This is expected to boost the trust-building process and assumptions about the exchange of socioemotional resources. Conversely, and based on the literature reviewed above, we expect inconsistent treatment (e.g., the demonstration of fair behaviors toward employees but a lack of concern for external constituents, or vice versa) to be psychologically confusing to employees. This will stunt the trust-building process and thus be similar in effect to consistent poor treatment in terms of its influence on subsequent LMX. For employees more ambivalent regarding leader perceptions (both justice and LMX), witnessing leader-driven CSR may shift both justice and LMX perceptions depending on various factors. Employees perceiving a leader's CSR participation as a diversion of resources (time or financial) may resent the "misappropriation," thereby decreasing justice perceptions and leading to lower LMX quality. Conversely, an employee who sees CSR as an opportunity to engage with a leader (directly or indirectly), or who endorses the witnessed CSR behaviors, may form positive perceptions, leading to higher-quality LMX.

Individual Differences

Additionally, we predict that employee individual differences will influence the extent to which leader-driven CSR policies and actions influence perceived LMX with the focal leader.

Moral identity. As implied by the name, individuals with high moral identity see acting in a self-defined "moral" way as a deep part of their self-conception (Aquino & Reed, 2002). Such individuals describe themselves using moral terms (e.g., fair, honest, compassionate), often without being prompted. Because identity is largely about behaving in ways that are consistent with the self-concept (Blasi, 1980), it should not be surprising then that moral identity predicts a wide range of morally motivated behaviors, such as volunteerism (Aquino, Freeman, Reed, Lim, & Felps, 2009), philanthropy (Aquino & Reed, 2002; Reynolds & Ceranic, 2007), prosocial behavior (Aquino, McFerran, & Laven, 2011), and ethical leadership (Mayer, Aquino, Greenbaum, & Kuenzi, 2012). Recent empirical work demonstrated that the positive relationship

between CSR perceptions and organizational citizenship behaviors is stronger among individuals high in moral identity (Rupp, Shao, et al., 2013).

In the context of the theoretical model presented herein, we propose that the effect of employees' perceptions of leader-driven CSR on their subsequently perceived LMX with that leader will be most pronounced among employees high in moral identity. This is due to the moral nature of CSR and its consistency with the moral values of those who identify as being moral. In other words, employees high in moral identity will self-identify with values such as honesty, kindness, compassion, and generosity—which can also be perceived as the driving motives of CSR (e.g., help others in need, protect the public, sustain environmental resources). If CSR actions taken by a firm are attributed to a particular leader, it is likely that employees will similarly associate the leader with these moral values. Through a sense of value congruence, attraction, trust, and mutual respect are cultivated, leading to perceptions of LMX and/or parasocial LMX.

Of course, the direction of this moderating effect (i.e., moral identity amplifying CSR–LMX relationships) is dependent on the extent to which the employee perceives the leader's CSR behaviors to be authentically motivated (McShane & Cunningham, 2012). Myriad scholars have written about the instrumentality of CSR in gaining legitimacy, competitive advantage, and profit (Bansal & Roth, 2000). Obviously the effect of CSR on LMX would backfire if a high moral identifier viewed a leader's CSR behaviors as instrumental and lacking a moral or ethical motive of any kind, in that this would break down the value congruence we predict to catalyze the engenderment of LMX.

Cultural values. We also expect cultural values to impact the extent to which perceived leader-driven CSR behaviors influence LMX. This is because varying cultural values play a large role in dictating the types of behaviors followers expect from leaders, as well as with what sorts of leader behaviors followers are comfortable. For example, the cultural value of *femininity* (in contrast to masculinity) largely surrounds a concern for the weak (Hofstede, 2001). Individuals with such values (and potentially regions of the world in which such values are in greater concentration, e.g., Finland) may be likely to identify more strongly (and consequently perceive higher LMX) with those leaders displaying CSR behaviors due to the congruent values most often associated with CSR (e.g., charity and social justice).[3]

The cultural value of *uncertainty avoidance* might also be of relevance here. This value pertains to the extent to which individuals are comfortable with ambiguity. Individuals high in this value seek security in their work environments and prefer them to be generally predictable (Hofstede, 1993; Vitell, Nwachukwu, & Barnes, 1993). Individuals high in uncertainty avoidance (or in regions associated with this value, e.g., Turkey) would most likely be quite intolerant of signals of instability or inconsistency. Thus, leaders displaying high levels of CSR may be valued and identified with due to their broad concern for social welfare, which might be seen by employees as predictive of the consistent treatment of others.[4]

In contrast, the cultural value of *power distance* concerns whether an individual is more or less tolerant of unequal distributions of power (Hofstede, 2001; Lam, Schaubroeck, & Aryee, 2002). Individuals who value power distance (or employees in regions in which power distance is known to be valued culturally, e.g., China) may be less influenced by variance in leader behaviors (e.g., leader-driven CSR) in that such individuals show great deference to leaders regardless of the leaders' specific actions or the employee's interactions with them (e.g., exposure to the leader through participation in CSR).

Of course, these values are not held in isolation, and will no doubt interact with one another in influencing how leader-driven CSR behaviors affect LMX. For example, although we argue that power distance may attenuate this effect, we might also argue that individuals high in collectivism (which can commonly co-occur with power distance values) may value CSR initiatives due to their focus on social harmony. Shao, Rupp, Skarlicki, and Jones (2013) considered the extent to which profiles of cultural values influenced employees' sensitivity to first-party justice. Using meta-analysis to aggregate 495 employee samples collected over 32 countries (n = +190,000), they found that justice effects were stronger among employees in nations known to value individualism, femininity, uncertainty avoidance, and low power distance. Countries that resemble this profile would be nations such as Finland and Norway, whereas regions such as China and Hong Kong would have the opposite profile.

It is important to note that this meta-analysis pertained to first-person (self-focused) justice and not CSR perceptions, and outcomes included an aggregation of social exchange, attitudinal, and behavioral outcomes.[5] It is unclear how these results would differ if leader-driven CSR was the target perception and LMX (with the same leader) was the outcome of interest. Some tangential evidence has been offered by Rupp, Shao, Skarlicki, Kim, and Nadisic (2013) that is suggestive of more complex interactions among cultural values, the social context, and CSR perceptions. They showed, using employee data collected in five distinct nations, that the positive relationship between employee CSR perceptions and employee engagement was strongest when employees valued individualism and had the autonomy to participate in CSR activities. Together, this research suggests a need for much more fine-grain theorizing with regard to the interactive effects of individual and contextual moderators of CSR–LMX relationships.

Conclusions

In this chapter, we have presented a model by which CSR can affect the development and quality of LMX between employees and leaders at multiple points in the organizational hierarchy. We have proposed that highly visible, leader-driven CSR presents the opportunity for mutual and/or parasocial LMX relationships to develop between leaders and followers at any level, regardless of their direct interaction. We have also spoken to the predicted moderating effects of individual differences and extant justice perceptions. Aspects of many of these propositions have already received support from empirical research, although our specific propositions remain untested. Although our overall model is not likely to be directly testable in a single study, individual components may be examined through future research. We are hopeful, however, as LMX has been shown to be a testable phenomenon both within experimental laboratory settings (e.g., Omilion-Hodges & Baker, 2013; Wayne & Ferris, 1990) and via field research (Erdogan et al., 2004; Liden et al., 1993; Mansour-Cole & Scott, 1998). Much headway has also been made in the study of employee-level CSR perceptions (Greening & Turban, 2000; Jones et al., 2013; McShane & Cunningham, 2012; Rupp, Shao, et al., 2013). We look forward to future research that directly tests the potential role of CSR perceptions on the LMX formation process. Under certain more complex conditions, researchers may even test multilevel, parasocial, and cascading LMX effects.

Although we are eager for these propositions to be tested, we would urge practitioners to consider the implications of our model as CSR programs are developed and implemented (and perhaps allow for collaborative evaluation studies). CSR has already demonstrated that it is an impactful resource for attracting, retaining, and empowering employees. By increasing the visibility of CSR activities, and the role of leaders in their implementation, positive effects may be amplified, ultimately driving positive social change for the greater good of all stakeholders involved.

Notes

1. Ironically, although often misinterpreted, Friedman did not truly disavow corporations' involvement with civil society insomuch as their actions increased their profits. More precisely, Friedman was speaking against what he called the "fundamentally subversive" label of "social responsibility," which ultimately, he argued, is often actually just good business sense.
2. Similarly, Treadway et al. (2009) argued that in order for followers to trust and identify with their leaders, leaders' actions must be seen as both consistent over time and authentic (e.g., not indicative of ulterior motivations; Brouer et al., 2009; Jones et al., 2013).
3. Note here too, the perceived authenticity of the leader's CSR motives would also be quite relevant.
4. This would also suggest a three-way interaction among justice, CSR, and uncertainty avoidance, in which the highest perceived LMX would be expected for individuals high in uncertainty avoidance who have been treated fairly and perceive their leader as engaging in socially responsible behaviors toward others.
5. When only LMX was considered, significant moderating effects were found only for individualism and power distance.

References

Adams, J. S. (1965). Inequity in social exchange. In L. Berkowitz (Ed.), *Advances in experimental social psychology* (Vol. 2, pp. 267–299). New York: Academic Press.

Agle, B. R., Mitchell, R. K., & Sonnenfeld, J. A. (1999). Who matters to CEOs? An investigation of stakeholder attributes and salience, corporate performance, and CEO values. *Academy of Management Journal, 42*(5), 507–525.

Aguilera, R. V., Rupp, D. E., Williams, C. A., & Ganapathi, J. (2007). Putting the S back in corporate social responsibility: A multilevel theory of social change in organizations. *Academy of Management Review, 32*(3), 836–863.

Aguinis, H., & Glavas, A. (2012). What we know and don't know about corporate social responsibility: A review and research agenda. *Journal of Management, 38*(4), 932–968.

Aquino, K., Freeman, D., Reed, A., II, Lim, V. K., & Felps, W. (2009). Testing a social-cognitive model of moral behavior: The interactive influence of situations and moral identity centrality. *Journal of Personality and Social Psychology, 97*(1), 123–141.

Aquino, K., McFerran, B., & Laven, M. (2011). Moral identity and the experience of moral elevation in response to acts of uncommon goodness. *Journal of Personality and Social Psychology, 100*(4), 703–718.

Aquino, K., & Reed, A., II. (2002). The self-importance of moral identity. *Journal of Personality and Social Psychology, 83*(6), 1423–1440.

Balmer, J. M., Fukukawa, K., & Gray, E. R. (2007). The nature and management of ethical corporate identity: A commentary on corporate identity, corporate social responsibility and ethics. *Journal of Business Ethics, 76*(1), 7–15.

Bansal, P., & Roth, K. (2000). Why companies go green: A model of ecological responsiveness. *Academy of Management Journal, 43*(4), 717–736.

Bhattacharya, C., Sen, S., & Korschun, D. (2008). Corporate social responsibility as an internal marketing strategy. *Sloan Management Review, 49*(2), 37–44.

Blasi, A. (1980). Bridging moral cognition and moral action: A critical review of the literature. *Psychological Bulletin, 88*(1), 1–45.

Bohlander, G. W., & Kinicki, A. J. (1988). Where personnel and productivity meet. *Personnel Administrator, 33*(9), 122–130.

Bolino, M. C., & Turnley, W. H. (2009). Relative deprivation among employees in lower-quality leader-member exchange relationships. *The Leadership Quarterly, 20*(3), 276–286.

Brouer, R. L., Duke, A., Treadway, D. C., & Ferris, G. R. (2009). The moderating effect of political skill on the demographic dissimilarity—leader–member exchange quality relationship. *The Leadership Quarterly, 20*(2), 61–69.

Carmeli, A., Gilat, G., & Waldman, D. A. (2007). The role of perceived organizational performance in organizational identification, adjustment and job performance. *Journal of Management Studies, 44*(6), 972–992.

Cogliser, C. C., & Schriesheim, C. A. (2000). Exploring work unit context and leader-member exchange: A multi-level perspective. *Journal of Organizational Behavior, 21*(5), 487–511.

Colquitt, J. A. (2004). Does the justice of the one interact with the justice of the many? Reactions to procedural justice in teams. *Journal of Applied Psychology, 89*(4), 633.

Creyer, E. H. (1997). The influence of firm behavior on purchase intention: Do consumers really care about business ethics? *Journal of Consumer Marketing, 14*(6), 421–432.

Cropanzano, R., & Byrne, Z. S. (2000). Workplace justice and the dilemma of organizational citizenship. In M. Van Vugt, M. Snyder, T. R. Tyler, & A. Biel (Eds.), *Collective problems in modern society: Dilemmas and solutions* (pp. 142–161). New York: Routledge.

Cropanzano, R., & Mitchell, M. S. (2005). Social exchange theory: An interdisciplinary review. *Journal of Management, 31*(6), 874–900.

Cropanzano, R., Prehar, C. A., & Chen, P. Y. (2002). Using social exchange theory to distinguish procedural from interactional justice. *Group & Organization Management, 27*(3), 324–351.

Dansereau, F., Graen, G., & Haga, W. J. (1975). A vertical dyad linkage approach to leadership within formal organizations: A longitudinal investigation of the role making process. *Organizational Behavior and Human Performance, 13*(1), 46–78.

Davis, K. (1973). The case for and against business assumption of social responsibilities. *Academy of Management Journal, 16*(2), 312–322.

DeCremer, D., & Hiel, A. V. (2006). Effects of another person's fair treatment on one's own emotions and behaviors: The moderating role of how much the other cares for you. *Organizational Behavior and Human Decision Processes, 100*(2), 231–249.

De Gilder, D., Schuyt, T. N., & Breedijk, M. (2005). Effects of an employee volunteering program on the work force: The

ABN-AMRO Case. *Journal of Business Ethics*, *61*(2), 143–152.

Derrick, J. L., Gabriel, S., & Hugenberg, K. (2009). Social surrogacy: How favored television programs provide the experience of belonging. *Journal of Experimental Social Psychology*, *45*(2), 352–362.

Derrick, J. L., Gabriel, S., & Tippin, B. (2008). Parasocial relationships and self-discrepancies: Faux relationships have benefits for low self-esteem individuals. *Personal Relationships*, *15*(2), 261–280.

Dulebohn, J. H., Bommer, W. H., Liden, R. C., Brouer, R. L., & Ferris, G. R. (2012). A meta-analysis of antecedents and consequences of leader-member exchange integrating the past with an eye toward the future. *Journal of Management*, *38*(6), 1715–1759.

Eisenberger, R., Huntington, R., Hutchison, S., & Sowa, D. (1986). Perceived organizational support. *Journal of Applied Psychology*, *71*(3), 500–507.

Elkington, J. (2004). Enter the triple bottom line. In A. Henriques & J. Richardson (Eds.), *The triple bottom line: Does it all add up* (pp. 1–16). London: Earthscan Publications Ltd.

Erdogan, B. (2002). Antecedents and consequences of justice perceptions in performance appraisals. *Human Resource Management Review*, *12*(4), 555–578.

Erdogan, B., Kraimer, M. L., & Liden, R. C. (2004). Work value congruence and intrinsic career success: The compensatory roles of leader-member exchange and perceived organizational support. *Personnel Psychology*, *57*(2), 305–322.

Erdogan, B., Liden, R. C., & Kraimer, M. L. (2006). Justice and leader-member exchange: The moderating role of organizational culture. *Academy of Management Journal*, *49*(2), 395–406.

Ford Motor Company. (2012). Sustainability 2012/13. Retrieved February 4, 2014, from http://corporate.ford.com/microsites/sustainability-report-2012-13/blueprint-strategy

Friedman, M. (1962). *1982, Capitalism and freedom*. Chicago: University of Chicago Press.

George, J. M. (2013). Compassion and capitalism implications for organizational studies. *Journal of Management*, *40*(1), 5–15.

Gerstner, C. R., & Day, D. V. (1997). Meta-analytic review of leader–member exchange theory: Correlates and construct issues. *Journal of Applied Psychology*, *82*(6), 827–844.

Glavas, A., & Piderit, S. K. (2009). How does doing good matter? Effects of corporate citizenship on employees. *Journal of Corporate Citizenship*, *36*, 51–70.

Goodwin, V. L., Bowler, W. M., & Whittington, J. L. (2009). A social network perspective on LMX relationships: Accounting for the instrumental value of leader and follower networks. *Journal of Management*, *35*(4), 954–980.

Graen, G. B. (1976). Role-making processes within complex organizations. In M. D. Dunnette (Ed.), *Handbook of industrial and organizational psychology* (pp. 1201–1245). Chicago: Rand McNally.

Graen, G. B., Cashman, J. F., Ginsburg, S., & Schiemann, W. (1977). Effects of linking-pin quality on the quality of working life of lower participants. *Administrative Science Quarterly*, *22*(3), 491–504.

Graen, G. B., & Scandura, T. A. (1987). Toward a psychology of dyadic organizing. *Research in Organizational Behavior*, *9*(1), 175–208.

Graen, G. B., & Uhl-Bien, M. (1995). Relationship-based approach to leadership: Development of leader-member exchange (LMX) theory of leadership over 25 years: Applying a multi-level multi-domain perspective. *The Leadership Quarterly*, *6*(2), 219–247.

Grant, A. M. (2012). Giving time, time after time: Work design and sustained employee participation in corporate volunteering. *Academy of Management Review*, *37*(4), 589–615.

Grant, A. M., & Mayer, D. M. (2009). Good soldiers and good actors: Prosocial and impression management motives as interactive predictors of affiliative citizenship behaviors. *Journal of Applied Psychology*, *94*(4), 900–912.

Greening, D. W., & Turban, D. B. (2000). Corporate social performance as a competitive advantage in attracting a quality workforce. *Business & Society*, *39*(3), 254–280.

Guler, I., Guillén, M. F., & Macpherson, J. M. (2002). Global competition, institutions, and the diffusion of organizational practices: The international spread of ISO 9000 quality certificates. *Administrative Science Quarterly*, *47*(2), 207–232.

Hayibor, S., Agle, B. R., Sears, G. J., Sonnenfeld, J. A., & Ward, A. (2011). Value congruence and charismatic leadership in CEO–top manager relationships: An empirical investigation. *Journal of Business Ethics*, *102*(2), 237–254.

Henderson, D. J., Liden, R. C., Glibkowski, B. C., & Chaudhry, A. (2009). LMX differentiation: A multilevel review and examination of its antecedents and outcomes. *The Leadership Quarterly*, *20*(4), 517–534.

Henderson, D. J., Wayne, S. J., Shore, L. M., Bommer, W. H., & Tetrick, L. E. (2008). Leader-member exchange, differentiation, and psychological contract fulfillment: A multilevel examination. *Journal of Applied Psychology*, *93*(6), 1208–1219.

Hofstede, G. H. (1993). Cultural constraints in management theories. *Academy of Management Executive*, *7*(1), 81–94.

Hofstede, G. H. (2001). *Culture's consequences: Comparing values, behaviors, institutions and organizations across nations*. Thousand Oaks, CA: Sage.

Horton, D., & Wohl, R. R. (1956). Mass communication and para-social interaction: Observations on intimacy at a distance. *Psychiatry*, *19*(3), 215–229.

Ilies, R., Nahrgang, J. D., & Morgeson, F. P. (2007). Leader-member exchange and citizenship behaviors: A meta-analysis. *Journal of Applied Psychology*, *92*(1), 269–277.

Jones, D. (2010). Does serving the community also serve the company? Using organizational identification and social exchange theories to understand employee responses to a volunteerism programme. *Journal of Occupational and Organizational Psychology*, *83*(4), 857–878.

Jones, D. A., & Rupp, D. E. (in press). Social responsibility IN and OF organizations. An exploration of the psychology of corporate social responsibility. In N. Anderson, D. S. Ones, H. K. Sinangil, & C. Viswesvaran (Eds.), *Handbook of industrial, work, and organizational psychology* (2nd ed.). Thousand Oaks, CA: Sage.

Jones, D., Willness, C., & Macneil, S. (2009). *Corporate Social Responsibility and Recruitment: Testing Person-Organization Fit and Signaling Mechanisms*. Paper presented at the Academy of Management Proceedings.

Jones, D., Willness, C., & Madey, S. (2013). Why are job seekers attracted by corporate social performance? Experimental and field tests of three signal-based mechanisms. *Academy of Management Journal*, *57*(2), 383–404.

Kahneman, D., Knetsch, J. L., & Thaler, R. H. (1986). Fairness and the assumptions of economics. *Journal of Business*, *59*(4), S285–S300.

Knight, G., & Greenberg, J. (2002). Promotionalism and subpolitics Nike and its labor critics. *Management Communication Quarterly*, *15*(4), 541–570.

Kozinets, R. V., & Handelman, J. M. (2004). Adversaries of consumption: Consumer movements, activism, and ideology. *Journal of Consumer Research*, *31*(3), 691–704.

Kray, L. J., & Allan Lind, E. (2002). The injustices of others: Social reports and the integration of others' experiences in organizational justice judgments. *Organizational Behavior and Human Decision Processes*, *89*(1), 906–924.

Lam, S. S., Schaubroeck, J., & Aryee, S. (2002). Relationship between organizational justice and employee work outcomes: A cross-national study. *Journal of Organizational Behavior*, *23*(1), 1–18.

Lavelle, J. J., Rupp, D. E., & Brockner, J. (2007). Taking a multifoci approach to the study of justice, social exchange, and citizenship behavior: The target similarity model. *Journal of Management*, *33*(6), 841–866.

Lavelle, J. J., Rupp, D. E., Manegold, J. G., & Thornton, M. A. (2015). Multifoci justice and target similarity: Emerging research and extensions. In R. S. Cropanzano & M.L. Ambrose (Eds.), *The Oxford Handbook of Justice in the Workplace*. Oxford University Press: New York: NY (pp. 335–350).

Leventhal, G. S. (1980). *What should be done with equity theory?* In K. Gergen, M. S. Greenberg, & R. H. Willis (Eds.), *Social exchange* (pp. 27–55). New York: Springer.

Liden, R. C., & Graen, G. (1980). Generalizability of the vertical dyad linkage model of leadership. *Academy of Management Journal*, *23*(3), 451–465.

Liden, R. C., Wayne, S. J., & Stilwell, D. (1993). A longitudinal study on the early development of leader-member exchanges. *Journal of Applied Psychology*, *78*(4), 662.

Lin, C. P., Lyau, N. M., Tsai, Y. H., Chen, W. Y., & Chiu, C. K. (2010). Modeling corporate citizenship and its relationship with organizational citizenship behaviors. *Journal of Business Ethics*, *95*(3), 357–372.

Mansour-Cole, D., & Scott, S. (1998). Hearing it through the grapevine: The influence of source of layoff information and leader-member-relations on survivors' justice perceptions. *Personnel Psychology*, *51*(1), 25–54.

Margolis, J. D., Elfenbein, H. A., & Walsh, J. P. (2009). Does it pay to be good . . . and does it matter? A meta-analysis of the relationship between corporate social and financial performance. Unpublished manuscript.

Margolis, J. D., & Walsh, J. P. (2003). Misery loves companies: Rethinking social initiatives by business. *Administrative Science Quarterly*, *48*(2), 268–305.

Martin, R., Epitropaki, O., Thomas, G., & Topakas, A. (2010). A review of leader-member exchange research: Future prospects and directions. In G. P. Hodgkinson & J. K. Ford (Eds.), *International review of industrial and organizational psychology* (pp. 35–88). London, UK: Wiley-Blackwell.

Masterson, S. S., Lewis, K., Goldman, B. M., & Taylor, M. S. (2000). Integrating justice and social exchange: The differing effects of fair procedures and treatment on work relationships. *Academy of Management Journal*, *43*(4), 738–748.

Matten, D., & Moon, J. (2008). "Implicit" and "explicit" CSR: A conceptual framework for a comparative understanding of corporate social responsibility. *Academy of Management Review*, *33*(2), 404–424.

Mayer, David M, K. Aquino, R. L. Greenbaum, and M. Kuenzi. (2012). Who displays ethical leadership, and why does it matter? An examination of antecedents and consequences of ethical leadership. *Academy of Management Journal*, *55*(1): 151–71.

McShane, L., & Cunningham, P. (2012). To thine own self be true? Employees' judgments of the authenticity of their organization's corporate social responsibility program. *Journal of Business Ethics*, *108*(1), 81–100.

Minter, S. G. (1991). Creating the safety culture. *Occupational Hazards*, *53*(8), 17–21.

Myerson, P., & Hamilton, R. D. (1986). Matching corporate culture and technology. *Advanced Management Journal*, *51*(1), 8–13.

Neumann, S., & Hadass, M. (1980). DSS and strategic decisions. *California Management Review*, *22*(3), 77–84.

Olson-Buchanan, J. B., Bryan, L. L. K., & Thompson, L. F. (Eds.). (2013). *Using industrial organizational psychology for the greater good: Helping those who help others*. New York: Routledge.

Omilion-Hodges, L. M., & Baker, C. R. (2013). Contextualizing LMX within the workgroup: The effects of LMX and justice on relationship quality and resource sharing among peers. *The Leadership Quarterly*, *24*(6), 935–951.

Orlitzky, M., Schmidt, F. L., & Rynes, S. L. (2003). Corporate social and financial performance: A meta-analysis. *Organization Studies*, *24*(3), 403–441.

Reed, A., Aquino, K., & Levy, E. (2007). Moral identity and judgments of charitable behaviors. *Journal of Marketing*, *71*(1), 178–193.

Reed, A., & Aquino, K. F. (2003). Moral identity and the expanding circle of moral regard toward out-groups. *Journal of Personality and Social Psychology*, *84*(6), 1270–1286.

Reynolds, S. J., & Ceranic, T. L. (2007). The effects of moral judgment and moral identity on moral behavior: An empirical examination of the moral individual. *Journal of Applied Psychology*, *92*(6), 1610–1624.

Rodgers, R., Hunter, J. E., & Rogers, D. L. (1993). Influence of top management commitment on management program success. *Journal of Applied Psychology*, *78*(1), 151–155.

Rupp, D. E. (2011). An employee-centered model of organizational justice and social responsibility. *Organizational Psychology Review*, *1*(1), 72–94.

Rupp, D. E., Bashshur, M., & Liao, H. (2007). Justice climate: Consideration of source, target, type, specificity, and emergence. *Research in Multi Level Issues*, *6*, 439–459.

Rupp, D. E., Ganapathi, J., Aguilera, R. V., & Williams, C. A. (2006). Employee reactions to corporate social responsibility: An organizational justice framework. *Journal of Organizational Behavior*, *27*(4), 537–543.

Rupp, D. E., & Mallory, D. B. (2015). Corporate social responsibility: Psychological, person-centric, and progressing, *Annual Review of Organizational Psychology and Organizational Behavior*, *2*, 211–236.

Rupp, D. E., Shao, R., Jones, K. S., & Liao, H. (2014). The utility of a multifoci approach to the study of organizational justice: A meta-analytic investigation into the consideration of normative rules, moral accountability, bandwidth-fidelity, and social exchange. *Organizational Behavior and Human Decision Processes*, *123*(2), 159–185.

Rupp, D. E., Shao, R., Skarlicki, D., Kim, T.-Y., & Nadisic, T. (2013). Corporate Social Responsibility and Employee Engagement: The Moderating Role of Self-Determination and Individualism. Paper presented at the Annual Meeting of the Academy of Management, Lake Beuna Vista, Florida.

Rupp, D. E., Shao, R., Thornton, M. A., & Skarlicki, D. P. (2013). Applicants' and employees' reactions to corporate social responsibility: The moderating effects of first party justice perceptions and moral identity. *Personnel Psychology, 66*(4), 895–933.

Rupp, D. E., Skarlicki, D., & Shao, R. (2013). The psychology of corporate social responsibility and humanitarian work: A person-centric perspective. *Industrial and Organizational Psychology, 6*(4), 361–368.

Rupp, D. E., & Thornton, M. A. (2014). The role of employee justice perceptions in influencing climate and culture. In B. Schneider & K. Barbera (Eds.), *The oxford handbook of organizational climate and culture*. New York: Oxford University Press (pp. 360–381).

Ryan, A., & Ford, J. K. (2010). Organizational psychology and the tipping point of professional identity. *Industrial and Organizational Psychology, 3*(3), 241–258.

Scandura, T. A. (1999). Rethinking leader-member exchange: An organizational justice perspective. *The Leadership Quarterly, 10*(1), 25–40.

Schiappa, E., Gregg, P. B., & Hewes, D. E. (2005). The parasocial contact hypothesis. *Communication Monographs, 72*(1), 92–115.

Seers, A. (1989). Team-member exchange quality: A new construct for role-making research. *Organizational Behavior and Human Decision Processes, 43*(1), 118–135.

Sen, S., & Bhattacharya, C. B. (2001). Does doing good always lead to doing better? Consumer reactions to corporate social responsibility. *Journal of Marketing Research, 38*(2), 225–243.

Shao, R., Rupp, D. E., Skarlicki, D. P., & Jones, K. S. (2013). Employee justice across cultures: A meta-analytic review. *Journal of Management, 39*(1), 263–301.

Sias, P. M., & Jablin, F. M. (1995). Differential superior–subordinate relations, perceptions of fairness, and coworker communication. *Human Communication Research, 22*(1), 5–38.

Skarlicki, D. P., & Kulik, C. T. (2004). Third-party reactions to employee (mis) treatment: A justice perspective. *Research in Organizational Behavior, 26*, 183–229.

Smith, J. (2013, October 10 2013). The Companies With the Best CSR Reputations. Forbes.com. Retrieved February 4, 2014, from http://www.forbes.com/sites/jacquelynsmith/2013/10/02/the-companies-with-the-best-csr-reputations-2/

Spencer, S., & Rupp, D. E. (2009). Angry, guilty, and conflicted: Injustice toward coworkers heightens emotional labor through cognitive and emotional mechanisms. *Journal of Applied Psychology, 94*(2), 429.

Starbucks Corporation. (2011, September 15, 2011). Starbucks Qatar Hosts Iftar For Dhreima Qatar Orphanage Foundation. Retrieved February, 2, 2014, from http://mena.starbucks.com/en/news/starbucks-qatar-hosts-iftar-for-dhreima-qatar-orphanage-foundation.html

Sully de Luque, M., Washburn, N. T., Waldman, D. A., & House, R. J. (2008). Unrequited profit: How stakeholder and economic values relate to subordinates' perceptions of leadership and firm performance. *Administrative Science Quarterly, 53*(4), 626–654.

Treadway, D. C., Adams, G. L., Ranft, A. L., & Ferris, G. R. (2009). A meso-level conceptualization of CEO celebrity effectiveness. *The Leadership Quarterly, 20*(4), 554–570.

Turban, D. B., & Greening, D. W. (1997). Corporate social performance and organizational attractiveness to prospective employees. *Academy of Management Journal, 40*(3), 658–672.

Turillo, C. J., Folger, R., Lavelle, J. J., Umphress, E. E., & Gee, J. O. (2002). Is virtue its own reward? Self-sacrificial decisions for the sake of fairness. *Organizational Behavior and Human Decision Processes, 89*(1), 839–865.

Van den Bos, K., & Lind, E. A. (2002). Uncertainty management by means of fairness judgments. *Advances in Experimental Social Psychology, 34*, 1–60.

Viswesvaran, C., Deshpande, S. P., & Milman, C. (1998). The effect of corporate social responsibility on employee counterproductive behavior. *Cross Cultural Management: An International Journal, 5*(4), 5–12.

Vitell, S. J., Nwachukwu, S. L., & Barnes, J. H. (1993). The effects of culture on ethical decision-making: An application of Hofstede's typology. *Journal of Business Ethics, 12*(10), 753–760.

Waddock, S., & Bodwell, C. (2004). Managing responsibility: What can be learned from the quality movement? *California Management Review, 47*(1), 25–37.

Waddock, S. A., & Graves, S. B. (1997). The corporate social performance. *Strategic Management Journal, 8*(4), 303–319.

Walumbwa, F. O., Cropanzano, R., & Goldman, B. M. (2011). How leader–member exchange influences effective work behaviors: Social exchange and internal–external efficacy perspectives. *Personnel Psychology, 64*(3), 739–770.

Wayne, S. J., & Ferris, G. R. (1990). Influence tactics, affect, and exchange quality in supervisor-subordinate interactions: A laboratory experiment and field study. *Journal of Applied Psychology, 75*(5), 487–499.

Wayne, S. J., Shore, L. M., & Liden, R. C. (1997). Perceived organizational support and leader-member exchange: A social exchange perspective. *Academy of Management Journal, 40*(1), 82–111.

Weiss, H. M., & Rupp, D. E. (2011). Experiencing work: An essay on a person centric work psychology. *Industrial and Organizational Psychology, 4*(1), 83–97.

Wood, D. J. (1991). Corporate social performance revisited. *Academy of Management Review, 16*(4), 691–718.

Relational Leadership through the Lens of International LMX Research

Ekin K. Pellegrini

Abstract

Over the past decade, a substantial body of research on leader–member exchange (LMX) has emerged from the international context. International LMX is a developing research area with some intriguing findings; however, this emerging literature is still in its infancy and much work remains to be done for a strong theoretical foundation with sound practical implications. This article provides a comprehensive assessment of international LMX research. It then highlights theoretical and methodological gaps and suggests promising directions for future international LMX research.

Key Words: leader–member exchange, LMX, leadership, international, cross-cultural

Introduction

Multinational business organizations are increasingly experiencing dynamic cross-cultural work arrangements due to technological advances such as teleconference, live chat, online hangouts, video conferencing, and an increasing reliance on email in lieu of face-to-face communication. In multinational companies, business is commonly conducted in multicultural work groups specifically via virtual work and expatriation. Accordingly, the twenty-first century has been referred to as "the century of international management research" (Tsui, Nifadkar, & Ou, 2007, p. 427).

Recent changes in organizational structures toward an increasingly multicultural work environment are accompanied by an accelerated interest in management research across cultures. This interest is evidenced by major reviews within the past few years (e.g., Gelfand, Erez, & Aycan, 2007; Kirkman, Lowe, & Gibson, 2006; Rockstuhl, Dulebohn, Ang, & Shore, 2012; Tsui et al., 2007). There is growing excitement among management scholars on cross-cultural research and it is clear from the review articles that sufficient research has accumulated to merit comprehensive reviews.

However, previous reviews of international research focused broadly on international management and organizational behavior and did not aim to provide an in-depth study of specific areas, such as leader–member exchange (LMX), where a substantial amount of international research has accumulated specifically over the past decade. To date, the meta-analysis of Rockstuhl et al. (2012) is the only review of international LMX research; however, they focused specifically on six outcome variables [i.e., task performance, organizational citizenship behavior (OCB), justice perceptions, job satisfaction, organizational commitment, and turnover intentions] and two antecedents (transformational leadership and leader trust).

Despite flourishing research in international LMX, the field is in need of a review of diverse findings. Thus, the purpose of this article is to provide a thorough examination of recent advances in international LMX research and identify theoretical and methodological gaps in the current state of the literature. LMX theory will advance only when diverse perspectives from the international context are integrated to provide a more complete theoretical framework.

Theoretical Background

According to LMX theory, leaders develop unique relationships with each follower (Scandura & Graen, 1984; Graen & Uhl-Bien, 1995). The quality of these LMX relationships falls on a continuum ranging from low-quality relations characterized by economic exchange to high-quality relations characterized by social exchange. LMX is grounded in social exchange theory (Blau, 1964), which posits that unlike economic exchanges, social exchange relations are more flexible and complex and cannot be reduced to a single calculative exchange scale. Social exchange relations involve unspecified obligations in return for received favors and they rarely involve explicit bargaining. In a high-quality relationship, followers receive support, encouragement, visibility, and developmental assignments from their leaders and they reciprocate the favor in more generalized terms (e.g., work harder) as opposed to immediate reciprocity in economic exchange (Liden, Sparrowe, & Wayne, 1997). As LMX matures from low-quality relations that are characterized by transactional exchanges specified by the employment contract to high-quality exchanges beyond work requirements, members stop keeping count of favors since the relationship evolves into one characterized by mutual trust, obligation, respect, and loyalty. The quality of a member's exchange relation with the leader has been shown to be positively related to performance, OCB, organizational commitment, job satisfaction, and justice perceptions and negatively related to turnover, perceptions of politics, role ambiguity, and role conflict (Gerstner & Day, 1997; Ilies, Nahrgang, & Morgeson, 2007; Dulebohn, Bommer, Liden, Brouer, & Ferris, 2012).

Definition

This review of over three decades of international research suggests a general consensus in the field with respect to the definition of LMX. According to Graen and Scandura (1987), effective leadership occurs when leaders and followers maintain a high-quality LMX relationship characterized by mutual trust, respect, and obligation. Graen and Uhl-Bien (1995) also endorse this definition. Dienesch and Liden (1986) conceptualized LMX as a multidimensional construct composed of affect, contribution, and loyalty. Later, Liden, and Maslyn (1998) conducted interviews to serve as guidelines for item generation and based on these interviews, they proposed a five-dimensional model of LMX composed of three dimensions originally proposed

by Dienesch and Liden (1986) and two new dimensions: trust and professional respect. They defined trust as "the perception of the degree of genuine concern for the best interest of the other member of the dyad as reflected in supportive behavior and honesty" (p. 49). However, trust (a central tenet of social exchange theory) was later dropped and loyalty dimension was revised to include notions of trust. Empirical analyses demonstrated support for a four-dimensional model that included affect, contribution, loyalty, and professional respect as currencies of exchange. Liden and Maslyn (1998) suggest LMX relations may be based primarily on one, two, three, or all four dimensions. For example, affect may develop quickly, perhaps during the employment interview; however, loyalty may take considerable time to grow.

A multidimensional conceptualization of LMX is especially significant in cross-cultural research as different LMX domains may lead to different outcomes (Liden & Maslyn, 1998). Furthermore, the relative importance of exchange currencies may vary considerably across cultures. However, current definitions of LMX used in international research are limited by a strictly etic (cultural-universals) perspective due to the conceptualization of LMX meaning based on interviews solely with U.S. samples.

Based on inconsistent LMX findings from the international context, Anand, Hu, Liden, and Vidyarthi (2011) suggested that LMX dynamics may operate differently in non-Western contexts. Inconsistent findings of these studies include, but are not limited to, a nonsignificant relation between LMX and OCB in China (Loi & Ngo, 2009), a nonsignificant association between LMX and turnover intentions in India (Mehta, 2009), and a significantly weaker association between transformational leadership and LMX in Saudi Arabia and Jordan as compared with Australia (Pillai, Scandura, & Williams, 1999). Given that these associations are well-established in the Western context, controversial findings from international research prompted Rockstuhl et al. (2012) to conduct a meta-analysis of international LMX research.

In their meta-analysis from the international context, Rockstuhl et al. (2012) observed a significantly weaker association between LMX and outcome variables as compared with established findings from the U.S. context. For example, the relationships among LMX and OCB, justice perceptions, job satisfaction, turnover intentions, and leader trust were all significantly stronger in Western (i.e., horizontal/individualistic; HI) contexts (e.g., United States, England, Canada, Australia) compared to vertical/collectivistic (VC) cultures (e.g., China, India, Turkey, Colombia, Malaysia, Singapore). They suggest that the underlying reason for weaker associations between LMX and outcome variables in the international context is that employees in VC cultures are influenced by role-based obligations; due to their stronger respect for authority, attitudes and behaviors of members in VC cultures are therefore less likely to be influenced solely by leader treatment. They further suggest that the weaker associations in non-Western contexts may be due to cross-cultural differences in the underlying mechanisms of LMX and they call for research that examines LMX content in the international context. Furthermore, they state that "change in construct meaning across cultures is an alternative explanation" for attenuated relationships (p. 1104). In this review, we also argue for a critical need to incorporate emic (cultural-specific) conceptualizations of LMX in international research.

Measurement

This current review of international LMX research suggests three commonly used measurement instruments to assess LMX perceptions (see the Appendix). Of the 93 studies reviewed, 48 (52%) used the 7-item, unidimensional LMX-7 scale (Scandura & Graen, 1984; Graen & Uhl-Bien, 1995). Another commonly used scale is the 12-item multidimensional LMX-MDM scale (Liden & Maslyn, 1998), which assesses four LMX dimensions: affect, loyalty, contribution, and professional respect. Although LMX-MDM is a multidimensional scale, notwithstanding a few exceptions (e.g., Ansari, Hung, & Aafaqi; 2007; Lee, 2005; Wang, Law, & Chen, 2008), international research using LMX-MDM mostly examined LMX as a higher-order construct, rather than studying the dimensions' differential relations with outcomes.

A common reliance on these validated scales produces the benefit of consistency and comparability of empirical LMX studies within and across cultures. However, LMX is a complex and multidimensional exchange relationship and we may be trading rigor for relevance (Hiller, DeChurch, Murase, & Doty, 2011; Staw, 1995) by not seeking to understand cultural variations in LMX meaning via in-depth interviews and focus groups for further theoretical refinement. A more complete conceptual understanding of LMX in non-Western contexts is essential for construct validity and will ultimately aid in advancing both theory and practice.

A call for international studies that examine indigenous LMX dimensions is long overdue. A common and troubling reliance on measurement scales based on Western conceptualizations may limit our ability to understand the varied cultural nuances in LMX relationships. The current review of the international literature suggests that the four LMX-MDM dimensions are theoretically and empirically meaningful across cultures. However, there may be additional, indigenous facets of LMX relationships that research has yet to identify.

For example, in Confucian cultures, *guanxi* describes dyadic relationship quality and it is the key driver of work relations. Confucian relationalism characterizes personal relations as the basic unit of social systems and Chinese society is so relationship oriented that *guanxi* is pursued for its own sake (Chen, Chen, & Huang, 2013; Hwang, 2009). *Guanxi* relationships are holistic in that they involve care and concern for the social, psychological, and economic (i.e., on the job and off the job domains) welfare of the other member (Chen, Friedman, Yu, Fang, & Lu, 2009). Recently, Chen, Yu, and Son (2014) suggested that the focus of LMX research has long been on Western LMX theory and that research needs to move beyond Western conceptualizations and identify indigenous LMX components that involve an off-the-job personal relationship. Almost two decades ago, House and Aditya (1997) suggested that LMX theory reflects U.S. cultural preferences for a separation between work and personal relations; however, research has still yet to extend LMX theory beyond the Western business context.

To delineate the distinction of *guanxi* from LMX, Law, Wong, Wang, and Wang (2000) defined leader–member *guanxi* (LMG) in non-work-related social exchanges, such as gift giving and dinner invitations. The major difference between Chinese LMG and Western LMX is that whereas LMX is limited to work-related exchanges, LMG includes non-work-related social exchange (Chen et al., 2013). Given that Chinese leader–member relationships involve both work and off-the-job domains, an overarching framework depicting leader–member exchange quality in the Chinese context should include both LMX and LMG to thoroughly assess relationship quality. In fact, due to the limited ability of LMX to capture indigenous cultural nuances in leader–member exchange relations (Hui & Graen, 1997), Chen et al. (2009) developed a scale to assess supervisor–subordinate *guanxi* quality encompassing both work and non-work-related aspects of the dyadic relationship, which is conceptually similar to LMX in the Western context (Chen et al., 2013). Recently, in the Chinese context, Chen et al. (2013) found that LMX differentiation was not significantly related to job satisfaction or turnover intent; however, LMG differentiation was negatively related to job satisfaction and positively related to turnover intent. Thus, *guanxi* may be a key aspect of LMX in the Chinese context. In assessing LMX quality, it is time that researchers integrate the broader social context and incorporate culturally significant exchange norms into measurement instruments. LMX will represent an overarching framework for the study of social exchange relationships at work only when indigenous perspectives are also integrated into theoretical development.

Similar to the significance of *guanxi* in Chinese LMX relationships, dominant Confucian values—hierarchy and relationalism—suggest another significant indigenous construct in high-quality exchange relations. Paternalistic leadership has been at the forefront of indigenous dyadic leadership theories and has received growing interest within the past decade (Aycan, Schyns, Sun, Felfe, & Saher, 2013; Chen, Eberly, Chiang, Farh, & Cheng, 2014; Cheng et al., 2014; Pellegrini & Scandura, 2010). Paternalism combines discipline and authority with fatherly benevolence (Farh & Cheng, 2000). Benevolence refers to a holistic concern for subordinate's well-being and people in authority consider it an obligation to take a personal interest in the follower's off-the-job lives to promote welfare (Gelfand, Erez, & Aycan, 2007). Subordinates show loyalty and deference out of respect and appreciation for the leader's care and protection (Aycan, 2006). Paternalistic leaders are also authoritative (as opposed to authoritarian) and they exercise control to promote the subordinate's welfare (Aycan, 2006). Subordinates know the rules are for their advancement and respect and willingly comply with the leader's decisions. Research suggests that in paternalistic business contexts, such as Turkey, India, China, and Mexico (Aycan et al., 2000; Pellegrini & Scandura, 2008), paternalism may be a key component in defining high-quality LMX relations. Aycan et al. (2013) recently suggested that paternalism is commonly practiced in VC cultures of Asia, the Middle East, Latin America, and Africa and that it represents leadership dynamics in the majority of the world. Incorporating emic management practices into LMX measurement instruments will broaden the scope and representativeness of LMX theory.

Regarding the established LMX dimensions (i.e., affect, contribution, loyalty, respect), what is interpreted as positive behavior may not have a similar connotation in another culture. For example, one item from Liden and Maslyn's (1998) *affect* scale is "My supervisor is the kind of person one would like to have as a friend." The definition of 'friend' may vary considerably across cultures. In a cross-cultural study in Hong Kong, Smith, Misumi, Tayeb, Peterson, and Bond (1989) found that when an employee encounters difficulties, the discussion by the supervisor of the employee's personal problems with other team members in the absence of the employee is considered "considerate behavior," whereas respondents from the United States regard talking "behind the back" of this person as inconsiderate. Thus, future research needs to delve deeper into culturally accepted as well as culturally questionable behaviors for LMX dimensions to provide a solid and practical theory for business leaders in cross-cultural work contexts.

Similarly, loyalty may have different connotations across cultures. According to Liden and Maslyn (1998), *loyalty* refers to "the expression of public support for the goals and the personal character of the other member of the LMX dyad" (p. 50). However, in paternalistic societies loyalty goes beyond simple expressions of public support. Unquestioning obedience and deference to the leader are essential elements of loyalty in leader–member relations in paternalistic work environments (Pellegrini & Scandura, 2006). Therefore, the definition of "loyalty" may have additional emic aspects that have yet to be identified in LMX research.

Furthermore, Liden and Maslyn (1998) initially conceptualized trust as a separate, fifth dimension of LMX. However, their findings suggested that trust and loyalty were not easily distinguishable and they decided to include trust in the loyalty dimension and to drop the separate trust dimension. However, trust is a central tenet of social exchange theory, and given the significance and salience of trust in relationship-oriented, VC business contexts, trust as originally conceptualized by Liden and Maslyn (1998) may appear as an additional LMX dimension in non-Western business contexts.

Antecedents of LMX in the International Context

The current review suggests a disproportionate attention devoted to outcomes rather than antecedents; however, there is still ample research on antecedents of LMX from the international context. Of the 93 studies reviewed, 32 (34%) studied one or more antecedents of LMX. To provide a reference for the reader, Table 19.1 presents a list of the studies identified as examining LMX in an international context. This list was constructed by performing a search of the key terms LMX, leader–member exchange, international, and cross-cultural in the PsychINFO database. Additional studies from the references lists of the identified articles were also added.

Table 19.1 lists the studies reviewed, including antecedent and outcome variables, LMX measurement instruments used, source of ratings (e.g., member, leader, personnel records), as well as sample information.

The majority of studies examining LMX antecedents in the international context employed cross-sectional/same source (45%) and cross-sectional/multisource (39%) methods followed by time-lag/multisource (6%) designs. Specifically, research that examines leader–member similarity (e.g., organizational tenure, value, personality, gender, age, national origin similarity) as LMX antecedents (Ashkanasy & O'Connor, 1997; Bhal, Ansari, & Aafaqi, 2007; Loi & Ngo, 2009; Schaubroeck & Lam, 2002; Pelled & Xin, 2000; Testa, 2009) predominantly adopted cross-sectional designs. These studies suggest subordinates in high-quality exchanges are more similar to their leaders on gender, national origin, values, and personality. For example, in China, Loi and Ngo (2009) found that male subordinates with female supervisors reported the lowest LMX quality, whereas male subordinates with male supervisors reported the highest LMX. However, given the cross-sectional design in all these studies, we still do not know much about the longitudinal effects of similarity. For example, at early stages of LMX development, demographic similarities may be more salient predictors of LMX quality. However, as LMX matures into a high-quality relationship, non-work-related predictors (e.g., demographics) may no longer be salient in determining LMX quality. Thus, these relations should be examined at more than one time point with a sufficient time lag to allow LMX relationships to mature.

In addition, international research should incorporate the broader social, historical, and political context into LMX theory building. For example, Waismel-Manor, Berger, and Dikstein (2010) studied Ashkenazi Jews and Mizrahi Jews in Israel and found LMX to be more strongly related to OCBs in similar dyads. Gong, Farh, and Chattopadhyay (2012) found shared dialect identity (e.g., Mandarin, Hakka, Mingnan) to be a predictor of LMX in Taiwan. One similarity variable that may be a significant predictor of LMX quality in the Middle Eastern business context is political affiliation. Numerous Middle Eastern countries are currently experiencing political turmoil and examining value similarity or congruence in political affiliation as a potential LMX antecedent is a relevant and timely endeavor. For example, in the Turkish business context, a leader affiliated with AKP (Justice Development Party; a right-wing party developed from the tradition of Islamism) and a member affiliated with CHP (Republican People's Party; a center-left party endorsing social liberalism) may report significantly lower LMX compared to dyads congruent in political values.

Another untapped research avenue includes leader–member similarity on implicit leadership theories (ILTs) and implicit followership theories (IFTs) (Engle & Lord, 1997; Sy, 2010). In a longitudinal study in the U.K., Epitropaki and Martin (2005) found that leader–member differences in prototypic ILTs (e.g., sensitivity) negatively influence LMX, whereas differences in antiprototypic ILTs (e.g., tyranny) positively influence LMX quality. Furthermore, in the U.S., Sy (2010) found leaders' followership prototype (e.g., enthusiasm) to be positively related to LMX, whereas leaders' followership antiprototype (e.g., conformity) was negatively related to LMX. However, these definitions originated in the Western context and therefore ILTs and IFTs as LMX antecedents should be examined carefully in an international business context. This research stream is promising for international LMX research since leaders and members may have culturally ingrained notions of the definition of an ideal leader and follower and uncovering indigenous ILTs and IFTs may provide a more in-depth understanding of LMX antecedents. Given the limited number of LMX studies on ILTs and IFTs, the potential for theory development in international LMX research is significant (Epitropaki, Sy, Martin, Tram-Quon, & Topakas, 2013).

Another promising avenue in studying LMX antecedents is that the studies examining antecedents in extant research measured LMX from the subordinate's perspective. To date, little progress has been made in incorporating the leader's perspective [i.e., supervisor leader–member exchange (SLMX)] in examining predictors of LMX quality. A central tenet of LMX theory is that LMX

Table 19.1. Antecedents and Outcomes of LMX (Non-U.S. Context)

Author(s)	LMX Dimensions	Antecedent(s) and Source*	Outcome(s) and Source*	Sample Characteristics Size/ Source Country	LMX Measure and Source[1]
Harris, Li, & Kirkman (2014)	Overall LMX		Organizational citizenship behavior (L) Turnover intention (M)	223 employees matched with 60 supervisors China	8 items adapted from Bauer & Green (1996) (M)
Chen, Yu, & Son (2014)	Overall LMX		Job satisfaction (M) Organizational commitment (M) Turnover intention (M) Co-worker helping behavior (M)	228 employees in 60 work groups from 12 companies China	LMX-7 (Scandura & Graen, 1984) (M)
Liu, Lin, & Hu (2013)	Overall LMX		Unethical behavior (M) Job satisfaction (M)	249 employees from four finance companies China	LMX-7 (Scandura & Graen, 1984) (M)
Liu, Cai, Li, Shi, & Fang (2013)	Overall LMX		Organizational identification (M) Turnover intention (M)	190 leader–member dyads Hong Kong China	LMX-7 (Graen & Uhl-Bien, 1995) (L)
Bakar & Sheer (2013)	Dyadic LMX agreement		Team-member exchange (TMX) (M) Cooperative communication (M) Group cohesion (M)	375 employees matched with 48 managers Malaysia	LMX-MDM (Liden & Maslyn, 1998) (M) and SLMX-MDM (L)
Volmer, Spurk, & Niessen (2012)	Overall LMX		Creative work involvement (M, Time 2)	144 employees Germany	LMX-7 (Graen & Uhl-Bien, 1995) (M, Time 1)
Zhou, Wang, Chen, & Shi (2012)	Overall LMX	LLX (leader–leader exchange) (L; Time 1)	Empowerment (M, Time 1) Job satisfaction (M, Time 2) Job performance (L, Time 2)	577 bank employees nested within 104 managers China	8 items adapted from Scandura & Graen (1984) by Bauer & Green (1996) (M; Time 1)

Study	LMX type	Moderator/Mediator	Outcome	Sample	Country	LMX measure
Brunetto, Shacklock, Bartram, Leggat, Farr-Wharton, Stanton, & Casimir (2012)	Overall LMX		Psychological empowerment (M) Affective organizational commitment (M)	1283 nurses	Australia	LMX-7 (Graen & Uhl-Bien, 1995) (M)
Hu, Ou, Chiou, & Lin (2012)	Overall LMX	Team knowledge sharing (M)	Team service innovation performance (M)	466 employees from 35 hotels	Taiwan	LMX-7 (Scandura & Graen, 1984) (M)
Joo & Ready (2012)	Overall LMX		Career satisfaction (M)	232 employees	Korea	LMX-7 (Scandura & Graen, 1984) (M)
Gajendran & Joshi (2012)	Overall LMX		Member influence on team decisions (M)	167 members in 40 globally distributed teams	Europe, Japan, Korea, Australia, United States	7 items adapted from Scandura & Graen (1984) by Janssen & Van Yperen (2004) (M)
Gong, Farh, & Chattopadhyay (2012)	Overall LMX	Shared dialect identity (M, L)		179 subordinates nested within 76 supervisors	Taiwan	LMX-7 (Scandura & Graen, 1984) (M, L)
Zhang, Waldman, & Wang (2012)	Overall LMX		Member's emergence as an informal leader (peer team members)	361 employees in 74 teams	China	LMX-7 (Graen & Uhl-Bien, 1995) (M)
Volmer, Niessen, Spurk, Linz, & Abele (2011)	Overall LMX	Job satisfaction (M; Time 1)	Job Satisfaction (M, Time 2)	279 employees from a large IT company	Germany	LMX-7 (Graen & Uhl-Bien, 1995) (M; Time 1 and Time 2)
Yousaf, Sanders, Torka, & Ardts (2011)	Overall LMX		Affective organizational commitment (M) Satisfaction with human resources practices (M)	122 doctoral students	Netherlands	15 items adapted from Liden and Maslyn (1998) (M)
Karim (2011)	Overall LMX	Emotional intelligence (M)	Distributive justice (M) Procedural justice (M)	106 employees	Pakistan	LMX-7 (Scandura & Graen, 1984) (M)

(continued)

Table 19.1. Continued

Author(s)	LMX Dimensions	Antecedent(s) and Source*	Outcome(s) and Source*	Sample Characteristics Size/ Source Country	LMX Measure and Source[1]
Venkataramani, Green, & Schleicher (2010)	Overall LMX	Perceived leader status (M)	Job satisfaction (M) Turnover intentions (M)	184 employees nested within 42 managers / India	8 items adapted from Scandura & Green (1984) by Bauer & Green (1996) (M)
Pellegrini, Scandura, & Jayaraman (2010)	Overall LMX		Paternalistic leadership (M) Affective organizational commitment (M) Job satisfaction (M)	207 employed MBA students / India; 215 employed MBA students / U.S.	LMX-MDM (Liden & Maslyn, 1998) (M)
Anand, Vidyarthi, Liden, & Rousseau (2010)	Overall LMX		Organizational citizenship behavior (L)	231 subordinate–supervisor dyads / India	LMX-MDM (Liden & Maslyn, 1998) (M)
Kim, Lee, & Carlson (2010)	Overall LMX		Turnover intent (M)	232 nonsupervisory and 88 supervisory employees / South Korea	LMX-7 (Scandura, Graen, & Novak, 1986) (M)
Liao, Liu, & Loi (2010)	Overall LMX		Self-efficacy (M) Creativity (HR department)	828 employees / China	LMX-7 (Graen & Uhl-Bien, 1995) (M)
Huang, Chan, Lam, & Nan (2010)	Overall LMX		Burnout (M) Work performance (supervisor, peers, customers)	493 leader–member dyads / China	LMX-7 (Graen & Uhl-Bien, 1995) (M)
Li, Liang, & Crant (2010)	Overall LMX	Proactive personality (M)	Job satisfaction (M) Organizational citizenship behavior (L)	200 employees matched with 54 supervisors / China	8 items adapted from Scandura & Graen (1984) (M)
Brunetto, Farr-Wharton, & Shacklock (2010)	Overall LMX		Morale (M) Affective organizational commitment (M)	1064 nurses / Australia	LMX-7 (Graen & Uhl-Bien, 1995) (M)

Study	LMX measure	Outcomes	Sample	Country	Scale
Erdogan & Bauer (2010)	Overall LMX	Job satisfaction (M) Affective organizational commitment (M) Satisfaction with co-worker relations (M) Helping behavior targeting co-workers (L)	276 employees nested within 25 managers	Turkey	LMX-7 (Scandura & Graen, 1984) (M)
Eisenberger, Karagonlar, Stinglhamber, Neves, Becker, Gonzales-Morales, & Steiger-Muller (2010)	Overall LMX	Affective organizational commitment (M) In-role performance (L) Extra-role performance (L)	346 subordinate–supervisor dyads 251 employees matched with 79 supervisors	Portugal United States	LMX-MDM (Liden & Maslyn, 1998) (M)
Joo (2010)	Overall LMX	Affective organizational commitment (M) Turnover intention (M)	516 employees	South Korea	LMX-7 (Scandura & Graen, 1984) (M)
Waismel-Manor, Berger, & Dikstein (2010)	Overall LMX	Organizational citizenship behaviors (L)	163 supervisor–subordinate dyads	Israel	11 items from LMX-MDM (Liden & Maslyn, 1998) (M)
Lo, Ramayah, Min, & Songan (2010)	Affect Loyalty Contribution Respect	Organizational commitment (M)	156 employees from 11 companies	Malaysia	LMX-MDM (Liden & Maslyn, 1998) (M)
Botero & Van Dyne (2009)	Overall LMX	Employee voice (M)	109 employees 138 employees	United States Colombia	6 items (Graen, Novak, & Sommerkamp, 1982) (M)
Bhal, Gulati, & Ansari (2009)	Affect Perceived contribution	Job satisfaction (M) Organizational commitment (M) Loyalty (organizational citizenship behavior) (M)	306 software professionals	India	10 items (Bhal & Ansari, 1996) (M)

(continued)

Table 19.1. Continued

Author(s)	LMX Dimensions	Antecedent(s) and Source*	Outcome(s) and Source*	Sample Characteristics Size/ Source Country	LMX Measure and Source[1]
Loi, Mao, & Ngo (2009)	Overall LMX		Organizational social exchange (M) Organizational economic exchange (M) Affective organizational commitment (M) Intention to leave (M)	239 employees China	LMX-7 (Scandura & Graen, 1984) (M)
Loi & Ngo (2009)	Overall LMX	Gender dissimilarity (M, L) Organizational tenure dissimilarity (M, L) Age dissimilarity (M, L) Education dissimilarity (M, L) National origin dissimilarity (M, L)		239 supervisor–subordinate dyads China	LMX-7 (Scandura & Graen, 1984) (M)
Testa (2009)	Overall LMX	Leader–member national origin similarity (M)		520 employees from two U.S. cruise lines 66 countries (predominantly from United States, England, Italy, India)	LMX-7 (Scandura & Graen, 1984) (M)
Li & Hung (2009)	Overall LMX	Transformational leadership (M)	Task performance (M) Organizational citizenship behavior (M)	1040 teachers from 52 elementary schools Taiwan	LMX-7 (Graen & Uhl-Bien, 1995) (M)
Chen, Friedman, Yu, Fang, & Lu (2009)	Overall LMX		Affective organizational commitment (M) Turnover intention (M) Procedural justice (M)	209 employees from 12 companies China	LMX-MDM (Liden & Maslyn, 1998) (M)

Ishak & Alam (2009)	Overall LMX	Organizational citizenship behaviors (L) Self-esteem (M)	300 employees matched with 118 supervisors	Malaysia	LMX-MDM (Liden & Maslyn, 1998) (M, L)
Hsiung & Tsai (2009)	Overall LMX	Performance (L) Employee relative job breadth (M, L) Leader–member congruence on job content (M, L)	184 supervisor–subordinate dyads	Taiwan	LMX-7 (Graen & Uhl-Bien, 1995) (M)
Liao, Hu, & Chung (2009)	Overall LMX	Organizational commitment (M) Job satisfaction (M)	303 employees from 24 international hotels	Taiwan	6 items adapted from Fielder, Chemers, & Mahar (1977)
Yifeng & Tjosvold (2008)	Overall LMX	Cooperative goals (M) Competitive goals (M) Independent goals (M)	Organizational commitment (M) Performance (M) Leader effectiveness (M) Future collaboration (M) Open-minded discussion (M) Innovation (M)	199 employees (99 had American managers, 100 had Japanese managers)	China	5 items adapted from Graen et al. (1982) (M)
Van Dyne, Kamdar, & Joireman (2008)	Overall LMX	Helping (supervisor focused) (L) Voice (organization focused) (L)	218 employees matched with 34 supervisors	India	LMX-MDM (Liden & Maslyn, 1998) (M)
		Helping (supervisor focused) (L) Voice (supervisor focused) (L) Helping (organization focused) (L) Voice (organization focused) (L)	234 employees matched with 36 supervisors	Singapore	LMX-MDM (Liden & Maslyn, 1998) (M)
Asgari, Silong, Ahmad, & Samah (2008)	Overall LMX	Organizational citizenship behavior (L)	220 employees	Iran	LMX-7 (Scandura & Graen, 1984) (M)

(continued)

Table 19.1. Continued

Author(s)	LMX Dimensions	Antecedent(s) and Source*	Outcome(s) and Source*	Sample Characteristics Size/ Source Country	LMX Measure and Source[1]
Ozer (2008)	Overall LMX		Job performance (L) Job satisfaction (M)	243 supervisor–subordinate dyads	China, Hong Kong, Taiwan, Singapore, South Korea	LMX-7 (Scandura & Graen, 1984) (M)
Wang, Law, & Chen (2008)	Affect Contribution Loyalty Professional respect		Task performance (L) Contextual performance (L)	168 employees matched with 87 managers	China	16 items adapted from Liden and Maslyn (1998) by Wang et al. (2001) (M)
Dulac, Coyle-Shapiro, Henderson, & Wayne (2008)	Overall LMX		Psychological contract breach (M, Time 2) Psychological contract violation (M, Time 2) Affective organizational commitment (M, Time 2) Intentions to quit (M, Time 2)	152 employees	Belgium	LMX-7 (Scandura & Graen, 1984) (M, Time 1)
van Dam, Oreg, & Schyns (2008)	Overall LMX		Information (M) Participation (M) Trust in management (M)	235 employees	Netherlands	LMX-7 (Scandura & Graen, 1984) (M)
Chen, Tsui, & Zhong (2008)		Psychological contract breach by the subordinate (L)		273 supervisor–subordinate dyads	China	LMX-7 (Scandura & Graen, 1984) (M)
Lam, Huang, & Snape (2007)	Overall LMX	Feedback-seeking behavior (L)		209 employees matched with 70 supervisors	China	LMX-7 (Graen & Uhl-Bien, 1995) (M)
		Negative feedback-seeking behavior (L)	Performance (personnel records)	240 employees matched with 84 supervisors	China	LMX-7 (Graen & Uhl-Bien, 1995) (M)

Study	LMX dimension	Moderators/Mediators	Outcomes	Sample	Country	Measure
Chen, Lam, & Zhong (2007)	Overall LMX		Negative feedback-seeking behavior (L), Subjective in-role performance (L), Objective in-role performance (personnel records)	238 supervisor–subordinate dyads	China	LMX-7 (Scandura & Graen, 1984) (M)
Chen & Tjosvold (2007)	Overall LMX		Constructive controversy (M)	163 employees (68 reported to U.S. managers, 95 reported to Chinese managers)	China	5 items adapted from Graen et al. (1982) (M)
Bhal, Ansari, & Aafaqi (2007)	Affect, Perceived contribution	Gender match (M), Supervisor support (M), LMX tenure (M)	Perceived organizational support (M)	201 employees	Malaysia	10 items (Bhal & Ansari, 1996) (M)
Bhal & Gulati (2007)	Affect, Perceived contribution		Voice (M)	306 employees	India	10 items (Bhal & Ansari, 1996) (M)
Bhal & Ansari (2007)	Affect, Perceived contribution		Job satisfaction (M), Organizational commitment (M), Distributive justice (M), Voice (M)	295 employees	India	10 items (Bhal & Ansari, 1996) (M)
Schyns, Torka, & Gössling (2007)	Overall LMX		Turnover intention (M), Preparedness for change (M)	326 employees, 85 employees	Germany, Netherlands	LMX-7 (Graen & Uhl-Bien, 1995) (M), 10 items adapted from LMX-7 (Graen & Uhl-Bien, 1995) (M)

(*continued*)

Table 19.1. Continued

Author(s)	LMX Dimensions	Antecedent(s) and Source*	Outcome(s) and Source*	Sample Characteristics Size/ Source Country		LMX Measure and Source[1]
Ansari, Hung, & Aafaqi (2007)	Affect Contribution Loyalty Professional respect		Affective organizational commitment (M) Normative organizational commitment (M Continuance organizational commitment (M Turnover intentions (M) Procedural justice climate (M)	224 employees	Malaysia	LMX-MDM (Liden & Maslyn, 1998) (M)
Boies & Howell (2006)	Overall LMX (at the team level)		Team conflict (M) Team potency (M)	132 soldiers from 35 military teams	Canada	LMX-7 (Graen & Uhl-Bien, 1995) (M)
Erdogan, Liden, & Kraimer (2006)	Overall LMX	Interactional justice (M) Distributive justice (M) Organizational culture (peer)		516 teachers from 30 high schools	Turkey	LMX-MDM (Liden & Maslyn, 1998) (M)
Erdogan & Liden (2006)	Overall LMX	Interactional justice (M) Distributive justice (M)		100 employees	Turkey	LMX-MDM (Liden & Maslyn, 1998) (M)
Pellegrini & Scandura (2006)	Overall LMX		Paternalistic leadership (M) Delegation (M) Job satisfaction (M)	185 employees	Turkey	LMX-MDM (Liden & Maslyn, 1998) (M)
Schyns & Croon (2006)	Overall LMX		Satisfaction with supervisor (M) Satisfaction with colleagues (M) Satisfaction with task (M) Satisfaction with job conditions (M)	319 employees	Germany	LMX-7 (Scandura & Graen, 1984) (M)

Study	LMX dimensions	Antecedents/Moderators	Outcomes	Sample	Country	LMX measure
Aryee & Chen (2006)	Overall LMX	Supervisor control of rewards (M) Work unit climate (M)	Empowerment (M) Job satisfaction (M) Psychological withdrawal behavior (M) Task performance (L)	192 employees nested within 66 supervisors	China	LMX-7 (Liden, Wayne, & Stilwell, 1993) (M)
Graen, Dharwadkar, Grewal, & Wakabayashi (2006)	Overall LMX		Career progress (over 23 years) (personnel records)	65 employees	Japan	12 items (Graen et al., 1990) (M)
Lapierre, Hackett, & Taggar (2006)	Overall LMX	Family interference with work (M) Job enrichment (M)		381 government employees	Canada	LMX-6 (Schriesheim, Neider, Scandura, & Tepper, 1992) (M)
Bhal (2006)	Affect Perceived contribution		Loyalty (organizational citizenship behavior) (M) Distributive justice (M) Procedural justice (M) Interactional justice (M)	306 employees from 30 software companies	India	10 items (Bhal & Ansari, 1996) (M)
Yagil (2006)	LMX (M)	LMX (L) Interactional justice (M) Procedural justice (M)	Job satisfaction (M)	152 supervisor–subordinate dyads	Israel	LMX-7 (Scandura & Graen, 1984) (M, L)
Lee (2005)	Affect Loyalty Contribution Professional respect	Transformational leadership (M) Transactional leadership (M) Passive-avoidant leadership (M)	Organizational commitment (M)	201 research and development employees	Singapore	LMX-MDM (Liden & Maslyn, 1998) (M)

(continued)

Table 19.1. Continued

Author(s)	LMX Dimensions	Antecedent(s) and Source*	Outcome(s) and Source*	Sample Characteristics Size/ Source Country	LMX Measure and Source[1]
Martin, Thomas, Charles, Epitropaki, & McNamara (2005)	Overall LMX	Internal locus of control (M)	Intrinsic job satisfaction (M) Extrinsic job satisfaction (M) Work-related well-being (M) Organizational commitment (M)	404 employees 51 employees	Midlands, United Kingdom LMX-7 (Graen & Uhl-Bien, 1995) (M) South Wales, United Kingdom
Wang, Law, Hackett, Wang, & Chen (2005)	Overall LMX	Transformational leadership (M)	Task performance (L) Organizational citizenship behaviors (L)	162 employees matched with 81 supervisors China	LMX-MDM (Liden & Maslyn, 1998) (M)
Schyns, Paul, Mohr, & Blank (2005)	Overall LMX	Relationship tenure (M) Span of supervision (M)	Delegation (M) Organizational commitment (M) Occupational self-efficacy (M)	Four different employee samples ranging from 76 to 326 Germany	LMX-7 (Scandura & Graen, 1984) (M)
Epitropaki & Martin (2005)	Overall LMX	Implicit–explicit leadership traits difference (M)	Job satisfaction (M) Organizational commitment (M) Job-related well-being (M)	439 employees United Kingdom	LMX-7 (Scandura & Graen, 1984) (M)
Chen & Tjosvold (2005)	Overall LMX	Cooperative goals (M) Competitive goals (M) Independent goals (M)	Leader effectiveness (M) Organizational commitment (M) Future collaboration with the leader (M)	230 employees (68 managers were from the United States, 95 were local Chinese, 43 were from Hong Kong and Taiwan, and 24 managers were from Japan) China	5 items (Graen, Novak, & Sommerkamp, 1982) (M)
Wat & Shaffer (2005)	Overall LMX		Trust in supervisor (M) Psychological empowerment (M) Organizational citizenship behaviors (L)	183 employees matched with 32 managers Hong Kong	LMX-7 (Scandura & Graen, 1984) (M)

Study	LMX dimensions	Outcomes	Sample	Country	Measure
Perizade & Sulaiman (2005)	Affect Contribution	Job satisfaction (M) Organizational commitment (M) Attitude to change (M)	613 employees matched with 126 managers	Indonesia	10 items (Bhal & Ansari, 1996) (M, L)
Janssen & Van Yperen (2004)	Mastery orientation (M) Performance orientation (M)	In-role job performance (L) Innovative job performance (L) Job satisfaction (M)	170 employees matched with 14 managers	Netherlands	7 items adapted from Scandura and Graen (1984) (M)
Hui, Lee, & Rousseau (2004)	Overall LMX	Organizational citizenship behavior (L) Affective organizational commitment (M)	605 supervisor–subordinate dyads	China	LMX-7 (Scandura & Graen, 1984) (M)
Hung, Ansari, & Aafaqi (2004)	Affect Loyalty Contribution Professional respect	Affective organizational commitment (M) Normative organizational commitment (M) Continuance organizational commitment (M)	224 employees	Malaysia	LMX-MDM (Liden & Maslyn, 1998) (M)
Erdogan, Kraimer, & Liden (2004)	Overall LMX	Job satisfaction (M) Career satisfaction (M)	520 teachers from 30 high schools	Turkey	LMX-MDM (Liden & Maslyn, 1998) (M)
Gupta & Krishnan (2004)	Overall LMX	Self-confidence (M)	102 supervisor–subordinate dyads	India	6 items (Graen, Novak, & Sommerkamp, 1982) (M)
Krishnan (2004)	Overall LMX	Upward influence strategies (M) Value system congruence (M) Transformational leadership (M)	281 employees	India	LMX-7 (Scandura & Graen, 1984) (M)
Chi & Lo (2003)	Overall LMX	Procedural justice (M) Distributive justice (M)	104 employees from 15 companies	Taiwan	8 items adapted from Scandura & Graen (1984) by Bauer & Green (1996) (M)

(continued)

Table 19.1. Continued

Author(s)	LMX Dimensions	Antecedent(s) and Source*	Outcome(s) and Source*	Sample Characteristics Size/ Source Country	LMX Measure and Source[1]
Tierney, Bauer, & Potter (2002)	Overall LMX		Extra-role behavior (M) Organizational commitment (M)	100 employees	Mexico	8 items adapted from Scandura & Green (1984) by Bauer & Green (1996) (M)
Schaubroeck & Lam (2002)	Overall LMX	Subordinate (M)–supervisor (L) personality similarity	Promotion decisions (Promotion Committee) Performance (L)	386 bank tellers nested within 76 supervisors 185 bank tellers nested within 36 supervisors	Hong Kong United States	LMX-7 (Graen & Uhl-Bien, 1995) (M)
Law, Wong, Wang, & Wang (2000)	Overall LMX		Performance rating (L) Job assignment (L) Promotability (L) Bonus allocation possibility (L)	189 supervisor–subordinate dyads	China	LMX-7 (Scandura & Graen, 1984) (M)
Pelled & Xin (2000)	Overall LMX	Leader (personnel records)–member (M) gender similarity Leader (personnel records)–member (M) age similarity		195 employees 90 employees	Mexico United States	6 items (Graen, Novak, & Sommerkamp, 1982) (M)
Pillai, Scandura, & Williams (1999)	Overall LMX		Procedural justice (M) Distributive justice (M) Job satisfaction (M)	160 employees 80 MBA students 85 employees 190 employees 192 MBA students	Australia India Colombia Saudi Arabia and Jordan United States	LMX-7 (Scandura & Graen, 1984) (M)

Study	LMX Measure	Other Variables	Sample	Country	Scale
Howell & Hall-Merenda (1999)	Overall LMX	Follower performance (company records, Time 3) Transformational leadership (M, Time 1) Contingent reward leadership (M, Time 1) Management by exception (M, Time 1)	317 employees matched with 109 managers	Canada	4 items (Graen & Schiemann, 1978) (M, Time 2)
Epitropaki & Martin (1999)	Overall LMX	Organizational commitment (M) Job satisfaction (M) Job-related well-being (M)	73 employees of an academic institution	United Kingdom	LMX-7 (Graen & Uhl-Bien, 1995) (M)
Hui, Law, & Chen (1999)	Negative affectivity (M)	In-role performance (L) Organizational citizenship behavior (L)	386 employees matched with 126 managers	China	LMX-7 (Scandura & Graen, 1984) (M)
Law & Wong (1999)	Overall LMX	Job satisfaction (M) Turnover intention (M)	224 business school alumni	China	LMX-7 (Scandura & Graen, 1984) (M)
Ashkanasy & O'Connor (1997)	Leader–member value congruence (L, M)		160 employees nested within 30 supervisors	Australia	4 items (Liden & Graen, 1980) (M)
O'Driscoll & Beehr (1994)	Overall LMX	Psychological strain (M) Job satisfaction (M) Turnover intention (M) Role ambiguity (M) Role conflict (M)	136 employees (123 employees from New Zealand analyzed in combination with 113 employees from the United States)		13 items adapted from Leader Behavior Description Questionnaire (LBDQ) (Stogdill, 1963)

(continued)

Table 19.1. Continued

Author(s)	LMX Dimensions	Antecedent(s) and Source*	Outcome(s) and Source*	Sample Characteristics Size/ Source Country	LMX Measure and Source[1]
Graen, Wakabayashi, Graen, & Graen (1990)	Overall LMX	Organizational commitment (M)	LMX after 10 years (M, L) Performance (L) Speed of promotion (personnel records) Promotability (personnel records) Job satisfaction (M) Satisfaction with supervision (M) Management resources (M, L)	71 supervisor–subordinate dyads	Japan	12 items developed for this study (M)
Steiner (1988)	Overall LMX	Intrinsic work values similarity (M) Extrinsic work values similarity (M)		125 postsecondary students 156 college students	France United States	5 items (Graen, Liden, & Hoel, 1982) (M)

* M = variable assessed based on Member reports; L = variable assessed based on Leader reports.

development is a three-stage process and in the first stage (i.e., role taking), the leader may offer opportunities to the member based on the leader's perceptions of the member's abilities (Graen & Scandura, 1987). Therefore, leaders' perceptions may significantly influence initial LMX quality starting from the *stranger* (low-quality) phase through the *maturity* (high-quality) phase. Furthermore, given the power distance in the leader's favor, leaders likely play a more significant role in LMX relationship quality (Dulebohn, Bommer, Liden, Brouer, & Ferris, 2012), and it is surprising that research has yet to examine antecedents of LMX quality from the leader's perspective.

Research examining antecedents of LMX in the international context has predominantly emerged from China (28%), followed by Taiwan (9%) and Turkey (6%). There is a significant need for studies from Latin America, the Middle East, and non-Confucian Asia to gain a more thorough understanding of what drives LMX quality universally as well as locally.

Finally, meta-analytic findings suggest that the strength of the influence of transformational leadership in predicting LMX does not show cross-cultural variations (Rockstuhl et al., 2012). On the other hand, results suggest a significantly weaker association between leader trust (as an antecedent) and LMX quality in VC cultures as compared to HI cultures. This is an important finding given the significance of trust in LMX theory. Rockstuhl et al. attributed this attenuated association to the moderating effect of national culture (i.e., HI vs. VC); however, we argue that the weaker association may be due to insufficient LMX construct validity in international contexts. The association between leader trust and LMX may be stronger in the Western context because LMX meaning and dimensions originated from the Western context. Also, in the meta-analysis of Rockstuhl et al. (2012), numerous VC countries (e.g., China, India, Turkey) are studied as one group; however, business relations in each of these countries are influenced by different norms. For example, in China, *guanxi* may be a more significant predictor of LMX, whereas in Turkey paternalism may be more salient in predicting LMX quality. Each VC context has unique political, historical, and cultural perspectives and there is a significant need to identify additional, emic dimensions to adequately capture LMX construct meaning. We certainly do not suggest a separate LMX theory for each country, which would move the field away from parsimony and away from a unifying theory of LMX (Liden, 2012). However, as Liden (2012) recently suggested, LMX research from an international context needs to incorporate cultural contextual moderators between LMX and antecedents as well as outcomes. Research from the international context needs to move beyond a predominantly U.S.-based perspective and address LMX construct validity by integrating local cultural nuances into the studies.

Outcomes of LMX in the International Context

International research on LMX predominantly focused on outcomes as compared to antecedents and of the 93 studies reviewed, 83 (89%) examined one or more outcomes of LMX. Consistent with Rockstuhl et al. (2012), the current review suggests an overwhelming interest specifically in five outcome variables. A majority of the studies examined follower organizational commitment (32%), follower performance (25%), follower turnover intentions (16%), follower job satisfaction (15%), follower OCB (14%), and follower justice perceptions (14%). This attention in a limited set of outcomes may limit the development of international LMX theory. We suggest that additional outcomes relevant to cross-cultural social exchange relations, such as cultural intelligence and participative decision making, warrant research attention.

The meta-analysis of Rockstuhl et al. (2012) did not find cross-cultural variations in relationships of LMX with followers' task performance and organizational commitment. However, relationships of LMX with OCB, justice perceptions, job satisfaction, and turnover intentions were all significantly stronger in Western contexts than in VC (e.g., Asian) contexts. Although Rockstuhl et al. suggest the moderating influence of national culture (i.e., HI vs. VC) as an explanation for attenuated relationships, we suggest that it is a construct validity issue and that research has yet to identify significant emic LMX dimensions that may be relevant to these particular outcomes. Relationships between LMX and these outcomes may be weaker in the international context because research has yet to make an effort to clearly understand the conceptual meaning of the LMX construct and appropriately measure its construct domain in the international context.

Furthermore, extant international research on LMX has focused exclusively on follower outcomes. There is a significant need for studies that examine the benefits as well as potential disadvantages for leaders in high-LMX relationships. For example, Harris and Kacmar (2006), almost a decade ago, showed that high-LMX involved high levels of stress for followers; however, we still do not know much about stressors for leaders in high-LMX relationships. International research that examines the influence of high-LMX on leader outcomes is long overdue and results from this research stream are essential to effectively support high-quality LMX relationships and prevent early leader exit. There is also a significant need for studies that examine the benefits of high LMX relationships that accrue to organizations. Specifically, tangible organizational effectiveness outcomes as outlined by Hiller et al. (2011), such as sales growth, return on invested capital, and profit, have yet to be examined in the international LMX literature.

The majority of the research examining LMX outcomes in an international context measured LMX with LMX-7 (57%) (Scandura & Graen, 1984; Graen & Uhl-Bien, 1995), followed by LMX-MDM (19%) (Liden & Maslyn, 1998), predominantly from the follower's perspective (95%). The majority of studies employed cross-sectional/common source (58%), cross-sectional/multisource (32%), followed by longitudinal/multisource (6%) research designs. An overreliance on quantitative, cross-sectional studies in LMX research not only limits our understanding of the cultural nuances in LMX meaning but is also an unfitting design choice in studies that imply causal connections (i.e., outcomes research).

In addition, of the 83 studies we reviewed, more than half were from China (32%), India (12%), Malaysia (7%), and Taiwan (6%). There is a significant need in international LMX research to extend theory development beyond Asia, specifically into Latin American and Middle Eastern business contexts.

Despite two decades of research since Liden and Maslyn (1998) introduced LMX-MDM, out of 83 studies examining LMX outcomes, only 6% assessed LMX as a four-dimensional construct. As previously suggested by Liden and Maslyn (1998), these studies found that different LMX dimensions were differentially associated with outcome variables. For example, in Malaysia (with a predominantly Chinese sample), Ansari et al. (2007) found affect and professional respect were more salient currencies of LMX relationships. In India, Lee (2005) found that all four dimensions were positively related

to transformational leadership; however, only loyalty was significantly related to transactional leadership. More recently, in Malaysia, Lo et al. (2010) found a two-dimensional LMX-MDM measurement model in which affect and loyalty loaded on the first dimension and contribution and respect items loaded on the second dimension. There is a significant research gap in examining LMX as a multidimensional construct. The potential influence of the cultural context on which LMX dimensions may be more salient to individuals in international settings warrants research attention.

Directions for Future International LMX Research

This current review of 93 studies in international LMX, suggests three major limitations that characterize this body of research. First, all of these studies failed to integrate emic LMX dimensions into their studies. Cultural context influences leadership prototypes and to advance knowledge, research needs to move beyond a predefined Western conceptualization of LMX and attend to the meanings and perspectives that emerge from international research. Current LMX theory may depict an oversimplification of LMX relationships in non-Western cultures (Khatri, Tsang, & Begley, 2006). An indigenous focus on LMX nuances in international contexts should be a priority to advance LMX theory. Therefore, future research employing qualitative research designs to identify indigenous meanings is warranted.

The second limitation is a predominantly unidimensional conceptualization of LMX in current LMX research. This may be a significant limitation in international LMX studies since the priorities ascribed to different LMX dimensions may differ across cultures. An overall LMX quality is certainly an appropriate operationalization depending on the research question; however, multidimensional conceptualization of LMX specifically in the international context would be informative and should be given increasing research attention.

Third, extant LMX research in international contexts predominantly focused on LMX relationship quality and has paid almost no attention to examining relational dynamics and processes (Uhl-Bien, 2006). LMX meaning is limited by the sociocultural context and future research needs to integrate the broader local, historical, and political contexts in examining relational dynamics in LMX. Research findings from international contexts are specifically apt to contribute in-depth information toward a more comprehensive framework integrating LMX relationships and relationship dynamics. It is also essential that future research moves beyond cultural values and provides richer insight into the processes and local context.

During the past decade, LMX research has increasingly incorporated the broader relational social context into LMX theory building. There is flourishing international research examining social comparison processes in single-leader contexts, such as LMX social comparison (LMXSC; Vidyarthi et al., 2010), relative LMX (RLMX; Henderson et al., 2008), and LMX relational separation (Harris et al., 2014). However, to date, there is no international research from dual leader contexts in which each LMX relationship exists within the context of the other relationship (Vidyarthi et al., 2014).

Furthermore, there is increasing research interest in examining LMX relationships within the context of co-worker exchange (CWX), SLMX, and LLX (leader–leader exchange) relations and a fruitful research direction would be to add another dyadic relationship to the current nomenclature (Erdogan & Bauer, 2014). We suggest that a follower's exchange relationship with his or her formal (organizationally assigned) mentor (formal mentor-member exchange; FMMX) is a fruitful, emerging research direction. Mentoring and LMX relationships are embedded in the same organizational context and it would be interesting and informative to examine the influence of conflicting career advice from the mentor and leader on follower and organizational outcomes.

Finally, organizations are increasingly witnessing digital lifestyles along with technology-driven work models. We suggest a better understanding of LMX in these newly emerging work structures. This is specifically relevant for international research since traditional LMX theory is built on a foundation of hierarchical, face-to-face interactions and may not adequately represent LMX relationships in emerging work models mediated through technology, such as e-leadership (Avolio, Sosik, Kahai, & Baker, 2014) or a more recent, flatter organizational structure referred to as holacracy (Denning, 2014). International LMX research in emerging, alternative work structures represents an area of considerable opportunity for future studies to make pioneering scholarly and practical contributions.

Conclusions

We hope that this timely review will serve as a useful guide in future inquiries into the emerging body of literature in international LMX and will help to advance the field to a more in-depth exploration of LMX meaning and relational context.

References

Anand, S., Hu, J., Liden, R.C., & Vidyarthi, P.R. (2011). Leader-member exchange: Recent research findings and prospects for the future. In A. Bryman, D. Collinson, K. Grint, B. Jackson, & M. Uhl-Bien (Eds.), The Sage Handbook of Leadership, Thousand Oaks, CA: Sage.

Anand, S., Vidyarthi, P. R., Liden, R. C., & Rousseau, D. M. (2010). Good citizens in poor quality relationships: Idiosyncratic deals as a substitute for relationship quality. *Academy of Management Journal, 53*, 970–988.

Ansari, M. A., Hung, D. K. M., & Aafaqi, R. (2007). Leader-member exchange and attitudinal outcomes: Role of procedural justice climate. *Leadership and Organization Development Journal, 28*, 690–709.

Aryee, S., & Chen, Z. X. (2006). Leader-member exchange in a Chinese context: Antecedents, the mediating role of psychological empowerment and outcomes. *Journal of Business Research, 59*, 793–801.

Asgari, A., Silong, A. D., Ahmad, A., & Samah, B. A. (2008). The relationship between leader-member exchange, organizational inflexibility, perceived organizational support, interactional justice and organizational citizenship behavior. *African Journal of Business Management, 2*, 138–145.

Ashkanasy, N. M., & O'Connor, C. (1997). Value congruence in leader-member exchange. *Journal of Social Psychology, 137*, 647–662.

Avolio, B. J., Sosik, J. J., Kahai, S. S., & Baker, B. (2014). E-leadership: Re-examining transformations in leadership source and transmission. *The Leadership Quarterly, 25*, 105–131.

Aycan, Z., Kanungo, R. N., Mendonca, M., Yu, K., Deller, J., Stahl, G., & Kurshid, A. (2000). Impact of culture on human resource management practices: A 10-country comparison. *Applied Psychology: An International Review, 49*, 192–221.

Aycan, Z. (2006). Paternalism: Towards conceptual refinement and operationalization. In K. S. Yang, K. K. Hwang, & U. Kim (Eds.), *Scientific advances in indigenous psychologies: Empirical, philosophical, and cultural contributions* (pp. 445–466). London, England: Sage.

Aycan, Z., Schyns, B., Sun, J. M., Felfe, J., & Saher, N. (2013). Convergence and divergence of paternalistic leadership: A cross-cultural investigation of prototypes. *Journal of International Business Studies, 44*, 962–969.

Bakar, H. A., & Sheer, V. C. (2013). The mediating role of perceived cooperative communication in the relationship between interpersonal exchange relationships and perceived group cohesion. *Management Communication Quarterly, 27*, 443–465.

Bauer, T. N. & Green, S. G. (1996). The development of leader-member exchange: A longitudinal test. *Academy of Management Journal, 39*, 1538–1567.

Bhal, K. T. (2006). LMX-citizenship behavior relationship: Justice as a mediator. *Leadership and Organization Development Journal, 26*, 106–117.

Bhal, K. T., & Ansari, M. A. (1996). Measuring quality of inter-action between leaders and members. *Journal of Applied Social Psychology, 26*, 945–972.

Bhal, K. T., & Ansari, M. A. (2007). Leader-member exchange-subordinate outcomes relationship: Role of voice and justice. *Leadership and Organization Development Journal, 28*, 20–35.

Bhal, K. T., Ansari, M. A., & Aafaqi, R. (2007). The role of gender match, LMX tenure, and support in leader-member exchange. *International Journal of Business and Society, 8*, 63–80.

Bhal, K. T., & Gulati, N. (2007). Pay satisfaction of software professionals in India. *Vikalpa, 32*(3), 9–21.

Bhal, K. T., Gulati, N., & Ansari, M. A. (2009). Leader-member exchange and subordinate outcomes: Test of a mediation model. *Leadership and Organization Development Journal, 30*, 106–125.

Blau, P. (1964). *Exchange and power in social life*. New York: Wiley & Sons.

Boies, K., & Howell, J. M. (2006). Leader-member exchange in teams: An examination of the interaction between relation-ship differentiation and mean LMX in explaining team-level outcomes. *The Leadership Quarterly, 17*, 246–257.

Botero, I. C., & Van Dyne, L. (2009). Predicting voice: Interactive effects of LMX and power distance in the U.S. and Colombia. *Management Communication Quarterly, 23*, 84–104.

Brunetto, Y., Farr-Wharton, R., & Shacklock, K. (2010). The impact of supervisor-subordinate relationships on morale: Implications for public and private sector nurses' commitment. *Human Resource Management Journal, 20*, 206–225.

Brunetto, Y., Shacklock, K., Bartram, T., Leggat, S. G., Farr-Wharton, R., Stanton, P., & Casimir, G. (2012). Comparing the impact of leader-member exchange, psy-chological empowerment and affective commitment upon Australian public and private sector nurses: Implications for retention. *The International Journal of Human Resource Management, 23*, 2238–2255.

Chen, C. C., Chen, X. P., & Huang, S. (2013). Chinese guanxi: An integrative review and new directions for future research. *Management and Organization Review, 9*, 167–207.

Chen, X. P., Eberly, M. B., Chiang, T. J., Farh, J. L., & Cheng, B.S. (2014). Affective trust in Chinese leaders: Linking paternalistic leadership to employee performance. *Journal of Management, 40*, 796–819.

Chen, Y., Friedman, R., Yu, E., Fang, W., & Lu, X. (2009). Developing a three-dimensional model and scale for supervisor-subordinate *guanxi*. *Management and Organization Review, 5*, 375–399.

Chen, Y., Yu, E., & Son, J. (2014). Beyond leader–member exchange (LMX) differentiation: An indigenous approach to leader–member relationship differentiation. *The Leadership Quarterly, 25*, 611.

Chen, Y. F., & Tjosvold, D. (2005). Cross cultural leader-ship: Goal interdependence and leader-member rela-tions in foreign ventures in China. *Journal of International Management, 11*, 417–439.

Chen, Y. F., & Tjosvold, D. (2007). Guanxi and leader mem-ber relationships between American managers and Chinese employees: Open-minded dialogue as mediator. *Asia Pacific Journal of Management, 24*, 171–189.

Chen, Z., Lam, W., & Zhong, J. A. (2007). Leader-member exchange and member performance: A mew look at individual-level negative feedback-seeking behavior and team-level empowerment climate. *Journal of Applied Psychology, 92*, 202–212.

Chen, Z., Tsui, A. S., & Zhong, L. (2008). Reactions to psy-chological contract breach: A dual perspective. *Journal of Organizational Behavior, 29*, 527–548.

Cheng, B. S., Boer, D., Chou, L. F., Huang, M. P., Yoneyama, S., Shim, D., Sun, J. M., Lin, T. T., Chou, W. J., & Tsai, C. Y. (2014). Paternalistic leadership in four East Asian societies. *Journal of Cross-Cultural Psychology, 45*, 82–90.

Chi, S., & Lo, H. (2003). Taiwanese employees' justice per-ceptions of co-workers' punitive events. *Journal of Social Psychology, 143*, 27–42.

Denning, S. (2014, January 15). Making sense of Zappos and holacracy. *Forbes*. Retrieved from http://www.forbes.com/sites/stevedenning/2014/01/15/making-sense-of-zappos-and-holacracy/.

Dienesch, R. M., & Liden, R. C. (1986). Leader-member exchange model of leadership: A critique and further devel-opment. *Academy of Management Review, 11*, 618–634.

Dulac, T., Coyle-Shapiro, J. A.-M., Henderson, D., & Wayne, S. (2008). Not all responses to breach are the same: A lon-gitudinal study examining the interconnection of social exchange and psychological contract processes in organiza-tions. *Academy of Management Journal, 51*, 1079–1098.

Dulebohn, J. H., Bommer, W. H., Liden, R. C., Brouer, R., & Ferris, G. R. (2012). A meta-analysis of the antecedents and consequences of leader-member exchange: Integrating the past with an eye toward the future. *Journal of Management, 38*, 1715–1759.

Eisenberger, R., Karagonlar, G., Stinglhamber, F., Neves, P., Becker, T. E., Gonzales-Morales, M. G., & Steiger-Mueller, M. (2010). Leader-member exchange and affective organiza-tional commitment: The contribution of supervisor's orga-nizational embodiment. *Journal of Applied Psychology, 95*, 1085–1103.

Engle, E. M., & Lord, R. G. (1997). Implicit theories, self-schemas, and leader-member exchange. *Academy of Management Journal, 40*, 988–1010.

Epitropaki, O., & Martin, R. (1999). The impact of relational demography on the quality of leader-member exchanges and employees' work attitudes and well-being. *Journal of Occupational and Organizational Psychology, 72*, 237–240.

Epitropaki, O., & Martin, R. (2005). From ideal to real: A longi-tudinal study of implicit leadership theories, leader-member exchanges and employee outcomes. *Journal of Applied Psychology, 90*, 659–676.

Epitropaki, O., Sy, T., Martin, R., Tram-Quon, S., & Topakas, A. (2013). Implicit leadership and followership theories "in the wild": Taking stock of information-processing approaches to leadership and followership in organizational settings. *The Leadership Quarterly, 24*, 858–881.

Erdogan, B., & Bauer, T. N. (2010). Differentiated leader-member exchanges: The buffering role of justice cli-mate. *Journal of Applied Psychology, 95*, 1104–1120.

Erdogan, B., & Bauer, T. N. (2014). Leader-member exchange (LMX) theory: The relational approach to leadership. In D. Day (Ed.), *Oxford Handbook of Leadership and Organizations*. Oxford, UK: Oxford University Press.

Erdogan, B., Kraimer, M. L., & Liden, R. C. (2004). Work value congruence and intrinsic career success: The compensatory roles of leader-member exchange and perceived organiza-tional support. *Personnel Psychology, 57*, 305–332.

Erdogan, B., & Liden, R. C. (2006). Collectivism as a moderator of responses to organizational justice: Implications for leader-member exchange and ingratiation. *Journal of Organizational Behavior, 27,* 1–17.

Erdogan, B., Liden, R. C., & Kraimer, M. L. (2006). Justice and leader-member exchange: The moderating role of organizational culture. *Academy of Management Journal, 49,* 395–406.

Farh, J. L., & Cheng, B. S. (2000). A cultural analysis of paternalistic leadership in Chinese organizations. In J. T. Li., A. S. Tsui, & E. Weldon (Eds.), *Management and organizations in the Chinese context* (pp. 85–127). London, England: Macmillan.

Fielder, F. E., Chemers, M. M., & Mahar, L. (1977). *Improving leadership effectiveness: The leader match concept.* New York: John Wiley.

Gajendran, R. S., & Joshi, A. (2012). Innovation in globally distributed teams: The role of LMX, communication frequency, and member influence on team decisions. *Journal of Applied Psychology, 97,* 1252–1261.

Gelfand, M. J., Erez, M., & Aycan, Z. (2007). Cross-cultural organizational behavior. *Annual Review of Psychology, 58,* 479–514.

Gerstner, C. R., & Day, D. V. (1997). Meta-analytic review of leader-member exchange theory: Correlates and construct issues. *Journal of Applied Psychology, 82,* 827–844.

Gong, Y., Farh, J. L., & Chattopadhyay, P. (2012). Shared dialect group identity, leader–member exchange and self-disclosure in vertical dyads: Do members react similarly? *Asian Journal of Social Psychology, 15,* 26–36.

Graen, G., Dharwadkar, R., Grewal, R., & Wakabayashi, M. (2006). Japanese career progress over the long haul: An empirical examination. *Journal of International Business Studies, 37,* 148–161.

Graen, G. B., Novak, M. A., & Sommerkamp, P. (1982). The effects of leader-member exchange and job design on productivity and satisfaction: Testing a dual attachment model. *Organizational Behavior and Human Performance, 30,* 109–131.

Graen, G. B., & Scandura, T. A. (1987). Toward a psychology of dyadic organizing. In L. L. Cummings & B. M. Staw (Eds.), *Research in organizational behavior* (Vol. 9, pp. 175–208). Greenwich, CT: JAI Press.

Graen, G.B. & Schiemann, W. (1978). Leader-member agreement: A vertical dyad linkage approach. *Journal of Applied Psychology, 63,* 206–212.

Graen, G. B., & Uhl-Bien, M. (1995). Relationship-based approach to leadership: Development of leader-member exchange (LMX) theory of leadership over 25 years: Applying a multi-level multi-domain perspective. *The Leadership Quarterly, 6,* 219–247.

Graen, G. B., Wakabayashi, M., Graen, M. R., & Graen, M. G. (1990). International generalizability of American hypotheses about Japanese management progress: A strong inference investigation. *The Leadership Quarterly, 1,* 1–23.

Gupta, V., & Krishnan, V. R. (2004). Impact of socialization on transformational leadership: Role of leader-member exchange. *South Asian Journal of Management, 11,* 7–20.

Harris, K. J., & Kacmar, K. M. (2006). Too much of a good thing: The curvilinear effect of leader-member exchange on stress. *The Journal of Social Psychology, 146,* 65–84.

Harris, T. B., Li, N., & Kirkman, B. L. (2014). Leader-member exchange (LMX) in context: How LMX differentiation and LMX relational separation attenuate LMX's influence on OCB and turnover intention. *The Leadership Quarterly, 25,* 314–328.

Henderson, D. J., Wayne, S. J., Shore, L. M., Bommer, W. H., & Tetrick, L. E. (2008). Leader-member exchange, differentiation, and psychological contract fulfillment: A multilevel examination. *Journal of Applied Psychology, 93,* 1208–1219.

Hiller, N. J., DeChurch, L. A., Murase, T., & Doty, D. (2011). Searching for outcomes of leadership: A 25-year review. *Journal of Management, 37,* 1137–1177.

House, R., & Aditya, R. (1997). The social scientific study of leadership: Quo vadis? *Journal of Management, 23,* 409–474.

Howell, J. M., & Hall-Merenda, K. E. (1999). The ties that bind: The impact of leader-member exchange, transformational and transactional leadership, and distance on predicting follower performance. *Journal of Applied Psychology, 84,* 680–694.

Hsiung, H., & Tsai, W. (2009). Job definition discrepancy between supervisors and subordinates: The antecedent role of LMX and outcomes. *Journal of Occupational and Organizational Psychology, 82,* 89–112.

Hu, M. M., Ou, T., Chiou, H., & Lin, L. (2012). Effects of social exchange and trust on knowledge sharing and service innovation. *Social Behavior and Personality, 40,* 783–800.

Huang, X., Chan, S. C. H., Lam, W., & Nan, X. (2010). The joint effect of leader-member exchange and emotional intelligence on burnout and work performance in call centers in China. *The International Journal of Human Resource Management, 21,* 1124–1144.

Hui, C., & Graen, G. (1997). Guanxi and professional leadership in contemporary Sino-American joint ventures in mainland China. *The Leadership Quarterly, 8,* 451–465.

Hui, C., Law, K., & Chen, Z. X. (1999). A structural equation model of the effects of negative affectivity, leader-member exchange, and perceived job mobility on in-role and extra-role performance: A Chinese case. *Organizational Behavior and Human Decision Processes, 77,* 3–21.

Hui, C., Lee, C., & Rousseau, D. M. (2004). Employment relationships in China: Do workers relate to the organization or the people? *Organization Science, 15,* 232–240.

Hung, D. K. M., Ansari M. A., & Aafaqi, R. (2004). Fairness of human resource management practices, leader-member exchange and organizational commitment. *Asian Academy of Management Journal, 9,* 99–120.

Hwang, K. K. (2009). *Confucian relationalism: Cultural reflection and theoretical construction.* Beijing: Beijing University Press. (in Chinese)

Ilies, R., Nahrgang, J. D., & Morgeson, F. P. (2007). Leader-member exchange and citizenship behaviors: A meta-analysis. *Journal of Applied Psychology, 92,* 269-277.

Ishak, N. A., & Alam, S. S. (2009). Leader-member exchange and organizational citizenship behavior. The mediating impact of self-esteem. *International Journal of Business and Management, 4,* 52–61.

Janssen, O., & Van Yperen, N. W. (2004). Employees' goal orientations, the quality of leader- member exchange, and the outcomes of job performance and job satisfaction. *Academy of Management Journal, 47,* 368–384.

Joo, B. K. (2010). Organizational commitment for knowledge workers: The roles of perceived organizational learning culture, leader-member exchange quality, and turnover intention. *Human Resource Development Quarterly*, *21*, 69–85.

Joo, B. K., & Ready, K. J. (2012). Career satisfaction: The influences of proactive personality, performance goal orientation, organizational learning culture, and leader-member exchange quality. *Career Development International*, *17*, 276–295.

Karim, J. (2011). Emotional intelligence, leader-member exchange, organizational justice, and outcome variables: A conceptual model. *International Journal of Leadership Studies*, *6*, 390–411.

Khatri, N., Tsang, E. W. K., & Begley, T. M. (2006). Cronyism: A cross-cultural analysis. *Journal of International Business Studies*, *37*, 61–75.

Kim, B. C. P., Lee, G., & Carlson, K. D. (2010). An examination of the nature of the relationship between leader-member exchange (LMX) and turnover intent at different organizational levels. *International Journal of Hospitality Management*, *29*, 591–597.

Kirkman, B. L., Lowe, K. B., & Gibson, C. B. (2006). A quarter century of culture's consequences: A review of the empirical research incorporating Hofstede's cultural value framework. *Journal of International Business Studies*, *37*, 285–320.

Krishnan, V. R. (2004). Impact of transformational leadership on followers' influence strategies. *Leadership and Organization Development Journal*, *25*, 58–72.

Lam, W., Huang, X., & Snape, E. (2007). Feedback-seeking behavior and leader-member exchange: Do supervisor-attributed motives matter? *Academy of Management Journal*, *50*, 348–363.

Lapierre, L. M., Hackett, R. D., & Taggar, S. (2006). A test of the links between family interference with work, job enrichment and leader-member exchange. *Applied Psychology: An International Review*, *55*, 489–511.

Law, K. S., & Wong, C. S. (1999). Multidimensional constructs in structural equation analysis: An illustration using the job perception and job satisfaction constructs. *Journal of Management*, *25*, 143–160.

Law, K. S., Wong, C. S., Wang, D., & Wang, L. (2000). Effect of supervisor–subordinate guanxi on supervisory decisions in China: An empirical investigation. *International Journal of Human Resource Management*, *11*, 751–765.

Lee, J. (2005). Effects of leadership and leader-member exchange on commitment. *Leadership and Organization Development Journal*, *26*, 655–672.

Li, C., & Hung, C. (2009). The influence of transformational leadership on workplace relationships and job performance. *Social Behavior and Personality*, *37*, 1129–1142.

Li, N., Liang, J., & Crant, J. M. (2010). The role of proactive personality in job satisfaction and organizational citizenship behavior: A relational perspective. *Journal of Applied Psychology*, *95*, 395–404.

Liao, S. H., Hu, D. C., & Chung, H. Y. (2009). The relationship between leader-member relations, job satisfaction and organizational commitment in international tourist hotels in Taiwan. *International Journal of Human Resource Management*, *20*, 1810–1826.

Liao, H., Liu, D., & Loi, R. (2010). Looking at both sides of the social exchange coin: A social cognitive perspective on the joint effects of relationship quality and differentiation on creativity. *Academy of Management Journal*, *53*, 1090–1109.

Liden, R. C. (2012). Leadership research in Asia: A brief assessment and suggestions for the future. *Asia Pacific Journal of Management*, *29*, 205–212.

Liden, R.C. & Graen, G. (1980). Generalizability of the vertical dyad linkage model of leadership. *Academy of Management Journal*, *23*, 451–465.

Liden, R. C., & Maslyn, J. M. (1998). Multidimensionality of leader-member exchange: An empirical assessment through scale development. *Journal of Management*, *24*, 43–72.

Liden, R. C., Sparrowe, R. T., & Wayne, S. J. (1997). Leader-Member Exchange theory: The past and potential for the future. *Research in Personnel and Human Resources Management*, *15*, 47–119.

Liden, R. C., Wayne, S. J., & Stilwell, D. (1993). A longitudinal study on the early development of leader member exchanges. *Journal of Applied Psychology*, *78*, 662–674.

Liu, S., Lin, X., & Hu, W. (2013). How followers' unethical behavior is triggered by leader- member exchange: The mediating effect of job satisfaction. *Social Behavior and Personality*, *41*, 357–366.

Liu, Z., Cai, Z., Li, J., Shi, S., & Fang, Y. (2013). Leadership style and employee turnover intentions: A social identity perspective. *Career Development International*, *18*, 305–324.

Lo, M. C., Ramayah, T., Min, H. W., & Songan, P. (2010). The relationship between leadership styles and organizational commitment in Malaysia: Role of leader-member exchange. *Asia Pacific Business Review*, *16*, 79–103.

Loi, R., Mao, Y., & Ngo, H. Y. (2009). Linking leader-member exchange and employee work outcomes: The mediating role of organizational social and economic exchange. *Management and Organization Review*, *5*, 401–422.

Loi, R., & Ngo, H. Y. (2009). Work outcomes of relational demography in Chinese vertical dyads. *International Journal of Human Resource Management*, *20*, 1704–1719.

Martin, R., Thomas, G., Charles, K., Epitropaki, O., & McNamara, R. (2005). The role of leader-member exchanges in mediating the relationship between locus of control and work reactions. *Journal of Occupational and Organizational Psychology*, *78*, 141–147.

Mehta, A. (2009). Examining the role of personal, social exchange, and contextual fit variables in employee work outcomes under continuous change: A field investigation (Doctoral dissertation). Available from ProQuest Dissertations and Theses database. (UMI No. 3386211)

O'Driscoll, M. P., & Beehr, T. A. (1994). Supervisor behaviors, role stressors and uncertainty as predictors of personal outcomes for subordinates. *Journal of Organizational Behavior*, *15*, 141–155.

Ozer, M. (2008). Personal and task-related moderators of leader–member exchange among software developers. *Journal of Applied Psychology*, *93*, 1174–1182.

Pelled, L. H., & Xin, K. R. (2000). Relational demography and relationship quality in two cultures. *Organization Studies*, *21*, 1077–1094.

Pellegrini, E. K., & Scandura, T. A. (2006). Leader-member exchange (LMX), paternalism and delegation in the Turkish business culture: An empirical investigation. *Journal of International Business Studies*, *37*, 264–279.

Pellegrini, E. K., & Scandura, T. A. (2008). Paternalistic leadership: A review and agenda for future research. *Journal of Management*, *34*, 566–593.

Pellegrini, E. K., Scandura, T. A., & Jayaraman, V. (2010). Cross-cultural generalizability of paternalistic leadership: An expansion of leader-member exchange theory (LMX). *Group and Organization Management*, *35*, 391–420.

Perizade, B., & Sulaiman, M. (2005). Leader-member exchange and leadership effectiveness of chief executive officers in South Sumatra, Indonesia. *Business Review, 4*, 331–337.

Pillai, R., Scandura, T., & Williams, E. (1999). Leadership and organizational justice: Similarities and differences across cultures. *Journal of International Business Studies, 30*, 763–779.

Rockstuhl, T., Dulebohn, J. H., Ang, S., & Shore, L. M. (2012). Leader-member exchange (LMX) and culture: A meta-analysis of correlates of LMX across 23 countries. *Journal of Applied Psychology, 97*, 1097–1130.

Scandura, T., & Graen, G.B. (1984). Moderating effects of initial leader-member exchange status on the effects of leadership intervention. *Journal of Applied Psychology, 69*, 428–436.

Scandura, T. A., Graen, G. B., & Novak, M. A. (1986). When managers decide not to decide autocratically: An investigation of leader-member exchange and decision influence. *Journal of Applied Psychology, 71*, 579–584.

Schaubroeck, J., & Lam, S. S. K. (2002). How similarity to peers and supervisor influences organizational advancement in different cultures. *Academy of Management Journal, 45*, 1120–1136.

Schriesheim, C. A., Neider, L. L., Scandura, T. A., & Tepper, B. J. (1992). Development and preliminary validation of a new scale (LMX-6) to measure leader-member exchange in organizations. *Educational and Psychological Measurement, 52*, 135–147.

Schyns, B., & Croon, M. A. (2006). A model of task demands, social structure, and leader- member exchange and their relationship to job satisfaction. *International Journal of Human Resource Management, 17*, 602–615.

Schyns, B., Paul, T., Mohr, G., & Blank, H. (2005). Comparing antecedents and consequences of leader-member exchange in a German working context to findings in the US. *European Journal of Work and Organizational Psychology, 14*, 1–22.

Schyns, B., Torka, N., & Gössling, T. (2007). Turnover intention and preparedness for change: Exploring leader-member exchange and occupational self-efficacy as antecedents of two employability predictors. *Career Development International, 12*, 660–679.

Smith, P. B., Misumi, J., Tayeb, M. H., Peterson, M., & Bond, M. H. (1989). On the generality of leadership style across cultures. *Journal of Occupational Psychology, 30*, 526–537.

Staw, B. (1995). Repairs on the road to relevance and rigor: Some unexplored issues in publishing organizational research. In L. Cummings & P. Frost (Eds.), *Foundations for organizational science* (pp. 85–98). Thousand Oaks, CA: Sage Publications.

Steiner, D. D. (1988). Value perceptions in leader-member exchange. *The Journal of Social Psychology, 128*, 611–618.

Stogdill, R. (1963). *Manual for the Leader Behavior Description Questionnaire-Form XII.* Bureau of Business Research, University of Ohio, Columbus.

Sy, T. (2010). What do you think of followers? Examining the content, structure, and consequences of implicit followership theories. *Organizational Behavior and Human Decision Processes, 113*, 73–84.

Testa, M. R. (2009). National culture, leadership and citizenship: Implications for cross-cultural management. *International Journal of Hospitality Management, 28*, 78–85.

Tierney, P., Bauer, T. N., & Potter, R. E. (2002). Extra-role behavior among Mexican employees: The impact of LMX, group acceptance, and job attitudes. *International Journal of Selection and Assessment, 10*, 292–303.

Tsui, A. S., Nifadkar, S. S., & Ou, A. Y. (2007). Cross-national, cross-cultural organizational behavior research: Advances, gaps, and recommendations. *Journal of Management, 33*, 426–478.

Uhl-Bien, M. (2006). Relational leadership theory: Exploring the social processes of leadership and organizing. *The Leadership Quarterly, 17*, 654–676.

van Dam, K., Oreg, S., & Schyns, B. (2008). Daily work contexts and resistance to organizational change: The role of leader-member exchange, perceived development climate and change process characteristics. *Applied Psychology: An International Review, 57*, 313–334.

Van Dyne, L., Kamdar, D., & Joireman, J. (2008). In-role perceptions buffer the negative impact of low LMX on helping and enhance the positive impact of high LMX on voice. *Journal of Applied Psychology, 93*, 1195–1207.

Venkataramani, V., Green, S. G., & Schleicher, D. J. (2010). Well-connected leaders: The impact of leaders' social network ties on LMX and members' work attitudes. *Journal of Applied Psychology, 95*, 1071–1084.

Vidyarthi, P. R., Erdogan, B., Anand, S., Liden, R. C., & Chaudhry, A. (2014). One member, two leaders: Extending leader-member exchange theory to a dual leadership context. *Journal of Applied Psychology, 99*, 468–483.

Vidyarthi, P. R., Liden, R. C., Anand, S., Erdogan, B., & Ghosh, S. (2010). Where do I stand? Examining the effects of leader-member exchange social comparison on employee work behaviors. *Journal of Applied Psychology, 95*, 849–861.

Volmer, J., Niessen, C., Spurk, D., Linz, A., & Abele, A. E. (2011). Reciprocal relationships between leader-member exchange (LMX) and job satisfaction: A cross-lagged analysis. *Applied Psychology: An International Review, 60*, 522–545.

Volmer, J., Spurk, D., & Niessen, C. (2012). Leader-member exchange (LMX), job autonomy, and creative work involvement. *The Leadership Quarterly, 23*, 456–465.

Waismel-Manor, R., Tziner, A., Berger, E., & Dikstein, E. (2010). Two of a kind? Leader-member exchange and organizational citizenship behaviors: The moderating role of leader-member similarity. *Journal of Applied Social Psychology, 40*, 167–181.

Wang, H., Law, K. S., & Chen, G. (2008). Leader-member exchange, employee performance, and work outcomes: An empirical study in the Chinese context. *International Journal of Human Resource Management. 19*, 1809–1824.

Wang, H., Law, S. K, Hackett, R., Wang, D., & Chen, Z. (2005). Leader-member exchange as a mediator of the relationship between transformational leadership and followers' performance and organizational citizenship behavior. *Academy of Management Journal, 48*, 420–432.

Wang, H., Law, K.S., Wang, D., & Chen, Z. (2001). The Linkage Role of LMX: A mediating effect of LMX on the relationship between transformational leadership and followers' performance and OCB. Paper presented at the Annual Academy of Management Meeting. Washington, DC, 3–8 August.

Wat, D., & Shaffer, M. A. (2005). Equity and relationship quality influences on organizational citizenship behaviors: The mediating role of trust in the supervisor and empowerment. *Personnel Review, 34*, 406–422.

Yagil, D. (2006). Perceptions of justice within leader-employee dyads. *International Journal of Organization Theory and Behavior, 9*, 291–306.

Yifeng, N., & Tjosvold, D. (2008). Goal interdependence and leader-member relationship for cross-cultural leadership in foreign ventures in China. *Leadership and Organization Development Journal, 29,* 144–166.

Yousaf, A., Sanders, K., Torka, N., & Ardts, J. (2011). Having two bosses: Considering the relationships between LMX, satisfaction with HR practices, and organizational commitment. *The International Journal of Human Resource Management, 22,* 3109–3126.

Zhang, Z., Waldman, D. A., & Wang, Z. (2012). A multilevel investigation of leader-member exchange, informal leader emergence, and individual and team performance. *Personnel Psychology, 65,* 49–77.

Zhou, L., Wang, M., Chen, G., & Shi, J. (2012). Supervisors' upward exchange relationships and subordinate outcomes: Testing the multilevel mediation role of empowerment. *Journal of Applied Psychology, 97,* 668–680.

Appendix

Most frequently used leader–member exchange (LMX) scales listed in descending order of publication date.

LMX-MDM (Liden & Maslyn, 1998)

Seven-point Likert scale ranging from 1 (strongly disagree) to 7 (strongly agree).

Affect:

1. I like my supervisor very much as a person.
2. My supervisor is the kind of person one would like to have as a friend.
3. My supervisor is a lot of fun to work with.

Loyalty:

4. My supervisor defends my work actions to a superior, even without complete knowledge of the issue in question.
5. My supervisor would come to my defense if I were "attacked" by others.
6. My supervisor would defend me to others in the organization if I made an honest mistake.

Contribution:

7. I do work for my supervisor that goes beyond what is specified in my job description.
8. I am willing to apply extra efforts, beyond those normally required, to meet my supervisor's work goals.
9. I do not mind working my hardest for my supervisor.

Professional Respect:

10. I am impressed with my supervisor's knowledge of his/her job.
11. I respect my supervisor's knowledge of and competence on the job.
12. I admire my supervisor's professional skills.

LMX-7 and SLMX-7 (Graen & Uhl-Bien, 1995)

1. Do you know where you stand with your leader.... do you usually know how satisfied your leader is with what you do? (Does your member usually know)

Rarely	Occasionally	Sometimes	Fairly Often	Very Often

2. How well does your leader understand your job problems and needs? (How well do you understand)

Not a Bit	A Little	A Fair Amount	Quite a Bit	A Great Deal

3. How well does your leader recognize your potential? (How well do you recognize)

Not at All	A Little	Moderately	Mostly	Fully

4. Regardless of how much formal authority he/she has built into his/her position, what are the chances that your leader would use his/her power to help you solve problems in your work? (What are the chances that you would)

None	Small	Moderate	High	Very High

5. Again, regardless of the amount of formal authority your leader has, what are the chances that he/she would "bail you out" at his/her expense? (What are the chances that you would)

None	Small	Moderate	High	Very High

6. I have enough confidence in my leader that I would defend and justify his/her decisions if he/she were not present to do so. (Your member would)

Strongly Disagree	Disagree	Neutral	Agree	Strongly Agree

7. How would you characterize your working relationship with your leader? (Your member)

Extremely Ineffective	Worse than Average	Average	Better than Average	Extremely Effective

Note: Continuous scale of sum of 5-point items (1 left to 5 right). Leader's form consists of the same seven items asked about member (leader in parentheses).

LMX-7 (Scandura & Graen, 1984)

1. Do you usually feel that you know where you stand, do you usually know how satisfied your immediate supervisor is with what you do?

1	2	3	4
Never know where I stand	Seldom know where I stand	Usually know where I stand	Always know where I stand

2. How well do you feel that your immediate supervisor understands your problems and needs?

1	2	3	4
Not at all	Some but not enough	Well enough	Completely

3. How well do you feel that your immediate supervisor recognizes your potential?

1	2	3	4
Not at all	Some but not enough	As much as the next person	Fully

4. Regardless of how much formal authority your immediate supervisor has built into his or her position, what are the chances that he or she would be personally inclined to use power to help you solve problems in your work?

1	2	3	4
No chance	Might or might not	Probably would	Certainly would

5. Again, regardless of the amount of formal authority your immediate supervisor has, to what extent can you count on him or her to "bail you out" at his or her expense when you really need it?

1	2	3	4
No chance	Might or might not	Probably would	Certainly would

6. I have enough confidence in my immediate supervisor that I would defend and justify his or her decisions if he or she were not present to do so.

1	2	3	4
Probably not	Maybe	Probably would	Certainly would

7. How would you characterize your working relationship with your immediate supervisor?

1	2	3	4
Less than average	About average	Better than average	Extremely effective

Diversity and LMX Development

Caren Goldberg *and* Patrick F. McKay

Abstract

The management of diversity in organizations will require social exchanges between members of various social/demographic groups. Yet, high-quality leader–member exchanges (LMX) are built upon the presumption of competence and trust between supervisors and their subordinates. To the extent that members of stigmatized groups endure negative stereotypes of competence (and warmth), the initial role-taking and subsequent role-making stages of LMX development may be compromised. In this chapter, we consider the potential impact of highly visible characteristics such as age, gender, race-ethnicity, and obesity on initial role-taking, as well as the influence of less visible characteristics such as disability and sexual orientation on the later role-making stage of LMX development. After laying the groundwork regarding the content of various group stereotypes, we discuss the implications of leader–member similarity/dissimilarity on LMX formation. Finally, we conclude with directions for future research linking diversity and LMX.

Key Words: diversity and LMX, leader–member similarity, competence stereotypes, demographics and LMX, competence and LMX, stereotypes and LMX

Introduction

Over the past decade, the workforce has become more demographically diverse than any time in history. Minorities and women have represented 75% of new workplace entrants (Toossi, 2007), four generational groupings (i.e., Traditionalists, Baby Boomers, Generation Xers, Millennials) are working side by side (Westerman & Yamamura, 2007), yet organizations must grapple with how to manage such diversity effectively. This seemingly straightforward task is complicated by several notions. First, minorities and women are often underrepresented in supervisory and leadership posts, especially at top levels (Eagly & Chen, 2010; Ragins, 1997). Consequently, members of these groups, in all likelihood, will be supervised by someone who is of a different demographic group. Second, negative stereotypes exist that may serve to disfavor racial–ethnic minority groups (Cuddy, Fiske, & Glick, 2007; Fiske, Cuddy, Glick,

& Xu, 2002), women (Duehr & Bono, 2006; Heilman & Eagly, 2008), older adults (Garstka, Schmitt, Branscombe, & Hummert, 2004; Goldberg, Finkelstein, Perry, & Konrad, 2004; Kite, Stockdale, & Whitley, 2005), obese individuals (Finkelstein, Frautschy, Demuth, & Sweeney, 2007), gay, lesbian, bisexual, and transgendered (GLBT) people (Button, 2001; Ragins & Cornwell, 2001), and the disabled (Colella & Bruyère, 2011; Schur, Kruse, Blasi, & Blanck, 2009). Findings suggest that members of these disparaged groups enter organizations with the burden of overcoming negative views of their competence, character, work ethic, likability, etc. Finally, leader–member exchange (LMX) research, concerned with the nature of the supervisor–subordinate relationship, has emphasized the importance of such dyadic relations for work attitudes (Gerstner & Day, 1997; Settoon, Bennett, & Liden, 1996), job performance (Gerstner & Day, 1997; Lam, Huang, & Snape,

2007; Wayne, Shore, & Liden, 1997), the performance of prosocial work behaviors (Settoon et al., 1996; Wayne et al., 1997), retention (Gerstner & Day, 1997), and ultimate career success (Harris, Kacmar, & Carlson, 2006).

Despite the relevance of demographic diversity to LMX, little research has considered the implications of increasing workplace diversity on how supervisors and subordinates interact in the conduct of their work. Existing research has focused on whether supervisors and subordinates either share (similarity) or do not share (dissimilarity) demographic group membership, and how this impacts LMX. Generally speaking, relative to dissimilarity, demographic similarity between supervisors and subordinates is associated with higher LMX (Green, Anderson, & Shivers, 1996; Vecchio & Bullis, 2001) and enhanced perceptions of role clarity and career support (Tsui & O'Reilly, 1989); however, these studies have focused primarily upon race–ethnicity and gender, to the exclusion of other forms of diversity such as age, sexual orientation, and disability status (see Collela & Varma, 2001, for an exception). Furthermore, the confluence of members of previously underrepresented demographic groups in the workplace sets the stage for greater instances of demographic dissimilarity between supervisors and subordinates. A key focus of this chapter is to broaden consideration to these lesser-studied groups, while providing a theory-based review of the dynamics that are likely to influence the development of LMX among these personnel and their supervisors. Our presentation is targeted toward employees from stigmatized groups (i.e., racial–ethnic minorities, women, older adults, GLBT individuals, and the disabled) in relation to their presumably dissimilar supervisors (e.g., those who are nonminority, male, in the prime working age range of 35–44 years, heterosexual, and nondisabled). These latter groups are likely to be considered typical employees relative to their respective stigmatized counterparts. Moreover, we explore the consequences of LMX relationships, and highlight a number of research needs that could enhance the understanding of LMX processes, particularly in regard to diverse labor forces.

In our presentation, we follow Harrison and Klein's (2007) conceptualization of diversity as "variety," namely the extent to which members of different categorical groupings are present in a work context. Variety is minimal when all of the people in an environment come from one demographic group (e.g., all whites), whereas variety is maximal when all possible groups are present in the setting (e.g., one white, black, Hispanic, Asian, and Native American member of a project workgroup). In addition, we consider Harrison, McLaughlin, and Bell's (1998) surface-level diversity and deep-level diversity distinction. Surface-level characteristics include those aspects of the individual that are easily observable (e.g., demographics), whereas deep-level diversity emphasizes differences in attitudes, values, and beliefs. The bulk of dyadic LMX research has explored surface-level diversity; therefore, our review will lean more heavily toward research involving race–ethnicity, gender, and age.

In the following sections, we provide an overview of LMX, paying particular attention to how these relationships form and evolve. Then, we discuss demographic concerns of relevance to the LMX process, and review their prospective impact on LMX development and related outcomes. Finally, we close the chapter by highlighting several areas in need of future research to further illuminate the LMX process, especially within diverse work contexts.

Leader–Member Exchange Development and Outcomes
LMX Development

LMX theory posits that supervisor–subordinate relationships develop through a series of social exchanges between leaders and employees (Dienesch & Liden, 1986). Typically, LMX forms through a process of relationship testing whereby the supervisor conveys role expectations and the subordinate responds to them. The degree to which the member fulfills these role expectations determines the succeeding roles he or she receives and, thus, defines the quality of the subsequent exchange relationship. In addition, due to the reciprocal nature of the supervisor–subordinate relationship, other researchers have argued that LMX quality is a consequence of subordinate performance (Bauer & Green, 1996; Lam, Huang, & Snape, 2007). For example, Bauer and Green (1996) found that performance predicted LMX and changes in LMX, and noted that LMX development is "an exchange of resources and testing of competence" (p. 1541).

The role episode model is a useful framework for conceptualizing the LMX development process. According to the model, the LMX development process consists of three stages: role-taking, role-making, and role-routinization (Graen & Scandura, 1987; Graen & Uhl-Bien, 1995). The first stage, role-taking, represents the initial encounter between a newcomer and her or his supervisor. The establishment of mutual respect is paramount during this stage, and this determination is made from initial samplings of supervisors' and subordinates' behaviors. Consequently, the outcome of this initial stage is role-taking, or the extent to which parties to the LMX dyad view each other as able to contribute meaningfully to the relationship. The quality of early supervisor–subordinate interactions dictates whether the relationship will either develop into a high-quality LMX relationship or remain at the initial stage. Because the supervisor and subordinate are almost strangers at this point, surface-level characteristics such as supervisor–subordinate demographic similarity and subordinates' perceived similarity to their supervisors could influence subordinates' early impressions of LMX (Dienesch & Liden, 1986; Green et al., 1996; Vecchio & Bullis, 2001). Moreover, some scholars have highlighted the effects of supervisor–subordinate matching on other variables such as personality (Bauer & Green, 1996; Dulebohn, Bommer, Liden, Brouer, & Ferris, 2012; Nahrgang, Morgeson, & Ilies, 2009) and interpersonal factors between the two parties (e.g., liking, ingratiation, and delegation) as antecedents of LMX (Dulebohn et al., 2012; Maslyn & Uhl-Bien, 2001; Wayne & Liden, 1997).

Upon the establishment of mutual respect, the second LMX stage, role-making, will emerge. At this juncture, the supervisor and subordinate begin to mutually influence one another's attitudes and behaviors. This is a period in which supervisors begin to delegate work assignments to subordinates who are viewed as competent and able to perform. If the subordinate accepts and completes the assignments successfully, then she or he will become a trusted and respected assistant of the supervisor. Consequently, such subordinates garner the trust, respect, and endorsement of their supervisors in exchange for her or his successful performance. Mutual trust between supervisors and subordinates is the outgrowth of successful role-making, wherein supervisors support their subordinates' performance efforts and subordinates fulfill their supervisors' role demands effectively.

The third LMX stage, role-routinization (or commitment), is evidenced when a sense of mutual obligation forms between a supervisor and her or his subordinate. At this point, a supervisor and subordinate share a history, in which each party has performed on behalf of and supported the other. Subsequently, the two parties of the relationship develop a shared understanding of organizational norms and goals and sense their career trajectories as interdependent. Ultimately, the two share a level of predictability that promotes mutually beneficial role behaviors, thereby precipitating high performance expectations. Because entry into this third stage emerges as a result of success in the role-taking and role-making stages and because demographic characteristics carry greater meaning early in the dyadic relationship (Harrison, Price, & Bell, 1998), the following discussion of the effects of demographic group membership on LMX development focuses primarily on the first two stages of the role episode model.

In general, the literature largely has been supportive of role episode model predictions. For instance, follower characteristics such as high levels of competence (Dulebohn et al., 2012; Gerstner & Day, 1997; Graen & Scandura, 1987), positive affectivity (Bauer & Green, 1996; Dulebohn et al., 2012), conscientiousness (Bernerth, Armenakis, Feild, Giles, & Walker, 2007), extraversion (Dulebohn et al., 2012; Nahrgang et al., 2009; Phillips & Bedeian, 1994), emotional stability (Bernerth et al., 2007), openness (Bernerth et al., 2007), and internal locus of control (Kinicki & Vecchio, 1994) are positively related to subordinates' and/or supervisors' perceptions of LMX. Leader characteristics and behaviors that enhance LMX include high levels of extraversion (Nahrgang et al., 2009), contingent reward behavior (Wayne, Shore, Bommer, & Tetrick, 2002), transformational leadership (Wang, Law, Hackett, Wang, & Chen, 2005), and leader expectations of follower success (Dulebohn et al., 2012; Liden, Wayne, & Stilwell, 1993; Wayne, Shore, & Liden, 1997). Finally, several interpersonal factors between leaders and subordinates are predictive of LMX (in a positive manner). These factors consist of high levels of perceived similarity (Bauer & Green, 1996; Dulebohn et al., 2012; Liden et al., 1993; Phillips & Bedeian, 1994), liking (Wayne et al., 1997), ingratiation reported by supervisors or subordinates (Colella & Varma, 2001), self-promotion (Lam et al., 2007), and leader trust (Gomez & Rosen, 2001).

The above review indicates that the LMX development process is based largely upon the extent that supervisors and subordinates establish mutually beneficial working relationships. The formation of high-quality supervisor–subordinate relations is more likely when the two parties are viewed as competent, trustworthy, motivated, and likable. These perceptions are facilitated when leaders and members perceive one another as similar on demographic characteristics and personality. As we discuss later, the extant LMX literature has given very little consideration to how well the above conclusions generalize across members of various demographic groups. Potentially, existing status differentials between groups could act as boundary conditions of the correlations between LMX and its antecedents.

LMX Outcomes

LMX quality has been theorized to influence worker experiences through the role-making, role-taking, and role-routinization processes. Essentially, the nature of the supervisor–subordinate relationship determines the degree to which a worker will be viewed as a competent contributor who can be entrusted with enriching, meaningful work demands. These conditions further influence the depth of exchanges a worker will have with her or his supervisor, which can have a profound impact on how the person experiences her or his job role. Based on the preceding logic, it is not surprising that LMX has been linked to a host of worker outcomes. To organize these constructs, we utilize Dulebohn et al.'s (2012) scheme that includes behavioral outcomes (e.g., turnover intentions, actual turnover), attitudinal outcomes (e.g., affective commitment, job satisfaction), perceptual outcomes (e.g., procedural justice, empowerment), and role states (i.e., role conflict and role ambiguity). High-quality LMX is associated with reduced turnover intentions (Dulebohn et al., 2012; Gerstner & Day, 1997), voluntary turnover (Dulebohn et al., 2012; Gerstner & Day, 1997), role ambiguity (Dulebohn et al., 2012; Gerstner & Day, 1997), enhanced affective organizational commitment (Dulebohn et al., 2012; Kinicki & Vecchio, 1994; Wayne et al., 2002), perceived organizational support (Dulebohn et al., 2012; Wayne et al., 1997, 2002), job satisfaction (Dulebohn, 2012; Gerstner & Day, 1997), supervisor satisfaction (Dulebohn, 2012; Gerstner & Day, 1997), job performance (Gerstner & Day, 1997; Lam et al., 2007; Wang et al., 2005; Wayne et al., 1997, 2002), organizational citizenship behaviors (Dulebohn et al., 2012; Settoon et al., 1996; Wang et al., 2005; Wayne et al., 1997, 2002), procedural justice (i.e., fairness of process; Dulebohn et al., 2012; Erdogan & Bauer, 2010), distributive justice (i.e., fairness of outcomes; Dulebohn et al., 2012; Erdogan & Bauer, 2010), and psychological empowerment (Dulebohn et al., 2012; Gomez & Rosen, 2001).

The above results suggest that LMX is significantly related to subordinates' behavioral, affective, and perceptual outcomes and role states. These outcomes are of critical importance to effective organizational functioning, thus underscoring the pivotal role of supervisor–subordinate relations to firm success. Despite the increased inflow of underrepresented women and minorities into the workforce over the past decade (Toossi, 2007), and labor projections of increased age diversity in firms (Westerman & Yamamura, 2007), there is uncertainty concerning the influence of such diversity on LMX development. Accordingly, over the next few sections we review diversity-related theory and research in an attempt to consider the prospective effects of demographic diversity on LMX development.

Stereotypes and LMX Development

Because the Role Episode Model posits that dyad member's perceptions of one another in the initial stage of role-taking influence the subsequent role-making and role routinization stages (Graen & Scandura, 1987; Graen & Uhl-Bien, 1995), the consideration of how these initial impressions are formed (i.e., group stereotypes) is paramount to our understanding of the role-taking stage. As Pettigrew (1979) noted, we do not form stereotypes of individuals, per se; rather, we stereotype individuals as members of a certain group. Thus, much of the following section is dedicated to discussing the content of the stereotypes of various groups.

Group Stereotypes

Stereotyping is a cognitive shortcut that allows a perceiver to place targets in categories and organize her or his internal knowledge structures in an efficient manner (Ford & Stangor, 1992). As Lord and Maher (1993, p. 35) note, "Physical features of people are so salient that they provide a powerful set of indexing cues." Although they are not completely insurmountable, stereotypes are quite resistant to disconfirming evidence (Brewer & Miller, 1984). Furthermore, Brewer and Kramer (1985) found that people are more apt to attend to stereotype-consistent information and recall information that is related to category-based stereotypes than to information that is unrelated to the stereotype.

In considering how demographic group membership (and the stereotypes associated with various groups) may affect the development of LMX, we rely on Status Characteristics Theory (SCT), which emphasizes the importance of group stereotypes in newly formed dyads. According to SCT (Berger, Rosenholtz, & Zelditch, 1980), societies place relative value on membership in particular social identity groups. Based upon these status differences, members of social groups endure varying expectations of competence, particularly in group settings (Berger et al., 1980). Thus, in this section, we examine some of the stereotypes that have been associated with various groups, with consideration given to how these stereotypes may affect the LMX relationship. Because perceptions of group status are widely shared, the effects of stereotypes should be more pronounced during the initial role-taking stage; however, in addition to coping with the lower expectations that others have of their competence, members of low-status groups may also internalize these lower expectations for themselves (Berger et al., 1980). Consequently, they may approach tasks with less confidence and contribute less to group tasks, thereby reinforcing the negative stereotypes and hindering their ability to engage in high-quality exchanges with their supervisors later in the LMX development process (i.e., role-making and role-routinization).

The notion that individuals who belong to negatively stereotyped groups may inadvertently reinforce negative group stereotypes has been well-supported in the stereotype threat literature. For example, several researchers (Roberson, Dietch, Brief, & Block, 2003; Roberson & Kulik, 2009) have contended that because minorities are aware of the existence of competency stereotypes, irrespective of whether they see themselves as counterstereotypic, nonetheless, the threat that others will ascribe a negative stereotype to them looms. Stereotype threat is operative when members of a disparaged group (e.g., blacks, women) are put into a situation in which they may confirm the negative stereotype (e.g., low intellectual or mathematical ability) about their group. Steele and his colleagues (Steele, 1997; Steele & Aronson, 1995; Steele & Davies, 2003) developed a variety of experiments that demonstrate how stereotype threat negatively affects minorities' test performance in laboratory settings. Organizational research over the past decade has also shown the adverse effects of stereotype threat on performance in the context of employment testing (Chung, Ehrhart, Erhart, Holcombe, Hattrup, & Solamon, 2009; Gillespie, Converse, & Kriska, 2010; McKay, Doverspike, Bowen-Hilton, & Martin, 2002; Mayer & Hanges, 2003).

To simplify our treatment of the following sections on the nature of the stereotypes, our discussion focuses on how a subordinate's group membership likely influences the supervisor's perceptions of her

or him. However, it is important to note that as LMX is a two-way street, we would expect that the leader's membership in those groups would have a similar effect on the subordinate's perceptions of the leader. That is to say, the same stereotypes apply to both protégés and mentors. Furthermore, to emphasize the role of group stereotypes on the development of LMX, our focus here is on how an individual's group membership may hinder his or her ability to form a positive relationship with the other party of the dyad. Yet, although we explore dyadic similarity later in this chapter, for now we remind the reader that diversity is inherently a multiperson construct. When dissimilarities exist between the members of the dyad, the negative stereotypes generally are apt to have a more pronounced effect.

It bears noting that group stereotypes typically do not embody a single defining characteristic, but instead, they often include both positive and negative attributes. For example, Asians are perceived as intelligent (positive), but untrustworthy (negative) (Wilson, 1996). Yet, as the role-taking stage is largely concerned with initial perceptions of competence, stereotypes (particularly negative stereotypes) that may drive perceptions of competence are more likely to interfere with the formation of a favorable exchange. Thus, in the following discussion of group stereotypes, we focus particular attention on negative group perceptions that may be associated with initial assessments of competence.

The distinction between highly visible and less visible characteristics is important in understanding the relative impact of stereotypes at different stages of the role episode model. Because visible characteristics carry greater weight early in the acquaintance process (Harrison, Price, & Bell, 1998), when less performance-related information is available, demographic stereotypes, such as those related to age, race, gender, and obesity, should exert a stronger influence at the role-taking stage than at later stages. In contrast, because less visible characteristics are, by definition, less readily perceived, we postulate that attributes that can be concealed (e.g., nonphysical disabilities and sexual orientation) will exhibit a stronger effect on the LMX relationship during the role-making stage. In keeping with this distinction, we begin our discussion of stereotypes associated with visible characteristics.

Stereotypes Based on Visible Characteristics

Stereotypes of Older Workers. Stereotypes of older workers include views that they are less productive, flexible, creative, ambitious, harder to train (Kulik,

Perry, & Bourhis, 2000; Ringenbach & Jacobs, 1994; Sonnenfeld, 1978), and less economically beneficial to organizations (Finkelstein & Burke, 1998). In light of this cluster of negative stereotypes, it is not surprising that Fiske et al. (2002) showed that older individuals were perceived as low in competence compared to other groups that study participants were asked to evaluate (e.g., rich people, Southerners, Asians). This tendency to negatively evaluate older people led Shore and Goldberg (2004) to suggest that older workers are likely to be denied workplace opportunities. Indeed, studies using hypothetical incidents of younger and older employees depicted in identical circumstances demonstrated that stereotypes of older workers' resistance to change, disinterest in technological change, and skill obsolescence resulted in respondents providing them with less feedback and opportunity to improve substandard performance, and a lower likelihood of and less generous support for training (Posthuma & Campion, 2009; Rosen & Jerdee, 1976, 1977).

Although relational demography literature holds that similarity generally results in more favorable outcomes than dissimilarity (Chattopadhyay, George, & Lawrence, 2004), research on age similarity indicates that the effects of relational norms may overshadow positive similarity effects. In the workplace, the normative assumption is that those in roles of authority (i.e., managers) *ought to be* older than the individuals they supervise. Indeed, Lawrence (1984) has shown that organizations have implicit timetables for employees' achievement of particular organizational levels by a certain chronological age. Consistent with these timetables, researchers have found that managers' evaluations of employees' in-role and extra-role performance were higher when the dyad was consistent with relational age norms (old manager/young employee) than when members of the dyad were either similar in age (both old or both young) or defied the norm (young manager/old employee) (Shore, Cleveland, & Goldberg, 2003; Tsui, Porter, & Egan, 2002). These findings suggest that it may be particularly difficult for older personnel who have young supervisors to develop high-quality LMX early in the dyadic relationship. To the extent that they are able to do so, their incongruence with age timetables may impose obstacles to maintaining favorable relationships with their supervisors. In particular, Lawrence (1984) found that employees who were below the normative organizational level for their age (i.e., "behind time") early in their tenure were seen as "damaged goods" and thus were overlooked for future advancement opportunities.

To summarize, negative stereotypes about older worker competence are apt to impede their ability to foster favorable exchanges in the role-taking stage; this effect should be particularly pronounced for older workers who have young managers. Furthermore, because they are seen as "behind time," it will be difficult for older employees to maintain high-quality LMX throughout the role-making stage.

Stereotypes of Women. Although feminine stereotypes may evoke positive images of nurturing sympathetic friends, these communal attributes are inconsistent with perceptions of an ideal leader (Eagly & Karau, 2002) or general competence (Eagly, 1987). In contrast, agentic attributes such as self-confidence, assertiveness, ambition, and independence, which are positively related to perceptions of an ideal leader, are more commonly ascribed to men. Indeed, several researchers have argued that negative perceptions of women leaders are largely attributable to a perceived mismatch between stereotypes of women and stereotypes of leaders (Eagly & Karau, 2002; Powell, Butterfield, & Parent, 2002; Ritter & Yoder, 2004). As a consequence, female protégés in newly formed dyads are likely to be perceived as less able to fulfill the demands of their roles, thereby reducing their likelihood of forming early high-quality LMX.

Whereas we might postulate that engaging in counterstereotypic (i.e., masculine) behaviors, such as those perceived as necessary in leadership positions, might help female protégés overcome the obstacle of this initial perception of low capability, research suggests otherwise. Specifically, Eagly and Karau (2002) found that women who exhibit the masculine/leadership-consistent characteristics of self-confidence and assertiveness are often evaluated less favorably than their more stereotype-consistent feminine counterparts. These reactions to women's counterstereotypic behavior occur because they are violating their prescribed gender roles. Moreover, research on stereotypes has indicated that professional women, who are viewed as high in competence, are also rated as lower in warmth (e.g., viewed as less likable) than women in general (Fiske et al., 2002). These findings are reminiscent of Madeline Heilman's lack-of-fit theory (Heilman, 1983), which postulates that women are penalized for demonstrating stereotypically male behavior. Later studies, in fact, have shown that women are rated more favorably when they perform in female-typed (e.g., administrative staff) than male-typed jobs (e.g., line manager jobs; Lyness & Heilman, 2006). Notably, this "fit" bias phenomenon extends to the rating of performance dimensions, such that women receive higher ratings than men on more feminine dimensions (e.g., interpersonal sensitivity, communication), whereas men are evaluated more highly than women on more masculine dimensions (e.g., leadership, planning; Davison & Burke, 2000). Based on the above review, it is likely that women will encounter challenges to forming early LMX relationships, particularly in roles requiring the exhibition of male-stereotypic traits for successful performance.

Stereotypes of Nonwhites. Fiske et al. (2002) proposed that when a perceiver meets another person, she or he makes inferences about the person in terms of two focal dimensions, competence and warmth. Their work demonstrated that blacks and Hispanics are viewed as lower in competence compared to whites and Asians. Negative stereotypes regarding blacks' and Hispanics' competence may hinder their ability to forge high-quality LMX relationships during the role-taking stage; as expected and/or demonstrated, competence is the cornerstone of the development of high-quality initial supervisor–subordinate relationships (Dienesch & Liden, 1986). Consistent with this concern, a plethora of studies indicate that black and Hispanic managers alike report lower access to developmental and advancement opportunities (Cianni & Romberger, 1995; DiTomaso, Thompson, & Blake, 1988; Greenhaus et al., 1990; Sanchez & Brock, 1996), job discretion (DiTomaso et al., 1988; Greenhaus et al., 1990), career support (Greenhaus et al., 1990), and access to influential social networks (Ibarra, 1995) than their white counterparts.

In contrast to their black and Hispanic counterparts, Asians are perceived to be high in competence (Fiske et al., 2002). More specifically, research indicates that Asians are characterized by positive traits such as intelligent, capable, ambitious, and hard-working (Cuddy, Fiske, & Glick, 2007; Fiske et al., 2002; Ho & Jackson, 2001). Although positive competence stereotypes are apt to facilitate Asians' establishment of positive relationships with their supervisors during the role-taking stage, other negative stereotypes may hinder their ability to maintain high LMX through the role-making and role-routinization stages. Notably, research suggests that Asians are perceived to be untrustworthy, cunning, selfish, and unable to interact smoothly in social situations (Brambilla, Ravenna, & Hewstone,

2012; Cuddy et al., 2007; Fiske et al., 2002; Ho & Jackson, 2001; Lin, Kwan, Cheung, & Fiske, 2005). Consistent with these stereotypes, relative to whites, Asians experience underrepresentation and lower expectations of success in verbal-persuasive careers such as management (Chung-Herrera & Lankau, 2005; Leong & Hayes, 1990; Sue, 1975; Sue & Kirk, 1973). Thus, despite the support for the "model minority" competence stereotype, negative stereotypes regarding untrustworthiness and cunning may derail Asian subordinates' attempts to maintain favorable leader–member exchanges beyond the initial role-taking stage.

Stereotypes of Obese Employees. Despite the fact that over one-third of adults in the United States are considered to be obese (Bartels & Nordstrom, 2013), negative weight-related stereotypes abound. Owing to attributions of weight being a function of self-control, prejudice against the obese is considered more socially acceptable than are negative attitudes toward other groups (Crandall & Biernat, 1990; Finkelstein, Frautschy, Demuth, & Sweeney, 2007). Although both sexes exhibit antiobesity attitudes, men endorse significantly stronger antiobesity attitudes (obesity five-item scale composing of the following: Fat people are less sexually attractive than thin people; I would never date a fat person; fat people are lazier than thin people; fat people have only themselves to blame for their weight; and it is disgusting when a fat person wears a bathing suit at the beach) than women (Morrison & O'Connor, 1999). Furthermore, although weight bias has negative effects on both male and female applicants and employees (Roehling, 1999), Bartels and Nordstrom (2013) found that obesity-related stereotypes have a far stronger negative effect on the job suitability ratings of female applicants than on their obese male counterparts. The effect of gender on obese male and female candidates' ratings was stronger for jobs that were both highly visible and physically demanding (server) than for jobs that were low in visibility and high in physical demands (banquet worker), low in physical demands and high in visibility (concierge), or low in both physical demands and visibility (guest service agent).

Although the term "obese" may evoke a variety of perceptions, Morrison and Connor (1999) found that antiobesity attitudes are unidimensional and uniformly negative. Of particular interest in the work context, over one-fifth of participants in their study agreed that "on average, fat people are lazier than thin people" (p. 443). Likewise, earlier research (Larkin & Pines, 1979) reported that weight, alone, resulted in obese applicants being perceived as incompetent, indecisive, nonindustrious, and disorganized. The cognitive association between these characteristics and obesity has important ramifications for the prospects of LMX development. Particularly, as noted previously, given the centrality of competence perceptions in the formation of early LMX relationships (role-taking), obese protégés may endure stifled LMX development. In addition, even if an obese protégé can overcome these barriers in the role-taking stage, the transition to role-making is apt to be a rocky path because obese individuals are perceived to be lacking in self-control; thus, the trust and respect that define a high-quality exchange in a more mature dyad may be harder to achieve.

Stereotypes Based on Less Visible Characteristics

Aronson (2002) notes that stereotype-threatened people seek to distance themselves from a stereotype by acting in a manner contrary to it. To the extent that a negatively stereotyped person can conceal her or his stigmatized identity, this has significant implications for others' perceptions of her or him (Stone & Colella, 1996). Unfortunately, however, empirical evidence has demonstrated that such distancing efforts, alone, are insufficient to affect objective assessments of performance (Meyer, 2003). Generalizing these findings to the work setting, we infer that concealment of membership in a stigmatized identity group is unlikely to favorably impact a person's work performance. Indeed, concealment may, in fact, decrease task performance. That is, because concealing our membership in a negatively categorized group requires a great deal of effort, this coping strategy exerts inordinate stress on the stigmatized individual. For example, Goffman (1963) argued that stigmatized individuals approach interactions with others with anxiety because they believe that regardless of any expressed view to the contrary, others "will not really accept him and are not ready to make contact with him on 'equal grounds'" (p. 7). Furthermore, Miller and Major (2000) argue that concealing the stigma might often backfire and become stressful and anxiety producing. Notably, several studies have demonstrated that stress and anxiety heighten stereotype threat (Chung et al., 2010; Osborne, 2001; Ployhart et al., 2003; Steele & Aronson, 1995; Steele & Davies, 2003).

In addition to the stress created by the tangible effort required to conceal part of one's identity, Major and Gramzow (1999) found that the more a person tried to suppress his or her membership in a stigmatized group, the more likely he or she was to have intrusive thoughts about membership in that group (i.e., a stereotype suppression effect regarding one's own group membership). Thus, concealment efforts may result in decreased levels of objective performance because of the increased stress associated with this strategy, as well as the additional demands it places on the concealer's cognitive, affective, and physical resources.

Theory would suggest that the foregoing conclusions apply to individuals who belong to an infinite variety of negatively categorized groups for whom group membership is not readily discernible. However, as organizational diversity statements have recently (in most cases) expanded to include disability and sexual orientation, we focus our presentation on disabled employees and GLBT employees.

Stereotypes of Disabled Employees. The Americans with Disabilities Act (ADA) defines a disability as a "physical or mental condition that substantially limits a major life activity" (US Equal Employment Opportunity Commission, 2014). The literature in this area includes studies that discuss disabilities as a whole, as well as studies that classify disabilities into various categories. Although physical disabilities vary along a continuum of invisible (e.g., pancreatic cancer) to highly visible (e.g., paraplegia), for the purposes of this discussion, we assume that physical disabilities are generally more visible than nonphysical disabilities.

Despite the findings of several studies indicating that disabled workers perform as well or better than their nondisabled counterparts (e.g., Braddock & Bacheldor, 1994; Unger, 2001), negative stereotypes abound with respect to disabled workers' ability to perform their jobs. Stone and Colella (1996) proposed that stereotypes of disabled persons involve six dimensions: social and interpersonal competence, task competence, integrity, emotional adjustment, and potency or strength. Notably, the characteristics of each of these dimensions are either universally positive (e.g., the integrity dimension reflects descriptors such as "saint-like" and "honest") or universally negative (e.g., the task competence dimension reflects descriptors such as "helpless," "dependent," and "noncompetitive"). In contrast, Louvet (2007) has suggested that people often ascribe positive personality attributes to disabled persons to offset the guilt they experience due to the lack of empathy they feel based on their assumptions about the target's lack of competence. Importantly, observers presume that the negative dimensions (social and interpersonal competence, task competence, emotional adjustment, and strength/potency) are job relevant.

In light of these negative stereotypes, it is not surprising that Snyder, Carmichael, Blackwell, Cleveland, and Thornton (2010) found that disabled employees reported significantly higher levels of overt and subtle discrimination and lower levels of job satisfaction, procedural justice, and perceived organizational and supervisor support than their nondisabled counterparts. It is worth noting that these researchers also found that respondents with nonphysical disabilities (e.g., mental illness, intellectual impairment) reported significantly more subtle discrimination and significantly less procedural justice and perceived organizational support than those who had physical disabilities. This finding, which shows that perceptions of disabled individuals vary as a function of the type of disability, is consistent with prior research. Specifically, people with nonphysical disabilities are perceived more negatively than individuals with physical disabilities (Combs & Omvig, 1986). Moreover, treatment disparities evident between those with various types of disabilities indicate that (1) our understanding of the stereotypes of disabled workers will be improved by acknowledging that variations exist in reactions to various types of disabilities; and (2) the presence of a physical versus nonphysical disability could impact the nature of LMX development. Specifically, because physical disabilities are more likely to be visible and difficult to conceal, they are likely to impinge more heavily upon LMX development in the role-taking stage. During role-taking, negative task competency stereotypes held about the physically disabled could undermine a supervisor's view that the subordinate can make meaningful work contributions. In contrast, nonphysical disabilities, although more negatively perceived (Snyder et al., 2010), may play a smaller role in the role-taking stage than in the role-making stage. In latter stages of LMX development, mutual respect and trust are necessary for a supervisor to feel comfortable delegating important work tasks to a subordinate. Negative stereotypes about the trustworthiness of mentally disabled persons could hamper the role-taking process, as initially a mentally disabled subordinate may be viewed as dependent or untrustworthy.

Stereotypes of GLBT Employees. Although there is no federal legislation that protects employees on the basis of sexual orientation, as of 2014, there are currently 21 states that provide protection (Choksi, 2013). In addition, as of 2012, nearly all (96.6%) of Fortune 500 organizations include sexual orientation in their diversity statements. Despite this progress, a 2009 Catalyst study found that more than half of all GLBT employees surveyed indicated that their managers were not comfortable with GLBT employees. Similarly, Levine and Leonard (1984) reported that more than 60% of lesbian employees in their study expected to experience job discrimination (ranging from taunts and harassment to termination and violence) if their sexual orientation was known in their workplace. More recently, in a review of 15 GLBT survey studies, Badgett, Lau, Sears, and Ho (2007) found that between 15% and 43% of respondents reported some experience of discrimination based on sexual orientation. Notably, between 12% and 30% of heterosexual co-workers reported witnessing evidence of antigay discrimination against their GLBT colleagues (Badgett et al., 2007).

Interestingly, although negative stereotypes underlie barriers experienced by GLBT employees (Klie, 2009; Meyer, 2003), little work has focused on uncovering the content of these stereotypes. That is, contrary to the other stigmatized groups mentioned in this chapter that are ascribed specific competence-based stereotypes, perceptions of GLBT employees are quite vague. By and large, these views are based on the prevailing cultural norm of heterosexism. As Herek (1992) described, heterosexism is "an ideological system that denies, denigrates, and stigmatizes any non-heterosexual form of behavior, identity relationship, or community" (p. 89). Moreover, due to uncertainty about the extent of heterosexism in a particular organization, gay and lesbian employees may be reticent to disclose their sexual orientation (Griffith & Hebl, 2002; Ragins & Cornwell, 2001); thus, researchers find difficulty in assessing the impact of stereotypes on GLBT employees' work-related experiences.

Despite the limited understanding of GLBT stereotype content, theory suggests that these perceptions may negatively affect the development and maintenance of favorable leader–member exchanges. Indeed, prior research shows that contextual factors such as organizational policies and having GLBT co-workers influence GLBT employees' decision to disclose their sexual orientation at work (Chrobot-Mason, Button, & DiClementi, 2001). As part of sexual identity management processes, closeted individuals (i.e., those who have not openly proclaimed a GLBT identity) might experience discomfort engaging in deeper leader–member exchanges for fear of revealing their GLBT status. As Chrobot-Mason et al. (2001) observed, GLBT personnel reported significantly higher use of the avoidance strategy (i.e., being evasive about their sexual identity and situations that might reveal the hidden identity) in work climates viewed as antagonistic toward non-heterosexual personnel. By implication, GLBT personnel may fear negative treatment due to their sexual orientation and stifle the initial establishment of a high-quality leader–member exchange.

Previously, we noted that the choice to reveal less visible dimensions of diversity will have stronger implications for LMX quality during the role-making and role-routinization stages versus the role-taking stage of the dyadic relationship. Despite GLBT employees' fears about revealing their sexual orientation, Meyer (2003) argued that the emotional burden of nondisclosure precipitates anxiety, which undermines work performance. Griffith and Hebl (2002) provide empirical support for the disclosure–anxiety linkage. Namely, "closeted" gay and lesbian employees report higher levels of job anxiety than their openly gay and lesbian counterparts. Likewise, Day and Schoenrade (1997) showed that compared to their openly gay and lesbian counterparts, "closeted" gay and lesbian employees had significantly lower levels of job satisfaction, affective commitment, and perceived top management support, and significantly higher levels of role conflict, role ambiguity, and conflict between work and home. Thus, although hiding their sexual orientation might enable GLBT employees to forge LMX relationships that otherwise might be inhibited due to heterosexism, it seems likely that the toll of nondisclosure may impede their ability to stay focused on the job. Moreover, owing to trust being the defining characteristic of the role-making stage, disclosure may serve to foster positive interactions between the parties, which can improve the quality of the relationship in the role-making and role-routinization stages. Specifically, the decision to disclose one's previously concealed sexual orientation may be viewed as a gesture of trust by the other party in the dyad, who will likely reciprocate, in kind, by according more trust. Thus, disclosure might set the stage for a cycle of trust that will help the LMX relationship flourish in the long term.

Stereotypes and Dyadic Similarity/Dissimilarity

In the previous section, we briefly introduced the idea that negative stereotypes are apt to have a particularly pronounced effect when the leader and follower are dissimilar. Social identity theory (SIT) and the similarity–attraction paradigm both propose that dyadic similarity can enhance LMX quality. Social identity theory proposes that individuals classify themselves and others into social categories based on accessible characteristics (Gaertner & Dovidio, 2000; Hogg & Terry, 2000; Tajfel & Turner, 1986). The individual's knowledge of his or her memberships in these social categories or groups, together with the emotional significance of that knowledge, constitutes his or her social identity (Turner, 1981). As evaluating similar others more favorably than dissimilar others enhances our own identity, similar others are afforded ingroup status, whereas dissimilar others are relegated to outgroup status. Given that managers presumably view themselves as successful organizational members, they will likely favor subordinates who are demographically similar to themselves, with the expectation that these subordinates will fit in the organization (Goldberg, 2005; Judge & Ferris, 1991). Consistent with this view, Bauer and Green (1996) contended that dyadic similarity on demographic characteristics should have a stronger connection with LMX early in the relationship.

Because LMX quality is determined early in the supervisor–subordinate relationship, many researchers have suggested that similarity is an important predictor of LMX (Vecchio & Brazil, 2007; Green, Anderson, & Shivers, 1996). Dyadic similarity fosters a sense of shared history, trust, and cohesion, which are conducive to favorable exchanges. Indeed, research indicates that supervisor–subordinate sex similarity is associated with higher-quality LMX relationships (Vecchio & Brazil, 2007; Green et al., 1996). In contrast, differences between dyad members may create barriers to building the supervisor–subordinate relationship. For example, Thomas (2001) notes that many cross-race relationships suffer from what he terms "protective hesitation," in which both parties are reluctant to raise issues that may make race more salient. The result of avoiding this pink elephant is decreased trust, thereby compromising the quality of the relationship.

Summary and Directions for Future Research

The conceptual arguments regarding the effects of similarity on LMX have been well-supported by empirical evidence. Indeed, in their meta-analysis,

Dulebohn et al. (2012) found that similarity was among the best predictors of LMX quality, with correlation of .45. However, it bears noting that although meta-analysts must group together predictors in a parsimonious manner, the relational demography literature has consistently demonstrated that not all similarity is created equal. In our earlier discussion of age, we noted that dyadic dissimilarity may yield more favorable outcomes than similarity, when the dissimilarity is consistent with societal or organizational norms. Thus, norm-congruence/norm-violation represents an important boundary condition on the general expectation that similarity results in high-quality LMX.

Additionally, although either party in the dyad may be negatively stereotyped, we note here that the effect of dissimilarity on LMX quality likely differs depending on which member of the dyad is in the negatively stereotyped group. That is, although there is evidence that both leaders' and followers' LMX perceptions are influenced by their perceptions of the other party's actual or expected competence and trust (Bauer & Green, 1996; Liden et al., 1993; Nahrgang et al., 2009), it is probable that the repercussions of belonging to a negatively stereotyped group are more dire for subordinates than for managers. Whereas LMX is a two-way street, leaders typically have greater power and influence over followers' careers (through performance ratings, providing developmental opportunities, and recommendations for promotions) than subordinates have on supervisors' careers. Thus, although stereotypes and dissimilarity may provide obstacles to the development and sustenance of the dyadic relationship from both parties' perspectives, the outcomes of this decreased exchange quality have focused exclusively on followers. We believe this gap represents an omission in the literature that ought to be addressed in future LMX research.

Additionally, we note that the impact of dissimilarity potentially varies as a function of organizational demography. More specifically, individuals in the aforementioned negatively stereotyped groups are often in the numerical minority (particularly in positions of power and/or status) within the organization. Token status, in itself, has been shown to heighten stereotype salience (Jackson, Thoits, & Taylor, 1995; Kanter, 1977; Niemann & Dovidio, 1998). Yet, Fairhurst and Snavely (1983) found that tokens who are in low status groups (e.g., women) fare worse than tokens who are members of more valued groups (e.g., men). For example, Blau (1977) noted that when few members of the same

gender are available in an unbalanced gender context, the quality of social relationships experienced by the focal individual may be relatively low. That is to say, dissimilarity may have very different effects on members of negatively stereotyped groups, based on the extent to which members of their group are represented in the organization as a whole. For instance, LMX will likely develop quite differently for female employees with male supervisors in a male-skewed organization compared to female employees in a gender-balanced or female-skewed organization (e.g., Ely, 1994, 1995). We encourage researchers to examine the moderating role of organizational demographics on the relationships between group membership and dyadic (dis)similarity and LMX quality.

Related to our call to incorporate organizational demography into examinations of the diversity–LMX linkage, we note that diversity climate is another factor of relevance to the quality of supervisor–subordinate relations. Diversity climate involves employees' consensual perceptions of the extent to which their organization is fair and socially integrates all personnel into the organization (McKay, Avery, & Morris, 2008). Accordingly, in work contexts perceived as having supportive diversity climates, demographic group membership should have attenuated effects on work outcomes. Diversity climate research has shown, in fact, that racial–ethnic disparities in sales performance (McKay et al., 2008), retention (McKay et al., 2007), and absenteeism (Avery, McKay, Wilson, & Tonidandel, 2007) are minimized (amplified) when diversity climates are viewed as more (less) supportive. Applying this logic to diversity and LMX, we suspect that demographic dissimilarity between supervisors and subordinates should be less disadvantageous to LMX quality in prodiversity contexts, as differences in perspective are valued and appreciated. As Ely and Thomas (2001) showed, in workgroups that respected the differences between and perspectives of members from varying demographic groups (i.e., the learning-and-effectiveness paradigm), workgroup attachment and performance were higher. Most importantly, members of disparaged groups (e.g., minorities) reported feeling more highly valued in the above types of workgroups. The implication here is that people in work environments with supportive diversity climates should be more prone to appreciate differences across the supervisor–subordinate dyad, thereby reducing the influence of negative stereotypes during the role-taking stage of LMX. The above notions are speculative, and therefore should be investigated in further LMX research.

It is worth noting that the large majority of LMX studies have examined relationships with either leader perceptions or member perceptions, with very few including both perspectives. What is striking in the studies that have considered both parties' perspectives is the weak correlation between supervisor-rated and subordinate-rated LMX. For example, in the studies of Nahrgang et al. (2009), the four within-period supervisor LMX–subordinate LMX correlations ranged from .09 to .18. The lack of agreement between supervisors' and subordinates' perceptions of the relationship led Cogliser et al. (2009) to examine the outcomes of LMX agreement. They found that congruence was associated with performance, organizational commitment, and job satisfaction. We encourage researchers to continue this line of research, focusing on other outcomes as well as predictors of LMX agreement. Given that similarity fosters a sense of shared history and cohesion (Byrne, 1971), it is likely that dyadic similarity may serve to keep supervisors and subordinates "on the same page" regarding the quality of the relationship.

Finally, we concur with Dulebohn et al.'s (2012) call for more longitudinal LMX research. Our conceptualization of the way in which diversity influences LMX is largely predicated on the finding that stereotype-reliance is greatest when little individuating information is available to the perceiver (Harrison et al., 1998). As such, we have argued that visible characteristics and similarity on those characteristics should have the greatest influence on LMX in the role-taking stage. Moreover, we have stated that efforts to conceal less visible characteristics may mitigate the impact of negative stereotypes on early LMX formation; however, attempts to veil such characteristics may be deleterious to fostering a high-quality relationship through the role-making and role-routinization stages. Simply put, understanding the role of group membership and diversity on the leader–member exchange relationship requires an examination of how the LMX process unfolds over time.

References

Avery, D. R., McKay, P. F., Wilson, D. C., & Tonidandel, S. (2007). Unequal attendance: The relationships between race, organizational diversity cues, and absenteeism. *Personnel Psychology*, 60, 875–902.

Badgett, M. V. L., Lau, H., Sears, B., & Ho, D. (2007). *Bias in the workplace: Consistent evidence of sexual orientation and gender identity discrimination*. Los Angeles, CA: University of California, The Williams Institute.

Bartels, L. K., & Nordstrom, C. R. (2013). Too big too hire: Factors impacting weight discrimination. *Management Research Review*, 36, 868–881.

Bauer, T. N., & Green, S. G. (1996). Development of leader-member exchange: A longitudinal test. *Academy of Management Journal*, 39, 1538–1567.

Berger, J., Rosenholtz, S. J., & Zelditch, M. (1980). Status organizing processes. *Annual Review of Sociology*, 6, 479–508.

Bernerth, J. B., Armenakis, A. A., Feild, H. S., Giles, W. F., & Walker, H. F. (2007). Is personality associated with perceptions of LMX? An empirical study. *Leadership & Organizational Development Journal*, 28, 613–631.

Braddock, D., & Bachelder, L. (1994). The glass ceiling and persons with disabilities. US Department of Labor. Retrieved on April 10, 2014 from http://digitalcommons.ilr.cornell.edu/key_workplace/114/

Brewer, M. B., & Kramer, R. M. (1985). The psychology of intergroup attitudes and behavior. *Annual Review of Psychology*, 36, 259–271.

Brewer, M. B., & Miller, N. (1984). Beyond the contact hypothesis: Theoretical perspectives on desegregation. In N. Miller & M. B. Brewer (Eds.), *Groups in contact* (pp. 281–301). Orlando, FL: Academic Press.

Button, S. B. (2001). Organizational efforts to affirm sexual diversity: A cross-level examination. *Journal of Applied Psychology*, 86, 17–28.

Byrne, D. E. (1971). *The attraction paradigm*. New York: Academic Press.

Catalyst (2009). *Building LGBT-inclusive workplaces: Engaging organizations and individuals in change*. New York: Catalyst.

Chattopadhyay, P., George, E., & Lawrence, S. A. (2004). Why does dissimilarity matter? Exploring self-categorization, self-enhancement, and uncertainty reduction. *Journal of Applied Psychology*, 89, 892–900.

Chrobot-Mason, D., Button, S. B., & DiClementi, J. D. (2001). Sexual identity management strategies: An exploration of antecedents and consequences. *Sex Roles*, 45, 321–336.

Chung, B., Ehrhart, M. G., Ehrhart, K. H., Hattrup, K., & Solamon, J. (2010). Stereotype threat, state anxiety, and specific self-efficacy as predictors of promotion exam performance. *Group and Organization Management*, 35, 77–107.

Cogliser, C. C., Schriesheim, C. A., Scandura, T. A., & Gardner, W. L. (2009). Balance in leader and follower perceptions of leader-member exchange: Relationships with performance and work attitudes. *Leadership Quarterly*, 20, 452–465.

Colella, A., & Bruyère, S. M. (2011). Disability and employment: New directions for industrial/organizational psychology. In S. Zedeck (Ed.), *APA handbook of industrial and organizational psychology* (Vol. 2, pp. 473–504). Washington, DC: American Psychological Association.

Colella, A., & Varma, A. (2001). The impact of subordinate disability on leader-member exchange dynamics. *Academy of Management Journal*, 44, 304–315.

Combs, I. H., & Omvig, C. P. (1986). Accommodation of disabled people into employment: Perceptions of employers. *Journal of Rehabilitation*, 52, 42–45.

Crandall, C. S., & Biernat, M. (1990). The ideology of anti-fat attitudes. *Journal of Applied Social Psychology*, 20, 227–243.

Day, N. E., & Schoenrade, P. (1997). Staying in the closet versus coming out: Relationships between communication about sexual orientation and work attitudes. *Personnel Psychology*, 50, 147–163.

Dienesch, R. M., & Liden, R. C. (1986). Leader-member exchange model of leadership: A critique and further development. *Academy of Management Review, 11*, 618–634.

Duehr, E. E., & Bono, J. E. (2006). Men, women, and managers: Are stereotypes finally changing? *Personnel Psychology, 59*, 815–846.

Dulebohn, J. H., Bommer, W. H., Liden, R. C., Brouer, R. L., & Ferris, G. R. (2012). A meta-analysis of antecedents and consequences of leader-member exchange: Integrating the past with an eye toward the future. *Journal of Management, 38*, 1715–1759.

Eagly, A. H. (1987). *Sex differences in social behavior: A social-role interpretation*. Hillsdale, NJ: Erlbaum.

Ely, R. J. (1994). The effects of organizational demographics and social identity on relationships among professional women. *Administrative Science Quarterly, 39*, 203–238.

Ely, R. J. (1995). The power in demography: Women's social constructions of gender identity at work. *Academy of Management Journal, 38*, 589–634.

Erdogan, B., & Bauer, T. N. (2010). Differentiated leader-member exchanges: The buffering role of justice climate. *Journal of Applied Psychology, 95*, 1104–1120.

Fairhurst, G. T., & Snavely, B. K. (1983). A test of the social isolation of male tokens. *Academy of Management Journal, 26*, 353–361.

Finkelstein, L. M., & Burke, M. J. (1998). Age stereotyping at work: The role of rater and contextual factors on evaluations of job applicants. *Journal of General Psychology, 125*, 317–345.

Finkelstein, L. M., Frautschy Demuth, R. L., & Sweeney, D. L. (2007). Bias against overweight job applicants: Further explorations of when and why. *Human Resource Management, 46*, 203–222.

Fiske, S. T., Cuddy, A. J. C., Glick, P., & Xu, J. (2002). A model of (often mixed) stereotype content: Competence and warmth respectively follow from perceived status and competition. *Journal of Personality and Social Psychology, 82*, 878–902.

Ford, T. E., & Stangor, C. (1992). The role of diagnosticity in stereotype formation: Perceiving group means and variables. *Journal of Personality and Social Psychology, 63*, 356–367.

Gaertner, S. L., & Dovidio, J. F. (2000). *Reducing intergroup bias: The common ingroup identity model*. Oxford, UK: Psychology Press.

Garstka, T. A., Schmitt, M. T., Branscombe, N. R., & Hummert, M. L. (2004). How young and older adults differ in their responses to perceived age discrimination. *Psychology and Aging, 19*, 326–335.

Gerstner, C. R., & Day, D. V. (1997). Meta-analytic review of leader-member exchange theory: Correlates and construct issues. *Journal of Applied Psychology, 82*, 827–844.

Gillespie, J. Z., Converse, P. D., & Kriska, S. D. (2010). Applying recommendations from the literature on stereotype threat: Two field studies. *Journal of Business and Psychology, 25*, 493–504.

Goffman, E. (1963). *Notes on the management of spoiled identity*. Englewood Cliffs, NJ: Prentice Hall.

Goldberg, C. B., Finkelstein, L. M., Perry, E. L., & Konrad, A. M. (2004). Job and industry fit: The effects of age and gender matches on career progress and outcomes. *Journal of Organizational Behavior, 25*, 807–829.

Gomez, C., & Rosen, B. (2001). The leader-member exchange as a link between managerial trust and employee empowerment. *Group & Organization Management, 26*, 53–69.

Graen, G. B., & Scandura, T. A. (1987). Toward a psychology of dyadic organizing. *Research in Organizational Behavior, 9*, 175–208.

Graen, G. B., & Uhl-Bien, M. (1995). Relationship-based approach to leadership: Development of leader-member exchange (LMX) theory of leadership over 25 years: Applying a multi-level multi-domain perspective. *Leadership Quarterly, 6*, 219–247.

Green, S. G., Anderson, S. E., & Shivers, S. L. (1996). Demographic and organizational influences on leader-member exchange and related work attitudes. *Organizational Behavior and Human Decision Processes, 66*, 203–214.

Griffith, K. H., & Hebl, M. (2002). The disclosure dilemma for gay men and lesbians: "Coming out" at work. *Journal of Applied Psychology, 87*, 1191–1199.

Harris, K. J., Kacmar, K. M., & Carlson, D. S. (2006). An examination of temporal variables and relationship quality on promotability ratings. *Group & Organization Management, 31*, 677–699.

Harrison, D. A., & Klein, K. J. (2007). What's the difference? Diversity constructs as separation, variety, or disparity in organizations. *Academy of Management Review, 32*, 1199–1228.

Harrison, D. A., Price, K. H., & Bell, M. P. (1998). Beyond relational demography: Time and the effects of surface- and deep-level diversity on work group cohesion. *Academy of Management Journal, 41*, 96–107.

Heilman, M. E. (1983). Sex bias in work settings: The lack of fit model. *Research in Organizational Behavior, 5*, 269–298.

Heilman, M. E., & Eagly, A. H. (2008). Gender stereotypes are alive, well, and busy producing discrimination. *Industrial and Organizational Psychology, 1*, 393–398.

Ho, C., & Jackson, J. W. (2001). Attitudes towards Asian Americans: Theory and measurement. *Journal of Applied Social Psychology, 31*, 1553–1581.

Hogg, M. A., & Terry, D. J. (2000). Social identity and self-categorization processes in organizational contexts. *Academy of Management Review, 25*, 121–140.

Ibarra, H. (1995). Race, opportunity, and diversity of social circles in managerial networks. *Academy of Management Journal, 38*, 673–704.

Jackson, P. B., Thoits, P. A., & Taylor, H. F. (1995). Composition of the workplace and psychological well-being: The effects of tokenism on America's Black elite. *Social Forces, 74*, 543–557.

Kanter, R. M. (1977). Some effects of proportions on group life: Skewed sex ratios and responses to token women. *American Journal of Sociology, 82*, 965–990.

Kinicki, A. J., & Vecchio, R. P. (1994). Influences on the quality of supervisor-subordinate relations: The role of time-pressure, organizational commitment, and locus of control. *Journal of Organizational Behavior, 15*, 75–82.

Kulik, C. T., Perry, E. L., & Bourhis, A. C. (2000). Ironic evaluation processes: Effects of thought suppression on evaluations of older job applicants. *Journal of Organizational Behavior, 21*, 689–711.

Lam, W., Huang, X., & Snape, E. (2007). Feedback-seeking behavior and leader-member exchange: Do supervisor-attributed motives matter? *Academy of Management Journal, 50*, 348–363.

Larkin, J. C., & Pines, H. A. (1979). No fat persons need apply: Experimental studies of the overweight stereotype and hiring preference. *Sociology of Work and Occupations, 6*, 312–327.

Lawrence, B. S. (1984). Age grading: The implicit organizational timetable. *Journal of Occupational Behavior, 13*, 181–191.

Liden, R. C., Wayne, S. J., & Stilwell, D. (1993). A longitudinal study on the early development of leader-member exchanges. *Journal of Applied Psychology, 78*, 662–674.

Lord, R. G., & Maher, K. J. (1993). *Leadership and information processing: Linking perceptions and performance.* New York: Routledge.

Louvet, E. (2007). Social judgment toward job applicants with disabilities: Perception of personal qualities and competencies. *Rehabilitation Psychology, 52*, 297–303.

Lyness, K. S., & Heilman, M. E. (2006). When fit is fundamental: Performance evaluations and promotions of upper-level female and male managers. *Journal of Applied Psychology, 91*, 777–785.

Major, B., & Gramzow, R. H. (1999). Abortion as stigma: Cognitive and emotional implications of concealment. *Journal of Personality and Social Psychology, 77*, 735–745.

Maslyn, J. M., & Uhl-Bien, M. (2001). Leader-member exchange and its dimensions: Effects of self-effort and other's effort on relationship quality. *Journal of Applied Psychology, 86*, 697–708.

Mayer, D. M., & Hanges, P. J. (2003). Understanding the stereotype threat effect with "culture-free" tests: An examination of its mediators and measurement. *Human Performance, 16*, 207–230.

McKay, P. F., Avery, D. R., & Morris, M. A. (2008). Mean racial-ethnic differences in work performance: The moderating role of diversity climate. *Personnel Psychology, 61*, 349–374.

McKay, P. F., Avery, D. R., Tonidandel, S., Morris, M. A, Hernandez, M., & Hebl, M. (2007). Racial differences in employee retention: Are diversity climate perceptions the key? *Personnel Psychology, 60*, 35–62.

McKay, P. F., Doverspike, D., Bowen-Hilton, D., & Martin, Q. D. (2002). Stereotype threat effects on the Raven Advanced Progressive Matrices scores of African Americans. *Journal of Applied Social Psychology, 72*, 767–787.

Meyer, I. H. (2003). Prejudice, social stress, and mental health in lesbian, gay, and bisexual populations: Conceptual issues and research evidence. *Psychological Bulletin, 129*, 674–697.

Miller, C. T., & Major, B. (2000). Coping with stigma and prejudice. In T. F. Heatherton, R. E. Kleck, M. R. Hebl, & J. G. Hull (Eds.), *The social psychology of stigma* (pp. 243–272). New York: Guilford Press.

Morrison, T. G., & O'Connor, W. (1999). Psychometric properties of a scale measuring negative attitudes toward overweight individuals. *The Journal of Social Psychology, 139*, 436–445.

Nahrgang, J. D., Morgeson, F. P., & Ilies, R. (2009). The development of leader-member exchanges: Exploring how personality and performance influence leader and member relationships over time. *Organizational Behavior and Human Decision Processes, 108*, 256–266.

Niemann, Y. F., & Dovidio, J. F. (1998). Relationship of solo status, academic rank, and perceived distinctiveness to job satisfaction of racial/ethnic minorities. *Journal of Applied Psychology, 83*, 55–71.

Pettigrew, T. F. (1979). The ultimate attribution error: Extending Allport's cognitive analysis of prejudice. *Personality and Social Psychology Bulletin, 5*, 461–476.

Phillips, A. S., & Bedeian, A. G. (1994). Leader-follower exchange quality: The role of personal and interpersonal attributes. *Academy of Management Journal, 37*, 990–1001.

Posthuma, R. A., & Campion, M. A. (2009). Age stereotypes in the workplace: Common stereotypes, moderators, and future research directions. *Journal of Management, 35*, 158–188.

Ragins, B. R. (1997). Diversified mentoring relationships in organizations: A power perspective. *Academy of Management Review, 22*, 482–521.

Ragins, B. R., & Cornwell, J. M. (2001). Pink triangles: Antecedents and consequences of perceived workplace discrimination against gay and lesbian employees. *Journal of Applied Psychology, 86*, 1244–1261.

Ringenbach, K. L., & Jacobs, R. R. (1994). Development of age stereotypes in the workplace scale. Society of Industrial and Organizational Psychologists Conference, Nashville, TN.

Roberson L., Deitch, E., Brief, A. P., & Block, C. J. (2003). Stereotype threat and feedback seeking in the workplace. *Journal of Vocational Behavior, 62*, 176–188.

Roberson, L., & Kulik, C. T. (2009). Stereotype threat at work. *Academy of Management Perspectives, 21*, 24–40.

Roehling, M. V. (1999). Weight-based discrimination in employment: Psychological and legal aspects. *Personnel Psychology, 52*, 969–1016.

Rosen, B., & Jerdee, T. H. (1976). The influence of age stereotypes on managerial decisions. *Journal of Applied Psychology, 62*, 428–432.

Rosen, B., & Jerdee, T. H. (1977). Too old or not too old. *Harvard Business Review, 55*, 97–106.

Scandura, T., & Graen, G. B. (1984). Moderating effects of initial leader-member exchange status on the effects of a leadership intervention. *Journal of Applied Psychology, 69*, 428–436.

Settoon, R. P., Bennett, N., & Liden, R. C. (1996). Social exchange in organizations: Perceived organizational support, leader-member exchange, and employee reciprocity. *Journal of Applied Psychology, 81*, 219–227.

Shore, L. M., Cleveland, J. N., & Goldberg, C. (2003). Work attitudes and decisions as a function of manager age and employee age. *Journal of Applied Psychology, 88*, 529–537.

Shore, L. M., & Goldberg, C. B. (2004). Age discrimination in organizations. In R. L. Dipboye & A. Colella (Eds.), *Psychological and organizational bases of discrimination at work.* Bowling Green, OH: Lawrence Erlbaum—SIOP Frontiers Series.

Snyder, L. A., Carmichael, J. S., Blackwell, L. V., Cleveland, J. N., & Thornton, G. C. (2010). Perceptions of discrimination and justice among employees with disabilities. *Employee Responsibilities and Rights Journal, 22*, 5–19.

Sonnenfeld, J. (1978). Dealing with the aging work force. *Harvard Business Review, 78*, 81–92.

Steele, C. M. (1997). A threat in the air: How stereotypes shape intellectual identity and performance. *American Psychologist, 52*, 613–629.

Steele, C. M., & Aronson, J. (1995). Stereotype threat and the intellectual test performance of African Americans. *Journal of Personality and Social Psychology, 69*, 797–811.

Steele, C. M., & Davies, P. G. (2003). Stereotype threat and employment testing: A commentary. *Human Performance, 16*, 311–326.

Stone, D. L., & Colella, A. (1996). A model of factors affecting the treatment of disabled individuals in organizations. *Academy of Management Review, 21*, 352–401.

Thomas, D. A. (2001). The truth about mentoring minorities: Race matters. *Harvard Business Review, 79*, 98–107.

Toossi, M. (2007). Labor force projections to 2016: More workers in their golden years. *Monthly Labor Review, 130*, 33–52.

Tsui, A., Porter, L., & Egan, T. (2002). When both similarities and dissimilarities matter: Extending the concept of relational demography, *Human Relations, 8*, 899–932.

Tsui, A. S., & O'Reilly, C. A. (1989). Beyond simple demographic effects: The importance of relational demography in superior-subordinate dyads. *Academy of Management Journal, 32*, 402–423.

Unger, D. D. (2001). A national study of employers' experiences with workers with disabilities and their knowledge and utilization of accommodations. *Dissertation Abstracts International, 62/02*.

Vecchio, R. P., & Bullis, R. C. (2001). Moderators of the influence of supervisor-subordinate similarity on subordinate outcomes. *Journal of Applied Psychology, 86*, 884–896.

Wang, H., Law, K. S., Hackett, R. D., Wang, D., & Chen, Z. X. (2005). Leader-member exchange as a mediator of the relationship between transformational leadership and follower' performance and organizational citizenship behaviors. *Academy of Management Journal, 48*, 420–432.

Wayne, S. J., Shore, L. M., Bommer, W. H., & Tetrick, L. E. (2002). The role of fair treatment and rewards in perceptions of organizational support and leader-member exchange. *Journal of Applied Psychology, 87*, 590–598.

Wayne, S. J., Shore, L. M., & Liden, R. C. (1997). Perceived organizational support and leader-member exchange: A social exchange perspective. *Academy of Management Journal, 40*, 82–111.

Westerman, J. W., & Yamamura, J. (2007). Generational preferences for work environment fit: Effects on employee outcomes. *Career Development International, 12*, 150–162.

Wilson, T. C. (1996). Cohort and prejudice: Whites' attitudes toward blacks, Hispanics, Jews, and Asians. *Public Opinion Quarterly, 60*, 253–274.

Does Age Matter to LMX and its Outcomes?
A Review and Future Research Directions

Donald M. Truxillo *and* Gabriela Burlacu

Abstract

Age-related changes in industrialized countries have increased interest in how age differences play out in the workplace. However, little research has been done to uncover how age differences may influence the development and maintenance of leader–member relationships. Empirical and theoretical work that has been done in this area suggests that age may be a key demographic factor in understanding LMX, both as a direct and moderating influence. In this chapter we discuss age-related studies that build the case for the effects of age in LMX. We also examine developmental theories and stereotyping research that provide a foundation for understanding of how age differences between employees and supervisors may affect the relationships between them. The authors conclude with a set of research questions in each theoretical area to address in order to develop a comprehensive understanding of the influence of age on LMX relationships.

Key Words: age, age differences, leader–member exchange, leadership, aging workforce

Introduction

As the average age increases in many developed nations across the globe, the industrialized workforce is experiencing unprecedented demographic shifts. Overall, the workforce is aging, with people staying in the workforce beyond traditional retirement ages (Eurostat, 2012; Toossi, 2007, 2012). These trends are due to several factors, including the fact that people are living longer and staying healthier as they age (Vaupel, 2010). These factors have led to an increase of the official retirement age in some countries because their retirement systems must support people for a longer time period than was necessary at one time (Curl & Hokenstad, 2006). Moreover, people in many regions are finding they need to work longer, or to return to work after retirement, as a result of the economic downturn (Moen, 2012).

This has led to several changes in the age demographics of the workforce. First, the average worker is becoming older. Second, older and younger individuals are working together side-by-side across the spectrum of career stages and job levels. Third, and most relevant to the present chapter, there are increasing incidents of extreme age differences between workers and their supervisors. This means that leaders must more frequently supervise highly age-diverse teams of workers, with greater variability and disparity in the age differences of leader–member dyads (Mor-Barak, 2011). Further, the phenomenon of younger supervisors managing older workers is becoming more commonplace (Liebold & Voelpel, 2006).

The purpose of this chapter is to examine the implications of the changing age diversity in the workplace for leader–member relationships. Although a small amount of research has begun to focus on these issues, there is still a great deal that is unknown. In this chapter, we begin by examining the limited research on age differences in leadership in general, and in the dyadic relationships that develop between leaders and followers. Next, we briefly review findings regarding age-related changes in individual differences (personality, cognitive skills, and motivation), theoretical models that explain how people adapt to these age-related changes, and the social context for aging (age climate) that could affect how older and younger people respond to the workplace in general and to the relationships they build at work. We point out the needed future research along the way to help address how age diversity affects the leader–subordinate relationship.

Possible Age Effects on Leader–Member Exchange and Its Outcomes

Schriesheim, Castro, and Cogliser (1999) provided an overview of the leader–member exchange (LMX) literature through the 1990s, noting that parts of the LMX literature were confusing and not clearly developed. The same could be said today of the study of LMX theory in relation to the aging workforce: namely, that relatively little research has focused specifically on how age of the leader and subordinate can affect the relations between them. As with many areas of organizational psychology, age has only recently received much attention as a result of the aging workforce. Walter and Scheibe (2013) provide a detailed review of the literature on leader age and leader behavior and its outcomes, and they lament the confusing state of the current literature. Specifically, they note that there is inconsistent theorizing in the literature on age in leadership and that there are few consistent findings. The same could be said of the study of age in LMX literature.

Although there is relatively little research regarding age and LMX per se, there are streams of research that can help us to see our way through this challenging situation. We begin by discussing studies on the effects of leader age on performance ratings, followed by a discussion of the effects of age on leader behaviors and outcomes and a review of research on the effects of age congruence in dyadic relationships. We then discuss recent work that suggests that age alone may not affect the relations between leaders and individual followers, but that age interacts with other variables to affect the leader–member relationship. We conclude this section with a discussion of the issue of age versus "deep-level" variables that may affect LMX.

Age and Performance Ratings

Liden, Stilwell, and Ferris (1996) tracked the effects of supervisor and subordinate age on objective and subjective measures of performance. Using data collected over a period of 6 years (1980–1986) in a large U.S. corporation, they found that older employees performed better than younger employees on both objective and subjective measures, a finding that is consistent with other research on age-related performance differences (Ng & Feldman, 2008). In addition, however, the authors found that the subordinates of older leaders showed higher performance than the subordinates of younger leaders. These effects may be characteristic to the nature of the work, where older supervisors may provide greater opportunities such as sales for their subordinates. No effects were found for age differences or similarities in the supervisor–subordinate dyads. As much as anything, this study helped to identify some of the key issues and pointed out the need for greater theorizing regarding age and the supervisor relationship.

Effects of Age Congruence on Leader–Team Member Relationship

A number of studies have examined the effects of age congruence on the relationship between supervisors/leaders and followers. One of the key questions here is whether demographic differences, including age differences among team members, actually do affect perceptions and performance. The relational demography literature, which examines the effects of demographic similarities and differences among teams, is particularly relevant to understanding whether age differences between leaders and followers have similar effects on their dyadic relationships.

In an early study of the effects of demographic similarity in teams, Tsui and O'Reilly (1989) looked for the effects of relational demography in supervisor–subordinate dyads, examining the effects of demographic similarity and differences within the dyad. Specifically, using a sample of 272 supervisor–subordinate dyads, they found that demographic differences in dyads leads to lower ratings of perceived effectiveness by supervisors, less attraction between supervisors and subordinates, and increased perceptions of role ambiguity by subordinates. However, they also noted that the age effects were minimal: Age differences only had marginal effects on subordinate role ambiguity, and there were no effects on supervisor ratings of effectiveness. Moreover, later studies by Harrison and colleagues (Harrison, Price, & Bell 1998; Harrison, Price, Gavin, & Florey, 2002) showed that the effects of demographic differences on group relations and functioning can be largely erased over time as members come to know each other in more meaningful ways (e.g., personality, abilities) beyond the "surface" demographic characteristics such as gender and age.

Shore and Bleiken (1991) provide a study that may help to shed light on the effects of age in supervisor–subordinate relationships, examining the effects of age and supervisor–subordinate age congruence on performance ratings. Using a sample of 70 assemblers and their supervisors, they found inconsistent results for age bias and that bias may only be important for certain dimensions of performance ratings. Again, this is consistent with later research by Harrison et al. (1998, 2002) that found age had few effects on team relationships and functioning once team members had gotten to know each other at a deeper level.

Other studies have also found small or nonexistent effects of age in leader–member relations. Schaffer and Riordan (2013) found that age similarity in leader–member dyads in an insurance company was not significant in predicting the extent to which followers perceived discrimination or exclusionary treatment coming from their supervisor. Similarly, Epitropaki and Martin (1999) examined the combined impact of relational demography and leader–member interactions on employee attitudes and well-being and found that only similarity in tenure, combined with LMX, influenced positive employee outcomes. Age similarity was nonsignificant. Further, Perry, Kulik, and Zhou (1999) found in a sample of 35 groundskeepers that employees who were older than their supervisors had less absenteeism and more OCBs, suggesting that incongruence may not have negative effects.

Fagenson-Eland, Baugh, and Lankau (2005) examined the effects of age differences in mentor–protégé dyads. Using a sample of 27 dyads from two high-technology companies, they found that age differences within the dyad reduced agreement between the mentor and the protégé about the extent of mentoring provided. The authors suggested that one reason for this effect of age differences on perceptions of the relationship is that people from different age cohorts may have different expectations as a result of their differing social experiences. Of course, such differences may also be found because of the differences in accumulated experience of dyad members of different ages.

Though not directly related to LMX, Kearney (2008) examined whether age differences between leaders and followers affects the relationship between transformational leadership and group performance, primarily because of decreased perceived legitimacy on the part of a leader that is not older than the followers. As expected, Kearney found that the relationship between transformational leadership and team performance was positive when the leader was older than most team members, but the relationship was nonsignificant if the leader's age was close to the group mean.

In short, the effects found for age differences on within-group dyadic relationships, either among group members or between members and leaders, have been mixed. While some studies have suggested that such differences do not matter, others have suggested that they may matter under certain circumstances.

LMX as a Mediator Between Age and Leader–Follower Outcomes

Two studies by Gellert and Schalk (2012a, b) show how LMX may play a mediating role in understanding the relationship between age issues and important leader outcomes. First, using a sample of 152 workers in residential homes, they found that age-related attitudes of employees affected their LMX perceptions, which in turn affected self-reported employee performance and job satisfaction (Gellert & Schalk, 2012a). In a separate study of 150 workers in residential homes for the elderly, Gellert and Schalk (2012b) found that LMX mediated the relationship between employee age and job satisfaction, and partially mediated the relationship between employee age and performance. Taken together, these studies provide an interesting account of how both leader and follower age impact work outcomes through LMX. However, both of these studies were limited by cross-sectional designs and single-source data, perhaps inflating the relationship between the mediator (LMX) and the antecedents and outcomes.

Interaction of Leader Age with Other Variables on the Leader Relationship

A more compelling possibility is that age interacts other variables (either characteristics of the leader or of the follower) to affect the dyadic relationship. One study, although not strictly related to LMX, illustrates the impact of leader age on aspects of the organization. Zacher and Gielnik (2012) examined the effects of CEO attitudes on the age culture of an organization. Specifically, using a sample of 66 small and medium-sized organizations and 274 employees, they found that CEO age was related to a positive age culture when CEOs had a more positive attitude toward older workers. For CEOs with a less positive attitude, the relationship between CEO age and organizational age culture was nonsignificant. Given the importance of age climate to organizational outcomes such as turnover and productivity (e.g., Boehm, Kunze, & Bruck, in press; Kunze, Boehm, & Bruch, 2011), these findings point to the importance of leader age and attitudes in impacting the organization.

A second study by Zacher, Rosing, and Frese (2011) examined the interaction of age with a leader's "legacy beliefs" (the belief that one's work and actions will have a lasting impact on future generations) on leadership effectiveness. They used a sample of 106 German university professors and their research assistants to see the combined effects of leader legacy beliefs and age on leader effectiveness. Age was positively related to legacy beliefs such that the older a worker was, the more he or she felt that actions would have a lasting impact. But perhaps more interesting, older leaders with high legacy beliefs were rated as being more effective by their followers than those low in legacy beliefs. This bodes well for understanding not just whether age affects subordinates' perceptions of leader effectiveness, but also which characteristics make older leaders more or less effective.

Another study demonstrated that leader age may also interact with subordinate characteristics, namely, subordinate beliefs and stereotypes, to affect follower perceptions of the leader–follower relationship. Although not directly examining the effects of age on LMX, Zacher and Bal (2012) provide an example of how leader age *may* impact relationship quality. Using a sample of 128 professors and their research assistants—a case where there can be considerable differences in age between the leader and the follower—Zacher and Bal looked at whether leader age affected leader age-related work concerns (e.g., less interest in research; more awareness of exit) which in turn might affect research assistant ratings of passive–avoidant leadership and proactive leadership. They found that this mediated relationship was not supported. Instead, however, they found that leader age interacted with follower age stereotypes to affect follower perceptions, such that leader age only had detrimental effects on follower ratings of proactive leadership and passive–avoidant leadership when the follower had negative age stereotypes. In other words, individual followers only seemed to have negative views of their older leaders when they held negative age stereotypes themselves. This particular study suggests that not only leader characteristics but follower characteristics as well should be examined for its interactive effects with age on the LMX relationship.

Zacher, Rosing, Henning, and Frese (2011) examined the interactive effects of leader age with leader generativity, or the extent to which the leader establishes and guides members of future generations, and the key mediating role played by LMX. Using a sample of 128 university professors (leaders), each matched with one research assistant (follower), they found that leader age was related to leader generativity as rated by the research assistants, and that leader age was also negatively related to leader effectiveness. However, generativity moderated the effects of leader age, such that older leaders high in generativity showed little decrease in effectiveness. In other words, older leaders perceived to be high in generativity were about as effective as younger leaders. A key for LMX research is the finding that subordinate-rated LMX mediated the effects of this interaction. More specifically, the combined influence of supervisor age and generativity on leader effectiveness happened through LMX. In short, this study provides a deeper understanding of how age interacts with other characteristics to shape leader effectiveness. Moreover, it shows that characteristics sometimes associated with age (in this case, generativity) can actually interact with age. Finally, it shows how LMX can be an important mechanism to explain how this affects leader effectiveness.

Perhaps the complexity of interactions between leader and follower demographics and LMX is best shown in a study by Nishii and Mayer (2009). They examined the combined effects of demographic diversity and LMX, as well as LMX differentiation (the extent to which subordinates perceive varied leader–member relationships across their team), on turnover in 348 supermarket departments. They found evidence for a three-way interaction, such that there was only a significant interaction between demographic diversity and LMX differentiation when the LMX mean was high. Note, however, that the diversity variable was a combination of multiple demographics—age, gender, tenure, and ethnicity—such that the specific effects of age diversity could not be examined. However, these findings do show that demographic differences may play a role in LMX relationships. It is also possible that different levels of age differences between leaders and different subordinates in the group may play a role in LMX differentiation, although this is an area for future research. Most important, however, is that this study further illustrates that we might need to look less for simple age effects on LMX and more at the combination of age with LMX and with other variables.

Leader Age: Surface versus Deep Characteristics

As previously mentioned, some research has suggested that over time, demographic variables may become less salient in impacting attitudes and relationships. A number of authors have noted the importance of differentiating surface characteristics (in the case of the present discussion, age) from deep characteristics (see Harrison et al., 1998; Harrison et al., 2002) such as leadership skills. Harrison and colleagues (1998, 2002) have argued that surface demographic differences such as gender, ethnicity, and age are less likely to be problematic in groups or teams where people come to know each other in deeper ways (e.g., personality), as opposed to in situations where people do not know each other as well (e.g., in selection interview situations).

For these reasons, Klein and Wang (2010) argue that it is easily possible (and incorrect) for researchers to conflate two such characteristics (e.g., age and a particular leader behavior) simply because they may covary. For example, just because older leaders tend to exhibit certain leader characteristics (e.g., generativity), it doesn't mean that all older leaders will do so; in fact, there may be quite a bit of variability among older and younger leaders. The study by Zacher et al. (2011) described above is a good case in point: Although age was correlated with generativity, it was really the combined, interactive effects of age and generativity that impacted leader effectiveness.

Walter and Scheibe (2013) provide a detailed review of the literature on leader age and leader behavior and outcomes, presenting an emotion-based conceptual model that may help provide boundary conditions for *when* leader age matters. Specifically, they argue that the effects of leader age on leader behaviors and outcomes may be moderated by the leader's functional age (continued availability of physical and cognitive resources; Sterns & Scheibe, 1995) and psychosocial age (subjective perceptions of one's own age; Sterns & Miklos, 1995), as well as the cognitive and emotional demands of the particular work context. In short, the conceptual work presented by Walter and Scheibe (2013) has set the stage for a greater understanding of when leader age may affect leader behavior and the LMX relationship.

Summary

There has been relatively little work that specifically examines the effects of leader age on actual LMX, although several studies have examined age differences regarding dyadic relationship quality. Studies suggest that within groups and teams, age alone may not always have a strong effect on the supervisor–subordinate dyad. In fact, the effects of a surface characteristic such as age in the relationship may be attenuated over time, as members learn more important things about the leader and each other beyond their demographic characteristics. Further, a number of studies have shown that age may interact with other perceptions and characteristics of the leader and the follower to affect leader effectiveness, and recent models hold promise for understanding the boundary conditions within which leader age will matter.

Age-Related Changes That May Affect the LMX Relationship

Although relatively little research has been done to examine the effects of age on LMX, much theoretical and empirical work has been done to uncover the influence of age on work attitudes, behaviors, and motivation. This literature begins to provide some insight into *when* and *why* leader and employee age may be an important determinant of the quality of the leader–member relationship, which can then inform research in this area. In this section we discuss the application of several developmental theories to the workplace, exploring how the tenets of each may impact the development and maintenance of LMX. We also demonstrate how contextual variables, such as stereotypes, organizational climate, and employee and leader perceptions could influence the quality of the leader–member relationship. We identify research questions related to LMX as we examine these topics (see Table 21.1 for a summary of these).

Age and Changes in Personality

Although personality is generally considered to be stable, research also shows that there are significant changes in personality with age. For example, many dimensions of conscientiousness increase through adulthood, while neuroticism tends to decrease (e.g., Roberts, Walton, & Vichtbauer, 2006.) Relatedly, there is evidence that older persons may be better at emotion regulation (e.g., Blanchard-Fields, 2007; Carstensen, 1992; Scheibe & Zacher, in press). It is important to note, however, that while there may be some within-individual changes in personality,

Table 21.1. Streams for future research as to how LMX may be affected by leader and subordinate chronological age or age differences.

Empirical Finding or Theory Related to Age	Questions for LMX Research
Age-Related Changes	
Personality changes	• Do personality differences better prepare older and younger people for their roles as leaders and followers? • What is expected of different age groups in a leadership role? • Do differences in emotion regulation better prepare older people for leadership?
Age-related changes in motivation	• Do age-related differences in motivation (intrinsic/extrinsic, generativity motives) impact the LMX relationship? • Do differences in generational values affect LMX?
Lifespan Development Theories	
Selection, optimization, and compensation	• How do SOC strategies on the part of leaders or followers enhance (or hurt) the LMX relationship? • How might SOC-oriented interventions improve the leader dyad, especially for older leaders?
Socioemotional selectivity theory	• How do the aspirations of younger leaders (e.g., toward advancement) affect their subordinates and the quality of the leader–member relationship? • How do age differences within a dyad (with corresponding differences in the goals) affect LMX relationships?
Age Perceptions and Stereotyping	
Stereotypes of older and younger workers	• How do age stereotypes affect the expectations of an older or younger leaders and followers? • Do age stereotypes affect LMX once leaders and subordinates work with each other over time and come to know each other (cf., Harrison et al., 2002)? • How do "meta-stereotypes" regarding age affect the LMX relationship? • What is "old" or "young" for a leader in one profession versus another?
Organizational climate and age	• What are the effects of group or organizational age climate on the leader–member relationship?
Teams and age diversity	• What are the moderators that determine when age differences affect LMX? • Can organizations encourage positive intergenerational contact? Can we develop successful interventions?
Relative age and career timetables	• What are the career timetables for different jobs and how does this affect expectations of leader age and appropriate age differences between members and followers (including direction), and the LMX dyad? • Are career timetables changing? • Are there cultural differences in terms of career timetables and leader age expectations?

there is still considerable variability in personality for a given age group. Interestingly, research has also found that older and younger people (e.g., Wood & Roberts, 2006) and older workers specifically (Bertolino, Truxillo, & Fraccaroli, 2013; Truxillo, McCune, Bertolino, & Fraccaroli, 2012) are actually perceived to differ in terms of their personality. An important research issue, then, is whether these personality differences may better prepare older and younger people for their roles as leaders and followers, and what is expected of different age groups in these roles. Whether such differences result in the development of differential relationships between subordinates and leaders in different age groups is another issue to explore: deep-level differences such as personality that covary with age may better explain differences in leader behavior than a surface-level characteristic such as age by itself (see Klein & Wang, 2010).

Age-Related Changes in Motivation

The relationship between age and work motivation is complex, with increases in some types of motivation and decreases in others. In one study, Kanfer and Ackerman (2000) found that for 228 adults completing the Motivational Trait Questionnaire, age had a negative relationship with task mastery, other-referenced goals, and competitiveness. However, there were several motivational constructs such as emotionality, job absorption, and social potency that did not carry this negative relationship. Although some research has uncovered little to no variation across age groups in terms of work motivation (e.g., Jurkiewicz & Brown, 1998; Wong, Gardiner, Lang, & Coulon, 2008), a recent meta-analysis identified some differences across different age groups. Kooij et al. (2011) found that age was positively related to intrinsic motives (e.g., accomplishment, autonomy), but negatively related to extrinsic motives (e.g., compensation, promotion). Although such differences may be due to the development and experiences of older workers, other research by Twenge, Campbell, Hoffman, and Lance (2010) also suggests the existence of generational differences, with baby boomers (those born between 1946 and 1964) endorsing more intrinsic values and millennials (those born after 1982) endorsing more extrinsic values. The effects of any differences in generational values should be examined for effects on LMX.

Kanfer and Ackerman (2004) developed a model of aging and motivation that may help to explain age-related changes in motivation. They posited that as individuals age they experience loss, growth, reorganization, and exchange. Older adults may lose fluid intelligence abilities that allow them to quickly retain new information, but they tend to gain crystallized intelligence through their knowledge and experience. These losses and gains likely influence how individuals direct and focus their efforts (reorganization and exchange), such that older employees may have different motivations than their younger counterparts. Moreover, Kanfer and Ackerman point out that generativity motives (McAdams, St. Aubin, & Logan, 1993), or a focus on the next generation, begins in middle age. (Subsequent sections of this chapter will describe developmental theories that explain specifically how motivation changes across the lifespan.)

Although few studies have empirically explored the link between work motivation, age, and LMX, motivation differences may help explain the development of the LMX dyad. For example, Social Identity Theory (Brown, 2000; Tajfel & Turner, 1986) suggests that individuals have better attitudes and outcomes when working with someone with whom they relate, including the sharing of similar values. Because individuals' motivation changes over the lifespan, it is possible that wide variations in age within the leader–member dyad will negatively affect perceptions of LMX. Indeed, Ellemers, de Gilder, and Haslam (2004) proposed that factors that set a leader apart from his or her followers are likely to undermine leadership effectiveness and spur negative follower attitudes. In short, however, more research is needed to uncover whether age-related differences in motivation impact the LMX relationship. The previously mentioned study conducted by Zacher et al. (2011) shows the promise of this approach: Older leaders were able to maintain their leadership success when they had high generativity motives, and LMX actually mediated this effect.

Lifespan Development Theories

Lifespan development theories have developed to explain how people adapt to age-related changes, such as losses and gains, over time. These theories have also been applied to the workplace and may help to explain how age can factor into the dyadic relationship.

Selection, optimization, and compensation. Selection, optimization, and compensation theory (SOC theory; Baltes & Baltes, 1990; Baltes, 1987; 1997) suggests that as individuals age, they experience losses that compel them to reorganize their goal structures and behave in ways that allow them to select, optimize, and compensate according to these goal structures (Baltes & Baltes, 1990; Baltes, 1997). An individual that engages in *selection* chooses the direction of his or her goals and efforts in a systematic way, whether this decision is impacted by preference (elective selection) or necessitated by loss of resources (loss-based selection). An individual engaging in *optimization* allocates internal and external resources toward achieving improved functioning in those selected goals. An individual engaging in *compensation* substitutes processes to counteract losses impacting functioning in selected goals (Baltes & Heydens-Gahir, 2003; Freund & Baltes, 1998). An individual engaging in all three strategies will adaptively select goal structures, direct effort, and maintain functioning in the domains they perceive as important and most likely to lead to success (Freund & Baltes, 1998). As a simplified example, an aging construction worker might decide to focus on skills at which he can still maintain peak performance such as supervisory (nonphysical) skills (selection), look to ways to maximize his supervisory skills such as through development opportunities (optimization), and find ways to deal with any physical limitations, such as the use of special equipment (compensation).

Research has shown support for SOC theory. Indeed, with the exception of much older adults who likely have less control over biological and physical losses, individuals tend to exhibit more SOC behaviors as they age (Freund & Baltes, 1998; Freund & Baltes, 2002). Research has also shown that effective use of SOC behaviors and strategies is associated with more successful aging. For instance, Freund and Baltes (1998; 2002) showed that individuals engaging in SOC behaviors tend to have greater subjective well-being, more positive emotions, and a greater absence of loneliness than individuals not engaging in these behaviors.

Individuals who effectively use SOC strategies are able to engage in goal management activities that allow them to better adapt to change and workplace environmental constraints as they age (Zacher & Frese, 2011). Environmental and social constraints in the workplace are particularly salient for aging employees as they are consistently called upon to manage work and family responsibilities along with physical, cognitive, and health declines (Baltes & Heydens-Gahir, 2003; Ng & Feldman, 2008; 2010). Behaviors indicating effective use of SOC strategies at work (e.g., adapting to change, scheduling of time and energy, or using the help of others) predict a wealth of positive work- and relationship-related outcomes. Baltes and Heydens-Gahir (2003) found that the use of SOC strategies in both the work and family domains tended to lower stress in each domain, reducing work–family conflict. Research has also shown that SOC behaviors predicted unique variance in job performance (Bajor & Baltes, 2003) and global and work-specific well-being (e.g., Weise, Freund, & Baltes, 2000; Weise, Freund, & Baltes, 2002). SOC behaviors have also been shown to influence work motivation, with use of SOC strategies predicting greater focus on new goals, options, and possibilities ("focus on opportunities") in one's career, particularly for older adults (Zacher & Frese, 2011). Interestingly, research has found SOC strategies among older workers do not seem to negatively affect coworkers (i.e., by forcing them to take on additional tasks) but may have a positive impact on older workers' task performance (Weigl, Mueller, & Paoli, 2013).

Although some researchers have explored the possibility of applying SOC theory to leadership training and development (e.g., Mumford, Hunter, Eubanks, Bedell, & Murphy, 2007; Mumford & Manley, 2003), virtually no research has examined the link between SOC behaviors and the LMX dyad. However, given the positive outcomes for workers applying SOC strategies at work (e.g., Bajor & Baltes, 2003; Weise et al., 2000; Weise et al., 2002; Zacher & Frese, 2011), further research should examine how such strategies on the part of leaders and followers might enhance the LMX relationship, as well as how SOC-oriented interventions might improve the leader–member dyad, particularly for older leaders.

Socioemotional selectivity theory. While the validity of SOC theory has been demonstrated, the theory does little to explain or predict the types of goals older versus younger individuals will select. Socioemotional Selectivity Theory (SST; Carstensen, 1991; 1992) utilizes a time perspective framework to explain why older individuals are likely to select goals that create positive emotions and stronger social bonds, while younger individuals are likely to select goals centered around learning and future opportunities. Specifically, SST suggests that individuals tend to perceive time according to how much time they believe they have left in life. Younger individuals, who perceive time to be open-ended, tend to adopt a future-oriented perspective and focus on goals that promote their learning and advancement. Conversely, older adults, who perceive less time remaining, tend to adopt a present-focused perspective and focus on emotional regulation and the development and maintenance of meaningful social relationships.

Organizational studies have shown evidence of SST in the workplace, with older employees tending to exhibit more organizational citizenship behavior (Ng & Feldman, 2008) and generally exhibiting better attitudes toward others at work and work in general (Ng & Feldman, 2010). In the service industry, older workers have been found to use more "deep acting" and expression of felt emotions in dealing with customers, partially due to their increased likelihood to have greater trait positive affect than their younger counterparts (Dahling & Perez, 2010). In their comprehensive meta-analysis, Kooji, de Lange, Jansen, Kanfer, and Dikkers (2011) found a positive relationship between employee age and intrinsic work motivations, and a negative relationship between employee age and growth and extrinsic work motivations. Taken together, these studies indicate that individuals who are closer to the end of their working lives tend to exhibit the emotionally and socially focused goals of older individuals as posited by SST.

Very little research has examined the impact of socioemotional goals on the functioning and quality of a leader–subordinate relationship. However, as previously mentioned, some work has been done on investigating the impact of leader generativity on the LMX relationship (Zacher et al., 2011). While these findings offer some insight into how the aspirations of older leaders may impact LMX, much more is needed on SST behaviors and their effects within the supervisor–subordinate dyad. For example, little is known about how the aspirations of younger leaders (e.g., toward advancement) may affect their subordinates and the quality of the leader–member relationship, or how age differences within a dyad (with corresponding differences in the goals) may affect LMX relationships. An interesting research question, then, is how differences in SST behaviors might affect LMX quality and its outcomes.

Stereotyping and Other Age-Related Perceptions

Stereotypes of older and younger workers. One of the larger areas of research on the aging workforce is the examination of stereotypes of older and younger workers. A number of negative stereotypes have been attributed to older workers, including the pervasive idea that they are resistant to change and are more costly than their younger counterparts (e.g., Posthuma & Campion, 2009). This may lead to more negative HR decisions about them (Bal, Reiss, Baltes, & Rudolph, 2011). In addition, younger raters may hold more negative stereotypes of the performance of older workers (Finkelstein, Burke, & Raju, 1995). However, except for a decreased desire to learn, most negative older worker stereotypes have been shown to be untrue (Ng & Feldman, 2012). In addition, the stereotypes of older workers are sometimes positive and may be changing: Whereas earlier studies generally found more negative older worker stereotypes (e.g., Rosen & Jerdee, 1976), recent replications have found that there can be some positive older worker stereotypes as well (Weiss & Maurer, 2004), perhaps due to the aging of the baby boomer generation and greater familiarity with older people

in the workplace. Moreover, raters of all ages view older workers to be more conscientious, less neurotic, and higher in OCBs than younger workers (e.g., Bertolino et al., 2013; Truxillo et al., 2012), although the age of the evaluator plays a moderating role as well, which they explained as a type of intergroup bias. For example, Bertolino et al. (2013) found that while all respondents perceived older workers as more conscientious than younger workers, this was especially pronounced among older respondents. Finally, jobs can carry their own age stereotypes, such that certain types of jobs and professions are associated with certain age groups (e.g., older persons selling stamps and coins versus younger persons selling CDs, records, and tapes; Perry, Kulik, & Bourhis, 1996).

A recent topic with potential relevance to perceptions of older and younger leaders and their effects on leader behavior is the examination of meta-stereotypes (Vorauer & Kumhyr, 2001), or how different age groups perceive that that are seen by other age groups. Finkelstein, Ryan, and King (2012) found evidence that workers of different age groups may believe (often inaccurately) that coworkers in other age groups hold negative perceptions about them. Although the study of meta-stereotypes is relatively new in the context of the workplace, it raises another factor that may affect relations among different age groups at work.

At this point, there has been little research that directly addresses the effects of age stereotypes on LMX relationships. However, given the different ways older and younger workers may be perceived, there may be considerable differences in the expectations of an older or younger leader. Moreover, leaders themselves may hold different stereotypes of older and younger subordinates, leading to differential relationship quality and outcomes. However, one question that remains is the lasting effects of such age stereotypes once leaders and subordinates work with each other over time and come to know each other (cf., Harrison et al., 2002). In addition, what is considered "old" or "young" in one profession may not be in another (Perry et al., 1996.) For this reason, any examination of how age differences within a dyad affect LMX should consider the particular profession as a boundary condition.

Organizational climate and age. Another factor that may impact how employees perceive and react to age diversity within their own organizations is age climate. Organizational climate in general refers to shared perceptions among employees regarding some aspect of organizational functioning. Diversity climate in particular has been noted as an important area of study as the demographic composition of the workforce shifts (Kossek & Zonia, 1993). Diversity climate refers to shared perceptions among workers regarding the value the organization places on diversity, or the extent to which its policies and procedures fairly integrate underrepresented employees (McKay, Avery, & Morris, 2008). Research has shown that positive diversity climate promotes positive diversity-focused attitudes, and vice versa (McKay et al., 2008).

Pertinent to the LMX dyad, researchers have explored age diversity climate in particular as a predictor for age-related outcomes at work. Age diversity climate refers broadly to employees' shared perceptions of the value organizations place on different ages in the workforce, or perceptions of the fairness of organizational actions, procedures, and behaviors toward different age groups (Kunze et al., 2011). Organizations that send positive messages regarding the collaboration of individuals of different ages (through, for instance, job assignments, and performance evaluations) are likely to see better age-related outcomes and attitudes from their employees. However, these organizations will need to overcome significant challenges in employee perceptions and cognitions. Hertel and colleagues (2013) suggested that organizations need to develop processes to address ingroup favoritism, age norms, age discrimination, differences in communication styles, and age diversity attitudes in order to benefit from greater age diversity within teams. Indeed, Kunze and colleagues (2011) found that greater age diversity in organizations tends to predict greater age discrimination among employees, subsequently resulting in reduced affective commitment and firm performance. More recently, Boehm and colleagues (in press) examined the effects of age diversity climate across 93 German organizations and using multisource data. They found that age diversity in terms of perceived support for workers of all ages affected both organizational performance and turnover intentions through its effects on the collective perceptions of social exchange.

Although researchers have examined the impact of support climate, innovation climate (Tordera, Gonzalez-Roma, & Peiro, 2008), safety climate (Hofmann, Morgeson, & Gerras, 2003), empowerment climate (Chen, Lam, & Zhong, 2007), and affective climate (Tse, Dasborough, & Ashkanasy, 2008) and on LMX, very little research has examined age climate in particular as an important leader–member relationship construct. Studies have shown that leaders can impact diverse work groups through LMX, such that leaders promoting higher LMX among their diverse work teams can impact lower turnover rates (Nishii & Mayer, 2009) and better performance (Stewart & Johnson, 2009). However, no research to date has examined the opposite path, namely, the direct impact of age climate on the development and maintenance of LMX relationships. It is possible that in conjunction with the processes described in the developmental theories described in the preceding sections, age climate—either within the group or within the larger organization—has a strong effect on the extent to which individuals perceive a differently aged supervisor either negatively or as a valuable interpersonal asset.

Teams and age diversity. As mentioned earlier, one area that offers insights for understanding age and LMX is the examination of age and other team demographics and how these impact team effectiveness and functioning. First, individuals' age-based attitudes toward coworkers may mirror their age-based attitudes toward their supervisors to some extent (e.g., Liden, Wayne, & Sparrowe, 2000). Second, in many industries and organizations the concept of "leader" is changing—project managers, matrix managers, and emergent leaders can all be conceptualized as leaders in the LMX framework (Day, Gronn, & Salas, 2006) and work has begun to examine the role of having multiple leaders under such situations (Vidyarthi, Erdogan, Anand, Liden, & Chaudhry, in press).

Demographically based team research has sometimes used the lens of relational demography, based on the attraction–similarity paradigm, which suggests that the more similar people are, the higher the degree of attraction between them (Riordan, 2000). This suggests that people who are more similar to their coworkers in terms of demographic attributes such as age should have more positive attitudes toward those coworkers. A number of studies have found that increased group diversity in terms of age, tenure, education, sex, and race was associated with negative outcomes such as lower group attachment and perceived productivity and increased conflict and aggression (e.g., Drach-Zachary & Trogan, 2013; Pelled, 1996; Tsui, Egan, & O'Reilly, 1992).

As noted earlier, the evidence for the leader–subordinate dyad is mixed. Dyadic differences in factors such as age, gender, race, education, and company and job tenure have been linked to lower supervisor-administered performance ratings and supervisor liking of employees and higher employee role ambiguity (Tsui & O'Reilly, 1989), and decreased employee trust (Farh, Tsui, Xin, & Cheng, 1998). However, Perry et al. (1996) found that subordinates who were older than their immediate supervisor exhibited lower turnover and higher OCBs. Indeed, the relationship between demography and attitudinal outcomes may be more complex than simple similarities and differences (e.g., Geddes & Konrad, 2003; Lawrence, 1984; Tsui et al., 1992), and the negative effects of demographic differences may be reduced over time as team members come to know each other (Harrison et al., 1998; 2002).

Some team research has shown that while demographic similarity is important in predicting individual attitudes, this may be more or less salient depending on the situation. For instance, Timmerman (2000) examined the relationship between age diversity, racial diversity, and team performance in two settings with very different requirements for member interaction—basketball teams, requiring high interdependence for task completion, and baseball teams, requiring relatively low interdependence. Using archival data, this study showed that after controlling for team ability, age and racial diversity were negatively associated with team performance only when interdependence was high. These demographic disparities were unrelated to team performance when team interdependence was low. In their meta-analytic review, Bell, Villardo, Lukasik, Belau, and Briggs (2011) found that age diversity did not predict team performance when other demographic variables, such as functional and educational background, were taken into account.

Taken together, these studies indicate that researchers have not thoroughly plumbed the impact that age diversity has on work teams or on leader–member relationships. However, the relational demography literature does indicate the possibility of negative LMX outcomes in age-disparate leader–member dyads, at least under certain circumstances. One area for future research would be to examine *when* leader–member age differences affect outcomes. For example, it has been noted that demographic "faultlines" within teams may develop depending on the task at hand or during a task when a demographic difference is particularly salient (e.g., Jackson & Joshi, 2011.) The development of negative outcomes as a result of age differences between leaders and followers should be examined for moderators, that is, when such age differences may lead

to positive or negative outcomes. Iweins, Desmette, Yzerbyt, and Stinglhamber (2013) note that the encouragement of positive intergenerational contact within organizations may help to reduce negative results of in-group–out-group differences. The Iweins et al. study provides hope for interventions that may reduce the negative effects of age differences, both within a leader–member dyad and within organizations as a whole—a fruitful avenue for future research.

Relative age and career timetables. Inconsistent findings in relational demography research (e.g., Epitropaki & Martin, 1999; Perry et al., 1999; Schaffer & Riordan, 2013) have led to the examination of other ways in which demography impacts workplace outcomes. Such research has been extended to account for the possibility that demographic differences *in a certain direction* may have greater effects on individual attitudes and outcomes than general demographic differences.

Lawrence (1984) suggested that people form implicit timetables of normal career progression and tend to judge careers as being on or off schedule according to these perceptions. While these perceptions are not always accurate, they have been shown to influence employee work attitudes. For instance, perceptions of the adequacy of one's career stage have been linked to career and work motivation (Noe, Noe, & Bachhuber, 1990) and job satisfaction (Lawrence, 1984). Lawrence (1984) found that managers who perceived themselves as being "behind" in terms of their career progression experienced more negative work attitudes and were less oriented toward work, regardless of the accuracy of those perceptions. Not surprisingly, the most common marker by which people determine normal career progression is chronological age (Lawrence, 1984; Sofer, 1970), and research has shown that jobs often have an "age norm" associated with them (Perry et al., 1999). Further, Implicit Leadership Theories (ILT), which states that people possess implicit ideas of what a leader should be (Lord, DeVader, & Alliger, 1986; Lord, Foti, & DeVader, 1984; Offermann, Kennedy, & Wirtz, 1994), may also help to explain and predict how relatively younger or older supervisors will impact LMX.

For these reasons, researchers have begun focusing more directly on directional age differences within supervisor–subordinate dyads. Where the study of general age differences calls for an examination of the degree of difference or similarity in supervisor and subordinate ages (operationalized, for instance, as the absolute value of the difference between the two ages, e.g., Perry et al., 1999; Turban & Jones, 1988), studies examining directional age differences have operationalized these by explicitly asking employees to indicate whether they perceive their supervisor as being younger or older than themselves, or by subtracting supervisor chronological age from employee age and exploring patterns occurring on the positive and negative side of the difference (e.g., Perry et al., 1999; Shore, Cleveland, & Goldberg, 2003; Vecchio, 1993). The idea in this line of research is that if people use age as a marker for determining their place on their implicit career timetable, having a younger supervisor in particular should represent a violation thus should result in poorer employee outcomes.

Empirical evidence has largely supported this notion. Shore and colleagues (2003) found that employees who were older than their managers received more negative performance evaluations and fewer opportunities for training and development. Employees with younger managers were also found to have less favorable work attitudes (Shore et al., 2003), despite the generally positive relationship between employee age and job attitudes (Ng & Feldman, 2010). Collins and colleagues (2009) found that across various organizations and industries, older workers tended to have lower expectations of their younger supervisors, and in turn tended to rate younger supervisors' leadership behaviors lower. Although one study suggested that older employees reported better working relationships with younger supervisors and evaluated those supervisors more favorably (Vecchio, 1993), this study was conducted using a sample entirely comprised of high school faculty members, an occupational group in which career progression is not necessarily demarked by age (i.e., having the training and education necessary to become a teacher is not the same as what is necessary to become a principal or superintendent, so career progression does not occur linearly here). Perry and colleagues (1999) found that directional age differences in the dyad (i.e., having a younger supervisor in particular) were associated with greater OCBs and reduced absenteeism. Thus, although the research supports the idea that employees possess implicit age-driven expectations about career progression (Lawrence, 1984) and having a younger supervisor generally violates these expectations, this very likely depends on the type of job and other contextual issues, which is a useful path for future research. We also suggest that as the age diversity of the workplace as well as stereotypes of younger and older workers evolve (e.g., Weiss & Maurer, 2004), the effects of such career timetables and expected age of the leader may evolve over time, and that the LMX literature should examine such changes. Finally research should examine cultural differences in whether age differences in the dyad may affect outcomes.

Conclusion

This is the point in most chapters where authors make recommendations for research and practice. As noted, we have made a number of recommendations for future research, as highlighted throughout our review and shown in Table 1. However, we find it difficult to make confident recommendations for practice at this point given the relatively scant research on the topic of age and LMX. Nevertheless, we do note that to really understand how leader and subordinate age differences may affect LMX, the literature needs to develop a model that specifically addresses not only *if* age differences affect LMX and its outcomes, but *when* (e.g., Zacher et al., 2011) and *why*. In this chapter we have reviewed the literature on age and LMX and a number of theories that may explain how age differences could affect the dyadic relationship and that may help us to uncover when age differences matter in the leader relationship and the underlying mechanisms. We suspect that the growing interest in the aging workforce will continue to spur interest in age as a focal variable in understanding LMX.

References

Bajor, J. K. & Baltes, B. B. (2003). The relationship between selection optimization with compensation, conscientiousness, motivation, and performance. *Journal of Vocational Behavior, 63*, 347–367.

Bal, A. C., Reiss, A. E. B., Rudolph, C. W., & Baltes, B. B. (2011). Examining positive and negative perceptions of older workers: A meta-analysis. *The Journals of Gerontology, Series B: Psychological Sciences and Social Sciences, 66*, 687–698.

Baltes, P. B. (1997). On the incomplete architecture of human ontogeny: Selection, optimization, and compensation as foundation of developmental theory. *American Psychologist, 52*, 366–380.

Baltes, P. B. (1987). Theoretical propositions of life-span developmental psychology: On the dynamics between growth and decline. *Developmental Psychology, 23*, 611–696.

Baltes, P. B. & Baltes, M. M. (1990). Psychological perspectives on successful aging: The model of selective optimization with compensation. In P. B. Baltes and M. M. Baltes (Eds.), *Successful Aging: Perspectives from the behavioral sciences* (pp. 1–34). New York: Cambridge University Press.

Baltes, B. B. & Heydens-Gahir, H. A. (2003). Reduction of work-family conflict through the use of selection, optimization, and compensation behaviors. *Journal of Applied Psychology, 88*, 1005–1018.

Bell, S. T., Villado, A. J., Lukasik, M. A., Belau, L., & Briggs, A. L. (2011). Getting specific about demographic diversity variable and team performance relationships: A meta-analysis. *Journal of Management, 37*, 709–743.

Bertolino, M., Truxillo, D. M., & Fraccaroli, F. (2013). Age effects on perceived personality and job performance. *Journal of Managerial Psychology, 7/8*, 867–885.

Blanchard-Fields, F. (2007). Everyday problem solving and emotion. *Current Directions in Psychological Science, 16*, 26–31.

Boehm, S., Kunze, F., & Bruck, H. (in press). Spotlight on age diversity climate: The impact of age-inclusive HR practices on firm-level outcomes. *Personnel Psychology.*

Brown, R. (2000). Social identity theory: past achievements, current problems and future challenges. *European Journal of Social Psychology, 30*, 745–778.

Carstensen, L. L. (1991). Selectivity theory: Social activity in the life-span context. *Annual Review of Gerontology and Geriatrics, 11*, 195–217.

Carstensen, L. L. (1992). Social and emotional patterns in adulthood: Support for socioemotional selectivity theory. *Psychology and Aging, 7*, 331–338.

Chen, Z., Lam, W., & Zhong, J. A. (2007). Leader-member exchange and member performance: A new look at individual-level negative feedback-seeking behavior and team-level empowerment climate. *Journal of Applied Psychology, 92*, 202–212.

Collins, M. H., Hair, J. F., & Rocco, T. S. (2009). The older-worker-younger supervisor dyad: A test of the Reverse Pygmalion effect. *Human Resource Development Quarterly, 20*, 21–41.

Curl, A. L. & Hokenstad, M. C. T. (2006). Reshaping retirement policies in post-industrial nations: The need for flexibility. *Journal of Sociology and Social Welfare, 23*, 85–106.

Dahling, J. J. & Perez, L. A. (2010). Older worker, different actor? Linking age and emotional labor strategies. *Personality and Individual Differences, 48*, 574–578.

Day, D. V., Gronn, P., & Salas, E. (2006). Leadership in team-based organizations: On the threshold of a new era. *The Leadership Quarterly, 17*, 211–216.

Drach-Zahavy, A. & Trogan, R. (2013). Opposites attract or attack? The moderating role of diversity climate in the team diversity—interpersonal aggression relationship. *Journal of Occupational Health Psychology, 18*, 449–457.

Ellemers, N., de Gilder, D., & Haslam, S. A. (2004). Motivating individuals and groups at work: A social identity perspective on leadership and group performance. *Academy of Management Review, 29*, 459–478.

Epitropaki, O. & Martin, R. (1999). The impact of relational demography on the quality of leader-member exchanges and employee's work attitudes and wellbeing. *Journal of Occupational and Organizational Psychology, 72*, 237–240.

Eurostat (2012, August). Employment statistics. *European Commission.* Downloaded on January 29, 2014 http://epp.eurostat.ec.europa.eu/statistics_explained/index.php/Employment_statistics

Fagenson-Eland, E. A., Baugh, S. G., & Lankau, M. J. (2005). Seeing eye to eye: A dyadic investigation of relational demography on perceptions of mentoring activities. *Career Developmental International, 10*, 460–477.

Farh, J-L., Tsui, A. S., Xin, K., & Cheng, B-S. (1998). The influence of relational demography and guanxi: The Chinese case. *Organization Science, 9*, 471–488.

Finkelstein, L. M., Burke, M. J., & Raju, N. S. (1995). Age discrimination in simulated employment contexts: An integrative analysis. *Journal of Applied Psychology, 80*, 652–663.

Finkelstein, L., Ryan, K., & King, E. B. (2012). Stereotypes and metastereotypes of older, younger, and middle-aged workers. *European Journal of Work and Organizational Psychology.*

Freund, A. M. & Baltes, P. B. (2002). Life-management strategies of selection, optimization, and compensation: Measurement by self-report and construct validity. *Journal of Personality and Social Psychology, 82*, 642–662.

Freund, A. M. & Baltes, P. B. (1998). Selection, optimization, and compensation as strategies of life management: Correlations with subjective indicators of successful aging. *Psychology and Aging, 13*, 531–543.

Geddes, D. & Konrad, A. M. (2003). Demographic differences and reactions to performance feedback. *Human Relations, 56*, 1485–1513.

Gellert, F. J. & Schalk, R. (2012a). Age-related attitudes: The influence on relationships and performance at work. *Journal of Health Organization and Management, 26*, 98–117.

Gellert, F. J., & Schalk, R. (2012b). The influence of age on perceptions of relationship quality and performance in care service work teams. *Employee Relations, 34*, 44–60.

Harrison, D. A., Price, K. H., & Bell, M. P. (1998). Beyond relational demography: Time and the effects of surface- and deep-level diversity on work group cohesion. *Academy of Management Journal, 41*, 96–107.

Harrison, D. A., Price, K. H., Gavin, J. H., & Florey, A. T. (2002). Time, teams, and task performance: Changing effects of surface- and deep-level diversity on group functioning. *Academy of Management Journal, 45*, 1029–1045.

Hertel, G., Van der Heijden, B. I. J. M., de Lange, A. H., & Deller, J. (2013). Facilitating age diversity in organizations—pt. II: managing perceptions and interactions. *Journal of Managerial Psychology, 28*, 857–866.

Hofmann, D. A., Morgeson, F. P., & Gerras, S. J. (2003). Climate as a moderator of the relationship between leader-member exchange and content specific citizenship: Safety climate as an exemplar. *Journal of Applied Psychology, 88*, 170–178.

Iweins, C., Desmette, D., Yzerbyt, V., & Stinglhamber, F. (2013). Ageism at work: The impact of intergenerational contact and organizational multi-age perspective. *European Journal of Work and Organizational Psychology, 22*, 331–346.

Jackson, S. E., & Joshi, A. (2011). Work team diversity. In S. Zedeck (Ed.), *APA Handbook of Industrial and Organizational Psychology*, Vol. 1 (pp. 651–686). Washington, DC: American Psychological Association.

Jurkiewicz, C. L. & Brown, R. G. (1998). General comparisons of public employee motivation. *Review of Public Personnel Administration, 18*, 18–37.

Kanfer, R. & Ackerman, P. L. (2000). Individual differences in work motivation: Further explorations of a trait framework. *Applied Psychology, 49*, 470–482.

Kanfer, R. & Ackerman, P. L. (2004). Aging, adult development, and work motivation. *Academy of Management Review, 29*, 440–458.

Kearney, E. (2008). Age differences between leader and followers as a moderator of the relationship between transformational leadership and team performance. *Journal of Occupational and Organizational Psychology, 81*, 803–811.

Klein, K. M., & Wang, M. (2010). Deep-level diversity and leadership. *American Psychologist, 65*, 932–934.

Kooji, D. T. A. M., De Lange, A. H., Jansen, P. G. W., Kanfer, R., & Dikkers, J. S. E. (2011). Age and work-related motives: Results of a meta-analysis. *Journal of Organizational Behavior, 32,* 197–225.

Kossek, E. E. & Zonia, S. C. (1993). Assessing diversity climate: A field study of reactions to employer efforts to promote diversity. *Journal of Organizational Behavior, 14,* 61–81.

Kunze, F., Boehm, S. A., & Bruch, H. (2011). Age diversity, age discrimination climate and performance consequences—a cross organizational study. *Journal of Organizational Behavior, 32,* 264–290.

Lawrence, B. S. (1984). Age grading: The implicit organizational timetable. *Journal of Organizational Behavior, 5,* 23–35.

Liden, R. C., Stilwell, D., & Ferris, G. (1996). The effects of supervisor and subordinate age on objective performance and subjective performance ratings. *Human Relations, 49,* 327–347.

Liden, R. C., Wayne, S. J., & Sparrowe, R. T. (2000). An examination of the mediating role of psychological empowerment on the relations between the job, interpersonal relationships, and work outcomes. *Journal of Applied Psychology, 85,* 407–416.

Liebold, M. & Voepel, S. (2006). Managing the aging workforce: Challenges and solutions. Germany: Wiley Publishing.

Lord, R. G., De Vader, C. L., & Alliger, G. M. (1986). A meta-analysis of the relation between personality traits and leadership perceptions: An application of validity generalization procedures. *Journal of Applied Psychology, 71,* 402–410.

Lord, R. G., Foti, R. J., & DeVader, C. L. (1984). A test of leadership categorization theory: Internal structure, information processing, and leadership perceptions. *Organizational Behavior and Human Performance, 34,* 343–378.

McAdams, D. P., de St. Aubin, E., & Logan, R. L. (1993). Generativity among young, midlife, and older adults. *Psychology and Aging, 8,* 221–230.

McKay, P. F., Avery, D. R., & Morris, M. A. (2008). Mean racial-ethnic differences in employee sales performance: The moderating role of diversity climate. *Personnel Psychology, 61,* 349–374.

Moen, P. (2012). Retirement dilemmas and decisions. In J. W. Hedge and W. C. Borman (Eds.), *The Oxford Handbook of Work and Aging.* New York, NY: Oxford.

Mor-Barak, M. E. (2011). Managing diversity: Toward a globally inclusive workplace (2nd ed.) Thousand Oaks, CA: Sage Publishing.

Mumford, M. D., Hunter, S. T., Eubanks, D. L., Bedell, K. E., & Murphy, S. T. (2007). Developing leaders for creative efforts: A domain-based approach to leadership development. *Human Resource Management Review, 17,* 402–417.

Mumford, M. D. & Manley, G. G. (2003). Putting the developing in leadership development: Implications for theory and practice. In S. E. Murphy and R. E. Riggio (Eds.). *The Future of Leadership Development.* Lawrence Earlbaum, Mahwah, NJ.

Ng, T. W. H., & Feldman, D. C. (2012). Evaluating six common stereotypes about older workers with meta-analytic data. *Personnel Psychology, 65,* 821–858.

Ng., T. W. H. & Feldman, D. C. (2008). The relationship of age to ten dimensions of job performance. *Journal of Applied Psychology, 93,* 392–423.

Ng, T. W. H. & Feldman, D. C. (2010). The relationships of age with job attitudes: A meta-analysis. *Personnel Psychology, 63,* 677–718.

Nishii, L. H. & Mayer, D. M. (2009). Do inclusive leaders help to reduce turnover in diverse groups? The moderating role of leader-member exchange in the diversity to turnover relationship. *Journal of Applied Psychology, 94,* 1412–1426.

Noe, R. A., Noe, A. W., & Bachhuber, J. A. (1990). An investigation of the correlates of career motivation. *Journal of Vocational Behavior, 37,* 340–356.

Offermann, L. R., Kennedy, J. K., & Wirtz, P. W. (1994). Implicit leadership theories: Content, structure, and generalizability. *Leadership Quarterly, 5,* 43–58.

Pelled, L. H. (1996). Relational demography and perceptions of group conflict and performance: A field investigation. *International Journal of Conflict Management, 7,* 230–246.

Perry, E. L., Kulik, C. T., & Bourhis, A. C. (1996). Moderating effects of personal and contextual factors in age discrimination. *Journal of Applied Psychology, 81,* 628–647.

Perry, E. L., Kulik, C. T., & Zhou, J. (1999). A closer look at the effects of subordinate-supervisor age differences. *Journal of Organizational Behavior, 20,* 341–357.

Posthuma, R. A., & Campion, M. A. (2009). Age stereotypes in the workplace: Common stereotypes, moderators, and future research directions. *Journal of Management, 35,* 158–188.

Riordan, C. M. (2000). Relational demography within groups: Past developments, contradictions, and new directions. *Research in Personnel and Human Resources Management, 19,* 131–173.

Roberts, B. W., Walton, K. E., & Viechtbauer, W. (2006). Patterns of mean-level change in personality traits across the life course: A meta-analysis of longitudinal studies. *Psychological Bulletin, 132,* 1–25.

Rosen, B., & Jerdee, T. H. (1976). The nature of job-related age stereotypes. *Journal of Applied Psychology, 61,* 180–183.

Schaffer, B. S. & Riordan, C. M. (2013). Relational demography in supervisor-subordinate dyads: An examination of discrimination and exclusionary treatment. *Canadian Journal of Administrative Sciences, 30,* 3–17.

Scheibe, S., & Zacher, H. (in press). A lifespan perspective on emotion regulation, stress, and well-being in the workplace. In P. Perrewe', J. Halbesleben, & C. Rosen (Eds.), *Research in Occupational Stress and Well Being, Volume 11.* Emerald.

Schriesheim, C. A., Castro, S. L., & Cogliser, C. C. (1999). Leader-member exchange (LMX) research: A comprehensive review of theory, measurement, and data-analytic practices. *Leadership Quarterly, 10,* 63–113.

Shore, L. M., & Bleicken, L. M. (1991). Effects of supervisor age and subordinate age on rating congruence. *Human Relations, 44,* 1093–1105.

Shore, L. M., Cleveland, J. N., & Goldberg, C. B. (2003). Work attitudes and decisions as a function of manager age and employee age. *Journal of Applied Psychology, 88,* 529–537.

Sofer, C. (1970). Men in mid-career: A study of British managers and technical specialists. Great Britain: Cambridge University.

Sterns, H. L., & Miklos, S. M. (1995). The aging worker in a changing environment: Organizational and individual issues. *Journal of Vocational Behavior, 47*(3), 248–268.

Stewart, M. M. & Johnson, O. E. (2009). Leader-member exchange as a moderator of the relationship between work group diversity and team performance. *Group Organization Management, 34,* 507–535.

Tajfel, H. & Turner, J. C. (1986). The social identity theory of intergroup behavior. In S. Worchel & W. G. Austin (Eds.), Psychology of intergroup relationships (pp. 7–24). Chicago: Nelson-Hall.

Timmerman, T. A. (2000). Racial diversity, age diversity, interdependence, and team performance. *Small Group Research, 31,* 592–606.

Toossi, M. (2007). Labor force projections 2016: More workers in their golden years. *Monthly Labor Review, 130*, 33–52.

Toossi, M. (2012). Labor force projections to 2020: A more slowly growing workforce. *Monthly Labor Review, 135*, 43–64.

Tordera, N., Gonzalez-Roma, V., & Peiro, J. M. (2008). The moderator effect of psychological climate on the relationship between leader-member exchange (LMX) quality and role overload. *European Journal of Work and Organizational Psychology, 17*, 55–72.

Truxillo, D. M., McCune, E. A., Bertolino, M., & Fraccaroli, F. (2012). Perceptions of older versus younger workers in terms of big five facets, proactive personality, cognitive ability, and job performance. *Journal of Applied Social Psychology, 42*, 2607–2639.

Tse, H. H. M., Dasborough, M. T., & Ashkanasy, N. M. (2008). A multi-level analysis of team climate and interpersonal exchange relationships at work. *The Leadership Quarterly, 19*, 195–211.

Tsui, A. S., Egan, T. D., & O'Reilly, C. A. (1992). Being different: Relational demography and organizational attachment. *Administrative Science Quarterly, 37*, 549–579.

Tsui, A. S. & O'Reilly, C. A. (1989). Beyond simple demographic effects: The importance of relational demography in superior-subordinate dyads. *Academy of Management Journal, 32*, 402–423.

Turban, D. B. & Jones, A. P. (1988). Supervisor-subordinate similarity: Types, effects, and mechanisms. *Journal of Applied Psychology, 73*, 228–234.

Twenge, J. M., Campbell, S. M., Hoffman, B. J., & Lance, C. E. (2010). Generational differences in work values: Leisure and extrinsic values increasing, social and intrinsic values decreasing. *Journal of Management, 36*, 1117–1142.

Vaupel, J. W. (2010). Biodemography of human aging. *Nature, 464*, 536–542.

Vecchio, R. P. (1993). The impact of differences in subordinate and supervisor age on attitudes and performance. *Psychology and Aging, 8*, 112–119.

Vidyarthi, P., Erdogan, B., Anand, S., Liden, R. C., & Chaudhry, A. (in press). One member, two leaders: Extending leader-member exchange theory to a dual leadership context. *Journal of Applied Psychology*.

Vorauer, J., & Kumhyr, S. (2001). Is this about you or me? Self- versus other-directed judgments and feelings in response to intergroup interaction. *Personality and Social Psychology Bulletin, 27*, 706–719.

Walter, F., & Scheibe, S. (2013). A literature review and emotion-based model of age and leadership: New directions for the trait approach. *Leadership Quarterly, 24*, 882–901.

Weigl, M., Mueller, A., & Paoli, C. (2013). Employees' action strategies for successful ageing at work: SOC strategy use in the eyes of coworkers. Poster presented at the 2013 Age in the Workplace Conference, University of Trento, Italy.

Weise, B. A., Freund, A. M., & Baltes, P. B. (2000). Selection, optimization, and compensation: An action-related approach to work and partnership. *Journal of Vocational Behavior, 57*, 273–300.

Weise, B. S., Freund, A. M., & Baltes, P. B. (2002). Subjective career success and emotional well-being: Longitudinal predictive power of selection, optimization, and compensation. *Journal of Vocational Behavior, 60*, 321–335.

Weiss, E. M., & Maurer, T. J. (2004). Age discrimination in personnel decisions: A reexamination. *Journal of Applied Social Psychology, 34*, 1551–1562.

Wong, M., Gardiner, E., Lang, W., & Coulon, L. (2008). Generational differences in personality and motivation: Do they exist and what are the implications for the workplace? *Journal of Managerial Psychology, 23*, 878–890.

Wood, D., & Roberts, B. W. (2006). The effect of age and role information on expectations for Big Five personality traits. *Personality and Social Psychology Bulletin, 32*, 1482–1496.

Zacher, H., & Bal, M. (2012). Professor age and research assistant ratings of passive-avoidant and proactive leadership: The role of age-related work concerns and age stereotypes. *Studies in Higher Education, 37*, 875–896.

Zacher, H. & Frese, M. (2011). Maintaining a focus on opportunities at work: The interplay between age, job complexity, and the use of selection, optimization, and compensation strategies. *Journal of Organizational Behavior, 32*, 291–318.

Zacher, H., & Gielnik, M. M. (2012). Organisational age cultures: The interplay of chief executive officers' age and attitudes toward younger and older employees. *International Small Business Journal*. [Online download.]

Zacher, H., Rosing, K., & Frese, M. (2011). Age and leadership: The moderating role of legacy beliefs. *Leadership Quarterly, 22*, 43–50.

Zacher, H., Rosing, K., Henning, T., & Frese, M. (2011). Establishing the new generation at work: Leader generativity as a moderator of the relationships between leader age, leader-member exchange, and leadership success. *Psychology and Aging, 26*, 241–252.

Leader–Member Exchange Theory: A Glimpse into the Future

Berrin Erdogan *and* Talya N. Bauer

Abstract

This chapter serves as the conclusion to the edited volume *The Oxford Handbook of Leader–Member Exchange* and provides a path forward for future studies in Leader–Member Exchange (LMX) theory by highlighting important gaps and future avenues of investigation. Recommendations include extending the theoretical foundations of LMX theory beyond role making and social exchange theories, exploring antecedents of LMX by utilizing longitudinal methods and examination of trajectories, integrating the context of new dyad formation, examining outcomes from objective measures or measures that do not rely on manager or self-reports, further exploring the effects of LMX differentiation, social comparison, and social networks, and systematically investigating the degree to which LMX may have a dark side.

Key Words: leader–member exchange, LMX, relational leadership, dyadic leadership, social exchange

In this volume, thought leaders in our field of LMX have taken stock of the major developments in LMX theory over the past four decades. Each chapter in this edited volume contains a targeted summary of research relating LMX theory to a particular topic and provides directions for future research (Figure 22.1). As these chapters serve to attest, LMX theory remains one of the most active, comprehensive, and intensively researched theories of leadership. LMX quality seems to matter for employee job attitudes and behaviors, and it is the primary lens through which employees regard their work environment. Given the number and depth of past studies, it is easy to assume that leader–member relations are now a known quantity. *Is there anything left to be done? Is it time to move on to greener pastures, or are there assumptions to be challenged, questions to be answered, and gaps in the literature to be filled?*

After reading every chapter in this volume and considering the status of the literature, we anticipate just the opposite. It is our conclusion that there are a number of intriguing, theoretically, and practically important research questions that will keep LMX researchers busy over the next decade. In the following pages, we summarize some of the topics that we consider high priorities on the list of issues to be resolved and questions to be investigated. Many of these points were inspired and affirmed by the individual chapters in this volume. It is our hope that after reading the *Oxford Handbook of Leader–Member Exchange* that you are as inspired as we are.

Theoretical Background

To date, social exchange theory and role theory have been the most frequently used theories to explain how LMX quality develops and how employees respond to the quality of their LMXs. According to the role theory perspective (Dienesch & Liden, 1986), LMX quality develops as a result of a negotiated role. Mutual testing of the loyalty and competence of the exchange partner is viewed as key to the development of a high-quality exchange. According to social exchange theory (Wayne, Shore, & Liden, 1997), employees reciprocate the level and quality of support they receive from their leaders by

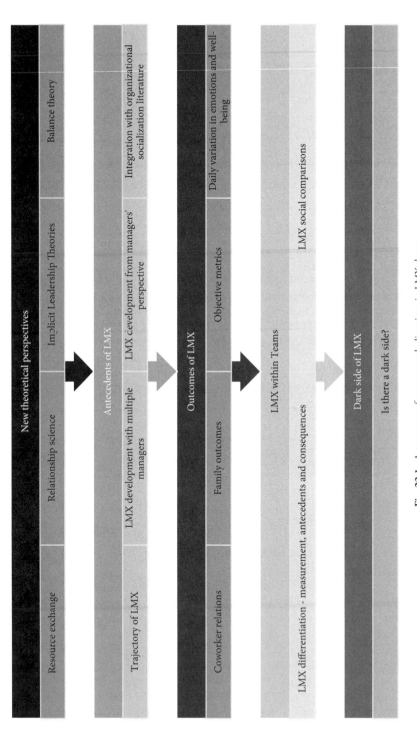

Fig. 22.1. A summary of new research directions in LMX theory.

behaving in ways that benefit the leader directly and indirectly. Although these theoretical bases explain a great deal about the formation of a relationship, we see room for further extension of our understanding of these exchanges. For example, what exactly is exchanged in relationships of different qualities? In this handbook Law-Penrose, Wilson, and Taylor (2015) discussed this important and oft neglected issue. More explicit focus on the resource exchange process should help researchers open up the "black box" of the exchange process. *What resources do employees receive from a high-quality exchange? What do leaders receive? Does resource exchange necessarily begin with the leader, or can employees be the initiators of the relationship by providing resources leaders value? If the leader is merely the provider of organizational resources, does this environment still contribute to the development of a high LMX quality?*

Integration of implicit leadership and followership theories into the LMX literature has been rare; nevertheless, it remains important. Individuals typically hold implicit leader theories (ILT) in their mind, listing the attributes of who they believe is an effective leader and what an effective leader does. The fit between the leader's attributes and employee ILTs will have implications for LMX quality, just as the leader's implicit followership theories, or expected attributes from effective employees, will (Engle & Lord, 1997). Scholars have theorized about the integration of ILT literature with LMX literature (e.g., Epitropaki & Martin, 2005; Thomas, Martin, Epitropaki, Guillaume, & Lee, 2013; van Gils, van Quaquebeke, & van Knippenberg, 2010), and more work in this area would be beneficial. Furthermore, in addition to the leadership and followership prototypes, the prototypicality of the leader for the group as predicted by social identity theory of leadership would have implications for LMX development. Epitropaki and Martin (2015) discussed potential ways in which the social identity theory of leadership developed by Hogg and colleagues (2005) may be integrated into LMX research.

Heider's (1958) balance theory is another theoretical perspective with important implications for LMX theory. The theory predicts that when one person likes another person, that person will seek alignment between their own attitudes and values and those of the other person, which has implications for the process of LMX development. When a new employee joins an organization, his or her exchange quality with the leader will likely be affected by co-worker opinions about the employee and the quality of the exchange between the leader and existing employees. Thus, it will be unlikely for a leader to develop a high LMX relationship with a newcomer if current employees who have a high LMX relationship with the leader dislike the newcomer. Balance theory suggests that factors other than social exchange and role making operate in leader–member exchanges.

Finally, the LMX literature would benefit from explicit consideration and integration with perspectives from relationship science. Epitropaki and Martin proposed in their chapter that cross-fertilization with findings and theories of relationship science will move the LMX literature forward, and Thomas et al. (2013) discussed the connections between relationship science and LMX theory, which we believe has important implications for future research in this area. Processes such as social comparisons, attachment styles, and relationship prototypes can enrich the LMX literature and introduce further research questions.

Antecedents of LMX Quality

How do high-quality exchanges between leaders and employees develop? As Nahrgang and Seo (2015), as well as Schyns (2015), summarized in their chapters, this research topic has received much attention, yet it remains a fertile ground for future research. A key limitation of past research has been the cross-sectional designs and examining established instead of new dyads. To answer the question of how LMX develops, it is important to identify and examine new dyads early in the life of the relationship. Such studies are still extremely rare (for exceptions, see Bauer & Green, 1996; Liden, Wayne, & Stilwell, 1993). Furthermore, fully answering the question of how LMX develops requires researchers to utilize longitudinal approaches and model change in LMX quality over time. This approach has been underutilized to date (with the exception of Nahrgang, Morgeson, & Ilies, 2009). Examining the trajectory of LMX quality over time should help answer interesting and important questions. *What is the trajectory of LMX quality over time? Is the trajectory different for employees with different personalities such that the relationship develops faster for employees with certain personality traits (such as extraversion)? Is the trajectory more sustainable for some employees rather than others?* For example, we already know that influence tactics and impression management relate to LMX quality, as does job performance (Dulebohn, Bommer, Liden, Brouer, & Ferris, 2012), but is it possible that when LMX develops primarily through the work-related efforts of the employee, LMX quality remains positive over time, whereas if it develops primarily as a result of impression management behaviors of employees, LMX develops quickly but is less stable?

In their chapter Day and Mischenko (2015) highlighted the importance of longitudinal research and make the astute observation that leaders change over the course of a career, and the degree to which an employee (or a manager) is able to consistently develop high-quality exchanges with a series of leaders will drive his or her career success and other long-term outcomes. Therefore, in addition to understanding the development of a specific new relationship, it is important to investigate antecedents of a person's ability to establish relationships with multiple leaders, or the degree to which one high-quality exchange can be leveraged into developing a high-quality exchange with the next manager.

We still have limited understanding regarding what helps LMX development from the manager's perspective as opposed to the employee's perspective. Though the literature has often treated LMX quality measured from employees' and managers' perspectives as interchangeable, studies have also shown that LMX reported from these perspectives has little overlap (Liden, Wu, Cao, & Wayne, 2015). If this is the case, then it would seem reasonable to expect that LMX as assessed from the manager's perspective is a fundamentally different concept than LMX measured from the employee's perspective, with a different set of predictors. We believe that examining how LMX quality develops from the manager's perspective is of critical importance.

When investigating the development of LMX quality, it is also important to adopt an organizational socialization perspective (Zhou & Wang, 2015) and integrate the two literatures more fully. A new dyad may form in one of at least three ways: the employee may be new to an existing team, the leader may be new to an existing team, or both the leader and the member may be new to an existing team. Each of the ways in which a new dyad forms will have its unique challenges, and the process may be somewhat different for each variant. Perhaps the most common scenario is the first one, when the employee joins a team with an intact social network in place. In this case, the employee is developing a relationship with the leader as well as with new co-workers. As co-workers form their opinions about the newcomer, their opinions are likely to affect their leader's opinions about the newcomer.

The newcomer will ultimately be absorbed into the existing social network, and perhaps challenge and ultimately change the social network in the aftermath. In the case of a leader being new to a team, LMX development may follow a slightly different process. Because the leader is joining an existing network of employees, he or she will be simultaneously developing relationships with both his or her own supervisor and with all new subordinates. The leader will need to invest in relationship development with several subordinates at the same time and will be under greater time pressure to establish relationships while proving his or her own effectiveness. Finally, the third scenario, although likely uncommon, may facilitate the LMX development process by introducing a point of similarity between the leader and the member, and possibly enhance camaraderie. In short, examining LMX development without regard to the context surrounding the formation of the new dyad potentially misses important distinctions between the influences underlying each scenario.

Another way of conceptualizing LMX development is to consider whether the new dyad is also undergoing a process of organizational socialization. A new dyad may form because either the employee or the manager is a new hire to the organization or because of an internal move. In the case of an internal move, the new dyad may actually be a result of an employee who has been promoted from within the team and is now taking on a supervisory position among former colleagues. Technically, both circumstances produce new dyads, but each brings about its own set of unique challenges. In the case of internal hires, the person (either the leader or the employee) has a reputation, a history, and an existing social network within the organization, which should affect the LMX development process differently from the stranger-to-stranger exchange normally inherent to LMX theories. In other words, assuming that LMX development is a process in which two strangers come together to develop a relationship through a mutual testing process misses the actual richness and nuances possible in the process of relationship development.

Much of what happens before the newcomer is hired into the organization could also have implications for LMX development. If the newcomer is replacing a specific person who has left (as opposed to being hired to fill a new position), the characteristics of the former job incumbent may affect expectations of the new person, and the similarity to the previous employee may affect

LMX development. Factors such as whether the newcomer is hired after interviewing with only the future manager or as a result of a joint decision among co-workers, and whether the newcomer is joining the team after enthusiastic support of the manager or despite the objections of the manager, will likely influence how much support the manager provides to the newcomer, again shaping the entire LMX development process. As a result, we believe that there is much more work to be done with regard to exploring and understanding the process by which leaders and employees develop a high-quality relationship.

Finally, what disrupts a high-quality relationship? In their chapter Nahrgang and Seo (2015) noted the lack of literature addressing this topic as an important research gap. Currently, we know little about what causes changes in relationship quality. *How do psychological contract breaches affect high-quality leader–member relations? If a breach occurs, how is the damage repaired?* The study of breaches within the dyad is a potentially important issue that has received scant research attention (for an exception, see Shapiro, Boss, Salas, Tangirala, & Von Glinow, 2011). Furthermore, an important question we have not yet answered is whether it is possible to deliberately increase LMX quality. Are there behaviors employees or managers may be taught to display within the context of an existing, mature relationship that will improve the relationship quality? For example, we know that leadership style relates to LMX quality (Dulebohn et al., 2012), but is it possible for managers who are trained to display a particular leadership style to actually improve their LMX quality? Such questions have important practical implications and highlight the importance of developing interventions that would improve LMX quality in mature and presumably less malleable relationships.

Outcomes of LMX Quality

At first glance, the outcomes of LMX quality seem well known. As discussed in this volume, LMX quality is related to job attitudes (Epitropaki & Martin, 2015), stress (Sonnentag & Pundt, 2015), job performance and citizenship behaviors (Matta & Van Dyne, 2015), emotions (Tse, Troth, & Ashkanasy, 2015), career success and mobility (Kraimer, Seibert, & Astrove, 2015), and justice perceptions (Masterson & Lensges, 2015), and creativity (Tierney, 2015), among others. Are there outcomes that have not yet received sufficient research attention?

In our view, despite all the research conducted in this area, there is still work to be done. *First, how about co-workers? What is the nature of the relationship between LMX quality and the degree to which the focal person is socially accepted and valued among co-workers?* Recent work suggests that a positive link between the two is not assured. For example, Erdogan, Bauer, and Walter (2015) showed that LMX quality was positively related to centrality in co-worker advice network only when focal employees showed high levels of discreetness and high levels of helpful behaviors toward colleagues. It is possible to imagine a scenario in which a high-quality LMX turns the employee into a "teacher's pet," suggesting that positive co-worker relations are not necessarily guaranteed, even if the LMX quality is high.

Does LMX quality have relations to stress and well-being of others who are not part of the dyad? In fact, we know little about the effects of truly low-quality exchanges and how they affect the job attitudes of co-workers. Furthermore, an employee who is in a poor-quality exchange may transmit his or her stress to those with whom he or she cohabitates, such as family members and children. A focal employee's partner may be affected by the focal employee's LMX quality through affective events theory (Weiss & Cropanzano, 1996). For example, an employee who is supported, trusted, and valued by the manager may experience a more positive mood at home, whereas an employee who dislikes and lacks trust in the manager may display more aggression and negativity at home. A partner's LMX quality may act as a stressor for the other partner to the degree to which the member of the LMX relationship communicates worries and frustrations at home. Alternatively, in dual career couples, a partner's LMX quality may be a referent for the other partner, either helping appreciate their own relationship with their own manager, or helping the partner realize what he or she is missing. A partner's low LMX may contribute to the sense of job insecurity, affecting the well-being and life satisfaction of both the focal employee and the partner. In other words, LMX quality may have implications for the health and well-being of others who are not part of the dyad, which is an important possibility to investigate.

Does LMX quality really shape employee behaviors? One potentially problematic aspect of the majority of studies relating LMX quality to job performance, citizenship behaviors, or other types of behaviors is that the behavioral measures are typically rated by supervisors. As a result, these assessments may more readily reflect the quality of the relationship between the manager and the employee, rather than accurately representing whether the employee truly behaves in a particular way. Therefore, extending our measurement to include objective job performance or co-worker-rated performance or utilizing raters who are not part of the focal dyad is essential before we can accept with great confidence that high-quality LMX is a driver of pro-manager and pro-organizational behaviors. At the same time, when objective measures such as sales performance or actual turnover behavior are used, relationships are, not surprisingly, much weaker because such outcomes tend to have many other antecedents and some environmental, uncontrollable elements (Gerstner & Day, 1997). One way to increase confidence in these findings is to utilize experimental methodology and focus on observable behaviors. *Given a particular LMX quality, what is the likelihood that a person will respond to a request to help a co-worker or actually help out a newcomer?* These behaviors can be observed at the microlevel using experience sampling methodology or direct observations at the day level. Sonnentag and Pundt (2015) highlight the importance of day-level analyses in examinations of the connection between LMX and stress, and Tse et al. (2015) call for additional research utilizing this method to explore the connection between LMX quality and emotion variation at the day level. We would also add that the ability of LMX quality to predict day-to-day variations in helpfulness, productivity, absenteeism, idea generation, and biological metrics of stress will validate the typically unquestioned assumption that LMX results in behavioral outcomes.

LMX at the Team Level

The focus of LMX researchers has recently shifted from understanding the effects of individual perceptions of LMX quality to understanding the effects of LMX distribution within the team, or LMX differentiation. This topic is understudied and conclusive findings are hard to come by, and therefore there is still a need for further investigation. As Anand, Vidyarthi, and Park (2015) discussed in their chapter, there are many important questions to answer in relation to LMX differentiation.

• How should LMX differentiation be measured? Should we measure LMX differentiation statistically or by using employee perceptions?

Should we use manager or employee perspectives in these calculations?

• Are differentiated relationships always harmful to group cohesion, coordination, or effectiveness? What are the boundary conditions?

• What is the role of LMX differentiation in more novel organizational contexts such as virtual teams as opposed to teams that work face to face within the same office space?

A recent development in this line of research is the investigation of LMX configuration within the work group. For example, Li and Liao (2014) showed that when LMX quality was distributed in such a way as to split the group into two subgroups, team coordination was affected, resulting in poorer team performance. LMX differentiation as well as understanding the effects of LMX distribution remain important research topics, but examining the effects of LMX differentiation while controlling for the within-group average of LMX quality is not informative in capturing the reality of how LMXs are distributed or the particular challenges that exist within the group. Supplementing these studies by adopting a configurational approach may contribute more to this conversation.

In addition to LMX differentiation, the constructs of LMX social comparisons (LMXSC; the perceived degree to which a person's LMX quality is higher than his or her colleagues, Vidyarthi, Liden, Anand, Erdogan, & Ghosh, 2010) are timely developments considering the effects of the web of relationships surrounding the focal dyad. As Liden et al. (2015) observed in their chapter, perceived relative standing may be more important than the absolute possession of resources. The authors contended that LMX quality itself may take a backseat to LMXSC. When LMX scholars utilize the underlying rationale that LMX confers a special status on the members, what they are actually referring to may not be LMX quality, but LMXSC. Therefore, familiarity with this new addition to the literature may ensure more consistent and theoretically congruent ways of operationalizing the focal variable of interest in studies of LMX. Going one step further, Sparrowe and Emery (2015) discussed the need to consider the entire social network in investigations of LMX quality, and Pellegrini (2015) noted the importance of relational context in cultural settings in which relationships take a more prominent role in organizational life. In other words, it is reasonable to anticipate that future LMX studies will investigate the dyad within the context of an existing network of other leader–leader, member–leader, and member–member relationships.

Is There a Dark Side to High-Quality Relations?

When we spend decades embedded into a research field, it becomes easy to see the prescriptions of the theory as the solution to all ills in the world. Yet a balanced approach would necessitate explicit consideration of any potential downsides to having a high-quality exchange. *Is there a dark side to LMX quality? Are there problems high LMX members or leaders are likely to encounter, or any costs to the person, team, or organization as a result of having a high-quality exchange?*

This possibility has been recognized and discussed previously. In this volume, Matta and Van Dyne (2015) also discussed the exploration of any potentially negative outcomes as an important research direction, calling for research that examines the conditions under which LMX quality may negatively relate to job performance. Tierney (2015) examined the possibility that LMX may be a stifling force for creative behaviors under specific circumstances, given that creativity necessitates thinking beyond the status quo and questioning assumptions. However, scant research attention has been paid to this question. An obvious potential problem of high-quality LMX is the potential challenges for diversity management, as recognized by Scandura and Lankau (1996). These authors recognized that similarity–attraction may have a role in shaping the quality of exchange between managers and employees. For example, if race similarity, gender similarity, or religious similarity results in a higher-quality LMX, which is then translated into performance advantages and a better work situation for the high LMX member, high-quality LMXs may introduce concerns about discrimination or unfair advantages to the team.

High-quality LMX may also blind the employee toward controversial or unfair actions of leaders, creating an effective blind spot due to the potential halo of a high-quality relationship. There is some evidence that this can occur. In an experimental study Pelletier (2012) illustrated that high LMX members view their leader as less toxic if the victim of the leader was an outgroup member. This suggests that high-quality LMX may limit the degree to which employees question the leader, notice unethical actions of the leader, or even "blow the whistle" when the leader is engaged in questionable actions. Further research regarding the blinding effect of LMX quality is warranted.

LMX quality has also recently emerged as having both positive and negative effects on the degree of stress experienced by employees (Lawrence & Kacmar, 2012). Studies have shown that positive effects of LMX quality were mediated by increased levels of job involvement. This finding suggests that LMX quality may motivate the employee to the detriment of his or her well-being. The desire to not let the manager down, meet your perceived obligations, and support the manager may clearly be taken too far. This is an interesting possibility, suggesting that the sum total effects of LMX quality on employee health and well-being would benefit from further investigation.

Finally, Ballinger, Lehman, and Schoorman (2010) pointed out an important downside of high-quality LMX: when their leaders leave the organization, high LMX members are at greater risk of turnover. This could be because the organization may lose some of its attractiveness for high LMX members. The leader who leaves may also recruit former high LMX members into his or her new company, again motivating employees to leave. This suggests that LMX quality may create loyalty to the leader but not always to the organization. How organizations can turn a high-quality LMX into a high-quality relationship between the employee and the organization and leverage this relationship for the benefit of the organization is an important research question with theoretical and practical implications.

Bridging the Theory–Practice Gap

LMX theory is empirically valid, widely researched, and conveys a clear message to give to employees and managers alike: developing a trust, liking, and respect-based relationship with employees (or managers) matters. In fact, this is likely the key difference between successful and less successful managers. In their Project Oxygen (Bryant, 2011), Google scientists analyzed vast amounts of data to identify the characteristics of effective leaders. Their eight-point list is consistent with the prescriptions of the theory. For example, listening to employees, paying attention to their career goals, and expressing interest in team member success and well-being were all on the list. *Given its practical implications, how do we get LMX theory into the hands of practicing managers and employees?* The theory perhaps suffers from lacking a catchy, intuitive name such as "authentic leadership" or "charismatic leadership" and may seem like commonsensical advice for managers and students who are seeking the "next best thing" in leadership. It also seems easier to prescribe simple, short-term solutions to leaders such as "act confident," "improve your posture," and "remember people's names" as opposed to suggesting that they be fair, trustworthy, and supportive of employees. In contrast, the advice from LMX theory is longer term, with few absolutes, and the information does not come in easy to communicate "sound bites."

How can we address these difficulties? It seems to us that it is essential to expose practicing managers to LMX theory. This may necessitate publishing more research translations, articulating the practical implications more succinctly and clearly, and designing training programs to be used in disseminating the theory. Given its dyadic nature and the important role it assigns to followers, we can also more easily integrate LMX theory into college classes. We can teach our students to be more proactive and thoughtful in developing, managing, and maintaining the quality of the relationships they have with their managers and co-workers. This awareness would serve them well, increase their effectiveness at work, and be instrumental in helping them achieve their career goals.

Conclusions

In conclusion, we set out to bring together top scholars in the area of LMX to create a lasting resource for current and future scholars. It has taken several years to complete this work. At last, we have a research-based handbook that serves to preserve what is known and inspire further work on LMX theory. The future of the theory remains bright, and there is much work to be done. It is our hope that researchers will take the opportunity to take LMX research full-steam ahead.

References

Anand, S., Vidyarthi, P. R., & Park, H. S. (2015). LMX differentiation: Understanding relational leadership at individual and group levels. In T. N. Bauer & B. Erdogan (Eds.), *The Oxford handbook of leader–member exchange*. Oxford, England: Oxford University Press.

Ballinger, G. A., Lehman, D. W., & Schoorman, F. D. (2010). Leader-member exchange and turnover before and after succession events. *Organizational Behavior and Human Decision Processes, 113*, 25–36.

Bauer, T. N., & Green, S. G. (1996). Development of leader-member exchange: A longitudinal test. *Academy of Management Journal, 39*, 1538–1567.

Bryant, A. (3/12/11). Google's quest to build a better boss. *The New York Times*. Retrieved on January 20, 2015 from http://www.nytimes.com/2011/03/13/business/13hire.html?pagewanted=all&_r=0

Day, D., & Mischenko, D. (2015). Leader-member exchange (LMX): Construct evolution, contributions, and future

prospects for advancing leadership theory. In T. N. Bauer & B. Erdogan (Eds.), *The Oxford handbook of leader–member exchange*. Oxford, England: Oxford University Press.

Dienesch, R. M., & Liden, R. C. (1986). Leader-member exchange model of leadership: A critique and further development. *Academy of Management Journal, 11*, 618–634.

Dulebohn, J. H., Bommer, W. H., Liden, R. C., Brouer, R. L., & Ferris, G. R. (2012). A meta-analysis of antecedents and consequences of leader-member exchange: Integrating the past with an eye toward the future. *Journal of Management, 38*, 1715–1759.

Engle, E. M., & Lord, R. G. (1997). Implicit theories, self-schemas, and leader-member exchange. *Academy of Management Journal, 40*, 988–1010.

Epitropaki, O., & Martin, R. (2005). From ideal to real: A longitudinal study of the role of implicit leadership theories on leader-member exchanges and employee outcomes. *Journal of Applied Psychology, 90*, 659–676.

Epitropaki, O., & Martin, R. (2015). LMX and work attitudes: Is there anything left unsaid or unexamined? In T. N. Bauer & B. Erdogan (Eds.), *The Oxford handbook of leader–member exchange*. Oxford, England: Oxford University Press.

Erdogan, B., Bauer, T. N., & Walter, J. (2015). Deeds that help and words that hurt: Helping and gossip as moderators of the relationship between LMX and advice network centrality. *Personnel Psychology, 68*, 185–214.

Gerstner, C. R., & Day, D. V. (1997). Meta-analytic review of leader–member exchange theory: Correlates and construct issues. *Journal of Applied Psychology, 82*, 827–844.

Heider, F. (1958). *The psychology of interpersonal relations*. New York, NY: Wiley.

Hogg, M., Martin, R., Epitropaki, O., Mankad, A., Svensson, A., & Weeden, K. (2005). Effective leadership in salient groups: Revisiting leader-member exchange theory from the perspective of the social identity theory of leadership. *Personality and Social Psychology Bulletin, 31*, 991–1004.

Kraimer, M. L., Seibert, S. E., & Astrove, S. L. (2015). Consequences of high LMX: Career mobility and success. In T. N. Bauer & B. Erdogan (Eds.), *The Oxford handbook of leader–member exchange*. Oxford, England: Oxford University Press.

Law-Penrose, J. C., Wilson, K. S., and Taylor, D. (2015). Leader-member exchange (LMX) from the resource exchange perspective: Beyond resource predictors and outcomes of LMX. In T. N. Bauer & B. Erdogan (Eds.), *The Oxford handbook of leader–member exchange*. Oxford, England: Oxford University Press.

Lawrence, E. R., & Kacmar, K. M. (2012). Leader-member exchange and stress: The mediating role of job involvement and role conflict. *Journal of Behavioral and Applied Management, 14*, 39–52.

Li, A. N., & Liao, H. (2014). How do leader-member exchange quality and differentiation affect performance in teams? An integrated multilevel dual process model. *Journal of Applied Psychology, 99*, 847–866.

Liden, R. C., Wayne, S. J., & Stilwell, D. (1993). A longitudinal study on the early development of leader-member exchanges. *Journal of Applied Psychology, 78*, 662–674.

Liden, R. C., Wu, J., Cao, A. X., & Wayne, S. J. (2015). LMX measurement. In T. N. Bauer & B. Erdogan (Eds.), *The Oxford handbook of leader–member exchange*. Oxford, England: Oxford University Press.

Masterson, S., & Lensges, M. (2015). Leader-member exchange and justice. In T. N. Bauer & B. Erdogan (Eds.), *The*

Oxford handbook of leader–member exchange. Oxford, England: Oxford University Press.

Matta, F. K., & Van Dyne, L. (2015). Leader-member exchange and performance: Where we are and where we go from here. In T. N. Bauer & B. Erdogan (Eds.), *The Oxford handbook of leader–member exchange*. Oxford, England: Oxford University Press.

Nahrgang, J. D., Morgeson, F. P., & Ilies, R. (2009). The development of leader-member exchanges: Exploring how personality and performance influence leader and member relationships over time. *Organizational Behavior and Human Decision Processes, 108*, 256–266.

Nahrgang, J. D., & Seo, J. J. (2015). How and why high leader-member exchange (LMX) relationships develop: Examining the antecedents of LMX. In T. N. Bauer & B. Erdogan (Eds.), *The Oxford handbook of leader–member exchange*. Oxford, England: Oxford University Press.

Pellegrini, E. K. (2015). Relational leadership through the lens of international LMX research. In T. N. Bauer & B. Erdogan (Eds.), *The Oxford handbook of leader–member exchange*. Oxford, England: Oxford University Press.

Pelletier, K. L. (2012). Perceptions of and reactions to leader toxicity: Do leader-follower relationships and identification with victim matter? *Leadership Quarterly, 23*, 412–424.

Scandura, T. A., & Lankau, M. J. (1996). Developing diverse leaders: A leader-member exchange approach. *Leadership Quarterly, 7*, 243–263.

Schyns, B. (2015). Leader and follower personality and LMX. In T. N. Bauer & B. Erdogan (Eds.), *The Oxford handbook of leader–member exchange*. Oxford, England: Oxford University Press.

Shapiro, D. L., Boss, A. D., Salas, S., Tangirala, S., & Von Glinow, M. A. (2011). When are transgressing leaders punitively judged? An empirical test. *Journal of Applied Psychology, 96*, 412–422.

Sonnentag, S., & Pundt, A. (2015). Leader-member exchange from a job-stress perspective. In T. N. Bauer & B. Erdogan (Eds.), *The Oxford handbook of leader–member exchange*. Oxford, England: Oxford University Press.

Sparrowe, R. T., & Emery, C. (2015). Tracing structure, tie strength, and cognitive networks in LMX theory and research. In T. N. Bauer & B. Erdogan (Eds.), *The Oxford handbook of leader–member exchange*. Oxford, England: Oxford University Press.

Thomas, G., Martin, R., Epitropaki, O., Guillaume, Y., & Lee, A. (2013). Social cognition in leader-follower relationships: Applying insights from relationship science to understanding relationship-based approaches to leadership. *Journal of Organizational Behavior, 34*, S63–S81.

Tierney, P. (2015). LMX and creativity. In T. N. Bauer & B. Erdogan (Eds.), *The Oxford handbook of leader–member exchange*. Oxford, England: Oxford University Press.

Tse, H. H. M., Troth, A. C., & Ashkanasy, N. M. (2015). Leader-member exchange and emotion in organizations. In T. N. Bauer & B. Erdogan (Eds.), *The Oxford handbook of leader–member exchange*. Oxford, England: Oxford University Press.

van Gils, S., van Quaquebeke, N., & van Knippenberg, D, (2010). The X-factor: On the relevance of implicit leadership and followership theories for leader-member exchange agreement. *European Journal of Work and Organizational Psychology, 19*, 333–363.

Vidyarthi, P. R., Liden, R. C., Anand, S., Erdogan, B., & Ghosh, S. (2010). Where do I stand? Examining the effects of leader-member exchange social comparison on employee work behaviors. *Journal of Applied Psychology, 95*, 849–861.

Wayne, S. J., Shore, L. M., & Liden, R. C. (1997). Perceived organizational support and leader-member exchange: A social exchange perspective. *Academy of Management Journal, 40*, 82–111.

Weiss, H. M., & Cropanzano, R. (1996). Affective events theory: A theoretical discussion of the structure, causes and consequences of affective experiences at work. *Research in Organizational Behavior, 18*, 1–74.

Zhou, L., & Wang, M. (2015). Leader-member exchange and newcomer adjustment. In T. N. Bauer & B. Erdogan (Eds.), *The Oxford handbook of leader–member exchange*. Oxford, England: Oxford University Press.

INDEX

A

Aafaqi, R., 70, 318t, 320
Abele, A. E., 199, 243
Ability, 90
Abstract resource, 56
Abusive supervision, 160
Ackerman, P. L., 403
Actual network, 294
Adams, G. L., 342
Adams, J. S., 68, 267
Adaptive performance, 159, 165–166
Adaptor employees, 177
Aditya, R., 353
Affect, 62, 62t, 132, 190
Affective Events Theory (AET), 210–211
Affective revolution, 210
Affect scale, 354
Affiliation
    definition of, 58
    demographics as proxy for, 59
    as resource, 55–65 (See also Resource
        exchange perspective)
Affiliative extra-role behavior, 159, 162–164
Age, 397–408
    demographics of, 397
    on leader–team member relationship,
        398–399
    lifespan development theories on, 402t,
        403–405
    on LMX exchange and outcomes,
        398–401
    on motivation, 402t, 403
    on performance ratings, 398
    on personality, 401–403, 402t
    relative, and career timetables, 402t,
        407–408
    selection optimization and
        compensation theory and, 403–404
    socioemotional selectivity theory and,
        404–405
    stereotyping and, 402t, 405–408
Age, leader, 399–401
Aggregate climate, 312
Aggression, workplace, 195–196
Agreeableness
    consensus and, 129
    on creativity, 177
    of followers, 124
    of leaders, 120–121
Aguinis, H., 244
Ahmad, U. N. U., 313t, 314
Ahmed, I., 313t, 314

Alden-Anderson, R., 200
Allen, D., 319t, 324
Alon, P., 73, 126
Alters, 294
Ambady, N., 221
Amor, I., 73, 126
Anand, S., 168, 215–216, 264, 286t, 288,
    352, 418
Anderson, S. E., 143, 162–163
Andrews, M. C., 195, 196
Ang, A., 326S.
Anger, 217
Angerer, P., 194
Ang, S., 61, 70, 164
Ansari, M. A., 70, 318t, 320
Antecedents, of LMX, 6, 68, 87–114. *See
    also specific topics and antecedents*
    attributes in, leader and member,
        90, 91t
    attributes in, leader and member
        similarity of, 90, 92t–94t, 107–108
    attributes in, of relationship, 95t–97t,
        108–110
    contextual characteristics in,
        105t–106t, 112
    emotional intelligence in, 214–215
    high and low LMX relationships in, 87
    implications and future directions in,
        112–113
    international research on, 354–371,
        356t–370t
    justice in, 69–74
    leader actions and behaviors in,
        98t–100t, 110–112
    LMX differentiation in, 265f
    LMX quality in, 415–417
    LMX relationship development over
        time in, 88–89, 88f
    member actions and behaviors in,
        101t–104t
    meta-analysis of, 88
    newcomer–supervisor LMX in,
        228–231, 228f
    organizational climate in, 317–323,
        318t–320t
    organizational culture in, 313–314
    resources as, 57–59
Appraisal
    primary, 212
    secondary, 212–213
Appraisal Theory of Emotion, 212–213
Armenakis, A., 35, 132

Aronson, J., 388
Aryee, S., 58, 59–60, 111, 142, 313t, 314, 328
Ashforth, B. E., 150
Ashkanasy, N. M., 209–222, 320t, 324
Asim, A. I., 319t, 323
Astrove, S. L., 7, 417
Athanasiadou, M., 122
Attachment style
    consensus and, 129
    of follower, 125
    of leader, 122–123
    in leader–follower interaction,
        126–128, 128f
    self-evaluations and, 129
Attitudes. *See also specific types*
    behavior from, 140
    job, 16
    work (*See* Work attitudes)
Attitudinal similarity, 21
Attributes. *See also specific types*
    leader, 90, 91t
    member, 90, 91t
Attribute similarity, leader and member,
    90, 92t–94t, 107–108
    attitudinal, 21
    demographic, 90, 92t–93t, 107
    perceived, 93t, 107
    personality, 94t, 107–108
Attributes of relationship, 95t–97t, 108–110
    expectation in, 95t, 108
    liking in, 95t–96t, 108–109
    trust in, 96t–97t, 109–110
Atwater, L., 63, 197
Average leadership style approach, 12, 29
Axtell, C. M., 38
Aycan, Z., 354

B

Badgett, M. V. L., 389
Bagger, J., 201
Bai, Y., 268
Bakker, A. B., 191, 197
Bal, A. C., 400
Balanced reciprocity, 231
Balance theories, 231, 270, 415
Ballinger, G. A., 251, 419
Bal, M., 400
Bal, P. M., 193, 197
Baltes, P. B., 403–404
Barbuto, J. E., 110
Barksdale, K., 35
Barrett, L. F., 217

Barsade, S. G., 210, 211, 212
Bartels, L. K., 387
Basu, R., 162
Bauer, T. N., 3, 58–59, 71, 89, 107, 110,
    111, 150, 161, 163, 168, 196, 210, 220,
    229, 234–236, 251–253, 256, 267,
    268, 272, 288, 319t, 324–325, 356t,
    358t, 359t, 367t, 368t, 390, 417
Baugh, S. G., 399
Becker, J. A. H., 197
Bedeian, A. G., 107
Beeri, I., 165
Belau, L., 407
Bell, M. P., 382, 385
Bell, S. T., 407
Benenuto, M., 217
Benevolence, 354
Bennett, N., 60, 71, 160
Benson, G. S., 166, 234
Berger, E., 355, 359t
Berger, J., 384–385
Bernas, K. H., 200
Bernerth, J. B., 35, 121, 124–125, 129, 132
Bertolino, M., 405
Bettencourt, L. A., 164
Beutell, N. J., 191
Bhal, K. T., 70, 163, 165
Bhattacharya, C., 341, 343
Bialosiewicz, S., 267
Bian, Y. J., 33
Bidirectional perspective, 56
Bies, R., 58
Big Five personality traits, 17–18
    consensus and, 129
    of followers, 124–125, 126f
    of leaders, 120–122, 123f
"Black box," LMX, 7, 140, 142–143,
    143f, 415
Blackwell, L. V., 389
Blau, P. M., 36, 56
Bleiken, L. M., 399
Boehm, S., 406
Boies, K., 271
Bolino, M. C., 144, 168, 199, 267, 337
Bommer, W. H., 72, 415
Bond, M. H., 354
Borghatti, S. P., 293
Botero, I. C., 164
Bowler, W. M., 121
Brands, R. A., 303, 307
Brass, D. J., 293
Brazil, D. M., 107
Breland, J. W., 252–253
Brewer, M. B., 384
Brief, A. P., 210
Briggs, A. L., 407
Brockner, J., 72–73
Bronkhorst, B. A. C., 200–201
Brotheridge, C. M., 218
Brouer, R., 198, 415
Brower, H. H., 109
Bruce, R. A., 165, 318t, 321
Brunetto, Y., 200

Bryant, A., 419
Buch, R., 35, 132
Budhwar, P. S., 58, 59–60
Burlacu, G., 7
Burnout, 191, 197–198
Burris, E. R., 164
Burton, J. P., 74, 161, 163, 167
Burt, R. S., 231, 233, 234, 294
Byrne, Z. S., 198, 203, 245, 252, 253, 337

C
Cai, Z. Y., 315
Camerman, J., 73
Campbell, S. M., 403
Cao, A. X., 416
Career mobility and success, 7, 241–258
    career motivation theory on, 248t
    career success typologies in, 242–244,
        244t, 245f
    conservation of resources theory on,
        31, 248t, 256
    dyadic-exchange theory on, 248t
    extrinsic and objective career
        outcomes in, 244–245, 246t–250t,
        250–252
    extrinsic and subjective career
        outcomes in, 252–254
    future research on, 255–257
    gender role orientation theory
        on, 248t
    gender role theory on, 248t
    guanxi and, 249t, 253
    impression management social
        information processing theory
        on, 247t
    intrinsic and objective career
        outcomes in, 254
    intrinsic and subjective career
        outcomes in, 254–255
    job embeddedness theory on, 247t,
        248t, 249t, 251–252, 255–256
    LMX "leader as substitute" theory on,
        247t, 248t, 253
    role-making theory on, 248t
    social capital theory on, 246t, 247t,
        252–253, 256
    social categorization theory on, 249t
    social exchange theory on, 241–242,
        248t, 249t, 250t, 251
    social network perspective on, 250t
    social support theory on, 248t
    tournament theory on, 242, 244–245,
        250t, 252, 253, 255
Career motivation theory, 248t
Career success
    definition of, 242
    intrinsic vs. extrinsic, 242–243,
        244t, 245f
    objective vs. subjective, 243–244,
        244t, 245f
    typologies of, 242–244, 244t, 245f
Career timetable, relative age and, 402t,
    407–408

Carioppo, J., 211
Carley, K., 307
Carlson, D. S., 253
Carmeli, A., 63, 197
Carmichael, J. S., 389
Carmona-Lavado, A., 318t, 320
Cashman, J., 29–30, 88–89, 295–296, 295f
Castro, S. L., 398
Centrality, 38
Chang, C.-H., 168, 195–196
Change-oriented extra-role behavior,
    159, 164–165
Chan, S. C. H., 198
Chattopadhyay, P., 355, 357t
Chaudhry, A., 33, 70
Cheema, L. J., 319t, 323
Chelladurai, P., 110
Chen, G., 161, 236, 313t, 314, 319t, 324
Chen, K. W., 150–151
Chen, T., 353, 356t
Chen, Y., 33–34, 353–354
Chen, Z., 161
Chen, Z. G., 319t, 325
Chen, Z. X., 58, 59–60, 62–63, 111, 142,
    160, 162, 328
Chiu, R. K., 71, 163, 319t, 324
Chongsen, Y., 214
Chow, I. H. S., 163, 319t, 324
Chow, I. H. W., 71
Christensen, T. C., 217
Chrobot-Mason, D., 389–390
Chuang, A., 60–61
Chung, H.-Y., 253
Citations, article
    by frequency count, 4, 5f
    most cited, 10, 11–12, 11f
    most cited, 30 highest, 12, 13t–15t
    most cited, "Big 4," 11, 11f
    most cited, by year, 12, 15f
    by year, 4, 4f
Citizenship, on performance, 164
Clegg, C. W., 140
Cleveland, J. N., 389
Climate
    aggregate, 312
    diversity, 391–392, 406
    safety, on performance, 164
Climate, justice, 72
    procedural, on performance, 164, 165
Climate, leadership, on performance, 161
Climate, organizational, 311–312,
    317–328
    age diversity on, 402t, 405–406
    as antecedent of LMX quality, 323
    constructs of, 312
    definition of, 312
    empirical studies on, 317, 318t–320t
    future research on, 326–327
    history of, 317
    LMX quality as antecedent of,
        317–323
    LMX quality as antecedent of,
        high-level, 318t–320t, 321–323

LMX quality as antecedent of, individual-level, 317–321, 318t–319t
LMX quality–organizational culture integration with, 327–328, 327f
as moderator, 323–325
studies on, and their limitations, 325–326
Climate, psychological, 194, 312
Climate, work, 105t–106t, 112
Climbers, 243
Cogliser, S., 146, 168–169, 317, 318t, 321, 392, 398
Cognitive networks, 294–308
accuracy and, 307
activated, 303
definition of, 294
LMX mental representations as, 302–303
LMXSC and, 305–306, 305f
PLMXD and, 303–304
RLMX and, 304–305, 305f, 306f
Cohen-Charash, Y., 68–69, 73
Colella, A., 388
Collectivism-oriented Human Resource Management, 315
Collins, M. H., 408
Colquitt, J. A., 69, 73–74, 77, 78
Commitment, organizational
components of, 141
vs. identification, 150
on performance, 163
on work attitude, 150–151
work attitudes in, 141–142
Communication frequency
on agreement, 108, 143f
on outcomes, 63
on performance, 162
Compensation, 403–404
Competence
emotional, 217
employee, 143, 269
empowerment and, 195, 254
experts on, 243
of future work, newly formed dyads on, 108
leader and member, 31, 69, 90, 91t, 382, 413
leader's trust in, cultivating, 113
manager view of, 109
negative views of, stereotypes, 381, 385–388, 391
newcomer, 235
in promotion focus, 199
in trust, 36-37
in well-being, 195
Concrete resource, 56
Confirmatory factor analysis, 31
Congruence
age, on leader–team member relationship, 160
on performance outcomes, 168–169
proactive personality, 160
Conlon, E. J., 72, 204

Conscientiousness
consensus and, 129
of followers, 124
of leaders, 121
leader traits in, 129–130
Consensus, 128–129
Consequences, 7, 68
Conservation of resources theory (COR), 55
on career mobility and success, 248t, 256
Contagion, emotional, 218
Contempt, 217
Context, on creativity, 178
Contextual characteristics, 105t–106t, 112
on performance, 162
span of supervision in, 105t, 112
work climate in, 105t–106t, 112
Contextual schools of leadership, 18–20
Contribution, 9–10, 62, 132, 190
Côte, S., 212
Coworker exchange (CWX)
definition of, 18
on performance, 162
quality of, 320–321
on work attitudes, 146
workgroup on, 18
Crain, E. C., 90
Crant, J. M., 125, 164
Creative performance, 165
Creativity, 7, 165, 175–185
agreeableness on, 177
context on, 178
embeddedness of LMX on, 182–183
employee identity on, 180–181
employee motivation on, 180
employee self-efficacy on, 178–179
employee sensemaking on, 179–180
enabling of, 176–177
freedom on, 178
future of, 184
leader–leader exchange on, 182–183
LMX as destructive for, 183–184
LMX as natural catalyst for, 175–177
for LMX development, 181–182
LMX differentiation on, 183
mediating mechanisms of, 178–181, 179f
motivation on, 176
practical implications of, 184–185
when LMX matters most in, 177–178
Cropanzano, R., 56, 72, 76–78, 161, 210, 213, 337, 338, 417
Crosby, F., 144, 267
Culbertson, S. S., 200, 201
Cultural values, corporate social responsibility in, 345–346
Culture, national, 18–19
Culture, organizational, 311–317
as antecedent of LMX quality, 313–314
constructs of, 311–312
definition of, 311
empirical studies on, 312, 313t

future research on, 315–316
integrating LMX quality and organizational climate with, 327–328, 327f
LMX quality as moderator of, 314–315
as moderator, 314
origins and basic idea of, 312
studies on, 315
Culture strength, 317

D

Dadhich, A., 165
Dansereau, F., 11, 12, 29–30, 89, 112, 119–120, 159
Dark triad, 129–132
followers in, 131
leaders in, 130–131
similarity in, 131–132
toxic triangle in, 132, 132f
Dasborough, M. T., 145, 151, 210–211, 213, 214, 216, 320t, 324
Davidovitz, R., 122–123, 125, 128
Davis, D. D., 200
Davis, K. E., 127
Davis McCauley, K., 128
Day, D. V., 4–5, 9–12, 13t, 16–18, 20, 22–24, 31, 90, 128, 141, 146, 168, 194, 233, 251, 296, 416, 418
Day, N. E., 390
DeConnick, J. B., 251
De Dreu, C., 212
de Gilder, D., 403
Degoey, P., 77
de Lange, A. H., 404–405
de la Rosa-Navarro, M. D., 318t, 320
Delegation, 98t, 110
Deluga, R. J., 111–112, 160
DelVecchio, S. K., 90, 110
Demands, job, on job stress, 196
Demerouti, E., 191
Demographics, leader-member similarity of, 90, 92t–93t, 107
Density, 38
Desmette, D., 407
Detachment, psychological, on performance, 164
Deviation LMX, 30
Diefendorff, J. M., 217–218
Diener, E., 191
Dienesch, R. M., 6, 30, 36, 38, 61–62, 88–89, 112, 132, 190, 294, 296, 312, 352, 414
Differentiation, LMX, 263–268, 312
as antecedent of justice, 70–71
antecedents of, 265f
on creativity, 183
definition of, 312, 336
drivers of, 287
four configurations of, 301
group level, 268–269, 268t
moderating effects of, 266f
organizational justice theory in, 267–268, 268f

Differentiation, LMX (*Cont.*)
perceived, 145
psychological experience of,
variations, 301–302
relative deprivation theory in, 267
research on, 3, 17, 68
social comparison theory in, 264, 267
social networks and, 301–306
work groups and well-being in, 199
Differentiation research, LMX, 268–289
criticisms of, 273, 287–289
group level, 271–273
individual level, 269–270
meso level, 270–271
overview of, 268–269
summary of, 273, 274t–286t
Dihn, J., 139–140
Dikkers, J. S. E., 404–405
Dikstein, E., 355, 359t
Dimou, N., 122
Disabled employees, 388–389
Discrete emotions, 216–217
Disgust, 217
Dissimilarity. *See also* Diversity;
Stereotypes
dyadic, stereotypes and, 390
impact of, demography on, 391
Diversity, 381–392
future research on, 390–392
LMX development and, 382–383
LMX outcomes and, 384
Status Characteristics Theory on,
384–385
stereotypes in, 384–390 (*See also*
Stereotypes)
on supervisor–subordinate
interactions, 381–382
as variety, 382
in workforce, 381
Diversity climate, 391–392, 406
Dockery, T. M., 58, 90, 111
Doherty, M. L., 317, 318t, 319t, 322, 326
Dries, N., 243
Duchon, D., 162, 318t, 321
Dulebohn, J. H., 61, 68, 70, 141,
164, 253, 326, 342, 384, 391, 392,
415, 417
Duncan, P., 313t, 314
Dunegan, K. J., 162, 318t, 321
Dyadic dispersion LMX, 273
Dyadic-exchange theory, 248t
Dyadic theory, 3, 9
on work attitude, 146–147, 147f
Dyads. *See also* Vertical dyad linkage
(VDL) theory; *specific topics*
extending domain beyond, 299–300
in networks, relationship quality and,
296–299, 297f, 298f
relationship duration on performance
of, 162
similarity/dissimilarity in, stereotypes
and, 390
Dysvik, A., 35, 132

E
Eagly, A. H., 386
Economic exchange measure, 35, 48–49
Economic LMX (ELMX), 35
Edwards, J. R., 287, 326–327
Ee, F. E., 71
Effort, member, 101t, 111
Egan, T. D., 302
Ego, 294
Einarsen, S., 218
Ekman, P., 216, 217
El Akremi, A., 73
Elderly worker stereotypes, 385–386,
402t, 405–408
Elfenbein, H. A., 221
Elicker, J. D., 164
Ellemers, N., 403
Ely, R. J., 391
Embeddedness, job, 151, 233
on career mobility and success,
247t–249t, 251–252, 255–256
on creativity, 182–183
on newcomer adjustment, 233
on performance, 161, 163
Embeddedness, organizational, on work
attitudes, 151
Emery, C., 301, 418
Emotional contagion, 218
Emotional Contagion Theory, 211–212
Emotional intelligence, 213–216
Emotional intelligence, LMX and
as antecedent to LMX, 214–215
fundamentals of, 213–214
future research on, 220–221
on job performance, 214
outcomes on, 215
Emotional labor, 217–219
leaders' use of, 220
leading with, 215
Emotional regulation, 22, 150
Emotion in organizations, 209–213
Affective Events Theory in, 210–211
Appraisal Theory of Emotion in,
212–213
Emotional Contagion Theory in,
211–212
Emotion in organizations, LMX and,
213–222
discrete emotions in, 216–217
emotional intelligence in, 213–216
emotional labor in, 217–219
future research on, 219–221
history of research on, 209–210
theory/measurement/analysis
misalignment in, 221–222
Emotions interface, 7
Emotions, negative, 217
Empathy, 38
Employees. *See also specific topics*
extraversion of, on performance, 161
growth need strength of, on
performance, 161
identity of, on creativity, 180–181

justice perceptions of, in social
responsibility, 344–345
motivations of, on creativity, 180
self-efficacy of, on creativity, 178–179
sensemaking in, on creativity, 179–180
socialization of, 7
Empowerment
on competence, 195, 254
on performance, 160–161
psychological, 254
on role stressors, 195
Enabling, in creativity, 176–177
Enders, J., 142, 161, 167
Engle, E. M., 90
Ensher, E., 123
Epitropaki, O., 90, 107, 142–144,
270–271, 355, 366t, 369t, 399, 415
Eplion, D., 125
Equity theory, Adams, 68
Erdogan, B., 3, 71–73, 139, 141–145,
149–150, 161, 167, 210, 220, 251,
253, 264, 267, 268, 272, 288, 313t,
314–316, 319t, 323–325, 359t, 364t,
367t, 417, 418
Erez, A., 211
Eudaimonic perspective, 191
Evolution, construct, 10–17
in 1970s, 12, 15
in 1980s, 15–16
in 1990s, 16
in 2000-present, 16–17
by article citations, by year, 4, 4f
by article citations, frequency
count, 4, 5f
by articles most cited, 10, 11–12, 11f
by articles most cited, 30 highest, 12,
13t–15t
by articles most cited, "Big 4," 11, 11f
by articles most cited, by
year, 12, 15f
by scholarly impact, 11
"Exchange" in LMX, locating, 299–300
Expatriate adjustment, newcomer,
233–234
Expectation
in newcomer adjustment, 229–230
in relationships, 95t, 108
Experience sample method, for
emotions, 221
Experts, 243
Exploratory measures
leader–member *guanxi*, 33–34
LMX-24, 33, 47
supervisor–subordinate
guanxi, 47–48
Extra-role behavior
affiliative, 159, 162–164
change-oriented, 159, 164–165
Extraversion
consensus and, 129
employee, on performance, 161
of followers, 124
of leaders, 121

Extrinsic and objective career outcomes, 244–245, 246t–250t, 250–252
Extrinsic and subjective career outcomes, 252–254

F

Fagenson-Eland, E. A., 399
Fairhurst, G. T., 391
Fairness heuristic theory, 74
Fang, Y. Q., 313t, 315
Farh, J., 33, 355, 357t
Farr-Wharton, R., 200
Feild, H. S., 132
Fein, E. C., 319t, 323
Feldman, D. ., 404, 405, 408
Felt obligations, on performance, 164–165
Female stereotypes, 386–387
Ferris, G. R., 108–109, 111, 160, 342, 398, 415
Festinger, L., 264
Field, J. S., 35
Finkelstein, L., 405
Fischer, A., 212
Fisher, C, D, 221
Fiske, S. T., 386, 387
Fisk, G. M., 218
Fletcher, T. D., 200
Foa, E. B., 56, 58, 62, 144
Foa, U. G., 56, 58, 62, 144
Foley, C., 195
Folkman, S., 212
Follower Machiavellianism, 131
Follower narcissism, 131
Follower personality, 124–126, 126f
    attachment style in, 125
    Big Five in, 124–125
    consensus in, 128–129
    self-evaluations and proactivity in, 125–126
Follower psychopathy, 131
Ford, J. M., 31, 271, 288, 319t, 322–323
Formal mentor-member exchange (FMMX), 373
Fraley, R. C., 131
Freedom, on creativity, 178
Frese, M., 192, 400
Freund, A. M., 403–404
Friedman, M., 347, 348
Friesen, J. P., 218
Frijda, N. H., 212
Future research, on LMX, 22–24, 413–420. See also specific topics
    on antecedents of LMX quality, 415–417
    balance theories in, 415
    bridging theory–practice gap in, 419–420
    on dark side to high-quality relations, 419
    implicit leadership theories in, 415
    on LMX at team level, 418–419
    on outcomes of LMX quality, 417–418

relationship science in, 415
role theory in, 413–415
social exchange theory in, 413–415
summary of, 414f

G

Gaddis, B., 131, 211
Galatea effect, 229
Gardner, W. L., 128, 168–169, 219
Gavin, M. B., 212, 221
Gellert, E. J., 399
Gender role orientation theory, 248t
Gender role theory, 248t
Generalized reciprocity, 230–231
Generativity, leader, age on, 400
George, J. M., 213, 214, 216
Germano, L. M., 200
Gerras, S. J., 60, 320t, 324
Gerstner, C. R., 10, 17, 31, 141, 146, 168, 194, 233, 251, 418
Ghosh, S., 264, 418
Gielnik, M. M., 399–400
Giles, W. F., 35, 132
Glaser, J., 194
Glasø, L., 218
GLBT employee stereotypes, 389–390
Glibkowski, B. C., 33, 70
Gobdel, B. C., 160
Goffman, E., 388
Goldberg, C. B., 381, 386, 390
Golden, T. D., 145–146, 161, 200
Goldman, B. M., 58, 60, 160, 338
Gong, Y., 355, 357t
González-Romá, V., 194, 268, 273, 287, 312, 317, 318t, 319t, 320–322, 325–327
Goods, as resource, 55–65. See also Resource exchange perspective
Goodwin, V. L., 121, 300–301, 306
Gooty, J., 144–145, 146, 210–212, 221, 273
Gouldner, A. W., 57–58, 143–144
Graen, G., 29–32, 56, 88–89, 108, 109, 142, 159–161, 190, 194, 209–210, 232, 294–299, 297f, 298f, 304, 307, 352, 356t–370t
Gramzow, R. H., 388
Grandey, A. A., 218
Granovetter, M., 231, 293–294, 306–307
Graves, L. M., 197
Graves, S. B., 339, 340, 340t
"Great man" perspective, 17–18
Greenhaus, J. H., 191, 252
Green, S. G., 58–59, 89, 107, 110, 111, 143, 146, 162, 196, 229, 234–236, 270, 390
Greguras, G. J., 31
Griffin, M. A., 158
Griffith, K. H., 390
Grijalva, E., 131
Gross, J., 217
Group Affective Tone, 219
Group level of analysis, on work attitude, 146, 147f

Group level personality, and consensus in follower personality, 128–129
    leader traits predicting, 129–130
Group stereotypes, 384–385
Guanxi, 33–34, 47–48, 249t, 253, 353–354, 371
    leader–member, 33–34
    supervisor–subordinate, 47–48
Guenzi, P., 165
Gurunathan, L., 73

H

Hackett, R. D., 60, 62–63, 121–123, 125, 128, 160, 194, 201
Hadži, O., 313t, 316
Haerem, T., 35, 132
Halbesleben, J. R. B., 197
Hall-Merenda, K. E., 160
Hall, R. J., 164
Han, G., 252
Hanges, P. J., 140
Han, H. G., 268
Hansbrough, Keller, 125
Harms, P. D., 131
Harris, K., 55, 125, 198, 202, 204, 251, 253
Harrison, D. A., 229, 234, 302, 382, 385, 398–399, 401
Harris, R., 125
Harris, T. B., 270, 271, 302, 304–305
Haslam, S. A., 403
Hatfield, E., 211
Hebl, M., 390
Heider, F., 270, 415
Heilman, Madeline, 386
Help-seeking behavior, costs of, 162–163
Henderson, D. J., 70, 270, 302, 304, 337
Henning, T., 400
Henriques, 73P. L.
Herrera, R., 313t, 314
Hertel, G., 406
Heyden-Gahir, H. A., 404
High distributive justice climate, 72
High LMX relationships, 39, 71, 87. See also Differentiation, LMX
    antecedents of, 87–114 (See also Antecedents, of LMX)
    on career mobility and success, 241–258 (See also Career mobility and success)
    challenging task assignment in, 263, 287
    on climate perception, 319t, 322
    in coworkers, 270
    creativity in, 176–184 (See also Creativity)
    dark side to, 419
    definition of, 194
    detrimental personality in, 163
    diversity and turnover in, 282t
    diversity on, ethnic, 387
    favorable effects of, 283t, 284t
    future research on, 165–167, 169
    at group level, 271–273, 274t

High LMX relationships (*Cont.*)
  on individual *vs.* group, 269
  international studies of, 372
  job satisfaction and organizational
    commitment in, 147
  on leader–member exchange, 67, 68
  leader positive emotion on, 216
  as moderator, 316
  in resource allocation, 267
  resource exchange process on, 415
  social exchange theory on, 161
  trust in, leader, 268
High procedural justice climate, 72
Hiller, N. J., 353, 372
Hinojosa, A. S., 128
Hochschild, A. R., 217
Hochwarter , W., 198, 203
Ho, D., 389
Hoel, W., 304
Hoes, M., 269
Hoever, I. J., 177, 184
Hoffman, B. J., 403
Hofmann, D. A., 60, 164, 320t, 324
Hogg, M. A., 148–149, 415
Holes, structural, 231
Hollensbe, E. C., 76
Holmvall, C. M., 214, 215
Hooper, D. T., 34, 145, 199, 301–302
Hornung, S., 194
House, R., 353
Howell, J. M., 160, 271
Hsiung, H.-H., 71, 165, 319t, 324
Huang, X., 146, 160, 198, 215
Huan, X., 270
Hubristic pride, 217
Hu, D.-C., 253
Huffman, A. H., 200
Hui, C., 162
Hu, J., 270, 302, 304
Hu, K., 352, 356t, 357t, 361t
Human Resources Management policies, 311
Humphrey, R. H., 216–220
Hung, D. K. M., 70, 318t, 320
Hussain, N. M., 319t, 323

I

Identification, organizational, 150–151
Identity. *See also* Social identity
    theory (SIT)
  on creativity, 180–181
  leader relational, on performance,
    162, 163
  moral, in social responsibility, 345
  social relations on, 180
Ilies, R., 164, 169
Implicit leadership theories (ILTs), 21,
    90, 148, 355, 407, 415
Impression management social
    information processing theory, 247t
Individualized leadership, 119–120
Individual-level personality
  follower, 124–126
  leader, 120–124

Individually targeted citizenship, on
    performance, 164
Influence behaviors, member, 102t–104t,
    111–112
Influencers, 243
Information, as resource, 55–65. *See also*
    Resource exchange perspective
Information Processing school, 21–22
In-group, 87, 149, 190. *See also* High
    LMX relationships
Inhibitory-remedial pattern, 177, 178
Initial interactions and behaviors,
    98t, 110
Initial offer, 190
Innovator employees, 177
Interactional justice, 160
  on performance, 163
Intergroup leadership, on work
    attitudes, 149
International LMX research, 351–373
  antecedents in, 354–371, 356t–370t
  definitions in, 352–353
  future research on, 372–373
  measurement in, 353–354
  outcomes in, 371–372
  theoretical background on, 352
Interpersonal justice, in creativity, 181
Interpersonal Reactivity Index (IRI),
    37-38, 52
Intrinsic and objective career
    outcomes, 254
Intrinsic and subjective career outcomes,
    254–255
Ishaq, M. I., 319t, 323
Islam, T., 313t, 314
Iweins, C., 407
Izsak, R., 122

J

Jablin, F. M., 269, 288, 343
Jackson, S. E., 191
James, William, 212
Jansen, P. G., 404–405
Janssen, O., 143, 160
Jaworski, R. A. A., 233–234
Jian, G., 194
Jiang, J. W., 196, 198
Job attitudes, 16
Job demands, on job stress, 196
Job demands-resource model, 55
Job embeddedness. *See*
    Embeddedness, job
Job performance. *See* Performance
Job satisfaction, 140–141. *See also* Work
    attitudes
Job stress. *See* Stress, job
Johnson, J. W., 158
Johnson, O. E., 271
Johnson, R. E., 161–162, 163, 168
Johnson, T., 74
Jones, D. A., 77, 78, 344
Jones, K. S., 346
Joo, B., 253, 313t, 314

Jordan, P. J., 213–214, 219
Joseph, D. A., 33
Judge, T. A., 140, 160
Justice, 67–81
  on creativity, 181
  future research on, 78–79
  history of, 67
  integration with LMX in, current
    knowledge, 78–79
  integration with LMX in, model,
    74–78, 75f
  interactional, 160
  LMX and, 68
  LMX–justice relationship in, 69–74
    (*See also* LMX–justice relationship)
  next steps in, 79–81
  organizational, 68, 339–340, 340t
  on performance, 163
  procedural, 68
Justice climate, 72
Justice perceptions, 68–69
  employee, in corporate social
    responsibility, 344–345
  in social exchange theory, 74

K

Kacmar, K. M., 195, 196, 198, 202, 204,
    253, 419
Kafetsios, K., 122
Kahn, R. L., 88, 90, 209
Kamdar, D., 124, 163, 168
Kammeyer-Mueller, J. D., 140
Kanfer, R., 319t, 324, 403–405
Karoly, P., 36
Karriker, J. H., 162
Katz, D., 209
Kauppila, O.-P., 195
Kearney, E., 399
Kelly, J. R., 211, 212
Kenny, D. A., 146–147
Kent, A., 110
Khan, S. R., 313t, 314
Kilduff, M., 303
Kim, T.-Y., 346
Kimura, T., 142
Kim, W., 70
King, E. B., 405
Kinicki, A. J., 196, 203
Kirkman, B., 270, 319t, 324
Kirkpatrick, L. A., 127
Klein, K. J., 302, 382
Klein, K. M., 401
Klimoski, R. J., 236
Kooij, D. T., 403, 404–405
Korschun, D., 341
Kozlowski, S. W. J., 317, 318t, 319t,
    322, 326
Krackhardt, D., 38, 231, 294, 303, 307
Kraimer, M. L., 63, 73, 162, 163, 165,
    233–234, 243, 247t, 248t, 250t, 253,
    255, 256
Kramer, R. M., 384
Kulik, C. T., 399

Kun, T., 214
Kunze, F., 406
Kuvaas, B., 132
Kuvaas, V., 35
Kwan, H. K., 164

L

Labianca, G., 293
Labor, emotional, 215, 217–219
Lack-of-fit theory, 386–387
Lam, C. K., 146, 160, 270
Lam, L. W., 150–151
Lam, S. S. K., 245, 251
Lam, W., 161, 198, 319t, 325
Lance, C. E., 403
Lankau, M. J., 194, 197, 399, 419
Lapierre, L. M., 201
Larkin, J. C., 387–388
Laschinger, H. K. S., 63
Latitude, 98t, 110
Lau, H., 389
Lavelle, J. J., 72–73
Law, K. S., 60, 62–63, 160, 162, 196, 253,
     353, 362t, 366t, 368t, 369t
Lawler, E. J., 209
Law Penrose, J. C., 415
Lawrence, B. S., 386, 407, 408
Lawrence, E. R., 419
Lawrence, S. A., 146, 270
Lawthom, R., 140
Lazarus, R. S., 212
Leader actions and behaviors, 98t–100t,
     110–112
   delegation/latitude, 98t, 110
   initial, 98t, 110
   leadership, 98t–100t, 110–111
   performance, 100t, 111
"Leader as substitute" theory, LMX,
     247t, 248t, 253
Leader attributes, 90, 91t. See also
     specific types
   on performance, 161–162
Leader Behavior Description
     Questionnaire (LBDQ), 29
Leader downward influence, on
     performance, 163
Leader-follow dyad, 9–10
Leader–follower relationship
   age on, 400
   measures of (See Relationship
     measures, leader–follower)
   personality interaction in, 126–128
   personality similarity in, 18
Leader–leader exchange (LLX), on
     creativity, 182–183
Leader Machiavellianism, 130
Leader–member agreement, 33
Leader–member exchange (LMX). See
     also LMX; specific topics
   as antecedent of justice, 69–70
   concept of, 189–190, 263–264
   definitions of, 68, 352–353
   development of, 382–383

four-dimensional, 13t, 31, 62, 62t, 132,
     190, 372
   measurement of (See Measurement)
   as moderator of justice–outcome
     variables relationship, 74
   outcomes of, 384
   relationship development over time
     in, 88–89, 88f
   as resource, 61–62, 62t
   role development in, 382–383
Leader–member exchange (LMX) scale,
     44. See also LMX entries
   12-item, 30
   13-item, 30–31
   supervisor version, 31–32
Leader–member exchange (LMX)
     theory, 3–7
   articles on, 10–11
   consequences of, 7, 68
   emerging issues in, 7
   focus of, 3
   history of, 29–30
   importance of, 3
   meta-analyses on, 9
   research progress in, 3
   unique features of, 10
   from vertical dyad linkage theory,
     15–16, 29–30
Leader–member guanxi (LMG), 33–34,
     353–354
Leader–member similarity
   demographic, 90, 92t–93t, 107
   perceived, 93t, 107
   personality, 18, 94t, 107–108
Leader–member social exchange
     (LMSX), 35–36, 50
Leader narcissism, 131
Leader performance, 100t, 111
Leader personality, 120–124, 123f
   attachment style in, 122–123
   Big Five in, 120–122
   predicting consensus in LMX from,
     129–130
   self-evaluations and proactivity in,
     123–124
Leader psychopathy, 131
Leader relational identity, on
     performance, 162, 163
Leadership behaviors, 98t–100t, 110–111
Leadership climate, on performance, 161
Leader's point of view, 119–120
Le Blanc, P. M., 268, 273, 287
Lee, J., 69
Lee, M. J., 70
Legacy beliefs, 400
Lehman, D. W., 251, 419
LePine, J. A., 169
Levels of analysis
   definition of, 144
   in work attitudes, 144–147
Lewin, K., 317
Lewis, K., 58, 60, 160
Li, A. N., 201, 301, 418

Liang, J., 125, 164
Liao, H., 301, 418
Liao, P.-Y., 201, 253, 272, 288
Liden, R. C., 30–39, 33, 37, 58, 60–62,
     62t, 70–73, 107, 108, 112, 132, 142,
     145, 159–161, 168, 169, 190, 215–216,
     229–231, 234–235, 251, 253, 256,
     264, 268, 270, 272, 288, 294, 296,
     299–301, 302, 304, 319t, 323, 352,
     354, 356t–362t, 364t–367t, 369t,
     370t, 371, 398, 413–415, 416, 418
Life satisfaction, on work attitude, 150
Lifespan development theories, 402t,
     403–405
Li, J., 313t, 315
Likert, R., 295
Liking, in relationships, 95t–96t,
     108–109
Li, N., 125, 164
Lind, E. A., 77, 78, 88–89
Linking pin, 295
Linz, A., 199
Lippit, R., 317
Litwin, G. H., 317
Liu, J., 164, 272
Liu, Z. Q., 313t, 315
LMX-7, 31, 44–45, 53–54, 378–379
   international, 372
   supervisor version, 32, 44–45, 53–54
LMX-8, 45
LMX-24, 33, 47
LMX differentiation. See
     Differentiation, LMX
LMX–justice relationship, 69–74
   justice as antecedent of LMX, 71–74
   justice as moderator of
     LMX–outcome variables in, 71
   LMX as antecedent of justice, 69–70
   LMX as moderator of
     justice–outcome variables in, 71–74
   LMX differentiations as antecedent of
     justice, 70–71
LMX "leader as substitute" theory, 247t,
     248t, 253
LMX relational separation (LMXRS),
     270, 271, 301–302
   cognitive networks and, 305–306, 305f
   definition of, 301
LMX social comparison (LMXSC),
     34–35, 48, 264, 270, 301–302
Lock, E. A., 140
Loi, R., 55, 150–151, 272, 355, 358t, 360t
Lord, R. G., 21, 90
Louvet, E., 388–389
Low LMX relationships, 87
   avoidance in, 128, 129
   benefits and resources in, 251
   climate perception in, 319t, 321, 322
   creativity in, 183, 185
   dissimilarity in, 143
   distributive injustice in, 20
   group level, 272, 280t, 282t
   highly balanced, attitudes and, 146

Low LMX relationships (*Cont.*)
  leader–member exchange in, 69
  member turnover in, 250t, 251, 252
  organizational justice theory on, 268
  of partner, in job insecurity, 417
  performance goals and career
    satisfaction in, 253
  performance in (*See* Performance)
  relative deprivation theory on, 144,
    199, 267
  RLMX on, 304–305
  task challenge in, 175, 264
  team level, 219
  team life cycle and, 287
  as transactional, 242
  unfairness in, 268–269
  unfairness in, on coworker exchanges, 19
Loyalty, 62, 62t, 132, 190
Luciano, M. M., 197
Lukasik, M. A., 407
Lusky, L., 319t, 323
Lynch, P., 35
Lyons, B. J., 195–196

M

MacCurtain, S., 212
Machiavellianism
  follower, 131
  leader and follower, 131–132
Mael, F. A., 150
Major, B., 388
Major, D. A., 143, 145, 200, 201, 255,
  313t, 314, 316
Ma, L., 70–71, 273, 287
Mallory, D. B., 338, 339
Manager adjustment, new, 234
Manogran, P., 72
Mansfield, L., 150
Mao, Y., 164
Martin, R., 34, 90, 107, 139, 141–145,
  147, 148, 150, 199, 267, 270–271,
  301–302, 328, 355, 366t, 369t,
  399, 415
Maslach, C., 191
Maslyn, J. M., 31, 36, 62, 62t, 110, 132,
  296, 352, 354, 356t–362t, 364t–367t
Masterson, S. S., 58, 60, 67, 69, 71–72,
  75–80, 143, 160, 162
Mastery orientation, 160
Matta, F. K., 419
Matthews, R. A., 195
Mayer, D. M., 251, 253, 271, 400
Mayer, J. D., 213–214
Mayer, R. C., 37
McAllister, D. J., 37
McKay, P. F., 385, 391, 406
Means efficacy, on job stress, 196
Measurement, 31–39. *See also specific types*
  exploratory measures, 33–34
  future research on, 23–24, 38–39
  of leader–follower relationship, 34–39
    (*See also* Relationship measures,
    leader–follower)

leader–member agreement, 33
LMX-7, 31, 44–45, 53–54, 378–379
LMX-7, international, 372
LMX-7, supervisor version, 32,
  46–47, 54
LMX-MDM, 30, 45, 53, 62–63, 378
LMX-MDM, international, 353, 372
LMX-MDM, supervisor, 32, 46–47,
  62, 62t
overview of, 31
supervisor versions in, 31–32
vertical dyad linkage in, 30–31
Mediator, LMX as, 142–143
Mehra, A., 293
Member actions and behaviors,
  101t–104t
  effort, 101t, 111
  influence, 102t–104t, 111–112
  performance, 101t–102t, 111
Member attributes, 90, 91t. *See also*
  specific types
Member effort, 101t, 111
Member influence behaviors, 102t–104t,
  111–112
Member performance, 101t–102t, 111
Mentoring, 373
Meyer, I. H., 390
Miao, Q., 160
Miklos, S. M., 401
Mikulincer, M., 122
Miller, C. T., 388
Mischel, W., 322
Mischenko, D., 4–5, 416
Misumi, J., 354
Mitchell, M. S., 56, 251, 255
Mitchell, T. R., 151
Moag, J. S., 58
Mobility, career. *See* Career mobility and
  success
Moderators
  climate, 323–325
  emotional intelligence, 215
  justice, 71
  of justice–outcome relationship, 74
  LMX, 142–143
  LMX differentiation, 266f
  LMX quality, 314–315
  organizational culture, 314
  on organizational culture, 314–315
  for performance, new, 166
  for work, 142–143
Money, as resource, 55–65. *See also*
  Resource exchange perspective
Moral identity, corporate social
  responsibility in, 345
Moral intensity, on performance, 165
Morgeson, F. P., 60, 146, 168, 169,
  320t, 324
Morrison, E. W., 233
Morrison, T. G., 387
Morrow, P. C., 252
Mossholder, K. W., 37
Motivation

age on, 402t, 403
  in creativity, 176, 180
Mowday, R. T., 141
Muldoon, J., 195
Multidimensionality
  of LMX, 61
  in resource exchange, 57
Multidimensional LMX (LMX-MDM),
  31, 45, 53, 378
  empirical research with, 62–63
  international, 353, 372
  supervisor version (SLMX-MDM),
  32, 46–47, 62, 62t
Multiple networks, 307
Murphy, S. M., 72, 123

N

Nachreiner, F., 191
Nadisic, T., 346
Nahrgang, J. D., 87–90, 100t, 102t, 109,
  111–114, 121, 124, 146, 168, 169, 392,
  415, 417
Naidoo, L. J., 272
Nan, X., 198
Narcissism
  follower, 131
  leader, 131
  leader and follower, 132
National culture, 18–19
Nawaz, M. M., 319t, 323
Neal, A., 158
Nedeljkovi, M., 313t, 316
Negative affect, 217
  on performance, 162
Negative feedback-seeking, on
  performance, 161
Negative reciprocity, 231
Negative traits, 120, 129–132, 132f. *See
  also* Dark triad
Negotiating latitude, 30, 42–43
Negotiating latitude/VDL scale, 30
Neider, L. L., 143
Neocharismatic approaches, 20–21
Networks
  actual, 294
  cognitive, 294–308 (*See also* Cognitive
    networks)
  multiple, 307
  structure of, on newcomer
    adjustment, 230–231
  task interdependency alignment
    with, 299
Networks, social
  analysis and measures of, 3,
    38–39, 250t
  on career mobility and success, 250t
  on newcomer adjustment, 233
Neuroticism
  consensus and, 129
  of followers, 124
  of leaders, 121
Newcombe, M. J., 213, 216, 217
Newcomer adjustment, 227–238

antecedents of LMX in, 228–231, 228f
dynamic processes in, 234–236, 235f
embeddedness in, 233
expatriate adjustment in, 233–234
expectation in, 229–230
future research directions in, 234–237
LMX on, 231–233
network structure on, 230–231
new manager adjustment in, 234
organizational context in, 236–237
organizational socialization in, 227–228
overview of LMX in, 227–228, 228f
role development in, 231–232
similarity in, 229
social aspect of, 227
social exchange in, 232–233
social network in, 233
supervisor socialization tacts in, 230
task aspect of, 227
team context in, 236
New Leadership school, 20–21
New manager adjustment, 234
Newman, D., 131
Ngo, H. Y., 355, 360t
Ng, T. W. H., 243, 404, 405, 408
Nickell, S., 140
Niessen, C., 199
Nikoli, M., 313t, 316
Nishii, L. H., 251, 253, 271, 400
Nodes, 294
Nonwhites stereotypes, 387
Nordstrom, C. R., 387
Novak, M. A., 142

O

Obese employee stereotypes, 387–388
Obligations, felt, on performance, 164–165
O'Connor, W., 387
O'Hair, H. D., 197
Ok, C., 70
Older worker stereotypes, 385–386, 402t, 405–408
One-With-Many (OWM) model, 147
Openness
consensus and, 129
of followers, 124–125
of leaders, 121
Optimization, 403–404
O'Reilly, C. A., 302, 398
Oren, L., 73, 126
Organizational citizenship behavior (OCB), 176
affective commitment in, 339
as affiliative extra-role behavior, 162
beginnings of, 16–17, 70 (See also specific contexts)
Bhal's model on, 70
corporate social responsibility and, 339, 345
creativity and, 176
ELMX and, 35

in high-quality LMX, 337
in horizontal-individualistic contexts, 164
international research on, 356t, 358t–361t, 365t–367t, 369t
job embeddedness in, 163
leader relationship identity and, 163
LMX-MDM on, 63
LMX on, 21, 58, 69, 77, 159, 160, 384
negative affectivity on, 162
in older employees, 404
organizational commitment on, 141
outcome favorability in, 163
in performance, 157
procedural justice climate and, 164, 323
relative LMX on, 34
RLMX and, 270, 302
SLMX-MDM on, 32
Organizational climate. See Climate, organizational
Organizational culture. See Culture, organizational
Organizational identification, 150–151
Organizational justice, 68
corporate social responsibility as, 339–340, 340t
Organizational justice theory, 267–268, 268f
Organizational level, 19–20
Organizationally targeted citizenship, on performance, 164
Organizational politics
on job stress, 195
perceptions of, on performance, 165
Organizational socialization, 194, 227–228
Organizational support, on performance, 161–162
Othman, R., 71
Outcome favorability
definition of, 328
on performance, 163
Outcomes. See also specific topics
emotional intelligence on, 215
of LMX, resources as, 59–61
research on, 139 (See also specific types)
Out-group, 87, 149, 190. See also Low LMX relationships
Ozer, M., 142

P

Palachy, O., 319t, 323
Pan, W., 71, 163, 319t, 324
Paparoidamis, N. G., 165
Parasocial LMX, 342
Parasuram, S., 252
Parker, S. K., 38, 158
Park, H. S., 418
Particularistic resource, 56
Paternalism, 354
Patterson, M., 140
Pattie, M., 166, 234

Peiró, J. M., 194, 317, 318t, 320, 321, 325
Pelled, L. H., 107
Pellegrini, E. K., 109–110, 354, 358t, 364t, 418
Pelletier, E. K., 419
Perceived LMX differentiation (PLMXD), 145, 301–302
cognitive networks and, 303–304
definition of, 301
Perceived LMX variability, 34–35, 48–49
Perceived organizational support (POS), 14, 18–19, 21, 38
work attitudes in, 142
work climate in, 112
Perceived similarity, leader-member, 93t, 107
Perceived supervisor support (PSS), 36–37, 51
Performance, 7, 157–170
adaptive, 159, 165–166
affiliative extra-role behavior in, 159, 162–164
age on ratings of, 398
change-oriented extra-role behavior in, 159, 164–165
contextual factors on, 162
creative, 165
definition of, 158–159, 158f
emotional intelligence on, 214, 215
employee characteristics on, 161
empowerment on, 160–161
future research on, 166–169, 167f
importance of, 157
individual differences on high LMX in, 158
leader, 100t, 111
leader characteristics on, 161–162
LMX congruence on outcomes in, 168–169
LMX in, 158f
member, 101t–102t, 111
mitigating negative effects of low LMX in, 168
moderators for, new, 166
multiple mediators on, 161
negative feedback-seeking on, 161
negative relation to, conditions for, 166–168
supervisor liking on, 160
systematic reviews of, prior, 157
task, 158–162 (See also Task performance)
time and, 169
Perry, E. L., 399, 407–408
Perry, J. T., 111–112
Personality, leader and follower, 119–133. See also specific levels
age on, 401–403, 402t
future directions in, 129–132
group level in, 128–130
individualized leadership in, 119–120
individual level in, 120–126

Personality, leader and follower (*Cont.*)
  interaction rather than similarity
    in, 130
  leader-member similarity of, 94t,
    107–108
  leader's point of view in, 119–120
  negative traits in, 120, 129–132, 132f
    (*See also* Dark triad)
  on performance, 163
  relationship level in, 126–128
  similarity in, 126
Personal resource, 56
Perspective taking, 38, 53
Peterson, M., 354
Pettigrew, T. F., 267, 384
Phillips, A. S., 107
Piccolo, R. F., 74
Pillai, R., 69–70
Pines, H. A., 387–388
Pippin, G. M., 267
Point of view, leader's, 119–120
Politics, organizational
  on job stress, 195
  perceptions of, on performance, 165
Popper, M., 122
Porter, L. W., 141
Positional resource, 56
Positive attributions, making, 38
Potter, R. E., 163
Powell, G. N., 191
Pratt, M. G., 150
Price, K. H., 385
Pride, 217
  hubristic, 217
Proactive personality congruence, 160
Proactivity
  in follower personality, 125–126
  in leader personality, 123–124
Procedural justice, 68
  on performance, 163
Procedural justice climate
  perceptions of, on performance, 165
  on performance, 164
Process models, future research on, 23
Project Oxygen, 419
Psychological climate, 194, 312
Psychological detachment, on
  performance, 164
Psychopathy
  follower, 131
  leader, 131
  leader and follower, 132
Pulakos, E. D., 159, 165, 166
Pundt, A., 418
Pygmalion effect, 229

Q
Quality, LMX
  future research on, 415–419
  moderators of, 314–315
  organizational climate in, 317–323,
    318t–320t (*See also* Climate,
    organizational)

Quinn, R. E., 316
Qu, Q., 70–71
Qu, W., 273, 287

R
Raja, R., 210, 221
Ramsay, S., 200
Randolph-Seng, B., 128
Ranft, A. L., 342
Rapson, R. L., 211
Ready, K. J., 253
Reciprocity, 36, 230–231
  balanced, 231
  generalized, 230–231
  measures of, 36, 50
  negative, 231
  norm/principle of, 57–58, 60
Ree, M., 313t, 314
Relational identity, creativity and, 181
Relational leadership theory
  evolution of, 9
  individual and group level (*See*
    Differentiation, LMX)
Relational perspective, 10, 17–22
  contextual schools of leadership
    in, 18–20
  future LMX research on, 415
  Information Processing school
    in, 21–22
  New Leadership school in, 20–21
  trait theories of leadership in, 17–18
Relationship attributes, 95t–97t, 108–110
  expectation, 95t, 108
  liking, 95t–96t, 108–109
  trust, 96t–97t, 109–110
Relationship duration, dyadic, on
  performance, 162
Relationship level personality
  leader–follower personality
    interaction in, 126–128
  similarity in, 126
Relationship measures,
    leader–follower, 34–39
  Interpersonal Reactivity Index,
    37–38, 52
  leader–member social exchange,
    35–36, 49
  LMX social comparison, 34–35
  perceived LMX variability, 34–35, 48–49
  perceived supervisor support,
    36–37, 51
  perspective taking, 38, 53
  reciprocity, 35–36, 50
  relative LMX, 34
  social and economic exchange, 35
  social LMX and economic LMX, 35
  social network analysis and
    measures, 38
  test of negative social exchange, 36, 50–51
  trust, 36–37, 51–52
Relationship quality, dyadic networks
    and, 296–299, 297f, 298f
Relationships, workplace, 189

Relative deprivation theory
  in LMX differentiation, 267
  on work attitudes, 144
Relative LMX (RLMX), 21, 30, 34, 145,
    301–302
  cognitive networks and, 304–305,
    305f, 306f
  contingency approach to, 270–271
  definition of, 145, 264, 301, 302
  divergence approach to, 270
  operationalization of, 270
  performance and citizen behaviors
    in, 270
  on work attitudes, 145
Research, LMX. *See also* Citations,
    article; *specific topics*
  progress of, 3
Research, LMX, future, 22–24, 413–420.
    See also Future research, on LMX
Resource exchange perspective, 6, 55–65
  bidirectional perspective in, 56
  history of, 55–56
  key theoretical pieces in, 56–57
  literature on, 57, 57t
  LMX as resource itself in, 61–62, 62t
  multidimensionality and LMX
    measurement in, 57
  positional and personal
    resources in, 56
  research on, 62–65
  resource outcomes from exchanges
    with members in, 56–57
  resources as antecedents of LMX
    in, 57–59
  resources as outcomes of LMX
    in, 59–61
  social exchange in, 56
Resources, 56. *See also specific types*
Resource theory of social exchange, 144
Respect, professional, 62, 62t, 132, 190
Rhoades, L., 37
Richards, D. A., 122, 125, 128
Riketta, M., 140
Riordan, C. M., 399
Rockstuhl, T., 61, 142, 164, 326,
    351–353, 371
Rodell, J. B., 77, 78
Role Episode Model, 61, 88–90, 88f,
    231–232, 413
  on career mobility and success, 248t
  in diversity, 382–383
  in newcomer adjustment, 231–232
  role expectations in, 108
  stereotypes in, 384–390 (*See also*
    Stereotypes)
Role identity, creativity and, 180–181
Role making, 15, 89, 179, 182, 383
Role perceptions, on performance,
    163, 165
Role receiver, 88, 88f
Role routinization, 89, 182, 383
Role stressors

empowerment on, 195
LMX and, 194–195
Role taking, 88f, 89, 182, 382–383
Role theory. *See* Role Episode Model
Rosen, B., 319t, 324
Rosenbaum, J. E., 242, 244, 252, 255
Rosen, C. C., 74
Rosing, K., 400
Rotundo, M., 158
Rousseau, D. M., 168, 194, 202
Ruehlman, L. S., 36
Runciman, W. G., 267
Rupp, D. E., 72, 336, 338–340, 340t, 343–346
Russell, J. A., 216
Ryan, K., 405
Ryff, C. D., 191

S

Saavedra, R., 212
Sablynski, C. J., 161, 163, 167
Sackett, P. R., 158
Safety climate, on performance, 164
Sahlins, M., 230–231
Salovey, P., 213–214
Salvaggio, A. N., 140
Satisfaction, life, on work attitude, 150
Scandura, T. A., 56, 69, 88–89, 108–110, 143, 168–169, 194, 245, 256, 268, 294–299, 297f, 298f, 352–355, 356t–369t, 371–372, 419
Schaffer, B. S., 399
Schaffer, M. A., 163
Schalk, R., 399
Schaubroeck, J., 245, 251
Schaufeli, W. B., 191
Scheibe, S., 398, 401
Scherer, L. R., 212
Schiemann, W., 30
Schneider, B., 140
Schoenrade, P., 390
Schoorman, F. D., 251, 419
Schriesheim, C. A., 143, 168–169, 245, 256, 317, 318t, 320, 321, 398
Schyns, B., 120–123, 125, 128–130, 132, 271, 415
Scott, S. G., 165, 318t, 321
Sears, B., 389
Sears, G. J., 121, 123, 125, 194, 214, 215, 288
Seeking help, costs of, 162–163
Seers, A., 145, 271, 319t, 322–323
Seibert, S. E., 242, 243, 248t, 256
Sekiguchi, T., 161, 163, 167
Selection optimization and compensation theory, 403–404
Self-determination, in well-being, 197
Self-efficacy, employee, in creativity, 178–179
Self-evaluations
attachment styles and, 129
of follower, 125–126
of leader, 123–124

Self-realizers, 243
Sen, S., 74, 341
Sensemaking, employee, in creativity, 179–180
Seo, J. J., 415, 417
Services, as resource, 56–65, 62t. *See also* Resource exchange perspective
Settoon, R. P., 60, 71, 160, 162
Shacklock, K., 200
Shaffer, M. A., 234
Shanock, L. R., 37, 72
Shao, R., 344, 345, 346
Shared leadership, 9–10
Shared leadership capacity, 9–10
Shared realty theory, 273
Sharoni, G., 73, 126
Shaver, P. R., 122
Shen, C., 60–61
Sherman, K. E., 251
Sherony, K. M., 146, 270
Shi, J., 123, 142, 229
Shi, J. Q., 160
Shi, N. L., 71
Shi, S.P., 313t, 315
Shivers, S. L., 143
Shore, L. M., 35, 58, 60, 61, 70, 72, 142, 160, 164, 326, 386, 399, 408, 413–415
Sias, P. M., 269, 288, 343
Similarity
attitudinal, 21
dyadic, stereotypes and, 390
interaction *vs.*, 129
leader-follower personality, 18
leader-member attributes, 90, 92t–94t, 107–108 (*See also* Attribute similarity, leader and member)
in newcomer adjustment, 229
in relationship level personality, 126
Similarity attraction paradigm, 214–215, 390
Simmelian ties, 231
Sin, H. P., 33, 146, 168, 204
Skarlicki, D. P., 77, 78, 346
Sleebos, E., 150
Sluss, D. M., 110, 230
Smith, D. B., 140, 267
Smith, P. B., 354
Snavely, B. K., 391
Snyder, L. A., 389
Social capital theory, 246t, 247t, 252–253, 256
Social categorization theory, 249t
Social comparison theory, 264, 267
Social/economic exchange, 35, 48–49
Social/economic LMX, 49–50
Social exchange, 56
definition of, 56
in newcomer adjustment, 232–233
Social exchange measure, 35, 48–49
Social exchange theory, 61, 413–415
on career mobility and success, 241–242, 248t, 249t, 250t, 251

justice as antecedent of LMX in, 72–74
justice perceptions and outcome variables in, 74
on newcomer adjustment, 232
on work attitudes, 143–144
Social identity theory (SIT), 22, 390
principles of, 148
on work attitudes, 148–149
Socialization
organizational, 194, 227–228
supervisor tactics for, on newcomer adjustment, 230
Social LMX (SLMX), 35
Social networks
analysis and measures of, 3, 38–39, 250t
in newcomer adjustment, 233
Social networks, LMX differentiation, 301–306
mental representations of, as cognitive networks, 302–303
psychological experience of, variations, 301–302
Social responsibility, corporate, 3
background on, 336–337
boundary conditions in, 343–346
cultural values in, 345–346
employee awareness of, 343
employee justice perceptions in, 344–345
employee participation in, 344
historical foundations of, 338–339
importance of, 335–336
individual differences in, 345–346
leadership as driver of, 341–342
LMX and, 336–338
moral identity in, 345
new era of, 339
as organizational justice, 339–340, 340t
perceptions of, shifting focus of, 340–341
strengthening LMX and reducing differentiation in, 342–343
theoretical model of, 336, 336f
trickling down of culture of, 341–342
Social structure, informal. *See* Structure, informal
Social support theory, 248t
Socioemotional selectivity theory (SST), 404–405
Soetjipto, B. W., 63, 163
Sommerkamp, P., 60, 142
Son, J., 353, 356t
Sonnentag, S., 73, 191, 192, 197, 202, 418
Span of supervision, 105t, 112
Sparr, J. L., 73, 234–235
Sparrowe, R. T., 32, 38–39, 60, 63, 142, 145, 163, 167, 230–231, 253, 256, 294–296, 299–301, 418
Spataro, S. E., 210
Spector, P.E., 68–69, 73

Spurk, D., 199
Srikanth, P. B., 73
Status, as resource, 55–65. *See also* Resource exchange perspective
Status Characteristics Theory (SCT), 384
Staudigl, L. F., 125
Stauffer, J., 72
Steele, C. M., 385
Steers, R. M., 141
Steiner, D. D., 58, 90, 111, 370t
Stereotypes, 384–390
   of disabled employees, 388–389
   distancing by threatened stereotype in, 388
   dyadic similarity/dissimilarity and, 390
   of GLBT employees, 389–390
   of groups, 384–385
   of nonwhites, 387
   of obese, 387–388
   of older workers, 385–386, 402t, 405–408
   of women, 386–387
   of younger workers, 405
Sterns, H. L., 401
Stewart, M. M., 271
Stilwel, D., 58, 169, 398
Stinglhamber, F., 407
Stone, D. L., 388
Stress, job, 7, 189–204. *See also specific stressors*
   core concepts of, 190
   on creativity, 177
   future practice in, 204
   future research in, 202–204
   stressors in, 190–191
   well-being in, 191, 197–199 (*See also* Well-being)
   work–family interface in, 191, 200–202 (*See also* Work–family interface)
   workplace relationships and, 189
Stress, job, LMX and, 192–196, 193f
   concept of LMX in, 189–190
   direct relationship in, 192–193, 193f
   job demands in, 196
   job stressors in, 193–194
   leaders' time-based stress in, 196
   means efficacy in, 196
   organizational politics in, 195
   research findings on, 191–192, 192f
   role stressors in, 194–195
   workplace aggression in, 195–196
Stressors, job, 190–191
   LMX and, 193–194
Stressors, role, 194–195
Stringer, R. A., Jr., 317
Strong ties, 231, 233, 293–295, 297, 299
Structural holes, 231
Structure, informal, 293–308
   dyadic networks and relationship quality in, 296–299, 297f, 298f

"exchange" and domain extension beyond dyad in, 299–300
networks and task interdependency alignment in, 299
origins and history of, 294–295
overview of, 294
recent empirical research on, 300–301
refining LMX relationship in, 296
in Vertical Dyad Linkage, 295–296, 295f
Sturges, J., 243
Success, career mobility and. *See* Career mobility and success
Sufang, G., 214
Sun, J. J. M., 196
Sun, L.-Y., 71, 163, 319t, 324
Supervision. *See also specific topics*
   abusive, 160
   span of, 105t, 112
Supervisor liking, on performance, 160
Supervisor LMX (SLMX), 355, 371
Supervisor LMX-7 (SLMX-7), 34, 46–48
Supervisor perceived organizational support, on performance, 161–162
Supervisor socialization tacts, in newcomer adjustment, 230
Supervisor–subordinate *guanxi* (LMG), 49–50
Supervisor versions, measures
   LMX, 31–32
   LMX-7, 31, 44–45, 53–54
   multidimensional LMX, 32, 46–47, 62, 62t
   multidimensional LMX-7, 32, 46–47, 62, 62t
Synergistic diminishing gains, 177, 178
Sy, T., 212, 355

T
Taggar, S., 201
Tajfel, H., 390
Takeuchi, R., 143, 162
Target similarity framework, 340
Task challenge, on performance, 162
Task i-deals, 194–195
Task interdependencies, network alignment with, 299
Task performance, 158–162
Tayeb, M. H., 354
Taylor, D., 415
Taylor, M. S., 57t, 58, 60, 143, 160
Team-level LMX
   age diversity on, 402, 406–407
   emotion on, 219–220
   evolution of LMX differentiation in, 287–288
   future research on, 418–419
   newcomer adjustment to, 236
Team member exchange (TMX), 272–273
   definition of, 145
   on work attitudes, 145–146
Tee, E. E., 216

Tekleab, A. G., 143, 252
Tepper, B. J., 164
Terek, E., 313t, 316
Test of negative social exchange (TENSE), 36, 50–51
Tetrick, L. E., 35, 72
Thomas, C. H., 197
Thomas, D. A., 390
Thomas, G., 127, 146–147, 149–150, 194, 415
Thomas, J. S., 212–213
Thompson, B. S., 110, 230, 318t, 321–322
Thornton, G. C., 389
Tierney, P., 163, 175–185, 318t, 321, 419
Ties, 294
Tie strength, 34, 38, 293–301, 306–307
   definition and origin of, 293–294
   dyadic networks and relationship quality in, 296–299, 297f, 298f
   "exchange" and domain extension beyond dyad in, 299–300
   future research on, 306–307
   hierarchy-free conceptualization of, 306–307
   multiple networks in, 307
   networks and task interdependency alignment in, 299
   origins and history of, 294–295
   recent empirical research on, 300–301
   refining LMX relationship in, 296
   in Vertical Dyad Linkage, 295–296, 295f
Time-based stress, leaders', on job stress, 196
Timmerman, T. A., 407
Token status, 391
To, M. L., 221
Tordera, N., 194, 318t, 319t, 320, 322, 324, 325–327
Tournament theory, 242, 244–245, 250t, 252, 253, 255
Toxic triangle, 132, 132f
Traditional leadership theory, 12
Trait theories of leadership, 17–18
Transformative leadership, 20–21, 160
Treadway, D. C., 342, 347
Triandis, H. C., 316
Troth, A., 212–214, 217, 218, 219, 221
Trust
   definition of, 352
   measures of, 36–37, 51–52
   on performance, 163
   in relationships, 96t–97t, 109–110
Truxillo, D. M., 7, 150, 402, 405
Tse, H. H. M., 216, 217, 219, 220, 221, 270, 304, 320t, 324, 418
Tse, H. M., 145, 146, 151, 209–213, 222
Tsui, H. H., 302, 398
Tummers, L. G., 200–201
Turner, J. C., 390
Turner, R. J., 242
Turnley, W. H., 144, 168, 199, 267, 337
Twenge, J. M., 403
Tziner, A., 73, 126, 319t, 323, 355, 359t

U

Uhl-Bien, M., 31–32, 36, 110, 162, 190, 210, 295, 299, 307, 352, 356t, 358t, 360t–364t, 366t, 368t, 369t, 372
Unsworth, K., 184

V

Vadera, A. K., 164–165
Values, corporate social responsibility and, 345–346
Van Breukelen, W., 269, 273
Vancouver, J. B., 235, 235f
Vandenberge, C., 73
van den Bos, K., 77, 78
Van Der Leeden, R., 269
Van Dyne, L., 124, 158–159, 163–165, 168, 169, 419
Van Knippenberg, D., 148–149, 150
Van Vianen, A. E. M., 60–61
Van Yperen, N. W., 160
Variance, 29
VDL/LMX, 30
Vecchio, R. P., 107, 160, 196, 203, 390, 408
Venkataramani, V., 59, 300–301, 306
Vertical dyad linkage (VDL) measures negotiating latitude in, 30, 43
VDL/LMX in, 30
Vertical dyad linkage (VDL) theory, 3, 11, 12, 15
formulation of, initial, 294–295
history of, 29
LMX transition from, 15–16, 29–30
structure and tie strength in, 295–296, 295f
Vertical Exchange, 43
Vidyarthi, P. R., 33, 88, 144–146, 168, 215–216, 221, 264, 270, 273, 286t, 302, 305, 352, 358t, 418
Vigoda-Gador, E., 165
Villardo, A. J., 407
Visionary leadership, 20–21
Volmer, J., 199
Vukonjanski, J., 313t, 316

W

Waddock, S. A., 339, 340, 340t
Waismel-Manor, R., 355t, 359t
Wakabayashi, M., 30
Walker, H. J., 132
Walker, J. J., 35
Wall, T. D., 140

Walter, F., 398, 401
Walter, J., 417
Walumbwa, F. O., 73, 161, 163, 165, 166, 196, 338
Wang, D., 60, 62–63, 110, 142, 160, 353, 366t, 368t
Wang, H., 60, 62–63, 160, 162, 353, 362t, 366t, 368t
Wang, M., 123, 160, 227–229, 232, 237, 401, 416
Wat, D., 163
Wayne, S. J., 30–31, 33, 35, 39, 58, 60, 72, 108–109, 111, 112, 142, 145, 160–162, 169, 233–234, 245, 251–253, 413–415, 416
Weak ties, 231, 293
Weigl, M., 194
Weiss, H. M., 210, 213, 243, 417
Well-being, 7, 191–192, 192f. *See also* Stress, job
LMX and, 197–199
Wesselius, W., 269
West, M., 140, 212
White, R. K., 317
Whittington, J. L., 121
Wilke, H. A. M., 77, 78
Wilk, P., 63
Williams, L. J., 162–163
Williams, M. L., 162
Wilson, K., 56–62, 64, 144, 204, 415
Within-group variance, 268
Witt, L. A., 146
Women, stereotypes of, 386–387
Wong, C. S., 353, 368t, 369t
Wong, K. F. E., 162
Work attitudes, 7, 139–151
"black box" of LMX and, 7, 140, 142–143, 143f, 415
cultural characteristics in, 142
direct relationships to, 140
dyad analysis of, 146–147, 147f
future research on, 150–151
group analysis of, 146, 147f
history of, 139–140
individual analysis of, 145–146, 147f
individual variables in, 142
intergroup leadership on, 149
job satisfaction and, 140–141
levels of analysis in, 144–147
LMX as mediator/moderator in, 142–143
organizational commitment on, 141–142

organizational embeddedness on, 151
organizational variables in, 142
relationship science on, 149–150
relative deprivation theory in, 144
research on, 139–142
resource theory of social exchange theory in, 144
social exchange theory in, 143–144
social identity theory on, 148–149
Work climate, 105t–106t, 112
Work–family interface, 200–202
enrichment in, 191
interference in, 191–192
job stress and, 191
LMX as predictor of work–family variables in, 200–201
on performance, 164
predicting LMX by work–family variables in, 201–202
research findings on, 191–192, 192f
Workgroup level, 19
Workplace aggression, 195–196
Wormley, W. M., 252
Wu, J., 416

X

Xanthopoulou, D., 197
Xiaqi, K., 214
Xin, K. R., 107
Xu, E., 160, 162

Y

Yagil, D., 73
Yammarino, F. J., 119–120, 146, 221, 273
Yang, J., 37
Yoder, R. J., 235, 235f
Younger worker stereotypes, 405
Yperen, N. W., 143
Yu, E., 353, 356t
Yun, S., 162
Yzerbyt, V., 407

Z

Zacher, H., 399–401, 403, 405, 408
Zhang, Z., 107–108, 123, 125, 126, 142, 160, 229
Zhong, J. A., 161, 319t, 325
Zhou, J., 177, 399
Zhou, L., 232, 416